EUROPE'S GHOST

Tolerance, Jihadism, and the Crisis in the West

Michael Radu

ENCOUNTER BOOKS  NEW YORK • LONDON

Copyright © 2009 by Michael Radu

First American edition published in 2009 by Encounter Books,
an activity of Encounter for Culture and Education, Inc.,
a nonprofit, tax exempt corporation.
Encounter Books website address: www.encounterbooks.com

Manufactured in the United States and printed on
acid-free paper. The paper used in this publication meets
the minimum requirements of ANSI/NISO Z39.48—1992
(R 1997) (Permanence of Paper).

FIRST AMERICAN EDITION

LIBRARY OF CONGRESS CATALOGING-IN-PUBLICATION DATA

Radu, Michael.

Europe's ghost : Tolerance, Jihadism, and the crisis in the West / by Michael Radu.

p. cm.

Includes bibliographical references and index.
ISBN-13: 978-1-59403-262-2 (hardcover : alk. paper)
ISBN-10: 1-59403-262-9 (hardcover : alk. paper)
1. Toleration—Europe.
2. Multiculturalism—Europe.
3. Islamic fundamentalism—Europe.
4. Islam and politics—Europe.
5. National security—Europe.
6. Europe—Ethnic relations.
7. Europe—Race relations. I. Title.

HN380.Z9M847 2009

305.6'97094—dc22

2009018974

CONTENTS

The Islamization of Europe

Will tourists in the year 2109 visit the Eiffel Minaret in Paris and the Westminster Mosque in London?

It is not a far-fetched question. After decades of massive immigration, and supine and impotent responses from European leaders to increasing Muslim restiveness, some Muslims in Europe and elsewhere are openly boasting about accomplishing today what they failed to accomplish at the time of the Crusades: the Islamic conquest of Europe.

In April 2008, Islamic cleric and Hamas parliamentarian Yunis al-Astal declared in a sermon that "very soon, Allah willing, Rome will be conquered, just like Constantinople was, as was prophesied by our Prophet Muhammad. Today, Rome is the capital of the Catholics, or the Crusader capital. . . . This capital of theirs will be an advanced post for the Islamic conquests, which will spread through Europe in its entirety, and then will turn to the two Americas."[1] Likewise, the leader of one of the largest and most influential Islamic organizations in the world, the Muslim Brotherhood, declared in 2004: "I have complete faith that Islam will invade Europe and America, because Islam has logic and a mission."[2]

How realistic are these boasts? The respected historian Bernard Lewis forthrightly told the German newspaper *Die Welt*: "Europe will be Islamic by the end of the century."[3]

Indeed, if demographic trends continue, France, the Netherlands, and other Western European nations could have Muslim majorities by mid-century. It was a sign of how much things have changed in Europe, and will continue to change, when the Nordgård-skolen in Aarhus became Denmark's first Dane-free school: The students now come entirely from Denmark's fastest-growing constituency, Muslim immigrants.[4]

Meanwhile, these growing Muslim minorities are increasingly assertive and disruptive. Sweden's third-largest city, Malmö, has become a Middle Eastern outpost in Scandinavia. A quarter of the city's population is now Muslim, and that number is rapidly growing. Nor are the Muslims of Malmö inclined to be peaceful and tolerant. Even the police are afraid: "If we park our car it will be damaged—so we have to go very often in two vehicles, one just to protect the other vehicle," a police officer reported. Ambulance drivers will not enter some areas of Malmö unless police accompany them.[5] Islamic enclaves of this kind are springing up all over Europe.

The official response to Islamic assertiveness and aggressiveness has amounted essentially to appeasement. In 2004, Pakistani Muslim leader Qazi Hussain Ahmed gave an address at the Islamic Cultural Center in Oslo. He was allowed into the country despite the fact that, according to Norway's *Aftenposten*, he "has earlier made flattering comments about Osama bin Laden, and his party, Jamaat-e-Islami, also has hailed al-Qaeda members as heroes."[6] In Norway, he declined to answer questions about whether or not he thought homosexuals should be killed.[7] No one in Norway seemed particularly concerned about standing up for Western values in the midst of all this. The old model of requiring that immigrants assimilate and adopt the customs and mores of their new country has given way to a multiculturalist model that envisions immigrants maintaining their own practices and cultural habits.

In the case of Islam, since Islamic law contains a complete model for society and governance that is considered to be divinely inspired and superior to all its rivals, multiculturalist accommodation is short-sighted at best; at worst, it is tantamount to cultural suicide. And given that Islam also is unique among the religions of the world in containing a developed doctrine, theology, and legal system that mandate warfare against unbelievers, this accommodation is difficult to distinguish, either in intention or in effect, from outright appeasement.

Case Study: Britain

The nation in which this policy stands most vividly exposed as appeasement pure and simple is Britain. Many of its cultural accommodations border on the risible. For example, British officials reoriented prison toilets so that they wouldn't face Mecca (Islam forbids Muslims to face Mecca or turn their back to it when urinating or defecating).[8] In another instance, a non-Muslim teacher disciplined two schoolchildren after they refused to participate in classroom exercises that involved reciting Islamic prayers. The mother of one of the boys commented: "This isn't right, it's taking things too far. I understand that they have to learn about other religions. I can live with that, but it is taking it a step too far to be punished because they wouldn't join in Muslim prayer. Making them pray to Allah, who isn't who they worship, is wrong, and what got me is that they were told they were being disrespectful." Another parent remarked: "The school is wonderful but this one teacher has made a major mistake. It seems to be happening throughout society. People think they can ride roughshod over our beliefs and the way we live."[9] The teacher was suspended and then fired.

Many Muslims have spoken about their intention to impose, as soon as they are able to do so, Islamic law, Sharia, upon the non-Muslim populations of Western countries. They are beginning to do this today by portraying accommodation of Islamic law as a matter of "civil rights" and "diversity." This effort got a tremendous shot in the arm in Britain in July 2008, when the Lord Chief Justice, Lord Phillips of Worth Matravers, said in an address at the London Muslim Centre that "it is possible in this country for those who are entering into a contractual agreement to agree that the agreement shall be governed by law other than English law."[10] Including Islamic law? Yes: "There is no reason why principles of sharia, or any other religious code, should not be the basis for mediation or other forms of alternative dispute resolution."[11]

At first glance there was nothing remarkable in this. The Lord Chief Justice was calling simply for the voluntary application of Sharia in private arbitration, and he emphasized that the decisions of such arbitration would be subject to British law: "So far as the law is concerned," he explained, "those who live in this country are governed by English and Welsh law and subject to the jurisdiction of the English and Welsh courts."[12] As such, "it must be recognised . . . that any sanctions for a failure to comply with the agreed terms of the mediation would be drawn from the laws of England and Wales."[13]

What's more, Lord Phillips decisively rejected the idea that the notorious Sharia penalties of stoning for adultery and amputation for theft would be implemented in Britain: "There can be no question of such sanctions being applied to or by any Muslim who lives within this jurisdiction."[14]

If he hedged his statement about the use of Sharia for private arbitration so carefully, why were the Lord Chief Justice's remarks a victory for the advance of Sharia in Europe? The answer to this lies in the nature of Sharia itself. In Islamic law, private matters are not so easy to separate from public ones. If a woman is judged in a private Sharia court to be guilty of adultery, the Sharia penalty is stoning. The Lord Chief Justice spoke coolly of not allowing such punishments, but once the principle that Sharia can be applied in Britain is accepted, calls to increase its scope will begin immediately. The next step will be challenges to the principle Lord Phillips stated, that whenever British law and Sharia come into conflict, Sharia must give way. And given the prevailing multiculturalist relativism, soon enough that principle will give way also.

In his address, Lord Phillips praised the Archbishop of Canterbury, Rowan Williams, who famously said in February 2008 that it was "inevitable" that Sharia would come to Britain. An approach to law that simply said, "there's one law for everybody . . . —I think that's a bit of a danger," said the Archbishop.[15] He had apparently forgotten, if he ever knew, that the idea of "one law for everybody" was one of the great achievements of Judeo-Christian civilization, and was rooted in the idea of the dignity of all human beings as created in the image of God. Once a society discards the principle of "one law for everybody," it lays the groundwork for protected and privileged classes, and ends up inevitably with a tyranny in which some groups are denied basic rights.

If Muslims ever came to power in Britain, they themselves would enforce one law for everybody—a law that would reduce Lord Phillips, Archbishop Williams, and their fellow Britons to a second-class status of institutionalized discrimination. Meanwhile, they will, before too long, find that those they have been so earnestly accommodating are not mollified at all by their concessions, but have come up with new lists of demands. As there is always more Sharia to accommodate, at a certain point they will have to draw the line—or else consent without a struggle to the conquest of Britain.

The same blindness that afflicts Lord Phillips and Archbishop Williams now darkens the sight of all of Europe, as Michael Radu demonstrates in chilling detail in these pages. Europe is blind to its own Islamization and to its new concomitant status as an exporter of Islamic terrorism. As Western Europe becomes more and more Islamized, that new export will increasingly make itself known in America, as it already did on 9/11. "For the United States," Radu writes, "and especially its political elites, the fact that Europe is now a major incubator and exporter of Islamist terrorism should be a wake-up call."

"The Atlantic Ocean," Radu continues, "is wide." Yet maybe, given the harrowing truths that Radu brings to light in this book, not quite wide enough.

Robert Spencer is the director of Jihad Watch, a program of the David Horowitz Freedom Center, and the author of the *New York Times* best-sellers *The Politically Incorrect Guide to Islam (and the Crusades)* and *The Truth about Muhammad*.

INTRODUCTION

We might have expected, after the 9/11 attacks, that there would be a significant and growing number of academic studies on the issue of the radical and violent Islamist presence in the West—generally defined here as Western Europe and the United States. In fact, however, English-speaking academia still has little to say about the problem, even as popular volumes on Islam, Muslims, and the Muslim presence in the West multiply.

On the other hand, in continental Europe, especially in France, academics, journalists, former intelligence analysts, and politicians are all very active and interested in such issues and have produced a massive literature on them—too little of which has been translated into English.

This volume is intended to fill a gap in the American public's understanding of Islam and Islamism in the West. It draws from the author's decades of study of political violence in Latin America, sub-Saharan Africa, Turkey, and Western Europe; his European background; and his general conviction that political correctness, lack of practical field experience, and extreme specialization are all pernicious in the study of Islamist terrorism.

The most relevant bibliography is in European languages, and this raises complications as to the transliteration of Muslim names and terms. I have generally presented those names and terms as they are most frequently rendered in English. All translations from Spanish, French, and Italian, unless otherwise indicated, are the author's.

Terms like *jihad* and *Salafi* and their derivatives are usually used in this book in the sense understood by those associated with them. Thus, while the meaning of *jihad* is a much-debated issue, and the word has multiple meanings for Muslims, it has only one meaning for radical Islamists: acts of war in defense of true Islam. It is used herein exclusively in that sense. Salafism, most often defined as a literalist interpretation of Islam as it was during its first decades, is similarly used in that sense, which is agreed upon by most of its followers. This is important, because for radicals such definitions are a matter of belief, not of rational or logical argument. Some Arabic words (*takfir, jihad,* etc.) are not translated, either because they have already entered Western languages or because there is no satisfactory translation.

As a general proposition, it is unhelpful to engage in a protracted debate over the "correct" or "orthodox" meaning of such concepts, since for the radicals they have a very clear meaning, theologically and historically debatable though it may be. To debate meaning would be like arguing over the philosophical correctness of the various self-proclaimed Marxist-Leninist sects compared to Karl Marx's *Das Kapital*. That does not mean that attempts within the Muslim community to demonstrate the falsity of radical Islamists' interpretation of the faith are irrelevant or unnecessary, but only that they are not useful for the purpose of this study.

Nor, for similar reasons, is it very useful to engage in a debate over the link between the Islamic faith, in all its forms, and the beliefs and actions of jihadists. While it is abundantly clear that those beliefs are not shared by a majority of Muslims, it is also clear that for a growing minority they are seen as compatible with Islam's tenets.

As for the European Context, for at least three centuries the word "European" has not been simply a geographical term but has referred to an intellectual tradition, rooted in a combination of Greco-Roman, Christian, and Enlightenment elements and characterized by individualism and rationalism. Major deviations like Nazism, Fascism, and Communism notwithstanding, it is also associated with political democracy. To be sure, one may argue (and many do) that some of the intellectual traditions that long defined "Europe," primarily the Classical and Christian, have been lost in recent decades, to be replaced with a postmodern culture defined by agnosticism, multiculturalism, and a consequent loss of cultural identity.

Meanwhile, a growing number of Muslims are living in this changing Europe. Furthermore, many of these Muslims, if not a majority, in most European countries see themselves as living in, rather than being part of, "Europe." The distinction is important, if often avoided for reasons of political correctness. Thus, the British media's outcry over the phenomenon of British-born Muslim terrorists murdering "fellow Britons" is misplaced. The terrorists did what they did precisely because they did not see themselves as "Britons" but as true Muslims at war with the "infidel" country in which they lived. Thus, throughout this volume the term "European Muslims" has been avoided in favor of "Muslims in Europe." That is simply to recognize that in all European countries the integration, let alone the assimilation, of resident Muslim communities is, at best, a work in progress rather than a fact of life.

Finally, a geographical definition: By "Europe" this study means Western Europe alone, defined as the pre-2004 membership of the European Union plus non–EU members Norway and Switzerland. If this is "Eurocentrism," so be it.

CHAPTER ONE

Europe's Islamic Problem

"The jihadists regard Europe as an important venue for attacking Western interests. Extremist networks inside the extensive Muslim diasporas in Europe facilitate recruitment and staging for urban attacks, as illustrated by the 2004 Madrid and 2005 London bombings."

—From the U.S. National Intelligence Estimate, April 2006[1]

The culture of Islam—alien to most of Europe but proliferating there in recent decades—has seen its influence grow to the point that Islam is now sometimes called the second largest religion in Europe. In fact, in some countries (England being a notable example), practicing Muslims may be greater in number, and certainly in fervor, than practicing Christians.

Until the traumatic events of September 11, 2001, only in hushed, discreet tones was it admitted that Europe had an "Islamic problem." Analysis by most academics and journalists, not to mention politicians, was gingerly and scarce. Since then, and especially following the Madrid train bombings in March 2004, the slaying of Dutch filmmaker Theo van Gogh in November 2004, and the London Tube bombings in July 2005, public discourse spanning the range of the political spectrum has grown less fearful and even insistent.

In the United States, as in Europe, a number of popular articles and books proclaiming the decline, indeed the Islamization, of Europe have been published recently. Some choice examples are Claire Berlinski's *Menace in Europe: Why the Continent's Crisis Is America's Too* (Crown Forum, New York, 2006) and Bruce Bawer's equally heartfelt but better executed *While Europe Slept: How Radical Islam Is Destroying the West from Within* (Doubleday, New York, 2006). While these, along with voting patterns in the Netherlands, Germany, Denmark, and France (particularly in 2002 but also in 2007), point to a growing awareness of the problem in Europe, they have had very little impact on American academic commentary, as European cultural and political influence in the United States has generally declined.

Still, within Washington policy, intelligence, and military circles, there is increasing recognition that Europe's Islamic problem affects North America too. This is seen both in the support given by European nongovernmental organizations (NGOs) to American groups that oppose the U.S. government's handling of suspected terrorists, and in the real threat of terrorists landing on U.S. soil after having been "birthed" by European-based movements.

Europe is already wrestling with an internal cultural conflict, precipitated by slow economic growth, steeply declining birthrates, and what is looking more and more like a failed social model—the welfare state. Adding to this brew the tensions implicit in having accepted into their societies, in a relatively short span of time, a large number of adherents of a religion that has been at historic odds with Christendom was bound to result in mounting discord.

The sovereignty of the European nations is under attack both from above, by supranational institutions such as the EU and its associated arms (notably the European Court) and even the UN, and from below, in the form of regional secessionisms, particularly in Spain, Belgium, and the UK. The European Court in Strasbourg is problematic for national sovereignty because individuals may appeal the decisions of the courts of their own country, delaying justice and overriding national tradition, custom, and law—as well as, often, common sense.

This is the context in which I have undertaken this study. Europeans are increasingly discomfited by the specter, especially on their soil but also abroad, of Islam's adherents growing more and more numerous, militant, and assertive. When the growth of Islam is combined with Europe's loss of the religious foundation upon which its societies and identity were built, it is not surprising that the relative amity which prevailed until recently has become uneasy, even precarious. French journalists Eric Conan and Christian Makarian make the point that

> Between immigration and conversion, the Islamic religion acquires more and more adherents on the Old Continent. For decades the countries have counted on their power to attract and integrate so that new believers base themselves on their models. Now they realize that some demands question their own values. In France and her neighbors one has to analyze a confrontation that turns upside down a number of received ideas.[2]

The European Context

European analyses of Islamism are shaped by the changing economic, social, political, cultural, and demographic conditions and trends of the past four decades.

Like those of the United States and every other developed country, Europe's economies have changed from heavy industry to high technology and services, placing a higher premium on a better-educated work force. Thus Finland, previously known as a major exporter of timber, is now the home of the world's largest cell-phone maker, Nokia. The traditional coal mines of Belgium's Walloon region and northern France are now closed, as are most of those in Wales. Spain, once famous for Valencia oranges, Basque-country steel, and Asturian coal, is now known, especially in Latin America, for its omnipresent banks and telecommunication companies. Norway, once the land of fishermen and cross-country skiers, has become, ever since the great oil field was discovered in the North Sea in the late 1980s, one of the world's top oil exporters. The UK itself, the original land of the coal-based Industrial Revolution, is also a major oil exporter, from its side of that same oil field as Norway's. France is still a major exporter of wine, cheese, fashion, and cultural sophistication (real or imagined), but now also of nuclear-power technology, weapons, and aircraft.

A continuing problem in terms of efficiency and competitiveness is that a disproportionate number of companies are still state owned or controlled in most countries, France in particular. Combine that with the fact that in some countries—France, again, is a perfect example—a large part of the labor force is employed in the public sector, and the inevitable intersection of economics and politics becomes more obvious than anywhere but the poorest Third World countries.

Taxation in Europe remains very high—unsurprisingly, since it must pay for both the costs of running a massive welfare state, and the resulting inefficiency, bureaucracy, waste, and corruption. Tellingly, many European companies (including even some state-owned ones) are looking to move to cheaper, lower-taxed, and less regulated environments, like the new EU members, the Third World, and even the United States. Thus BMW, Mercedes, and Volkswagen have established plants in non-union, low-tax states like Tennessee, Georgia, and Alabama.

The welfare state in Europe has reached levels that might appear excessive even to the most "progressive" American liberal. Until very recently, an artist in the Netherlands had the right to have his work bought by the government, without regard to merit. A German could retire because of a medical condition, a psychological condition, and collect a large pension wherever he lived—hence the recent scandal of a retired, "depressed" bankrupt businessman living in Florida and having his apartment, maid, and golf-club membership fee paid by Berlin. The insistence of French public-sector unions on privileged retirement ages (as low as fifty) demonstrates the same kind of problem. Naturally, all higher education is, for all practical purposes, free in virtually all European countries.

Since all the European countries are functioning democracies, none of the above could have happened without the approval of a majority of voters over the course of many elections. The Swedish Socialists have been in power, with a few brief interruptions, since the 1920s. Communist parties were in the government, or supporting it, in France until a few years ago, and still are in Italy. Socialists or Social Democrats are or were recently among the major parties in Austria, Belgium, the Netherlands, Finland, Denmark, and Norway. In most of these countries, left-of-center parties are allied with, or depend on the votes of, highly organized and disciplined labor unions, always controlled by Socialists or, in France, Spain, and Italy, by Communists and Socialists.

THE EUROPEAN IDENTITY CRISIS

While radical Islamism threatens the peace and security of Europe, it simultaneously is threatened by the very identity of Europe, even if what exactly that identity is has become a critical and elusive question.

Europe is undergoing a massive debate about identity. During the past three decades, Western Europe—meaning Norway, Switzerland, and the 15 members of the pre-2004 European Union—has changed dramatically. It has changed in its demography, its social and political arrangements, and its cultural makeup.

The French and Dutch referenda defeating the proposed EU Constitution in 2005 were the most obvious examples of the recognition that there has been a profound change in Europe. The people of the Netherlands and France were registering in those referenda their frustration with the EU structure's having failed to address their concerns regarding the relationship between their national identities and the EU's position on immigration.

The cultural change in Western Europe can be attributed to the trend toward secularism, which is a matter of objective fact, whatever one's feelings about it. Christian Europeans have largely opted out of religious practice. The native forms of Christianity (Anglicanism in the UK; Lutheranism in Scandinavia, part of Germany, and the Netherlands; Catholicism everywhere else) are dying in Europe. The trend was noted in the results of a 2004 Europoll:

> Comparing the answers to the question "Do you identify with a particular religion, or do you associate with any religion?" between the age cohorts of 14–29, 30–49, and 50+ the answers clearly demonstrate a steady decline in religious identification strongly correlated to age—the younger the respondent, the less identification. Thus, for Western Europe as a whole, religious identification goes down from 76 percent among the over-50 respondents to 58 percent among the youngest.[3]

The number of French who say they attend church regularly has shrunk to 7.7 percent. Though 90 percent of Italians call themselves Catholic, fewer than 30 percent go to Mass. Only

14 percent of young Spaniards are churchgoers, a 50-percent decline in less than four years. The statistics from Brussels confirm this religious gap: More than a third of northern Europeans declare themselves without religion, compared to 1 percent among Turkish immigrants; among Western European believers only 25 percent of Catholics, Jews, and Protestants declare themselves practicing, compared to 72 percent of Muslims.[4]

Cardinal Cormac Murphy-O'Connor, former Archbishop of Westminster, has said that Christianity in Britain is "almost vanquished."[5] Cardinal Adrianis Simonis of Utrecht has stated that the "spiritual vacuity" of Dutch society has left the Netherlands open to an Islamic cultural takeover and that "Today we have discovered that we are disarmed in the face of the Islamic danger." When he linked this to "the spectacle of extreme moral decadence and spiritual decline" that Europe offered to young people,[6] he echoed what many Dutch conservatives—and many more Muslims—think. A salient difference between conservative Christians and radical Muslims is that the dwindling number of European Christians are hampered by a backward-facing view, while Muslims can look to a future of radical Islam, which seems to be on a global offensive.

When former French President Valéry Giscard d'Estaing was drafting the (ultimately rejected) European Constitution, he omitted any references to Christianity in the account of the making of Europe. No doubt his being French—"*Vive la laïcité!*"—had something to do with this. But equally without doubt, political correctness made such references untenable (even if history makes them obvious). That is, mentioning Pascal, Abelard, Abbot Suger, and Saint Louis—not only all Frenchmen, but also all Catholics—or the Catholic (though non-French) thinkers Aquinas, Bonaventura, Francis of Assisi, and so on, would have aggrieved atheists, secularists, and Muslims alike.

The Multicultural Ideal

The prevailing alternative to tradition is multiculturalism, which is intrinsically undemocratic, since it seeks to undermine the prevailing, majority culture. Europe's elites often adhere to the multicultural ethos, as evidenced by the protest by Renzo Guolo, sociologist and professor at the University of Padua. "We never thought of immigrants as people who would stay and live here for the future," Guolo wrote. "We just don't know how to build a society of different ethnic groups." He suggests allowing them easier access to citizenship. "How can we expect them to follow the law, unless we give them something to make them feel part of the nation?"[7]

Citizenship, then, is seen by such elites as an encouragement to newcomers to become part of the nation in which they live, rather than a reward for having proved adherence to prevailing values. However, not everyone in European public life accepts this view. One French member of parliament wrote:

> Our society changes, and that is good. Let us grant that she gets richer from the contributions of those who wish to live with us and whom we freely accept! But it must not be forgotten that living with us also means living like us. The first duty of immigrants is to respect the culture of the country that has received them. And this is not negotiable. . . . We are, we remain, "Gauls." Thus, it must be possible to affirm that to freely practice one's religion in places of worship does not mean the power to build new minarets, symbols of a conquering Islam and a sharia opposed to the laws of the Republic.[8]

A striking example of the unilateral concessions demanded by multiculturalism is the controversy over the cathedral at Córdoba. The Socialist mayor of Córdoba supported the petition of local Muslims to pray in the cathedral—at roughly the same time as the Socialist mayor of Granada, in the face of local opposition, allowed the construction of a mosque near the Alhambra. The bishop of Córdoba refused the demand, and quoted an explanation given in an interview by the Vatican's Archbishop Michael Fitzgerald, president of the Pontifical Council for Inter-Religious Dialogue, in 2004, when a similar demand was made:

> [Fitzgerald:] The Holy Father visited the Umayyad Mosque in Damascus, praying in front of the tomb of St. John the Baptist. But he did not ask to celebrate mass in the mosque. It is difficult to have Christians and Muslims mixing and sharing a common (civic and religious) life, despite being driven by wanting to go back in time or take some form of vengeance. One has to accept history and go forward....
>
> [Cervellera:] Government authorities in Córdoba suggest that the Church allow the Cathedral to be used also by Muslims—thus respecting, they say, "the building's universal value" and showing a Catholic Church which is "open and dialogical." What do you think?
>
> [Fitzgerald:] Spain's government authorities are trying to please all sectors of society. But perhaps they have not the necessary theological sensitivity to understand the Church's position. We, too, want to live in peace with persons of other religions. However, we don't want to be pushed, manipulated and go against the very rules of our faith.[9]

The axiom that Muslim demands for rights in Europe ought to be matched by an acceptance of corresponding obligations does not enjoy much support among the elites. The fact that mosques have gone up like mushrooms after a rainstorm from one end of the continent to the other has been tolerated, and no one asks whether the money to build them might have come from Saudi Arabia—where simply being a Christian is officially a crime.

The Muslim Dilemma

Islamic tradition has always been leery of the very idea of large numbers of Muslims leaving the *Dar al Islam*, "the abode of Islam," for the *Dar al Harb*—the rest of the world, translated literally as "the abode of war." The sheer numbers of those now living in the *Dar al Harb*, and particularly the fact that they do so of their own accord, are unprecedented.

Only a few times in the long history of Islam have large numbers of Muslims been forced to live under non-Muslim rule—in Spain at the end of the *reconquista*, between the 13th and 16th centuries, as Moriscos (converts, however unwilling, to Christianity[10]), and in the 20th century in the lost Balkan territories of the Ottomans (Bosnia, Albania), in Israel, and in India. In all those places, they were forced by military defeat to live in the *Dar al Harb*. Not so today, when the paradigm is of Muslims emigrating to the *Dar al Harb* of their own free will (or being born to parents who had emigrated).

In all those earlier cases, under the usual interpretations of Islamic law, Muslims were allowed a choice between (temporary) submission to their non-Muslim conquerors and emigration to Muslim countries. In Spain, most chose, or were forced to "choose," emigration. This was also the case in the parts of the Balkans where Muslims lived after World War I (Atatürk himself was born in Thessalonica, which today is Greece's second-largest city, and one with zero Muslim population) and in most parts of the British Raj in India.

Against this background rages the debate within Islam between the Salafists, fueled by Saudi Wahhabi oil money, and the moderates, who are numerous among older Muslims in Europe but who have few influential spokesmen. There is the Swiss-based scholar Tariq Ramadan (a grandson of Hassan al-

Banna, the founder of the Muslim Brotherhood), who favors a "European Islam" and whose ideas are popular with educated Muslims. (It is highly symbolic that his first name is the same as that of Tarik ibn Ziyad, the conqueror of Visigothic Iberia in 711 A.D.) Bassam Tibi, of the University of Göttingen in Germany, is a student of the conflicts between fundamentalism and modernity in Islam and is also well regarded by moderate, integrated Muslims.[11] The Qatar-based Yusuf al-Qaradawi, a leading member of the Muslim Brotherhood, opposes integration into the cultural majority, but he equally opposes jihadism.

But such voices are few, while the extreme Salafi model has gained ground among alienated Muslim youths who were born in Europe of non-European parents. Native Europeans fear that the Salafists are winning the hearts and minds of their enormous Muslim populations.

THE MUSLIM POPULATION IN EUROPE

Estimates of the number of Muslims in Europe range from official estimates of 12 million up to 20 million.[12] These Muslims have been described, routinely, as belonging to their adopted country's "second-largest religion," although that description is debatable. Muslims seem to have overtaken Jews two decades ago as the chief non-Christian minority in France, the Netherlands, Belgium, and Denmark.

While Portugal and Ireland still have insignificant numbers of Muslims, one million out of the Netherlands' 16 million people (nearly 6 percent) are Muslims, and some estimate France's Muslim population at 10 percent. By contrast, and outside our area of analysis, Muslims in the Czech Republic make up some 0.2 percent of the population and in Slovakia 0.01 percent.[13] So, clearly, the Muslim population is unevenly distributed throughout the European Union, as it is within individual Western European countries. Muslims are concentrated in a few regions in France—Ile de France/Saint-Denis in Greater Paris, Lille, Lyon, and Marseille. They are concentrated in Berlin and Ulm in Germany; in Greater London and Manchester in the UK; in Catalonia and Andalusia in Spain; in northern Flanders in Belgium; in Milan in Italy; and in the Netherlands' two largest cities, Amsterdam and Rotterdam. In some of these places Muslim children are already the majority in schools.

Some crucial caveats are in order. A Muslim in Europe is not necessarily a practicing Muslim, let alone a religious fundamentalist, Salafi or Wahhabi. The devotion to their faith of Muslims in Europe varies according to their national origin, the colonial past of their country of origin, their reasons for having emigrated, and their class and educational background. Here is a brief sketch of some of the differences:

- In the UK, the overwhelming majority of Muslims come from the Indian subcontinent—today's Pakistan, India, and Bangladesh. Among other things, that means that their radical elements are Deobandi. This movement, which originated in India in the latter part of the 19th century, advocates puritanism and the purging of Western influences, including the education of girls beyond the age of eight; its adherents include the Taliban. The traditions of Muslims from the subcontinent include arranged marriages and disdain/ hatred toward Hindus (a situation aggravated recently by the rise of Hindu fundamentalism in India).

- In France, the overwhelming majority of Muslims come from the Maghreb (the Islamic West—i.e., Morocco, Algeria, Tunisia, Mauritania, and Libya) and from Central/West Africa. The sub-Saharan Muslims, mostly

Malians, are far more likely to engage in female genital mutilation and polygamy than Maghrebis.

- In Germany, the Muslim community is largely divided between ethnic Turks and Kurds—both "Turkish" in national origin, but mutually hostile. Ethnic Turks, under Ankara's influence, tend to be moderate; Kurds are far more religiously conservative, and are more likely to engage in honor killings.

The Muslim reluctance to accept European values and customs *in Europe* makes for a dangerous cultural admixture. As I have said, I normally avoid the terms "European Muslims" and "European Islam." Some Muslim scholars, notably Bassam Tibi and Tariq Ramadan, do suggest that Muslims in Europe must adapt their faith to a different environment and establish a "European Islam" willing and able to live within the parameters of Europe's increasingly secular culture. They hope for (Tibi) or advocate (Ramadan) some temporary acceptance of local cultural habits. Many ordinary Muslims, perhaps a majority, already do live this way. But most Muslim organizations are more interested in imposing acceptance of their values and beliefs upon the host countries, usually under the pretext of "tolerance" and multiculturalism. Hence, in the most optimistic scenario, a "European Islam" is a work in progress—a very slow progress. For now, we are mostly talking about Muslims in Europe rather than European Muslims.

THE CULTURAL CHALLENGE OF ISLAMISM

Islamist battles, in matters not concerning Europe directly, were first fought on French soil in 1979, immediately following Ayatollah Khomeini's return to Iran from his Parisian exile, when loyalists of the Shah were targeted for assassination

in Paris. Since then, Muslims have committed further terrorist acts in Europe (the bombings in Madrid and London); have
volunteered to fight on behalf of Muslims in Bosnia, Kosovo,
Chechnya, Palestine, India, and Iraq; and have exported violence to non-European Western targets, such as the 9/11 attacks
against the United States. The majority populations in Europe
have finally begun to apprehend the existence of a problem.
Now, the issue has assumed political importance in several
countries.

A thorough look at this issue requires that one contend with
the problem from a cultural perspective, since ultimately, the
nexus of issues relating to the Muslim presence in Europe—
immigration, integration, and radicalization—is less a matter
of politics and policies than one of cultural attitudes. In fact,
the "root cause" of radical Islamism, as it has been expressed in
violence, is cultural—and not a reaction to the oft-cited racism,
poverty, discrimination, legacy of colonialism, etc. Terrorist acts
have been threatened or have taken place in the Netherlands,
Denmark, and England, among the most permissive and tolerant societies on earth. Indeed, so tolerant are Europeans that
they offer a safe haven to Islamists trying to escape secularism
at home, *viz.* the Turkish Islamist woman who was prohibited
from wearing the *hijab* in a university at home,* but who was
able to do so in an Austrian university.[14]

THE ISLAMIST CHALLENGE TO INTEGRATION

In Islam—whether one is discussing its Salafi, Sufi, Sunni, or
Shia interpretations—no distinction can be drawn, at least in
theory, between faith, law, and politics. Thus, the separation of
church and state is a profoundly alien idea to most Muslims. A

---

* In February 2008 Turkey's Parliament voted to lift this ban, but Turkey's highest
  court struck down the legislation.

major exception was the nationalist Mustafa Kemal Atatürk, who established the modern Turkish Republic on secular terms. But he and his successors are regarded as apostates by fundamentalist Muslims; idem the Tunisian regimes, starting in 1957, of Bourguiba and Ben Ali.

The basic concept that unites and motivates Muslim communities across national, even continental, boundaries is that of the *ummah*, the worldwide community of the Islamic faithful. In fact, the idea of a Caliphate—an Islamic state reaching from Indonesia all the way to Europe and beyond—is the very thing that drives Islamist radicals to commit such atrocities as the London bombings. It is also the concept of *ummah* solidarity that largely explains the frustrating (for non-Muslims) relative silence of Islamic moderates when faced with the brutality of the radicals in their midst.

Indeed, the very concept of a nation-state, based on common traditions, history, ethnicity, and language, is alien to many (though far from all) of Islam's followers, for whom only the *ummah*—rather than their country, their government, or their own local historical traditions—deserves their fealty. In spite of the many cases of inter-Muslim conflicts, both historically and in the present, the *ummah* is an idea that has rapidly gained adherents among Muslims in the West. In fact, there are two phenomena that can be observed among Muslim communities in Europe: (1) reluctance to condemn and act against Islamists, and (2) among Islamists, a close cooperation across ethnic lines (e.g., between Algerians and Moroccans in Spain and France).

THE ISLAMIST CHALLENGE TO DEMOCRACY

For Islamists like Yusuf al-Qaradawi of the Muslim Brotherhood and Ayman al-Zawahiri of Al-Qaeda, democracy itself is anti-Islamic, because of Islam's tenet that the laws of God supersede the laws of man. Even among more moderate Muslims, democracy has not been widely embraced. Turkey aside, there is not and never has been a lasting democratic system in a country with a Muslim majority. The democratic credentials of such countries as Pakistan, Bangladesh, Malaysia, and Indonesia are insecure at best. Even the few secular Muslim countries such as the People's Democratic Republic of Yemen (South Yemen, now defunct), Somalia under Siad Barre, and socialist Algeria and Tunisia were far from democratic.

In view of this historic and abiding dissonance between Islam and the Western democratic, secular model, it might be unrealistic to expect Muslim minorities in the West to be strong defenders of democracy. In any case, full cultural integration into the majority of Europe remains an elusive ideal, as we shall see.

The Culture Gap

The culture gap between Europeans and Muslims in Europe has grown, as has the economic one, at a frightening rate. For instance, the unemployment rate of UK Muslims is twice the national average, whereas among UK Hindus it is lower than the national average. The same applies to the Netherlands, where the rate of unemployment among the foreign-born (who are largely Moroccan or Turkish) is more than twice as high as for natives.[15]

Generally speaking, with a few exceptions—such as England's East African Indian community, forced into exile by Idi Amin's regime in the late 1970s—Muslim immigrants to Western Europe, and their sons and grandsons, tend to have consistently lower levels of employment and education than other immigrant groups and than the native populations.

There is a great disparity between Muslims and Surinamese in the Netherlands, between Muslims and Hindus in Britain, and even between Muslim and non-Muslim sub-Saharan blacks in France, suggesting that differences of religion, rather than class and social differences, or simple "racism," are to blame.

Islamic views of fundamental moral values are, simply, incompatible with those of contemporary Western European societies. Whether the issue is punishment for crime, including capital punishment, the status of women and homosexuals, freedom and equality of religion, or freedom of expression (especially when it comes to Islam itself and the Prophet Muhammad), Muslim—not just Islamist—values are in direct conflict with those of a secular, tolerant, increasingly amoral West. Conservatives in the West may agree with Muslims that their own culture is decadent and self-indulgent, but, especially in some European countries, that culture is in reality supported, democratically, by the majority.

Secondary issues, such as polygamy and female genital mutilation, are indeed secondary, because they are not essential to Islam. The problem, in Western eyes, is that the people usually associated with such practices are Muslims, and that adds to the general perception of Islam itself as alien and threatening.

While the European Left still avoids the question of whether Muslim beliefs and practices are in conflict with those of the native majority, or whether they should be celebrated as "diversity," the Right agrees with the Islamists in this respect: "It is not just the extreme right which considers Islam inassimilable in the European societies, but Islamists who proclaim that the application of egalitarian common law is impossible."[16]

Western Responses to Islamism

EUROPEAN RESPONSES

In a country that had not known politically motivated murder since the shooting of Willem van Oranje in 1584, the Dutch were jolted by two spectacular political assassinations at the turn of the 21st century. In 2002 the Netherlands' most popular politician, Pim Fortuyn, was shot to death by a Dutch animal-rights militant who cited as his reason Fortuyn's "scapegoating" of Muslims. (Fortuyn had called Islam a "backward culture" and favored closing the door to further immigration.) Then in 2004 Theo van Gogh was stabbed to death by a Muslim Moroccan immigrant. (Van Gogh's film *Submission* had chronicled the treatment of women in Muslim-majority societies.) Van Gogh's murder stirred up the normally placid Dutch into unheard-of acts: a few attacks against mosques (followed by more numerous Muslim retaliations against churches) and proposals for draconian legislation against radical Muslim clerics and mosques. The Netherlands, one of the world's most permissive and tolerant countries, entered a period of intense self-examination, the main conclusion of which, shared by Socialists, Liberals, and others, seems to be that multiculturalism has failed to integrate recent (mostly Muslim) immigrants.

For France and the United Kingdom, both until recently imperial powers in the Muslim world, contacts with Muslims—as enemies, as colonial subjects, and more recently as immigrants—go back for many years. Thus, their treatment of Muslims has been largely tolerant and accepting. From time to time, tensions have erupted, but the official line remained one of acceptance. British-born Muslims have been involved in suicide terrorism in Israel and have been killed or captured while fighting on the Islamist side in Afghanistan, Chechnya, and

Iraq, as have French-born Muslims, and citizens of both countries have been involved in attempted attacks on the United
States. Belgian-based Islamic terrorists, with help from British-
based clerics, assassinated the leader of the anti-Taliban forces
in Afghanistan, Ahmed Shah Massoud, just prior to September
11; and for a number of years imams based in the UK provided
religious cover and legitimacy via *fatwas* (authoritative statements by recognized religious scholars) for atrocities committed by Islamist groups in Algeria and Yemen.

A series of Iranian-sponsored assassinations of exiled opponents of the Islamist regime in Tehran plagued France for several years starting in 1970, and another wave of Islamist terrorism in metropolitan France followed the beginning of the civil
war in Algeria between Islamists and the military in the mid-
1990s. These acts of violence grabbed the international media
spotlight. Nevertheless, apart from a handful of journalists and
intelligence experts, there was, until recently, little mention of
the link between Muslim communities in Europe and Islamist
terrorism.[17] Politicians, especially those of mainstream political
parties, have consistently avoided discussing, let alone acting
on, the security problem raised by the growing Muslim presence in Europe. Their negligence led directly to the spectacular
9/11 attacks in the United States.

AMERICAN POPULAR RESPONSES

The 9/11 attacks were planned in Hamburg, Germany, by a multinational group of Arab Muslims, most of whom had lived
there for a number of years, either as students or posing as students. Following the attacks, American Muslims initially feared
a violent backlash, a fear that was not borne out—although,
in a grisly case of mistaken identity, an American of Sikh origin was killed in Arizona a few days after the event. Although

generally the American population remained silent on the subject of whether Muslims in the United States belonged to the
Islamist strain, the subject of Islamism made its way into the
official dialogue in October 2006 when Senator Rick Santorum
(R. Pa.) warned against the dangers of "Islamic fascism," a color-
ful description that drew support from his traditionalist base
and ridicule from moderates and leftists. Although Santorum
later lost his seat, the term he coined became commonly used
by U.S. conservatives—and by President Bush.

Still, for most Americans, if they consider the issue of
Muslims in Europe at all, it is in the context of national security. For the European countries, it poses a far more extensive
set of problems and dilemmas, having to do with national culture, inter-ethnic relations, and a new role for religion in societies where religion has been growing less and less relevant for
many decades.

One reason for the difference is the orders of magnitude of
the Muslim populations on the two sides of the Atlantic. The
pre-2004 EU countries have around 15 million Muslims, in a
population of some 320 million; the United States, with 300 million inhabitants, has a Muslim population generally estimated
at 3 to 4 million. Most Muslims in Europe are immigrants or
descendants of immigrants from Muslim majority countries;
American Muslims include a very large percentage of native
black converts. In Europe, Arabs are assumed to be Muslim;
not so in the United States: There are perhaps twice as many
Catholic (including Maronite) as Muslim Arab-Americans. In
the U.S., non-black Muslims tend to be among the most successful immigrant groups in terms of education and income,
while in Europe, with some exceptions in the UK, they tend
to be at the bottom of the social, economic, and educational

heap. Finally, the Muslim region of North Africa is a neighbor to Europe, the same way that Mexico is to the United States, while the United States is separated from the Muslim world by an ocean on either side.

Historically, the pre-9/11 popular perceptions of immigrant Muslims in the United States were not that different from perceptions of any other immigrant group—whether Irish, Poles, or Jews. That is clearly not the case in most of Europe.

DIVERGENT ANALYSES OF ISLAMISM

The asymmetry in the magnitude of the Muslim communities on the two sides of the Atlantic also explains the enormous differences in the attention given to the issue in America and in Europe. Whereas in the United States, at least prior to 9/11, native Muslims were seldom seen, heard, or examined by politicians and academics, in Europe the question has received much official and academic, as well as popular, comment. The quantity of academic, media, and political research on the two continents bears directly on its quality.

Prior to 9/11, U.S. academic research on Islamist radicalism was scant—much as was academic research on Eastern European Communism prior to 1989, and for the same reasons: ideological bias, fear of losing access, and the wish to avoid running afoul of political correctness. In France, on the other hand, serious academic study was prompted by past events on French soil, the presence of Muslim academics, and concerns of the government—whose funds pay for virtually all research. That fact explains why this study has so many more French-language bibliographical citations than English-language.

Even today—years after 9/11, and with a number of disturbing events in the interim—American academics are mostly silent about radical Islamism in Europe (or at home). The bulk of research on these issues is being carried out in think tanks rather than in academia.

The lack of serious examination of the role and impact of Islam in Europe is due in large part to a deliberate effort by the elites—politicians, media, academics, and the array of NGOs whose influence extends over them all—to keep these issues out of the public discourse. The opinions of the person in the street are neither sought nor seriously considered, and when they emerge in the press or in political debate, the citizens' views are usually described as ignorant and racist. Because the elites view measures such as limiting the numbers of immigrants, or calling for integration, as being *ipso facto* racist, intolerant, and biased, parties and politicians advocating them are automatically labeled as such—whatever might be their true program.

Academic study of this subject, furthermore, is fraught with concerns of political correctness. A good example of the inanity that is sometimes seen in academic discourse is the following pearl from a website on international migration maintained by the University of California at Davis:

> There is no obvious relationship between the percentage of foreigners in European populations and the unemployment rate—Portugal had relatively few foreigners (one percent) and a low unemployment rate (four percent), while Belgium had about nine percent foreigners, and 10 percent unemployment. These examples imply that the more foreigners, the more unemployment.[18] [Emphasis added.]

CHAPTER TWO

Immigration and Integration

"Of generosity, of respect of fundamental rights, of international solidarity, there is no question any more. The only thing that matters is the egoist interest of France."

—L'Humanité *on illegal immigrants* [1]

Muslim Immigration to Europe

LATE-20TH-CENTURY HISTORY

It is impossible to separate the issue of Islam and Islamism in Europe from that of immigration. Virtually all Muslims in Europe are relatively recent immigrants, or their immediate descendants. These communities are a favorite recruiting ground for Islamists, and make up a significant element in terrorist operations in Europe.[2] The country of origin, size, and degree of integration of an immigrant population are directly related to the degree to which that population displays extremist tendencies. The greater the numbers of immigrants of a given population, the greater the difficulties of integrating them into the larger society—as evidenced by the case of Hispanic immigration to the United States.

The epigraph for this chapter is from the newspaper of the French Communist Party, but it typifies an attitude that was commonly held until just a few years ago throughout Europe: The "rights" of immigrants, legal or otherwise; woolly notions of "international solidarity"; and rejection of "egoist" national interests were the dominant concepts in immigration policy— together with a promiscuous definition of political asylum. In France until 2006 the *official* immigration policy was to grant permanent legal residence, leading to citizenship, to illegal immigrants who had somehow managed to evade the law for ten years.

Across Europe, also until just after 9/11, the very idea of restrictions on immigration, especially from Third World countries, was considered the province of the politically unsavory "far Right"—and thus, *ipso facto*, "racist" and "discriminatory." Yet economic, social, political, and security considerations have forced a slow but inexorable scrutiny of immigration policy.

Third World immigration to Europe had its roots in the labor shortage of the 1960s, when rapid economic growth outpaced domestic labor supplies, especially in sectors requiring unskilled labor: construction, manufacturing, and domestic work. When economic conditions changed during the 1970s, economic immigration stagnated and regressed, almost to the point of ceasing altogether. The paradigm of immigration as the solution to Europe's labor needs was supplanted by immigration based on humanitarian considerations, such as political asylum and family reunification—all intended, perhaps, to cleanse Europe from the stain of the recent past of totalitarian abuses of minorities. Whatever the motivating force of these changes, they brought about a large-scale *de facto* tolerance of non-economic, often illegal immigration, even in massive numbers. For a variety of reasons, such as the colonial past (France, the United Kingdom) or geographical proximity (Germany), most such immigrants were Muslims.

FALLACIES CONCERNING IMMIGRATION

Two basic assumptions regarding Muslim immigration to Europe have both been proven wrong. The first was that immigrants would choose to return home, eventually; the second, that later waves of immigrants would follow essentially the same course as earlier, non-Muslim ones—i.e., that North Africans and Turks would assimilate in much the same fashion as Portuguese or Italians did in France. The latter assumption, which Claude Imbert of *Le Point* called "historical blindness,"[3] is closely related to the tenets of multiculturalism, which holds that, all cultures being equal, one must expect that members of all cultures will behave in the same way.

The standard wisdom in the 1960s—of the media, in academic discourse (in both Europe and America), and among the immigrants themselves—was that these economic immigrants were being invited to Europe for a temporary stay; they were even called "guest workers." Yet, so far from returning, these Muslim immigrants have brought large numbers of their extended families to the lands of the infidels. Or, as a German saying put it, "We wanted labor and we got people."

A 2005 Pew study of Muslims in Europe examined the misunderstandings underlying most European analyses of Muslim immigration:

> Muslims still only make up a small portion of Europe's population, no more than about 5 percent of the EU's more than 425 million people. But most demographers predict that that number will increase dramatically in the coming decades—to 10 percent as early as 2020. Indeed, if the past is any guide, that estimate may be low, since the size of the European Muslim community has tripled in the last 30 years.

This rapid growth is caused both by immigration and by high Muslim birthrates. . . .

"Given the age spread of the Muslim population, their numbers would grow quite a bit even if immigration stopped tomorrow," says Furman University Professor Brent Nelsen, an expert on religion in Europe.

Meanwhile, low native birthrates throughout the continent will further increase the Muslim share of the entire population. . . . With Europe's aging population putting an increasing strain on the continent's generous health and pension schemes, much greater immigration may be necessary to maintain a workforce large enough to pay benefits to retirees.

Waiting to fill this need are an estimated 300 million Muslims under the age of 20 who are living along the Mediterranean's "southern rim"   —North Africa and the Middle East.[4]

Looking at the Numbers

Prior to 1986, the number of Polish, Spanish, or Portuguese immigrants to the EU—whether professionals, laborers, or domestic personnel—was limited to tens of thousands per year, as was the number of "Yugoslav" (i.e., Croat, Serb, Kosovar Albanian) immigrants to Germany. By contrast, today, the numbers of Muslim immigrants, legal or otherwise, are in the hundreds of thousands annually, and many millions are already settled.

In Italy, the 2003 Fini-Bossi law regularized 690,000 illegal immigrants; in 2006 the new leftist Italian government did the same with another 517,000 non-EU illegals[5]—most of them North Africans. Similarly, the 2005 Spanish amnesty involved some 700,000 people (mostly Ecuadorans, Romanians, and Moroccans).[6] The following table gives some approximate idea of the numbers involved—approximate because the figures, especially for illegal immigrants, are inevitably unreliable and rapidly outdated.

TABLE I. EUROPE'S MUSLIM COMMUNITIES

Country	Muslim Population as of 1990	Percentage of Total Population	Principal Countries of Origin	Muslim Population as of 2005	Percentage of Total Population	Growth
Belgium	335,000	3.4	Morocco, Turkey	371,000	3.6	+36,000
Denmark	55,000	1.0	Morocco, Somalia, Turkey	114,000	2.1	+59,000
France	4 million	7.0	Algeria, Morocco	5 million	8.2	+1 million
Germany	2.9 million	3.6	Turkey	3.7 Million	4.5	+800,000
Italy	600,000	1.1	Morocco, Albania	1 million	1.8	+400,000
Netherlands	533,000	3.6	Turkey, Morocco	804,000	4.9	+271,000
Spain	170,000	0.5	Morocco	427,000	1.0	+257,000
Sweden	137,000	1.6	Turkey, SE Asia	179,000	2.0	+42,000
UK	1.05 million	1.9	Africa, SE Asia, Middle East	1.64 million	2.2	+590,000

Source: "Europe's Muslim Communites," *Wall Street Journal* online

There are some striking elements in these figures. First, the spectacular growth in the total numbers of Muslims in all countries—more than double in Spain; by roughly a million people in France. Second, the significant increase in their general share of the total population—at a time when most of the countries of Western Europe, except France, have negative or, at best, stagnant natural growth rates. Even in France, most of the growth is due to the natural growth of the Muslim population. According to Eurostat, the total population of the EU will reach 470 million in 2025, but *the increase will be almost entirely due to foreign migration. Without it, by 2025 deaths would outnumber births by 5 million a year.* Eurostat anticipates a reduction of the EU population after 2025, to 450 million in 2050. In countries like Denmark and Sweden, where virtually the entire

Muslim population is made up of asylum and refugee cases—rather than, as in France, the UK, or the Netherlands, of immigrant descendants—the immigration impact will be greater still.[7] While that does not mean that some rather panicky projections of a Muslim-majority Western Europe within the next decades are credible,[8] for reasons developed below, neither is the frequent disregard of the importance of demography a realistic approach.

EUROPEAN RESPONSES TO IMMIGRATION

The questions being asked by more and more European voters and some governments are essentially these: In *economic* terms, does Europe need more Kurds, Turks, North Africans, or Pakistanis? In *financial* terms, can Europe afford them and their families? In *cultural* terms, could Europe integrate more? In *moral* terms, does Europe have an obligation to take them? And, finally, in *practical* terms, what can be done about the extraordinary levels of abuse of such concepts as political asylum and refugee status?

As for immigration now, here is the case of Malta, reported by the BBC:

> The islands of Malta are small, but full. Almost 400,000 people live there, making it the third most densely populated country on earth. The buildings are full of newly arrived immigrants, their washing hanging from the windows. The grounds are packed with military tents housing more of the asylum-seekers. In the first 10 months of 2005, more than 1,500 have come from Africa. . . . The increase of 1,500 is the equivalent of almost a quarter of a million arriving in the United Kingdom in 10 months. That is why the Maltese government is asking for help.[9]

A similar phenomenon has taken place in the Italian island of Lampedusa and in the Spanish Canary Islands, which have also seen quantum leaps in the numbers of (mostly Muslim) people who hope to settle in the EU. The issue in these islands—and in the Spanish enclaves of Ceuta and Melilla, located across the Strait of Gibraltar in Morocco—is not local. The invaders seek access not to Fuerteventura, Ceuta, or Lampedusa but to continental Spain and Italy, or to France or Belgium. Worse still—but easy to understand, considering the sympathetic Third Worldism of European academics and left-of-center politicians—the most articulate illegal migrants convince themselves that they have a right to break European laws.

Hence, a Senegalese illegal immigrant in Mauritania complaining about obstacles to his entering the EU: "Why do Europeans come to Senegal for vacations, sexual tourism, with corrupt companies, but we cannot go to work in Europe?"[10] For him and many like him, European investments in Senegal's few resources—tourism most of all ("sexual" tourism in Muslim Senegal is this individual's convenient fantasy)—are not a reason to stay at home and help one's own country, but a pretext to seek the welfare state of the "colonialist" Europeans. Even more ironic is the fact that for many Europeans investment in and tourism to Africa are seen as means to reduce poverty and emigration there. But help becomes a reason for guilt.

That immigrants often need, and obtain, access to the EU's generous welfare system is understood by any serious student of this subject, and manipulated by the "progressive" ones. As a British journalist put it:

> [M]ost immigrants who arrive in Britain from outside the EU, and who hope to settle permanently here, are not highly skilled. Some have no skills at all. Many female immigrants do not want to work in paid employment, or are actively discouraged from seeking it by their spouses and families.[11]

The picture is quite similar in most European countries. Hence the increasingly similar responses to the problem throughout Europe.

In **France** the 2005 clash over then Interior Minister Nicolas Sarkozy's proposed reform of immigration laws—conditioning family reunification on the immigrants' ability to make a living from work rather than welfare checks and giving preference to skilled immigrants—was ultimately a battle between ideologies. Jean-Pierre Richer, president of Secours Catholique, along with assorted human-rights spokesmen, argued that the reform proposals were "utilitarian"[12] rather than ethical, and that they did not take into account that the immigration problem is international rather than peculiarly French. As if there were no ethical dimension to the prospect of admitting more unskilled workers in a country with 9.6 percent unemployment and with an already overextended welfare state, not to mention the cultural impact of more Third World immigrants! Sarkozy was focusing on concerns such as the national interest and the economic well-being of France, while the opposition disguised its disregard for those goals behind a vague emotional solidarity with the Third World.

In the **Netherlands**, on March 15, 2006, the government introduced new requirements for would-be immigrants, including a large application fee and a compulsory viewing of a video of life in the Netherlands—gays kissing and nude women included. The reaction from some multicultural quarters was significant. "This isn't education, it's provocation," said Abdou Menebhi, chairman of Emcemo, a Moroccan Muslim interest group in Amsterdam. "The new law has one goal: to stop the flow of immigrants, especially by Muslims from countries like Morocco and Turkey."[13] In so stating, he confirmed the very reasons that led the government to introduce the film.

At about the same time, the **German** state of Hesse introduced a questionnaire about German culture for would-be
immigrants, including "name three German philosophers; a
poem by Goethe; a German Nobel Prize winner; and the doctor
who discovered the cholera virus." That's because, as Volker
Bouffier, the state's interior minister, said, "Anyone who wants
to acquire German citizenship should have gone through an
extensive consideration of our country and our system of values and have accepted them. The government has to make certain that applicants want to be German citizens—and not just
outsiders who live at home in a parallel society." This opinion was shared by Chancellor Angela Merkel: "The state can
ask whether citizenship choice is a conscious choice or not."[14]
However, national immigration rules can be decided only by
consensus among the *Länder*, and it is unlikely that the rules
proposed by Hesse (and Baden-Württemberg) will be accepted at the national level or in the states with a strong Social
Democratic presence, like Schleswig-Holstein.

Political Asylum: Europe's Achilles' Heel

In an absurd turn of events, radical Islamists forced to flee their
own countries because of their jihadist views and actions have
consistently found refuge in Europe. The cases of the Kurdish
Mullah Krekar—founder of the Ansar al-Islam terrorist group—
in Norway and of the Egyptian Abu Hamza, the Jordanian Abu
Qatada, and the Syrian Omar Bakri—all deeply involved in
terrorist activities—in the UK are only the most prominent;
there are many others in other countries. Furthermore, known
or suspected practitioners of jihad—veterans of Afghanistan,
Bosnia, Chechnya, Algeria, Egypt, Kashmir, Turkey—have also
found safe haven by the hundreds in Europe, again as refugees
or asylum seekers.[15]

Article 1 of the 1951 United Nations Convention Relating to the Status of Refugees defines a refugee as "A person who is outside his/her country of nationality or habitual residence; has a well-founded fear of persecution because of his/her race, religion, nationality, membership in a particular social group or political opinion; and is unable or unwilling to avail himself/ herself of the protection of that country, or to return there, for fear of persecution."[16]

British courts in particular have repeatedly failed to notice the all too common connection between asylum abuse and terrorism. The cases of two of the perpetrators of a second, failed terrorist attack on London's transportation system (on July 21, 2005, two weeks after the 7/7 Tube bombings) are far from unique. The convicted leader of the group, known as Osman Hussain, a naturalized British citizen, turned out to be not a Somali refugee, as he had claimed when entering the UK, but an Ethiopian whose real name was Hamdi Isaac. However, since the protracted chaos in Somalia has attracted international attention and sympathy, he manipulated those circumstances and posed as Somali.[17]

The case of Yacine Hassan Omar is equally revealing. Hassan Omar is a Somali who arrived in Britain in 1992 at age 11 with his elder sister and her husband, all seeking asylum. The following year he was taken into the care of social services. After spending the next seven years in various foster homes, Omar was assessed as a "vulnerable young adult." Under a "leaving care" scheme operated by social services, at age 18 he was given a one-bedroom flat in north London.[18] In other words, Hassan Omar had lived on public welfare for nearly half his life, and all efforts at "integration" had failed.

The United Nations—an entity taken far more seriously in Europe than in the United States—plays a large role in encouraging such abuse of the asylum and refugee provisions, always to the advantage of the Third World majority of its members. Thus, General Assembly resolution 2312 of 1967 claimed:

> Mindful of the Universal Declaration of Human Rights, which declares in article 14 that: "1. Everyone has the right to seek and to enjoy in other countries asylum from persecution" . . . [n]o person . . . shall be subjected to measures such as rejection at the frontier or, if he has already entered the territory in which he seeks asylum, expulsion or compulsory return to any State where he may be subjected to persecution.[19]

This kind of language, combined with modern political correctness, has led to EU legislation encouraging, indeed mandating, asylum abuse. In 2005 a gang of Somali asylum seekers murdered one British policewoman and seriously wounded another. Four were arrested and put on trial, but a fifth, known as Mustaf Jama, escaped arrest and fled the country wearing a *niqab*—the garb (once supported in court by Tony Blair's lawyer wife) that covers the body and the entire face except the eyes, not allowing even for gender distinction. Jama was described as a Somali asylum seeker who had gained entry to Britain on a false passport. He had not been deported because Somalia was considered to be too dangerous a place for him, even though he had served four jail terms in the six years since his arrival in the UK and had 21 criminal convictions there, for, among other things, firearms offenses. Hence, as a British journalist put it, "his own safety was clearly given a higher priority than that of the potential victims of his criminality."[20] Interestingly, Jama fled to . . . Somalia, where his influential clan protected him. He was recently captured, returned to Britain, and imprisoned.[21] So much for asylum and the ban on compulsory return!

Such cases are all too common. In early 2003, Wali Khan Ahmadzai, a former Taliban intelligence officer and son of a senior minister of the deposed Taliban regime, was given indefinite leave to remain in Britain after entering the country illegally, hidden in a container ship. The reason? "He told the Home Office that his position in the Taliban made it impossible for him to return to Kabul without fear of torture and even death." To help with his case, he received "free" (i.e., at taxpayers' expense) legal aid. Nor was he alone. Lawyers disclosed that at least two other Taliban fighters' asylum applications were being processed, at a time when British soldiers were dying in Afghanistan fighting against remnants of the Taliban.[22] One may seriously ask whether such legal reasoning would be applied if the applicants had been Nazis from Paraguay.

Still, when it comes to Third World refugees, few questions are raised. As Minoo Jalali, the director of Refugee Action, a charity that assists asylum seekers, correctly described the law: "If they can prove that they face a risk of persecution and torture in their home country then they could get asylum here. . . . The law states that they are entitled to it. It is irrelevant what their beliefs are, by law we cannot send someone back if they are in danger of their life."[23] Ahmadzai himself does not try to hide the contradictions. He told a reporter, "I live here but I still think America and Britain are enemies of the Afghanistan people and Muslim people. . . . But I don't want to fight anymore. I just want the chance to live in peace and safety and to be a good Muslim." So he is saying that it is easier for him to be "a good Muslim" in the country of the enemy than in Afghanistan. The obvious irony that British soldiers were dying fighting the comrades of Wali Khan Ahmadzai in Afghanistan, while paying taxes to keep him happy in Britain, was clearly missed in London.

Also illustrative is the case of the Franco-Algerian citizen officially known only as "MK." Actually MK is Rachid Ramda, a member of the Algerian GIA (*Groupe Islamique Armé*). Ramda had fled to the UK in 1992, after being convicted in France of terrorist activities. He was protected by English courts since 1995 despite his known ties with Al-Qaeda, his training in Afghanistan and Pakistan, and proven close ties with at least 12 suspected extremists in Britain since 1999. Finally, in 2006, authorities moved to deport him to France. When Sir Herman Ouseley, head of the Special Immigration Appeals Commission, asked MK why he objected to deportation, his answer was that it would "disrupt my life."[24] Inconvenient indeed!

It is politically incorrect to attempt to assess the seriousness of a claim for asylum, and even worse to make distinctions on the basis of the immigrant's background.[25] Why would an Iranian ask for asylum in Europe? He may well be a victim of the Islamist theocratic regime—either as middle class, or as Christian or Bahai, and so on. On the other hand, Somalis, coming from a dysfunctional political culture, are disproportionately involved in violence, welfare dependent, and likely to exhibit adaptation problems anywhere—whether Britain, the Netherlands, or . . . Minnesota. The superior ability of Iranians to adapt has much to do with their social status and education back home, and less to do with their religion, as is also the case with East African Asians in Britain—but that is considered irrelevant. Finally, why would Algerians ask for asylum in cold, rainy Britain rather than France, where millions of their compatriots live? Perhaps because the French know and care who many of them are—remnants of the defeated, genocidal GIA—and the British do not?

Obstacles to Integration and Assimilation

"I do not identify myself as a Dane or an Algerian. I identify myself as a Muslim, and I will shoot anybody who fights against the cause of Allah on the battlefield."

—Slimane Hadj Abderrahmane, Danish citizen,
former Guantanamo detainee[26]

"I understood that I was different, that I was not French, that I would never become French and that I had no business trying to become French either . . . I was proud of my new Muslim identity. Not to be French, to be Muslim, just that: Algerian too, but, above all, Muslim. I was rid of the malaise from which I had suffered and all of a sudden I felt good about myself: no more impossible dreams, no more desire to become part of this France that did not want me. And, above all, I started to nourish a tremendous hatred toward the Fascist regime that had rejected the vote of the Algerian people for Islamic rule."

—"Ousman," an Algerian-born Islamist in French prison[27]

"I am not French, I'm a sworn enemy of France; I am a Muslim."

—Convicted Al-Qaeda terrorist Zacarias Moussaoui[28]

Such sentiments are increasingly common among Islamists, indeed among Muslims of various origins and backgrounds living in Europe. However, it is also true that there are many claims like that of Mohammed Mumtaz Tanweer, the father of one of the 7/7 London suicide bombers, Shehzad Tanweer, at his son's funeral (in a Pakistani village): "My son was more British than anything. God knows why he carried out this act." Mumtaz Tanweer declared that he and his family remained "mystified" by his son's motivation. However, he also accused the British media of "highly biased" and "treacherous" accounts of the bombings and of "hate reporting" against Muslims: "They have called us murderers, killers, slaughterers and assassins. What worse can they do?"[29] Indeed. That reaction suggests that among the older generation of Muslims in Europe, their children's rejection of integration remains misunderstood, or is missed altogether. It is also a rather typical mixture of defiant Muslim rejection of Europeans as the "others" ("They"), loud claims to victimhood, and offense at any accusation that there is any, any link at all between Islam and Islamist terrorism. All of which raises the obvious question: How integrated are Muslims in Europe, including the "moderates"? A question which has not one clear answer but many. It depends on how the question is posed, and on what group of Muslims and what country it is asked about.

Among the reasons for lack of integration, some are traditional, applying to immigrants in general. For example, in many cities there are large "islands" of unassimilated immigrants—and, one may add, those islands are spreading with the growing numbers of recent arrivals.[30] In the case of Muslims in Europe there is also the religious identity of the group. Their countries of origin tend to have relatively homogeneous religious environments, leading to a lack of contact with or understanding of religious diversity and tolerance. This factor is often reproduced in the European diaspora.

Second, while second-generation immigrants learn the local language, that often separates them from their parents, but this in itself is not usually enough to bring them closer to the mainstream.

There are many reasons for the difficulties in integration, let alone assimilation, including the conservatism of many Muslim communities and the lack of pressure from the majority cultures to adapt and change. Recently, another powerful element has intervened to make integration even more difficult: revivalist currents in Islam in general, and Salafist trends in particular. Moreover, that element has proven to be effective in recruiting and indoctrinating Muslims in Europe for violent action. It also has an impact on existing Muslim organizations not normally considered radical, making them less supportive of integration.

Even the Muslim Council of Britain (MCB), seen by the British government as its main ally in combatting Islamist terrorism, has a less than unambiguous view of Muslim integration. Indeed, in a recent paper it stated that "Muslims balance a sense of allegiance to the global Muslim community with responsibilities of citizenship to their nation state—the *ummah* and *qawm* respectively in Islamic terminology."[31] Balance? How should an ordinary Muslim in Brixton, Birmingham, or London's Tower Hamlets interpret that, other than that he has a dual identity, loyalty, and allegiance?

None of that is surprising, since Muslim ideologues receive powerful support from European "experts." For example, German psychoanalyst Horst-Eberhard Richter has written: "The West should desist from engaging in all provocations that produce feelings of debasement and humiliation . . . We should show greater respect for the cultural identity of Muslim countries. . . . For Muslims, it is important to be recognized and respected as equals." The German journalist Henryk Broder counters:

> Richter neglects to describe what this partnership might look like. Does achieving such equality mean that we should set up separate sections for women on buses, as is the custom in Saudi Arabia? Should the marrying age for girls be reduced to 12, as is the case in Iran? And should death by stoning be our punishment for adultery, as Shariah law demands? What else could the West do to show its respect for the cultural identity of Islamic countries? Would it be sufficient to allow Horst-Eberhard Richter to decide whether, for example, a wet-T-shirt contest in a German city rises to a level of criminal provocation that could cause the Muslim faithful in Hyderabad to feel debased and humiliated?[32]

Nor is increased integration of Muslims in Europe encouraged when, for example, on February 10, 2008, in front of a Turkish crowd of 20,000 in Cologne, Turkish Prime Minister Recep Tayyip Erdogan told the multitude: "I understand that you are sensitive about the issue of assimilation. . . . No one can demand that from you. . . . It is your natural right to teach your children their mother tongue."[33] This provoked a direct riposte from German Chancellor Angela Merkel: "If they are citizens. . . their loyalties are then to the German state."[34] But Erdogan is not unique, as was pointed out on Radio Netherlands:

> It's beginning to take on the appearance of a trend. While European immigration ministers emphasize the need for migrants to integrate—and preferably even assimilate— politicians from their countries of origin underline the need for migrants to preserve their cultural identity. [Moroccan Minister for Moroccan Communities Abroad Mohammed] Ameur recently revealed Morocco's new migrant policy. "The Moroccan community abroad," he argued, "should be regarded as our country's 17th province."[35]

Dutch officials, and even some Moroccans in the Netherlands, especially those of Berber origin, complained, but the fact remains that nothing is done, by Germany or the Netherlands, to convince the countries of origin of their Muslim immigrants that the latter are now living in Europe—and thus need to adapt to the cultural and legal realities there.

ALIEN ORTHODOXY IN SECULAR SOCIETIES

Diasporas tend to be more culturally and politically conservative than the majority in the countries they originated from—a universal phenomenon, applicable to Eastern European refugees in the West during the Cold War and to Cubans in the United States today. To some extent that is self-preservation in a culturally alien environment, an attempt to retain group identity, and to some extent, in the West, a manifestation of greater freedom of expression. The Muslims in the European diaspora are no exception. They are often more openly orthodox and conservative than their cousins in their countries of origin—Turks and Tunisians are two obvious examples. The difference is that, unlike most Third World or ex-Communist diasporas, second- or third-generation Muslims in Europe are more attached to their religious (as distinct from ethnic) identity than their parents or grandparents.

There are two main reasons for this phenomenon. First, most Muslims in Europe came from the more conservative (or backward) areas of their original countries, be it Eastern Anatolia, Kashmir, or the Rif of Morocco—pushed out, in a vicious circle, by the poverty produced, in large part, by cultural conservatism.[36] This fact was recognized by then Dutch Foreign Minister Bernard Bot in January 2006 when he observed that "The problem is that the Turks who settled in the Netherlands in the '60s were the poorest in their country of origin . . . a bit underdeveloped and poorly educated."[37]

Many observers ignore this fact, but it is extremely important in explaining the persistence among Muslims in Europe of customs and traditions long rejected in the urban areas of their countries of origin. Indeed, it is often more accurate to understand practices such as polygamy, clitorectomy, arranged marriages, "honor" killings, or even the wearing of the *burqa* as matters of rural conservatism than as "Islamic" tradition. Similarly, when second- or third-generation Muslims in Europe try to "return" to what radical imams encourage them to believe is "pure Islam," they often look back to their Rif, Diyarbakir, or Kashmir grandparents' practices, rather than those prevailing in Casablanca, Istanbul, or Karachi.

Second, multicultural Europe has long tolerated, even encouraged, practices not tolerated in some of the countries of origin. Thus, while wearing the *hijab* in public institutions in Turkey or Tunisia is forbidden by law—and that prohibition has been deemed legitimate even by the European Human Rights

Court in 2005—it is still perfectly legal in England. Forced or arranged marriages (and not just for women), mistreatment of girls and women, and the wearing of the *hijab* everywhere are more tolerated in Kiel or Brussels than in Ankara or Tunis. A 2004 study for the German Federal Ministry for Family Affairs found that 17 percent of Turkish women surveyed considered their marriage forced, and a similar figure (13 percent) was mentioned among Turkish women in Belgium.[38] The most outrageous case of official tolerance of practices going against any policy of integration may have occurred in Germany in 2007. A (female) divorce-court judge in Frankfurt denied a fast divorce to a battered woman because husband and wife were both from Morocco. "It's a religion thing," she argued, citing the Quran.[39] One may point out that a woman in those circumstances would have received better treatment in Morocco itself, after the most recent changes in the family code there.

TIES ABROAD

One of the self-inflicted problems facing European governments is their own tolerance and, at times, outright encouragement of foreign governmental influence among their Muslim populations. Thus, for years, successive French governments have encouraged Algiers to subsidize the Grand Mosque in Paris, on the premise that an Algerian secular—even if, until the late 1980s, pro-Soviet and socialist—regime would ensure moderation of the mosque's leadership.[40]

The Egyptian-born Italian journalist Magdi Allam (himself a Muslim until his conversion to Catholicism in 2008) has pointed out that

> In Italy, in the case of marriage between an Italian and a Muslim woman, Sharia prevails over the laws of the state. Even countries normally considered secular, like Algeria,

Tunisia, Morocco or Egypt, demand that a non-Muslim, to be able to marry one of their citizens, must necessarily convert to Islam, which is a *sine qua non* condition to release a certificate granting permission to marry, without which the Italian authorities do not authorize the marriage.[41]

After a very close election in 2006, and after protracted negotiations, a Christian Democrat–Labor government was formed in the Netherlands, including, for the first time, two Muslim junior ministers: Ahmed Aboutaleb at Social Affairs and Nebahat Albayrak at Integration—ironically, because both have dual citizenship, Moroccan and Turkish respectively. Moreover, a newly elected Labor MP, Khadiya Arib, also a dual citizen, is an adviser to the King of Morocco.[42] In fact, Arib is a member of King Mohammed VI's Advisory Council on Human Rights, an organization specifically established to reinforce the Moroccan identity among the diaspora. She disingenuously claimed, "If I served in an advisory council in Nepal, you probably wouldn't even consider it an issue."[43] She misses the fact that a large Nepalese community with fundamentalist networks is not a real problem in Amsterdam.

Nor is the Dutch case unique. Ali Dizaei is a chief superintendent in the London police and a legal adviser to the National Black Police Association. He holds dual Iranian and British citizenship and is a frequent visitor to the Iranian embassy, and he has repeatedly and publicly accused the Metropolitan Police of "racism" for daring to investigate his background and activities. Although he was acquitted on charges of misconduct in public office and perverting the course of justice, he has since posed as a victim of "racial discrimination"—a claim contradicted by the very high rank he has obtained. No one seems to find anything odd in a senior police officer holding the citizenship of a state known for its extensive support for terrorism, and having extensive contacts with its government.[44]

A different form of tie to the country of origin is prevalent among Bangladeshis in Britain. According to *The Observer*,

> Wealth from Britain has transformed Taherpur [in the district of Sylhet]. Grandiose mosques and markets dot the approach road, and brick houses—a status symbol that is a rarity in other Bangladeshi villages—in kitschy green and red colours are commonplace. Some are built in the style of country homes with pitch roofs, terraces and sprawling grounds, lying empty for most of the year, except when their owners come to visit from the UK.

> "All the wealth you see here is from money sent from London," said local journalist Ahmed Azad, explaining that "London" is the generic term used to describe Britain. Located 90 miles northeast of the capital, Dhaka, property prices in Taherpur and surrounding areas are rising every year. "There is a race among our people who live in the UK for who can buy the best property back home and build the most lavish house on it," Azad said. He believes that at least 50,000 people from this district alone have struck gold in the restaurant business in "London." "Almost every family here has at least one son or daughter living in the UK, and receives about £500 every few months," he said. Such an amount is a fortune in a country where the average annual income is £200.[45]

From this pattern one could only conclude that many Bangladeshis in Britain intend to return to their native country, at least upon retirement—which does not suggest a great desire to integrate.

Thus the claim of Abdullah Ismail, 33, an immigration-law consultant and son of a Birmingham imam, that "the government is saying to us to integrate into society but, because of the foreign policy in Iraq and Afghanistan, it is more difficult for the Muslim community in 2006 than it was in 1992"[46] should be taken very cautiously. In fact, post-2001 British policy in Iraq or Afghanistan would seem to have much less to do with the failure of Bangladeshis to integrate in "London" than the decades-long pattern of marriage with people back home and heavy investment in Sylhet as opposed to in the UK.

The price of emigration to "London" can be high, as demonstrated by the story of Musammat Mumtahana, who in 2006, at the age of 22, hanged herself after killing her two young boys. She "was educated, she had passed her [school-leaving] exams, and she was pious and beautiful.... She loved to watch TV and in the afternoons she would teach her brothers and sisters to read the Koran." In Birmingham, where she arrived in 2003 after marrying a British resident from her native area, she lived in an £85,000 flat inside a converted house, thus apparently fulfilling her mother's hopes: "We wanted her to live in happiness and peace, to not ever be poor again. London is the kingdom of dreams—how could we know she would not find peace there?" Obviously, she didn't. According to neighbors, she was mostly alone, and her husband verbally mistreated her. "There are places she could go for help, but she wouldn't have known about them. She couldn't speak English, she couldn't go out and do anything, so she seems to have gone over the top and killed herself."[47] How common this is there is no way to know with any precision, but abusive treatment is certainly widespread among such families. And marriage abroad is also widespread: more than 10,000 British South Asians brought home foreign brides in 2005 alone.[49]

The Case of Finland: An Instructive Example

Finland is not known for a history of large immigration. Rather, it is an ethnically homogeneous country, aside from the historic Swedish minority. Only recently, following its EU membership in 1995, did it come in contact with what that membership now implies—including becoming a target of asylum seekers and refugees. Its reactions to those developments are thus quite instructive.

Until a year or so ago, recent immigrants to Finland were, with few exceptions, Muslims, defined by high illiteracy, large families (implying high costs for education), drastic language differences, and cultural habits illegal and/or unknown in Finland—sexual mutilation of girls, polygamy, arranged marriages of minors. Hence it was inevitable that there were what the UN diplomatically calls "integration challenges."

In Finnish analyses of the immigration problem there is the typical non sequitur—"immigration as a solution to the aging population." As in all European countries, Finland's population is growing older, with the bulk of the baby-boomers expected to retire in the coming five to seven years. A 2004 government study offers interesting insights:[49] more than 500,000 people will retire, which is every fifth or sixth person currently in the active workforce. Unless compensating measures are systematically deployed, population decline will inevitably occur starting in 2025. The speed of the decline may be slowed by more immigration. On the one hand, "With the government granting several thousand long-term residence permits and naturalizing 2,000 to 3,000 people each year, many well-integrated, skilled immigrants could compensate for possible future labor shortages." But on the other hand, "statisticians and economists debate over whether there will be a consistent need for skilled or unskilled foreign labor in the first place. Some argue that immigration would not solve the problem because even many current immigrants still lack Finnish language skills and occupational expertise. As a result, they have not become full participants in the labor market and everyday life."[50]

All this rather confusing analysis was subsidized by the Finnish government.[51] However, it appears that Helsinki now believes that large numbers of asylum seekers and refugees from the Third World are not a satisfactory solution to labor shortages—hence its 2007 decision, alone with Sweden among EU member states, to open widely its labor markets to workers from newly admitted EU members Bulgaria and Romania.

The problem is not what the Finns—people of a fairly small EU country—think about immigration in general or Muslim immigration in particular, but how representative that thinking is for EU elites—and how logical. How could one rationally think that Somalis, Kurds, and Kosovar Albanians could, at least in the short or medium term, fix Finland's (or Europe's) demographic problems and welfare-state cost deficits? Even if in the long term that might be possible—and there is of course no guarantee that future generations of Danish Somalis or Finnish Kosovars will be financially successful—the EU nations have a financial and demographic problem *now*—one that does not allow spectacularly more spending for an uncertain future generation of Third World Muslims, who may or may not assimilate the values of the present taxpayers. This is a bet that European elites were prepared to take, but the voters of Western Europe are less and less convinced.

LOW SKILLS, BIG PROBLEMS IN FRANCE

Toulouse, November 2005: "On Wednesday, groups of social workers called for an outdoor meeting to appeal for peace. A couple of young men began to harangue the workers. 'Go home. You're European. You don't belong here. You have nice jobs. Go back to France,' one said. The young men cheered as a stolen car buzzed by, its passengers on their way to torch the kindergarten."[52]

Paris, December 2005: At the Gare Montparnasse, three youths—one of Moroccan origin, another of Tunisian origin, the third native French—talk about the (left-wing) Human Rights League's mock vote on the issue of giving foreigners the right to vote in local elections. The event was supported by the Paris City Hall (controlled by the Socialists). All three of the young men are in favor of the idea, which has divided the political scene, with all the Left and, perhaps surprisingly, Nicolas Sarkozy (at that point already the front-runner in the polls for the 2007 presidential elections) in favor, and then President Chirac opposed. The Moroccan, Anouar, age 19, claims that "One should not forget that the immigrants have built France." He cannot understand why his parents, who arrived in France twenty years ago, still cannot vote. "If the old ones could vote that would change the [political] balance and push back the extreme Right. . . . .If Sarkozy is elected I would launch myself in a civil war." Another bystander, Christian, age 50 and a supporter of illegal immigrants, or *sans-papiers*, claims: "I know Spaniards established here who have the right to vote. Then, why not the people from Maghreb and the others? In this increasingly racist France, it would be a good means for them not to feel anymore outside."[53]

These examples illustrate the crux of the problems facing France and its immigrant population—and by extension quite a number of other European countries. First, the widespread and obviously wrong belief that "immigrants have built France." That is true only if one assumes that illiterate, unskilled Third World workers in the 1960s "built" (or rebuilt) France, rather than skilled Frenchmen (with American aid through the Marshall Plan). Second, perhaps Anouar's parents could not vote because they never bothered to apply for French citizenship, even after living in France for twenty years. Third, the assumption is, correctly, that the immigrant vote is a vote for the Left—which explains at least in part why it is the Left that supports extensive "rights" for illegal immigrants. Fourth, Christian exhibits the Pavlovian reflex of the Left to "explain" any form of distinctions applied to non-Europeans as "racism." Perhaps, if he was informed or sincere, he would remember that Spanish immigrants to France generally applied for naturalization and, since Spain is a now a European Union member—while the Maghreb countries are not—all its citizens living in any other EU country could automatically vote in local elections. Fifth, and most disturbing, it is clear that Anouar has assimilated the political culture of the radical Left rather than that of liberal Western Europe—hence his strong belief that if elections go against his opinion, violence is natural.

All of this is anecdotal, but as the 2005 riots in France proved—as did previous ones in Britain, Germany, and Belgium—Anouar and his buddies are far from isolated cases. Indeed, as an older Frenchman stated to *Libération* on that very occasion, "In light of the recent events in the banlieues, I believe that foreigners cannot truly understand the stake in municipal elections." [54]

WHY THE U.S. PICTURE IS DIFFERENT

Most observers, even in Europe, compare Europe's recent experience with integrating immigrants unfavorably to that of the United States. Writing in *The Economist* in 2005, commentator Charlemagne noted that "Whether Europe or America really has the better record on accommodating ethnic minorities is an issue that may be debated ad infinitum. But the riots in France point to one particular area in which Europe has been unusually bad: integrating immigrant families from the second and third generations."[55] He concluded that two factors are essential in understanding why assimilation of immigrants is more advanced in the United States than in Europe: jobs and house ownership. That is certainly true, but insufficient as an explanation. The culture of the bulk of the immigrants is probably an even more important factor.

For a Guatemalan or Mexican legal immigrant to the United States, the culture shock is mostly defined by language, work habits, free-market capitalism, and the relatively small role of government. The language problem is mitigated by the existence of large enclaves of Spanish-speakers in most large cities; work habits change rapidly, as employers insist on punctuality as a condition of employment; at their level in the job market immigrants have little competition from the natives; and the state, especially after the welfare reforms of the late 1990s, does not encourage staying on the public dole.

By contrast, in Europe the culture shock for the mainly Muslim immigrants and their children is far less economic than it is religious and cultural. For the Catholic majority of U.S. immigrants, the separation of church and state in their country of origin is not that different from the situation in the United States. For Muslims in Europe, Turks and Tunisians aside, that is far less true, given Islam's dominant role in their countries of origin.

Peculiar Problems and "Muslim" Practices

In all European countries "family reunification" is by now the main highway for legal Muslim immigration—larger than asylum and much larger than economic migration. To give just one example, France officially stopped receiving economic migrants from the Maghreb (or elsewhere) in 1974—but its Muslim population has exploded since, and not, at least not primarily, because of natural growth. It is the issue of family reunification—i.e., marriages with foreigners, who then join the spouse in Europe—that in France and elsewhere explains both the rapid growth in the number of Muslims and the growing difficulty in assimilating them. Simply put, Muslims in Europe, whether second- or third-generation, increasingly

choose to marry spouses from the countries of their parents—
both an indication and a reinforcement of the general rejection
of the very idea of assimilation. First-generation immigrants
in the 1960s and '70s, who were almost exclusively males, had
a cultural and demographic reason to seek spouses back home,
but that does not apply to their children and grandchildren.
Another problem is the way many such marriages take place,
in direct opposition to European traditions and laws. And that
is only one of the cultural habits, not necessarily Islamic but
widespread among certain groups of Muslims, that are incompatible with European laws and values.

Arranged marriages. Most Muslims newly arriving in the
Netherlands are doing so on the basis of marriage. At the beginning of 2005, of 55,600 outstanding requests for a residence
permit, 75 percent gave family reunification as a reason. A quarter of those were from Turks and Moroccans. The total requests
for marriage abroad in 2005 stood at "only" 32,000, probably
because of new, stricter legal demands. In order to get a residence permit for family-reunification reasons, one must now
be 21, and one's Dutch partner must earn at least 120 percent of
the minimum wage.

Why is this important? Because the pattern of marriages
among Muslims in Europe is the most obvious example of their
lack of integration and, more importantly still, of the bleak
prospect of that changing any time soon.

Thus, an exhaustive Dutch study, with a sample of 81,000, or
virtually 100 percent of Turks and Moroccans married and living in the Netherlands by 2000, revealed that "marriages with
indigenous partners are rare in this group (4 percent of the total). Around 18 percent of the study population are married to a
partner of the same ethnic origin who was already residing in
the Netherlands, but no fewer than three-quarters of all Turks

and Moroccans found their partner in the country of origin."[56] Other official figures suggest that only 10 percent of Turks and Moroccans in the Netherlands marry native Dutch, compared to over 40 percent of Surinamese and Indonesians.[57]

In Britain, among residents of Indian-subcontinent origins, the figures are similar. A 2003 study by Migration Watch UK found that in Bradford, a heavily Muslim city in West Yorkshire, "60 percent of Pakistani and Bangladeshi marriages . . . were with a spouse from the country of origin." The result?

> International arranged marriages are a major factor in the formation of ghettoes in Britain. Even in the second generation, a high proportion of immigrants from certain countries enter arranged marriages with spouses from their county of origin. This sets back integration by a generation. The flow of spouses and fiancées from the Indian Sub Continent (ISC) doubled between 1996 and 2001. Now nearly half of ethnic Indian and three-quarters of ethnic Pakistani and Bangladeshi children aged 0–4 have a mother born in her country of origin. 30 percent of all children born in Bradford are born to foreign mothers; in Tower Hamlets the figure is 68 percent. And the Pakistani population of Manchester, Birmingham and Bradford increased by about 50 percent between 1991 and 2001.[58]

In Germany between 21,000 and 27,000 family-reunification visas are granted annually to Turkish citizens on the basis of marriage. In Denmark, until new restrictive legislation was enacted in 2002, 62.7 percent of first- and second-generation immigrants from non-Western countries (overwhelmingly Muslims) married persons living abroad. The proportion has since fallen to 43.2 percent.[59]

These patterns have a number of very important implications. First, the fact that they persist beyond the first generation of immigrants clearly indicates a collective reluctance to integrate. Second, integration is continually pushed into the future, as the newly arrived spouses—overwhelmingly women—are in the same position as the original immigrants themselves in regard to the receiving society. Furthermore, since in all Muslim communities it is the women who are exclusively in charge of raising the children, the latter tend to be less integrated than their own fathers. That factor is exacerbated by the fact that the imported brides are overwhelmingly more religious and less educated than Muslim women born in Europe. Among Muslims of rural Pakistani background the arranged-marriage problems are compounded by the fact that many are between first cousins, with the unsurprising result that children of Pakistani background are disproportionately affected by genetic defects. Medical research suggests that while British Pakistanis are responsible for 3 percent of all births in Britain, they account for one in three British children born with genetic defects.[60]

Arranged marriages have been virtually banned in Norway since 2003, when their legal acceptance was conditioned on the right of the bride to divorce. In Britain, they are illegal for minors but recognized in other cases, even when undertaken under Sharia, except in ill-defined circumstances where to do so would be "repugnant to public policy."[61] In July 2006 the British government dropped a proposal to ban arranged marriages out of "concern . . . that the new law would stigmatize Muslims." Some organizations complained that it would "increase racial segregation," and the Muslim Council of Britain warned that such a law might become "another way to stigmatize our communities."[62]

How banning the importation of brides from the Muslim world would "increase racial segregation" is not explained. Nor is the danger of "stigmatization" balanced against the heavy burden such arrangements place on the women—suicide rates among young Asian women in Britain are more than three times the national average.

How serious is the problem? According to official figures, between 2003 and 2005, 518 forced marriages were recorded in London, and in 2005 more than 140 were recorded in Bradford.[63] In Germany, arranged marriages make up half of the total within the Turkish community, with most of the brides imported from Eastern Anatolia.[64]

Arranged marriages are central to the problems of Muslim families in many parts of Europe. Other cultural habits relating to the treatment of women are less pervasive, but even more disturbing when they occur.

Polygamy. In February 2008 it became public knowledge that the British government implicitly recognizes polygamous families if such marriages were contracted in countries where they are legal. Furthermore, "Income support for all of the wives may be paid directly into the husband's bank account, if the family so choose. Under the deal agreed by ministers, a husband with multiple wives may also be eligible for additional housing benefit and council tax benefit to reflect the larger property needed for his family." As Chris Grayling, the shadow work and pensions secretary, accurately noted, "This sets a precedent that will lead to more demands for the culture of other countries to be reflected in UK law and the benefits system." All the government could say in reply was that there are perhaps no more than one thousand polygamous marriages in the country.[65]

The Quran does not recommend polygamy but allows it, within the limit of four wives if the man is capable of providing for them. In many Muslim countries today, polygamy is officially frowned upon (Morocco and Jordan), banned outright (Turkey and Tunisia), or simply less and less common. Thus, by no means can the practice be described as "Islamic." Polygamy is still prevalent in sub-Saharan countries like Mali, however, and is brought to Europe by immigrants from those areas. It is also illegal throughout Europe. However, as with other such issues, it is not just *de facto* tolerated in places like France, it is publicly subsidized. Why? Because, the practitioners being black, the accusation of "racism" is more likely to stick—and no politician wants *that*.

How important is the matter? Geneviève Oger reports that somewhere between 150,000 and 400,000 people live in polygamous "marriages" in France. They get around the fact that polygamy is illegal by undergoing a formal "separation." However, this has no practical meaning other than the state providing separate housing for the various "ex-wives," who, however, do not see themselves as divorced, nor do they act as such.[66] Mamalea Bapuwa, Intercultural Mediator at France's Association of African Women, says, "It's a question of choice. We can't push people in this direction. Once a woman has made up her mind and has decided she wants to de-cohabitate [i.e., formally move to separate housing], she comes to see us."[67] Even for Bapuwa, who understands the problems raised by polygamy, it doesn't occur to her that "choice" at the expense of the taxpayers and against the law is not legitimate. The result?

> Fatima Camara, 39, is a Malian mother of five and the second wife in a polygamous marriage. She was living in Mali with her family when her cousin came to visit from France in 1987. He was already married, but Camara's family told her to marry him anyway, as is the custom in many Muslim communities in Mali. "I couldn't really say no to my parents. So I said that I would agree to whatever they decided. We went ahead with the marriage."
>
> She said that things worked out wonderfully until her children became older. But three adults and 10 children in a three-room

apartment grew increasingly more difficult to handle. Camara finally moved into a six-room apartment she was assigned in the spring of 2004. But she continues to live in semi-polygamy; her husband and the children belonging to his first wife come over every day. And she's happy with the set-up.... The French government, however, wants Camara to go a step further—to divorce her husband. Only then would she receive a 10-year residence permit. But Camara would rather be forced to renew her permit every year. She says she loves her husband and wants to stay married to him.[68]

Polygamous families in France typically live in crowded public housing, so crowded that many children live mostly on the street, where they are particularly vulnerable to becoming criminals or victims of crime. In polygamous families—estimated at between 12,000 and 30,000—there are on the average 12 persons. According to French MP Jacques Kossowski, polygamous marriages cost the authorities between €150 and €300 million a year.[69]

Following the 2005 urban riots in France, the government and some lucid intellectuals noted that polygamy played an important role. Although the Left promptly shouted "Racism!" they succeeded in opening this long-avoided issue to public debate. Gérard Larcher, delegate employment minister, stated that polygamy was one of the causes of the riots, and the ruling party's president in the National Assembly, Bernard Accoyer, claimed that "polygamy is the negation of the rights of the person, of the rights of the woman, . . . and also the inability to bring the education necessary in a organized society." Even the "experts" dealing with the problem had trouble responding. "It is a problem but one does not need to instrumentalize it," said Isabelle Faye, of the Group for the Abolition of Sexual Mutilation.[70] The Movement against Racism and for Friendship between Peoples (MRAP) tried to cut off the debate by the usual means: "Blaming such a complex problem on polygamy among a minority of African families is blatant racism. We will consider whether to bring legal actions against these people [Larcher and Accoyer]."[71]

In fact, many of the youths detained during the riots were of polygamous African origin.[72] Polygamous families tend to be poorer and living in the worst neighborhoods. There are cases like one in Vaulx-en-Velin, near Lyon, of a family with four wives and thirty children living in a single apartment. Such areas are completely dysfunctional, according to police, with the African custom of having the entire village take care of the children serving as a pretext for the parents to neglect them. Such areas serve as the perfect Petri dish for radicalization.

Polygamy is not limited to France. In Britain, a radical preacher and convert, Abdur-Raheem Greene, acknowledged in 1997 that he had "two wives, both British-born Muslims of Indian origin, and six children." He could do so, he said, despite polygamy's being illegal, because "those who practice bigamy can protect the second marriage under the provisions of 'common law wives.' Under this children out of such marriages are legitimate and wives inherit property."[73]

"Honor" killings. The murder of young women by their own relatives, typically the father or a brother, for breaking "the code of honor" is a widespread phenomenon in parts of the Muslim world and, now, in muslim enclaves in Europe, especially among Pakistanis, Bangladeshis, and Kurds. There were 45 known honor killings in Germany from 1996 to 2004; the phenomenon has also been seen in the Netherlands, Denmark, and Italy.[74] In the United Kingdom, Nazir Afzal, the lead prosecutor for the Crown on honor-based violence, stated:

> In some northern towns there are real horror stories—from places like Blackburn, where people say that you might as well

be in rural Kashmir for all the way that women are seen and treated.... Substantial numbers of the community actually did not assist and support prosecutors. Instead they supported the family members who were responsible for the killing.[75]

The scenario among Muslims in Europe usually involves a young woman falling in love with a person, even if he is also a Muslim, whom the family objects to, instead of accepting an arranged marriage. In some cases, the victim has also decided to work, has had European friends, and has adopted local dress and other non-Islamic habits, and thus has pushed the integration process beyond family acceptance.

This phenomenon demonstrates the rejection of integration by the entire family, including the young woman's mother, and including young males born in Europe, even when the family has lived there for decades. However, the relatively rare occurrence of "honor" killings among North African immigrants suggests that such extreme forms of gender discrimination are not inextricably linked to Islam, but have a closer relationship with conservative, rural, clan-based cultural traditions.

Rape. Paradoxically, the same Islamic teachings on the treatment of women that explain the very low incidence of rape in Muslim countries also account for its disproportional incidence among Muslims in Europe. While Islam teaches respect, however that is defined, for Muslim women, it does not have the same attitude toward non-Muslim ones. At the beginning of 2005 Danish police statistics showed that 68 percent of all rapes in the country were committed by immigrants, mostly second- or third-generation Muslims. In Norway 65 percent of rapists were of non-Western backgrounds, and a 2007 study of rapists in Oslo (data for 2004) indicated that 110 of 150 rapists were immigrants, with Somalis represented at 3.5 times their percentage in the population, and Iraqis at 10.39 times.[76]

That is perhaps not surprising when Shahid Mehdi, a Copenhagen imam, stated that women who do not wear headscarves "are asking" for rape—an opinion implicitly shared by Danish criminologist Flemming Balvig, who claimed that the second-generation Muslims' disproportionate involvement in rape is a reaction to "an increased tendency to marginalize and alienate immigrants." Similarly, Norwegian anthropologist Unni Wikan (a woman) stated: "Norwegian women must take their share of responsibility for these rapes" because Muslim men found their manner of dress provocative, and "Norwegian women must realize that we live in a multicultural society and adapt themselves to it."[77]

In the Netherlands, Sweden, and France there has been an increase in the use of headscarves by girls (even non-Muslims in certain areas), due to fear of rape or other violence, like "immodest" girls having acid thrown in their faces. In Britain the BBC was asked by police to pull a documentary about the high incidence of European women raped by Muslims—for fear of increasing ethnic tensions.[78] In 2005, after two Swedish girls were "assaulted, raped and beaten half to death by four Somali immigrants [of various legal statuses], Sweden's largest newspaper [*Aftonbladet*] presented the perpetrators as 'two men from Sweden, one from Finland and one from Somalia.'"[79]

It is in France that the general political correctness and academic opinion *à la* Balvig or Wikan has come under the most open and public attack—from secular Muslim women. Their organization, *Ni Putes, ni Soumises* (Neither Whores nor Submissives), makes it difficult for the authorities to push the issue under the rug.

Female genital mutilation. Like polygamy, female genital mutilation (FGM) is not "Islamic," and it is illegal in Europe, either under laws prohibiting bodily injury or by specific prohibition (in the UK, Sweden, Norway, Belgium, Denmark, Italy, and Spain). It has also been criminalized in many African nations. However, it is still practiced in many sub-Saharan and Pakistani communities. A 1998 study found that almost half of health-care providers in the UK had encountered FGM complications. While more than 90 percent of them said they would never perform an FGM procedure, the British Medical Association estimated that some three thousand procedures were performed in the UK each year. Prosecuting FGM is difficult, because FGM is often carried out abroad, on visits to the parents' native country.[80] Parents living in Europe often send their girls to undergo the mutilation in Djibouti, where the most severe form is used, under the pretext of "vacations."

In Europe, there are cases in every country. In Italy, "female circumcision is . . . a horrifyingly widespread secret practice"; according to *Corriere della Sera*, there are some 25,000 women with mutilated genitals living in Italy.[81]

A case in Norway is a good indication of attitudes toward this practice. When Kadra, a Somali woman living in Norway, asked three local imams for advice, all three advised her to have the operation done—all of this being secretly filmed by a Norwegian TV crew. When Kadra told one of the Gambian imams that the practice was prohibited in Norway, she was told:

> As I am sure you'll understand, we Muslims must be careful with what we say here in Norway. It is not necessary to include too many in these matters. I myself, for instance, have two wives. That is also prohibited in Norway. When my wife visits me from The Gambia, I tell the Norwegian government that it is my sister or my aunt. The same discretion should go for what you are bringing up. [82]

The imams denied these words until confronted with the footage, after which one of them, Gambian imam Ebrahim Sahidi, publicly apologized to Kadra and the Norwegian people.

General mistreatment of women. Female genital mutilation grabs headlines, but ordinary day-to-day mistreatment of women probably has a greater impact on the key problem of Muslim integration in Europe.

In November 2004, Mohammed Kamal Mostafa, a "respected" imam in Andalusia, was jailed for writing a book, *The Islamic Woman,* which advised Muslim men on how to beat "rebellious" women without leaving visible signs of injury. Mostafa's advice covered matters such as how to avoid incriminating bruises and scar tissue, and how to "inflict blows that are not too strong nor too hard, because the aim is to make them suffer psychologically and not to humiliate them or mistreat them physically." Mostafa's 12-month jail sentence was reduced to 20 days, and the imam was ordered to complete a training course in human rights.[83]

Problems in male–female relations both are caused by and result in serious social and cultural challenges within Muslim communities in Europe. To begin with, Muslim women born in Europe are generally more likely to integrate than their male counterparts—whether in terms of personal relationships or, more common, and more important, in terms of education, language skills, and career prospects. For instance, in the Netherlands, 60 percent of Moroccan women and 50 percent of Turkish women starting university studies in 1995 had completed them by 2001, but only 40 percent of Moroccan and Turkish men did. That means tensions within the family as the traditional male domination in Islam is challenged. It partly explains the tendency of the less educated, skilled, and adapted

Muslim males to seek more obedient, more conservative, and less skilled spouses in the home countries. It also partly explains why, in 2001, 59 percent of women seeking refuge in shelters were non-ethnic Dutch, mostly Muslim.[84]

Ironically, it seems that the relatively higher ability of Muslim women in Europe to integrate and adapt makes Muslim men less willing or able to do so. As Antoine Sfeir has pointed out, relations between the sexes is a big factor in the re-Islamization of second-generation Muslims in Europe. As the old patriarchal structures are upset, the young men acquire a strong incentive to reassert the old order.[85]

Meanwhile, some Muslim women in Europe are on the forefront of integration largely because they are the main victims of some of the customs described above, such as forced marriages and generally inferior treatment by their community and family. Seyran Ates, a lawyer and the author of *The Great Journey into the Fire,* Necla Kelek (*The Foreign Bride*), and Serap Cileli (*We're Your Daughters, Not Your Honor*) in Germany, Hirsi Ali in the Netherlands, Fadela Amara and her colleagues in *Ni Putes ni Soumises* in France are such examples, and they all bear scars. Kelek was threatened by her father with a hatchet, Ates survived a shooting attack on the women's shelter she founded in Kreuzberg, and Cileli tried to kill herself at age 13 to escape her first forced marriage; she was later married against her will in Turkey, from where she fled to Germany with two children to escape her father's violence.[86]

Social Pathologies

As we have seen, allegations of "discrimination" and "racism" are popular explanations for the general Muslim economic backwardness in Europe. In fact, several interrelated social pathologies play a major role.

Lower educational performance. Muslims everywhere in Europe, and especially Muslim males—a few ethnic groups (Iranians, East Africans) aside—are generally less educated than natives and perform worse on tests than other racial or ethnic minorities as well. In the Netherlands, for instance, the differences between Muslims and native Dutch are significant, in terms of both duration of schooling and level attained. In the 18–20 age group, 53 percent of the Dutch but only 28 percent of Turks and 23 percent of Moroccans are university students. After high school most non-Dutch go for vocational training instead of university, with 45 percent of students on that track being of immigrant background. The dropout rate for immigrants is 20 percent, compared to 8 percent for Dutch kids. Non-Dutch students have lower scores than their Dutch classmates. Figures from 2003 show a difference of 8 points in universities and 12 points in vocational training schools. In pre-university education 95 percent of Dutch students passed their exams, while only 83 percent of Moroccans and 73 percent of Turks did so, although among the second generation the figure for Moroccans was 89 percent and for Turks 85 percent.[87]

In Germany, according to a study from the Goethe Institute:

> In the 2001/2002 academic year, school leavers with foreign passports accounted for 9.6 percent of students graduating with the *Abitur*—the certificate entitling them to a place at a German university—and 19.5 percent of them did not even obtain a lower secondary school-leaving certificate. The figures for German nationals were 25.1 percent and 8.2 percent respectively. . . . There are striking discrepancies in the field of vocational training as well: the proportion of foreign nationals in the 14–17 age group who had secured a training contract in 2000 or who were taking vocational qualifications at a mainstream school stood at just 60 percent; this means that 40 percent of foreign nationals in this age group failed to obtain any further training after completing their

compulsory education (9th grade). By contrast, the figures
for their German peers were 85 percent and 15 percent. And
at universities, too, very few students come from immigrant
communities. . . . Migration-specific factors also come into
play: difficulties at school tend to increase proportionately
with later immigration.[88]

Education, skills, and habits are also closely related to
health—and in Europe, where health care is generally social-
ized, Muslims tend to be disproportionate beneficiaries, as is
the case, for instance, in Britain:

> British Muslims are known to have higher levels of
> coronary heart disease, diabetes, obesity, perinatal mortality,
> psychological distress, respiratory problems and tuberculosis
> than any other religious groups. Some of the differentials
> may be explained biologically, as is the case with diabetes,
> but some, such as those relating to heart disease and mental
> illness, are also rooted in socio-economic inequalities. . . . Crack
> and heroin are a growing problem among second- and third-
> generation Bangladeshis in Tower Hamlets, as they are among
> Muslim youth nationwide.[89]

Criminality. The form of social pathology that is most directly linked to Islamism and terrorism is criminality. In the
Netherlands, 37.5 percent of crime suspects in 2002 were non-
Dutch (though not all of these were Muslims), twice their
proportion in the total population.[90] In the UK, where ethnic
minorities make up only about 8 percent of the population,
24 percent of the male prison population comes from those
groups, and 28 percent of the female prison population. In
France, with a Muslim population of approximately 8 percent,
Muslims make up almost half the prison population, with close
to 80 percent Muslims in some jails on the outskirts of Paris.
Fourteen percent of Italy's prisoners are Muslims, 98 percent

of whom are foreign nationals, while Muslims account for less than 2 percent of the total population.[91]

One consequence of this is a shortage of officially sanctioned imams in the prison systems (in Nanterre, there are only eight chaplains for roughly 20,000 prisoners), with the result that lay prisoners, often radicalized ones, end up playing the role of prayer leaders. Britain's situation is no better than that of continental countries, nor are the results different: Richard Reid, the "shoe bomber" of Jamaican descent now imprisoned in the United States for trying to blow up a Paris-to-Miami flight in 2001, and London bomber Muktar Said Ibrahim, an Eritrean immigrant who obtained British citizenship despite having served a five-year prison sentence for armed robberies, were both converted to Islam in the same penitentiary.[92] A story in *The Guardian* reports: "In the wake of 9/11 the Home Office became alarmed at the recruitment of young Muslims inside prison by extremist organizations and took some steps to ensure that moderate imams led prayer meetings. Three imams working in Feltham, Aylesbury, and visiting eight other prisons in southeast England were suspended in the wake of 9/11 for 'unprofessional behavior'—making overtly anti-U.S. statements and spreading the views of the extremist cleric Abu Hamza."[93] Further complicating the picture is the immigrants' illegal drug use. As noted above, in England, crack and heroin are a major problem among second- and third-generation immigrant Bangladeshis. As of June 2000 one-fourth of the 4,000 Muslim inmates in the country had been convicted of drug-related offenses.[94] In Spain, Moroccan immigrants are dominant in the hashish trade, while throughout Europe the heroin business is largely controlled by Turkish Kurds and Muslim Albanians (from both Kosovo and Albania proper).

Socioeconomic factors. As already shown, the integration of Muslim immigrants in Europe is made more difficult by their low levels of education and low skills. These, in turn, are related to socioeconomic factors, some of them practical, most cultural.

One of the problems is the large families typical among Muslims. As Hugues Lagrange of the French National Scientific Research Center has pointed out, "The larger the family, the more chances for the children to fall behind and slip into delinquency."[95]

A related factor is Muslim women's limited role in the workplace. For most Muslims the primary role of the woman is to stay home and take care of the children. In a Europe where feminism is *à la mode* and the labor pool is shrinking, keeping half of adult family members out of gainful employment thwarts public policy and is a recipe for relative poverty. This in turn leads to a growing sense of collective victimhood, and invites anti-Muslim attacks from the extremist fringes of the dominant culture.

Thus, in Denmark, where an extensive network of free day-care facilities is in place in order to allow women to work, many Muslim women still insist on staying home and caring for their children—while receiving the Danish welfare state's lavish social benefits. Moreover, as then Integration Minister Rikke Hvilshøj complained, when Muslim children start school, their knowledge of Danish—the most difficult Scandinavian language—is "clearly inferior" to that of other students,[96] in many cases because their mothers themselves do not speak the language. That leads to high numbers of dropouts and, subsequently, complaints of "discrimination" in the labor market.

Just as the initial reasons for Muslim immigration to Europe were related to an economic environment that does not exist any more, so Muslim communities today, more than any other, have largely failed to adapt to those changes. As *The Economist* put it,

> Even in Britain, where anti-discrimination laws are relatively stringent, Muslims tend to be poor. Of all religious groups, they are the least likely to own their own homes. They are also the least likely to hold professional jobs and the most likely to be out of work. Just 48 percent of British Muslims reported that they were economically active in 2001, compared with 65 percent of Christians, 67 percent of Hindus and 75 percent of those who professed no religion. Lack of jobs in the areas where Muslims have settled is part of the problem, but another reason is that *women are less likely to do paid work. Four out of ten look after home and family, compared with little more than one in ten women in Britain as a whole.* [Emphasis added.] In one sense, the Muslim household is resilient—many fewer children are brought up in one-parent families than is the case among non-Muslims—but there is, literally, a price to be paid.[97]

Other figures suggest that in the UK the unemployment rate among Muslims is twice the national average, while among Hindus it is lower than among native English. Nor is this a peculiarity of Muslims in England: A study of comparable Somali groups in Sweden and Minnesota found that less than a third of working-age Somalis in Sweden had jobs, half the share of Somalis in Minnesota.[98] A Dutch government study of unemployment in nine cities in January 2006 assessed the national level at 9 percent, compared to 27 percent for Moroccan immigrants, 22 percent for Turks, and 21 percent for those from the Caribbean and Surinam. About 500,000 Turks and Moroccans in the Netherlands did not speak Dutch in 2004 (out of a combined population of around 700,000), and joblessness in some Moroccan communities there approached 40 percent.[99] On the other hand, while in 1994 there were 21,000 businessmen of foreign origin in the Netherlands, the number in 2005 was 58,000, suggesting that some immigrants, anyway, have entrepreneurial instincts (at least at the level of the small family business), as any visitor to Amsterdam could testify.[100]

SPECIFIC CULTURAL BACKGROUND AND WELFARE DEPENDENCY

Most Muslim immigrants to Europe were originally peasants from the rural Maghreb, the Balkans, Turkey, or the Indian subcontinent, and faced a multiple challenge in adapting to an alien religious, cultural, linguistic, economic, and physical urban environment.

This background has direct implications, as noted by Ahmed Aboutaleb, an Amsterdam councilman of Moroccan background: "Muslims are not used to focusing on sensitive issues within their own religion. . . . They are very rural populations here. They see the debate as an attack on their personal identity."[101]

The case of Turks in Germany is typical. There were one million immigrants from Turkey (actually about half of them Kurds, not ethnic Turks) in Germany in 1975, 1.5 million in 1981, and over 2 million by 2000—and the growth took place despite the post-1983 official German policy of encouraging them to return to Turkey.[102] The first wave of immigrants, prior to 1980, were mostly from western Turkey and were ethnic Turks. The second came after the 1980 military coup and the 1984 beginning of the PKK (Kurdistan Workers Party) terrorist campaign; most of these were from the Kurdish eastern provinces. It is important to note that this second wave included not only a more rural, conservative population, but also various radical elements—Marxist (Kurdish or not) and Islamist—and that it concentrated in the largest cities: The largest single concentration of "Turks" in Europe is the Kreuzberg sector of Berlin. Similarly, a third of "Turks" in Austria and Belgium live in Vienna and Brussels respectively, and half of those of Sweden live in Stockholm.[103] This pattern meant that the usual cultural shock experienced by all Muslim immigrants was greatly magnified by the sharp contrast between life in a small village in Eastern Anatolia and life in Berlin or Vienna.

The Netherlands is one of Europe's, indeed the world's, most tolerant countries, and historically so. For centuries it served as a refuge to persecuted Spanish Jews (like Spinoza), English dissenters (like the pilgrims, later of Massachusetts), and French Huguenots. Thus it offers a good example of the problems linked to mass Muslim immigration and of the changes in popular and political attitudes it has engendered.

The Dutch author Leon de Winter wrote that, after the cultural and sexual revolutions of the 1960s and '70s, the other important phenomenon shaping the Netherlands in the late 20th century was Moroccan immigration:

> The second simultaneous change in Dutch life was the recruitment of young men from the Rif Mountains of Morocco, most illiterate and many with only a rudimentary grasp of spoken Dutch, to work in Holland's rapidly expanding industries. When they came to the country, often under long-term government work visas, they were faced with a highly educated but apparently decadent society in the grip of a cultural revolution. Many were astonished: was this country some sort of freak show?

> No, it certainly wasn't. Under the effusive "anything goes" exterior, the majority of Dutch people held onto their disciplined Calvinist values. To the immigrants, however, this core was all but invisible.

> For a while, the immigrants did the dirty work for which no training was needed, and the two factions lived amicably. But

during the technology- and service-oriented economic boom of the 1980s and '90s, the demand for unskilled work declined. The "guest workers" were no longer needed in such numbers, but they were also not required to return to Morocco. Instead they were given extensive social benefits and their families were allowed to come from Morocco to join them. It was the birth of the ethnic-religious ghettoes that surround our affluent cities and towns.[104]

The result, inevitably, was that while the Netherlands' culture and values moved into a "postmodern" phase and the practice of Christianity died, the Muslim immigrant masses did not move at all or, as it is increasingly apparent, moved in the opposite direction—rejection of secular mores and tolerance, and increased appeal of Islam. De Winter's description of the process in his country applies, with some variations, to most other European countries.

MUSLIMS AND THE WELFARE STATE

The problem is exacerbated by the fact that the European governments are all struggling to fund their social-welfare programs. For instance, the reunited Germany:

Germany has also spent 1.4 trillion euros to rebuild the former East Germany. As the state goes broke, its reputation for high-quality social services wanes. The country had its Sputnik moment in 2003, when the Program for International Student Assessment (PISA) ranked the German education system near rock-bottom of 32 developed countries surveyed. To add to the problem, Germans are having children at half the rate they were when the socialist state was built up in the 1950s and 1960s. Since pensions and health care, the most expensive parts of the social system, are pay-as-you-go, battles over the role of the state increasingly pit the old against the young.[105]

Ironically, besides being increasingly unaffordable, the welfare state is a major obstacle to the assimilation or integration of Muslims. On the one hand, it protects, and thus encourages, the very customs mentioned above that keep many Muslims in relative poverty. On the other hand, by protecting public employees, and long-term employees in general, from competition from cheaper, lower-wage workers, the welfare state, and especially the French "social model," helps insure that disproportionately large numbers of Muslims remain unemployed, and thus fuels resentment, which in turn fuels Islamist recruitment activities.

Islamism, like Communism in times gone by, is now a magnet for all sorts of personal or collective frustrations, failures, and false hopes. Jailbirds and bored youths, anti-social types, the unemployed and unemployable, and adventurers often find in Islam, or what they think is Islam, the ultimate solution to their problems.

THE PITFALLS OF PUBLIC DISCUSSION OF IMMIGRATION ISSUES

Whereas during the early period of immigration from Muslim countries, European authorities considered it natural and normal to expect immigrants to respect the legal, cultural, and political rules of the countries in which they were now living, that is less and less the case. Instead, in many EU states, the very idea of assimilation has become taboo—a form of "colonialism," "Eurocentrism," etc. Increasingly, as we have seen, Muslim communities expect and demand a right to engage in the religious, cultural, and political habits of their countries of origin—even when those are in direct conflict with European traditions or law. Witness Abu Jahjah, founder of the European Arab League (LAE) in Belgium, organizing "patrols" in Antwerp to watch over the "racist" police. The country, he says, "must accept the reality of multiculturalism," and it is only natural to "simply demand our rights to housing, employment . . . while preserving our Arab-Muslim identity."[106]

In a similar vein, in 2007 Abdullah Gül—then Turkey's foreign minister, now its president—criticized the German immigration bill, which requires spouses coming to Germany to have a basic knowledge of the German language. Gül fashionably claimed, "I wish that all Turks in Germany could speak German. But making it compulsory is against human rights. And it doesn't solve the problem."[107] Why it doesn't solve the problem, he did not say.

Nevertheless, the European attitude toward Muslim immigration and demographics is still largely dominated by political convenience and prevailing intellectual winds, rather than scientific research. Thus, some fundamental types of information about immigrants in general and Muslims in particular are incomplete or even officially unavailable in some EU member states: the total numbers of immigrants and their religion; the number and percentage of illegal versus legal immigrants; and immigrant crime participation. The political, cultural, and economic implications of South-North migration are enormous and increasingly difficult to deal with, but until recently serious public debate has been artificially limited. Culturally, because of the very fact that virtually all immigrants in Europe are African, Arab, or Asian rather than Caucasian, any difficulty their numbers or customs may involve has tended to be explained away as caused by the innate "racism" of the receiving countries.

In recent years, however, the increasingly obvious negative social and cultural impact of multiculturalism has led to the rise of anti-immigration political parties, some operating outside the political mainstream but many, and increasingly so, reaching the mainstream.

Concerns over political correctness have started to ebb, as demonstrated by the Dutch government's attempt to deal with the related issues of immigration, asylum abuse, welfare dependency, and integration, largely motivated by public pressure following the assassinations of Pim Fortuyn and Theo van Gogh. Similar measures have since been introduced in Denmark and are widely discussed elsewhere.

According to a 2005 academic study, reforms were approved in the Netherlands after 9/11, "when it became clear that the profile of the ideal, highly skilled migrant (highly educated, multilingual and able to socially adapt to local circumstances) matched the profile of a terrorist." New laws were passed, and existing laws began being strictly enforced.

Thus, a tougher new "led to a dramatic drop in applications. In 2004, less than 10,000 people applied for asylum in the Netherlands, a 30 percent drop from 2003."[108] Labor-migrant regulations had already been tightened, leaving family reunification as almost the only legal way for non-EU nationals to be admitted to the Netherlands. That was controlled too, as a November 2004 Royal Decree required that spouses being brought to the Netherlands had to be 21 years of age or older, and that the sponsor had to earn at least 120 percent of the minimum wage (a net monthly income of €1,319). Since a majority of even second-generation Turks and Moroccans in the Netherlands still look for wives from their country of origin, these groups were the most affected. In 2004, only 2,900 Moroccans entered the country, compared to 4,900 in 2003, and the number of Turkish immigrants fell from 6,700 to 3,900. In the first three months of 2005, there were 7,600 marriage applications (mostly from Turks and Moroccans), compared to 10,800 in the same quarter in 2004. Furthermore, in 2005 the Dutch government passed a bill strengthening the Newcomers Integration Act of 1998, which had required new immigrants to take a civic integration course; the 2005 bill requires all immigrants, both newcomers and settled (as many as 450,000), to take the integration exam.[109]

There has actually been in recent years a small reverse migration. Since 2003, for the first time since the 1950s, the Netherlands has witnessed net emigration—16,000 in 2004 and 20,000 in 2005—and this despite a large immigrant influx from the new EU members.[110] Between January and November 2005, 110,000 people left the country, half of them Turks, Moroccans, and Surinamese, and the others mostly young professionals influenced by the political and cultural crisis that followed the Fortuyn and van Gogh assassinations.[111]

WHY IS THE MUSLIM CASE SO PROBLEMATIC?

Only a few decades back, Islam was still seen throughout Europe as a distant and exotic religion, with no European roots except in backward places like Albania, Bosnia, or the marginally European, and now officially secular, Turkey. Immigration, overwhelmingly Muslim, has introduced two powerful, related challenges to the European reality: *a strong religiosity in a post-religious environment* and *a historically alien religion and culture.* That is factually true and is certainly so perceived, even in the case of France (where analysis is the most comprehensive although, ironically, the data are the least reliable). There, perhaps as many as half of young, locally born Muslims are non-practicing in any meaningful sense. Indeed, they treat Islam more as a social/cultural tradition than as a demanding faith. Ramadan is not widely respected, mosques are not frequented, and many Muslims smoke and drink alcohol.[112] On the other hand, many young Muslims actually become more religious than their parents, and thus vulnerable to current Islamist influence and recruitment.

The gap between the levels of religious practice among Europeans and Muslims in Europe is well understood by both. A 2006 Pew poll, *"The Great Divide: How Westerners and Muslims View Each Other,"*[113] found the following:

DO YOU ASSOCIATE THEM WITH THE TRAIT "DEVOUT"?

Asked of Non-Muslims about Muslims:

	YES	NO
Great Britain	84	8
France	69	29
Germany	85	13
Spain	86	8

Asked of Muslims about "People in Western Countries":

	YES	NO
Great Britain (Muslims)	37	46
France (Muslims)	26	70
Germany (Muslims)	36	54
Spain (Muslims)	26	62

Given the general decline of Christianity and the growing attraction of Islam among previously non-practicing or only occasionally practicing Muslims in Europe, such perceptions are accurate on both sides. Furthermore, they capture, perfectly, Muslim alienation, best defined by Yusuf al-Qaradawi, a Sunni theologian held in high regard among Europe's Muslims, who stated: "We condemn the excessive materialism of the West. We deplore the loss of solidarity and brotherliness, the decay of morals and the daily violations of human dignity. God has disappeared—almost nobody in the West talks about Him anymore."[114]

The same Pew study also sheds interesting light on the attitudes of Muslims in Europe on the issue of integration and their position in the host societies. Here are some results:

RELATIONS BETWEEN
MUSLIMS AND WESTERNERS

	Generally Good	Generally Bad
U.S.	32	55
Germany	23	70
France	33	66
Spain	14	61
Great Britain	28	61
Russia	18	53
British Muslims	23	62
German Muslims	29	60
French Muslims	41	58
Spanish Muslims	49	23
Turkey	14	64
Egypt	31	58
Jordan	39	54
Indonesia	39	53
Pakistan	30	25
Nigerian Muslims	10	77
Nigerian Christians	24	52

To begin with, Britain stands out. While 28 percent of Britons in general consider relations with Muslims to be good, only 23 percent of Muslims in Britain share that opinion—in clear contrast with the situation in Germany, France, and Spain, where Muslims had a more positive view of those relations than the population as a whole. Also interesting is the fact that Muslims in Britain are more negative regarding those relations than Muslims in Egypt, Jordan, Indonesia, and Pakistan. Even more interesting, while Turks in Turkey are by far the most pessimistic, Muslims in Germany, most of whom are from Turkey, are twice as optimistic as their co-nationals back home.

Indeed, in regard to the two cases—Turkey and Pakistan—where Pew has assessed the views both of emigrants to Europe and of those who stayed in the native country, the picture is complex but revealing. The Turkish case is exceptional, in that Turkey is undergoing an increasingly tension-filled process of membership negotiations with the EU. At the time of the poll it was passing through an unusual outburst of anti-Americanism (mostly related to the Iraq issue); it is not surprising that respondents in Turkey were among the most pessimistic, or that the "Turkish" minority in Germany, while more positive, was still second only to Muslims in Britain in pessimism.

In the case of the UK and Pakistan, two elements are worth considering: first, that Muslims in England are mostly of Indian-subcontinent origin, at a time when Pakistan and Bangladesh are undergoing a dangerous and rapid Islamic radicalization; and second, that there are numerous recently arrived Algerians in Britain (many avoiding or rejected by France on suspicion of Islamist allegiances). Hence, that Pakistanis in Pakistan and Muslims in Britain are among the most negative regarding Muslims' relations with the West is also less than surprising.

While this is only one poll, its results suggest a number of important elements *vis-à-vis* Muslims in Europe. The most important is that country of origin is an essential factor influencing Europe-based communities. The vehicles for the transmission of mentalities and attitudes are examined elsewhere, but suffice it here to mention two: the continuous migratory flow from Turkey and Pakistan/Bangladesh and, closely related, the nature of that flow— spouses (almost always wives) from those countries. Combine this with the uncontrolled arrival of

imams and "imams" in England—to which one may add the influence of Algerian radicals promiscuously granted asylum—
and you have a clear explanation of higher levels of hostility
by Muslims in England and Germany.

On the other hand, France, often accused of heavy-handed
assimilationist policies, has one of the least unhappy Muslim
populations—indeed, more Muslims in France than French natives think bilateral relations are good. In Spain, where natives
are very unhappy with their Muslim neighbors, the reverse
is, extraordinarily, not true. This may, once again, have something to do with the country of origin and its influence—in
this case Morocco, which is engaged in an intensive, and so
far successful, campaign against local Islamism. However, it
probably has more to do with the extreme accommodationism
on the part of the present Socialist government in Madrid and
its twin in Catalonia, the other region with a heavy Muslim
concentration. These governments are strongly supportive of
Muslim demands, even ones as preposterous as the requests to
"share" the cathedral of Córdoba and to build a large mosque in
Granada. These are enough to explain the huge difference between majority Spaniards' dim view of relations with Muslims
and the Muslims' own optimistic view.

WHO ARE THE "MUSLIMS" IN THE EUROPEAN CONTEXT?

While there is obvious analytical utility in talking about
"Muslims in Europe," one should be wary of excessive general-
izations, *ummah* solidarity notwithstanding. Muslim communities in Europe are increasingly caught between their common
characteristics—not only religion, but also social pathologies
and perceived inferior status—and their ethnic, sectarian, and
social differences.

The overwhelming majority of Muslims in Europe are Sunnis, but there are also smaller Shia and Ismaili communities, which have different attitudes and behavior. Shias are closer to Iran—the only large country with a Shia majority—but also far less critical of the conflict in Iraq (of which their coreligionists are the main beneficiaries) than are the Sunni communities. Ismailis, regarded as heretics both by Sunnis and by most Shias, are far better integrated in their countries of adoption, usually quite prosperous, and generally aloof from politics. Thus, in general terms, the problematic issues regarding Muslims in Europe tend to be linked to the Sunni communities.

However, the Sunni communities themselves are far from homogeneous, and the differences are multiple: ethnic/national, linguistic, and historical. The four largest Sunni communities in Europe—Algerians, Moroccans, Turks, and Pakistanis—are not homogeneously spread through the various countries; there are few Turks in the United Kingdom and few Pakistanis in Germany and France. Nor are their levels of commitment to Islam similar. The majority of Turks, many served by moderate, Ankara-appointed imams, are generally less likely to support radical interpretations of Islam, while Pakistanis and Algerians are more likely to be influenced by Salafist thinking spread by radical preachers.

Turks in Europe tend to maintain traditional attitudes *vis-à-vis* Arabs and Iranians—contempt for the former, mistrust for the latter—and tend to avoid mixing with other Muslims or to join non-ethnic Islamic organizations, an attitude encouraged by linguistic differences. A trip through the Muslim neighborhoods of Brussels, for instance, demonstrates this clearly. Turkish neighborhoods are quite distinct from Moroccan or sub-Saharan ones, less integrated and more self-segregated.

North Africans in France, even the first generation, have less of a language problem with the natives than other immigrant groups, since French is still spoken widely in Tunisia, Algeria, and Morocco. On the other hand, the longstanding rivalry between Algiers and Rabat is directly reflected in France, with the former supporting the Grand Mosque of Paris and the latter the largest Muslim organization in France, the *Fédération Nationale des Musulmans de France* (FNMF). In Germany ethnic Turks and Kurds from Turkey do not see themselves as alike—any more than they do back home. The Kurds in Europe are often supporters of the PKK, a secessionist, Marxist, and secular terrorist group, hated by Turks everywhere. In addition, the Kurdish and Turkish languages are unrelated. A good case could be made that Kurds from Turkey living in Europe (mostly in Germany, the Netherlands, and Belgium) are less "Turkish" than Kurds in Turkey itself, mostly because the assimilationist policies of Ankara do not reach Berlin or Amsterdam.

As for the South Asian Muslim communities, the Pakistani, Indian, Bangladeshi, and East African Muslims, who live mainly in Britain, also differ among themselves in ethnicity, language, and customs. To begin with, there are the basically urban East African Muslims (most of them of British Indian descent) who took refuge in the UK following Idi Amin's outbursts of violent racism in Uganda during the 1970s. They soon reverted to middle- or even upper-class status in terms of both income and educational achievement, thanks to a specific culture unique to them and not repeated among other Muslim groups in England. In contrast, Pakistanis from Kashmir and Bangladeshis are doing poorly. Moreover, "Black African Muslim men . . . are three times as likely to be unemployed as white British men and almost twice as likely as Indian Muslims, who in turn are much more likely to be jobless than Sikhs or Hindus."[115]

It is said in the Netherlands that "Iranians integrate well." Among the four largest groups of asylum seekers—Iraqis, Afghanis, Iranians, and Somalis—40 percent of Iranians work, compared to only 25 percent of Somalis, and Iranians, boys and girls alike, have higher grades in school than the average among non-Western immigrants, Muslim or not.[116]

We have discussed the ethnic diversity of the "Turks" in Germany and the Netherlands. A rather similar situation exists in the cases of Moroccans and Algerians, many of whom are Berbers. Berbers *(Imazighen)*, a significant minority in Algeria and Morocco, are not Arab. In fact they are ethnically and linguistically quite distinct—and have become even more so in the European diaspora, where, unlike in Algeria or Morocco, they can freely manifest their separate identity.

Finally, there are the sub-Saharan Muslims, most of them living in France and originating from the Sahel states: Mali, Niger, Burkina Faso, Chad, and Senegal. They are culturally, and of course racially, distinct from the larger Arab, Pakistani, and Turkish communities; they are also different among themselves. The Senegalese are generally members of moderate Sufi brotherhoods: Mourides, Tidjanya, the Khadirya. That reality, plus their generally better education and knowledge of French, makes the Senegalese one of the most successful sub-Saharan immigrant groups in France. (The first, and long-serving, president of Senegal, Léopold Sédar Senghor, was a Christian married to a white Frenchwoman, and a poet and philosopher who wrote in French.) On the other hand, Malians—the largest group of migrants in proportion to their home country's population, and the Muslim community in France with the highest incidence of polygamy—are one of the poorest. Finally, the Somalis, large communities of whom exist in Italy and the UK (and now the United States), are, in all three countries, among the most welfare-dependent groups as well as far more likely to be religiously militant than any other sub-Saharan community. That was demonstrated, for instance, by their roles in the failed bombings in London on July 21, 2005, led by a Somali Eritrean named Muktar Said Ibrahim, with the support of fellow Somali Hamdi Adus Isaac, a.k.a. Osman Hussain, who was found among the Somali community in Italy during his brief period of refuge there.

Indeed, Somalis provide perhaps the best case study of an immigrant group whose native culture, imported to Europe and the United States, leads to exacerbated social pathologies. Somalis are notable underachievers in Western schools, and Somali boys are more involved in violence and delinquency than other immigrant groups. The usual academic explanations—overcrowding, language difficulties, and of course "racism"—are, as usual, off the mark. Why is it that in Wales Somali students are by far the worst, especially as they advance in grades, while Caribbean blacks are at levels close to those of native Welsh? Or why in Denmark are they, again, the worst performers in school, while Poles, Pakistanis, Vietnamese, and Iranians do much better? Perhaps there are cultural traits among Somalis that explain both the chaos in their country and their behavior in the diaspora, but that is not the kind of question even asked, let alone researched. The author of a study on Somali children in British schools stated that although "this study did not find racism in particular to be a cause for the underachievement of Somali pupils," he felt compelled to mention it because other academics did so![117]

INTEGRATION AND GLOBALIZATION

Integration is a term that is becoming acceptable in Europe—as opposed to the politically very incorrect *assimilation*. It is still undefined, but it suggests, at a minimum, acceptance of certain rules (also uncertainly defined) applicable in European states. As we have seen, the concept has met with resistance among the Muslim populations for various reasons, to which we may add globalization, or democratization of information. Any traveler to Muslim neighborhoods in Brussels, Paris, London, or Amsterdam can't avoid noticing the enormous number of satellite dishes in even the poorest housing complexes. This is an example of why global access to communications does not necessarily lead to integration, let alone common ways of thinking. To the contrary, Muslims in Europe—whether Turks watching Ankara's TV stations, Kurds watching the PKK's own Media TV, any Muslim watching Al Jazeera's repeats of Al-Qaeda's every statement, Indo-Pakistanis watching the mostly Islamist Pakistani networks—all keep in touch with a world distant and distinct from the one in which they live.

Add to such daily influences some prevailing European attitudes and policies, particularly the general acceptance of dual citizenship, which in the case of Muslims in Europe does not simply mean that individuals have two or more passports but that, for all practical purposes, they remain under the influence of their (or their parents') country of origin, and resistance to integration becomes easy to understand. Furthermore, it seems normal to many European governments that persons of Moroccan (or Algerian or Turkish) origin, even third-generation born in Amsterdam, Brussels, or Paris, remain citizens of a country they may never have visited. Even the French, normally so sensitive to any real or perceived threat to their sovereignty, seem to have no problem accepting, and indeed co-operating with, Muslim organizations widely known to be financed and controlled by the regimes in Rabat and Algiers. That also applies in Germany's case *vis-à-vis* Ankara.

Muslim communities' ties to the countries of origin are probably the most important variable in their degrees of radicalization, Islamist infiltration, and support for terrorism. For instance, a Kurd from Turkey living in Germany or the Netherlands is far more likely to be influenced by the PKK[118] than by Islamism in general and Arab Islamism in particular.

Even among Arab communities in Europe the differences are often acute. Thus Moroccans and Algerians in France, Italy, or Spain do not really get along well, as we have seen, and both are resentful of Saudi attempts to weaken their governments' control over diaspora communities via Muslim Brotherhood–influenced organizations, such as the UOIF (*Union des Organisations Islamiques de France*) and UCOII (*Unione delle Comunità ed Organizzazioni Islamiche in Italia*).

THE ROLE OF BLACKS

While most attention on Muslims in Europe is focused on Arabs, Turks, and South Asians, the reality is that blacks, especially sub-Saharan ones, as well as a few Caribbean converts to Islam, also play a role in Europe's Islamic problem.

Caribbeans, or West Indians, have until recently been by far the largest black group in the UK (though now numerically surpassed by African migrants). Traditionally Christian, a number of them have been converted to Islam in Britain and have participated in Islamist violence. We have mentioned "shoe bomber" Richard Reid, born in Britain to a British mother and a Jamaican father. Jihadist preacher Abdullah el-Faisal (né Trevor William Forest) was active in Britain prior to his 2007 deportation to his native Jamaica. And Germaine Lindsay, a British-born Jamaican with a white wife, was one of the four suicide bombers of July 7, 2005. While this list is not very long, it is significant.

In France, the blacks from the huge swath of former African colonies are overwhelmingly Muslim—albeit generally Muslims with a historically syncretic and moderate outlook. Once in France, however, blacks of the second or third generation tend to associate with, and often imitate, Arabs from the Maghreb in both behavior and religious tendencies.

France, of course, is in a peculiar position among European states, since it still does have its overseas *départements* and territories—such as Guadeloupe, Martinique, and Mayotte—which all have large black majorities. Muslim Mayotte aside, these areas are Christian and fall outside the topic of this study. However, race does play a role—hence the creation in November 2005 of the *CRAN (Conseil Réprésentatif des Associations Noires,* the Representative Council of Black Associations), led by a pharmacist, Patrick Lozès, and claiming to bring together African and West Indian blacks. Another prominent leader is Fodé Sylla, a former president of the human-rights organization *SOS Racisme* and a European Parliament MP, who ominously stated: "One must let the people express themselves, otherwise we will have in France a Louis Farrakhan. Right now, we are still at [the stage of following] Martin Luther King."[119]

During the riots in France in the fall of 2005, many black youths participated as a group. Police statements in many areas suggest that more and more young troublemakers are African. Blacks are tending to replace the more socially mobile Maghrebi Arabs in the poorest public-housing projects.[120] In such areas customs such as polygamy and genital mutilation of girls are common and reinforce a vicious circle of poverty, hostility to law, and resentment, often with racist overtones. Thus in 2003 blacks violently infiltrated demonstrations against high-school reforms; in 1995 they threatened "to break all white [stuff]"; in 1998, during the soccer World Cup, the *Renseignements Généraux,* the police intelligence division, sounded the alarm signal in a report titled: "Gangs of blacks, a disturbing community regression."[121]

Vaulx-en-Velin, near Lyon, has a history of criminality and riots going back to 1981—and a similarly long history of conversions to Islam by young Africans.[122] The black racist and anti-Semitic comic Dieudonné M'Bala M'Bala (himself half European) is seen by the youths of the area as their spokesman. Such social "microclimates" have their own slang—Europeans are *keufs* and *cistras* (racists)—and the trend is toward such neighborhoods becoming increasingly homogeneous in terms of ethnicity and religion—what some French sociologists call "the lost territories of the Republic." Islamist preachers recruit in places like Vaulx-en-Velin or Vénissieux (another suburb of Lyon) because they are a fertile ground already, as demonstrated by the arrests of members of Salafist terrorist cells in the area during the past few years.

While black/Muslim relations in France are not controversial, since many if not most blacks are Muslims, in Britain that is not the case, and relations are far from simple or peaceful. In May 2006 three Pakistanis were jailed for the "racist" murder of a young black in Birmingham—although whether the incident was racial or arose from inter-gang conflict is not clear.

SELF-SEGREGATION

The combination of all these identity contradictions, but especially the ultimate solidarity with the *ummah* rather than with any other group, such as family or country of birth, and the generally tolerant tone of the surrounding culture have led to the progressive development of the opposite of integration—segregation, and especially self-segregation. This is the case in virtually every European country, regardless of official policies and efforts—whether British *laissez-faire* or French assimilationism.

Thus, British government ministers became troubled that "the normal patterns of immigrant settlement have gone completely haywire. The so-called 'third generation' of Muslim Britons—those young enough to have grandparents who migrated here—ought, in theory, to be the most westernized and the most comfortable about the rich diversity of their heritage. In many cases, this is precisely what has happened. But paradoxically, it is also true that the third generation is the most radicalized to date: turning, as the young bombers from West Yorkshire did, to Islamist ideology, in search of certainty, purpose and prestige."[123]

The officials were right to be worried. As the BBC noted,

> An investigation for *Today* has found disturbing evidence that Asian youths in parts of Oldham are trying to create no-go areas for white people. Last year the police investigated record levels of racist attacks in Oldham. Of the 572 cases, 60% turned out to be white victims. Pakistanis make up the majority on the Glodwick estate just west of the town centre. Some youths speak the language of racial hatred. It's not clear whether this is bravado but their message is blunt . . . white people keep out.[124]

Shakeel Meer, director of the Leeds Racial Harassment Project, noted, in regard to local Muslim youths, that "They've developed their own very different culture within Islam, and they're not totally Pakistani or totally Islamic, and they're not totally British, either. These kids face quite an identity crisis. They're fighting to assert themselves not on one or two fronts, but in three or four different directions."[125] This view is confirmed by an informed outsider, Professor Akbar Ahmed, chairman of Islamic studies at the American University in Washington and formerly Pakistan's High Commissioner in Britain. Ahmed believes that "this new generation of British Muslims, especially with a South Asian/Pakistani background . . . have grown up suspended between two cultures and not really feeling they have dominated either. . . . So while they play cricket, enjoy western pop music, and speak with a northern accent, they are still susceptible to notions of Islam 'under siege.'"[126]

The British were not the only ones who were anxious about Muslim self-segregation. Similar complaints elsewhere in Europe have become more frequent, especially among women government officials. Thus, Lisa Prokop, then Austria's interior minister, in 2006 "told reporters that as many as 45 percent of Austria's Muslims are resisting integration, and that their insistence on living separate lives was 'a ticking time bomb.'"[127] Norwegian Minister of Local Government and Regional Development Erna Solberg stated that "Islam must be modernized" and that "Muslims living in Norway must accept that they're a minority in a progressive, egalitarian-oriented society."[128] Rita Verdonk, the Netherlands' outspoken former Integration and Immigration Minister, was relentless in her criticism of Muslims' resistance to accepting Dutch values.

Writing in the *Turkish Daily News*, Elif Safak, a Turkish journalist, described her experience in London's mostly Turkish neighborhood of Harringay:

> I walk around in Harringay. You know, that part of London where all the greengrocers are Turkish, where the white cheese is all imported from Turkey, and where the doner kebab sellers are more than you can count. Barbers, restaurants, "kahve" houses (a special café where Turkish males gather to drink tea, smoke, talk politics, etc.), newspaper sellers, corner stores: they are all run by Turks speaking Turkish in Harringay. It is a neighborhood where, if you had a problem, you could find a sympathetic ear without having to speak a word of English. . . . An evening out with a group of British women at

a Turkish restaurant in Harringay. They are speaking English, as is natural. They ask something about the menu, inquiring about the soup. The owner of the restaurant speaks not a word of English, though. He never learned any, so he calls over his daughter. She, a 13-year-old, speaks very good English as, after all, she was born, bred and educated here. Here is how the restaurant owner calls his daughter: "Oh daughter, could you come over here a second, some tourists have come to our restaurant, come tell me what they are asking for!" And so, the Turkish merchant who calls the Brits "tourists" in their own land lives comfortably on, without ever having to leave Harringay.[129]

Nor is Turkish integration more advanced in Germany or the Netherlands, where,

When exploring Turkish shops, one will notice at first sight how the Turkish buyers only deal with Turkish salespeople, despite the high prices. In return, the merchants are always keen on displaying Turkish goods. The shops have names like Istanbul, Ankara, Amra, Mulana, Turkeya, and display the same quantity and types of goods supplied in Turkey...

No immigrant Turkish home lacks satellite dishes configured to receive homeland Turkish channels. The satellite Channel 7, TRTint Channel, which addresses the Turkish community abroad, and Channel 5, which favors the Turkish Sa'ada Party, attract the majority of immigrant Turkish viewers because they telecast discussions (*iskelesenjak*) on the various home and immigrant Turkish issues. These channels also transmit music and Sufi Mawaweel (songs in praise of the Prophet Muhammad).[130]

One should note that these large "islands" of unassimilated immigrants are spreading. However, one should also point out that self-segregation among Muslims in Germany, Belgium, the Netherlands, or Britain is not just based on faith differences, but also on ethnic ones. Muslim neighborhoods in Brussels, for instance, are not distinct just because of the number of minarets or of women wearing the *hijab*, but also because some are homogeneously Turkish, some Moroccan, some sub-Saharan— and the lines are quite clear. Bangladeshi or Pakistani areas in London are similarly defined, as are the ethnic differences between the faithful in Spanish mosques—if a mosque is Algerian, one will hardly find Pakistani or Moroccan worshippers.

MUSLIM VIEWS OF INTEGRATION

For many Muslims in Europe, integration is both undesired and unnecessary.

> Necla Kelek sums it up this way in *The Foreign Bride:* "The guest workers turned into Turks, and the Turks turned into Muslims." . . . Kelek asked a group of Turkish "import brides" who had been living in Germany for years how they had actually prepared for their future in Germany. Their answer: incredulous laughter. Prepare? How and for what? "But how can you stand living here?" Kelek went on. "You don't have anything to do with this country, you despise its culture and the way people live here." But we have everything we need here, was the answer; we don't need the Germans.[31]

This hostility to the West is far from unique:

> Karim Traida, a stylish Algerian film director with a nomination for a Golden Globe [for *The Polish Bride* (1998)], says, "So there is the risk of a clash. The clash is already in the mind. Muslims fear that, if they open up, they'll wind up like the Christians— very decadent. So when Islam looks at Christian history, it's worried by what goes with liberalism. They think of the decadence of European society."

> Islam in Europe, he adds, "has no roots yet. It's unstable, a new phenomenon, and the mosques want to stay secret. Parents are afraid that their children will go into decadent Dutch society, so they bring them back to Islam."

> "The young are open to everything," says Uzeyir Kabaktepe, the vice president of the Turkish Milli Görüs mosque in Amsterdam. "If you give them pure Koran, they become

extremist. All doors close for them. 'Everything else is black,' they think, 'but I'm white and I'm going to paradise.' Those who see black and white think they are angels, they think they are flying. If a Dutchman speaks to them on the street, they think 'he's a Zionist' or 'he's a Satan'. We give the Koran, not pure, but with explanations. We make them debate with each other. We show them that some of the dark ones, the infidels, are religious people too."

The Moroccans, he says, are different. "They brought their ideas to Europe with them, and they don't budge," he claims. "Democracy for Arabs is Satanic, it's from the West, against God's word. Idiot imams came who said the Dutch and everything to do with them—schools, society—are devils. They said: get a second wife, from abroad, so the devils pay the social money for them. The Middle East plays a big role for the Arabs, it goes into the second and third generation. A child of 10 gets pictures on the internet of Americans in Iraq, mosques burnt down, prisoners. They say, why am I here? As a young Muslim? The internet can do big damage."

Safiyeh M, a Dutch Moroccan divorcee with two children, says there is "one little group that won't adapt. It's always 'damn Dutch, damn Jews, damn infidels'. They can't do anything in Morocco. They'd get squashed. So they try it here."[132]

Muslims in the West as a whole, including "mainstream" organizations, are increasingly disinclined to accept assimilation or integration. Instead, they have adopted, with strong encouragement from the Left, a politically correct approach, labeling any measure to control Muslim immigration and radicalism as "racist" or "Islamophobic." Thus, when France banned the *hijab* in schools and the Netherlands expelled false asylum seekers, Alaa Bayoumi of the Council on American-Islamic Relations (CAIR), the largest U.S. Muslim organization, said:

The new regulations unjustly infringe on the civil rights of millions of law-abiding Muslim immigrants by: forcing Muslim women and girls to choose between their religiously mandated attire and available public educational opportunities; sending Muslim refugees to countries where their lives may be endangered; and limiting Muslims' access to religious leaders and education. They also disregard historical and contemporary Muslim contributions to the advancement of Europe. During the colonial era, the Islamic world provided major pools of cheap labor and natural resources necessary for the advancement of industrial Europe. After World War II, France and Britain turned towards their former Muslim colonies in North Africa and South Asia to seek badly needed workforce to help their economic recovery, while the Germans sought the help of the Turks, their former allies.

Today, more than 15 million Muslims create an integral part of Europe. Some of them are highly educated immigrants and converts, while many are underprivileged workers who help fill blue-collar jobs, have little political access, if any, and face frequent discrimination, especially in the post–Sept. 11 era. In Britain, where 1.6 million Muslims live, a London-based Islamic human rights group reported 344 incidents of anti-Muslim violence in the year after Sept. 11, including the stabbing of a Muslim woman.

Instead of confronting the post–Sept. 11 anti-Muslim phobia, these new laws will find scapegoats in Muslims for the real problems dwindling Europe's ability to build on its traditions of multiculturalism and tolerance, its need for economic and political reform, and the rise of the extreme right.[133]

In other words, the problem is not the Muslims who committed the 9/11 atrocities, but the West's reactions to them. Bayoumi goes on to claim that

Europe's proposed anti-Muslim laws will create a false solution for serious problems, impeding Europe's multiculturalism. This will hinder Muslim integration in European society, as well as damage Europe's image in the Muslim world. Instead, European countries should seek creative approaches to fully engage their Muslim communities in the struggle for economic reform and ideological moderation.[134]

Not surprisingly, given the continuing and, in fact, increasing ties between Muslims in Europe and Muslims in the countries of their or their parents' or grandparents' origins, their view of what integration means is not that of either left-wing or conservative Europeans.

Instead, for more and more Muslims in Europe, the notion of integration is close to that offered by the Dublin-based European Council for Fatwa and Research (ECFR), led by the Muslim Brotherhood's most influential cleric, the Egyptian-born Yusuf al-Qaradawi. Given his enormous influence, it is worth an extensive quote:[135]

Fatwa (1)

Q) Could the Honourable scholars, members of the ECFR, give us their Fatwa on whether it is permissible for a Muslim to settle and reside permanently in non-Muslim countries. We would be grateful if the answer was supported by evidence from the Holy Quran, the Prophetic heritage (Sunna), and the statements of scholars and individuals of knowledge.

A) The issue of a Muslim's permanent residence in non-Muslim countries is one which has been discussed and debated at length. We have heard extremely strict views which call for all Muslims to leave these countries immediately, based upon a Hadith which decrees the disownment of all Muslims who live amongst non-Muslims (Mushriks), the meaning and degree of authenticity of which will be discussed later. However, it remains that these views caused great difficulty and inconvenience for many Muslims.

Our opinion is that a Muslim must never live amongst non-Muslims whilst compromising or even discarding his or her Islamic identity, unless that individual is one who is entirely overpowered and has no other option to choose. The reason for this is based upon the issue of whether or not the Muslim individual is able to protect himself, his religion and that of whomever he is responsible for, i.e. his wife and children. Therefore, if the environment in which the Muslim finds himself is one which threatens his life, religion and those for whom he is responsible, it is upon him to migrate to a land which does not pose such a threat, as it is unlawful for him to remain in an environment which threatens his life and religion.

Allah (swt [Subhanahu wa ta'ala--Glorious and exalted is he]) states in the Holy Quran:

"When angels take the souls of those who die in sin against their souls, they say: In what plight were you? They replied: Weak and oppressed were we in the earth. They say: Was not the earth of God spacious enough for you to move yourselves away from evil? Such men will find their abode in Hell; what an evil refuge! Except those who are really weak and oppressed—men, women and children who have no means in their power, nor a guide-post to direct their way. For these, there is hope that God will forgive: For God does blot out sins and forgive again and again. He who forsakes his home in the cause of God finds in the earth many a refuge, wide and spacious: should he die as a refugee from home for God and His apostle, his reward becomes due and sure with God: and God is oft-forgiving, Most merciful" (4:97-100).

This verse clearly states that it is an injustice for one to accept living under conditions of humiliation, whilst possessing the ability to move to another land which offers freedom, security and means of a dignified life. The only group of people excused from this judgment are those who possess no such power nor means of deciding such matters. *Thus, a migration is correct, in fact compulsory, if the destination allows the Muslim more means of performing religion than the land of origin.* [Emphasis added.] The migration of the weaker Muslims of Mekka to Abyssynia (Al-Habasha [Ethiopia]) with the permission of the Prophet (peace and prayers of Allah be upon him), is a worthy example. Those Muslims were told to migrate from an environment of infidelity and injustice to another, non-Muslim land, but which offered those who lived on it justice and security. The Muslims lived among Christians who treated them well and therefore managed to preserve their religion and to save their lives, until the day came when Allah (swt) supported his Prophet and bestowed upon the Muslims victory over the enemies of Islam. Only then did they migrate to Medina, and when they did so, they did it by virtue of their own will and not by any command or order of the Prophet (ppbuh).

Therefore, the issue here is the ability to maintain one's religion as well as to preserve and protect lives from death, injustice and oppression. It is lawful for one to find such a safe refuge in non-Muslim countries, as did the earlier Muslims who migrated to Abassynia (Al-Habasha). [136]

This *fatwa* implies that Europe "allows the Muslim more means of performing religion than the land of origin," a claim often made by radical Islamists like Mullah Krekar or Abu Hamza to justify their living among the infidels (and receiving welfare payments from them). However, life among the infidels is conditioned upon the understanding that, if forced to chose between Islam and the rules of the nonbelievers, the good Muslim always has to choose the former—since "it is unlawful for him to remain in an environment which threatens his life and religion." In a nutshell, this apparently moderate *fatwa* implies that Muslims should live in Europe only if their freedom to practice their religion is *greater* than in a Muslim country, and then only insofar as the laws and circumstances in the European country do not contradict Islam—in other words, only under their own conditions. None of this is exactly an encouragement to integration.

Indeed, for many Muslims, living in the West raises important dilemmas. Thus, for English convert and radical preacher Abdur-Raheem Greene,

The Western psyche emphasizes one's individuality. This is at variance with Islam. Any sincere Muslim feels disturbed. He or she is constantly bombarded by sex and sexuality. Most girls lose virginity by 13 and it is normal for girls to have three to four boyfriends.... The dilemma before Muslims in the West is as to how to integrate with a society so steeped in sex, drugs, drinks and sexual intimacy. And if no integration, then how to save themselves from ghettoisation.[137]

The founder of the Belgian-based Arab European League (AEL), Dyab Abu Jahjah, who obtained citizenship despite admitting that he cheated twice—once via a marriage of convenience and once by lying about his ties with *Hizbollah*—openly engages in anti-Semitism (although some would quibble with the term, as Arabs are also Semites) and supports terrorist groups, all in the name of freedom of speech, while complaining about European "hypocrisy":

> Europeans think that freedom of speech is guaranteed in Europe, and that they are defending it against Islamic pressure. This is a view that is widely propagated and defended by groups from across the political spectrum. Reality, however, presents us Muslims living in Europe with another experience. Muslims and others in Europe can not say everything they often want to say and they risk being arrested and prosecuted if they do. Muslims and other religious people can not express their disgust for homosexuality and clearly state that they believe it's a sickness and a deviation without being persecuted for being homophobic. . . . Not only Muslims are not allowed to voice all their opinions. . . . the French parliamentarian Christian Vanneste was sentenced in court to a heavy fine because he had stated that "homosexual behaviour endangers the survival of humanity" and that "heterosexuality is morally superior to homosexuality." Earlier last month a majority in the European Parliament called for sanctions against Poland and the Baltic states because their governments are said to be "homophobic." In the Netherlands access to certain jobs in the civil service is effectively denied to anyone religious (be it Christian or Muslim) who refuses to participate in concluding same-sex marriages. And the EU wants to force doctors to perform abortions and euthanasia because, it says, the right to conscientious objection is not "unlimited." . . . Yesterday, a Turkish Muslim wrote us: ". . . So Please look at the Denmark. They shows that Mohammed married many times. This not

true. One thing is true and all the world knows that a man can marry with a man in Denmark, Holland and Norway. They lost their heart and mind."[138]

Veteran British journalist and Professor of European Studies Timothy Garton Ash seems to agree about the reasons for the alienation of Muslims in Europe:

> Another possible reason is that Britain now has one of the most libertine societies in Europe. Particularly among younger Brits in urban areas, which is where most British Muslims live, we drink more alcohol faster, sleep around more, live less in long-lasting, two-parent families, and worship less, than almost anyone in the world. It's clear from what young British Muslims themselves say that part of their reaction is against this kind of secular, hedonistic, anomic lifestyle.[139]

EQUALITY OR SPECIAL TREATMENT?

A common example of logical contradiction is simultaneously insisting that Muslims be treated equally under the national law, and demanding concessions to specific Islamic customs and attitudes. Thus,

> The Dudley Metropolitan Borough Council (Tory-controlled) has now announced that, following a complaint by a Muslim employee, all work pictures and knick-knacks of novelty pigs and "pig-related items" will be banned. Among the verboten items is one employee's box of tissues, because it features a representation of Winnie the Pooh and Piglet. And, as we know, Muslims regard pigs as "unclean," even an anthropomorphized cartoon pig wearing a scarf and a bright, colourful singlet. . . . Mahbubur Rahman is in favor of the blanket pig crackdown. "It is a good thing, it is a tolerance and acceptance of their beliefs and understanding," he said. That's all, folks, as Porky Pig used to stammer at the end of Looney Tunes. Just a little helpful proscription in the interests of tolerance and acceptance.[140]

After British Muslim inmates complained that jail toilets were facing Mecca, the construction of Islamically correct toilets is now spreading throughout England. The Manchester Methodist Housing Association has developed a housing estate in North England with "bathrooms that face away from Mecca."[141]

When an anti-immigrant group in Strasbourg prepared pork soup for the homeless, Mayor Fabienne Keller was outraged. "Schemes with racial subtexts must be denounced," she claimed, and banned the soup distribution, because it "excluded" Muslims and Jews.[142] Considering that Strasbourg is a French border city known for its German-style *charcuterie* and beer, it is clear that if discrimination was at issue here, it was the mayor's discrimination against the local majority and their culinary traditions.

British bureaucrats or French Socialist mayors perhaps may be seen as feeble or opportunistic, but there are also the supposedly sophisticated intellectuals who willingly deny the obvious, as witness Ian Buruma of Bard College in New York State, in a debate with the French political writer Pascal Bruckner. When Bruckner complained about policies followed by an Islamic hospital in Paris and about beaches reserved for Muslim women in Italy, Buruma claimed that such phenomena are no different from kosher restaurants or Catholic hospitals. This earned his a sharp rebuke from Necla Kelek: "Whether it is headscarves or gender-specific separation of public space, political Islam is trying to establish apartheid of the sexes in free European societies. A Muslim hospital is fundamentally different from a Catholic hospital. In a Muslim hospital, patients are separated according to gender. Men may be treated only by men, women only by women. Muslim female nurses, for example, may not wash male patients; they may not even touch them."[143]

In France, *laïcité* is virtually the national credo and is understood as meaning that all religions are equally separated from public life, meaning education, politics, and government support. Nevertheless, the law banning Islamic scarves—but also other religious symbols, such as crosses and stars of David—was seen as "anti-Muslim," because it denied Muslims special treatment.

One cannot understand the Muslim problem in Europe without understanding the political correctness dominating the mentality and vocabulary of Brussels and the European elites behind it. Even in ostensibly ultra-secular France any criticism of Islam—though not of the Catholic Church or Christianity in general—is legally banned under the label of "racism" and "religious hatred." The French novelist and filmmaker Michel Houellebecq and the Italian journalist Oriana Fallaci were sued, the latter also in Italy, for "insulting Islam"—but no one was sued for supporting Ayatollah Khomeini's *fatwa* sentencing to death Salman Rushdie, the author of *The Satanic Verses*.

When, following the assassination of Theo van Gogh, the Dutch elites admitted that assimilation of Muslims in the Netherlands had failed, they were correct—and they could have been speaking for most European countries. Indeed, if assimilation or integration is the declared official goal (although in many countries it is not), it has failed throughout Europe. A 2006 Pew poll is revealing in this respect.[144]

WHAT DO YOU CONSIDER YOURSELF FIRST?

Muslims in:	A citizen of your country	A Muslim/A Christian
Great Britain	7	81
Spain	3	69
Germany	13	66
France	42	46
Pakistan	6	87
Jordan	21	67
Egypt	23	59
Turkey	19	51
Indonesia	39	36
Nigeria	25	71
Christians in:		
United States	48	42
Germany	59	42
Great Britain	59	42
Russia	63	42
France	83	42
Spain	60	42
Nigeria	43	42

It appears that French *laïcité* does have an impact on Muslims in that country, who are the only ones living in the West for whom the gap between feeling oneself to be a citizen and feeling oneself to be Muslim is not very great. In the other cases the distance is enormous. Among Muslims in Britain the Islamic identity is stronger than among Muslims in overwhelmingly Islamic countries like Jordan, Egypt, or Turkey—but close to the situation in Pakistan, where many of them originated.

Such figures are, or should be, disturbing to those seeking the integration of Muslims in Europe. Scottish historian and Harvard professor Niall Ferguson stirred up a revealing debate when he predicted that the growing number of Muslims could lead to "the death of Europe" within fifty years and its trans-formation into "a hybrid called Eurabia," a term initially coined and publicized by the Egyptian-born Jewish writer Bat Ye'or.[145] Ferguson noted that "A creeping Islamization of a decadent Christendom is only one of the conceivable scenarios: while the old Europeans get even older and their religious faith gets even weaker, the Muslim colonies within their cities get larger and more overt in their religious observance."[146]

These views are echoed, with glee, by radical Islamists en-sconced in Europe's comfortable welfare system, like Norway's Mullah Krekar: "We're the ones who will change you. . . . Just look at the development within Europe, where the number of Muslims is expanding like mosquitoes. . . . Every western woman in the EU is producing an average of 1.4 children. Every Muslim woman in the same countries are producing 3.5 chil-dren. . . . By 2050, 30 percent of the population in Europe will be Muslim."[147]

These statements are given added force by the figures pro-vided by the Pew poll, suggesting that only 7 percent, 3 per-cent, and 13 percent of Muslims in Britain, Spain, and Germany, respectively, consider themselves primarily citizens of those countries, as opposed to being Muslims first. Even so, the gen-erally lucid *Economist*, perhaps being too faithful to its title, has a very sanguine attitude toward Muslim integration in Europe. "Give them jobs, education and a seat on the city council" it believes, and all will be well.[148]

Perhaps, but the evidence appears to be to the contrary. For example, a youth worker from Somalia, Aydarus Yusuf, 29, admitted that when a group of Somali youths in Woolwich, southeast London, were arrested on suspicion of stabbing an-other Somali teenager, the victim's family told the police the matter would be settled out of court, and the suspects were released on bail. A "hearing" was convened, and elders ordered the assailants to compensate their victim. "All their uncles and their fathers were there.... So they all put something towards that and apologized for the wrongdoing."[149] While it has been noted already in this book that Somalis have more difficulties in integrating than most other Muslim groups, it is important to note that British authorities went along with this arrangement—and nobody knows how many such cases occur and go unreported.

With integration failing, and Islam increasingly important as a personal identifier, it is unsurprising that "In European countries, some Muslims—*especially the younger generation* [emphasis added]—are faced with an identity crisis. They do not feel Western even though they were born in the West and are European citizens. But they do not feel Arab either. So they choose a new nationality: Islamist."[150] The attitude of some of the friends of one of the London terrorists of July 7, 2005, is quite typical.

> At Beeston's Cross Flats Park, in the center of this now embattled town [Leeds], Sanjay Dutt and his friends grappled Friday with why their friend Kakey, better known to the world as Shehzad Tanweer, had decided to become a suicide bomber.
>
> "He was sick of it all, all the injustice and the way the world is going about it," Mr. Dutt, 22, said. "Why, for example, don't they ever take a moment of silence for all the Iraqi kids who die?"
>
> "It's a double standard, that's why," answered a friend, who called himself Shahroukh, also 22, wearing a baseball cap and basketball jersey, sitting nearby. "I don't approve of what he did, but I understand it. You get driven to something like this, it doesn't just happen."[151]

What do their words mean? First, that they believe that for Englishmen, their fellow citizens, to mourn the victims in London rather than those in Iraq is a "double standard." This suggests that these young Muslims in Britain (obviously, not British Muslims) have absolutely no loyalty to the country in which they were born and educated. They feel for fellow Muslims on another continent rather than for Englishmen on their street.

The leader of the Islamist *Hizb ut-Tahrir* (HuT—Party of Liberation) in the UK, Imram Waheed, claims, "We know that the killing of innocents is forbidden. . . . But we don't see two classes of blood; the blood of Iraqis is just as important to us as English blood." He emphasized that HuT in no way condoned the bombings. "But when you understand things from that perspective, why should we condemn the bombing?"[152] Why indeed, especially as *Hizb ut-Tahrir* advocates a world Caliphate and the rejection of Western, or all non-Islamic, values, laws, and behavior—although, it claims, through nonviolent means.

From such attitudes, shared by many ordinary Muslims— and not just in Britain—as well as by prominent religious figures, combining a strong, and growing, sense of Islamic identity with an equally strong sense of cultural victimhood, comes a vicious circle of false perceptions and alienation that is both the result and the cause of self-segregation from the surrounding community.

MUSLIMS IN EUROPE AND IN COUNTRIES OF ORIGIN

"Marseille is closer to Algiers than Lille."   —Rachid Kaci[153]

What are the relations between the various Muslim communities in Europe and their original homelands? Which way is the strongest influence going—from North Africa and the Indian subcontinent to Paris and London, or in the opposite direction? A number of facts have to be analyzed, including the following:

- The governments of the countries of origin of some of the largest Muslim immigrant groups in the EU retain major influence over the religious activities of their former citizens and even of their children and grandchildren. That is clearly true for the governments of Morocco and Algeria in the cases of France and Belgium, of Turkey in the case of Germany, and so on.

- At the same time, EU-born Muslims, especially the "*beurs*" (Muslims of Maghrebi origin born in France), as well as Pakistani, Bangladeshi, and Indian Muslims in Britain, often tend to lose their original national identity in favor of a communitarian Islamic one, a key ingredient in understanding the ability of groups like Al-Qaeda or the Algerian GIA to establish networks whose members are of different origins: Tunisians and Egyptians, Moroccans and Pakistanis, etc.

Ties abroad are of various types, including, as we have seen, taking a bride from the home country and receiving one's news from there via satellite dishes. One issue that is seldom linked to the poverty of Muslim communities in Europe is that of remittances. European Muslim remittances to Morocco, Algeria, and the West Bank are vital for those areas' economies (not unlike those from the United States to Mexico and Central America). One may also wonder whether the low rate of home ownership among Bangladeshis in Britain is not, in part, explained by the rapidly growing number of what are, by local standards, luxurious homes in Silhet, built by émigrés out of savings that have *not* been used to build or buy a home in Britain. That helps explain the huge proportion of people of

Bangladeshi origin in Britain who are living in overcrowded conditions, at three times the average.[154]

Politically, the policies of Spain and France *vis-à-vis* Rabat and Algiers are clearly influenced by the large numbers of North Africans living and voting in Europe. And the number of Muslims in Europe has influenced, if not determined, the EU's sympathetic position toward the Palestinians.

Following the Parliament's approval of his immigration legislation, then Interior Minister Sarkozy began a trip to the African countries most likely to be affected. In Mali, local MPs asked for the trip to be canceled, and the *Info-Matin* newspaper in the capital city, Bamako, warned of "A racist within our walls." In Cotonou Guy Mitokpe, president of the *Fédération Nationale des Etudiants du Bénin* (FNEB), opined that "The new Sarkozy law says that only the best will be accepted [in France]. Like yesterday, when the slave traders were choosing slaves among able men and women." That is rich in irony, coming from the African country whose rulers in earlier times, the kings of Abomey, played by far the largest role in the capture and sale of black slaves to the European traders. Not surprisingly, though, the "racist" label and phony analogies with the slavery of an earlier day, borrowed from the French Left, are used instead of rational arguments.[155]

Belgium has a long history of encouraging the governments of Islamic countries with a large diaspora there to influence, indeed control, those communities. Thus, in 2003, at the request of the Executive of Muslims in Belgium (EMB), Moroccan preachers vetted by the official Hassan II Foundation for Moroccans Living Abroad, as well as a "delegation of academicians, scholars and Koran readers" from Rabat, arrived in Brussels for Ramadan, to "explain the holy precepts of Islam" in the 45 mosques in and around the capital.[156] In 2004, Françoise

Schepmans, a prominent Walloon politician visiting Rabat, proposed a joint endeavor toward the creation of an Islamic theological institute in Belgium and regretted the fact that, contrary to the case with Catholicism and Judaism, there are no teachers of Islam in Belgian public schools. In response, the Moroccan minister-delegate in charge of Moroccan expatriates, Nouzha Chekrouni, deplored the "amalgam between immigration, Islam, and terrorism" and called for the Moroccan expatriates to participate in the ongoing democratic process in the Kingdom.[57]

When Rita Verdonk, then Dutch Integration and Immigration Minister, visited Morocco "to obtain permission from her counterparts for the Dutch wish to abolish Moroccan citizenship for Moroccans who have become Dutch citizens, she was met with unbelief and incredulity by Moroccan authorities. A government official in Morocco said at the time that Moroccan citizenship is an 'inalienable right' which is not up for discussion." In a follow-up visit, then Foreign Affairs Minister Bernard Bot admitted in Rabat that "They [the Moroccans] have taken a position, as have we. The theme, however, is on the table for discussion." According to Bot, "We believe it is best for children of the second or third generation that dual citizenship be abandoned." He added: "The Moroccan Government in Rabat believes Moroccans in the Netherlands have a right to their religion, their language and their cultural background. We believe that if they are to integrate they must adjust to Dutch customs and mores. We are now looking for an acceptable compromise."[58]

Apart from their own countries of origin, by far the most important and relevant outside influence on the European Muslim communities is that of Saudi Arabia, with its Wahhabi interpretation of Islam. From Sarajevo to Rome one can see Saudi-built mosques, with their tasteless shapes, and one can find organizations subsidized by Riyadh or the other Gulf states. The most important is the French UOIF (Union of Islamic Organizations in France), paid for by Saudis and ideologically part of the Muslim Brotherhood's global structure, the best organized and second most powerful Muslim NGO in France. Then Interior Minister Sarkozy found out where the UOIF's sympathies lie when he was booed by the crowd at its annual meeting at Le Bourget in April 2003 for advocating the ban on the *hijab*.[159]

CHAPTER THREE

The Islamic Presence

"One minister said, 'There are 5 million Muslims in France.' I asked, 'Mr. Minister, how did you arrive at that figure when we don't inquire about people's religion?' He said, 'I took an average. The Imams say 6 million; the ones who are against them say 3.5 million.' I said, 'With all due respect, Mr. Sarkozy, the average between two phony numbers does not make a real number."

—French scholar Gilles Kepel [1]

The Impact of Muslims in Europe

The numbers and impact of Muslims in Europe are still a matter of debate and conflicting assessments, and the language used to examine such issues is heavily tainted by concern for political correctness. In some countries, such as France and Belgium (similar legislation has been proposed in the United Kingdom), it is a criminal offense to express critical opinions on Islam or Muslims, as prominent authors Oriana Fallaci and Michel Houellebecq, philosopher Alain Finkielkraut, Danish MP Jesper Langballe, and Dutch MP Geert Wilders have learned. In fact, it is risky even to mention that there could be a Muslim problem in Europe, let alone a problem with Islam.

No similar prohibition applies when the topic is Christianity, Judaism, or any other religion or set of beliefs. Does this suggest that the alarmists warning of "Eurabia," the slow-motion Islamization of Europe, are correct? The answer is yes if the claim is that too many Europeans are still unaware of the Islamist problem, that all European governments are similar in their reactions, or that democracy has difficulty coping with the problem. It is also true if one assumes that the *angélisme* (hopeless naïveté and denial of the problem) typical among academics, political elites, and the media of most European countries is shared by those countries' electorates. Such assumptions, however, miss important differences among countries and between voters and elites—as demonstrated by the success of anti-immigration parties and personalities in places like the Netherlands, Denmark, and France.

European countries have a centuries-old tradition of dealing with organized religion. Since the Westphalian treaties of the 17th century, government and religion have had established institutional arrangements, with tolerance being a prominent feature. Some countries (Germany, the Scandinavian states, the UK) have official state religions (in the case of Germany, both Lutheranism and Roman Catholicism enjoy that status), while France is a secular state whose religious institutions are completely independent, and matters such as marriage, church building, etc. are a matter of individual or community choice. That arrangement, with occasional modifications regarding newer religious denominations, has lasted for a long time, everywhere in Western Europe. Islam, however, which is only recently a major claimant to some form of legal recognition, is neither organized nor institutionalized in the sense that Catholicism, Lutheranism, or most other Christian denominations have long been. To complicate matters further, the very size of Muslim communities is hard to assess with any accuracy, despite state efforts to arrive at an official tally.

The Numbers

The total number of Muslims living in Europe is spoken of in the media as "between 15 and 20 million," making it obvious that official sources are basically in the dark. The result is that, in general, figures regarding Muslims in Europe are approximate and should be so interpreted.

This is especially true of France. That country has by far the largest Muslim population, but census questions regarding ethnicity and religion are forbidden by law, so hard numbers are unavailable. In 2003, demographer Michèle Tribalat assessed the number of "possible Muslims" in France at 3.7 million, a figure much lower than the one usually mentioned, proving once again that the figure is one with "variable geometry," as *L'Express* put it. Indeed, a 1989 study assessed the number of Muslims at 2.5 million; in 1993 an official study mentioned a figure of 3 million; in 1996 the *Secrétariat des Relations avec l'Islam* mentioned 4.2 million, and, the same year, then Interior Minister Charles Pasqua claimed that there were 5 million Muslims in France, of whom 1 million were practicing, 50,000 were fundamentalists, and probably 2,000 were radicals; in 2003 then Interior Minister Sarkozy claimed that the number was between 5 and 6 million—and the xenophobic *Front National* has an estimate of 8 million.[2]

There are many reasons for the uncertainty. First, in countries like France where census questions regarding religion are prohibited by law, attempts are made to approximate the number of Muslims according to the percentage of Muslims in various immigrant groups' countries of origin. For example, it is assumed that people of Moroccan, Algerian, or Turkish origin, being from countries with more than 98 percent Muslim populations, are all Muslims. That is a largely accurate assumption as far as it goes, but one that does not apply in every case. Thus in Albania 80 percent of the population is Muslim, whereas in Bosnia-Herzegovina, 45 percent are Muslims and in Lebanon more than 60 percent are Muslims. The Palestinians in the West Bank are 92 percent Muslim, but in Gaza the figure is almost 100 percent.[3] Moreover, at least in the cases of the Lebanese and Palestinians, the European diaspora is not representative of the religious distribution in the country of origin, because a disproportionately high number of Lebanese and Palestinian Christians have emigrated to Europe and the United States, a major cause of the decline of Christianity in the Middle East.

Second, even where there are official figures based on the census, one must see them as a conservative minimum because of illegal immigration. It is virtually impossible to assess the number of illegal immigrants accurately; all we can say for certain is that they represent a sizeable number in all countries. Any serious study of, for instance, Maghrebi emigration to France, Spain, and Italy suggests the facility with which illegal migrants have entered those countries during the past two decades—although it appears that it has become somewhat more difficult recently. In addition, the size of the illegal-immigrant population varies greatly from country to country, because of factors like geography, effectiveness of border controls, and the existence of a settled immigrant group (which can facilitate the absorption of illegal newcomers). It is far easier for a Moroccan to cross from Tetuan to Algeciras or for a Tunisian to go from Tunis to Italy than for either of those to go to Finland. However, the abolition of border controls among the 12 EU member states that are signatories of the Schengen Accords makes it possible for an illegal immigrant to move from Algeciras or Ceuta to Helsinki—at least in theory. The European immigration figures are no better than the notoriously unreliable American ones.

Thus, "According to experts working for the Catholic Church, there are some 1 million illegal immigrants in [Germany], with at least 200,000 in Berlin alone."[4]

Third, even within the most frequently used and largely accepted definition of a "Muslim" (i.e., a follower of Islam) there are good reasons to be wary—especially when it comes to individuals born in Europe. At least in France, where the available sociological data are better, it seems that a large proportion of young *beurs* (French-born Muslims) are not practicing at all, or not much more than the native French, most of whom are anything but practicing Catholics. At least one author estimates that only 15 percent of the Muslim population of France goes to a mosque; among Muslim youths, this author believes, 5 percent are fundamentalists and 2 percent fanatics, but most are "*comme tous les Français*."[5] Recent polls also suggest sharp differences between Muslims in France and those elsewhere, especially in Britain. Thus, when asked, "How often do you pray?" a sample of Muslims in Britain answered as follows: 49 percent, five times a day; 22 percent, one to three times a day; 5 percent, never. Moreover, 66 percent claimed that religion is the most important thing in their life.[6] That is quite different from a sample of Muslims in France who, when asked, "Do you read the Quran?" answered as follows: 30 percent, never; 26 percent, less than once a year; 20 percent, at least once a week. To the question, "Do you go to the mosque?" the reply was: 49 percent, never; 16 percent, less than once a year; 17 percent, at least once a week.[7] The difference between Moroccans and Albanians, the two largest Muslim communities in Turin, is also revealing. Whereas only 10 percent of Albanians claim to pray or observe any Islamic ritual, one-third of Moroccans believed in a society controlled by Sharia and 60 percent did so on specific issues, such as wearing the veil or cutting a hand off for thievery.[8]

Some young Muslims may pay attention to some Ramadan restrictions, but mostly out of respect for their parents, and may participate in demonstrations for the "rights of Palestinians," and so on, but Salafism is the model for their way of life. In the case of Albanians and Bosniaks, their level of Islamic orthodoxy is quite low even in the home countries—and presumably less so in Europe. Why is this important? Because Bosniaks and Albanians, despite the latters' massive involvement in organized crime, are simply not—so far—vulnerable to Salafist recruitment. Indeed, few if any Bosniaks or Albanians have been known among any Islamist cell in Europe so far.

DIVERSITY OR DIVISIONS?

Even within the overwhelmingly dominant Sunni group in Europe, Muslim religious views are far from uniform. This leads to a difficulty for European governments seeking credible formal interlocutors within Muslim communities. From the UK to France to Germany to the Netherlands, governments are caught in a dilemma. On the one hand, Muslim activists issue strident demands that Islam be treated at least in the same manner as any other religious denomination, while on the other hand Muslim communities in Europe are inherently unable to present a common and legitimate representative in their dealings with officialdom. Indeed, as Carolyn M. Warner and Manfred W. Wenner have abundantly argued,[9] Islam, especially Sunni Islam, is by nature and history diverse and decentralized; in Europe it is also ethnically splintered.

There are four Sunni schools of jurisprudence (*madhab*), each distinct from the others, with the adherents of some being far more likely to fall under the influence of Islamists, and far more capable of organization, than others. The Hanafi is prevalent among Turks and Balkan Muslims, the Maliki among

North Africans, and the Shafi among Kurds and Egyptians; the most fundamentalist school, the Hanbali, which has Saudi adherents and is related to Wahhabism, is attracting increasing numbers of jihadists everywhere.

These schools are significant because they shape Muslim countries' national policies toward their diaspora, viz. Morocco's official insistence on forcing émigrés to remain Moroccan nationals, and thus Maliki adherents, under Rabat-influenced imams. Likewise, and despite occasional denials, the Saudis' financial beneficence regarding the building of mosques in Rome, Granada, Seville, and Berlin is paralleled by the appointment of Wahhabi imams and, in Spain and Italy, financial support for organizations competing with the older and more moderate ones that European governments prefer.

Despite these obvious difficulties, because of the sheer numbers of Muslims in their countries, European governments have consistently tried to treat Islam like any other religion by "organizing" or "recognizing" Muslim institutions, as if they were similar to Christian denominations, despite the fact that any such attempt is necessarily artificial. As a result, in France, for example, the government has essentially invented an Islamic body, the French Council of the Muslim Faith (CFCM), which it has designated as the official embodiment of Islam in France, both with the aim of engaging Muslims in a formal dialogue and as a means for crafting an Islam à la française. Initially, the CFCM had the approval of a great number of Muslims. Very soon, however, the CFCM's representativeness, legitimacy, leadership, and membership were drawing criticism, even from within the organization, as its component elements jockeyed for influence. The organization lacks, furthermore, the endorsement of youths from the banlieues, who are often in thrall to the local caids (gang leaders). These youths see established organizations like the CFCM as controlled by a government they perceive as hostile. Nor is the CFCM able to compete at the grass-roots level with alternative organizations such as HuT, or with a plethora of radical freelance preachers.

Elsewhere, Muslim groups have tried to join forces, in order to gain legal and formal recognition (which often brings with it state subsidies). The best funded and organized groups—the Saudi-supported Muslim Brotherhood in Italy, the Netherlands, Spain, and Germany being a good example—have received significant resulting advantages. Other groups, such as the Turkish *Dyanet* and the Grand Mosque in Paris, formally financed by Algiers, have been subsidized heavily by Ankara and Riyadh.

It thus appears that while the generally liberal governments of Europe are perfectly willing, indeed eager, to seek Islamic interlocutors and are prepared to treat them as they treat Catholics, Protestants of various hues, and Buddhists, Sikhs, or Waldensians, they are faced with the problem of how best to engage with Islamic representatives, in a manner suiting not only Muslims but the exigencies of government bureaucracies.

The Status of Muslims by Country

For the reasons described above, most figures are approximate and fluctuating; they should be seen as conservative and should be used only as points of reference—and very cautiously. Even basic terms such as "mosque" are still debated. Thus, while the figure most often circulated is that there are 735 mosques in Italy, some claim that there are actually only three: in Rome, in Catania, and in the Milan suburb of Segrate. All the rest are more or less makeshift places of worship located in basements, garages, or old factory buildings.[10] Such informal mosques as are mentioned below are establishments that are known and *de facto* recognized by authorities—inevitably a small minority of the existing ones.

Similarly, the term "imam" is debated and, in Europe, highly debatable. In the context of this study "imam" is defined as the prayer leader of a mosque, but even such a narrow understanding presents problems, since it may mean a theologically trained professional (the meaning used in most Muslim states), or it may mean a freelance, self-declared individual with no religious education whatsoever—and both can be highly influential. In this chapter the term is narrowed to refer only to religiously trained and officially recognized fulltime professionals.

Austria[11]

Total population: 8.2 million
Muslim population: 400,000 (data from 2006)—4.9 percent
Mosques: c. 200
National representative organization: *Islamische Glaubensgemeinschaft in Österreich* (Islamic Religious Community in Austria)

Despite historical ties—Austria formerly ruled over Bosnia-Herzegovina, and as long ago as 1912 the Emperor paid to build a mosque for his Bosniak subjects in Vienna—the significant Muslim presence in Austria is recent, and mostly due to the 1990s events in the Balkans and the waves of refugees and asylum seekers they produced. The number of Muslims in Austria increased 18-fold between 1971 and 2006—from 22,200 to around 400,000.[12] An Austrian government study concluded that 45 percent of Muslims in Austria are unwilling to integrate.[13]

The largest concentration of Muslims is in Vienna, where they make up some 15 percent of the population. The only officially recognized (since 1979) mosque is the Islamic Center in Vienna. The Islamic Academy in that city, sponsored by Al-Azhar University in Cairo, prepares teachers and imams,

and more than 40,000 pupils receive Islamic religious education from one hundred teachers under the supervision of the
Islamic Administration of Religious Education, with government financial support.[14]

Belgium[15]

Total population: 10.3 million
Muslim population: 400,000 (data from 2003)—3.9 percent
Imams: 300
Mosques: 328 (as of 2004)
National representative organization: *L'Exécutif des Musul-
mans de Belgique* (Muslims' Executive of Belgium)

The two largest groups are Moroccans (125,000) and Turks
(70,000), with smaller numbers of Algerians, Tunisians, Bosniaks,
Pakistanis, Lebanese, Iranians, Syrians, and Egyptians. There is
a high degree of self-segregation amongst these groups, and
between them and the Belgian society. The most obvious case
is that of the Turks, who seldom mix either with other Muslims
or with Belgians, are settled mostly in Flanders, remain a very
close-knit community, maintain many of their rural traditions
(e.g., choosing spouses from their parents' villages), master
the country's languages less well than the Moroccans, and do
worse in school. The Moroccans, established mostly in Brussels
and Wallonia, appear to be better integrated, having a higher
rate of mixed marriages with Belgians,[16] as are the Bosniaks,
who see themselves as Europeans,[17] and the Lebanese, many of
whom are Christians.

Demographics:

As of 2003, 35 percent of the Turks and Moroccans in Belgium
were 18 years old or younger, compared with 18 percent of
the native Belgians. One-quarter of Brussels's population un-

der 20 years old is of "Muslim origin," and in 2002 in the region of Brussels the most popular names given to babies were Mohammed and Sarah.[18]

Belgian scholar Brigitte Maréchal[19] claims that 113,842 people from the "Muslim countries" had acquired Belgian citizenship between 1985 and 1997—by European standards a very high rate. In addition, every year at least 8,000 Moroccans and 6,000 Turks receive Belgian citizenship. The number of converts is between 3,000 and 15,000.

It is important to note that many Muslims in Belgium (Turks aside) have historically preferred to settle in the French-speaking areas, rather than the Flemish, for a simple reason: The growing Flemish nationalism is at least as hostile to Muslims as it is to French (Walloon) culture. That fact, in turn, has implications for the Muslims' economic status, since the Walloon region has been in economic decline for decades, and in demographic decline (in both absolute terms and relative to the Flemings) for even longer. Francophone Brussels, because of its role as "the capital of Europe" (headquarters of both the EU and NATO) and its service economy, is the exception that explains the growing concentration of Muslims there.

Major Muslim Organizations:

L'Exécutif des Musulmans de Belgique—the **Muslim Executive Council (EMB).** Islam has been a legally recognized faith in Belgium since 1974, but for a long time Muslim organizations could not agree upon a representative structure, and the government's strict criteria for participation in dialogue further complicated efforts to find agreement. Nevertheless, in December 1998 Belgium's Muslims elected their umbrella organization, the EMB, an idea borrowed from France but, at that time, still unsuccessful there. As in France, the goal was to establish a legitimate partner in discussions with the government. However, the organization's exclusion of radicals and domination by the two largest ethnic groups (Moroccans and Turks), and especially its mainly Turkish leadership, raised doubts about its representativeness.[20]

The organization was responsible for managing Muslim worship in Belgium. It played the role of mediator between the state and Muslim communities. Its responsibilities ranged from training imams and providing religious education at schools to appointing Muslim chaplains in hospitals and prisons. The EMB was made up of 17 members: seven Moroccans, four Turks, three converts, and three of other nationalities—representing the four categories (colleges) of Muslims in Belgium.[21] The EMB received state subsidies since 2001. In 2002 the state supported the organization with €420,000, while the Catholic Church was given €350 million. Even so, in February 2008 the EMB went into receivership. It was replaced by another Executive Council, which is subject to many of the same criticisms.

Islamic Cultural Centre of Belgium (**ICCB**). Until the establishment of the EMB, this was the *de facto* representative of Muslims in Belgium. The ambassador from Saudi Arabia is head of its board of trustees. The land for the Centre was handed over to King Faisal in 1967, as a gift in exchange for donations he had made. The Centre was built with the financial support from the Muslim World League—a Saudi (i.e., Wahhabi-) dominated organization.

Arab European League (**AEL**).[22] This organization claims to defend "the civic rights of Arabs in Europe." It has attracted a following of thousands of jobless, frustrated young immigrants, and its leader, Dyab Abou Jahjah—a Lebanese former *Hizbollah* member, often portrayed by the media as Belgium's

Malcolm X—is a charismatic debater with an MA in international politics and fluency in four languages. The AEL now has branches in France and the Netherlands.

The AEL is fundamentally opposed to integration ("cultural colonization") and is aggressively Arab-centered, verging on racism, as suggested by its self-definition:

> The AEL is a political and social movement that stands for the Rights of the Arab and Muslim communities in Europe and the Arab causes in general. The AEL stands also for solidarity with all Muslim peoples and communities and all the oppressed peoples of the world. The member of the AEL declares hereby to abide and strive for the following 19 principals [sic] and goals:

> We declare as Arab Shatat (Diaspora) our belonging to the Arab Nation while being worthy and law abiding citizens of Europe. We demand the right to foster our Arab cultural identity while engaging actively as European citizens in the countries of residence, with equal rights and treatment.

> We declare that we will promote and restore our Arab language as a spoken lingua franca between our people all across Europe.

> We declare that we will establish structural ties between the Arab Diaspora in Europe in order to form one community all across the continent. And we will strengthen the bound [sic] between our Diaspora and the Arab Nation.

> We reject the Zionist project in Palestine and we call for the dismantling of the Zionist entity and the establishing of a united Palestinian democratic state in all historical Palestine. A state where Arabs and Jews can coexist peacefully enjoying equal rights without any discrimination. This includes the return of all Palestinian refugees to their original homes with compensation.

> Aramaic-Arabs, Assyrian-Arabs and Amazigh-Arabs especially are to be recognized as protected components of our nation.

Rif, Sous and Kabilya can become each a federated Arab
province enjoying internal autonomy while being parts of the
Arab federal state.[23]

Note here that Arameans and Berbers ("Amazigh-Arabs") are
considered Arabs, certainly a description they would strongly
reject. The AEL's extremism has been openly manifested in its
support for Saddam Hussein ("a legitimate ruler"), the Syrian
position in Lebanon, Palestinian terrorism, and a ferocious
anti-Americanism. Although secular, its position on violence
within Europe is similar to that of many Islamist groups, as
demonstrated by its reaction to the murder of Theo van Gogh.
After "condemning the murder as criminal and irresponsible,"
it went into a long complaint about alleged Islamophobia,
compared the murder with the Nazis' arranged Reichstag arson in 1933, compared the "verbal war" against Muslims with
Kristallnacht, and claimed that "Islamophobia is also a form
of anti-Semitism; obviously, some European countries did not
learn a thing from their history." Even Belgian Muslim leaders,
such as Senator Mimount Bousakla, were accused by AEL of
"Islam-bashing" for "mixing up issues like integration of immigrants with fundamentalism, and linking both these issues
with terrorism."[24]

Mouvement des Jeunes Musulmans—**Movement of Young
Muslims (MJM).** Like the AEL, the MJM also created a political
party. Its *Parti Citoyenneté et Prospérité* achieved a strong vote
(but no seats in the municipal council) in the local elections in
Brussels in May 2003.

Relations with the State:

Belgium has a Napoleonic legal system in which there is a formal link between state and church, or rather religious bod-

ies. The government accords "recognized" status to Roman Catholicism, Protestantism, Judaism, Anglicanism, Islam, and Orthodox Christianity.

By law, each recognized religion has the right to provide teachers at government expense for religious instruction in schools. The government also pays the salaries, pensions, and lodging costs of ministers and subsidizes the construction and renovation of places of worship. The administrations of recognized religions have legal rights and obligations, and the municipality in which they are located must pay any debts that they incur. Some subsidies are the responsibility of the federal government, while the regional and municipal governments pay others. According to an independent academic review, government at all levels spent $523 million (23 billion Belgian francs) on subsidies to recognized religions in 2000 (3.5 percent of these funds went to Muslims). In 2001 the EMB applied for subsidies for the first time. In 2002 the government recognized 75 mosques and started to pay salaries to imams assigned to these mosques.

One of the most important recent pieces of legislation regarding Muslims in Belgium concerns anti-discrimination. In December 2002 Parliament enacted a new law banning discrimination on all grounds specified in Article 13 of the EU's proposed Constitutional Treaty. In fact, the Belgian law is even wider than the ban in the proposed treaty, as the Belgian law not only covers employer/employee relations, but also bans discrimination in the general provision of goods and services, in relations between government and civilians, and in "any other public activity."[25]

Following the general pattern of Belgian politics, which tend to imitate French developments, there is a growing debate on the *hijab* and *burqa*, especially in Flanders. In one municipality near Brussels the mayor banned the *burqa*, and there were isolated cases in which women and girls wearing traditional dress or headscarves were insulted in public. In January 2001, the Court of Cassation, the nation's highest court, ruled that municipal authorities could not deny an identification card to a woman wearing a headscarf.

The country has taken various steps in order to integrate its foreign population. For instance, in January 2000, Belgium began its second immigrant-regularization campaign.[26] This lasted until the end of 2002, and in the course of it 60,000 illegal migrants applied for legal status. In November 2003 the Senate's Home Affairs Committee adopted a legislative proposal that non-EU nationals who had lived in Belgium for at least five years should be able to vote in local council elections, though without the right to run in these elections themselves.

The country's second-largest city and the capital of Flanders, Antwerp, is the center of persistent conflicts between Muslims and both native Flemings and the city's large Jewish community, some of whom now vote for the fast-growing ultranationalist and anti-Muslim party, *Vlaams Belang* (Flemish Interest).

Denmark[27]

Total population: 5.4 million
Muslim population: c. 270,000—5 percent
Imams: c. 90
Mosques: 50 (many informal)
Muslim private primary schools: 12
National representative organization: None officially recognized. The *Muslimernes Landsorganization* (Muslims' National Organization) and the (Wahhabi) Islamic Union in Denmark are the best known.[28]

In the 1970s Muslims arrived from Turkey (the largest group), Pakistan, Morocco, and Yugoslavia to work. In the 1980s and '90s there were new waves of Muslim arrivals, refugees and asylum seekers from Iran, Iraq, Somalia, and Bosnia; these now account for 40 percent of Denmark's Muslims, of whom just a minority have citizenship.

Popular reactions, especially following 9/11, led to a sharp decline in the number of asylum and refugee claimants admitted. A study by Oslo's Institute for Social Research shows that Denmark's share of asylum applications in the Scandinavian countries fell from 31 percent in 2000 to 9 percent in 2003, while Sweden's rose from 41 percent to 60 percent, and Norway's from 28 percent to 31 percent. That trend upset Sweden, whose Social Democrat–led government accused the Danes of undermining Scandinavian solidarity. In addition, restrictive Danish laws have been attacked by the UN High Commissioner for Refugees and by Europe's human-rights commissioner.[29]

Demographics:

Most Muslims in Denmark settled in the largest cities, Copenhagen and Aarhus. Their assimilation and integration levels are quite low, and so are their education and skill levels. Welfare dependency is concomitantly high. The most important ethnic groups are Moroccans, Somalis, and Turks. There is an acute crisis within the Muslim community between moderate and radical imams. The latter are mostly former asylum claimants, such as those from Copenhagen's *Islamisk Trosssamfund* mosque, who were the originators of the cartoon crisis of early 2006. As a result of that crisis Islam has taken a hit in public opinion, even among former liberals. Thus, polls in 2006 showed that 48 percent of Danes believe that Islam is incompatible with democracy (vs. 34 percent who believe it is compatible).[30]

That there was Muslim support for the radical position of the late Ahmed Abu Laban only increased public anxiety. Laban, a cleric and leader of the Islamic Society in Denmark, maintained that there could be no compromise on the cartoon issue ("We are not against freedom of speech but the Prophet Mohamed has unique status"[31]). All this in one of the world's most open, and open-minded, societies.

France[32]

Total population: 62.3 million
Muslim population: 5 to 6 million—8 to 9.6 percent
Mosques and prayer halls: c. 1,600. This number has multiplied from only about one hundred in 1970.
Imams: 1,000 to 1,500, but only about 600 live permanently in the country
National representative organization: *Le Conseil Français du Culte Musulman*—French Council of the Muslim Faith (CFCM)

The Muslim population of France, the largest in Europe, is predominantly of North African origin, with Algerians the largest group, closely followed by Moroccans (both likely in the 2-million range), with fewer Tunisians. There are also over 100,000 from various Middle Eastern countries, particularly Lebanon and Syria, some 300,000 from Turkey, 100,000 South Asians,[33] a very large sub-Saharan population, and somewhere between 30,000 and 100,000 converts.

Major Muslim Organizations:

Muslim associations have formed several distinct and often antagonistic federations to identify and represent common interests *vis-à-vis* the state. For the moment, these associations are more or less united under the umbrella of the CFCM, established in 2002 and led by the Paris Mosque's rector, Dalil Boubakeur. There are three principal organizations making up the CFCM:

La Fédération Nationale des Musulmans de France—the **National Federation of the Muslims of France (FNMF)**—was established in 1985, and aims to meet the religious, cultural, educational, social, and humanitarian needs of Muslims. Until 1993, it was financed by Saudi Arabia; today it is funded by the financial contributions of its members (a majority of whom are of Moroccan origin), and is closely affiliated with the Moroccan government.

The Muslim Institute of the Paris Mosque, established in 1926, numbers more than 500 local associations among its members. Like the FNMF, it was financed by Saudi Arabia until 1993; today it is funded by and closely affiliated with the Algerian government. It has always been closely associated with various initiatives of the French government.

L'Union des Organisations Islamiques de France—the **Union of the Islamic Organizations of France (UOIF)**— is the most powerful and influential branch of the Muslim Brotherhood's Union of the Islamic Organizations in Europe. The UOIF (established in 1983) manages the European Institute of Social Sciences of Saint Léger de Fougeret (Nièvre) and has a massive annual festival at Le Bourget, near Paris.

When the CFCM was established, the elections leading to its formation were disappointing for those, like then Interior Minister Sarkozy, who sought a "domesticated" Islam *à la fran-çaise*. Of the total of 41 seats in the CFCM's leadership, the FNMF had 16, the UOIF 13, the Paris Mosque six, and others, including the Turks and secularists, six.[34] Since the UOIF is Islamist, and the FNMF is infiltrated by Islamist elements, the election (or rather, the appointment under government pressure) of the moderate Dalil Boubakeur as leader, clearly a minority element, was not popular. Not only did the Turks and secular Muslims feel marginalized, but Boubakeur's small vote, despite the Algerians' majority among Muslims in France, suggests that even among them Islamism is gaining ground over ethnic solidarity.

Another major actor within the Muslim community is the *Tablighi Jamaat* (Proselytizing Group), with European headquarters in Dewsbury, England. Operating in France as the "Faith and Practice" association from its *merkez* (national headquarters) in Saint-Denis, it is very active among the youth in the *banlieues* of Paris and other major cities. It is also seen by intelligence and police organizations as a gatekeeper for Islamism and therefore the antechamber of terrorism, a suspicion regularly reinforced by the arrest of many of its former (and present) members.

Germany

Total population: 82.5 million
Muslim population: c. 3.2 million—3.8 percent
Imams: 1,500
Mosques: More than 1,000
Muslim private primary schools: 1
National representative organization: *Koordinationsrat* (Coordination Council)

In 2007 three established umbrella organizations, the *Islamrat für die Bundesrepublik Deutschland* (Islamic Congress in the Federal Republic of Germany, based in Cologne); *Zentralrat für die Muslime in Deutschland* (Central Congress of Muslims in Germany, based in Bonn), *and Islamische Konzil Deutschland* (Islamic Council in Germany), founded a joint *Koordinationsrat* (Coordination Council) to speak with one voice with the state on such issues as religious instruction in public schools.[35] The Turkish Directorate of Religious Affairs (the *Diyanet*), closely controlled by the Turkish government, is heavily involved in the religious affairs of Muslims in Germany, both through its attachés in a number of major cities (Berlin, Düsseldorf, Essen, Frankfurt, Hamburg, Hanover, Cologne, Karlsruhe, Munich, Nuremberg, Stuttgart, Münster, and Mainz), and through the numerous imams it sends to serve in Germany.[36]

Of the Muslim population of about 3.2 million, about 732,000 are citizens. The majority—as many as 2.2 million—are from Turkey, both ethnic Turks and Kurds. The latter are more religiously conservative, tend to avoid imams sent from Turkey, and often support the PKK.[37] The second-biggest group comes from Balkan countries (Bosnia-Herzegovina and Albania), and the third group is of Middle Eastern origin: refugees and students from Lebanon, Palestine, and Iraq. A rather large group of secular Muslims came at the beginning of the Eighties from Iran.

On the regional level (the German Länder, or states), coalitions of local Muslim communities now appear which, in contrast to the national umbrella groups, claim the status of religious communities, taking advantage of the fact that the German constitution stipulates that religion formally falls within the responsibility of the *Länder*, with the Berlin government having only an informal function of issuing directives. Among the most important of these coalitions are the *Islamische Religionsgemeinschaft Hessen* (Islamic Religious Association of Hessen), *Shura Hamburg* (Hamburg Council), and *Islamische Föderation Berlin* (Islamic Federation of Berlin).

The Turkish Community in Germany—*Türkische Gemeinde in Deutschland* (TGD)—is active throughout the country.

In Hamburg, Muslims also run an Islamic Academy Germany (*Islamische Akademie Deutschland*, and an Academy of World Religions (*Akademie der Weltreligionen*).[38]

Radical or unorthodox groups that are banned or restricted at home, such as Turkey's *Milli Görüs*, are free to operate, and they compete, often successfully, with the more established, Ankara-controlled organizations.

Italy[39]

Total population: 58.4 million

Muslim population: 805,000 to 1,000,000 (c. 1.5 percent), including some 10,000 influential Italian-born converts

Imams: NA

Mosques: 3

Prayer halls: 200

Muslim private primary schools: None official

National representative organization: *Centro Islamico Culturale d'Italia* (Islamic Cultural Center of Italy)

Most of Italy's Muslims are from the Balkans (Bosniaks and Albanians), Morocco, Tunisia, Senegal, and Somali. The largest concentrations are in Rome and the industrialized north, mostly in Milan, Genoa, Turin, and Bologna. Most arrived from the 1980s onwards, many of them as students.

The national representative organization, the Islamic Cultural Center of Italy (*Centro Islamico Culturale d'Italia*), attached to the Grand Mosque of Rome, was recognized as a religious legal entity in 1974, but it has not obtained equal legal status with other religious denominations.

Whereas even such small denominations as the Waldensians (1984), Assemblies of God (1986), Seventh-Day Adventists (1986 and 1996), and Christian Congregation of Jehovah's Witnesses (2000)—not to mention the Roman Catholic Church through various concordats and agreements with the Italian state since 1929—have all established clear legal frameworks in their relations with Rome,[40] Islam has not. This is because Muslim organizations in Italy are badly split, and assert rival claims to exclusive official recognition. In addition, none is plausibly representative of all, or even most, Muslims in Italy. Equally important, the rivalries among Muslim organizations in Italy are exacerbated by the direct interference of foreign governments, especially Saudi Arabia and Morocco, which control "their" organizations and use their political influence on the Italian government to promote the legitimacy of these organizations.

Besides the *Centro Islamico*, other Muslim organizations operate legally but are not formally recognized, the most important being the following:

***L'Unione delle Comunità ed Organizzazioni Islamiche in Italia*—the Union of Islamic Communities and Organizations in Italy (UCOII)**—established in 1992, is led by Hamza Roberto Piccardo, a convert who is also the spokesman of the European Muslim Network, although the membership is overwhelmingly North African and Middle Eastern. It claims to be the most representative Muslim organization in Italy, controlling as many as 80 percent of mosques and associations,[41] but its own internal polls suggest that the great majority of Muslims in Italy belong to no organization. UCOII is closely associated with the Muslim Brotherhood.

***La Comunità Religiosa Islamica*—Islamic Religious Community (Coreis)**—established in 1993, has a mostly convert membership

L'Associazione Culturale Islamica Zayd ibn Thabit—Islamic Cultural Association Zayd ibn Thabit—is led by convert Hamza Massimiliano Boccolini, who is also president of the Piazza del Mercato mosque in Naples and leader of the Italian section of the Saudi-created and -funded World Muslim League, an organization led (from Rome) by Mario Scialoja, a former Italian ambassador to Riyadh and another convert to Islam.

L'Unione Musulmani d'Italia (or *l'Unione Musulmani Italiani*—Union of Italian Muslims)—is led by Adel Smith, a Scottish-Italian convert and radical. Italian scholar Magdi Allam claims that its active members number "four or five," or perhaps only two—Smith and secretary Massimo Zucchi—"occasionally reinforced by a dozen Albanian sympathizers."[42] However, characteristically, and not just for Italy, this group has attracted a disproportionate level of media and political attention during the past few years, on the "squeaky-wheel-gets-the-grease" principle. Smith sued, in part successfully, the Vatican and the Italian state over the presence of crucifixes in schools. He gained notoriety for suing the late journalist Oriana Fallaci over "insults to Islam," and, most significantly, has managed never to get sued himself over his description of crucifixes as "cadavers."

L'Associazione dei Musulmani Italiani—Association of Italian Muslims (AMI)—is led by Sheikh Abdul Hadi Palazzi, a.k.a. Massimo Palazzi, who is also co-founder and a co-chairman of the Islam-Israel Fellowship.

The Netherlands[43]

Total population: 16.3 million
Muslim population: c. 1 million—5.8 percent
Imams: 500
Mosques: 450

Muslim schools: 46 primary and secondary schools, with a total of c. 10,000 students

National representative organizations: *Contactorgaan Moslims en Overheid* (Contact Body for Muslims and Government) and *Contact Groep Islam* (Islamic Contact Group)

Some 85 percent of Muslims in the Netherlands are of either Turkish/Kurdish or Moroccan origin (350,000 and 300,000 respectively), with groups of Surinamese, Iraqis, and Somalis, who were given refugee status, forming significant communities. Most are concentrated in Amsterdam, Rotterdam, The Hague, and Utrecht. As in Denmark and Belgium, there is a high degree of self-segregation, especially in the case of Turks.

Muslim Associations:

After many attempts and much wrangling, the government pressured Islamic organizations to unify themselves into the *Contactorgaan Moslims en Overheid* (CMO); however, one organization within it refused to admit the Ahmadiyya (a movement founded in the 19th century) on the grounds that they are not true Muslims. The *Nederlandse Moslim Raad* (NMR) then left the CMO, and together with Alevis (a subgroup among Turkish and Kurdish Muslims) and Ahmadiyya founded the *Contact Groep Islam* (CGI)—basically a collection of unorthodox sects.[44]

The CMO, with a membership of over 500,000, and the CGI, with some 115,000 followers, were officially recognized as consultation partners by the government, on November 1, 2004, and January 13, 2005, respectively.

The older organizations that formed these umbrella groups are clearly drawn on ethnic and national lines.

The **Union of Moroccan Muslim Organizations** controls some 100 mosques.

The Moroccan-dominated **Council of Muslim Representatives in the Netherlands** is popular among the "*probleem jongeren*" (problem youth), who are ambiguous at best about integration. The Council's deputy chairman, Dris Boujoufi, believes that "Linking integration to speaking Dutch in the street is nothing but an attempt to turn a blind eye to certain realities on the ground."[45] The Turkish community is separately organized, with the *Diyanet*-controlled **Islamic Foundation Netherlands**, the largest Turkish organization, in charge of 140 mosques. The Islamist **Milli Görüs** is in control of 30 mosques and 60 organizations for youth or women. The Sufis of the *Süleymanci* sect dominate 30 Islamic centers through the **Islamic Centre Foundation**. Alevis dominate 30 local organizations and a federation under the umbrella of the **Federatie van Alevitische Verenigingen in Nederland—Federation of Alevi Associations in the Netherlands**.

There are also smaller clusters of mosques, in which movements like the *Jamaat al-Tabligh* or the Muslim Brotherhood are influential. The World Islamic Mission, with a Surinamese and Pakistani membership, controls 30 mosques.

Norway[46]

Total population: 4.6 million
Muslim population: 115,000 (2004 data)—about 2 percent
Mosques: One purpose-built, with many others in modified buildings
Islamic schools: None approved

Most Muslims in Norway are refugees or their descendants. Pakistanis, Iraqis, and Somalis are the largest groups; Iranians are the oldest, most established, and best integrated. The main Muslim organizations are the **Islamic Council**

Norway—*Islamsk Råd Norge* (IRN)—and the **Supreme Islamic Council (SIC)**.

Spain[47]

Total population: 43.1 million

Muslim population: c. 1.5 million (2.3 percent), including some 20,000 converts, the largest percentage (2 percent) of the total number of Muslims in any European country

Imams: NA

Mosques: 12 purpose-built, more than 400 others. Madrid's "M-30" mosque (officially the *Centro Cultural Islámico*—Islamic Cultural Center) is the largest in Europe. Other large mosques are in Madrid (Tetuán), Córdoba, and Granada.

Islamic schools: While none is controlled by local groups, Saudi Arabia and Iraq under Saddam Hussein established a few. The Averroes (Ibn Rushd) Islamic University, founded in 1995 in order to train students in Arabic Philology, Islamic Sciences, and Andalusian Studies, is not recognized by the government.

National representative organization: *Comisión Islámica de España* (Islamic Commission of Spain)

Spain has probably the most rapidly growing Muslim population in Europe—and one of the hardest to count, since many, if not most, of the immigrants are illegal, entering the country through the North African enclaves of Ceuta and Melilla, or through the Canaries, and many of them stay in Spain only briefly before moving on to other European Union states.

The overwhelming majority of Muslims in Spain are Moroccan, with a large (perhaps 10 percent) Algerian group, and smaller Tunisian and sub-Saharan (mostly Malian, Guinean, and Mauritanian) groups. In addition, there are some Middle Eastern elements, and most recently there is a growing Pakistani community in Catalonia.

A special case is that of the North African enclaves of Ceuta and Melilla, where close to a majority of the total population of 140,000 is Muslim and Moroccan.[48]

Major Muslim Organizations:

Spain has recognized the *Islamic Commission of Spain* (**CIE**) as the official interlocutor since 1992, affording it a number of privileges, including teaching Islam in schools and overseeing religious holidays. However, the recognition remains without much practical result, since Madrid insists on dealing with only one Muslim organization, but community divisions prevent established Muslim organizations from working with it.

The *Federación Española de Entidades Religiosas Islámicas*—**Spanish Federation of Islamic Religious Entities** (**FEERI**)—is the largest organization, widely known as being supported by Saudi Arabia and various Gulf states.

The *Junta Islámica en España*—Islamic Council of Spain— dominated by Mansur Escudero since its inception, is mostly made up of converts. It has a regional chapter in Catalonia and a youth organization. It is the most vocal in demanding "historic" rights, and thus is more controversial than most. For instance, commenting on the CIE's demand to be given praying areas and time in the Córdoba cathedral, CIE spokeswoman Isabel Romero was careful to say, "In no way is this request about reclaiming our rights—far less any kind of reconquest. Instead, we want to give our support to the universal character of this building."[49]

For Abdennur Prado, secretary of the *Junta*, the main problem between Muslims and the West is not jihadism. Rather,

> The problem of Islamophobia is an urgent reality in countries like the United States, France, Germany, the Netherlands, Belgium, or Spain. In all of these one has lived through

attacks against Muslims for the simple fact of being such—representatives of this "other" who is not accepted on one's "own" territory. The fascist tide grows under the shelter of institutions, too preoccupied in the fight against a hypothetical Islamist fundamentalism to realize that the most urgent problem of the West is Islamophobia.[50]

Mansur Escudero claims to be a moderate and has complained about Saudi influence—leading to his expulsion from the CIE in 2006—while at the same time making controversial statements. For instance, as late as 2007 he was claiming that there is no proof that the March 2004 terrorists were Muslim, and he claims that the cathedral of Córdoba is a "mosque–cathedral" because UNESCO described it that way.[51]

The *Unión de Comunidades Islámicas de España*—**Union of Islamic Communities in Spain (UCIE)**—is close to the Muslim Brotherhood. It is centered in the Tetuán mosque of Madrid.[52]

Al-Murabitun is a Sufi group with puritanical leanings.

The Spanish state's relations with these Muslim groups have varied according to the party in power. The conservative *Partido Popular* under Prime Minister José Maria Aznar was mostly indifferent to the Islamic organizations, and during its years in power (1996–2004) no minister met with the Islamic Commission's leadership. By contrast, in October 2004, the Socialists created the Pluralism and Living Together Foundation (*Fundación Pluralismo y Convivencia*), seeking to contribute to programs of social integration for non-Catholic confessions. This included for the first time direct government subsidies, including pensions for imams, satisfying a Muslim demand of long standing.[53]

The case of Spain is in many ways revealing, among other things in demonstrating the difficulty governments face in collecting information, let alone in controlling the activities going on inside Muslim communities or in competing with outside influences for that control. Thus, of the approximately 250 mosques in Greater Madrid, all but two are unrecognized, i.e., have no permit to function as such, the majority being small, "garage mosques" in rented rooms, outside the control of state authorities or even Muslim religious organizations. Officially there are 62 Islamic communities in the city, revolving around the two major mosques: the "M-30" (so-called because it is next to the M-30 motorway) and that of Tetuán, led by Syrian imam Riay Tatary, president of the UCIE.[54] In Spain as a whole there are over 800 mosques and prayer halls for the million and half Muslims believed to live in the country (the official figure is only 900,000), generally serving separate ethnic groups: Moroccans, Algerians, Pakistanis, and sub-Saharans. However, the Ministry of Justice's *Dirección General de Asuntos Religiosos* has only registered 360 Islamic communities (although *Junta Islámica* knows of 427). Hence, almost half of Spain's Muslim places of worship are not legally recognized.

As the authorities do not know how many Muslim establishments exist, neither do they have a clear idea who finances them. *Junta Islámica*'s Mansur Escudero, a strong supporter of the ruling Socialists, claims that he prefers all mosques to be paid for by domestic, including government, sources; the reality is very different.

Of the 11 large mosques in Spain (two each in Madrid, Melilla, and Ceuta; three in the Málaga province; one each in Valencia and Granada), at least seven are supported by Saudi sources, including the M-30; the one in Valencia and Tetuán in Madrid are financed from Syria; and the one in Granada and the ones projected for Córdoba and Sevilla are supported by the United

Arab Emirates, which also pays for the Andalusian mosques of Málaga, Fuengirola, and Marbella.

With funding comes influence, and it is important to note that Saudi and, to a lesser and milder extent UAE, money means Wahhabism, while Syrian help implies Muslim Brotherhood. The case of Valencia (where the Muslim population is almost 100,000) is significant: in the city's *Centro Cultural Islámico*, which is moderate and allows the participation of women, there is a growing Wahhabi presence, deplored by local Muslim leaders.[55]

Although the big mosques' imams and leadership seldom engage in openly radical activities (those are generally planned in the garage mosques), they set the general tone of discourse and exert an indirect influence on the orientation of Muslims in Spain. In addition, the political power that is wielded by those who generously provide funds encourages and reinforces demands for official recognition and privileges.

Sweden

Total population: 9 million

Muslim population: c. 300,000 (3 percent) (censuses do not register religious affiliation)

Mosques: There are four Sunni mosques, in Malmö, Uppsala, Västerås, and Stockholm; one Shiite mosque in Trollhättan; and one Ahmadiyya mosque in Göteborg. Further, there are at least 150 Muslim prayer rooms.[56]

National representative organizations: *Förenade Islamiska Församlingar i Sverige* (United Islamic Communities in Sweden), *Islamiska Kulturcenterunionen i Sverige* (Union of Islamic Centers of Culture in Sweden), and *Sveriges Muslimska Råd* (Muslim Council of Sweden)

The Muslim population in Sweden is diverse, with significant groups from Turkey, Bosnia, Kosovo, Iraq, Iran, Lebanon, and Syria. Representative bodies receive state funding. Sweden favors multiculturalism, and immigrants can become citizens after only five years.

Between 1984 and 1993, 48 percent of the non-Scandinavian immigrants to Sweden, most of them Muslims, came as refugees, 46 percent came under family reunification, and only 6 percent came for other reasons.

The Muslim concentrations are mostly in large urban areas like Stockholm, Göteborg, and Malmö.[57]

Major Muslim Organizations:

The Commission for State Grants to Religious Communities (*Samarbetsnämnden för statsbidrag till trossamfund*—SST) "has the task of creating communication between the State and the different communities in Sweden. Recognizing Muslims as a religious community, SST gives each community some financial support according to the size of the community."

The three organizations listed above are supported by the government through the SST. They are all umbrella organizations for local communities, and among them they speak for about 75 percent of all Muslim communities in Sweden.

As elsewhere in Europe, the state demanded that Muslims form a national organization that would communicate with the government and distribute economic support to the different local communities. *Förenade Islamiska Församlingar i Sverige* (**FIFS**) was formed in 1974 to meet this need. FIFS organized all kinds of Muslim communities, including Shias, Sunnis, and communities of different ethnic backgrounds. The only exception was the Ahmadiyyas (largely considered as unorthodox or un-Islamic by both Sunnis and Shias), who split from FIFS and formed a separate organization, *Sveriges Förenade Muslimska Församlingar*—**United Muslim Communities of Sweden (SMuF)**.

In 1990, a new split occurred, leading to the creation of the *Islamiska Kulturcenterunionen i Sveriges*—**Union of Islamic Centers of Culture in Sweden (IKUS)**. IKUS has a *Suleymanci* Sufi orientation and is anti-Shia. Its members are mostly Turkish, but they also include a few Somali communities that are mainstream enough to be opposed to female circumcision and the chewing of *Khat*.

The *Sveriges Muslimska Råd*—**Muslim Council of Sweden (SMR)**—was formed in 1990 by FIFS and SMuF to be their active arm in their relations with the Swedish majority society. The most active person in the SMR is Mahmoud Aldebe, who has also held the chairmanship of SMuF for quite a while. The specific mission of the SMR is to found and maintain mosques and Islamic schools, and offer information about Islam to the non-Muslims of Sweden.

In addition to the organizations recognized by the SST, there are a few that exist outside its reach—partly because FIFS, IKUS, and SMuF oppose the establishment of possible rivals, and partly because they are ethnically or theologically distinct, such as a Bosnian association and a Shiite organization.

Switzerland[58]

Total population: 7.4 million
Muslim population: 310,800 (4.2 percent)
National representative organizations: *Musulmans et Musulmanes de Suisse* (Muslims of Switzerland) and *La Ligue des Musulmans de Suisse* (the League of Muslims of Switzerland)

The largest Muslim groups are Albanians, Turkish Kurds, and Bosniaks. Official figures suggest the Muslim population has doubled in recent years, but some sources say there are also about 150,000 Muslims in the country illegally. The first Muslims arrived as workers in the 1960s, mostly from Turkey, Yugoslavia, and Albania. They were joined by their families in the 1970s and, in recent years, by asylum seekers and refugees. Only 36,481 Muslims have Swiss nationality. Of those, half are converts,[59] a proportion quite similar to that of Italy and Spain.

Major Muslim Organizations:

There are some 35 generic Muslim associations, four Muslim youth associations, three Muslim women's associations, and four Muslim assistance associations.

Given Switzerland's federated system, most Muslim or Islamic unions operate at the cantonal level, such as the Union of Muslim Associations of Fribourg, giving them more weight to discuss important local issues (e.g., cemeteries, swimming pools, construction of mosques).

At the national level, there are two main structures, but neither has a legal status comparable to that of the French CFCM. They are *Musulmans et Musulmanes de Suisse* (MMS) and *La Ligue des Musulmans de Suisse* (LMS). They have their own publications, such as *Er-Rahma—Die Barmherzigkeit* (irregular, perhaps five times a year) and *Bulletins du Centre Islamique de Genève* (three times a year).

Most other groups are virtual, present only via Internet sites. The importance of such sites and virtual groups is primarily due to their ability to attract individuals and small groups banned or controlled elsewhere in Europe.

United Kingdom[60]

Total population: 58.8 million

Muslim population: 1.6 million (2.8 percent)

Imams: 2,000, mostly immigrants from South Asia and the Middle East. There are, however, two institutions dedicated to the training of imams: the Muslim College in London (established in 1981) and the Markfield Institute of Higher Education in Leicestershire (established in 2000).

Mosques: 500 mosques with official registration (which implies tax benefits and the right to perform recognized marriage ceremonies) and at least 2,000 overall

Muslim private primary schools: 60

National representative organization: The Muslim Council of Britain

At least 50 percent of the current Muslim population in the UK was born there. The overwhelming majority are of Pakistani, Bangladeshi, or Indian origin. Significant communities with links to Turkey, Iran, Iraq, Afghanistan, Somalia, and the Balkans also exist. The 2001 census showed that one-third of the Muslim population was under 16—the highest proportion of any group in Britain.

Major Muslim Organizations:

The main organization is the **Muslim Council of Britain** (**MCB**), which claims to represent some 70 percent of all Muslim associations in the United Kingdom. It describes itself as

> . . . an umbrella organization dedicated to the common good, to the betterment of the community and country. It was inaugurated—after several years of wide-ranging consultation and careful planning—on November 23, 1997, at the Brent Town Hall in Wembley by representatives of more than 250 Muslim organizations from all parts of Britain including Northern Ireland. The recent fifth annual general meeting (April 28, 2002) affirmed the MCB's status as a vibrant coalition of grassroots organizations and institutions and individual talent and skills that is making a positive and constructive contribution to meeting the needs and the aspirations of the Muslim community in a period of recurring crises and anxious optimism.[61]

In fact, these claims are increasingly challenged—by outside observers, by rival, often more radical groups, and by young Muslims in Britain. While many still consider the MCB moderate and mainstream, the main "voice" of British Muslims,[62] and while its stated purpose is to promote cooperation, consensus, and unity, some post-9/11 public statements by its leaders raise questions about its true goals and moderation. MCB claims to condemn "all" acts of terrorism—but not those that take place in Israel or Kashmir. It has always claimed that Maulana Mawdudi, one of the most important proponents of 20th-century Salafism and jihadism, was a moderate, and that *Hizb ut-Tahrir* is a peace-loving organization. Of the Israeli killing of Hamas's founder, it declared that "the Muslim Council of Britain condemns in the strongest terms Israel's criminal assassination of Shaykh Ahmad Isma'il Yasin, the renowned Islamic scholar and founder of the leading Palestinian Resistance Movement—Hamas."[63]

The most prominent of the MCB's rivals are the following:

Muslim Association of Britain (MAB). A new, younger, more radical group of Muslim activists, the MAB is linked to the Muslim Brotherhood and its Pakistani counterpart, *Jamaat-e-Islami*, and has links with left-wing British political groups, including George Galloway's Respect Party. One of its leaders is Dr. Azzam Tamimi, a Palestinian-born political scientist and supporter of Hamas. Although the MAB did condemn the 2005 London bombings, some spokesmen have made highly suspect remarks about suicide bombings in general and those in Israel in particular. Tamimi claimed that "What may be seen as a glorification of terrorism by one person might be seen as an explanation of the causes of terrorism by another person."[64] That was "interpreted" by MCB leaders—to no avail.[65]

Islamic Human Rights Commission. This is a London-based "civil rights" NGO promoting the notion of Muslim victimhood and complaining about "Islamophobia" everywhere, mostly in order to avoid debate over Islamist attitudes and actions. It states openly that "Our inspiration derives from the Koranic injunctions that command believers to rise up in defence of the oppressed." Its chairman is Massoud Shadjareh.

Muslim Parliament. After the 1989 Salman Rushdie affair and the violent events surrounding it, this body was founded to fight "Islamophobia"—defined as any form of critical comment on Islamic and Islamist behavior. Its main campaigns are against "discriminatory" laws against terrorism, forced marriages, and extremism. Its leader is Dr. Ghayasuddin Siddique.

Islamic Society of Britain. A relatively moderate and non-campaigning vehicle for the promotion of Islam and Islamic values, this group claims that "working for Islam is not just about campaigning for Muslim rights, but also about sharing Islam's view on God, life and society." Led by Dr. Munir Ahmed, it claims that "The Islamic Society of Britain totally condemns the vicious and indiscriminate attacks" of 2005.

Hizb ut-Tahrir (HuT). This group is a pan-Islamic political party open to all Muslims ("regardless of whether they are Arab or non-Arab, white or colored") seeking the creation of an Islamic state worldwide and the imposition of strict Sharia law. Its spokesman in Britain (where its European headquarters are located) is Qasim Khawaja. It claims to be nonviolent, but it has been banned from campuses since 1995 and, as previously mentioned, is widely seen, especially outside Britain, as a pathway to jihadism.

Al-Muhajiroun (The Emigrants). This group, now officially dismantled, but in fact replaced by another group, *Al-Ghurabaa (The Strangers)*, with identical membership and ideology, was set up by the extremist imam Omar Bakri Mohammed (now self-exiled) after he split off from *Hizb ut-Tahrir* in 1996. It is closely linked, ideologically and otherwise, to Islamist radicals, Al-Qaeda included, and has supported terrorism in the United States, Israel, and elsewhere.

Council of Imams and Mosques. An influential training group for imams, the Council is linked to the MCB. It advised the Home Office to have stricter entry visas and to introduce training for foreign imams. Its longtime chairman was Dr. Zaki Badawi (d. 2006), an Egyptian-born scholar and principal of the Muslim College in London. Badawi, an Al-Azhar alumnus and teacher at various Islamic universities from Malaysia to Singapore to Nigeria, condemned the 2005 London bombings, but was seen by the U.S. as associated with Islamist circles and banned entry.

There are also literally hundreds of smaller Muslim groups, some centered in major mosques (in Birmingham, Leeds, Manchester, etc.), mostly Sunni, with a few Sufi or Shia.

The Imam Question

The above analysis of Islam's legal organized presence in Europe demonstrates a number of common characteristics. The most important is that almost everywhere the governments have made efforts, often strenuous and occasionally heavy-handed, to engage the Muslim communities in the institutional and legal framework of their countries, thus opening the way for treating Islam on an equal footing with European religious denominations. When there were difficulties, these were often

caused by Islam's lack of institutionalization and sectarian frag-
mentation, by local Muslims' divisions (ethnic or otherwise), or
by the interference of foreign governments.

Another common characteristic is that all the established
organizations have difficulties dealing with an increasingly
alienated Muslim youth or competing with more radical, and
effective, groups like *HuT* or even some more extreme. To a
large extent, recognized Muslim organizations have the problem common to many large institutions—communicating with
and reflecting the concerns of a constituency rapidly growing
in number and diversity. It is for this reason and in this context, as well as because of some peculiarities of Islam, that the
role of the imams is essential. They are the most direct link
between ordinary Muslims, established Muslim organizations,
and society as a whole.

The role of imams and the organizations they lead or represent is ultimately the decisive factor for the future of Islam
in Europe. As such, these two factors—organized Islam and
imams—are the key to understanding the environment that
most Muslims in Europe live in, and that most governments
have to deal with.

Louis Caprioli, until March 2004 the head of counter-terrorism at the French Directorate of Territorial Security (*Direction
de la Surveillance du Territoire*—DST), once stated, "There is always a preacher at the origin of the passage to the terrorist
act."[66] It would be hard indeed to overstate the role of preach-
ers/imams in the creation and development of Islamism, including terrorism, in Europe, and there is little question that
the present and future nature of Islam in Europe will be largely
decided by them.

In 2005, then Interior Minister Sarkozy stated that Imam
Abdelkader Bouziane's statements regarding the proper Islamic

way of beating a woman were "not the Islam of France [but] Islam in France, and that we do not want."[67] Sarkozy's remarks were typical of the French approach to the issue of Islam's relationship to the native culture. That means support for "French Islam," defined as a type of Islam that is integrated and respects French laws; as against "Islam in France"—alien, global, Salafist, and violent. Herein lies the dilemma facing Paris, and indeed all European governments. Is Islam just another religion to be dealt with through accommodation, negotiation, and tolerance, on the post-Westphalia pattern, which made various Christian denominations legally equal, or is it too alien to accommodate? The legal, political, and intellectual debates suggest that the issue is still unresolved, and the Islamist terrorist threat remains to be assessed and dealt with.

In Bouziane's case, he was expelled to Algeria, but then he sued in France, where a court allowed him to come back. The court decided that what Bouziane did was to read the relevant Quranic texts—a perfectly legitimate act for a person in his position, never mind that he had no formal religious training (which keeps him in good company among imams in France). He was then expelled again, this time for good—but only after a change in French law. That makes France different from most other European countries, as quite a number of imams have been expelled for statements contrary to French laws and mores, usually incitements to violence against Jews, women, homosexuals, or indeed the state itself.

More important than the fate of one self-proclaimed imam in Vénissieux is Sarkozy's distinction between French Islam and Islam in France, a dichotomy applicable elsewhere. Is it an apt distinction, and does it operate in real life?

Belatedly, some European countries are beginning to realize the threat the imams pose to their security, and to address the closely related matter, raised by Sarkozy's distinction, of their Muslim communities' ability and/or willingness to integrate, if not assimilate. Belatedly, because some of them, especially Britain, have long tolerated activities by UK-based imams that have led directly to murder, first abroad and since 2005 in Britain as well. Abu Qatada, a Palestinian who, until his arrest in 2005, was based in London (Britain wants to deport him to Jordan, but so far the courts have prevented this), gave religious cover to the Algerian GIA and its atrocities, which produced some 150,000 deaths. The London-based Abu Hamza legitimized the GIA and planned and encouraged (including by sending his own son to participate in) the kidnapping and murder of foreign Christian tourists and locals in Yemen. Omar Bakri Mohammed, also based in London, recruited volunteers for Islamist terrorism in Bosnia, Chechnya, Iraq, and elsewhere. As will be seen below, all three had ties, direct or ideological, with Al-Qaeda.

The imam situation in Europe is quite disturbing to counterterrorism experts. Only 10 percent of France's 1,000 to 1,500 imams are believed to be citizens, less than half speak French, and "probably a majority" are illegal immigrants. Moreover, according to Abdellah Boussouf, an imam from Strasbourg, "the majority of imams preaching in France are self-taught or have had no formal religious education."[68] The situation is probably worse in Britain, where, at least until recently, immigration visas were freely given to Pakistani imams, a majority of whom had no formal religious training, and few, if any, spoke English or, for that matter, bothered to learn it once in the United Kingdom.

In Germany, where the majority of Muslims are of Turkish origin, many but not most imams are sent from Turkey—a secular Muslim country—and vetted by Ankara's Religious Affairs Directorate; they are thus unlikely to be inclined to fundamentalism. That said, however, there are dissident, anti-Ankara Turkish organizations actively proselytizing in Europe, ranging from *Milli Görüs*—the external branch of a former governing party in Turkey, the *Rafah* (Welfare) Islamist Party—and the smaller but dangerous Cologne-based *Khilafat* (Caliphate), the organization of followers of Metin Kaplan, seeking an Islamic state in Turkey (in October 2004 Germany finally extradited Kaplan to Turkey).

The present legitimizers of Islamism, as Caprioli suggested, are religious figures, even if its principal ideologues (such as Hassan al-Banna, Sayyid Qutb, Osama bin Laden, and Ayman al-Zawahiri) seldom were. Without the radical imams, the entire ideological, political, and psychological edifice of Islamism would crumble. Indeed, as demonstrated below, no jihadist terrorist act has ever been committed or planned in Europe (or anywhere else, for that matter) without some kind of theological sanction from a cleric. It thus follows that any long-term solution to the threat of Islamist terrorism has to start with Islam's radical clerics—especially in the West, where they are more free to operate than in most Muslim countries. The terrorist operatives themselves, most obviously those willing to commit suicide, are expendable, since their motivators and recruiters can always produce more—as they always do.

While imams and religious leaders in general have an obvious influence throughout Islam, especially among the Shias, there are a number of reasons why that influence is stronger still among Muslims in Europe. To begin with, the latter, especially those born there, know much less about their faith than Muslims who live in Muslim-majority countries, where Islam has permeated everyday life for centuries and its fundamentals are socially, officially, and often legally enforced. This means that for a Muslim in France, the Netherlands, or Britain the imam (supplemented, among the young, by the Internet) is the main vehicle for introduction to Islam. Furthermore, in Europe the "mosque," however defined, more often than not plays a major role in maintaining the cultural cohesion of ethnic groups, especially the smaller ones. It establishes small-group cohesion, which could easily produce a terrorist cell. Ironically, multiculturalist policies that encourage the preservation of ethnic and cultural distinctiveness also, at least indirectly, magnify the influence of imams over the Muslim population.

Few of these imams are locally trained—at least in part because of the generally lower educational level of Muslims in Europe. Language is also an obstacle—a trained imam is expected to read and know the Quran in its original Arabic. This difficulty is heightened further by the fact that Turks and South Asians do not understand Arabic, and most young Arabs born in Europe do not speak Arabic, or speak it poorly. The inevitable result of this reality is that the overwhelming majority of imams in Europe are at best immigrants themselves and at worst temporary imports from the countries of immigrants' origin, unfamiliar with Europe's cultural surroundings and often unable even to speak the language of their new flock. As for the relatively few Muslims from Europe who do train as imams abroad, far too often they do so in places like Saudi Arabia,[69] attracted by financial incentives and the presence of the Holy Places, or Pakistan—the two major sources of radical Islamism.

Islam, and especially Sunni Islam (85 percent of Muslims are Sunni), does not have a clergy in the strictest sense of the word.

In theory any Muslim man is entitled to lead Friday services at the mosque. In practice, learned, professional scholars of Islam are more highly respected and influential than a self-taught Ali or Osman claiming to be an imam. Some institutions, most prominently Al-Azhar University in Egypt, therefore have a large pan-Islamic influence, and their graduates may be more respected—but they do not have any ultimate authority over all Muslims.

Until recently, however—with the major exception of France—the imam issue was not taken seriously by most governments, for a variety of reasons. In Germany, for instance, the fact that most of the imams serving the Turkish communities were sent from secularist Turkey created a false sense of safety, suddenly shaken by the revelation that 9/11 was planned by a cell in Hamburg, made up of Arabs recruited and indoctrinated locally by Arab radicals.

The difficulty of handling the problem is common to all democracies. Where does freedom of expression and religion stop and incitement to murder start? What is the responsibility of a Muslim cleric who has never personally committed a violent act but has "only" recruited, indoctrinated, and motivated the actual murderers?

But those in the West who have long been serious about fighting Islamist ideology are now less alone. The French were the first and still the most effective in tackling this problem—especially under the leadership of their ambitious interior minister, now president, Nicolas Sarkozy. No matter how long they have lived in France, Islamist clerics are now being routinely expelled—usually to Algeria—under Sarkozy's "zero tolerance" approach to such things as legitimizing violence against women, calling Jews "apes," or inciting to jihad.

Even traditionally tolerant Belgium has created a *plan mos-*

qué, placing mosques under police surveillance; in Germany, "spiritual inciters of disorder" are to be prosecuted; in Austria, radical imams can now be expelled for "speeches threatening public security"; in Italy, radical imams can be expelled by the interior minister.[70] The UK is finally dealing with the radical imams on its territory, by proposing criminalization of incitements to violence, with conviction followed by extradition or expulsion, even to countries like Egypt, Jordan, or Saudi Arabia, traditionally the taboo "human-rights violators" of the powerful NGO lobbies and their supporters in the judiciary.

Even when they do receive some government financial help—and that is not the case in all European countries—legitimate imams have a number of disadvantages compared with the radical freelance operators like the London trio mentioned above, all of whom were on welfare. The Moroccan Mohamed Bouzakoura, who lived in a small Flemish town for 25 years, describes some of the problems:

> My inability to communicate with the young Muslims is my biggest frustration.... In Morocco there would be four people to perform what I do on my own. I lead every prayer, I am khatib, I am muezzin, I am a listening ear, I try to solve problems, and I try to understand Belgian society. However I still do not speak Dutch because I do not have the time to attend classes. Not speaking the language is a major obstacle in dealing with our young generation. Unlike their parents, they do not speak Arabic fluently and do not understand me well. We have to bridge two gaps: one of language and one of generation. I do think that new imams should be able to communicate in Dutch or French and understand the problems that our second and third generations face in this society.[71]

The issue of language is also deemed important by Tahir al-Tujani, an imam in Antwerp, for similar reasons:

> I don't speak Dutch and as a result I am losing touch with the new generations. During my *khutbah* [the sermon delivered

before Friday prayers and after Eid prayers], I mainly address the older generation and encourage them to try to understand the new context in which their children are raised. Living together in peace is so important for a kid. We, the old generation, have to set the example. I think that my inability to communicate with the young Muslims is my biggest frustration. We need new imams.[72]

Leave aside the problem of a person who, after living in a country for a quarter of a century, still does not speak the language for "lack of time," despite being aware that without doing so he cannot perform his function. The reality is that because most trained imams have only limited contact with young Muslims born or growing up in Europe, the ones who do have influence with the young are mostly radicals.

The issue of imams, like the related ones of youth radicalization and Islamist terrorism, was forced on the attention of most European governments by 9/11, and was made more salient by the subsequent attacks in Madrid and London. In general, European governments have tried two parallel approaches to the issue: in the short term, surveillance (and when possible expulsion of radicals—whether trained imams or freelancers); and in the long term, the formation of a new generation and type of imams in Europe.

The crackdown on Islamist imams has been most regularly pursued by France, starting even before 9/11. Between September 2002 and mid-2005 France expelled 40 radicals, including 10 imams; in the first 10 months of 2006 alone 11 Islamists were expelled, following the 12 thrown out in 2005.[73]

In 2005 Germany expelled Abdelghani Mzoudi to Morocco, after he was acquitted of charges of aiding the Hamburg cell behind 9/11; the same year, Italy expelled eight Palestinian radicals.[74] Italy has expelled several other radicals over this period. Abdel Qadir Fadlallah Mamour, an imam in Carmagnola, near

Turin, was expelled after supporting the murder of Italian soldiers in Iraq; Algerian-born Mahamri Rashid, the 34-year-old imam of a mosque in Florence, was expelled in May 2004. The Moroccan Bouriqui Bouchta of Turin was expelled in 2005; Mourad Trabelsi, the former imam of a mosque in Cremona, in 2003; and the Senegalese Imam Mamour in the fall of 2004.[75] The process of expulsion was made easier by new legislation passed after one of the Somalis implicated in the second, failed attack in London in 2005 fled to Italy.

In the Netherlands, in February 2005, then Immigration Minister Rita Verdonk began deportation proceedings against three Muslim imams (from Bosnia, Egypt, and Kenya) accused of being a threat to public order and national security. A few months later a Turkish professor of theology was also expelled.[76]

In Denmark, the imam problem was already beginning to be dealt with two years before a group of imams directly provoked the cartoon crisis. In 2004, Prime Minister Anders Fogh Rasmussen stated: "Access to obtaining a Danish residence permit for foreign missionaries has been too easy up until now." He introduced new legislation requiring any person coming to Denmark on a religious visa to show that he is a "worthy" candidate, educated, financially self-supporting, and connected with one of 200 recognized religious communities. Even apart from the cartoon affair—which rocked this country that had always valued freedom of the press—there were good reasons for such a measure. Thus, Abu Bashar, a Syrian cleric working as a prison chaplain at Nyborg State Prison, was fired after complaints from inmates that he engaged in Salafist propaganda. The Lebanese imam Raed Hlayhel of the Grimhøjvej mosque in Jutland, a graduate of Medina University, advocated the wearing of *burqas* by Muslim women in Denmark and claimed that Danish women's habits "invite rape"; his mosque was found to have among its regulars a suspected jihadist cell and Slimane Hadj Abderrahmane, a former Guantanamo inmate. Hlayhel voluntarily returned to his native Lebanon, in November 2006. But others like these two—such as the Lebanese Ahmed Akkari and the Palestinian Ahmad Abu Laban, both directly involved in instigating the cartoon controversy—have remained in Denmark. In fact Akkari, then visiting Lebanon, was rescued from there in the summer of 2006 by the Danish government.[77]

In Germany, Imam Mohamed Fizazi of the Al-Quds mosque in Hamburg—which was frequented by three of the 9/11 pilots—made the mistake of returning to his native Morocco, where in 2005 he was sentenced to 30 years for his role, as imam in Tangiers, in the 2003 Casablanca bombings, and for his ties to the Madrid terrorists of 2004. Following new legislation in January 2005, making it easier to expel or deny entry to non-German preachers of hate, Germany refused return visas to two Egyptian imams in September of that year.

However, denying entry to radicals is one thing, expelling those already in Germany is another. That was demonstrated by the complications following attempts to expel an Afghan imam in Frankfurt and the Lebanese Salem al-Rafei of Berlin's Al-Nur mosque, both of whom incited suicide bombings. Indeed, when Annette Schavan, minister of education of Baden-Württemberg, demanded that imams be permitted to preach only in the German language, and Joerg Schoenbohm from Brandenburg called for revoking the German citizenship of imams who preach hatred, both ideas were shot down as unconstitutional.[78] For such reasons most efforts are directed against foreign imams visiting Germany, rather than those already there and enjoying refugee status or even citizenship.

In Norway the imam problem is as serious as elsewhere, or worse. Indeed, people like Imam Zulqarnain Sakandar Madni, the leader of the United Ulama of Norway (*Jamiat Ulama-e-Norway*), Imam Hafiz Mehboob-ur-Rehman of the Islamic Cultural Center, and Imam Syed Ikram Shah of the World Islamic Mission all still claimed, as late as 2006, either that the 9/11 perpetrators were "not Muslims" or that nobody could prove they were.

Statements by Muslim clergy denying Islamist terrorism are not limited to Norway. In July 2005 Dr. Mohammad Naseem, chairman of the Birmingham Central Mosque, went further and stated that "Muslims all over the world have never heard of an organization called al-Qaeda."[79]

However, Norway has, in theory at least, more freedom to act against radical imams than EU member states. Indeed, as the British government has complained to the European Parliament at least since 2005, the European Convention on Human Rights makes it almost impossible to expel radical imams—a complaint that has led nowhere. As seen above, other countries, France most prominently, have been able to take advantage of the fact that most imams there are not citizens: 40 percent of the imams in France are from Morocco, 24 percent from Algeria, 16 percent from Turkey, and 6 percent from Tunisia.[80] However, most radical clerics in Britain are there as refugees or asylum seekers, or have British citizenship. Following diplomatic agreements with Jordan and Egypt, London is finally preparing to expel or extradite some of its radicals—against ferocious opposition from groups like Amnesty International.

EUROPEAN ISLAM?

Almost all European governments, with France in the forefront,[81] are attempting to ensure that the imams help establish a European Islam, rather than the present Islam in Europe—hence the Netherlands' and Denmark's new insistence on imams' proficiency in those countries' languages, training in European institutions, and familiarity with local/national traditions, including oaths of loyalty to the countries' respective monarchs.

Regarding the formation of imams in Europe, with the natural goal of creating a group of leaders who know the language, laws, and customs of their country of residence, France has expended the amplest efforts, with few results. At Saint-Leger de Fougeret in Burgundy, a grandly named European Institute of Human Sciences (*Institut Européen des Sciences Humaines*— IESH), to prepare imams *à la française,* was approved by the French Ministry of Youth and Sports as long ago as 1992. By 2004 it had produced only 30 alumni. And at that, it was funded by Saudi Arabia until after 9/11, and it is still controlled by the Muslim Brotherhood's UOIF, even having Yusuf al-Qaradawi on its "scientific council." In 1993, the Paris Grand Mosque opened a Theological Institute, like the Mosque itself under Algerian control, but it was closed two years later. Also in 1993, an Institute of Islamic Studies opened in Paris (later moved to Saint-Denis), under the auspices of the World Muslim League—a Saudi-controlled organization—but it closed in 2002.[82] Finally, almost in desperation, the rector of the Grand Mosque of Paris, Dalil Boubakeur, went to Egypt in October 2005 and reached an agreement in principle with Muhammad Sayyid Tantawi, the Grand Shaikh of Al-Azhar University, providing for the training of French imams at Al-Azhar and for Egyptian imams to teach in Quranic schools in France. The reason, according to Boubakeur's spokesman, was that "One has to face it . . . France is confronted with a mushrooming of imams coming from who knows where, preaching a fanatical Islam, such as Wahhabism. This project seeks to reinforce the cadres for a moderate Islam, of which Al-Azhar is the symbol."[83] Significantly, the intended formal cooperation with Al-Azhar is to be expanded to similar institutions in the Maghreb—all controlled by moderate or, in the case of Tunisia, secular regimes.

Ultimately, all this means is that the efforts to establish an *Islam de France*," as opposed to *"Islam en France*," have failed— UOIF trainees could hardly be expected to be either moderate or integrated—and Paris is back to square one, depending on friendly foreign regimes to control or manipulate its Muslim communities. That is better than having them under Muslim Brotherhood and/or Saudi influence,[84] but still far from the desired Islam *à la française*.

The role of the Boubakeurs family is interesting in this regard. As Frank Fregosi has pointed out,[85] personal and traditional ties between the Boubakeurs and important French politicians have ensured a prominent role for the Grand Mosque, although it is clearly unrepresentative of Muslims in France. Hamza Boubakeur was close to Socialist Prime Minister Guy Mollet during the 1950s, while his son and successor as rector of the Mosque, Dalil, is close to Jacques Chirac.

France's experience with the formation of imams has been repeated elsewhere. Thus the Austrian government has supported the creation of an Islamic Academy in Vienna, intended to prepare "future generations of teachers of religion and preachers," but the academy is officially sponsored by Al-Azhar University. However, there are Islamic secondary and preparatory schools in Austria, officially recognized and financed by the government, and certified by the Vienna Administration of Schools.[86]

Since September 2002 the Netherlands has required all imams coming into the country to complete a special series of preparatory classes on the Dutch language, the status of women and homosexuals, euthanasia, the role of Parliament, and Western culture in general. By 2005 only 12 Turkish and five Moroccan imams had finished those courses. Meanwhile, the Free University in Amsterdam has received a government grant to establish such a program for imams already in the country, but its content could not be agreed upon because of differences among various Muslim groups and between them and the university.[87]

Belgium has the Islamic Center in Brussels, financed by Saudi Arabia. However, the government—perhaps in recognition of the problems Wahhabism may pose or, more likely, of the fact that most Muslims in Belgium are of either Turkish or Moroccan origin—decided to look elsewhere for the training of imams. Thus Françoise Schepmans, chairwoman of the Walloon Parliament, during a 2004 visit to Rabat, asked for Moroccan help in establishing a theological institute for Belgian imams. They would then be teaching religion in schools, just as Catholic and Jewish teachers do.[88] The obvious question in the Belgian case is, Why is Brussels not interested in making a similar deal with the secular Turkish authorities? The answer may have a lot to do with the well-documented Belgian tolerance, if not sympathy, for the Kurdish terrorist group PKK—and the resulting cold relations with Ankara.

The problem of pay is very important, as is demonstrated by the ability of governments from Turkey to Saudi Arabia to control their radical clerics because they pay their salaries and are willing to use that leverage. In Europe that is far more difficult, for cultural reasons. First, even in the countries that do have a state religion (Anglicanism in England, Lutheranism in Scandinavia) and taxpayer-subsidized clergy, that clergy is free to act and express itself as it wishes—including, in some cases, going as far as denying basic tenets of their own religion,[89] with no fear of government reprisals.

Second, an imam in the Netherlands or Belgium whose salary was paid by the government would have little credibility in the eyes of the faithful. (In France the problem does not exist, since the law itself prevents the government from paying salaries for clergy of any sort.) However, donations from the imams' flock are often insufficient. In fact, some alumni of the Theological Institute in Paris had to study also at a secular university in order to be qualified for an additional job. Equally important, when imams depend on the donations of their flock they are afraid to adopt unpopular opinions.

Ironically, there is an alternative to accepting payment from the government specifically for religious activities. Many influential imams in Europe, including some of the most dangerous, live on the public dole. This allows them to dedicate full time to their religious activities and thus have the most influence and the largest followings. This is the case with the already-mentioned London trio. It is also true of the extremist mullah Najmuddin Faraj Ahmad, better known as Mullah Krekar (and his large family) in Norway. Even the now-expelled Abdelkader Bouziane of Vénissieux, a polygamist father of 16, received public assistance.[90]

None of the above is news to the governments of Muslim countries, which are perfectly aware of the threats that radical imams pose to their security and survival. In Turkey, whose population is 99 percent Muslim, imams are required to complete formal studies in institutions where the secular government establishes the curriculum, and they are allowed to preach only if they have a government-provided license. As a result, the Turkish diaspora in Western Europe, more than two million strong, is far less involved in Islamist activities than Arabs are. It should be pointed out, however, that the current Turkish government of Prime Minister Recep Tayyip

Erdogan of the Islamic Party of Justice and Development (a direct descendant of *Rafah*), which has been in power since 2003, is far less strict than its predecessors in its enforcement of secular policies—when not altogether reluctant to continue them. How that new reality will influence the Turkish diaspora remains unclear.

While world attention to Islamic terrorism has been concentrated on training camps in Afghanistan and elsewhere, the very nature of Islamic extremism, as we have seen, requires a legitimacy that can be given only by Muslim clerics. For obvious reasons, the governments of most Muslim countries do not encourage such activities, with the result that radical clerics have often found Western countries to be a more convenient location for their activities. When imams, legitimate or not, go beyond the limits tolerated by Muslim states, those governments take decisive action. Thus, when Muslim "scholar" Abdul Rehman of Pakistan organized a widely attended service for the London suicide terrorist Shehzad Tanweer, he was arrested. When Ali Belhadj, the former number two of the banned Islamic Salvation Front (FIS) of Algeria, publicly supported the murder of Algerian diplomats in Iraq, he was arrested. When Yemeni cleric Ali Yahya supported the rebellion led by the Zaidi cleric Sheikh Badr al-Din al-Huthi, he was sentenced to death.

IMAMS, TERRORISM, AND RESPONSIBILITY

Since major Islamist terrorist operations began in the West—with the 1993 bombing of the World Trade Center in New York—many of the methods developed and previously used elsewhere, including remote-controlled and suicide bombings and chemical attacks, have been introduced in Europe, and there are good reasons to believe that they will be attempted again in the United States. This is, whether the West likes to admit it or not, a civilizational conflict between a significant segment of Islam and the rest of the world. Nor, by the way, is the pernicious influence of radical imams on ignorant populations limited to terrorism: Their opposition to "Western" polio and measles vaccines in Nigeria has killed thousands throughout the world during the past three years—mostly through diseases contracted during pilgrimages to Mecca.

It is essential to keep in mind that Islamist terrorist groups and individuals are bound to act only under religious authority, which can be provided only by an imam—formally trained or self-declared. And because Sunni Islam lacks a universally recognized center of legitimacy, such as the Vatican for Catholics, there is no central body able to determine who is a "true" Muslim and who is not. This makes declarations to the effect that Islamist terrorist attacks are a "perversion of Islam" somewhat dubious, whether they come from moderate Muslims or from Western politicians. The Quran makes it clear that a Muslim is a Muslim once he makes a statement of his faith, and so no one who is not an open apostate can be denied the quality of Muslim. On what basis can Tony Blair, George Bush, or even Muhammad Sayyid Tantawi declare that Osama bin Laden is not a "true" Muslim or, indeed, an "imam"?

While in theory only formally trained imams have the right to issue *fatwas*—religious interpretations of legal cases, issues, or problems—in practice all sorts of individuals do so, bin Laden being only the most outrageous example. That is especially true in the West, where self-proclaimed imams abound and find willing followers owing to the fact that Western Muslims' knowledge of Islam is often skimpy or nil, despite growing interest.

There was an outcry when Sheikh Omar Abdel Rahman, 58 years old, blind and diabetic, got a life sentence for legitimizing the 1993 World Trade Center bombing. The "human-rights" groups ignore the crux of the matter, which is this: The fact that a blind or mutilated imam does not personally commit a violent crime, being physically unable to do so, but "only" recruits and encourages Islamist terrorists, is no excuse—nor should he be able to hide behind laws protecting freedom of speech or religion. The "blind sheikh" Omar Abdel Rahman, the crippled Ahmed Yassin of Hamas, and the handless Abu Hamza have all proved to be far more dangerous than any run-of-the-mill physically fit terrorist.

Thus, the French and Italian, as well as the American, legal systems are now moving toward applying the same conspiracy laws once limited to the Mafia and other criminal gangs to Islamist clerics. If "falsely shouting fire in a crowded theater" is not protected by the First Amendment, as Justice Oliver Wendell Holmes famously wrote, then calling for murder in the name of Islam is not protected, either.

CHAPTER FOUR

The Islamist Context

Islam "under Siege"

Even if European governments could persist in a policy of expelling radical imams—a far from certain proposition, considering the lack of consensus among EU member states and, most importantly, the powerful objections of well-established "human-rights" lobbies, which are more often than not supported by the European Court in Strasbourg—the fact remains that even the most poisonous imams are, ultimately, less dangerous than the long-term influence of recognized, active, and growing Islamist institutions already influential throughout the continent. While an Abu Hamza or an Abu Qatada can ultimately be dealt with (they are both now in custody), the cultural and social environment created and sustained by allegedly nonviolent organizations still provides the beginning of the path toward jihadist terror for thousands of young Muslims in Europe—often with direct or indirect government (i.e., taxpayer) support.

Muslim organizations in Europe are a transmission belt for the changing mentalities and attitudes of the *ummah* as a whole, and of its most influential elements—the Arab world and Pakistan—in particular. This is why, ultimately, the attempts by various European governments to encourage moderate, "representative" Muslim organizations have been less than successful.

To be sure, the very concept of "organized Islam," as distinct from Muslim organizations, is to some extent oxymoronic. In its very essence Islam, especially the Sunni variety, is incompatible with strong institutional organization in general and "national" organization in particular, especially if that implies cohabitation of distinct ethnic and sectarian groups. This is even truer for Salafis, but the very notion of "nation" is fundamentally alien to orthodox Muslims everywhere. "Nation" implies division (Arabic *finto*) of the *ummah* and thus conflict among Muslims. Being Muslim and nationally aware—as French, Dutch, or even Turkish or Moroccan—is, in the Salafist interpretation, impossible.

Thus, inevitably, all transnational Muslim organizations in Europe are pan-Islamic, and most advocate the re-creation of a unified Islamic state, the Caliphate. Some are legal, some not; some are tolerated, some subsidized, and some banned; and there are sharp, even murderous, differences among them in methods and theological backgrounds. They include the **Muslim Brotherhood** (*Ikwan el Muslimeen*), ***Tablighi Jamaat*** (Proselytizing Group—*Tabligh* or TJ), ***Hizb ut-Tahrir al-Islami*** (Islamic Party of Liberation—HuT), and ***Takfir-wal-Hijra*** (Excommunication and Exodus). They also include followers of Turkish Islamist Metin Hacaoglu, a.k.a. Metin Kaplan, the self-styled "Caliph of Cologne" and head of the (mostly diaspora) Turkish organization Union of Islamic Associations and Communities in Germany (ICCB, also present in France as the *Association Islamique de France*—AIF). The ICCB advocates a pan-Islamic state and has ties with the Muslim Brotherhood's largest European branch, the UOIF, as well as with Shia Iran.[1]

The European Context

The dominance of pan-Islamic groups in the organized Muslim scene in Europe is not happenstance nor solely reflective of these organizations' strength. It is also the natural result of a perverse cultural dynamic within Europe itself.

On the one hand, the advances of multiculturalism—here simply defined as an ideology which, beyond tolerance of cultural diversity, advocates legal equality based on ethnic, racial, religious, or cultural identity—and political correctness within Western societies have led to the creation of a myth of general Third World, or "color," victimhood, easily detectable in Western reactions to illegal mass migrations and Islamist terrorism. To this one has to add the unsettled situation of many Muslim societies in the post-decolonization and post–Cold War eras—what Samuel Huntington described as the "bloody borders of Islam," reinforced daily by Al Jazeera and rhetoric coming from places like Tehran and Gaza. Thus was a fertile ground created for many, even most, Muslims throughout the world to develop a collective sense of being under threat *as Muslims*. In the Islamic world, the enemy (when not a concrete and immediate neighbor, e.g., India, Russia, Israel) is a generic "West," with its Coca-Cola, advertising, and movies. In the West itself, uprooted masses of Muslims, many not truly Algerian or Pakistani any more but not French, Dutch, or English either, seek a new collective identity—and Islam is the most convenient and natural default expression of that identity. Hence the dialectic of international solidarity of Muslims, the sense of a global community—the Islamic *ummah*—pushing from below, being met by pan-Islamic organizations spreading their influence from above.

Ummah Solidarity

> "Islam is a single nation, there is only one Islamic law, and we all pray to a single God. Eventually such a nation will also become political reality. But whether that will be a federation of already existing states, a monarchy, or an Islamic republic remains to be seen."
>
> —Yusuf al-Qaradawi[2]

Qaradawi's view is shared by all Muslims, and even if some may not think of the *ummah* as a political as well as a faith community, many agree with Gilles Kepel's opinion that "The ummah, the community of believers, feels threatened by what it sees as a modern version of the crusades, and therefore perceives itself as the antipode of the West."[3]

To make sense of the changes in the attitudes of the Muslim communities in Europe, one must place them in the larger context of change in the Muslim world as a whole. Through the continuing flow of immigrants, the Internet, the media, and globalization in general, Muslims in Europe are not only a natural but an increasingly integral part of the *ummah*. As they become increasingly integrated into the *ummah*, Europe's Muslims become less and less integrated in Europe. Simultaneously, in a push-and-pull process, as Europe moves away from values compatible with Islamic values and traditions—as it becomes more and more accepting of homosexuality and lax about drugs and prostitution, thus more aggressively secular—more and more Muslims in Europe become in reaction more and more traditional or conservative in their values.

Here are some of the cultural trends in Western Europe during the past three decades or so. In the Netherlands, Belgium, and Spain, homosexual "marriage" is legal, and "civil unions" are accepted everywhere. In the Netherlands some drugs (marijuana) are freely sold and used. In quite a few European countries prostitution is legal (in the Netherlands it is even union-ized), and pornography is available everywhere. Secularism is triumphant everywhere, even in countries that still retain a state religion. By all measures, Western Europe is now in a "post-religious" era,[4] defined by the extremely small number of practicing Christians and the low level of respect for the con-tinent's Judeo-Christian tradition—a fact demonstrated by the exclusion of any mention of that tradition from the EU draft Constitutional Treaty of 2004. Meanwhile, Jews in Europe, at least until recently, have tended to be more of the Reform vari-ety than the Conservative or Orthodox.

In a cultural environment in which criticizing and/or mak-ing fun of Christianity or Jesus Christ or Moses is common, anachronistic examinations of history are also common, as demonstrated by the routine claims that the medieval Crusades were an act of Western imperialist aggression and the Crusaders were gangs of bloodthirsty barbarians, as evidenced by the 11th-century massacres in Jerusalem and Antioch, whereas Salahaddin was the "noble Muslim," known for his chivalry and generosity.[5] Such mistaken views, common among Western journalists and academics,[6] fit perfectly with Salafist propaganda seeking to justify violence against Christians by describing the Crusades as criminal enterprises and then tagging all present-day Christians as "Crusaders," and thus as legitimate targets.

To all of this, one should add the continent's persistent col-lective sense of remorse and guilt for its colonial past, with-out regard to the circumstances or actual results. Such feelings led to a widespread cultural habit of uncritical admiration for anything and everything coming from formerly colonial Third World areas. Typical of this cultural masochism among the intelligentsia of Europe was Jean-Paul Sartre's admiration for the anti-European, racist views of an obscure Caribbean psychiatrist, Frantz Fanon, who in *The Wretched of the Earth*[7] excoriated all that was European and legitimized violence against "whites." Once again, radical Islamists do not have to manipulate history (although they do that) to reinforce their claim to historic European persecution of Islam—all they have to do is quote the Europeans themselves.

In this context, it is natural for many Muslims in Europe to feel more solidarity with cultural trends in the Islamic world than in the lands that have become their homes. For Muslims everywhere and probably especially for those living in the West, the U.S. and allied military operations in Afghanistan and Iraq, not to mention Israeli operations in Gaza and the West Bank, constitute evidence of a global assault on Islam. This opinion is not limited to Islamists and their open apologists; rather, it is a widespread view among many Muslims in Europe, ranging from the Moroccan immigrants responsible for the Madrid bombings of 2004, to Muslim members of the House of Lords, to the radicals in the Paris *banlieues*. Some have used this to "explain" or even justify terrorism; others—the self-appointed "leaders"—to blame Tony Blair and George W. Bush for their own inability to control or moderate the young radicals.

Once again, quite significant segments of the Left in Europe and the United States also explain Islamist terrorism as the understandable, if extreme, reaction to Western attacks on Afghanistan and Iraq and Israeli attacks on *Hizbollah* and Hamas. There are many problems with such an approach, not the least of which is that the chronology of events does not fit with it. Events in Afghanistan in 2001, Iraq since 2003, or Lebanon in 2005 cannot explain attacks that preceded them, such as the 1993 World Trade Center bombing, the mid-1990s bombings of the French transportation system, the attacks on the U.S. embassies in East Africa, or the involvement of British-based Muslims in suicide attacks in Kashmir or Israel. Yet Afghanistan, Iraq, and Gaza are seen as persuasive evidence of Western enmity, even oppression of Islam in general.

Even allowing that reasonable persons, Muslim or not, could argue over the motivations, legality, or need for the overthrow of Saddam Hussein, no rational person could deny that the U.S.-British removal of the Taliban regime at the end of 2001 was a direct, natural, and legitimate response to Mullah Omar's longstanding harboring of Al-Qaeda and thus his shared responsibility for 9/11. As the French scholar Olivier Roy, among others, has pointed out, the very sequence of events contradicts the still popular Muslim view that 9/11 was a reaction to American attacks: "Attacks by al-Qaeda preceded U.S. action. The Americans intervened militarily in Afghanistan and Iraq after 9/11, not before it."[8] Nevertheless, Soumaya Ghannoushi, a highly educated Muslim—she is a researcher in the history of ideas at the School of Oriental and African Studies, University of London—claimed that "To Muslims, the caricatures [the Dutch cartoons of 2006] vividly brought back the scenes of Israeli bulldozers demolishing Palestinian homes in Jenin, the invasion of Afghanistan, the fall of Baghdad, terrors of Abu Ghraib and humiliations of Guantanamo Bay."[9]

That is not much different from the views of a radical like the Lebanese-born Dyab Abou Jahjah, currently living in Belgium: "Europe, and the 'new' and only world power, the United States, are still doing that. Whether it is Iraq, Afghanistan or Palestine, it is done to fight 'terrorism' and to bring 'freedom and democracy' to these 'peoples' who wouldn't know what freedom and democracy were if it struck them in the face."[10] It also echoes the opinion of Imam Abduljalil Sajid, a prominent Muslim theologian in Great Britain and, until 2002, chair of the Muslim

Council of Britain's Social Policy, Welfare, and Regeneration Committee:

> In most of the world's trouble spots, Muslims have been massacred and tortured and denied their most basic rights. Thousands of innocent people have died in Afghanistan and in the Iraq War. Not unnaturally Muslims feel that they have been treated unjustly by what is euphemistically called "the world community."[11]

The Muslim Association of Britain, linked to but distinct from the MCB, sees itself more as the *ummah's* representative in Britain than that of Muslims living in Britain: "What do we want? For Islamic issues world-wide to be recognized as just, fair and humane. For British Muslims to act as the first line of defence for Islam and Muslims all over the world."[12]

Among Muslims in Europe the opposition to the U.S. and British interventions in Iraq and Afghanistan was almost universal from the start, despite the fact that most Iraqis were supportive of the invasion, at least in the beginning, and most Afghans still are. On the other hand, in the Muslim world at large public opinion was thoroughly hostile. The logical conclusion is that most Muslims in Europe are in step with the generic *ummah*, share its reflexive anti-Americanism, and are not interested in the merits of those actions *per se*. While on Iraq their views do not diverge from European opinion in general, hostility toward the removal of the Taliban could only be interpreted as solidarity with *any* Islamic cause when in conflict with the West—and ultimately as a demonstration of massive cultural alienation.

Revealingly, upon the arrest in the UK of the alleged airplane-bomb plotters in August 2006, some local Muslims demonstrated in favor of the suspects, claiming that a suspect "was not a terrorist" and that police had used "excessive force"—all this before any information was available. This suggests, again, that there is support for whatever Muslims do, because they are all victims and victimized.

More dangerous, support or "understanding" for terrorism is not limited to "the Muslim on the street" in the UK. What is a young Muslim in Manchester to think when Afzal Khan, an attorney and former lord mayor of Manchester, Labour member of the City Council, and member of the central working committee of the MCB, asked to address terrorism, said:

> "The real issue is taking a step back and looking at the whole issue in a wider context. One side's terrorist is another side's freedom fighter. How do we bring about a just and fair world, so there are not any causes for terrorism? You have the Middle East. Then America comes into the game, and that brings in petrol. Quite frankly, it has been appalling. They didn't give a damn about the suffering of people. That's one thing that winds people up. . . . And another thing . . . There are many Muslims who have a question: How come America gets to decide who gets a nuclear weapon?"[13]

This is the real background of the persistent claim even by moderate Muslims in Britain, including members of Parliament, that recent U.S. and British foreign policy is the "cause" of Islamist terrorism. Taken to its ultimate logic, this leads to the attitude expressed by the leader of the 7/7 cell in London, Mohammed Sidique Khan, in a video made public after his death. Khan was born in Pakistan but raised, educated, and employed as a teacher's assistant in England. He was described by those who knew him well as "an exceptionally well integrated person. His anglicized name 'Sid' was just one symbol of his willingness to take on a British identity."[14] Nevertheless, he left behind a video, which was broadcast along with footage from Al-Jazeera of Ayman al-Zawahiri's approval for the crime. As AP reported it,

"Your [i.e., the British] democratically elected governments continuously perpetuate injustice against my people all over the world, and your support of them makes you directly responsible, just as I am directly responsible for protecting and avenging my Muslim brothers and sisters." ... He also said Prime Minister Tony Blair "not only disregards the millions of people in Iraq and Afghanistan, but he does not care about you as he sends you to the inferno in Iraq and exposes you to death in your land because of his crusader war against Islam."[15]

How can we explain this extraordinary gap between Sidique Khan's social persona in England and his private, and ultimately explosive, complete alienation from all things Western and English?

The first thing to note is his phrase "Your democratically elected governments." "Your," not "Our": For Khan, the British people, among whom he had lived most of his life, are alien. Next, repeating an often-used bin Laden and al-Zawahiri argument, because Britain (and the West in general) is democratic, all its citizens, whether or not a particular individual voted for a certain government, are collectively guilty—and hence legitimate targets. Women, children, the old are all part of a world hostile to "my Muslim brothers and sisters," for whose protection Khan is "directly responsible."

By mentioning Afghanistan as well as Iraq, Khan makes it clear that for him and his fellows, the issue is not the "legality" of the Western attack on Iraq. *Any* Western attack on *any* Islamic or Muslim country, for whatever reason, including self-defense, is a "crusade." That mentality, common among Salafists everywhere, is a permanent ideological presence among Islamist terrorists in Europe.

The notion among the Western intelligentsia that Islamic terrorism is a reaction to the Iraq war has led to a widespread view among citizens in Western countries that, at least in its present form, "the war on terrorism" is counterproductive. An ICM poll for *The Guardian* in August 2006 revealed that 72 percent of people in the United Kingdom think government foreign policy has made Britain more of a target for terrorists like Sidique Khan, and only 1 percent believe it has made Britain safer.[16]

What is important is less the obvious fallacy of the notion of "Islam under global siege"—after all, it was the West that saved Muslim lives in Bosnia, Kosovo, Kuwait, and Somalia, all episodes that have been conveniently forgotten—than the irrationality of that perception, which makes it almost impossible to counter. That is even more so when Muslims in the West are told daily, by their leaders and by the European establishment, that they are victims. A perfect example of official encouragement of a sense of victimhood among Muslims is the 2006 report by the EU-associated European Monitoring Centre on Racism and Xenophobia, based in Vienna: "Muslims, like other religious groups, remain inadequately recorded statistically, and even demographic data relies often on unofficial estimates that vary, sometimes substantially. More international survey research is therefore essential particularly in order to record attitudes and the extent of Muslims' victimization."[17] In other words, the authors admit lacking sufficient data but do know that there is Muslim "victimization." Or, as the Queen of Hearts in *Alice in Wonderland* put it, "Sentence first— verdict afterwards."

Mohammed Nasser, as chairman of Birmingham's Central Mosque, is that city's main Muslim religious leader. The British government considers him important in inter-community relations. But here is his reaction to the January 2007 arrest of men suspected of plotting to kidnap and behead a Muslim member of the British armed forces: "There is a fear about who is next.... People will need to know the facts, but there is a long-standing perception that this climate of terrorism is being maintained to further the political aims of the government." Selma Yahoo, a member of the Birmingham City Council, said: "There's a shock and disbelief that these arrests are being made in such a high-profile manner. People are very concerned about the social backlash."[18] For Yahoo, an elected official and a *hijab*-wearing activist member of George Galloway's radical Respect Party, any use of police force is "high profile" (the raids in Birmingham took place at 4 A.M.). When the "spiritual" and the elected leaders both pretend that police rather than terrorists are the problem, it seems naïve, to say the least, for British authorities to expect help from them in combatting Islamism.

Seeking an anchor while living in a West perceived as culturally and morally adrift, many (especially the young) find that the global persecution and oppression of the *ummah* is also a personally satisfying explanation of their own lack of economic and social success. That kind of refuge in a mythical, distant *ummah* is encouraged by some of those whom Muslims in Europe see as local guides. Thus Nasreddin Peyró, professor at the University of Seville, serves up a deft and trendy combination of anti-Americanism, anti-Westernism, and ignorance of history:

> What we Muslims call the *ummah* of Islam, which could be translated as the global Muslim community, is a single entity, without internal conflicts derived from its diversity, despite extending from Senegal to Indonesia or from Albania to Mozambique. Precisely because Islam is not an institution, a Church or a political organization, and does not have a "center" anywhere, its internal diversity is not a source of conflict.... There is no real confrontation in the Muslim world between Shias and Sunnis, as presented now by medias close to the American Administration. Islam is not similar with the case of Christianity, with its Catholics and its Protestants, and its St. Bartholomew's Eves.[19]

Simply put, if Muslims as a group and Islam as a whole are under attack everywhere, from Palestine to Kashmir to Iraq to Russia to China, it is obvious that we, the Muslims of Britain, France, Belgium, and Holland are also under attack, which explains why I, Ali, Mohammed, or Massoud, am poorer than Pierre, Hans, or John. How subjective this sense of persecution is is demonstrated by Muslim answers to the question whether Europeans are hostile to them: In Germany 51 percent answered in the affirmative, but only 19 percent had had a "bad personal experience" in this respect; in Britain the answers were 42 percent and 28 percent; in Spain, 31 percent and 25 percent.[20]

This deeply rooted sense of collective victimhood is both encouraged and taken advantage of by Islamists of all types. This is precisely the point used by radicals like HuT to recruit, indoctrinate, and radicalize young Muslims in the West—especially the majority whose knowledge of Islam's history, evolution, and scholarship is limited or nil:

> So, is it true that the Islamic Ummah, Arab and non-Arab, is weak in front of the state of the Jews? Certainly not! Impossible! The Islamic Ummah came forth from the Arabian peninsula which was fragmented into pieces and so she united it and conquered the empires of Rome and Persia. The light and Message of her state shone in the whole world and she remained the leading power in the world for a period of more than a thousand years. This Ummah has stumbled in this century and fallen—however, every horse has a fall—and she is returning to her origins and to her natural status for which Allah (swt [*subhanahu wa ta'ala*—glorious and exalted is he]) has prepared her with His saying:
>
> "*You are the best of peoples raised up for mankind, you enjoin the good (al-Ma'ruf) and forbid the evil (al-Munkar), and you believe in Allah.*" [TMQ (Translated Arabic Meaning of the Quran) 3:110]
>
> It is a disgrace for this Ummah to place herself as a rival to the Jews. She is a rival to America and Europe together. She is rival

> to Russia, China and Japan combined. She is the best Ummah
> and she carries the best Message to humankind. This is not an
> imagination, rather it is a fact which has filled history, which
> is ready now to fill the present and future history. It is this
> fact that the superpowers fear, a fact which they try to efface
> and mislead the Muslims from it so that they remain in a state
> of despair and submission.[21]

How is this vision of solidarity to be implemented? One relevant answer came from Mullah Krekar, asylum beneficiary in Norway and founder of the Iraqi terror group Ansar al-Islam: "The whole world must see that Jihad . . . is increasing in its scope with Allah's pardon . . . This trend represents solidarity in the Muslim community."[22]

Hence, *ummah* solidarity offers an explanation, a cause to fight for, a method, and an enemy—all fallacious, irrational, and ultimately self-destructive, but all attractive and tempting to those Muslims in the West who have lost their original roots in the Rif, Algeria, Anatolia, or Kashmir, but have not acquired new ones in Paris, London, Berlin, or Amsterdam.

While this is the general background creating a micro-culture of alienated Muslims throughout Europe, there is another important element to be considered: that for all practical purposes, most radicalized Muslims in Europe are *de facto* converts to Islam. We are not referring here to *de jure* converts—i.e., persons of Christian or Jewish background who have joined Islam, an issue discussed elsewhere. This is a very different phenomenon: the fact that the overwhelming majority of second- or third-generation "Muslims" in Europe who join the ranks of radical Islam previously knew and cared little about Islam. This was the case of Zacarias Moussaoui (known as the "20th hijacker" in the 9/11 plot), Mohammed Bouyeri (the killer of Theo van Gogh), and so many others. They move directly from ignorance to Salafism (often via *Tablighi* indoctrination), and for such a dramatic change, which amounts to conversion, they need a model, teacher, and mentor, one who offers everything they seek. That means someone reputed for Islamic scholarship, including knowledge of the Quran and of Arabic (a language most of them have lost or never knew), connections to the global *ummah,* and charisma—hence the decisive role of a few radical imams.

These dynamics among Muslims in Europe have often been missed by academic observers, but not by Islamist groups, who realized early on that in their global jihad against the nonbelievers they needed a strong "fifth column" in Europe. How well this effort works has been demonstrated repeatedly by the actions of Islamist terrorists recruited, indoctrinated, and led from Europe—such as those behind the 9/11 attack against the United States, the bombings in Madrid, Casablanca, and London, and the failed plots of such as Moussaoui and Richard Reid.

Without the growing sense of solidarity with Islamic causes everywhere, most terrorist actions by Europe-based jihadists could not be understood. Indeed, without *ummah* solidarity, how could one explain Xavier Djaffo, a.k.a. Massoud al-Benini, born in France to a Frenchwoman and a Beninois father, getting killed by Russian troops in Chechnya in 2004? Or his high-school friend Zacarias Moussaoui, trying to murder Americans in the United States? Why did the British Pakistani Mohamed Hanif blow himself up in a Tel Aviv café on April 30, 2003? Or why did the French-Tunisian Lotfi Rihani, Italy-based Tunisian Habib Waddani, and Moroccan Kamal Morchidi blow themselves up in Iraq in 2003?[23] In none of these cases (and there are many others like them) was there any personal or national reason for such actions—only complete allegiance to the perceived interests of the *ummah.*

For jihadis, this is convenient indeed. The concept of *nusra*, Islamic solidarity, is an operative fundamental for the structuring of jihadism. In practice it is manifested by radical Islamists involving the community and obtaining support from accomplices who donate funds, give hospitality, and receive jihadis in transit through European countries.[24] The main issue is that *ummah* solidarity is, beyond all distinctions among them, the common trait of virtually all Muslim organizations in Europe.

The Islamist Establishment

Pan-Islamic Organizations

As we have seen, the Muslim communities in Europe are characterized by extraordinary sectarian and ethnic diversity. This has opened the way for pan-Islamic ideologies and groups, most of them radical and some openly violent, including the Muslim Brotherhood, *Tablighi Jamaat, Hizb ut-Tahrir*, and *Takfir-wal-Hijra*. All but the first of these are secret or becoming so; hence any assessment of their membership, influence, or impact is bound to be incomplete and inaccurate. All share a pan-Islamic or global ideology, all have a continental presence in Europe, and all oppose Muslims' integration and assimilation in the European countries in which they live, by free choice or by birth. Theological details aside—and those are important enough to lead occasionally to violent clashes between them—and at the risk of oversimplifying matters, their differences are over means. There is *no* difference in their goal: the spread of Islam and Sharia throughout the world, usually associated with the idea of Caliphate.

We have discussed the general practice by European governments of attempting to treat Islam as any other religious denomination, and thus taking major risks: that groups legally recognized may not be representative of majority Muslim opinion, that legal recognition may bestow legitimacy upon radical groups (which tend to be better financed, mostly from outside Europe)—or both. This discourages or even discriminates against the large number of moderate Muslims, precisely the kind of people who are least likely to become radical or to oppose integration.

As Martin Bright, an astute British journalist and analyst of Islamism, has observed:

> [The] Foreign Office . . . is pursuing a policy of appeasement towards radical Islam that could have grave consequences for Britain. In making the television program I had the privilege of traveling around Britain to talk to some of the Muslim communities that feel shut out by the Government's bizarre dalliance with the Islamists. In London, Rochdale and Dudley people told me of their frustration with a Government that chooses to promote a highly politicised version of Islam. By contrast most ordinary Muslims believe their faith comes as a result of a personal relationship with Allah, not through lobbying for blasphemy laws.[25]

Nevertheless, it is to those organizations, many of them international in scope, that the European governments tend to turn. The most prominent and influential of these is the **Muslim Brotherhood (MB)**, also the main power behind the Saudi-based and funded World Muslim League. Nowadays the MB claims to be nonviolent, certainly in Europe, where is deeply rooted in France, Switzerland, the Netherlands, and Belgium. In the Arab world, where it is on the rise again via elections in Egypt and the Palestinian territories,[26] its tactics vary in time and by country between violence and legal activities. In most of Europe, the MB and its numerous associated groups and organizations are viewed with suspicion by intelligence agencies but generally tolerated—Russia aside, where the MB is banned, mostly because of its links to Riyadh.

It is common to exaggerate the Muslim Brotherhood's international unity. It is true that the organization has been, since its founding in Egypt in 1928, led by a succession of spiritual/ideological leaders in Cairo. The current supreme leader, Mohamed Akef, has a clear objective: the spread of Islam until it rules the world (he has ". . . complete faith that Islam will invade Europe and America, because Islam has logic and a mission").[27] However, the MB largely operates as a decentralized set of groups (it has branches in some 70 countries) with tactics changing depending on circumstances. It allows its various branches to take disparate positions in different locales—and retains the ability to distance itself from them when necessary. But, while it is meaningless to describe the organization as a whole as either violent or nonviolent, it is entirely appropriate to define it as Islamist.

Where approaching its goals is facilitated by elections (Algeria, Egypt, Jordan) it participates in the electoral process; where violence seems more promising (Algeria post 1991, Syria 1982) it has tried that; and in Europe, where Muslims are a minority, it tries both to promote a separate Muslim legal and cultural universe under the pretext of safeguarding human rights, and to present a "democratic" and peaceful face—allowing it to steadily penetrate and dominate established Muslim organizations, to kidnap the role of main representative of Muslims in negotiations with the state, and generally to present its goals as representative of the Muslims in Europe.

Furthermore, despite theological differences, since 1961 the Muslim Brotherhood has made an alliance with the Saudi regime—an arrangement that both limits its freedom of action and, most relevant in the European context, makes it by far the wealthiest Islamist structure on the continent.[28] That means independence from European (and also Moroccan, Algerian, and

Turkish) governments and additional credibility in the eyes of alienated young Muslims.

In Europe the MB controls many of the most influential Muslim organizations, directly or otherwise, but never under its own name or publicly. It has a very important spiritual and religious impact through the Dublin-based European Council for Fatwa and Research (ECFR), based in the Clonskeagh mosque in south Dublin. The ECFR is led by the Qatar-based Yusuf al-Qaradawi, probably the world's most influential and media-savvy Sunni theologian.

Ideologically the MB is the original source of most Islamist groups of today, violent or not. Some Salafist organizations have split from the MB because they disagreed with its tactical opportunism—such as electoral participation in some countries, temporary collaboration with Arab nationalism in others, etc. For some observers, the link between MB and Al-Qaeda is direct—for instance, Emmanuel Razavi sees the group "in the shadow of Al Qaeda."[29] In an ideological sense, that is a logical claim insofar as the writings of the Egyptian Sayyid Qutb, an MB member, had a decisive influence on fellow Egyptian Ayman al-Zawahiri, Al-Qaeda's second-in-command, and Abdullah Yusuf Azzam (1941–1989), Osama bin Laden's mentor in Pakistan, was also a Muslim Brother.[30] However, Al-Qaeda's ideology has other sources as well, some much older than MB, particularly Wahhabism.

As we saw in the country-by-country survey, many prominent Islamic/Muslim organizations in European states are controlled or heavily influenced by the Muslim Brotherhood, notably the UCIE in Spain, the UOIF in France, and the UCOII in Italy. It is characteristic of the intentional ambiguity of the Muslim Brotherhood that it consistently pretends to be open and "moderate," while at the same time opposing measures intended to diminish the risks of radicalization or to increase the level of Muslim integration. When the Italian government decided to imitate France and establish a foundation to manage funds for religious establishments, including the construction of mosques, the UCOII's secretary general, Hamza Roberto Piccardo, claimed that "The constitution says religious communities set themselves up according to their own statutes, and a secular state only needs to worry that everything is done legally"—in other words, no need for transparency. When the government stated its intention of checking on the teachers in Islamic schools in Italy, Piccardo denied that they even existed—according to him they are only language schools, teaching Arabic—fully aware that even other Muslim representatives complained of the activities of self-appointed Islamist imams.[31]

The ECFR claims to be the ultimate theological and legal authority for Muslims in the West, and considering Qaradawi's reputation and media activities—he is a regular presence on Al Jazeera TV and he created the influential IslamOnline.net—that is a plausible claim. Although it often interprets Islamic law selectively to suit specific circumstances in Europe—its leaders would not offer the same interpretation in Muslim-majority countries—it still takes distinctly ambiguous positions on key issues. Thus:

> Question: My question relates to the blind support the U.S. gives the Zionist State, Israel, even in killing innocent Muslims. Does that policy make the U.S. Dar Al Harb [House of War]?
>
> Answer: Sheikh Faysal Mawlawi, deputy chairman of the European Council for Fatwa and Research: Dar Harb is a juristic norm used by Muslim scholars in a certain epoch of time to refer to non-Muslim countries that have no peace treaty with Muslims. So, if we have what we call Dar Islam that adequately serves as a sine qua non for having Dar Harb. *But we have to assert that it is the Muslim ruler who possesses*

the authority of determining which place is Dar Harb and which one is Dar Al-Ahd [country that maintains peace with Muslims]. [Emphasis added.]

As for the case nowadays, most Muslim countries have slipped away from Shariah, confining its application to family cases, i.e., codes governing personal status. Some Muslim countries even refuse to apply Shariah in such cases, thus, giving in completely to man-made law to gain ground and govern everything, without exception.

Thereby, the notion of Dar Islam is hardly applied to many Muslim countries nowadays. But we prefer to consider countries whose populations are mainly Muslims Dar Islam—in essence that Islamic law should be the one to prevail in those countries, thus, drawing the attention of their rulers to the duty of accomplishing that task.

Given the aforementioned fact that the duty of determining places to be called Dar Al-Ahd is left with the rulers and the fact that most Muslim countries are now members of the UN, it has been agreed upon by all the Muslim rulers that *all the world countries now are Dar Al-Ahd, not Dar Harb.* [Emphasis added.]

But as we know, we, the subjects, are not obliged to give our rulers blind support in everything; we should not obey their orders that run counter to the ordinances of the Creator, Almighty Allah. Apart from that, we are to obey and support them in order to cater for the welfare of the society. Coupled with that is our constant advice to them and constructive criticism for some of their policies. Despite all the blind support that the U.S. gives Israel, it has not reached the extent of making explicit declaration of war against Muslims.[32]

The best interpretation of this is that the West, and the U.S. in particular, are not currently targets of war, but that is only because Muslim regimes of dubious orthodoxy say so. Individual Muslims, it is clearly implied, may legitimately think differently, an ambiguity that leaves open the possibility of legitimate attacks against the U.S. and other Western countries. The Council thus covers its bets against legal accusations of supporting violence, but does not go as far as to reject it. Similarly,

> Question: Some people say that the operations carried out by Palestinians are considered suicidal acts and not a kind of Jihad, is that true? Please tell me whether these acts are martyr operations and a kind of striving in Allah's Cause or not?
>
> Answer: Sheikh Faysal Mawlawi: *Martyr operations are not suicide and should not be deemed as unjustifiable means of endangering one's life.*[33] [Emphasis added.]

This is a characteristic Muslim Brotherhood (and Qaradawi) form of double-speak—the *fatwa* formally frowns upon suicide terrorism in general but considers it legitimate when the targets are Israelis. Once again, this is legalistic sophistry, since, once the principle of "martyrdom" is accepted, its application in various circumstances becomes just a matter of legitimate debate.

Thus, despite its pacific pretensions, the Brotherhood's Muslim weekly, *The Brotherhood Mission (Risalat al-Ikhwan)*, published in London, is used openly and actively by terrorist groups, such as Hamas, itself the Muslim Brotherhood's Palestinian branch, whose *Filisteen al-Muslima (Muslim Palestine)* publication is also distributed from London. The organization also supports anti-American terrorism in Iraq because, as the MB's deputy supreme leader, the Egypt-based Mahmud Ma'mun al-Hudaybi, explained,

> The American occupation of Iraq is a crude and obvious example of aggression against Iraq and the Arabic Islamic nation. Active resistance (*muqaawamah*) to the occupation and the use of any available means to resist it are a religious Muslim duty, a national duty and a natural right anchored in both international law and the United Nations Charter. Therefore, all Arab and Islamic nations and all free men

everywhere must stand side by side with the Iraqi people until the foreign forces [are forced to] leave and full [Iraqi] independence and sovereignty are reinstated.[34]

As Gilles Kepel has pointed out, the 1970s opening of an office in Paris by the Saudi-based World Muslim League marked a "turning point in the Islamization of France," because it brought together previously dispersed Muslim communities, paid for their mosques,[35] and through all this strengthened the Muslim Brotherhood, which was the channel used by the Saudis to expand their influence. Despite strong competition from the Algerian and Moroccan governments, both of which support rival groups in France and elsewhere in Europe, it is the Muslim Brotherhood, or specifically the UOIF and its foreign financiers, that is now the most influential Islamic organization in France.

It is not necessary for our purpose to examine the ideology of the MB in any detail, but a significant sample is provided by a brief quote from Mahmmud Ezet, the organization's secretary general:

> The Islamic ideology is comprehensive. It deals with all aspects of life; social, humanitarian, political, international relations, commercial relations . . . etc. The 77-year struggle of Muslim Brotherhood was to lay down that Islam is a religion that regulates the human life according to Allah's method and that the happiness of human beings is linked to a religion-controlled life. . . . The Islamic reform is gradual. It considers all necessary requirements to get the Islamic nation out of this civilization setback . . . The Islamic remedy begins with attaining the fundamentals, then the necessities, then the luxuries. Similarly, it is gradually concerned with the individual, the family, the community, and then the State which unifies, improves and urges the Muslims to carry out its role in the world civilization. . . . It is a peaceful ideology that rejects all forms of violence. But it uses the true and pure concept of jihad to clarify the truth of Allah by wisdom and gentle persuasion.[36]

Of course, the ideology Ezet calls "comprehensive" others may well call totalitarian—and at any rate, the point is that the ultimate goal is a transnational society ruled by Sharia. In the European context, this means that Muslims should not and cannot integrate, let alone assimilate. To the contrary, they have a duty, individually and collectively, to expand the reach of Islam—to be sure, by nonviolent, legal means. Ultimately, the Muslim Brotherhood's goal in Europe, and in other non-Muslim areas, is to start with *separation*, and move through missionary work (*dawa*) and other methods, toward an ultimately Muslim world. This explains the persistent demands of the MB for a status of Muslims in Europe that amounts to what Americans would call "separate but equal"—a situation in which Muslims take advantage of "human rights" in the West in order to retain and strengthen their collective religious identity. While this— minus the religious element—fits into the multicultural notions of the Western Left (which strengthens its impact), it is also a *Leitmotif* of virtually all legal Islamist groups in Europe as well as violent jihadist elements.

Tablighi Jamaat (TJ), or **Jamaat ut-Tabligh**, is an ostensibly nonviolent Islamic organization, and a fast-growing one at that, which walks a thin line between legality and advocacy of Islamism—a line that it has crossed in some countries, like Germany, where it is banned. Its members visit mosques and, it increasingly appears, college campuses in small missionary bands, preaching a return to "pure" Islamic values and recruiting Muslim men—often young men searching for identity—to join them for a few days or weeks on the road. *Tabligh* is both an organization and a certain way of interpreting Islam—hence its members easily join other groups while retaining ties with it and continuing to share its ideology. Aishah Azmi, the *niqab-*

wearing teacher in Dewsbury whose dismissal from her job in 2006 became a *cause célèbre*, was a member.

Mourad Amriou is a UOIF militant in the Paris *banlieue* of Torcy, and his path to Islamism is quite typical—he was "re-Islamicized" (his own word) by an itinerant *Tablighi* preacher after just two weeks of meetings. From there, in search of a more active form of strengthening his faith, he joined the Muslim Brotherhood.[37] This is far from an isolated case—indeed, *Tabligh* is credited with having been the group that first began the serious re-Islamization of young Muslims in France, during the mid-1980s in the Lyon region. Ahmed Merani, an early member of the Algerian Islamist FIS, began as a *Tablighi* preacher; Moussa Kraouche, an FIS propagandist in France in early 1990s, and Khaled Kelkal, a GIA terrorist in France in the mid-1990s, were initiated in radical Islamism by a *Tablighi* imam.[38]

Established in 1926 at Mewat, near Delhi, by Maulana Mohammad Ilyas (1885–1944), whose family still controls it, *Tabligh* is one of the largest and the most secretive Islamist mass organizations in the world. Its 1988 annual conference in Raiwind near Lahore, Pakistan, was attended by more than one million Muslims from all over the world; by now the Raiwind International Conference has become Islam's second largest congregation in the world, after the *Hajj*.[39] Centered in New Delhi and Dacca, it is active in some 90 countries, including those of Europe, plus Japan and the United States.

Theologically, mainstream Sunnis have an ambiguous attitude *vis-à-vis Tabligh*, with one asserting that "The biggest problem with the Jammat Tabligh is that they do not have enough scholars of true knowledge of Islam. The best part of the work of the Jammat Tabligh is that they do have so much enthusiasm and dedication to trying to make things better for the Muslims and to draw closer to Allah."[40] Shaykh 'Abdul-'Azeez bin Baaz, the late mufti of Saudi Arabia, declared that *Tabligh* has "many deviations . . . so it is not permissible to go with them, except for a person who has knowledge and goes with them to disapprove of what they are upon and to teach them [the truth]."[41]

Such criticism did not, however, prevent the Saudi-controlled World Muslim League from subsidizing the 1978 construction of the Dewsbury mosque.

To further obscure the issue, some Islamists have strong words for TJ's "pietism," which they associate with collaboration with the infidel:

> The thousands of members of the Tableeghi Jamaat are utilising all their energy exclusively inwards towards other Muslims and leaves the Kaafir powers to pursue their Godless exploitation of the Muslims completely unimpeded. . . . This is the reason why the Tableeghi Jamaat moves freely in Kufaar countries in Europe and the rest of the world, while other Muslims are being imprisoned, tortured, and killed on a daily basis.[42]

Paradoxically, that is an opinion shared by some reputed experts, who should be more cautious, including Gilles Kepel, who calls *Tabligh* "pietistic," and Olivier Roy, who claims that the group is completely nonviolent and apolitical.

The reality is that TJ's history and associations raise serious doubts in this respect. Thus, early in its history, *Tabligh* was directly involved in the 1926 assassination of Swami Shraddhananda, one of the few prominent Hindus to support Muslim efforts against the British in the 1920s;[43] military members of the group were behind a failed coup in Pakistan in 1995; and members of the allegedly "apolitical" *Tabligh* had high positions in the two Pakistani governments of Nawaz Sharif (1990–93, 1997–99), whose father was a prominent member and financier of the group.[44]

Even more significant is *Tabligh*'s connections with terrorist groups, such as the Pakistani *Harakat ul-Mujahideen*, and with Saudi Arabia—with one observer believing that there still is "large-scale Saudi financing of *Tablighi Jamaat*."[45] As *Tabligh* seems to have become more radical, access to Saudi and other similar financial support also makes it more dangerous. Not surprisingly, at least one member of the failed London airplane-bombing plot of August 2006 regularly attended camps run by *Tabligh*.[46]

Writing on *Tabligh*'s activities in Central Asia, the Turkish-American scholar Zeyno Baran described them as follows:

> The group claims to follow the Prophet's sunnah (way of life), which to *Tabligh* members means wearing long beards, robes, and leather shoes to replicate the Prophet's dress; the group firmly believes in outwardly showing that one is Muslim. Members are also required to conduct "*Tabligh*," that is, to try and convert others to Islam, on a regular basis. They each devote a certain amount of time to this *dawa* ("cause"), which, depending on the individual, could be one hour per day, one day per week, one week per month, or one month per year. Members can spend this time camping in small groups in order to preach "the Prophet's way" in mosques. In Central Asia, they also preach in bazaars.

> Often, local young men in search of an identity join the group for a few days or even for a few weeks. While the group does not involve itself in politics (and has been criticized by radical Islamists for being apolitical), over time *Tabligh* has become an international movement, active mostly in South and Central Asia.

> TJ has also succeeded in introducing Islamic networks to Europe and the U.S., and often functions in parallel to the Wahhabi Muslim World League. In recent years, like many other Islamic movements, TJ has also become radicalized. Consequently, those who learn about Islam via the TJ are today at risk of supporting or joining terrorist groups. The group has been accused of having indoctrinated its followers

to fight for the Taliban and al-Qaeda. TJ came to the attention of U.S. terrorism experts after it became known that American Muslim terrorist John Walker Lindh was inspired to go to Afghanistan after first traveling to Pakistan with *Tabligh*.

TJ can be easily infiltrated by terrorists. Al-Qaeda or other terrorist groups are believed to have used TJ as their cover to travel and smuggle operatives across borders; because the group is apolitical, TJ's members can fairly easily travel between countries. Other terrorist groups may have used the movement as a recruitment pool; its failure to discuss politics leaves room for others to provide a political message.

Today, TJ has offices and schools in Canada and the UK— though its main centers are on the Indian subcontinent. Its principal mosque and spiritual center is at Basti Nizamuddin, in New Delhi, while another major facility is located in the village of Raiwind, outside Lahore, Pakistan.[47]

Farad Esack, a South African Islamic scholar who says he spent 12 years with the group in Pakistan, recounted a favorite *Tablighi Jamaat* analogy that equates individual Muslims to the electricians who work to light up a village. Each person lays wire until one day, the mayor comes to switch on the lights. "For many people in *Tablighi Jamaat*," he said, "the Taliban represented God switching the lights on."[48]

Indeed, for many throughout the world *Tablighi* activities are the first step on the path to Islamic fundamentalism, and the results are by now clear. Michael J. Heimbach, deputy chief of the FBI's international terrorism section, stated in 2003: "We have a significant presence of *Tablighi Jamaat* in the United States, and we have found that Al-Qaeda used them for recruiting, now and in the past."[49] At least two Islamist terrorist cells in the United States—in Lackawanna, NY, and in Oregon—had close connections with *Tabligh* in Pakistan.

Similarly, French intelligence officials declared the group an "antechamber of fundamentalism" and believe that perhaps

80 percent of Islamist extremists in France come from *Tablighi* ranks.[50] For instance, an August 2003 report by French police intelligence considered the Essonne area south of Paris to be strongly infiltrated by *Tabligh*, described as a "powerful factor of conversion [to Salafism]," and assessed its membership in the region at about four hundred militants and active sympathizers. The report also stated that "While the ascetic life of the Tablighis and their not modern presentation may appear little related to the materialist aspirations of the urban youth, their sincerity and daily practice of their convictions, combined with a smooth discourse, end by imposing respect." Furthermore, "It is certain that converts, already impregnated by the religious fundamentalism of Tabligh, form a breeding ground where jihadist Islamists dip"—and indeed the two jihadi networks from Essonne, Ben Bellil's and Djamel Beghal's (the latter discussed more fully in Chapter 6) both included numerous converts.[51] How important is *Tabligh*? In France alone, of the 1,534 mosques and prayer halls known in 2004, it controlled 163—second only to the UOIF.[52]

What makes *Tabligh* so effective—and dangerous—is the simplicity and plasticity of its theology, perfectly adapted to an audience lacking a deep understanding of traditional Islam, such as second-generation Muslims in Europe. One of its six basic principles, "Honor the Muslim," seeks to reinforce *ummah* solidarity. The fact that in Pakistan many former senior military and intelligence officers are *Tablighi*[53] sheds some light on the phenomenon of swift transition from ostensible pietism to violent Salafism—one that is seen among Britain's Muslims of Pakistani origin.

Tabligh's main European base remains Britain, and its main mosque there, in Dewsbury, West Yorkshire, has attracted a number of Islamists who later became well known—including

Richard Reid, the "shoe bomber," and Sidique Khan and Shehzad Tanweer, the leaders of the 7/7 bombings in London.[54] None of this stops *Tablighi* spokesmen from appearing on the BBC, although the government did put at least a temporary hold on the group's plans to build Europe's largest mosque in London. In France and Belgium the organization operates under the name Association Faith and Practice of the Muslim Religion (*Association Foi et Pratique de la Religion Musulmane*) and is seen as a key factor in the re-Islamization of immigrants.[55] To conclude, while a case could be made that, at least for now and at least in Europe, a direct institutional link between *Tabligh* and Islamist violence is still to be made, its active roles in rejecting Muslim integration and in the radicalization of the youth cannot be disputed.

Although *Tabligh* is a secretive organization and, when circumstances dictate, so is the MB, they are both clearly different from the secret and violent *Hizb ut-Tahrir* (HuT) and *Takfir-wal-Hijra*, both of which should be treated separately from the other pan-Islamic organizations. The ultimate goal—a Caliphate ruled by Sharia—is the same, but their methods, and thus the threat they pose, are quite different. That is not just an analytical observation but one made, and acted upon, by literally thousands of Muslims in Europe, who first (re-)joined Islam via MB or *Tabligh* only to progress to jihadism via HuT or *Takfir*.

Hizb ut-Tahrir is a radical Islamist group, apparently based in London, with branches in a number of countries; it is especially active in Central Asia. Its website states:

> The Reason for the Establishment of Hizb ut-Tahrir was in response to the saying of Allah (swt), "Let there be among you a group that invites to the good, orders what is right and forbids what is evil, and they are those who are successful" [TMQ 3:104]. Its purpose was to revive the Islamic Ummah from the severe decline that it had reached, and to liberate it

from the thoughts, systems and laws of Kufr, as well as the domination and influence of the Kufr states. It also aims to restore the Islamic Khilafah State so that the ruling by what Allah (swt) revealed returns.[56]

Although claiming to be nonviolent (at least in its statements in Europe), HuT is in fact very active in inciting anti-Western resentments in Europe and, particularly, in the Muslim world. Its role following the publication in September 2005 of the Muhammad cartoons in Denmark—where the group was banned (as it is in Germany) after one of its spokesmen was found guilty of distributing racist propaganda—is characteristic of its approach. It described the cartoons as part of

a global Western conspiracy against Islam. The simultaneous publication across Europe means it was deliberately done to insult the Muslims in the context of the war on terror. All the talk of tolerance, pluralism, civilized people, etc. clearly means nothing when Muslims and people all over the world see this type of insult and abuse. Abu Gharib [sic], desecrating the Qur'an and now depicting the Prophet (swt) as a terrorist, confirm clearly what this war is about. It is not about security, it is about attacking Islam because it now stands as the only credible alternative to the decades of colonialism of the Muslim world. Furthermore Islam is the only viable opposition to the unstinting support to brutal dictators by hypocritical western governments.[57]

During the international controversy over the cartoons, which included violent reactions in Syria and Gaza, HuT demonstrated its reach by organizing protests in Bangladesh (where its local chief spokesman, Muhi al-Din Ahmad, claimed that "The terrorist West is conducting a crusade against Islam in the name of free speech and war on terror"), Karachi, Jakarta, and, twice, London. An HuT document at the time stated:

Hizb ut-Tahrir Britain is urgently contacting European ambassadors in London to express serious concerns over these

> provocative actions. We also encourage Muslims in Europe to contact the diplomatic missions of Muslim countries to demand that they take action against those who have undertaken and encouraged the publication of these caricatures. . . .
>
> Finally, we note the further decay of secular liberal societies who believe that it is perfectly acceptable to insult and defame religious communities whether they are Muslims, Christians or Jews. The Islamic Caliphate historically ensured that Muslims and non-Muslims were protected from such wanton disrespect.[58]

Such opinions were repeated by Hasan al-Hasan, deputy chairman of HuT in Britain, for whom the cartoons were a "false link in a wicked worldwide string whose goal is to humiliate Muslims, as seen in the desecration of the Quran in Guantanamo, the disrespect of Muslims in secret and open prisons and the destruction of mosques." Al-Hasan argued that such acts occurred because "the large majority of the Western public, specifically the Europeans—and among them the Scandinavians—is Atheist with no [holy] book and no religion and it sanctifies materialism, pleasure and egotism."[59] It should be mentioned that HuT was the only Muslim organization in Britain to openly support the suggestion made in 2008 by the Rt. Rev. Rowan Williams, Archbishop of Canterbury, that some aspects of Sharia should be legitimized in Britain, because it would let Muslims "live our lives according to Islam, in a personal space."[60]

The problem with HuT goes beyond the well-known fact that many of its members or former members became directly involved in terrorism. More importantly, its ideology and goal both inevitably channel its adherents toward such action. As pointed out by "Walid," a former HuT militant in Britain interviewed by the *New Statesman* in July 2005:

> "Groups like Hizb have really cultivated this idea of the Muslims being one body, this idea of the Ummah. I think that dynamic is very, very, important. It feeds the groups by allowing them to make you feel as though you are taking active, individual involvement . . . to alleviate the suffering of Muslims."[61]

Once that is done, the claim that such a solution is, or could be, nonviolent becomes logically untenable. In fact, HuT pursues (particularly in Pakistan) a policy of *nussrah* (seeking support among the military and security forces), and after 9/11 it re-established contacts with radical groups such as Omar Bakri's *Al-Muhajiroun*.[62] At that, though, HuT members often become frustrated because the organization is not active *enough*, and leave it to join even more militant groups. The *New Statesman* piece noted:

> Walid says that the UK contains "enough radical preachers who offer a violent vision," and makes the point that the British would-be bomber Omar Sharif, the 27-year-old from Derby who tried to help blow up a pub in Tel Aviv in 2003, graduated from reading Hizb literature to joining al-Muhajiroun, and then attempted his suicide mission. Hizb is the largest extreme Islamist group in Britain, but exact numbers have been hard to obtain. Walid says that, as far as he is aware, the organisation has between 2,000 and 3,000 members in the UK.[63]

In European countries, HuT usually targets the largest Muslim ethnic group—Turks in Germany and the Netherlands (the Dutch branch's leader is Okay Pala, a Turk), Pakistanis in the United Kingdom, and so on. Its strategy has been compared to that of the Trotskyites—entryism, the placement of members in strategic positions in the target society or social or ethnic group.[64]

HuT is banned in Pakistan and the Arab states, and in a number of European countries—in the former because it is correctly seen as subversive as well as theologically unorthodox,[65] in the latter because it is, again correctly, seen as a gateway to the indoctrination and recruitment of Islamist extremists.

In the U.S. and in Europe (except for Britain) HuT is a secretive organization, similar to the old Leninist groups in that it operates both through public fronts and as a highly disciplined underground structure. Its Western center is in Birmingham, and, as an analysis of its Spanish operations suggests, it concentrates its recruitment among converts and better-educated Muslim immigrants—precisely the most useful profile for would-be jihadists.[66]

Takfir-wal-Hijra (Excommunication and Exodus), originally an Egyptian radical splinter of the Muslim Brotherhood, is also active in Europe, especially in Britain, although banned in Germany, France, and Spain. It started as a structured organization, but after its leader, Mustafa Shukri, was executed in Egypt in 1978, it decayed into a loose network of floating cells, and now it is more a mentality than a coherent, autonomous group. It considers all Muslims outside its membership apostates, and thus legitimate targets. It is so extreme that it tried to kill bin Laden in Sudan in 1998 for not being Islamic enough, although since then at least some of its members have joined the efforts of Al-Qaeda's nebula in Europe. Kamel Daoudi and Djamel Beghal, the Madrid bombers, remnants of the GIA in Europe, and, according to some sources, even 9/11 leader Mohamed Atta were all linked with or strongly influenced by Takfir.[67] Azzam Tamimi, director of the Institute of Islamic Political Thought in London, is correct in thinking that the real ideological leader of Takfir today is Ayman al-Zawahiri: "He is their ideologue now.... His ideas negate the existence of common ground with others ... then and now, these men shared a common vocation—secret agents for an extreme vision of Islam."[68] At least one French source claims that as early as 1999 some Islamist terrorists prosecuted in France stated that members of *Takfir-wal-Hijra* networks in Europe, most of them refugees from the defeated Algerian GIA, had joined bin Laden's World Islamic Front, and that many had left France for Italy or the United Kingdom.[69]

It is not just ideas that bring *Takfir* close to Al-Qaeda. Their methods and mentality are also identical to those of Al-Qaeda's operatives, especially those active in Iraq during Abu Musab al-Zarqawi's leadership there:

> They were—and are—the ultimate infiltrators, unbound by moral restraint. These men are not subject to any meaningful cultural repercussions for their acts. Nor are they subject to an inner moral conflict. They are amoral machines by design, licensed to kill . . . An essential part of Takfiri religious practice is the infiltration of enemy societies, usually meaning Western society. . . . Takfiri members are permitted to take any measure necessary to assimilate, a stipulation which amounts to a blanket exemption from virtually every aspect of Islamic law. To outsiders, Takfiri can appear to be entirely secular, frequently engaging in sexual activity and drinking alcohol in order to hide their religious beliefs. This behavior has been seen repeatedly among key al-Qaeda operatives such as Yousef and Khalid Shaikh.[70]

Takfiris "don't have to go to mosques; they can even drink and use drugs to maintain their cover, [t]hey can commit crime to finance their activities, [i]t is like an intelligence service."[71] This explains both their usefulness and their prominence in the operations of Al-Qaeda's nebula in the West. Ultimately, as French expert Roland Jacquard put it, "Takfir is like a sect: once you're in, you never get out. The Takfir rely on brainwashing and an extreme regime of discipline to weed out the weak links and ensure loyalty and obedience from those taken as members."[72]

One may, perhaps, argue whether the description of *Takfir* as a sect is accurate. Perhaps it could better be described as a self-sustaining ideological group always ready to kill—not for money but for the sake of jihad alone, under whatever leadership is on offer. Europe's favorable legal and demographic environment has for over a decade allowed the remnants of nationally based Islamist terrorist groups to find refuge there, the most prominent and active being the Algerian GIA and GSPC and the Moroccan GICM. As proved, among other things, by the presence of members of *Takfir* in the groups behind the Madrid bombing, these fragments of defeated groups pool their resources and engage in joint operations.

NGOs

Nothing better demonstrates the favorable environment Europe offers for Islamists in general and jihadists in particular than their ability to operate in the guise of nongovernmental organizations—NGOs.

NGOs are generally seen in the West as "representatives" of civil society. Despite being unelected, they are admired and heavily subsidized by the same elected governments they criticize. They claim and enjoy rights and benefits seldom, if ever, matched by transparency regarding their finances, goals, and membership. This aspect of the NGO issue in general has yet to be seriously studied, but when it comes to the Islamic NGOs, it is highly relevant to the general problem of Islam, Islamism, and terrorism in Europe.[73] It is also very difficult to examine, because so many of the Islamic NGOs active in Europe are based elsewhere, in countries with little capacity and often less interest in supervising them—but also enjoying high levels of wealth, the states of the Persian Gulf being a prime example.

When the issue of Islamic NGOs is examined in the European context, one should see it in relation to the explosion in numbers and influence of NGOs in general. But just as Amnesty

International and Greenpeace are not representative of Western opinion, so Islamic NGOs such as those revolving around the Muslim Brotherhood are not representative of Muslim opinion in Europe. If anything, they are outside bodies, often instruments of foreign governments.

How is it that Muslim communities, some quite small and all claiming to be poor and discriminated against, are able to have huge mosques built in Granada, Rome, London, and Dewsbury, or to engage in massive demonstrations and media campaigns? The answer includes two elements: outside financing from the rich Muslim world, including governments, and the related organizational capacities of international Islamist groups active in Europe. A good example of how Islamist organizations and NGOs join forces was the opposition to the Blair government's 2005 attempts to tighten anti-terrorist legislation. As the press release issued by the Islamic Human Rights Commission (IHRC) put it:

> In a show of unprecedented unity, over 150 Islamic and Community-based organizations and individuals have added their name to a statement issued last month in response to the Government's latest anti-terror proposals. The original 38 signatories have now been joined by numerous community-based groups and individuals including a number of Councilors reflecting the mood of the Muslim community at a grassroots level. It is a clear signal to Tony Blair from the Muslim community that, irrespective of their various nationalities or political beliefs, they stand united against his draconian proposals. The massive number of signatories is evidence of the fact that Tony Blair's "consultation" with the community is virtually non-existent. . . .
>
> IHRC Chair Massoud Shadjareh stated: "Consulting task forces composed of a few unrepresentative individuals in the community will only further isolate the increasingly alienated Muslim masses. The Prime Minister must abandon his state of

denial if he truly wishes to build a more secure and peaceful Britain." In brief, the six points of the statement are:

—*The term extremism has no tangible legal meaning or definition and is therefore unhelpful and emotive.*

—*The right of people anywhere in the world to resist invasion and occupation is legitimate.*

—*Questioning the legitimacy of Israeli occupation is legitimate political expression.*

—*The proposal to ban the non-violent organization Hizb ut-Tahrir is unwarranted, unjust and unwise.*

—*Arbitrary closure of mosques may prevent legitimate political discourse in mosques, fuelling a radical sub-culture.*

—*Deporting foreign nationals to countries known for gross human rights abuses is abhorrent.*[74]

The London-based IHRC is characteristic of how some Muslim groups mimic Western NGOs' human-rights language to pursue radical, even violent Islamist goals. It has an annual "Islamophobia Award" for personalities it accuses of being "Islamophobic," covering the range from Vladimir Putin, Nicolas Sarkozy, and George W. Bush, to the American scholar Daniel Pipes, to Oprah Winfrey—and even to Abu Musab al-Zarqawi, the late Al-Qaeda serial killer of Shiites in Iraq. The presence of al-Zarqawi on that list may sound strange, until one learns that the IHRC is actually a Khomeinist front of Shia radicals in Britain, a fact underscored by Massoud Shadjareh's open calls for support for *Hizbollah*.[75] The fact that, like *bona-fide* human-rights NGOs, it opposes the extradition of terrorist suspects to Muslim states is a coincidence—the IHRC's interest is not in their "rights" but in their continued ability to operate. In short, the following description of the group is accurate:

The IHRC is a radical Islamist organization that uses the
language and techniques of a human-rights lobbying group
to promote an extremist agenda. Formed in 1997 by its current
chairman, Massoud Shadjareh, the IHRC supports jihad groups
around the world, campaigns for the release of convicted
terrorists and promotes the notion of a western conspiracy
against Islam. Shadjareh and the IHRC subscribe to the radical
Islamist belief that Jewish conspiracies are afoot to undermine
Muslims, and they compare Jews and Israelis to Nazis. Members
of the IHRC's board of advisors have even called on Muslims
to kill Jews.[76]

Not very different in essence, although rejecting all accusations of anti-Semitism, is the Muslim Public Affairs Committee
UK (MPACUK), another London-based Muslim NGO. It claims to
be fighting for more political involvement by Muslims, mostly
in order to combat "Zionism," but its real goal is the elimination
of Israel as a state. It defines Zionism as

a belief in a Jewish State in at least part of Biblical Israel,
in which Jews regardless of their place of birth could claim
citizenship—this is how the state of Israel currently defines
itself. We use the term zionist to describe those who actively
support the current Israeli state—its policies and its intrinsic
racism.[77]

Despite its generally anti-Sunni positions, the IHRC shares
some common traits with nonviolent Sunni Islamic groups
like the MB, the MPACUK, and the MCB (and on some key issues with most non-Muslim human-rights NGOs). They are all
trying to dilute the meaning of clear terms like terrorism or
extremism, under the guise of a "right to resist invasion and
occupation"—their standard reference to Israeli self-defense,
as well as to the Western efforts in Iraq and Afghanistan. They
have all resisted, in Britain, government attempts to strength-
en anti-terrorism legislation, both before and after the London
bombings; and everywhere in Europe (France, Germany, Italy,

the Netherlands) Muslim NGOs have opposed the banning of the *hijab* and even of the *niqab* and the *burqa*. The main reason given for these positions is that anti-terrorist and integrationist policies unfairly "stigmatize" all Muslims.

If this is the organized part of the religious, cultural, and political environment in which many Muslims in Europe live, how could one be surprised that more and more of them become attracted to radical Islam, and some go further than that, into violence?

By now all European governments realize that if they are to succeed in eliminating Islamist influence and the associated terrorism, and in integrating their Muslim communities, the cooperation of Muslims themselves and of their organizations is essential. But by seeking such cooperation they also implicitly admit that the threat comes mainly from within.

The greatest obstacle to gaining the support of Muslims in Europe in combatting Islamist terrorism is *ummah* solidarity. The very debate over Islamist terrorism has increasingly been framed by a majority of Muslim organizations as insulting to Muslims and their faith. It is now almost impossible to discuss Islamist terrorism without risking accusations of "Islamophobia" or "racism."

This, coupled with the common refusal of Muslim organizations to condemn the motivations, and not just the acts, of jihadist terrorists, only adds to the growing numbers of Europeans who believe that Islam *and* Muslims cannot or will not integrate. Nowhere is that more obvious than in England.

"Londonistan" as Producer and Exporter of Islamism

> "I am not surprised that you British are facing so many problems with extremists after what I saw in those mosques in Blackburn . . . What I saw . . . would not be allowed here in Iraq—it would be illegal."
> —Dr. Barham Salih, Iraqi deputy prime minister, 2005[78]

The British have traditionally, at least until the aftermath of 9/11, taken a live-and-let-live, benign-neglect approach to the issue of imams coming from the Arab world and the Indian subcontinent. That has attached to the UK the largely accurate label of "Londonistan" (sometimes referred to as "Beirut-on-Thames")—the European center of Islamic radical theology. Indeed, many of the most active and influential Islamist/Salafist theologians, all directly involved in indoctrinating, recruiting, and legitimizing terrorism elsewhere in Europe and in North Africa and Yemen, were based in London for many years. A distinction should be made between regular imams, who are attached to a specific mosque, and Islamist ideologues like those examined below, who may or may not have a permanent place of activity and who seldom perform the basic function of leading Friday prayers.

It is also important to note that the most prominent radical imams in Londonistan were given political asylum (and public welfare support) in the UK. That is because, according to the British courts' exceedingly strict interpretation of international law, a claimant for asylum only has to prove a "reasonable" fear of persecution in his own country—no matter what that fear is based on. Hence, political asylum was given even to people like Omar Bakri, expelled from Saudi Arabia for religious extremism. For all practical purposes, in the UK the reality behind political-asylum claims is irrelevant—just being, or even "feeling," persecuted elsewhere is enough. Such a loose interpretation of "persecution" and "asylum"—to some extent repeated in other European countries but firmly rejected in France—is a key to understanding the creation and continuing existence of Londonistan. But it is not enough.

From insiders like Omar Nasiri, to outside observers like Anglophobe Dominique Thomas, to British authors critical of their own country's establishment, like Melanie Phillips and Michael Gove,[79] the general view is that Britain, under both Labour and Tory governments, is too constrained by its legal traditions as well as by a precursor of modern multicultural-ism, going back to the country's history as the greatest colo-nial power. Thus, for the British establishment—intelligence services included—the issue of Islam in the UK as distinct from British Islam is irrelevant. Islam in the UK is allowed to flour-ish, as long as it does not threaten security. But whose secu-rity? That of British citizens, or also of the outside world?

According to these critics, non-assimilationist policies were too ingrained for the British government even to care about the impact of "Londonistan" on other countries—whether Yemen, France, or any other. Thus, although the United Kingdom's 1.6 million followers of Islam are not the largest Muslim commu-nity in Europe, and although the country is not the first or only European victim of Islamist terror, Britain does have the dubious distinction of having long been the main Western cen-ter of radical Islamism. Even after 9/11, and until the events of July 2005, England served as the R&R refuge of some of the most important Islamist ideologues, recruiters, and fundrais-ers anywhere.

It is no surprise that HuT's European base is in Birmingham, Tabligh's European center is in Dewsbury, and a whole plethora of radical Pakistani groups are active in the United Kingdom.

As already mentioned, understanding the role of imams is key to understanding the nature of the re-Islamization of the younger generations of Muslims in Europe. But imams are not all equal in influence, reach, charisma, or the degree of threat they pose to the governments in whose territories they oper-ate. How important is the role of the UK-based religious figures in legitimizing, recruiting, and providing logistical help for violent and militant Islamist groups in Europe, North Africa, the Middle East, and elsewhere? What is the national and educational background of the recruiters? What is the sociological profile of recruits to radical Islamist causes? Are there influential moderate Islamic leaders able to counter the radicals' influence among the Muslim population? The answers to these questions are relevant not only to the United Kingdom but to Europe as a whole, and to the United States as well.

The role of individual radical imams in radicalizing small groups of followers has been described above—as have been the authorities' attempts to deal with them. Most of those cases, however, were localized or of limited impact: Abdelkader Bouziane in Vénissieux mostly recruited his own sons and their friends; Abu Laban and his Copenhagen group brought international violence against Denmark on a specific issue. The London imams, however, have transformed Europe from an importer of Islamist radicalism into an exporter—the main center of "Eurojihadism" has long been the UK.

It is thus impossible to discuss Islam, Islamism, and Islamic terrorism in Europe without discussing "Londonistan." The term was coined by French analysts and intelligence operatives, infuriated with the British government's decades of tolerance for the open activities of Islamist terrorist recruiters. More recently the term was borrowed by British observers, themselves increasingly concerned with the trends within the Muslim community in their country.

Why "Londonistan" and not "Berlinistan" or "Parisistan"? After all, both Germany and France have far larger Muslim communities. There are at least two books with the title *Londonistan* and innumerable articles, including one by this author.[80] All refer to the same issue: the British government's and the English people's tolerating, if not actually encouraging, the transformation of London and a few other cities into Islamist indoctrination centers with a global reach, equal only to pre-2001 Afghanistan and to Pakistan and Saudi Arabia.

Is this an exaggeration? Consider that London-based Islamist ideologues were known to be the "spiritual" guides of internationally recognized (including by the British government) terrorist groups in Algeria (GIA and later GSPC) and Yemen (Islamic Army of Aden-Abyan). London imams recruited such prominent terrorists as Richard Reid, Zacarias Moussaoui, Mohamed Atta, Djamel Beghal—and the list could go on and on—who were involved in terrorist planning or attacks on five continents. European governments, particularly those of France and Spain, have consistently complained to London about its role as a protector and sustainer (most of the radicals there are or were on public welfare) of Islamists active in their countries, as have the United States, Morocco, Tunisia, Egypt, and Jordan.

True, after the London bombings of July 2005, the Blair government did try to wake up the public and Parliament on the "homegrown" Islamist security threat. But, by and large, it failed, not least because of resistance from the ruling Labour Party's own left wing. The opposition Liberal Democrats are also opposed to common-sense anti-Islamist measures, but even the supposedly law-and-order Tories opposed more stringent measures, apparently for the sake of being . . . in opposition. Hence the absurd debate about whether criminalizing advocacy of Islamist terror is compatible with freedom of speech. It is hard to avoid the impression that the implicit official assumption, at least prior to the London bombings, was that terrorist recruitment and incitement would "only" lead to the murder of people in faraway places (even if some of those were British tourists). Thus, whether actually true or not, Abu Hamza's claim in a London court—that "during his many meetings with the security services and anti-terrorism officers he believed a deal operated, whereby his activities would be tolerated as long as they had targets abroad"[81]—sounded all too plausible.

British activist judges are the most effective instrument of the powerful "human-rights" lobbies, both secular and Islamic, consistently using decisions by the European Court of Human Rights, as well as the Human Rights Act of 1998 (which integrates European legislation into British law), in favor of rights for terrorists.

Sometimes the courts' joustings with the Home Office reach almost comic levels, as in the case of Rashid Ramza, a known GIA operative already condemned in France, financier of the mid-1990s wave of bombings in Paris and elsewhere. His extradition from Britain took a decade—because British judges decided that he might be "mistreated" by the French. The High Court's Lord Hoffman illustrated this mentality when he stated, referring to the anti-terror laws proposed in the wake of the July 2005 London bombings, that "The real threat to the nation comes not from terrorism, but from such laws as these."[82]

While human-rights militants are influential throughout the Western world, in the UK their views are far closer to those of the media, academic, legal, and political establishments than elsewhere. In the United States the GOP, in France some Gaullists (now including President Nicolas Sarkozy), in the Netherlands and Denmark the ruling coalitions, all believe in some balance between a fundamentalist interpretation of "human rights" (such as Amnesty International's) and national security. In Britain, an increasingly isolated PM Tony Blair was effectively blocked by a tide of political correctness and judicial activism.

To be fair, not all prominent Islamist ideologues in Europe are based in England. One can find similar cases elsewhere, including some outrageous ones. Thus, the founder and "spiritual" leader of Ansar al-Islam—one of the oldest and most deadly terrorist groups in Iraq—Najmuddin Faraj Ahmad, better known as Mullah Krekar, is publishing and living well in Norway, openly using his welfare checks to incite the killing of Americans in Iraq. The German-based Metin Kaplan, a.k.a. the "Caliph of Cologne," was another (until he was finally extradited to Turkey in October 2004), and a plethora of smaller fry in France, Denmark, the Netherlands, and Italy fit the same pattern.

None, however, had the global reach or, most importantly, the subsidized infrastructure and official tolerance that the most important Salafi center in the world enjoyed in England. In this sense there is, indeed, a "British exception" from continental Europe—one recognized by the Islamist beneficiaries of British tolerance themselves. Abu Qatada admitted that "There is no doubt that one feels safe here, more so than at home, but it is obvious that there are some practices here that are not clean."[83] Omar Bakri declared in 1998 that there were no Islamist terror attacks in Britain because "I work here in accordance with the covenant of peace which I made with the British government when I got [political] asylum."[84] He may or may not have been sincere, but, at any rate, the existence of "Londonistan" gave birth to an entire universe of conspiracy theories suspecting all sorts of nefarious British intentions.

Why does Londonistan still exist? Here are some obvious practical reasons:

> Up to a dozen people suspected of being en route to join the fight against British forces in Iraq or Afghanistan, or to become suicide bombers overseas, have been detained by

one major police force alone in the past year. But because evidence gained by covertly intercepting conversations by phone or email is not admissible in British courts, they could not be charged with any serious offence. Patrick Mercer, the Conservative homeland security spokesman, said he was told by Greater Manchester police there was now a persistent pattern of such suspects, causing serious concern.[85]

There is also a legal loophole that allows banned radical Islamist groups to continue in existence by the simple device of changing their name. Thus, Omar Bakri's *Al-Muhajiroun*, which he allegedly dismantled in 2004, just a step ahead of being legally banned, immediately became two new groups, *Al-Ghurabaa* (The Strangers) and the Saviour Sect. When *those* were banned in 2006, there was already a replacement, *Ahlus Sunnah wal Jamaah* (Adherents to the Sunnah and the Community) ready to step in. It should not come as a surprise that all these groups had the same leadership: Anjem Choudary (Omar Bakri's right hand and the former UK head of *Al-Muhajiroun*), Abu Yahya, Abu Izzadeen, and Abu Uzair.[86]

The legal system is not the only problem. Even many high-ranking police in Britain have bought into this mentality. Blair tried to ban HuT, a group whose relatively "moderate" British branch claims that "to oppose the political destiny of the Muslim world being decided in Washington or London" is not extreme. The group, which is banned in countries as various as Pakistan, Russia, Germany, the Netherlands, and all Arab states, works for "the return of the Caliphate in the Muslim world—an Islamic system of government with an accountable leadership, chosen through the authority of the people, in which the rule of law would replace the tyranny that currently exists."[87] But Blair was dissuaded by . . . the police. Why? Because, as Rob Beckley, head of the Association of Chief Police Officers' group

for communities and counter-terrorism, put it, "If there was evidence for proscribing HuT, we would support a move to pro-
scribe it. But we think such a move would be counterproductive and not in the spirit of the government's [anti-terrorism]
legislation. It is not an offence to hold extreme views."[88] This
after HuT encouraged an undercover BBC researcher posing as
a recruit to commit crimes to "prove his loyalty" (HuT denied
this and said it intended to sue the BBC).[89]

Although by now outdated, Dominique Thomas's *Le Londonistan* is the most complete analysis of the role British policies
under successive Tory and Labour governments played in the
creation, expansion, and maintenance of a global Salafi terror
network. Her book largely blames a complex combination of
expansive definitions of freedom of speech and of the press,
paradoxically mixed with a peculiar respect, verging on self-
censorship, for "Muslim" sensitivities, as demonstrated in 2006
by then Foreign Secretary Jack Straw, who decried Danish "im-
prudence" during the cartoon dispute. Virtually alone in Europe,
the otherwise aggressive British press did not reproduce the
controversial cartoons depicting Muhammad. Despite Britain's
well-known coolness toward European integration, its courts
are far more influenced by the European Union's Convention
on Human Rights than those of pro-EU France.

Five Imams

Nothing demonstrates the perils of Londonistan more than the
activities of some its most prominent radical imams.

Five names are most frequently mentioned in this context:
Sheikh Yusuf al-Qaradawi, Sheikh Omar Bakri Mohammed,
Abu Hamza, Mohammad al-Massari, and Abu Qatada. They are
neither identical in their views nor personally close. Qaradawi
could be described as part of the global Islamic establishment

and is openly hostile to Salafis and HuT, while Abu Hamza and Abu Qatada were rivals in radical jihadist circles in London and abroad. Qaradawi influences Muslims in Europe from his perch in Qatar, and from Ireland through the ECFR; the others did so from London. Qaradawi understands that Muslims in Europe have a peculiar position that requires flexibility, and he advises them how to adapt while rejecting assimilation; the others, though living in Europe, not only opposed integration and assimilation, but also advocated rejection of European laws and values. While Qaradawi and the Palestinian Abu Qatada have well-established Islamic scholarly reputations, the Syrian Omar Bakri is a dropout of Al-Azhar University, the Saudi Mohammad al-Massari is a physicist by training, and Abu Hamza al-Masri ("the Egyptian") was trained as a civil engineer at the Brighton Polytechnic. It is important to note another difference: While Qaradawi numbered the then mayor of London, "Red Ken" Livingstone, as his most prominent non-Muslim fan in Europe,[90] Bakri is now in what amounts to exile in Lebanon, banned from returning to London; Abu Qatada awaits trial in England and extradition to Jordan; and Abu Hamza is serving a seven-year sentence in England and will be extradited to the United States upon its completion. Al-Massari is still active, but his ambitions were always more focused on overthrowing the Saudi monarchy than on pursuing global jihad.

Other similarities among this group bring us back to the practices of "Londonistan." Mohammad al-Massari was admitted as a "political refugee" from Saudi Arabia, but he openly states that "we are more inclined to move the masses toward some kind of revolt or popular uprising, perhaps along the lines of the French and Iranian revolutions,"[91] a position in direct violation of his formal status. Omar Bakri was expelled from Saudi Arabia for "religious extremism" and found refuge in

London, where he persistently violated his status for 19 years. Abu Qatada, expelled from Kuwait for supporting the Iraqi invasion of 1990, arrived in Britain with a forged UAE passport but claimed and received asylum on grounds of "religious persecution." Abu Hamza obtained his UK residence on the basis of a (bigamous) marriage of convenience.

For our purposes, they all were or are key influences in creating the spiritual and cultural context leading to re-Islamization, alienation from society, and support for Sharia—the key phenomena that ultimately lead to jihadism.

The general thinking of Abu Hamza, Omar Bakri, Abu Qatada, and Mohammad al-Massari[92] is well known, and any detailed analysis of their ideology/theology is superfluous, since it largely coincides with standard Salafi ideas, as enunciated by Ayman al-Zawahiri and others. However, their location in Britain makes their opinions on certain specific matters relevant to such issues as the attitudes of Muslims living in the West toward their host societies and the United States. Furthermore, these highly charismatic figures have had influence well beyond Europe, and their links with Islamist and terrorist groups are revealing for the role Europe is now playing in the Islamic world as a whole. A brief comparison of these important figures' views on issues relevant to Islamism and terrorism is instructive.

Sheikh Yusuf al-Qaradawi, a Qatar-based Egyptian imam and member of the Muslim Brotherhood, is different from the others, but that does not make him a "moderate" in any meaningful sense. He condemned both the 9/11 attacks and the 7/7 London bombings, but he defends suicide bombers in Israel and Iraq. After the London attacks in 2005, pressure was exerted on Charles Clarke, then Home Secretary, to refuse him entry, following Tony Blair's call for a clampdown on extremist preachers, but then Mayor Ken Livingstone considered him a friend and a moderate, and repeatedly invited him to visit. In fact, Qaradawi held a multiple-entry visa to the UK, which was revoked only in February 2008. On the other hand, Qaradawi has long been denied entry to the United States—precisely because of his advocacy of suicide bombings against Israelis and his association with the Al Taqwa Bank, suspected by the FBI of laundering funds for Al-Qaeda.

While a student in his native Egypt in the 1940s he studied under Hassan al-Banna, the founder of the Muslim Brotherhood; a few years later he volunteered to fight the British occupation of the Suez Canal, and in 1954 his connection to the MB led to the first of several arrests by Egyptian authorities. In 1962, Qaradawi moved to Qatar to become the director of a religious institute.

The 83-year-old imam is considered one of the most influential men in modern Sunni Islam. Through his weekly Sunday-night spot on Al Jazeera and his prolific use of the Internet, his *fatwas* touch the lives of tens of millions of Muslims every day. But it is through his positions as the leader of the European Council for Fatwa and Research, and as a member of the academic board of the UOIF's European Institute of Islamic Studies at Nièvre, that Qaradawi became the most influential theologian among Muslims in Europe, and one who is directly interested in their specific problems.[93]

Omar bin Bakri bin Mohammed, a.k.a. "the Tottenham Ayatollah," was born into a wealthy family of Aleppo, Syria, in 1959.[94] During adolescence he lived in Beirut, studied Sharia law in Damascus, and moved to Saudi Arabia for further Islamic education. After dropping out from Cairo's Al-Azhar, he settled in Saudi Arabia, from where he was deported in 1984. In what is a common path among Islamists, he was active in the Muslim

Brotherhood, found it too moderate and joined HuT, only finally to set up his own group, *Al-Muhajiroun* (The Emigrants) in 1996.[95] (As we have seen, he allegedly dismantled it in 2004, but actually split it into two new groups.) Once in Britain, he tried to establish a computer company, failed, and, with his wife and seven children, was on welfare until his departure for Lebanon in 2005. His charisma and powers of argument were well known; former HuT militant Ed Husain admits to being impressed by a Bakri speech at the London School of Economics.[96] As a resident in the UK, purportedly a "handicapped person" because of a childhood leg injury, he also received during his twenty years there £300,000 in social security and was even given a car worth £31,000 by the government. Not until August 2005 were his residence permit and asylum withdrawn.[97] Throughout his two decades of life in London, Omar Bakri had retained dual Lebanese and Syrian citizenship, but he never acquired British citizenship.

Mustafa Kamel Mustafa, a.k.a. Abu Hamza al-Masri, born in Alexandria, Egypt, in April 1958, arrived in London on a student visa in 1979. His British citizenship, illegally acquired through a marriage of convenience, was withdrawn in 2003. Although an engineer by training, for a while he held all sorts of low-skilled jobs, including hotel receptionist, bar bouncer, and doorman at a Soho peepshow, and never had serious theological training. He claims to have lost his hands and an eye fighting in Afghanistan in 1993, a claim disputed by many, and after that lived on disability benefits for many years. His justification? "I take back from them [the infidels] the booty they plundered from the Muslim lands, in accordance with my needs. This is money that originally belonged to Muslims. What they invest of this money in Muslims here [in Britain] is leftovers and crumbs of bread in comparison with the meat and honey that they eat in our land."[98]

In 1994 Abu Hamza founded the Supporters of Sharia (SOS—*Ansar al-Sharia*) which he claimed operated "under many other names in various parts of the world" and supported both *mujahedin* and refugees in Afghanistan, Bosnia, and Kashmir, "as well as the frontline soldiers." The group's aim was "to remove the oppression created by man-made laws, so that the whole of mankind can enjoy the freedom, purity and justice of living under Allah's laws—the Shariah."[99] A Yemeni newspaper described one SOS event as follows: "Over Christmas 1998, from December 24–26, SOS held its fourth Islamic Camp at Finsbury Park Mosque in north London. The list of activities included 'military training for brothers'. A picture of a hand grenade appeared on the publicity material. Admission was £20, with reduced prices for children and families."[100]

Abu Hamza was the religious guide of Islamist terror groups in Algeria, Egypt, and Kashmir, and especially the Islamic Army of Aden Abyan (IAA—*Jaysh Aden Abyan al-Islami*) of Yemen. He even had his son Mohammed go to that country, where he was arrested in 1998 for involvement in terrorist activities, including the kidnapping of Western tourists, and received a three-year jail sentence. Abu Hamza's connection with Yemen was established during his Afghan misadventure, when he met Abu Hassan al-Mihdar, a Yemeni radical and later the founder of IAA.

As (self-appointed) imam at Finsbury Park mosque, until fired in 2001, he attracted an ever-larger circle of sympathizers and recruits, including many former GIA militants later involved in terrorist operations in Europe, the Middle East, and the United States. Abu Hamza was on the list of Egypt's top 14 terrorists, and sympathizers of his were found among imams in British prisons, while one of the four 7/7 bombers, Germaine Lindsay, was an admirer, as were Richard Reid, Zacarias Moussaoui, and Xavier

Djaffo, a friend of Moussaoui's who died fighting in Chechnya. Arrested in May 2004, Abu Hamza was tried in London and sentenced to seven years in prison in 2006; in February 2008 the Home Secretary approved his extradition to the United States, where he is accused of being behind the jihadist cell found in Oregon.[101]

Omar Mahmoud Othman abu Omar al-Philisteeni, a.k.a. Abu Qatada, is a Palestinian born in 1960 in Bethlehem, who studied Islam in Jordan. He arrived in Britain in September 1993 and claimed asylum for himself, his wife, and their three children. Detained and kept under arrest between 2002 and 2005, he was released on a court decision and is now back in prison appealing extradition to Jordan, where he is under a life sentence *in absentia*, accused of participating in the planning of a massive terrorist attack during the millennium celebrations. Although under EU and British law he cannot be extradited because Jordan still has the death penalty, a new agreement between London and Amman may change that.

Abu Qatada was involved in the Afghan jihad since the mid-1980s. As an Islamic teacher in Peshawar, he met bin Laden in 1989. While not creating his own group (like Abu Hamza's SOS or Bakri's *Al-Muhajiroun*), he played the key role in providing the Algerian GIA and GSPC with a coherent doctrine and religious cover. For a number of years he delivered *fatwas* for the GIA and published the group's newsletter, *Al Ansar*, from London. After that his ideological recruitment to Salafi jihadism extended throughout Europe and beyond, from the likes of Mohamed Atta to Muslims in Thailand. Some of this was done through associates of his, like Abu Dahdah and Abu Musab al-Suri Setmariam in Spain. Videos of his sermons were found in Mohamed Atta's Hamburg apartment and in the homes of Casablanca suicide bombers. Djamel Beghal was one of his

recruits, and he is still wanted for terrorism by the governments of Spain, Italy, Germany, France, Algeria, and the United
States.[102] For years Abu Qatada has been seen as the *de facto*
gatekeeper for would-be *mujahedin* from Europe seeking to go
for training in Pakistan or the Middle East.[103] His role in jihadist circles in Europe was described by Spanish investigating
judge Baltasar Garzón as "spiritual leader and patron not only
of Al Qaeda but also of GIA, Tunisian Islamic Combatant Group,
GSPC, the mujahedin in Chechnya, Bosnia and Afghanistan, and
other Islamic fundamentalist groups"; he is seen by some as the
"spiritual father of Al Qaeda."[104]

More than any of the other most prominent London Salafi
imams, Abu Qatada has solid religious credentials; he has added legitimacy in *jihadi* eyes for his direct association with Al-
Qaeda. Not only did he train with well-known Muslim scholars
like Mohammed Nasir al-Din al-Bani and publish extensively,
but he participated in Al-Qaeda's "*fatwa* committee." It is likely
that this is what gave him religious authority over both the
GIA and the GSPC, and he was plausibly considered Al-Qaeda's
paymaster in Europe.[105] The fact that he dropped his support
for the GIA and transferred it to the GSPC at the time bin Laden
did the same seems to be more than a coincidence. Although he
denies any association with Al-Qaeda, at the time of his arrest
police found £180,000 in his hideout, even though he had been
on public welfare for the previous eight years, receiving only
£1,000 per month.[106]

Mohammad al-Massari, born in Saudi Arabia in 1951, claims
to be a "dissident" and has lived in Britain since the early 1990s.
In 1996, in response to Saudi protests, the British tried to expel
him to either Yemen or the Caribbean island of Dominica, but
both attempts were blocked by the courts, who agreed with
his claim that his life "may be in danger."[107] What makes al-

Massari interesting is the fact that, like Bakri, he is a critic of the Saudi regime from the radical Salafi perspective—in other words, for both of them the official Wahhabi doctrine as practiced by Riyadh is too moderate. In London he is the head of the Party for Islamic Renewal (PIR), in which his son, Majid (a U.S.-trained physicist who worked for a time as a computer expert in Seattle), is also a prominent member. Al-Massari runs his own website (www.tajdeed.org.uk/), which is used extensively for pro–Al-Qaeda manifestos and messages, and he is an advisor of the IHRC and the head of the Committee for the Defence of Legitimate Rights (CDLR). Al-Massari has also been chairman and president of the Global Jihad Fund (GJF), whose "main aim" was "to facilitate the Growth of various Jihad Movements around the World by supplying them with sufficient Funds to purchase Weapons and train their Individuals," and which, Evan Kohlmann claims, also provided actual "jihad military training" to willing volunteers located in continental Europe and in the United Kingdom.[108]

Here are some of the opinions of these influential clerics:

On Osama bin Laden

Omar Bakri: "Why would I condemn Osama bin Laden? I condemn Tony Blair. I condemn George Bush. I would never condemn Osama bin Laden or any Muslims . . . Bin Laden certainly believes he is fighting a defensive jihad. . . . And in the psyche of Muslims, anyone who dies in such a cause—especially against America—will be highly regarded and respected, no matter the civilian casualties."[109]

In fact, in 2004 Bakri's group, *Al-Muhajiroun*, tried to organize a celebration of the "Magnificent 19" perpetrators of September 11. That he had contacts with and probably direct ties to the Al-Qaeda nebula in Europe is suggested by his April 2004 prediction of a major bombing in London by Al-Qaeda and his July 15,

1999, letter to bin Laden, posted on the *Al-Muhajiroun* website: "The Islamic Movements have not used the real weapon yet. . . . Oh Osama . . . You and your brothers are now breathing life and dignity into the body of the Ummahh. Our main mission as Muslims is to carry the Islamic message to the entire world."[110] It was reported that Bakri was helping train Thai Islamist separatists in Malaysia, and he himself claimed to have encouraged Western Muslims to go and fight in Bosnia, Chechnya, and Iraq.

Al-Massari: "He's a fighter and fighting according to his beliefs. . . . Anyone who fights according to his beliefs is a hero." He also said: "Bin Laden is a military leader. He was appointed by the Afghans as Amir of the Arab Mujahedin. Because he has been engaged in fighting for decades, OBL and his followers have not had time to study recent developments and innovations in Islamic politics and philosophy. They have no detailed theory of the Islamic state in whose cause they are fighting. They believe in the Islamic state in a very general sense, and they have no real program. This is the essential difference between OBL and CDLR. Moreover, bin Laden's obsessive concentration on the U.S. is not really wise."[111]

Abu Qatada: "I have not met him, but it would not be a crime to do so. I would be honored, as a Muslim, if I did meet him."

After 9/11, Abu Qatada claimed that "Bin Laden was one of those people who witnessed the corruption of our governments and they are corrupt because of their connections with you and because of their contacts with the Americans, the British and the Europeans."[112]

On the July 7 London bomb attacks

Bakri: "I blame the British Government, the British public and the Muslim community in the UK because they failed to make the extra effort to put an end to the cycle of bloodshed which started before 9/11 and on July 7 was devastating for everybody.... The British people brought 7/7 on themselves by initiating a 'cycle of bloodshed' in Iraq."

(The latter opinion was echoed by then London Mayor Ken Livingstone: "We created these people" by assisting the *mujahedin* in Afghanistan.[113])

On 9/11

Bakri: "I believe September 11 was a direct response to the evil American policy in the Muslim world. We do not want another event like this in the West. If there is an attack by the British Government against Muslims abroad, then Muslims abroad have the right to retaliate and defend themselves ... We are giving sincere advice to the British Government and the British public so they understand the consequences of playing with fire."

Bakri even issued a "Fatwa Against General Musharraf-USA" for his government's support of the U.S. attack on the Taliban.[114]

Al-Massari: "When a regime is helping somebody like Israel attack you and if someone attacks you it is war.... If a Muslim decides he can do something about that and take retaliatory action, then why not? An eye for an eye, as an old book said."

Abu Qatada: From hiding, in his Internet manifesto "The Legal Vision for the September 11 Events," he wrote: "Bin Laden strongly imposed himself on the events of September 11, his name is on everybody's tongue and his statements are louder than planes. . . . America lost its glory after the September 11 events because of the importance and strategy of the two towers, which represented the American economy—the American economy that was stealing the economy of weak nations."[115]

After his capture, Abu Qatada argued that "It is not the size of the action that matters, it is the reason behind it which matters. . . . It would only be a bad act if there were no American bases in Bin Laden's country. He has got a problem because the Americans have military bases and control everything in his country, loot his country and control its politics and economics."[116]

For Abu Hamza, the United States is "United Snakes of America," and it was his notion that Yemen was the only Arabian Peninsula country that had not "surrendered" and could still "explode in the faces of the Snakes . . . this will hopefully trigger a domino effect in the peninsula."[117] That is what attracted him to that country. After 9/11 he stated:

> I do not condone what happened and I won't condemn it because I don't know yet who has done it. If somebody has done this just for earthly gain and political advancement then obviously it is a cheap cause. But if it was done because people are desperate and their lives have been threatened, then that is a respectable cause. . . . Then those people who carried out the attacks would be martyrs.[118]

In other words, the method and the nature of the victims are not essential—the motivation is.

On Iraq

In August 2002, Abu Hamza al-Masri, Mohammad al-Massari, Omar Bakri, and Yasser al-Sirri (another Egyptian radical, usually less open on such matters) issued a joint public warning to the British government regarding a possible attack on Iraq, providing "the uncompromising Islamic stance on the U.S. Crusade against Muslims in general and Iraq in particular" and denouncing the U.S. as "the head of Satan" and Iraqi opposition groups allied to the U.S. as Muslims who have "sold themselves to Satan." (They also called Saddam "Satan.")[119]

Al-Massari: "It will take a few years but they [the U.S.] will fail. They will begin to make blunders, like bombing whole cities, the kind of things they are doing in Afghanistan right now. But of course Iraq is much more sophisticated and they will not be able to cover up their crimes there.... On a religious and moral basis, it was settled long ago. Retaliation is justified by the embargo against Iraq and the destruction of the Iraqi civilian infrastructure.... If there is a further attack against Iraq, it will become even more evident."

He said Britain was unlikely to be targeted. "It is a practical issue. Al-Qaeda have limited resources and it is not worth the sacrifice of mujahideen to hit targets in Britain.... Britain is irrelevant. What would they hit? Big Ben?"

On suicide bombers in Israel

Bakri: "I knew [would-be bomber Omar Khan] Sharif very well and he used to attend regularly at my sessions. He was my brother and I am very proud of him and any Muslim who will do the same as he did.... Our duty is to work to establish an Islamic state anywhere in the world, even in Britain.... Life is protected under us. There will be no minorities and majorities as in America. Anti-Semitism in the U.S. is disgraceful. Synagogues and churches will flourish in the Khilafa as long as they adopt Islamic law. We restored life for Jews after the Crusades, and we plan to do so again."[120]

Abu Qatada: "The time of victory is near. All over the world, Muslims are sacrificing more and contributing more to the struggle. May Allah accept us all to be slaughtered."

On the Danish cartoon controversy

Bakri: "In Islam, God said, and the messenger Muhammad said, whoever insults a prophet, he must be punished and executed. . . . This man [the cartoonist] should be put on trial and . . . executed."[121]

The Kurdish jihadist imam Mullah Krekar, in an interview from his comfortable refuge in Norway, put the issue of the cartoons in a general Islamist perspective:

> The spread of democracy is just an excuse. The same with the hunt for Osama bin Laden—it's just an excuse. It is Islam that the West can't stand. . . . The attack on Islam is like a hand. One finger is the war in Iraq and Afghanistan. Another finger is the imprisonment of Muslims at Guantanamo Bay. The third finger is the publishing of the pictures of the Prophet Muhammad. We must see things as they are, and those pictures [of Muhammad] are one part of the military fight that the West is conducting against Islam.[122]

UNDERMINING THE WEST FROM WITHIN

It is interesting how Salafi "refugees" in Europe manipulate local legal conditions to their advantage. Prior to the July 2005 London bombings, but after September 2001, while still on welfare in London, Bakri claimed that "Muslims in Britain are not allowed to do anything. But I believe the Government must expect a lot of resistance from Muslims outside the UK." He was offering "sincere advice to the British Government and the British public so they understand the consequences of playing with fire," but he claimed that Muslims in Britain, who are under a "covenant" to respect British laws, are not permitted to carry out terrorist attacks.[123] However, suddenly, after leaving Britain, he declared that "I believe the whole of Britain has become Dar al Harb [abode of war]. The jihad is *halal* [acceptable] for the Muslims wherever they are."[124]

Mullah Krekar went further and claimed that "It is you and the West who should be telling us what [the West] can do for us. The West should protect Islam, and not the other way around." On the other hand, Muslims owe no loyalty to Western countries they live in:

> Muslims in the West and in Norway don't want to understand that this is not their country. The Muslim state will be their home, no matter where it is located. Muslims in the West are like the Jews were. We are homeless and weak, and will remain so until we create our own country. Life here has no value for Muslims.[125]

What all these radicals living in Europe preach is a general ideology manipulating Muslim alienation, resentment, and refusal to integrate. The common threads among these men:

- With the exception of Qaradawi (who has never been a permanent resident in Europe), they are first-generation immigrants, which may explain their minimal knowledge of and indeed interest in the actual causes of the situation of Muslims in Europe. To the contrary, they magnify the perceived victimhood of Muslims, usually helped by ever-complaining established organizations and their allies among a Left in perpetual search for an oppressed class. Paradoxically, that is precisely what makes these imams influential among second-generation Muslims and thus so dangerous. They have a global view of Islam; a clear ideological direction, in the purification of faith from its alleged departure from the true path; a strategic goal, in the establishment of a Caliphate; and a method: jihad.

- As Arabs, the people of the Prophet, speaking the language of the Quran, and in some cases as *bona-fide* Islamic scholars, they enjoy particular legitimacy and respect among the second and third generations of young Muslims in France, Britain, and the Netherlands, whose knowledge and understanding of Islam is in an inverse relationship to their growing interest in it.

The result is that, as Olivier Roy has pointed out, radical imams play on those youths' sense of alienation and uprootedness—indeed, they see the latter as "an advantage, since it removes them from the influence of the cultural and traditional Islam of their parents and countries of origin. These imams want to radicalize young Muslims in their countries of residence and enlist them in a worldwide jihad. And for that, anywhere will do. Let them go to Afghanistan, Kashmir or Yemen (the way that Abu Hamza's son did), or just stay in London."[126] Not only do the radical imams manipulate the cultural and generational alienation of many of the young Muslims of Europe, they have a vested interest in deepening it. Ultimately the most effective way to do this is to turn them against the very societies of their birth—hence the numerous terrorist plots uncovered since 9/11, including, most spectacularly, the 7/7 London bombings. Although Abu Qatada, Abu Hamza, and Bakri have for years preached, organized, and recruited for a civil war within Islam, their influence has more recently turned toward the provocation of a conflict within Europe itself—and their impact continues even if they themselves are now out of action.

To justify their dependence on infidel financial support and legal protection, the London-based Salafi imams, but also the likes of Mullah Krekar, found theological cover by dividing the world into areas that go beyond the traditional division into

Dar al Harb (abode of war) and *Dar al Islam* (abode of Islam), and proclaimed Europe as *Dar al Ahd* (realm of the pact, i.e., of non-aggression between Muslims and the infidel *kufr*) or *Dar al Hijra* (realm of exile).[127] That this distinction was tactical and pragmatic rather than theologically well rooted was demonstrated by Bakri's turnaround, once he was refused re-entry to Britain. Suddenly he stopped talking about a "covenant" with London and described the country as a little Satan to be attacked. More generally, it is demonstrated by the Madrid and London bombings, which could in part be seen as a Salafi reaction to the post-9/11 European tightening of anti-terrorist and immigration-control legislation.

MODERATE OR RADICAL?

Considering that Yusuf al-Qaradawi has long been closely associated with the Muslim Brotherhood, by far the largest, most powerful, and most protean Islamist organization in the world (whose supreme leadership he was apparently offered and declined), the extent to which he differs from an Abu Qatada is important. Judging by some of his statements, he clearly distanced himself from Al-Qaeda on key issues—but does that make him a moderate?[128]

On September 11

After 9/11 he co-signed a *fatwa* stating that "The terrorist acts, considered by Islamic law, [constitute] the crime of *hirabah* (waging war against society)."

On Bin Laden and terrorism

"The vast majority of Muslim scholars have condemned Bin Laden's deeds; only a small minority stand behind him. What helps his reputation even more than scholarly opinion is the injustice that befalls Muslims every day—above all in Palestine. You underestimate this in the West: The one-sidedness of American support for Israel has devastating consequences."

This is a standard position for "moderate" Islamists in Europe (and among their allies on the secular Left). It amounts to opposition to Al-Qaeda's terrorism but agreement with the "grievances" it uses to justify its acts: i.e., the cause is understandable, the method, at least in some cases, is not.

On whether Bin Laden and his people are Muslims

"We condemn their acts, but I am categorically opposed to the idea of expulsion [from the ranks of Muslims]. That would be committing the same sort of sin as these people themselves commit: They want to make us and their other critics out to be heretics. . . . The day will come when they will have to stand in front of the Kadi [Islamic judge], but at this point, we are not so far along. First we have to decide who should be their judges."[129]

Coming from such an authority and, incidentally, supported by Quranic texts, this statement, by itself, demolishes the common claim of most Muslims and politically correct non-Muslims that Islamist terrorism has nothing to do with Islam and Muslims. Moreover, on Qarawadi's reading, condemnable as their actions are, bin Laden and his group *should only be judged by fellow Muslims because they are Muslims.*

On terrorism in Israel

"I was the first who condemned the crimes of 9/11—even before it was clear to many that al-Qaida was behind the attacks. There is certainly a difference if violence is used in a blind terrorist act or if it is used in rebellion against a foreign occupying force. . . . The Israelis might have nuclear bombs but we have the children bomb and there human bombs must continue until liberation. . . . We must all realize that the Israeli society is a military society—men and women. We cannot describe the society as civilian . . . they are not civilians or innocent."

Once again the characteristic Muslim Brotherhood double-speak: 9/11 was a "blind terrorist act" but the murder of women (and children) in Israel is legitimate because all Israelis do military duty. Beyond its duplicity, this argument is precisely the one used by Hamas (an MB offshoot) and indeed applied by Al-Qaeda itself to all citizens of Western democracies. Thus bin Laden in 1998: "Every American man is an enemy—whether he fights us directly or pays his taxes. And perhaps you have heard . . . that the number of those who support Clinton's strike against Iraq is some three-quarters of the population! This is a people whose votes are won when he kills innocents." Or, in November 2001: "The American people should remember that they pay taxes to their government, they elect their presidents, their government manufactures arms and gives them to Israel, and Israel uses them to massacre Palestinians."[130]

It seems clear that the difference between Qaradawi and bin Laden in this respect is prudential more than ideological.

On suicide bombing in Israel

"It is not suicide; it is martyrdom in the name of God. I consider this type of martyrdom operation as an indication of the justice of Allah almighty. Allah is just. Through his infinite wisdom, he has given the weak what the strong do not possess, and that is the ability to turn their bodies into bombs as Palestinians do. . . . Clearly, Jews, or at least Israelis and 'Zionists,' are beyond the limits of peaceful coexistence—killing them is legitimate."

On jihad

"We will conquer Europe, we will conquer America!" (Judging

by other statements, Qaradawi means "conquer" through *dawa*—missionary work—rather than the sword, and for the long term.)

On nonbelievers

"It has been determined by Islamic law that the blood and property of people of Dar Al-Harb (non-Muslims) is not protected: Because they fight against and are hostile towards the Muslims, they annulled the protection of his blood and his property." On the other hand, referring to Muslims in Europe: "As head of the European Council for Fatwa and Research, we call on the faithful to obey the laws of the countries they live in."

On the Caliphate and ummah

"Islam is a single nation, there is only one Islamic law and we all pray to a single God. Eventually such a nation will also become political reality. But whether that will be a federation of already existing states, a monarchy, or an Islamic republic remains to be seen."

Obviously, since the Caliphate is the ultimate goal, Muslims, if not the entire world, belong to their own "nation"—not to the nations they live in.

Greater Londonistan

The persons examined above were the most influential among the radicals operating from London, but they were neither isolated nor alone; there were and are many other inhabitants of Londonistan who pursue goals similar to those of Abu Hamza, Bakri, or Abu Qatada.

Saad al-Faqih, a Saudi dissident who has been declared a "specially designated global terrorist" by the United States for his ties to Al-Qaeda, was associated with Mohammad al-Massari when he first came to London in 1991. They split up a few years later, and in 1996 al-Faqih formed the Movement for Islamic Reform in Arabia, which he still heads.

Yasser al-Sirri, an Egyptian given asylum in Britain, faces the death penalty in his own country after being convicted *in absentia* for his role in a bomb attack. He was also connected to the Al-Qaeda murder of Ahmed Shah Massoud in Afghanistan in September 2001. He runs the Islamic Observation Centre in London, and it was alleged that he received and distributed messages smuggled out from Sheikh Omar Abdel Rahman, jailed in the United States.[131]

Abdullah el-Faisal, born Trevor William Forest in a family of Salvation Army members in Jamaica, converted to Islam as a teenager. He studied Islam at university in Riyadh; upon his graduation in 1991, Saudi religious authorities sent him to Britain, where he became the imam of the Salafi Brixton mosque. He had a strong influence on Germaine Lindsay, one of the London suicide terrorists, and his mosque was also attended by Al-Qaeda operative Dhiren Bharot, a.k.a. Abu Eisa al-Hindi, and by Richard Reid and Zacarias Moussaoui. His radicalism was such that the Salafis controlling the Brixton mosque expelled him. In return he declared them *takfiris* (apostates) and called for their murder.

His career is quite interesting, and typical of many of the less well-known imams spread all over Europe. As a news report summarized it:

> From Brixton, El-Faisal and his second wife, Zubeida Khan, a British national of Pakistani origin, moved to Tower Hamlets, East London, where he began a study centre. America, he declared, was the great Satan. But Britain, France, Italy and Germany were also numbered among Islam's greatest enemies. In one sermon he advanced "19 reasons why there can never be peace with the Jews." According to the prosecution [at his

trial], El-Faisal suggested fuelling nuclear power stations with the bodies of Hindus to be slaughtered for their "oppression" of Muslims in Kashmir. The jury heard that he tried to recruit British schoolboys for terrorist training camps and promised them "seventy-two virgins in paradise," if they died fighting a holy war. On a tape called "Them Versus Us" he said: "There are two religions in the world today—the right one and the wrong one. Islam versus the rest of the world."[132]

El-Faisal, who was living on welfare throughout his stay in Britain, was convicted by a London jury in 2003 on three charges of soliciting murder and three of stirring up racial hatred. He received a sentence of nine years but in July 2007 was deported to Jamaica.

WESTERN GOVERNMENTS AS ENABLERS

It appears that the legitimizing and recruiting roles of Islamic radical clerics in Europe were systematically missed or minimized by the authorities. Norway's persistent refusal to withdraw asylum protection and expel Mullah Krekar, the "spiritual leader" of *Ansar al-Islam*, although his case has been in the courts for nearly six years, is well known. But that is just a particularly egregious example of what happens in much of Europe, with individuals openly, and for years, providing the absolutely necessary "Islamic" legitimacy to terrorist groups as far away as Algeria, Indonesia, and Yemen. The legitimizing roles of Abu Qatada and Abu Hamza for successive Algerian terrorist groups has been mentioned,[133] but a similar role has been played by Syrian Muslim Brotherhood refugees in Spain and Turkish Islamists in Germany, Belgium, and the Netherlands.

There may well be intelligence reasons for British (though certainly not Norwegian) tolerance for radical Islamist clerics. Indeed there were widespread but unproven rumors that

Abu Qatada was in fact an MI5 or MI6 agent. But the key questions remain. Why is it that radical Islamic clergymen, deemed dangerous even by governments like those of Saudi Arabia, are considered legitimate "asylum seekers" in London? Is there something that the British legal system and political culture do not really understand? Such as that murder, mutilation, and mayhem by self-proclaimed jihad warriors is absolutely dependent upon some sort of religious legitimacy, which can be provided only by recognized Islamic figures?

This is not to say that the GIA or IAA would not have committed murder, kidnappings, and other atrocities without Abu Qatada's or Abu Hamza's blessing. But for many Europe-based terrorists, the role of Islamist imams was decisive, particularly in the light of such individuals' poor education, knowledge of Islam, or both.

Both the European and the American media routinely describe characters like Sheikh Abdel Rahman, Abu Qatada, Abu Hamza, or Abdullah el-Faisal as "spiritual" guides or leaders of various terrorist groups or individuals. And, for the public, the images of a blind, old diabetic like Sheikh Abdel Rahman, or a handless, one-eyed Abu Hamza, may seem to prove that these two are *ipso facto* innocent, since they could not kill a fly. That, however, is like saying that a vegetarian dog lover and believer in traditional marriage could not be responsible for the Holocaust—but by now we know differently.

Not even the Israeli courts that tried Adolf Eichmann and sentenced him to death claimed that he, personally, killed anyone—Jews or Slavs or anyone at all. Nor is there any proof that Hitler, Stalin, Mao, Pol Pot, or Castro, some of the 20th century's worst mass murderers, ever personally killed anyone. Hence, why the widespread refusal to admit a link, any link, between religion and the self-described militants of Islam? Does that have to do with the contradictions of the multiculturalist ideology dominating Western culture and education?

Eurojihadis, Europe-based Islamic terrorists, have long been active internationally, albeit until recently mostly outside Europe. They have been involved in jihadi violence in Kashmir, Afghanistan, the United States, Pakistan, Israel, Algeria, Morocco, Singapore, Russia, and Iraq, using methods similar to those of native groups. These include suicide bombings, car bombings, use of mines and IEDs (improvised explosive devices), individual assassinations and mutilations, and massacres of noncombatants. Until recently, the whole phenomenon of Euro-Islamism has rarely been examined. Now, because of its growing presence and threat—especially after 9/11 and the subsequent attacks within Europe—it has to be.

While world attention to Islamic terrorism has been concentrated on training camps in Afghanistan and elsewhere, the very nature of Islamic extremism requires legitimacy that can be given only by Muslim clerics. For obvious reasons, the governments of Muslim countries do not encourage such activities, with the result that radical clerics who do provide such legitimacy for terror have increasingly found Western countries a more convenient and comfortable location for their activities. And, as we have seen, in some cases such clerics went beyond providing religious cover for terrorism and engaged in recruiting and even actually plotting terrorist activities.

The following is perhaps the best assessment of the duplicity of radical Islamist ideologues in the West and of their victims as enablers. Since the writer, Abd Al-Rahman Al-Rashed, Director General of the Saudi-funded Al-Arabiyya TV, cannot be accused of "racism" or "Islamophobia," it deserves a lengthy quotation:

> What makes Omar Bakri, who enjoys liberty in Britain, spread hatred [against Britain], fight its culture, and say obscenely

that [Britain] is a toilet in which he lives in order to defecate there? Does it make sense for someone like him to express a desire to return to Britain after everything he has said and done? As for Abu Qatada, he prefers to remain in prison and not to return to his homeland Jordan, just like [Osama Nasser], the imam from Milan, who is protesting about being taken to Egypt and about being imprisoned there. Not only is he protesting his abduction; he has also decided to sue for €20 million in damages. . . . It is blatantly obvious that all three are enjoying all the benefits of the [government] they despise: They want the financial aid, the security, the [rule of] law, the justice and the freedom of expression afforded by this government. Is this not the epitome of hypocrisy? When they preach, aren't they greatly deceiving their followers—[considering this discrepancy] between what they say and what they do?

It is some of the extremist hate-mongers living in the West who are inciting the Muslims in the East against Western countries. . . . Those [same] countries that have hosted them, given them protection and shelter, and in many cases also financed the education of their children, including their Islamic and Arabic language studies. It is also revolting to see writers denouncing the actions of [Western] governments that wish to get rid of the extremists by sending them back to their Islamic countries.

Instead of demanding that the Arab [countries] mend their legal and security deficiencies, they ask the [Western] countries that have thrown out these extremists to spare them and to tolerate the ideological damage that they inflict upon their societies.[134]

CHAPTER FIVE

Paths to Eurojihad

"I have a more technical point . . . I stand here as a French citizen. I want to make clear that I am not French and have no relation. I'm a sworn enemy of France. So I want to make this in the record that I'm not French, okay? I tell you I am a Muslim, and I have nothing to do with a nation of homosexual Crusaders. And I am not a frog. That's the first thing."

—Zacarias Moussaoui[1]

The most important development in the Muslim communities in Europe since the 1980s is the re-Islamization of significant numbers of second-generation Muslims. This phenomenon could be briefly defined as a nominal or mainstream-orthodox Muslim's conversion to radical and/or violent versions of Islam. Those undergoing this process identify themselves simply as "Muslims" rather than French, Danish, British, etc., and consider themselves loyal exclusively to the interests of the *ummah*, as they perceive them. This process is a necessary first step toward an individual's psychological and cultural separation and isolation from the surrounding society, its laws, customs, and traditions.

Young Muslims in Europe, or at least large numbers of them (especially males), are made vulnerable to extremist interpreters of Islam by their identification with a religion and culture they know little about. A huge majority of second-generation Arab Muslims in France do not speak vernacular Arabic, let alone understand the classical language of the Quran. As stated above, Salafi/jihadist ideology is so effective in terms of recruitment in the West (especially in prisons) because of its simplicity—or simplism. Manichean approaches to religion always have the upper hand against sophisticated, complex, and subtle ones, especially among the poorly educated young. That applies among the poor and illiterate in Karachi, Casablanca, or Aswan as much as among the alumni of increasingly dysfunctional Western educational systems.

Statements by detained Islamist terrorists in Europe and the United States often indicate that the subject traveled to Saudi Arabia, Pakistan, or Afghanistan at the time of the Taliban seeking to "learn Islam" or even to "learn Arabic," despite the fact that the latter two countries are not Arabic speaking. It is highly unlikely that Islamist thugs like Khaled Kelkal in France have ever read the Quran, certainly not in the original, and the same applies to many of those involved in the terrorist attacks in Madrid, London, or New York. Their understanding of Islam's basic tenets, such as it is, is completely second-hand, filtered through the interpretation offered by local authority figures, usually imams who are themselves immigrants and ignorant of or indifferent to European traditions and realities. In fact, some converts excepted, there is no known case of Europe-born and -trained imams, few as they are, being involved in Islamist radicalism.

Indeed, as British convert Dr. Tim Winter, a.k.a. Sheikh Abdul Hakim Murad, stated, "There is a struggle for the soul of Islam. . . . Even as young European Muslims seek new ways of living their religion, [Persian] Gulf embassies . . . spend tens

of millions of pounds to ensure that the most fundamentalist form of Islam prevails in schools and bookshops. . . . liberal Islam—economically, culturally, and socially—is crying in
the wilderness."[2]

Like all complex phenomena, Islamism and jihadism in
Europe cannot be explained by any single cause. A combination of outside influences, self-alienation, a permanent victim
complex, and the multiculturalism dominant in Western societies, all reinforcing one another, are the main causes. All these
factors are operating against a background of growing interest
in Islam among Muslims in Europe, especially the young second or third generation. Without this fertile ground the Abu
Qatadas and Omar Bakris of Londonistan would find fewer
followers beyond recent immigrants and veterans of jihad in
Algeria, Iraq, or Afghanistan. In fact, many of the thousands
of committed Islamists arrested throughout Europe during the
past few years were born or grew up there.

Re-Islamization

The phenomenon of re-Islamization as a reaction to the private
or assimilated form of practicing the faith was first identified,
and extensively examined, by French analyst Olivier Roy.[3] For
him it basically involves a drift by second- and third-generation
Muslim immigrants toward Islam as the identity default position, separating them from both their parents' nationality and
the nationality of their own present country of residence—i.e.,
Moroccan or French, Pakistani or British.

Jean Noël Ferrié defines re-Islamization as "The desire to restore a Muslim moral order based on [traditional] authority."[4]
Ferrié is talking about the situation in Egypt, where this may
be true enough. But it does not fully apply to the European
context, where most of those undergoing re-Islamization are

ignorant of the very basics of Islam, which suggests that the process starts before, and is independent of, a clear Muslim moral order; in other words, that we are dealing with a utopian project. Like all utopian projects, it only gains concrete substance later, in contact with real challenges to its fulfillment. Just as Communism had to find its real-life expression and found it in Stalinism or Maoism, so the return to the already romanticized "original Islam" finds its substance in the Caliphate and jihad—especially when there is an Abu Qatada to offer "scholarly" advice and a bin Laden as an example in action. In Europe the subject of re-Islamization moves directly from ignorance to the Salafi or other radical version of the faith. That is not true in the case Ferrié is discussing, that of Egypt, or in other areas where there is a local/national Islamic tradition and religious structure to resist rapid change. In the former Soviet republics of Central Asia, re-Islamization meant a return to pre-Communist freedom to practice (Sufi) Islam. In the Balkans (Bosnia, Albania/Kosovo) it had a similar meaning as an addition to recovery or discovery of ethno-national identity.[5] For Gilles Kepel, as early as 1994 it meant a return of Islam as an openly political counter to socialist and Arab nationalist ideologies[6]—all true enough, but inapplicable to Europe.

In a world of global communications, migration flows, and transportation, whatever happens in the Islamic world has an influence on Muslims in Europe. That influence is filtered by local circumstances in Birmingham, Liverpool, the *banlieues* of Paris, or Amsterdam. In Muslim-majority countries, re-Islamization is brought about by the growing influence of Islamist parties, movements, and organizations, often tolerated or encouraged by the governments themselves, as demonstrated in places as different as Turkey, Pakistan, the Palestinian areas, Egypt, Indonesia, Nigeria, and Bosnia.[7] Inevitably, it has reached Muslims in the West, in part through continuous mass immigration.

A 2004 Pew poll taken in several Muslim-majority countries suggested that among Turks (43 percent), Pakistanis (79 percent), Moroccans (70 percent), and Jordanians (63 percent) the trend is toward growing identification with Islam rather than nationality.[8] The percentage among Turks, the most secular of Muslims, is particularly significant (the percentage among Pakistanis is the most expected, since Pakistan was established precisely, and only, on the basis of the religion of its majority). The relevance of these figures, which are corroborated by additional data from most of the Muslim world, is that they are increasingly replicated among those countries' diasporas in Europe, especially among the youth. This phenomenon, called "de-territorialization" by Olivier Roy, is an extension of what he describes as the "privatization" of Islam[9]—the practice of the faith outside, or against, established institutions—with the anti-institutional Taliban given as an example.

In Europe de-territorialization is manifested by individuals' transfer of allegiance to the generic *ummah* at the expense of ethnicity and nationality. It also translates into a highly individual practice, seen as "orthodox" despite its combining of various interpretations of the Quran which are not supported by prestigious institutions like Al-Azhar. It is in this environment that Islamist radicals, whether ostensibly peaceful like *Tabligh*, violent like the *Takfiris*, or freelancers like Abu Qatada and Omar Bakri, find their support.

Thus, according to the *New York Times*, "Danish counterterrorism officials say more young Danish Muslims are being drawn to *Hizb ut-Tahrir*, or the Party of Liberation, which seeks the unification of all Muslim countries under one leader and Shariah, the Islamic legal code. The group, which distributes literature at mosques and on the Internet, is banned in most of the Muslim world, as well as in Russia and Germany."[10]

In the Netherlands, according to a story on Radio Netherlands, increasing numbers of young Muslims appear to be developing "a strong interest in orthodox Islam" (i.e., radical Islam). "On the streets, an increasing number of young men can be seen sporting long beards, while the number of young women wearing head scarves is also growing." A young professional, Youssef Azghari, tells that when he was a student at Nijmegen University in the late 1980s, he came into contact with Muslims who supported the "Taliban form of Islam":

> "They were set on having their own Islamic prayer space and refused to share a room with other student religious groups," he recalls. However, Islamisation at universities was much less visible than it is now . . . "Nowadays, Muslim students are open about their orthodox religious views, and they dress accordingly, too. I see a growing number of students in class with beards, short trousers or head scarves. . . . There's also a large number of girls who wear a headscarf and who follow a more liberal interpretation. Yet there are young Muslims, too, who wear a veil or grow a beard to make a political statement, and take their faith to the extreme." Nevertheless, he also sees a total revolution taking place in the way many young Muslims think: "Up to puberty, these young Muslims enjoyed all the benefits of a western lifestyle, but suddenly left all this behind them and turned against the west."

He sees a particular growth in interest for fundamentalism among young people whose parents come from Morocco, but who were themselves born and raised in the Netherlands and, significantly, notes that students who've only recently arrived from Morocco are much more modern: "Migrants' children do not choose orthodox Islam on the basis of conviction, but out of frustration." He knows young people of Moroccan descent who do not feel accepted in Dutch society and who try to set themselves apart with radical religious views: "They are lost, because when you are teenager you are looking for your roots and identity."[11]

It is by now a widely accepted sociological fact that "Alienation from both parental roots and country of origin, and the society in which they live, can lead to a desire to identify with a more motivating or powerful locus of identity."[12] Born in Europe, young Muslims lost their ties with the country of their parents, while at the same time Muslim families suffer the same phenomenon of disintegration as native ones, with parents losing control over their children, either to gangs or to Islamists—or both. Citing high unemployment as the explanation for Muslim violence and refusal to integrate misses the point—in fact, it misses more than one point. First, and most important, is that, as Jacques Myard put it, "these youths, French against their will, products of Arab-African immigration, intend to maintain their cultural and religious specificities. Far from wanting to mix and integrate in a scared France which confuses indulgence with tolerance, they continuously look to their close origins, due to modern means of communication, and refuse to come out from their identity ghetto."[13]

Second, unemployment is not primarily a result of "discrimination." Hugues Lagrange misses the irony when he claims that "the main reason for these [violent] tendencies lies in the unemployment of unskilled youths. This scourge touches almost a third of the children of immigration."[14] Could it be that they are unemployed because, instead of staying in schools, they prefer to burn them (as occurred in the November 2005 riots), and thus remain unskilled? One must also refer back to Antoine Sfeir's observation that relations between the sexes is a big factor in the re-Islamization of second-generation Muslim males in Europe. Because, as we have seen, young Muslim women often do better than men at adapting to the host society, young men acquire a strong incentive to reassert the old order that gives them control over women.[15]

A 2006 Dutch intelligence report noted that the dominant trend has been toward the autonomous radicalization of young Muslims, and the main vehicle for Islamization and "jihadization" in the Netherlands has shifted since 2003, from fundamentalist mosques and foreign extremists like Radwan al-Issa, to the Internet. Moreover, the report notes that "While radical Muslim women in other European countries are often invisible and play no more than a supporting role, they play a much more prominent part in the Netherlands.... It would appear to be just a matter of time before these women become actively involved in violent activities." The report links this phenomenon to the strength of feminism in Dutch society.[16]

The lengths to which re-Islamization can go are demonstrated by the fact that "More than 100 British Muslim families emigrated to Afghanistan before September 11 in line with the Koranic teaching called Hijrah [sic], meaning migration from a bad way of life for a good or more righteous way.... There are people who genuinely went there to live. They weren't fighters. They were just living there."[17] Obviously, when a Muslim from London moves to Taliban-ruled Afghanistan because it offers "a good or more righteous way," his cultural alienation is complete—and that is the certain path to jihad. Emigration to the medieval regime of Mullah Omar in Kandahar was an extreme case of re-Islamization, but the debate over the wearing of the headscarf (*hijab**) involves a majority of Muslims in Europe and

---

* Commonly in Europe and the U.S. the media refer to the *hijab* as the "veil" when in fact it covers just the hair and neck, unlike the *niqab*, which leaves only the eyes visible, and the *burqa*, which covers the entire face.

is a good indication of how far the process has advanced in many countries. Perhaps the best proof of this is the involvement in the debate of figures on the secular Left not otherwise known for their interest in feminine fashion.

THE *HIJAB* AS SYMBOL OF RE-ISLAMIZATION

Spiegel: But what is so objectionable about devout Turkish women wanting to wear the headscarf in universities?

Cig: It's quite simple. Secularism is not directed against religion, but it does call for a separation between the state and religion. In other words, the young women are welcome to wear the headscarf, but not on government premises. It so happens that the headscarf is a religious symbol. Besides, it is one that incorrectly invokes religion.

Spiegel: Can this be proven?

Cig: You won't find anything in the Koran that isn't ambiguous. I could explain to the female students in detail why the headscarf was never a religious necessity and that, if they were to obey all rules in Islam, they would first have to obey many other requirements. Islam is basically a very inconspicuous and individual religion, which can make do quite easily without demonstrative clothing regulations."

—Interview with Muazzez Ilmiye Cig,
93-year-old doyenne of Turkish archaeologists[18]

The pressure to "veil" has grown greatly in the past few years, and not just in Europe, as demonstrated by the intense debates over the issue in Tunisia and Turkey. Claude Moniquet of the European Strategic Intelligence and Security Center (ESISC) in Brussels claimed in congressional testimony:

Ten years ago, the Islamic veil was mainly worn by older women. Now at least half of the female Muslim population wear the veil. In some municipalities in France, the figure is about 80 percent. From field investigation we know that in most cases those girls and women didn't really choose to wear the veil but were "forced" to do so by family or community

> pressure. In some European cities, a Muslim girl who refuses to wear the veil leaves herself open to insults, physical aggression, sexual harassment and even collective rape.[19]

Indeed, one of the most obvious signs of re-Islamization among young Muslims in Europe is the growing trend of women wearing not just the *hijab* but increasingly even the *niqab* and *burqa*. While the former is traditional and, among older Muslim women, quite widespread, it is now increasingly worn by young women. It is important to point out that although the Quran and Hadith (the sayings of the Prophet) do not mention any of these, the same people who maintain, correctly, that female circumcision and honor killings are for that very reason "un-Islamic" also tend to claim that the *hijab* (at least) is a religious obligation.

It is also important to note that, unlike the *hijab*, the *niqab* and *burqa* present a clear security problem by making identification difficult. Hence those who oppose counter-terrorism legislation in general, usually Islamists and persons on the Left, tend to dismiss security considerations in this context—despite incidents like one of the Somali would-be London bombers of 2005 avoiding British police and border controls and fleeing to Rome wearing . . . a *burqa*; not to mention the well-documented increased use of women as suicide bombers by Al-Qaeda and associated groups.

While the *burqa* is still rare—in the Netherlands the number of wearers is estimated at less than 50—the use of the *niqab* is growing throughout Europe, and both have to be seen as a result of re-Islamization. The *niqab*, and even more so the *burqa*, by hiding the physical identity of the wearer, allows only one alternative: the Islamic identity. By wearing it, the woman declares that she is first and only Muslim, rather than an individual, let alone a French, English, or Dutch citizen. For a Muslim in the West it is a declaration of separation—as then Prime Minister Blair and Foreign Secretary Jack Straw noted when calling the *niqab* a "statement of separation," or as shadow home secretary David Davis did when describing it as "voluntary apartheid."[20] Generally speaking, the *hijab* debate in Europe is actually a debate over Muslim integration.

For any neutral observer, the explanation given by Ms. Muazzez Ilmiye Cig—a knowledgeable secular Muslim woman in a Muslim-majority country—should end the debate over whether the *hijab* is a religious choice, rather than an obligation. However, while all this may seem obvious, it is not obvious to certain prominent Muslim leaders, such as Daud Abdullah, the deputy secretary general of the Muslim Council of Britain, for whom the very debate over the *niqab* is "opportunism" and "incitement to violence," not to mention a diversion from the "real" problem: "The government's refusal for so long to recognize the link between its own disastrous foreign policy in the Muslim world and the extremism it was fomenting is now fuelling the flames of Islamophobia."[21]

Abdullah's goal is clearly to change the subject, not to contribute to the debate on Muslim integration, which is what the veiling issue is all about. Considering the MCB's general ambiguity on delicate issues, that is not surprising. Nor is it surprising when an official branch of the EU gives its official blessing to that attitude, as the European Commission against Racism and Intolerance (ECRI) did as late as February 2008:

> ECRI considers that the widely-discussed proposal (finally not adopted) to introduce a ban on the wearing of *burkas* and *niqabs* in public [in the Netherlands] has increased feelings of victimisation, stigmatisation and alienation among Muslims and raised once again majority and minority

communities against each other. Irrespective of its human rights implications, the proposed measure and the debate around it do not appear to ECRI to be in any way proportional to the situation the proposed measure aimed to address, as ECRI understands that only a few dozen women are reported to wear the garments in question in the Netherlands. Instead, it has been reported to ECRI that, in practice, the discussions around the proposed ban have opened new opportunities for further discrimination or exclusion of Muslim women generally in everyday life.[22]

Simply put, the ECRI's position is that the very fact of democratic political debate over the veiling issue is *ipso facto* proof of discrimination against Muslims, and, with Orwellian logic, opposition to the self-isolation represented by wearing the *burqa* is . . . exclusion. Thus, not only is the ECRI contradicting legal decisions of the European Human Rights Court, which declared the ban on the *hijab* legal in Turkey (and elsewhere), but it also pretends that its own interpretation of the ban's impact on Muslims' feelings trump law, security concerns, and indeed common sense. And that is precisely what Islamists seek—European legitimization of their claims, no matter what the opposing concerns.

What the MCB implies and the ECRI advocates is avoidance of any discussion, let alone debate, on any issue regarding integration of Muslims in Europe—and the tool used is accusations of "Islamophobia." This convergence of attitudes and values between European human-rights fundamentalists and Islamists, further examined below, is key to understanding the latter's earlier success in promoting their agenda.

Throughout Europe, and even, partially, in some Muslim-majority countries, many young people now see Islam, and particularly its political face, Islamism, as an instrument for fighting "the system"—i.e., any authority getting in the way of their attaining a sense of mission and identity or personal satisfaction. This is reminiscent of the gang culture through-out the West. In that sense, the only difference between the Hispanic *Mara Salvatrucha* gangs of Los Angeles and Central America, and the Moroccan hashish-trafficking gangs in Spain who are also involved in Islamist terrorism, is that the latter have been persuaded that they fight for a greater cause. At the center of re-Islamization as opposition to the "system" is the *hijab*, both because it is visible and because it attracts support from libertarians, leftists, and human-rights advocates. While veiling among the young is not always or only an indication of re-Islamization or radicalization—sometimes it is just adoles-cent rebellion or seeking for attention—it is spreading with the encouragement of Islamist groups.

In **Germany**, while in 2000 only 27 percent of resident Muslims thought women should cover their hair, the number had almost doubled, to 47 percent, five years later. A similar pattern emerged on the topics .of dual-sex sports classes and participation in coeducational school trips. Rejected by 19 percent in 2000, by 2007 such activities were rejected by 30 percent. Moreover, as a German teacher in a mostly Turkish neighborhood of Berlin complained, "If I say that headscarves are worn less in Turkey than here, they simply counter: 'That's why we came to Germany, so that we can openly practice our religion.'"[23] Indeed, many German judges, when having to de-cide between Islamic rules, such as those forbidding mixed education, sports, or field trips, and the girls' right to a normal German education, choose the former.

In **Belgium**, the dominant Muslim groups, Moroccans and Turks, display the re-Islamization trend in their daily behavior, as an article in the popular Flemish newspaper *Het Volk* suggests:

Hind Fraihi, a faithful Muslim woman, lived two months disguised as a sociology student in the heart of Molenbeek. "I am astonished about what I discovered. Many Brussels Muslims do not show the slightest intention to integrate. They look upon the Belgians as infidels and do not have any affection with our country. They consider Molenbeek not as a part of Belgium anymore but as an Islamic enclave where they make the rules as in an Islamic state and where Belgians are not welcome."[24]

And then there is **France**. In January 2006, *Le Figaro* noticed that one-third of the 25,000 Muslims from France doing the *Hajj* were under 30 years of age. It used to be that the *Hajj* was the monopoly of older, married Muslims, but since 2000 or so, younger, even unmarried couples made the pilgrimage in growing numbers.[25]

As the Europe-based American reporter Bruce Bawer wrote, "Many Muslims, wanting to enjoy Western prosperity but repelled by Western ways, travel regularly back to their homelands. From Oslo, where I live, there are more direct flights every week to Islamabad than to the U.S. A recent Norwegian report noted that among young Norwegians of Pakistani descent, family honor depends largely on 'not being perceived as Norwegian—as integrated.'"[26]

One associated element is the growing Muslim hostility to Christians and, especially, Jews—a sentiment now increasingly common in the countries of origin as well. A 2004 Pew poll found that

[P]eople in predominantly Muslim countries have mixed views of Christians and strongly negative views of Jews. In Lebanon, which has a large Christian minority, 91 percent of the public thinks favorably of Christians. Smaller majorities in Jordan and Indonesia also have positive views of Christians. However, in Turkey (63 percent), Morocco (61 percent) and Pakistan (58 percent), solid majorities express negative opinions of

Christians. Anti-Jewish sentiment is endemic in the Muslim world. In Lebanon, all Muslims and 99 percent of Christians say they have a very unfavorable view of Jews. Similarly, 99 percent of Jordanians have a very unfavorable view of Jews. Large majorities of Moroccans, Indonesians, Pakistanis and six-in-ten Turks also view Jews unfavorably.[27]

Obviously, the diaspora communities in Europe are influenced by such opinions in their countries of origin.

Meanwhile, significant and increasingly large majorities of Europeans are coming to perceive the Muslims in their midst as increasingly Islamic. Pew found that in Western countries with sizeable Muslim minorities, a majority of the native population believed that Muslims coming to their countries wanted to remain distinct from the larger country; that resident Muslims had a strong sense of Islamic identity; and that resident Muslims' sense of Islamic identity was growing. And, according to Pew's summary, "those who do [hold these views] see this as a negative development."[28]

Outside Influences

As we have seen, the multifaceted influence of the countries of origin, the growing radicalization of the global *ummah*, an abundance of freelance, often radical imams, and the European cultural environment, especially its multiculturalist bias, all have a powerful effect on Muslims in Europe. But outside influences also contribute heavily to re-Islamization, which in turn is a necessary ingredient in the creation and growth of Islamist terror groups. Some of these influences are more important culturally, some more immediately significant in a security sense. Ultimately however, the impact of the outside Islamic world on Muslims in Europe, furthered by elements like global transportation and the Internet, is a key ingredient explaining the rise of Islamism, including jihadism, in Europe—and its export to the rest of the world.

The impact of radical imams resident in Europe is often paralleled by that of outside actors, many from the Middle East or Pakistan, usually well financed and organized. Whether direct, as in the case of Qaradawi's or the Wahhabis' role in financing and supporting Islamism throughout Europe, or indirect but pervasive, as in the general sweep of revivalism, there is no barrier between Europe and the Muslim world. None of those influences is more relevant than that of Saudi or Gulf-sponsored Wahhabism. Indeed, the influence of Saudi Arabia and the Gulf states, whether direct or through the groups that they finance, such as the multiplicity of Muslim Brotherhood organizations, is one of the major obstacles to the integration of Muslims in Europe.

That influence is complex, ranging from the construction of huge mosques, which serve as poles of attraction for local Muslims seeking an Islamic identity; to political influence, such as the Saudi role in pressuring Denmark on the cartoons issue; to the subsidizing of Wahhabi imams.

As the Saudi oil company Aramco proudly claimed in 1979:

> European mosques also combine the traditions of the worshipers with those of their new environment. Near London's Regent's Park, the copper dome of a new mosque gleams above the treetops. Above a busy street in Almelo, The Netherlands, the shape of a minaret stands sharp against the sky. And in Munich and Manchester, Copenhagen and Coventry, new mosques announce to Europe the return of Islam. Even Rome, city of pagan ruins and Christian churches, is to have a mosque soon. These mosques, and others being constructed in other European cities, reflect not only the permanence of the Muslim presence in the West, but also a rapprochement between Christianity and Islam—whose

defenders once fought each other fiercely as an act of faith. They also suggest that some European authorities have finally recognized the needs of their Muslim residents and guests.[29]

It all came to pass, and more—with many of the new mosques being ugly and grandiose (as visitors to Sarajevo can testify), given Wahhabism's indifference to beauty. With them came the salaried imams, but secretly funded ones came too. It is no exaggeration to say that among young Muslims in Europe, or at least among the significant number of those attracted by re-Islamization, the struggle for hearts and minds is between the regulated Islam of Rabat, Algiers, Tunis, or Ankara and the wealthy (thanks to Gulf support) freelance radicals, often too radical to preach in their own countries—or even expelled from them for extremism. And the advantage of the latter, wealth aside, is that their countries have few emigrants in Europe; thus they can claim to support "Islam" rather than a specific diaspora. Many Islamic organizations' funding is opaque but widely suspected of being of Gulf origin, often funneled through obscure or secretive charities.[30] In France alone there are some 20 known Salafi—a term often used as synonymous with Wahhabi—mosques operating in the open. Most of these are in Paris or its suburbs, but there is also one in Roubaix (the Dawa mosque), near Lille, and one in Vénissieux, all Wahhabi-controlled and led by imams closely following the teachings of a handful of fundamentalist scholars: the late Great Mufti of Saudi Arabia, Abdulaziz Ibn Baz; the Albanian-born Sheikh Muhammad Nasiruddin al-Albani; and the Algerian-born Sheikh Abubakr al-Jezairi, whose book *The Muslim Way* has been translated into French (*La Voie du Musulman*) and is popular among the new adepts.[31]

While it is often said that there is a significant difference between reformist and "fighting" Salafis, as far as re-Islamization is concerned, this is a distinction without a difference. Many of those attracted by "reformist" Salafi preaching end up in jihadi ranks. It has been pointed out that "reformist Salafism has found favor among the unemployed youth in the suburbs of major cities . . . thanks largely to the proselytizing work carried out in certain European mosques by *Salafi* Imams who have enjoyed, and still enjoy, considerable backing from Saudi Arabia."[32]

More openly and directly, Saudi money produces radical imams in Europe through abundant offers of scholarships. A few hundred Muslims from France alone study in the Middle East at any given time. Some 30 Muslims from Europe, mostly recent converts, go each year to the Saudi universities of Riyadh, Mecca, and Medina, where they are encouraged to marry Muslims of other nationalities. Upon their return home they tend to form a support network for radicals. Their influence is enhanced by their training in the land of the Prophet. The University of Medina has a long-standing record of Islamist ideologues among its alumni, having produced Abu Muhammad al-Maqdisi, one of the most prominent jihadist ideologues and a mentor of the late Abu Musab al-Zarqawi; London's firebrand imam Abdullah el-Faisal; the equally radical Kenyan-born imam in the Netherlands, Mohammed Mahmoud (since expelled); a large number of GIA leaders; and convert Christian Ganczarski, a German jihadist implicated in the deadly bombing of Djerba in Tunisia.[33]

Moreover, the large number of Salafi imams exported to Europe by Saudi Arabia are mostly Medina University trainees and were actively recruited there. Once in Europe they pretend to ignore calls to jihad while in public, but encourage them in private, according to complaints by the well informed (if perhaps biased) Dalil Boubakeur, head of the French CFCM and rector of the Grand Mosque in Paris.[34]

The Extent of Re-Islamization

One should not exaggerate the level of re-Islamization of Muslims in Europe, or the number of incompletely integrated ones—a common habit among alarmist followers of the "Eurabia" scenario of Bat Ye'or. In reality, most Muslims in Europe are still in a stage of incomplete integration. They are not subjects of re-Islamization as a mass but only as distinct groups or as individuals. While that fact is no reason for complacency or optimism, it is a reason not to give way to defeatism or fatalism.

Re-Islamization, meanwhile, has led to the formation of a veritable no-man's-land. Millions of young Muslims have ceased to have real ties with their parents' national or ethnic origins, but have not created their own new identity in Europe. Young Muslims from Europe trying to "go back" to Rabat or Algiers, Kayseri or Lahore, often admit to finding there rejection or confusion—they are not seen as fully European, but neither are they "our own." That having been said, the fact that so many Muslims from Europe do manage to find brides in the lands of their parents suggests that for people there they are acceptable as family members—if only for economic reasons.

To (over)simplify: Some people, especially young people in Europe, see Islam (as they understand it) as the rejection of, or opposition to, the rules of the societies they live in. The following both describes well and underestimates the phenomenon:

> A poll for Policy Exchange last week found that about a third of younger Muslims [in Britain] would like to live under Sharia. Ask a stupid question. Ask these kids if they can explain the details of Sharia. When they can't, ask them what they're really upset about. British Muslims, usually of Pakistani or

> Bangladeshi origin, are the ethnic group most likely to be
> unemployed, poor and live in overcrowded homes. They're
> born angry, and now need a reason to be. Radical Islamism has
> become an off-the-peg label that young Muslims can wear to
> rebel against their dads and wider British society. Like punks
> before them, they'll grow up and grow out of it.[35]

Young people's rebelliousness is indeed natural, and it is not limited to Muslims; the difference is that punks, rap-music fans, and drug addicts do not usually blow themselves up—jihadists do. And ignorance of Islam or Sharia, far from being an argument to dismiss young Muslims' attraction to Islam as superficial and temporary nonsense, is precisely a major reason they are so vulnerable, and attracted to Islamism and jihadism. And that is the enormous difference between "re-Islamization" among Muslims in Europe and the genuine re-Islamization of entire peoples (Uzbeks or Bosniaks, Albanians or Tajiks) returning to their historic traditions.

The symptoms of re-Islamization among Muslims in Europe are not hard to notice—even among the comparatively better integrated, if not necessarily assimilated, Muslims of France. Thus, according to *Agence France Presse,* "Young French Muslims were less likely than their elders to hold liberal opinions on these topics: Conversion from Islam to other faiths was opposed by 56 percent of those aged 18–24, compared to 45 percent among all age groups. Among youths, 31 percent opposed interfaith marriage compared to 26 percent of all French Muslims."[36]

Among Muslims in Britain, 31 percent agreed with the statement, "I feel more in common with Muslims in other countries than I do with non-Muslims in Britain," and attachment to Britain was much weaker among the young—55 percent of those over 45 years of age but only 44 percent of those 18 to 24 years old declared Britain "my" as opposed to "their" country.[37]

One of the most lucid descriptions of the causes of re-Islamization of Muslim youth in Europe was provided by French Muslim sociologist, author, and former Justice Ministry official Dounia Bouzar:

> To [Bouzar], the attraction of radical Islam for young Muslims in France is a smokescreen for obtaining power and refusing to obey the law. The true faithful obey religious authorities, but such youths reject imams who contradict them. In reality, such radicalized youths seek power, superiority and ecstasy, and use a religious cover to solder their group, to impose themselves over the others. Nor is the phenomenon a matter of loss of social hope; some of the London terrorists were engineers and well integrated. . . .
>
> What these youths have in common is the feeling that they belong nowhere—they are neither Marseillais, nor Arab, nor Kabyle, nor Parisian, or Roubaisien. What they experienced as a wandering life is suddenly given value by the discourse of a Bin Laden. They are no more rootless beings but soldiers of the world revolution, superior to the others. They find a place and a role. All those interviewed said it: they consume Islam like a drug, just as their elders were addicts.[38]

As an aside, one may point out that if such a diagnosis were made by a "right-wing" non-Muslim, the accusations of racism and Islamophobia would follow as day follows night.

Still, the questions remain pertinent: Why is the re-Islamization of young Muslims in Europe occurring and why is it important?

First, because without it the entire phenomenon of jihadism in Europe could not happen. Although personal alienation, criminal background, and jail experience often play key roles in attracting European-born Muslims to radical Islam, it is radical Islam that provides the motivation for and legitimization of action. Alienated individuals and criminal elements are not a majority of jihadists in Europe, nor do they become jihadists simply because they are alienated or criminals. The common element among them is not their personal background, age, education, immigration status, or ethnicity, but a common ideology—Salafism in its various versions. Indeed, most European (or American) youths, not just Muslims, may feel themselves misunderstood by their parents or society, and at some point many engage in illegal activities, but only an infinitesimal minority become terrorists. Islamism exacerbates pre-existing dysfunctional characteristics of individuals and small groups.

One must note, moreover, that re-Islamization is taking place at a time when a large number of Muslims in Europe are increasingly secular or, at least, non-practicing. In France in 1995 studies found that only a third of Muslims were practicing; a year later the Interior Ministry estimated that share at only a fifth. In Germany, the estimates of Muslims regularly attending services at mosques vary between 40 and 50 percent. In Italy, surveys suggest that only 50 percent regularly attend services, and 30 percent identify themselves as non-practicing.[39]

All these figures may seem to contradict the argument that re-Islamization is a common phenomenon—but one has to look behind the figures. The lack of regular participation at Friday prayers should be interpreted with some care. It is in part a demonstration of secularization and privatization of faith, but it is also, in many instances, a rejection of traditional and orthodox Islam, itself a step toward radicalization. It is a standard practice of Islamists, especially *Takfiris*, to avoid mosques, both because they see them as not representative of true Islam and because they may attract the attention of the authorities. Hence, a case like that of Abdelhalim Badjoudj, a French Muslim who died in a suicide attack in Iraq. His uncle, Hicham, expressed confusion over his nephew's actions since Badjoudj could hardly speak Arabic and did not identify with Islamic culture: "Abdel drank beer, he smoked hashish a lot."[40]

Ultimately, the phenomenon of re-Islamization, combined with long-standing multiculturalist tolerance of radical groups and individual jihadi ideologues, led to the creation, in many states, of a peculiar and growing "European" form of violent Islamist microculture, intrinsically related to but distinct from its versions in the Islamic world. It is a microculture that made Europe first a rest-and-recreation area for global jihad, then an exporter of it, and finally, especially since 2003, a target.

Re-Islamization, essential as it is, remains a general phenomenon, which has to be understood as a background for more specific phenomena leading to the transformation of a "regular" Muslim immigrant in London, Madrid, or Amsterdam into a jihadi. The specifics of jihadi recruitment are various and need to be examined as such. The first and foremost such additional element is criminality.

Criminality and Islamism

> "When I ask Winston [a Muslim Boys gang member] whether he believes in Islam, he prevaricates. "Sort of," he says. "I converted when I was in prison. I found it relaxing, we got better food. Now we all go to mosque together. If I refuse, they blow [shoot] me, innit. I pray twice a day: before I do crime, and after. I ask Allah for a blessing when I'm out on the street. Afterwards, I apologise to Allah for what I done."[41]

If Islamist terrorism in Europe is directly linked to re-Islamization, the latter is most evident among Muslim delinquents and criminals, since it is in jail that victimhood, rebellion against "the system," and the search for personal redemption combine most intimately. The relationship between criminality and jihadism is a pull-and-push affair—criminals may feel attracted to radical Islam for the reasons described by the Muslim Boys gangster, but jihadists also look for criminal recruits out of concerns of practicality and convenience. For committed jihadis, it is their duty to continue their activities in jail. As Abdelkrim Bensmail, one of the leaders of the *Mártires por Marruecos* jihadi cell in Almeria, Spain, stated, "The brothers in the mountains fight with their bullets and their bombs and those in the prisons of the infidels fight through the preaching of Islam with their heart, tongue and pen."[42]

Muslims make up a significant majority of illegal immigrants in Europe, a situation that places many of them outside the law to begin with. Illegal status begets illegal employment or steady unemployment, which in turn partially explains and certainly serves as an excuse for criminality. As shown above, many Muslim immigrant groups, first- and second-generation, have much higher rates of criminality than the national average of the country in which they are living. And criminality and terrorism are increasingly linked, both because of changes in Islamist terrorist structures—specifically the trend toward the self-financing of terrorist cells—and because of the growing role of prisons in the indoctrination and recruiting of Salafis.

It is an ideological tenet of Salafis that Muslims have a legitimate right to obtain the property of infidels by violence, because such property will be used for the sake of Allah. An article on the jihadi website of *Sawt al Jihad* claims this, and a preacher in a Paris mosque claimed that "Allah will destroy their [the infidels'] state and their goods will be our booty." At any rate, Salafis claim, that booty was obtained through the "crusaders'" looting of the Islamic world's resources, and thus taking it back is legitimate.[43] For criminals of all kinds, this offers a religious justification for their activities.

The link between criminality and terrorism did not begin with jihadism, nor is it limited to it. The IRA in Ireland and Britain, the ETA in Spain and France, to mention only contemporary cases, have engaged in racketeering, robbery, and smuggling on a regular basis. One difference, however, is that in those cases imprisonment was the result of criminal activities engaged in on behalf of the terrorist organization, while in the cases of Islamists there are numerous instances of criminals joining terrorist cells as recruits while incarcerated—*after* committing their crime. In many cases, particularly in France, but also in Britain and the U.S.,[44] non-Muslim criminals convert to Islam and jihadism while in prison. By contrast, in the Muslim world, with a few exceptions (al-Zarqawi comes to mind), jihadis seldom have a criminal background prior to conversion, although there are known cases, such as Al-Qaeda's "emir of Samara" in Iraq, a Saudi missing three fingers—the result of Sharia punishment for banditry.[45]

One does not need to enter the complex relationship between Islamist terrorism and ordinary crime to observe that the link between the two is qualitatively different in Europe (and to some extent the United States) from what it is in the Muslim world. While it is true that the Taliban has often, albeit sporadically, lived from opium and heroin trafficking, and that Al-Qaeda did and still does the same in some measure, that is not the norm among Islamist terrorist groups in the Muslim world. Islamist terrorists in Europe, by contrast, are increasingly, and indeed almost naturally, involved in regular criminal activities: credit-card fraud, trafficking in drugs and persons, car theft, even prostitution.

There are a number of reasons for this difference, the most important being the post-2001 weakening of the control the Al-Qaeda central core exercises over significant sources of money, and thus of its ability to fund operations worldwide. The loss of the Afghan sanctuary means that Osama bin Laden does not write checks any more. That, combined with the concomitant communications and command-and-control problems facing bin Laden, al-Zawahiri, & Co., led to the decentralization of Islamist terrorism and forced various elements of what the French call the Al-Qaeda "nebula"—whether organizations such as the GSPC and GICM or individual cells—to become financially self-sufficient. The result is that cells seek funds in crime, as demonstrated by the spectacularly diverse criminal activities of Abu Hamza's followers operating from his Finsbury Park mosque,[46] or by the importance of drug trafficking in the operations of the cell responsible for the 2004 Madrid bombings.

Farhad Khosrokhavar claims that "Islam is becoming in Europe, especially France, the religion of the repressed, what Marxism was in Europe at one time."[47] This is a dubious analogy, since Marxism was an attraction for rebellious members of the middle and even upper classes, rather than what it pretended to be—the ideology of the proletariat. Nevertheless, it remains true that "despite making up only 10 percent of the population, Muslims account for most of [France']s inmates and a growing percentage of the prison populations in many other European countries."[48] Indeed, Spanish counter-terrorist judge Baltasar Garzón noted that members of a dismantled Islamist cell who had been planning to attack objectives in Madrid were recruited by a jailed militant serving time for credit-card fraud.

At the beginning of 2006 more than 50 percent of the French prison population were Muslims. In Belgium, as of March 2007, of 10,000 persons in jail, fully 10 percent were Moroccans.[49] In Britain, according to Theodore Dalrymple, a prison doctor and journalist, the number of Muslims in prison has risen sixfold over the past 15 years. Imam Abduljalid Sajid, chairman of the National Council for the Welfare of Muslim Prisoners, told him that there are about 7,500 Muslim prisoners in the system: "about 12 percent of all people in prison in Britain, even though Muslims only account for 2 percent of the population as a whole."[50] As Dalrymple observed,

> The politico-religious fanaticism of which we are rightly afraid is thus not the product of Islam alone, but of an amalgam of Islam with sociological ideas according to which people are victims of structural injustice, of the modern equivalent of djinns [the Qoranic equivalent of fallen angels or incarnations of Evil] such as institutionalised racism.[51]

Many first- and second-generation immigrant groups have higher rates of criminality than the national average, in every country and over a broad range of time. Americans have only to look back over the last century, at the Jewish Mafia of Meyer Lansky, the Italian Mafia, and the Russian, Chinese, and Vietnamese organized-crime groups of today. In this sense Muslims in Europe are no exception. What makes them different is that their goal is not personal enrichment but a global cause—the triumph of Islam over the infidels.

Pascal Mailhos, the ex-director of the French police intelligence service, pointed out that released prisoners are a serious concern. A dozen of the individuals convicted for participation in the terrorist wave of 1995–98, once released, left France and continued their activities elsewhere. Another of the 1990s prisoners, Safé Bourada, was released from jail in February 2003. He became the leader of a terrorist cell that was apparently planning attacks throughout France at the time police arrested him and eight colleagues in September 2005.[52]

The link between prisons, criminality, and recruitment for terrorism is by no means limited to France. In Scandinavia,

It is four times more likely that a known rapist is born abroad, compared to persons born in Sweden. Resident aliens from Algeria, Libya, Morocco and Tunisia dominate the group of rape suspects. According to these statistics, almost half of all perpetrators are immigrants. In Norway and Denmark, we know that non-Western immigrants, which frequently means Muslims, are grossly overrepresented on rape statistics. In Oslo, Norway, immigrants were involved in two out of three rape charges in 2001. The numbers in Denmark were the same, and even higher in the city of Copenhagen, with three out of four rape charges. Sweden has a larger immigrant, including Muslim, population than any other country in northern Europe. The numbers there are likely to be at least as bad as with its Scandinavian neighbors. The actual number is thus probably even higher than what the authorities are reporting now, as it doesn't include second-generation immigrants. Lawyer Ann Christine Hjelm, who has investigated violent crimes in Svea high court, found that 85 percent of the convicted rapists were born on foreign soil or to foreign parents.[53]

Figures quoted by the *New York Times* suggest that 26 percent of inmates in Swedish prisons are foreigners, a figure that hides the fact that even among the other 74 percent there are many naturalized individuals—which leads the newspaper to conclude that "the association of crime and immigration is not a figment of the Swedish imagination. The left-leaning tabloid *Aftonbladet* revealed that a number of Muslim extremist groups were recruiting in prisons. The largest is a group called Asir, perhaps named for the Saudi province from which four of the Sept. 11 hijackers came."[54]

The role of prisons as Islamist recruiting and indoctrination centers is reinforced by the lack of alternatives. France's prison population is served by only 66 imams (of whom only 40 were salaried). That compares with 505 Catholic chaplains (180 salaried), 266 Protestant and five Orthodox chaplains, 66 rabbis, and two Buddhists.[55] Missoum Abdelmadjid Chaoui, the imam responsible for the Nanterre prison, says there are only eight Muslim chaplains for the nearly 20,000 Muslim inmates in the Paris region alone. He handles nine of the area's 25 prisons himself, but works as a chaplain only part time. According to a report from *Renseignements Généraux* (RG—the French domestic intelligence service), 68 of France's 188 prisons are infiltrated by Islamist recruiters. Ten percent of Islamists in French prisons are Salafis, but many more belong to *Tabligh*, a movement that, as we have seen, officially denies supporting violence but is often associated with it.[56]

Similarly, Imam Abduljalid Sajid, chairman of the National Council for the Welfare of Muslim Prisoners in Britain, has long been aware of the problem of radicalization of Muslim prison inmates, and squarely blames the authorities: "Has the Home Office made any improvements? Yes . . . the Government has started bringing equality. There are 20 or 21 full-time imams now—but there are 179 prisons. The spiritual needs of Muslims are still not being met." Furthermore, he complained, the Home Office was refusing to pay imams in the same way as Anglican padres, which meant leaving the job to a bunch of volunteers of uncertain background and qualifications. So most prisons are still visited by 130-odd freelance spiritual leaders. "Most have their own mosques, and that means they can't go to the prisons on Fridays. They can't read one to one with the prisoners and can't offer the same solace."[57] Although "solace" isn't always what they want to offer: "Three imams working in Feltham [and] Aylesbury and visiting eight other prisons in south-east England were suspended in the wake of 9/11 for 'unprofessional behavior,' making overtly anti-US statements and spreading the views of the extremist cleric Abu Hamza."[58]

Jihadi recruiting in prisons often goes hand in hand with conversion (of nominal Muslims as well as of nominal Christians), for reasons well described by Khosrokhavar:

> Any prison time means a break propitious to spirituality. But Islam presents a characteristic that makes it especially attractive to inmates searching for dignity: it is the religion of the oppressed. Christianity, on the other hand, is the religion of former colonizers. Moreover, to become a Muslim is not difficult—it is enough to pronounce a sentence in front of witnesses, proclaiming the uniqueness of God and the truth that Mohammed is his prophet.[59]

Of course, many Muslim prisoners refuse the appeal of radicals—often because, as "Habib," a Tunisian quoted by Khosrokhavar,[60] stated, the jihadis "sell hashish in the suburbs and then advocate war against other religions." Even so, if the success ratio of the Islamists' conversion attempts is 20 out of 30, as French sources suggest, the phenomenon is significant.[61]

The French government is trying to address the problem by recruiting moderate imams to counter Salafi penetration in prisons. However, not until 2005 was the first Muslim national chaplain appointed by the CFCM—only to have the appointment die as a result of the usual internal conflicts in that organization. Nevertheless, the government persisted in trying the same approach, asking the CFCM to appoint 10 regional chaplains (nine for continental France, one for the Indian Ocean department of La Réunion). Just in case the Council proves ineffective again, the traditional policy of controlling radicalism through a special bureau of prison intelligence continues.[62]

One of the main characteristics of male converts is that most of them have a checkered past, often including criminal convictions, or come from dysfunctional families.[63] Upon release from prison, many Muslims are already isolated by social rejection on the part of family, mosque, and friends, and thus have passed the first necessary step toward recruitment to jihadism.[64]

"Atef el O," for instance (described more fully below), was a 22-year-old bachelor Tunisian immigrant from Aubervilliers, stuck in small jobs like pizza delivery and involved with the gangs of Seine-Saint-Denis; he ended up in Iraq in 2005. The 21-year-old Youssef, a Catholic convert from Normandy, born Antoine, was a school dropout with a military brother; he went to Yemen "to learn Arabic" and ended up in Iraq.[65] Both were petty criminals, brought into Salafism through their participation in street gangs. Youssef was influenced by his older brother, who converted before him but did not get involved in gangs—probably because of his military background and the discipline that comes with it. In both instances, it was the close connection between criminality and Islamism that led to Salafism and dedication to fighting the Americans in Iraq.

This is a common pattern among Europe's Islamists. As we have seen, the group responsible for the Madrid bombings of March 2004 included drug dealers and individuals involved in credit-card fraud. At least two of the Islamists sentenced in Germany in October 2005 for preparing attacks against the Jewish community were involved in drug dealing. Khaled Kelkal, the Islamist thug in France, is the archetypal case: a petty criminal involved in jihad, killed by police, transformed into a martyr by re-Islamized youths and into a victim of capitalist oppression by the radical Left.

The Moroccan GICM and *Salafia Islamia* have long had an advantage over their Algerian (GIA or GSPC) counterparts because they had access to Morocco's enormous hashish and heroin harvests,[66] and thus greater ability to finance their operations. Thus, the brothers Rachid and Mohammed Oulad Akcha—two of the plotters of the 2004 Madrid bombings and among those who blew themselves up in the cell's hideout in the suburb of Leganés rather than be taken prisoner—were also heroin traffickers.[67] Data from Spain, France, the Netherlands, and Belgium suggest that drugs are the main source of funds for Islamist groups throughout Europe, more than *"ganaem"* (booty) in the form of credit-card fraud, car theft, and robbery. It is interesting in this regard that most Moroccans arrested for terrorism in Europe come from the Tangiers or Tetuán areas—the very ones where most of Morocco's heroin is produced and whose residents, on the basis of a 1956 arrangement with Spain, do not need visas to enter the enclaves of Ceuta and Melilla.[68]

It is difficult, for obvious reasons, to collect detailed information on Salafist recruitment in European prisons. While bibliographies on the topic are limited,[69] we can nonetheless say confidently that the phenomenon is quite widespread in France, Italy, the Netherlands, and Spain.

In the Netherlands, the case of two members of the radical Islamist Hofstad Group—to which the killer of Theo van Gogh belonged—is instructive. Born in 1979, Jamal Eddin Barkour is a Dutch Moroccan criminal, a frequent offender who had spent five years in prison at the time of his release in March 2005. In the final months of his prison term, he met and recruited—or converted—another Dutch Moroccan, Bilal Lamrani, former pizza deliverer. Lamrani was clearly receptive: He was already in prison for an Internet posting offering a reward for the killing of the anti-Islamist member of Parliament Geert Wilders.

The incidence of jihadism in prisons is particularly acute in France. Pascal Mailhos noted in 2005 that "It is there, in prison, that a minority of radical Islamist terrorists (about 100) hook up with petty criminals who find their way back to religion under its most radical form." Other police officials have noted that among Muslim inmates "we observe a steady increase of Salafism, with two particularities: a strong rejection of Western values and the legitimacy of violence."[70] In fact, in 2005 the RG estimated the number of Salafis in French jails at 173. Police also noted that quite often the *caids* (crime bosses) are active in the radicalization of inmates, since claiming allegiance to jihad provides more prestige than being a drug seller or having beaten an old lady. The fact that most Muslims in French jails are young first- or second-generation Maghrebis, and under-educated, makes the appeal of radical Islam all the more potent, as does the extensive presence of *Tabligh* in prisons.[71]

While the Islamist recruitment problem in French jails is especially well known—mostly because of the work of Khosrokhavar, but also because the numbers involved are so much larger than elsewhere—it is far from unique. In Britain (England and Wales), more than 5,000 Muslims make up some 8 percent of the inmate population—almost four times their share of the total population. They include the largest number of Islamist terrorists in Europe—and they are not segregated from the general prison population, with the result that "The Prison Officers Association believes recruitment to extreme causes is going on, but is rendered helpless to stop it by circumstances ranging from language barriers to bureaucracy."[72] In Italy, Muslims are some 14 percent of the prison population (but only 1 percent of the country's population), and most of them are foreign-born.[73]

In Spain, a dozen Algerian and Moroccan inmates in the Topas jail in Salamanca formed an entire jihadist network, *Mártires por Marruecos*, under the leadership of Abderrahmane Tahiri, a.k.a. Mohammed Achraf, an Algerian GIA and *Takfir-wal-Hijra* member, jailed for credit-card fraud. Achraf's cells eventually recruited in 10 Spanish prisons; released members maintained contact with those still in jail. Members of the cells have ties with the group behind the 1993 World Trade Center bombing and were planning an attack on the *Audiencia Nacional* (the second-highest Spanish court) when they were arrested in the fall of 2004. Achraf managed to set up new cells every time he was arrested, often among GIA inmates.[74]

Perhaps the first major example of a thug becoming a jihadist—and a *cause célèbre*—was in France, mostly because of French intellectuals' genius for making a fundamental "issue" of everything and getting European and American academia to pay attention to it; and also because it signaled what later became a pattern: the *de facto* alliance between Islamism and the "progressive" Left. The case centered on Khaled Kelkal (see Chapter 6), whose terrorist misadventures and death led to an outburst of critical analysis of French society's treatment of young Muslims. Actually, the truth was much more banal: A petty thug saw the "light of Islam," which gave him a "higher" rationale. He moved from small-time criminality to jihad—the same trajectory later followed by bigger names like Samir Azzouz and Abdelhalim Badjoudj.

A number of other cases confirm the pattern—for instance Ahmed Ressam, the Algerian-French "millennium bomber." He was captured at the U.S.-Canadian border in December of 1999 on his way to California, intending to blow up Los Angeles International Airport on New Year's Eve. Born in 1967, by age 20 Ressam was a village troublemaker, described as "bitter" and "paranoid" about Algeria's military regime. In 1992, he was arrested and jailed for gun running. Upon release, he made his way to France and hooked up with GIA terrorists and associated gangsters raising money by bank robberies and hijackings for the holy war back home.[75] He ended up in Canada, taking advantage of the lax Canadian immigration rules and lack of counter-terrorism laws—and of the established GIA jihadi cells in Montreal and Toronto.[76]

Even more important jihadi figures in Europe have had some brushes with the law—a helpful experience later, when they recruited petty delinquents for important operations. Thus Mohammed Bouyeri, the murderer of Theo van Gogh and a central figure of the Hofstad terrorist group:

> Farid Zaari, spokesman for El Tawheed, a mosque that Bouyeri attended for a brief period and one of Amsterdam's most fundamentalist, said that young people like Bouyeri are vulnerable to recruitment by radicals. "He is not accepted by society, and he is not accepted at home, either," said Zaari, who also was born in Morocco. "Everyone is pushing him, and no one understands him. And he becomes an easy target for the extremist who uses religion as bait." The man who early in 2002 preached mutual tolerance and respect was by this fall [2004] comparing the Dutch police to the Nazis and saying that the American troops deserved to be beheaded. While studying accounting at a polytechnic, Bouyeri spent a lot of time hanging out on the streets of Slotervaart. At some point, friends told the *NRC Handelsblad* newspaper, he was arrested and imprisoned for seven months for a crime related to violence. The Dutch Justice Department is searching for a record of the conviction, which may have been expunged under the Netherlands' strict privacy rules, a spokesman said. [After his time in prison], he returned to school to study social work and later work at the Eigenwijks community center.[77]

> At an early age he was known to the police as a member of a group of Moroccan *problem jongeren* (problem youth). His sudden radicalization happened in the fall of 2003, when his mother died, his father re-married and the war in Iraq was continuing. Bouyeri grew a beard and began to wear a *djellaba*. He visited the El Tawheed mosque and came in contact with other radical Muslims, among whom the terrorism suspect Samir Azzouz.[78]

Samir Azzouz, born in the Netherlands in 1986 of Moroccan descent, shared a criminal background with Bouyeri:

> [He] grew up in a working class neighborhood and attended soccer games as a child. He converted to radical Islam at the age of 15 and attempted to join the jihad in Chechnya at 16. A year later, he purchased a gun, ammunition, silencer, night vision equipment and materials that could be used to make a bomb.... [I]n 2002 the Dutch investigators noticed that several Muslims with known or suspected links to jihad groups, including Samir, were meeting informally in homes and prayer rooms in Rotterdam, Amsterdam, and The Hague. They became increasingly concerned with the group, particularly because it brought together two categories of people who have not previously cooperated in the Netherlands: petty criminals and men such as Samir, whose arrest records for border or visa infractions were related to their support for the Islamist *jihad*. In October of 2003, police rounded up several members of the group, but, with little evidence, let them free. . . . According to the police, Samir's actions fit the pattern: In April 2004, he was alleged to have made off with about $400 by helping rob a grocery store where he worked.[79]

The list of accused, suspected, or condemned jihadis in Europe directly linked to ordinary crime is long and growing.[80] But at least as important is recruitment among Muslim youth gangs. The step from gang membership to terrorist cell is small and easy.

ISLAMISM AND GANGS

The issue of Islamist recruitment among gangs is related to the more general one of criminality and jihadism, with one significant addition: Gang members, once recruited, bring a ready-made group identity lacking in the case of individual criminals. Peter Varghese, head of Australia's Office of National Assessments, was referring to his country, but his observation applies to Europe as well:

> One thing we frequently see in the trajectory of terrorists is
> a conversion experience that occurs within a small, tight-knit
> group. The dynamics of such groups tend to reinforce personal
> conviction, especially among individuals whose other social
> networks have frayed or can't match the intensity of bonds
> forged in what is for them an existential struggle.[81]

It is not surprising, therefore, that the abundant youth gangs
of Europe's cities offer a major potential pool of recruits to jihad—although that potential has not yet been fully exploited.
Thus the riots in France at the end of 2005 were not "Muslim riots" in any meaningful sense, although most of the participants
were of Muslim background. Mohammed Rezzoug, a Muslim
caretaker at the municipal gymnasium and soccer field in Le
Blanc-Mesnil, a suburb of Paris hard hit by the disturbances,
claimed: "It's not a political revolution or a Muslim revolution.
There's a lot of rage. Through this burning, they're saying, 'I exist, I'm here'."[82] Turning René Descartes's dictum "Cogito, ergo
sum" (I think, therefore I am) into They burn, therefore they
are, Rezzoug well described the aimless and anarchic nature
of the riots. But Salafist recruiters can see the potential in the
numbers of rioters, ripe for the plucking.

Jean-Louis Debré, then Speaker of the National Assembly
and mayor of riot-torn Evreux, seemed to agree with Rezzoug,
claiming that "It is a true episode of urban guerrilla."[83] However,
as "Abdelkarim," one of the rioters in Aulnay-sous-Bois, put it,
"From my window I can see the Eiffel Tower. . . . But Paris is another world. This is Baghdad." Since street gangs in France's banlieues do regularly talk about "intifada," swear on the Quran, and
salute one another with Inshallah despite knowing no Arabic,[84]
and since one of "Abdelkarim's" buddies showed the media a
film of a Chechen guerrilla cutting off the head of a Russian
soldier, it is no surprise that a growing number of alienated
youths are ready for the most radical Islamist messages.

The other key ingredient—the "victimization" of Islam—is already there too. Thus, "Murad," a Muslim leader in Aulnay: "Islam has been insulted and nobody has yet asked forgiveness. . . . If there had been a tear gas canister in a church or synagogue, Sarkozy would have gone there to apologize."[85]

For the terrorist recruiter, uncontrolled rioting youths, just like individuals with criminal backgrounds, offer a number of advantages. To begin with, criminals and gang members have already taken a major step toward breaking ties with the surrounding community, family included. It is in this context that Belgian analyst Rik Coolsaet's accurate observation should be interpreted:

> In a vicious circle of frustration and dissatisfaction, youngsters from migrant communities choose the easiest way out and pose themselves as victims, projecting onto society whatever ill-fortune they encounter. They form the hard core of radical groups of Salafist Islamists and rapidly radicalise into self-declared local vanguards of the worldwide jihad, sometimes under the influence of a charismatic individual. By seemingly acting in community with a worldwide liberation struggle they develop a sense of self-esteem. This feeling of commonality with jihadi theatres of war is the ultra radicalised and polarising version of a more general sense of increased solidarity among Muslims worldwide, as revealed by surveys by the Pew Global Attitudes Project and Zogby International.[86]

Once again, if alienation is the push factor, active efforts by jihadi groups serve as the pull element.

The Jihadi Pool

Attempts to estimate the pool of potential jihadists in Europe are no more accurate than attempts to assess precisely the number of Muslims. At best they provide an order of magnitude whose reliability varies from country to country.

Of the about 1.6 million Muslims living in Britain, counter-terrorist sources have estimated that up to 0.5 percent—about 8,000—support Al-Qaeda's aims and have links to Islamist extremists. According to another report, "MI5 keeps very close tabs on more than 1,000 extremists; 14,000 British Muslims are considered potential terrorist threats."[87]

The French intelligence directorate uses a formula to assess the number of fundamentalists: In a given Muslim population, an average of 5 percent are fundamentalists, and about 3 percent of those could be considered dangerous. For a Muslim population of perhaps 6 million, that means some 300,000 fundamentalists, of whom 9,000 are potentially dangerous.[88]

On a regional level, on the other hand, intelligence agencies believe that at least 3,000 Europe-based Muslims have already been radicalized to the extent of participation in planning or execution of attacks. In many cases they are returnees from war zones like Afghanistan, Bosnia, Chechnya, or Iraq who form Al-Qaeda nuclei. All this is in addition to the large numbers of "refugee" members or sympathizers of North African or Middle Eastern terrorist groups already tied to Al-Qaeda—groups like the GIA, GSPC, GICM, Hamas, *Hizbollah*, etc. Terrorism experts largely concur that the numbers of hard-core jihad sympathizers are significant in almost all Western European countries. The range goes from about 300 in Germany to an estimated 1,000 in Great Britain.[89] Aside from Finland, Luxembourg, and Greece, there is at least some known Islamist terrorist presence in each and every European country—including non-EU members Norway and Switzerland.

We know that there is a well-established, multi-layered, and deeply rooted Salafist terrorist infrastructure, created over the span of two decades and extremely hard to eradicate, even in those countries (France, the Netherlands, Denmark) that finally have realized the magnitude of the problem and acted on it. That says little about other countries—notably Sweden and Norway—where even official political (as distinct from professional intelligence) recognition of a problem is basically nonexistent.

The main human components of the jihadi universe in Europe are ready-made immigrant radicals and local recruits. The two groups are not always easy to separate clearly, especially within families, where European-born members may be recruited by relatives coming from abroad. Almost every known terrorist cell found in Europe since the early 1990s includes both types, with the imported radicals usually in leading roles. The question then is how this fundamentalist subculture is formed, and by whom.

RECRUITMENT

If one assumes that jihadis in Europe go through stages of radicalization, beginning with joining an established aboveground organization and then "graduating" into fundamentalism and violence, one must not separate too sharply the Muslim Brotherhood, for example, and related groups, like *Tabligh* and *Hizb-ut-Tahrir*, from active jihadi cells. In fact, despite the conflicts between those groups, they are parts of a natural progression—whether they admit it or not.

That is well demonstrated by a 2002 plan for the penetration of the society at all levels, but especially among elites and university students, prepared for a network of some sixty cadres of the Movement of Muslim Students in France (EMF), which is linked with the UOIF. *L'Express* considered this "a fascinating insight into the strategies of Islamists."[90] The plan was detailed in a "lobbying manual," disguised as a pirated CD of Italian supermodel, songwriter, and singer Carla Bruni (now the first lady of France).

The network, codenamed "Veni, vidi, vici" (Caesar's famous words—"I came, I saw, I conquered"), with the text encrypted around a volume of Émile Zola, involved young university-educated Islamists from Lille, Strasbourg, Lyon, Marseille, Montpellier, Toulouse and Bordeaux. The group boasted about having succeeded in getting 39 sympathizers elected on various university councils and even a dozen UMP (the main governing party) deputies. While still admitting to being behind the secular Muslims "better established than us," the Islamists explain their relative success as owing to Muslim disillusionment with the Socialist politicians whose local policies led to ghettos and an end of the social mixing of the 1980s. As a model of successful political influence in the name of a religious community, to be learned from, they mention the Representative Council of Jewish Institutions in France and the Union of Jewish Students in France (UEJF). By contrast, the network avoids known extremists, such as the anti-Semitic *Parti musulman de France* of Mohammed Latrèche.

The means to be employed is re-Islamization, because, "by going back to orthodox religious practice, therefore re-Islamizing the neighborhoods, especially among the young, we would increase our political weight . . . with the additional advantage of marginalizing the secular [Muslims]."

The motifs of the propaganda would be "secular discrimination"—tolerance of the *kippa* but not the *hijab*, description of the state as a "racist oppressor," etc. For finances, the small shop owners of the Muslim neighborhoods, "who could not afford to appear less pious than their customers," are a major source, using the *zakat* as the instrument, but also "for certain activities we could put in place double accounts, obviously in exchange for a percentage of the difference."

In recruitment, priority is given to the universities, taking advantage of the weakening of traditional leftist student organizations. One way to do this is to force those organizations to condemn Jewish student groups for their pro-Zionist positions, which are unpopular among leftist students. In fact, the network notes, "With every accusation of anti-semitism we reinforce our non-Muslim electorate [among student organizations]. The abusive use of the accusation of anti-semitism banalizes it and makes it less condemnable among non-Muslims."[91]

While UOIF is active in French universities, the more radical *Hizb ut-Tahrir* is even more active in England. Here is an accurate description of its methods, from a hostile Islamic website:

> Hizb-ut-Tahrir is found in universities either in the Islamic societies, or under other "societies" such as Millennium Society, 1924 Society, Pakistan Society (sometimes). They normally create other societies after Islamic societies have banned them from preaching their deviant beliefs openly. On the Internet, they are found at their own web site or at www. muslimstudent.org.uk, where they take care not to mention Hizb-ut-Tahrir too much in order to trap Muslim students with their deviant beliefs under the pretext of an innocent Muslim student resource site.[92]

What activities does this sect engage in at universities?

> Study-circles (on Khilaafah and politics), Tafseer classes (on Khilaafah and politics), talks and lectures (on Khilaafah and politics), Jumuah khutbahs [Friday sermons] (on Khilaafah and politics) and small iftaar [evening meal] gatherings in Ramadan (on Khilaafah and politics). They also attend lectures and study-circles by other Muslims on other topics and ask questions about Khilaafah and politics at the end. In addition, they specialise in getting Islamic Society prayer rooms closed down and getting Muslim students expelled from University, e.g. Brunel, Imperial, Kingston and UCL, where, to this day, the Muslims have no prayer room.

What methods does *Hizb ut-Tahrir* use to recruit members at universities?

> Being very nice to new students, visiting them in Halls of Residences, accompanying them home on public transport

or offering lifts to them, offering to help them out, inviting them to small dinner gatherings. All these visits and informal "social" meetings are accompanied by discussions on Khilaafah, social, economic and political problems of the Muslims, and politics because they rarely speak about anything else. They also stress the point that their methods are based on "clear" evidences. However, the reality is that everything tends to be "clear" except their Aqeedah [creed], which they will try to refrain from discussing about, saying it is not a priority. If you are in doubt, you can always ask them if they work with Hizb-ut-Tahrir, or, if they will not give you a straight answer, ask other Muslims in the Islamic Society. Such interaction is only established for the sake of "Da'wah" and for working towards the re-establishment of Khilaafah. If they find that you are not responsive, the extreme care and attention that they have hitherto bestowed is immediately abandoned, and no further time and energy is wasted upon you.

Nor is the link between Islamism and universities limited to France and Britain. Seventy percent of the members of Spanish Islamist networks have some university education, the majority in technical fields, while in their countries of origin the proportion of university graduates barely reaches 5 percent.[93]

In British universities, according to Professor Anthony Glees—the author, with Chris Pope of the Royal United Services Institute, of a report on Islamist activities on 24 British campuses[94]—Islamist activities are "a serious threat. We have discovered a number of universities where subversive activities are taking place, often without the knowledge of the university authorities."[95] Indeed, the Glees–Pope study states that the Islamist groups *Hizb ut-Tahrir* and *Al-Muhajiroun*—which advocate a world caliphate, demand that Britain adopt the Sharia, and express a violent hatred for the West and Jews, and which are subject to a "no-platform policy" by the National Union of Students—are active on many campuses, often operating under different names. For instance, both *Hizb ut-Tahrir* and

Al-Muhajiroun have repeatedly tried to gain student converts at the University of East Anglia.[96] Other universities with Islamist activities mentioned in the study are Birmingham, Brunel, City, Coventry, Derby, Dundee, Durham, the Imperial College, Kingston, Leeds, Leicester, the London School of Economics, Luton, Manchester, Manchester Metropolitan, Newcastle, Nottingham, Reading, the School of Oriental and African Studies, South Bank, Sunderland, Swansea, and Wolverhampton.[97]

HuT, the most active Islamist organization on British campuses, was found to have been "recruiting under the name 'Stop Islamophobia' at University College London (UCL), the School of African and Oriental Studies [sic], Luton University and other institutions. . . . The National Union of Students has called for banning the group from campuses, accusing the party of 'supporting terrorism and publishing material that incites racial hatred'."[98]

While the Glees–Pope study was often abused in the media, accusations of "McCarthyism" being among the mildest, the Blair government, after the 2005 London bombings, did take the problem seriously and asked university authorities to watch for extremist activities. Moreover, Ed Husain's *The Islamist*—the confessions of one of HuT's best recruiters and propagandists, published in 2007—confirmed all of Glees–Pope's warnings and observations.

Recruitment efforts by Islamists among the young are a reaction to and reinforcement of the re-Islamization process described above. Indeed, European intelligence sources agree that would-be jihadists in Europe are getting younger. According to a Reuters report,

> "Radical Muslims are becoming younger," said a Dutch security source, who said some youths were being drawn into militant circles as early as the age of 14. "We think these young people

are not feeling at home here in this country. They are outsiders in our society, in our culture, and they also do not feel at home with their parents, who are guest workers from the 1960s and 1970s. . . . Radical Islam gives them a perspective they can be important, they can have a role, and gives them a feeling they can have a stronger identity."

In France, intelligence chief Pierre de Bousquet told *Le Monde* . . . that alongside experienced militants, there was a new danger from "boys with no combat experience" who were nevertheless radicalised and ready to take part in jihad, or holy war. The French jihadist is more unpolished, younger, but more radicalized and committed than a few years ago. The ease with which these young people can be brainwashed to go and serve as cannon fodder is worrying.[99]

How the process of recruitment operates is clearly illustrated by the case of the "shoe bomber," Richard Reid:

The Brixton Mosque, where 60 per cent of the 500-strong community are black converts, has a reputation for helping ex-offenders readjust to life outside. Richard Reid made progress at first. He renamed himself Abdel Rahim and learned Arabic. But, says Abdul Haqq Baker, the head of the mosque, he was "tempted away" by "individuals who set up a few years ago away from the mosque"—extremists who worked on "weak characters." Baker has also told CNN that Reid overlapped at Brixton Mosque, in 1998–99, with Zacarias Moussaoui, the Frenchman of Moroccan origin who has been charged in the US with conspiracy over the September 11 attacks. Moussaoui was expelled from Brixton Mosque for his extreme views and attempts to impose them on younger members. Reid also left. Baker calls Reid "very, very impressionable."[100]

The link between family ties and terrorist recruitment is well known. This is not only because family proximity facilitates frequent contacts and thus opportunities for indoctrination, but also because, from a purely operational standpoint, a cell centered on a family nucleus is difficult, if not impossible, to penetrate. While this phenomenon is far from unique to Islamist jihadis, it is true that, even in Europe, family plays a far more important role in Muslim communities than in any contemporary Western society.

The role of the family in recruitment is best demonstrated by cases like that of the Benchellalis in France.[101] Organized by the father, Chellali Benchellali, a self-proclaimed imam from Minguettes, near Lyon, the jihadist cell included the entire family and reached four continents. Chellali, born in southern Algeria in 1944, arrived in France in 1967, with no education or skills. He worked, occasionally, as a cleaning man or on construction sites. As the Soviet empire crumbled, he became obsessed with the Chechen issue. He was also involved in Bosnia, and actually tried to go there in 1993—only to be arrested by the Croatians and sent back to France. There he created a "charity" called *Ouverture* to collect funds for the Chechens, and, in a small room in the Lyon suburb of Vénissieux, he set up the Abou Bakr mosque with himself as the self-proclaimed imam. Chellali Benchellali was known for his anti-Bush, anti-Putin, and anti-Israel radical sermons. He made his living by selling tours to Mecca—in addition to his welfare payments.

His oldest son, Menad, was arrested in 2002 in connection with the "Chechen network"—a group of Maghrebi origin acting in support of Chechnya. In June 2006 he was sentenced to 10 years in jail for his role in the network's plot to blow up the Eiffel Tower, a supermarket, and other locations in Paris. Although Menad had never held a job, he was known as a frequent traveler to Georgia, Sudan, Mauritania, and England. His money came from armed robberies and fraud, and his ideological and organizational links were with the Algerian GIA.[102] He recruited his youngest brother, Mourad, a poor student rejected by the girl he wanted to marry; Mourad was later captured in Afghanistan and became a longtime resident in Guantanamo.

Upon his return to France he found time to write a pathetically self-serving version of his adventures for the *New York Times*.[103] The middle brother, Hafed, is a computer programmer. A sister was briefly expelled from high school for wearing the *hijab*, which was banned under French law. In January 2004 Chellali, Hafed, and Chellali's wife, Hafsa, were detained under suspicion of providing logistical support to Islamists, tried, and given prison terms equal to time under detention.

An interesting thing about the Benchellali case is that it combined two key elements of recruitment: the family and the mosque. Indeed, the radical mosque is perhaps the most frequent first step toward a jihadi career. Although a distinction should be made between a "real" mosque and improvised facilities, ranging from garages to private apartments, all prayer locations are a favored recruiting environment, at least in the initial stages.

In some instances, recruiters simply visit established mosques looking for possible recruits, as Basel Ghalyoun, a young Syrian involved in the March 2004 Madrid bombings, was known to do. In most cases, however, interested youths frequent mosques with an established reputation of radicalism. For a long time the most significant such mosques were in England, but there are others, some large, some "underground," in all European countries.

A case study:

Adda'Wa mosque, Rue de Tanger, was a makeshift adjunct to a hostel for North Africans in the Buttes-Chaumont area of Paris. The self-proclaimed imam there was Farid Benyettou, a 25-year-old French-born Algerian. The third of four siblings, from age 16 he lived with Youssef Zemmouri, his brother-in-law, a member of the Algerian GSPC. Under Zemmouri's influence and that of other Algerian Islamists, Farid left school and dedicated himself to the study of theology. Zemmouri was arrested and jailed in 1998 for involvement in the planning of attacks during the soccer World Cup in France. By then young Farid was ready to continue his mentor's work—although discreetly enough to avoid converting his younger brother, Mohammed, who, according to a friend, "smokes, drinks, goes to nightclubs, chases girls, like everybody else."

First at the mosque and later in his apartment, Farid was busy recruiting younger men from the neighborhood and preparing to join the jihad in Iraq—establishing what the French press calls the Buttes-Chaumont group. One of his followers was the orphan son of Algerian immigrants, Cherif Kouachi, who, until meeting Benyettou at age 20, "drank, smoked pot, slept with his girlfriend and delivered pizzas for a living," according to his lawyer, who speculated, "I think in Mr. Benyettou he found someone who could tell him what to do, like an older brother." Kouachi and Thamer Bouchnak, a 22-year-old Tunisian who admires Benyettou because "he knows the Quran from the tip of his fingers," were arrested, together with their leader, while on their way to Iraq; another group member, "Peter," was arrested and sentenced to 15 years by an Iraqi court.

Three of Farid's followers, all age 19, died in Iraq between July and October 2004: Redouane el-Hakim, killed in a U.S. air attack at Fallujah; Tarek Ouinis, shot by an American patrol; and Abdelhalim Badjoudj, dead in a suicide bombing. Redouane el-Hakim's brother, 21-year-old Boubakeur el-Hakim, was arrested by the Syrians on the Iraq border in August 2004.[104]

It thus appears that the Buttes-Chaumont group was, in part, self-recruited, a pattern also seen elsewhere. In Denmark, young Islamists, known as "little imams" or "little ayatollahs," add to the efforts of known radical imams like those behind the Danish cartoon affair. In the Netherlands, an indoctrinated young man often expands the circle independently of his original mentor/recruiter.

The migration of radicals to war zones is well known to the French authorities, as are some of its causes:

> Our suburban areas have become recruitment fishponds, from which hundreds of young French Muslims have already left to Bosnia, Chechnya, Afghanistan or Iraq to fight side by side with mujahideen and receive a terrorist training. These departures have been as much motivated by the specific sociological context of the immigrated third generation—to which a transit through jihadist camps seems to give a meaning to existence—as by the situation in the Middle East, where the Israeli-Palestinian conflict and Iraq occupation reinforce the radical Islamists' victimization.[105]

And then there is the Internet, whose role in the recruitment and indoctrination of young Muslims in Europe has been well studied and perhaps even exaggerated.[106] All this seems to confirm the description of the young jihadists of Europe as "*fanatiques autodidacts*," or "self-taught fanatics"—and that is indeed part of the story. As a French analyst observed, describing those *bébés bin Laden,*

> Many of these youth are content to become radical Islamists by improving their knowledge of Arabic and Islam. Others chose the path of jihad leaving for Iraq. Finally, others want to strike at the heart of their country. . . . It is with their own savings that the youths of Buttes-Chaumont paid their plane tickets to Damascus in order to go to Iraq, or those of Denmark bought components for explosives. In the Netherlands an Islamist student was discovered while preparing bombs from instructions found on the Internet.[107]

While all of this is true, one has to be careful, because ultimately both common sense and actual information strongly suggest that while the Internet, like the Islamist media so many

Muslims in Europe follow, may push identity-seeking, alien-ated youths toward Islamism, it is not sufficient to push them into action. Most importantly, it does not offer the logistics and training for action. Most jihadis in Europe did not take the path to violence via the Internet—they had an Islamist mentor, a real person, usually older, immigrant, and, at least apparently, versed in the Quranic texts.

Thus the importance of looking beyond Mohammed Bouyeri and the Hofstad Group and into the role of Syrian imam Redouan al-Issar, beyond Buttes-Chaumont and into the GSPC, beyond the London bombers of 7/7 and into *Lashkar-e-Toiba* (the "Army of the Pure" in Afghanistan/Pakistan).[108]

JIHADIS—"HOMEGROWN" OR IMPORTS?

Following the London bombings of July 2005, the British media were full of headlines decrying the fact that the terrorists were "homegrown," or that "our" boys could do such a thing. The BBC said the London bombers "were all British," and Sir Iqbal Sacranie of the Muslim Council of Britain talked about "our youth."[109] Even leaving aside the fact that the participants in the failed attempts of July 21 were all recent immigrants from the Horn of Africa, the description seemed questionable. From the statements of the leaders of the deadly July 7 attack, Mohammad Sidique Khan and Shehzad Tanweer, it should have been clear that they did not consider Britain their "home" or see themselves as its citizens. Nor were they radicalized (and trained) in the United Kingdom, but in Pakistan. In the videos released *post mortem*, both referred to "your government" and "your country" when addressing the British, and to "our peo-ple" or "our mothers" when mentioning Palestinians or Iraqis.

That said, many of the circumstances leading to such extreme separation from and hatred for the environment the terrorists grew up in are specifically European. The pertinent question, however, is not whether a particular Islamist terrorist made in Europe was indeed manufactured only there and out of all European parts, or whether he was largely made of imports. While at different times and in different places the balance between the local and the imported influences has changed, a jihadi, by definition, does not see himself as "of Europe," let alone "homegrown." In his mind he is part of and acts in defense of the *ummah*, against all things European.

While there is no single or universal pattern of recruitment or motivation, some occur more frequently than others. One constant remains the guru, the religious legitimizer who manipulates these youths and pushes them over.[110] A charismatic individual was, is now, and will remain necessary to transform numbers of alienated Muslim youths into soldiers of jihad. The important word here is "numbers," because jihadis in Europe seldom, if ever, act alone. It is within groups, organized along neighborhood lines or within specific establishments, that recruitment occurs most often. When Fadi Kassem, a Lebanese in Denmark, observed that the country's young, second-generation Muslim rioters of February 2008 "live in gangs, suffer in gangs, hunt in gangs," he could have also been describing life in jihadi cells.[111]

Thus, at least 10 of the 19 suspects in the 2006 plot to blow up transatlantic flights from England lived in the East London borough of Waltham Forest, an area long targeted by *Al-Muhajiroun* and by HuT, both of which were known to have leafleted the area heavily. Moreover several of the suspects were members of a local gym, Al Badr, which was owned by the brother of community leader Imtiaz Qadir.[112] It was also a gym, the one run by Mohammad Sidique Khan, that formed the nucleus of the July 7 London cell. In a similar pattern, Mohammed Hamid, the self-styled "Osama bin London," arrested in February 2008 as the head of a Pakistani-linked jihadi cell in England, was a volunteer youth worker and managed a Sunday football team. One of his cell members, Atilla Ahmet, was a soccer coach as well—the perfect disguise for a recruiter.[113]

Sometimes the local environment is decisive in combining the necessary elements for the formation of a jihadi cell. A perfect case is the situation in the Spanish North African enclaves of Ceuta and Melilla. The jihadi group found there in 2006 was formed during meetings in the small Darkawia mosque, dominated by a radical imam, and located in the Príncipe Alfonso district—a disadvantaged area of Ceuta, with high rates of unemployment and delinquency, where around 12,000 Muslims live. Up until the raids of December 12, 2006, the area was considered practically a no-go zone by local police. In the months preceding the operation, the local police had given up patrolling the neighborhood because of various threats, especially from ambushes by organized delinquent groups.[114] Here, then, we have the necessary ingredients for jihadi recruitment concentrated in a small area: criminality, alienation, Muslim majority, withdrawal of the state. These are the very ingredients observed in the French *banlieues* and in Copenhagen's Norrebro and Amsterdam's Slotervaart areas. Adding to those is the salient fact that Ceuta and Melilla, bordered by Morocco, are in direct contact with the Muslim world.

There is nothing "spontaneous" in the process leading to membership in the extremist community. Given a pervasive presence of radicalism, there is still always someone or something that unleashes the process. Osman Hussain, a Somali arrested in Rome for his participation in the failed bombing in London on July 21, 2005, told police: "More than praying we discussed work, politics, the war in Iraq . . . we always had new films of the war in Iraq ... more than anything else those in which you could see Iraqi women and children who had been killed by US and UK soldiers."[115] The question is not how the group came into possession of those videotapes—they are widely available, often distributed free on the streets or at radical mosques— but who made the selection and interpreted them, and why. In other words, what is the motivation of individuals taking advantage of the existing favorable environment?

MOTIVATION

There is no single answer but, diverse as they are, the motivations of the leaders of jihadi cells are seldom related to negative personal social or economic experiences. Those "root causes" still searched for by so many Western academics can, as we have seen, play a part in creating a receptive environment. But in many cases, rather than being caused by lack of opportunity, the attraction of jihad is partly the rejection of existing opportunities. Court statements by some of the jihadis returned to France in 2006 after a stay at Guantanamo are quite revealing:

> Imad Achhab Kanouni did not "like" his biology studies in Nice, moved to Germany and became influenced by Salafism at the radical Bangladeshi mosque in Frankfurt, where some told him that Afghanistan is a country where one could freely practice the faith. After a brief temptation he gave up the idea of fighting in Kosovo and went to Afghanistan. Why not Saudi Arabia? asked the judge, and Kanouni answered that he was young and "Afghanistan was in fashion."

Fellow defendant Redouane Khalid, an accountant who had served in the Algerian army, was convinced by a radical imam that a "good believer must pray in a Muslim country." The imam's "very friendly presence and knowledge of religious texts" did the rest—"by stages" Khalid gave up efforts to integrate in France, his studies, and his job.

Similarly, Nizar Sassi left Vénissieux for London, Islamabad, Peshawar, Jallalabad, Kabul, and Kandahar because, after being influenced by Menad Benchellali, who saw in him "a future fighter for jihad," he "had to face the challenge, for itself. Because something exciting was missing from my life."[116]

Boredom, the influence of a friend or a charismatic imam, "fashion," and ignorance led them to jihad, even though they were educated and, ostensibly, integrated. Moreover,

> Many of the members of such cells have little history of extremism—or of piety. The most pious are not necessarily those most likely to become terrorists. Indeed, one could argue that for some people it is their poor understanding of Islam—and for the young suicide bomber, perhaps even their naïveté—that has made them susceptible to extreme views.[117]

A 2004 British government document accurately describes the nature of the domestic Islamist terrorist recruitment but also explains the wide consensus among observers that it is difficult, if not impossible, to establish a profile of the volunteers of jihad:

> The link between social deprivation among British Muslims and extremism is not simple cause and effect. Case histories suggest that the British Muslims who are most at risk of being drawn into extremism and terrorism fall into two groups: a) well educated, with degrees or technical/professional qualifications, typically targeted by extremist recruiters and organisations circulating on campuses; b) under-achievers with few or no qualifications, and often a non-terrorist criminal background—sometimes drawn to Mosques where they may be targeted by extremist preachers and in other cases radicalized or converted whilst in prison. Moreover many of the UK's links to international terrorism are from expatriate communities and exiles from abroad, especially North Africa, who are motivated by an international agenda.[118]

The Islamists taking refuge in Europe are a case apart, and themselves a contributing factor to the radicalization of second-generation Muslims. But what do educated individuals, social losers, and criminal elements have in common, other than their religion? The most obvious, and mutually reinforcing, answers are age and a permissive social and cultural environment.

Youth and Jihad

With few exceptions, especially among leaders, "European"—or Europe-based—Islamists are young, mostly under thirty years of age. Most are male, a few with families; some were born abroad and came to Europe as children, some were born in Europe.

These data were confirmed in a 2006 study by the French intelligence service, "The Radicalization Process in the Islamist Movement," examined by *Le Figaro*, which also shed more light on Islamist recruitment methods.[119]

First, the group primarily targeted by radicals is the c. 200,000 practicing Muslim youths. The Salafis have some 5,000 militants in France, and one may assume that all are involved in recruitment at some level.

Second, the recruiters are nearly always older than their victims—30 years old on average—and tend to have studied in universities, often being employed in scientific professions. The recruitment process does not begin with religious arguments, but first concentrates on problems in daily life. The reason is that most of those targeted—who are getting younger every year, and among whom women are increasingly numerous—are North and sub-Saharan Africans, most affected by the stagnant economy. Converts are a major element—of the 1,610 converts detected in 2005, a quarter are Salafi converts.

Third, in a pattern by now familiar, the groups most involved in Islamist recruitment have connections with *Tabligh*, established in France in 1972 and especially active since 1997.

Fourth, the venue of recruitment tends to be mostly mosques, which provide meeting opportunities as well as financial resources, and prisons. In the latter, c. 2,000 of the total of 60,000 inmates in France are "dangerous Islamists," including 173 converts; common criminals are more active in recruitment than sentenced terrorists.

Finally, Salafis are beginning to build an alternative education system, including schools and kindergartens, on the notion that "it is not permitted to the faithful to abandon those most loved to infidel (women) teachers."[120] This latter effort has two aims: to avoid further integration and to socialize children into a "pure" version of Islam—preferably at home, by imported brides.

> A perfect example of a radical involved in both recruitment and organizing of cells—one might call him a multi-step producer of jihadis—was Safé Bourada. Arrested in 2005 for his role in a recruitment network of volunteers for Iraq, Bourada, born of Algerian parents in France in 1970, was the GIA activist who organized the logistics for the organization's terrorist wave in France in 1995–98. In 1998 he was sentenced to ten years in jail.

> While an inmate from 1998 to 2003, he recruited a dozen of his fellow prisoners—including Kaïs, the rapist; Samir, the murderer; and Stéphane, the petty criminal—some of whom he converted to Islam. He lectured them, commented on verses from the Quran (in an approximation of Arabic), and formed his own cell, Ansar al-Fath ("The Partisans of Victory"). Upon release, he visited Egypt in 2004 "to learn the language"—and probably to establish contacts with the Zarkawi network. Meanwhile, back at the prison he had spent time in, Val-de-Reuil, he continued the process. By the year of his release, Islamist detainees there refused to participate in classes given

by women, separated themselves from non-Muslim inmates, and wrote anti-Western "poems."[121]

It is significant that among Safé Bourada's prison recruits and followers on the path of jihad were a number of converts from Christianity. Converts—in the strict definition of persons who changed religions and adopted Islam, often in its radical forms—play a disproportionately important role in Islamist activities in Europe, and thus deserve a separate examination.

CONVERTS TO ISLAM

Virtually all known terrorist cells in Europe in the past decade include some converts to Islam. In fact, considering their still relatively small, albeit rapidly growing, number, converts' participation in terrorism is disproportionately large. As seen in the cases of the Roubaix and Beghal networks in France, the Hofstad group in the Netherlands, and the London bombers, converts tend to be present, often prominently, in most major attacks, as well as among Europe-based volunteers for jihad in Bosnia, Chechnya, Iraq, and elsewhere.

While the precise number of converts from Christianity (or nominal Christianity) to Islam in Europe is no better known than the number of Muslims, the available, fragmented data provide at least an order of magnitude. Thus, in Spain there were about 20,000 as of 2006; in France the figure varies between 30,000 and 100,000; one figure for Germany suggests that there are around 70,000; in Italy, the most commonly mentioned estimate is 25,000, and in Britain, about 14,000.[122] Any such figures are both unreliable and misleading, since the very definition of a convert is unclear. Thus, a convert could be anyone who marries a Muslim, since a woman who marries a Muslim man is required to convert, while Muslim women are prohibited from marrying non-Muslims. This prohibition is enforced by the governments of Muslim-majority countries (Tunisia, Morocco, Algeria, Egypt) even in the cases of their citizens who live in Europe.

Some European celebrities convert to Islam, apparently because it is "different," much as some Hollywood celebrities join Buddhism or Scientology. Some convert because of marriage, like soccer star Franck Ribéry. More relevant, however, are prominent figures in the political/ideological sphere, such as former Marxist philosopher and Communist Party Central Committee member Roger Garaudy. The list includes the Venezuelan-born terrorist Ilich Ramírez Sánchez, a.k.a. Carlos the Jackal, who tried to give his conversion an ideological spin.[123] Yussuf Galán is a former member of Batasuna (the Basque ETA's old legal front), who upon conversion founded an Islamist association with Syrian ties, named after Ibn Taymiyyah, the medieval ideologue of jihad. These cases of Marxist-Leninist converts (to which one can add a few Nazi sympathizers who are now supportive of radical Islamism) reinforce the argument that there is a natural compatibility among totalitarian ideologies, whether secular or religious: Nazism, Leninism, jihadism. This compatibility is strengthened by a shared anti-Americanism and anti-Semitism: Garaudy, a Holocaust denier, was found guilty of anti-Semitism in a French court, and "the Jackal" has a long track record of both.

The very term "convert" is also subject to practical interpretations. Is a previously secular or non-practicing person with a Muslim background a convert once he or she joins a Salafi or other fundamentalist mosque or organization? One could well argue, with the American counter-terrorism consultant Marc Sageman, that for all practical purposes, such a person is indeed a convert, just as a born-again Christian could be seen as one. Certainly, such individuals tend to exhibit typical convert behavior, particularly a more intense faith and militancy.

For non-Muslims, the reasons for conversion, generally speaking, vary between the attraction of Islam's moral simplicity or clarity, and an intense sympathy with the apparently oppressed and downtrodden. Again, a comparison has been made to the past attraction of Fascism and Communism. It is also true that many converts turned to Islam because they were already members of social groups that saw themselves as marginalized: e.g., those with criminal backgrounds and members of racial minorities. Germaine Lindsay and Richard Reid in Britain, Jean-Marc Grandvisir and Xavier Djaffo in France, and the Walters brothers in the Netherlands are all black.

The attraction of Islam's simplicity is often mentioned by converts, however poorly informed in the subtleties and details of their new faith that may prove them to be. Mary Fallot, a young Frenchwoman, is a recent convert. She told an American interviewer:

> "Islam demands a closeness to God. Islam is simpler, more rigorous, and it's easier because it is explicit. I was looking for a framework; man needs rules and behavior to follow. Christianity did not give me the same reference points." . . .

> The early stages of a convert's discovery of Islam "can be quite a sensitive time," says Batool al-Toma, who runs the "New Muslims" program at the Islamic Foundation in Leicester, England. "You are not confident of your knowledge, you are a newcomer, and you could be prey to a lot of different people either acting individually or as members of an organization," Ms. al-Toma explains. A few converts feel "such a huge desire to fit in and be accepted that they are ready to do just about anything," she says.[124]

In many instances, converts involved in jihadi activities, whether they are from a Christian background or were previously non-practicing Muslims, felt they had been leading a dissolute life, or had suffered some traumatic personal experience. Islam was seen as the absolute answer to intense emotional stress—part of the explanation for the frequency of prison conversions.

While conversion is, for someone who had not been a practicing Muslim, a necessary precondition to becoming a jihadi, it is not a sufficient one. For instance, while "Youssef," formerly Antoine, converted following the example of his older brother—and they came from a solid, practicing Roman Catholic family—Youssef was recruited in a Salafi mosque and ended up a "martyr" in Iraq, while his brother, perhaps because of the discipline inculcated while serving in the military, remained just an ordinary, peaceful Muslim. Similarly, Zacarias Moussaoui was radicalized in the Islamist environment of London's Finsbury Park mosque and joined the jihad, whereas his brother, Abd Samad Moussaoui, who did not frequent the same circles, formed a family and lives a normal life.[125]

The first and most important fact to be considered when examining the reason converts to Islam in Europe play a disproportionately large role in jihadi ranks is that the very act of conversion is by itself a manifestation of rejection of societal values. Thus, by converting to a non-Western, non-European religion, the convert "leaves" his culture and his country and willingly joins "the other side." The line between rejection of a set of values and opposition to them is very thin, if it exists at all. While, as has been pointed out, many nominal Muslims in the West who join the jihad could also be considered converts, there is a significant difference between them and those who have rejected an entire moral and cultural universe and chosen another. In a sense the change from nominal Islam to radical Islam is a matter of degree; the change from Christianity to

Islam is of a different order of magnitude, a radical rupture. Additional factors—such as the fact that many converts are already in conflict with their society—only add to the intensity of the break with both their own past and the culture and values into which they were born.

Magdi Allam, Italy's main expert on Islamism, notes that converts usually go through four stages on their way to full-fledged participation in jihad: first as logistical helpers; second as combatants, usually after ideological and military training in Afghanistan; third as participants in terrorist operations; and fourth, so far rarely, as leaders of cells.[126]

Allam's first point was confirmed by the French intelligence service, which underscored the fact that "converts are even more appreciated by radicals because their French nationality allows them to cross borders more easily, to serve as front men for placement of headquarters or leadership of (radical) associations, to give logistical aid on housing, transportation."[127]

The operational advantages that European converts offer terrorist networks should not be underestimated. Lionel Dumont, a French convert, traveled to Italy, Croatia, Slovenia, Hungary, Malaysia, Indonesia, Thailand, and Japan (where he was arrested). His friend Andrew Rowe, a British convert (and, like Dumont, a former soldier), was also a global traveler, visiting Afghanistan, Chechnya, Malaysia, Pakistan, Saudi Arabia, and Morocco over a seven-year period. One may ask whether an Algerian or Moroccan from Europe could have done the same without attracting attention—all without even speculating how much Pierre Robert's blond hair and blue eyes helped him establish his operations in Morocco undetected.

Al-Qaeda is in fact quite open in expressing its interest in recruiting Western Muslims. For instance, one of its virtual branches, "Al Qaeda's Voice on the Internet," posted a statement entitled "Al Qaeda's Future Soldier: Rakan Bin Williams," which explicitly stated that it is targeting white European converts rather than Middle Easterners or Asians.[128]

Not surprisingly, then, conversions are a major, if relatively recent, tool of Islamists throughout Europe, and they select their targets well. In this they are helped by the general cultural environment and the omnipresent trend, in the media and academia, of permanently reinforcing the perception of "racism" and collective post-colonial guilt. In this context, one can indeed "consider the converts to *jihad* as the children of the allegedly anti-racist and, really, guilt-creating discourse offered for years by now, to the youth of France and Europe."[129]

Among well-known cases of converts active as "combatants" or involved in terrorism (and in jihadi eyes there is no distinction between the two) are John Walker Lindh, the "American Taliban" captured in Afghanistan while fighting on Mullah Omar's side; the Australian David Hicks, formerly at Guantanamo; British citizen Richard Reid, the "shoe bomber" of 2001; the Puerto Rican José Padilla, convicted for attempting to conduct a "dirty bomb" attack in the United States; the Germans Christian Ganczarski, involved in the Djerba bombing in Tunisia, and Steven Smyrek, who offered to blow up an Israeli target for Hamas; and the Belgian Muriel Degauque, who in 2005 blew herself up in Iraq—the first European woman to do so.

The path of converts to jihad is perhaps best exemplified by three cases. **Christophe Caze**, born in 1971 in the northern French town of Roubaix, studied medicine for five years and apparently went to Bosnia for humanitarian reasons. Once there, however, he converted to Islam after meeting the London cleric Abu Hamza, handless but able to travel. The results were immediate and spectacular. At Zenica, the center of foreign jihadis during the Bosnia war, he had fun playing soccer with Serbians' heads he had cut off in the hospital where he treated wounded members of the El Moujahid group of international jihad volunteers. Such extreme violence was also characteristic of the Algerian GIA, which Abu Hamza was serving as "spiritual" adviser at the time. While in Bosnia, Caze also met Al-Qaeda's main recruiter, the Palestinian Abu Zubaida, and learned terrorist tactics from El Moujahid's leader, an Algerian GIA veteran, Abu al Maali. Equally important, Caze used his influence as a medic to recruit among his patients; this, combined with his macabre game, demonstrates again that for jihadis all moral values are to be rejected.[130] It was in Bosnia that Caze met, and probably recruited, another convert who had gone there on a humanitarian mission, Lionel Dumont.

Lionel Dumont was born in 1972, the youngest of eight siblings in a working-class Catholic family in Turcoing, close to Roubaix. Blue-eyed, he was described by his sister as "very sensitive, idealistic, a dreamer who could not tolerate injustice."[131] After one year of studying history at university, he served in the military in Djibouti and volunteered to help in a humanitarian mission in Somalia, where he converted to Islam and became "Bilal." Back in France, he joined *Takfir-wal-Hijra* and became a volunteer of the NGO Aide Directe—a front for the *Takfiris*—in Croatia. By 1994 he had met Christophe Caze. He joined al Maali's El Moujahid in Zenica, and married a 16-year-old Bosniak peasant girl. While in Bosnia, Caze and Dumont met another convert who, like them, would later become part of international jihad: Andrew Rowe.

Andrew Rowe, London born (1971) of Jamaican extraction, had a petty criminal record when, at age 19, he converted to Islam in West London, becoming "Yussef the Jamaican." He told the jury he had become a Muslim in the early 1990s after a drug-fueled conversation at a rave. He converted at the Central Mosque in Regent's Park, London, an event that "put meaning into my life." By 1995 he was in Bosnia on "humanitarian" missions. He met Dumont, was wounded, and joined El Moujahid. Never employed, he was arrested when traveling to Georgia with $12,000 in cash he had "volunteered to take as humanitarian assistance." He also traveled to Thailand, Malaysia—visits that coincided with Dumont's—and Morocco, where he was involved in the Casablanca bombings. Upon his arrest, British police found traces of high explosives on socks in his garage.[132]

At the end of the Bosnia war in 1995, the trio returned to Western Europe, surrounded by the prestige of participation in jihad. Caze became the leader of a cell including Dumont, operating in his native area of Roubaix. After a series of bank robberies and a final firefight with police, Caze was killed by Belgian police while crossing the border, but Dumont escaped. The authorities were shocked by the Roubaix gang's possession of and willingness to use weapons seldom found in France: Sten and Kalashnikov submachine guns, grenade launchers—all brought from Bosnia by Caze's jihadi network. That network, in fact, had ramifications on four continents, from Japan to Washington State to Morocco.[133]

The travels of Dumont after escaping from Roubaix and of Rowe demonstrate both the extent of the converts' insertion into the global network of terrorism, and their usefulness to it. Dumont traveled to Japan, where he tried to establish cells among the small Pakistani and Bangladeshi communities,[134] an attempt that, although it failed, would have been inconceivable for a foreigner without a Western passport. While in Malaysia, Singapore, and Indonesia, Dumont was helped by the local jihadi network, *Jamaa Islamiya*.[135] Upon his return to Europe, Dumont lived in Germany, aided by his new German wife. Rowe's ability to obtain a Georgian visa, and to move freely between Morocco and Thailand, without attracting suspicion was facilitated by his British passport.

These three cases present some interesting common characteristics. To begin with, the Bosnia experience occurred after the conversion to Islam—weakening the argument that Muslims in Europe became radicalized because of events like Bosnia.

In all three cases conversion was from the start associated with Islamist mosques: the Salafi Dawa in Roubaix, a GIA meeting point, for Caze; the "Moroccan" mosque at Ladbroke Grove in West London for Rowe; one of the many mosques in Somalia for Dumont. A journalist who knew Dumont from Bosnia thought that "Lionel needed a cause. . . . In other times he could have been anarchist, Maoist, Trotskyite. Islam was only coincidental in his itinerary."[136] But one may doubt that, considering that Europe does not lack for radical non-Muslim causes or groups he could have joined. The fact that both he and Caze were able to make such a rapid transition from "humanitarian" to jihadi demonstrate the effectiveness of jihadi recruitment techniques. To be sure, Caze, and probably the others as well, were personally indoctrinated in Zenica by Abu Hamza. In fact, Abu Hamza did more than recruit them—as late as 1996, just prior to the Roubaix events, he was allegedly sending hundreds of pounds to Caze.[137]

Besides their ability to travel freely without attracting undue attention, the three offered specific skills—medical in the case of Caze, military and martial-arts training for the other two.

In a pattern common among jihadis in Europe, none of the three ever had a stable source of income—or a job—but all were able to travel widely and often. Dumont declared himself in court "without profession or fixed address," Rowe was unemployed, and Caze was too busy organizing cells and robbing banks to hold a job. In other words, all three were full-time jihadis, supported by the international network they were members of—and by crime. Finally, the story of the Bosnia convert group also demonstrates, in a nutshell, the very direct ideological, operational, logistic, and indeed personal links between Londonistan, via Abu Hamza, and Al-Qaeda's Asian and North American tentacles.

Caze went through Magdi Allam's four phases in less than two years—between entering Bosnia and his death as a cell leader. Another French convert reaching Allam's last stage is Richard Pierre Antoine Robert, a.k.a. Abu Abderrahmane or Yacoub, also known as "the blond guy from La Ricamarie," who was accused, tried, and convicted in Morocco for his leadership of the three cells that perpetrated the Casablanca bombings in 2003.

Born in 1972 in a working-class but not poor family, he converted at age 17, married a Moroccan, and had a son and a daughter. Mediocre in school, he never kept a stable job, although he worked occasionally selling used cars. As a fresh convert Robert traveled to Konya, in Turkey, where he learned some Arabic, but he was dissatisfied with mostly secular Turkey and went on to Pakistan (where he was trained in explosives and weapons). He then established himself in Tangiers and joined Morocco's *Salafia Jihadia* network. As usual, those who had known him earlier claimed to be surprised. Ahmed Abdelouadoud, a member of the Al Qalam cultural center (run by the Muslim Brotherhood) in Saint-Etienne, said he was not surprised at Pierre's becoming a fundamentalist, but he "could not imagine" his joining a terrorist organization.[138]

In Tangiers, Pierre Robert proclaimed himself imam and claimed a mission to "Islamize a decadent society," while raising money by defrauding would-be illegal immigrants hoping to get to Spain by as much as $9,000 per head. His network had ambitious goals, including an attack on a French nuclear power plant. Although he had a reputation for excessive self-importance, it is quite clear that he was at the very least a significant figure—and a link between European and North African jihadi structures.

After the Casablanca bombings, the Moroccan General Directorate for the Surveillance of the Territory (DGST), pursuing leads from a captured Islamist computer expert, found that in 2001 a certain "Lhadj Abu Abderrahmane" was elected "emir" of a three-cell GICM-related network in Tangiers, Fez, and Casablanca—and that he was in fact Pierre Robert. He was keeping in touch with his followers via the Internet at a café, where he pretended to be a German tourist.

At his trial Pierre Robert professed innocence, offered the standard claim that he had been tortured, and even claimed to have worked for French intelligence. Nevertheless, in September 2003 a Moroccan court sentenced him to life in prison for planning attacks in Tangiers.

Belgian Arabist and policeman Alain Grignard makes an interesting analogy:

> [Converts] are often maladjusted youths, breaking with their society of origin. I've seen drug addicts, former bar girls, delinquents. They see in Islam a more just society, a strict framework in which they are taken into consideration. Without forgetting, of course, the militant dimension. In a certain way the situation reminds one of that of the 1970s, with the fascination for South American Marxist movements. At that time some admired Che Guevara and some, a minority, passed to action, joining the guerrillas. It is a little the same phenomenon today, with Bin Laden as the hero and Iraq as the operational theater. And then, you see, the convert will always be only the product of who converted him. There is always, at one moment or another, a person who plays the

> key role in the tipover. Say someone like a guru. In this sense, again, the situation is comparable with that of the movements of the extreme Left. The chief thinks for all. This resembles a sectarian dynamics, with a series of rituals pushing people on a certain path. Anything that could distance them from that path is neutralized by the invocations and certainties of the chief. Some say that drug addiction is the meeting of a product and a person in a certain context. Terrorism is the same thing.[139]

The analogy with the most sectarian aspects of Leninism is very plausible, and may well explain the conversions of a Garaudy, Galán, or Ramírez. Salafis see themselves as the equivalent of the "vanguard of the proletariat" without, in most cases, having anything to do with actual oppressed Muslims; the "revisionists" condemned by Lenin are today's apostates, and the "class enemy" is the infidel. Moreover, as Olivier Roy pointed out, "What is new is that with al Qaeda, converts are now considered full members . . . not just tools to get past security. It's a way for them to become a global movement. In just about every al Qaeda cell over the past eight years, we have seen converts. It's structural, not just accidental."[140]

Recruitment Patterns?

The previous analysis provided an overview of social groups vulnerable to jihadi recruitment and a few specific cases. Is there a regular pattern, supported by similar motivations facilitating the process? Are there similar factors explaining the recruitment of European converts and Muslims on the continent?

Prince Turki al-Faisal, then Saudi ambassador to the U.S. and former Saudi intelligence chief, in an address at Harvard on February 15, 2006, stated that the cause of Islamist terrorism is ideology, not poverty, etc. He added that new recruits first break with their families, then with society. Importantly, he

also stated that terrorists seldom claim local or personal grievances as their motivation.[141] He was presumably referring to
Saudi jihadists, citizens of one of the wealthiest countries in the
world—and in that respect similar to their brethren in Europe.

He was also correct in stating that family often plays the role
of incubator for jihadis—certainly in some Muslim countries
but also sometimes in Europe, as the Benchellali case shows.
However, in both instances, once the process of indoctrination
is completed the relationship between the radical and his family often changes, as does his general behavior. He either breaks
all ties or tries to impose new rules and behavior on family
members—he has in fact joined another "family."

Once the possible recruits are detected by observers in large
mosques, they are attracted into small circles that meet in private apartments or remote locations—the Madrid cell members
bonded on a isolated farm at Morata de Tajuña, where the planning also took place; the London bombers of July 2005 often
took trips to remote areas in Wales; French radicals have been
found doing physical and ideological preparation in the Alps,
Americans in remote locations in Oregon or Virginia. These locations both served a practical purpose and, by isolating the
participants, helped replace previous loyalties, allegiances, and
social environment with the narrow one of the cell itself.

While converts are, in one sense, self-recruited, for ordinary
cell members, certainly in Spain, the recruiters seek persons
with limited education, as being more susceptible to radicalization—often, as we have seen, inmates or former inmates.
The dismantled cell planning to blow up the Santiago Bernabeu
stadium in Madrid in 2004 was formed in prisons. When the
recruitment is made outside prisons, it could be in legitimate
mosques, where the most zealous faithful are observed and then
taken away from those mosques and moved to underground,

radical mosques, where the indoctrination process continues. Subsequently, the recruiter selects future operatives, some then sent for training abroad, or potential new recruiters, who repeat the process.[142]

The visible impact of recruitment is often dramatic. Bouchra El-Hor, a 24-year-old Moroccan woman from the Netherlands, was a member of the cell involved in the transatlantic plot in London. At her trial, Allal Kaddouri, a friend, testified that "She was a modern young girl." But when she converted, she "transformed so quickly from a fashion-conscious college student with a secular outlook on life into a *burqa*-wearing fundamentalist . . ."[143] It is typical for a male recruit to Salafism or other forms of fundamentalism to stop playing sports, begin to wear traditional Muslim garb, grow a beard and cut his hair, lose weight because of fasting, and start avoiding looking at women or shaking hands with them.[144]

These changes seem obvious and usually sudden, mostly because family members have missed or misinterpreted the signs that the process was ongoing, which explains in part (denial and insincerity are also common) why so many of the jihadis' relatives and friends are surprised when they hear the news.

An equally sudden change often occurs when the individual has a target and is on the brink of acting. In those circumstances the opposite type of behavior occurs, aiming to avoid attracting attention. Thus the soon-to-be terrorist may steal, drink alcohol, even frequent prostitutes. One could speculate that Takfiri's tolerance for such extremely un-Islamic behavior may explain, in part, its attractiveness to individuals previously involved in such behavior.

Whatever the individual causes of conversion or vulnerability to fundamentalist recruitment, they are never enough to explain both the radicalization of so many and their entry into continental or global terrorist networks. That requires recruiters with specialized expertise, psychological and sociological, and, most importantly, a coherent and attractive ideology, all of which could be provided only by an established infrastructure with deep roots in Europe.

THE IDEOLOGY OF JIHAD

It is often said that jihadism is more a political ideology than a specific form of religious belief, and some even deny the existence of any links with Islam and declare it "anti-Islamic." Hilary Benn, international development secretary in the Blair government, went so far as to claim that "In the U.K. we do not use the phrase 'war on terror' because we can't win by military means alone and because *this isn't one organized enemy with a clear identity and a coherent set of objectives.*"[145] (Emphasis added.) More recently, Home Secretary Jacqui Smith considers terrorism "anti-Islamic" and stated: "As so many Muslims in the UK and across the world have pointed out, there is nothing Islamic about the wish to terrorise, nothing Islamic about plotting murder, pain and grief."[146] While such opinions are not shared uniformly throughout Europe, they are supported by the European Union and by most, if not all, "mainstream" Muslim organizations, such as the MB and MCB.

As already mentioned, neither the Islamic tradition nor prominent contemporary theologians, such as Qaradawi, deny jihadis the quality of true Muslims. Thus, to deny organizations like the GIA or the Al-Qaeda Organization in the Islamic Maghreb (AQIM). The quality of "Islamic" when they claim it in their very names places British and Brussels politicians in the strange position of claiming to know better than Qaradawi or the jihadis themselves who they are and what they believe in. This is political correctness, not logical thinking. The Catholic

Church does not deny that Torquemada was a Catholic, nor do the Austrians deny that Hitler was Austrian, no matter how strongly they condemn their deeds. Nor do such statements help explain what makes jihadis tick, let alone help to combat them. The reality is that they have a strategic world vision, a defined set of goals, and a very well defined set of methods to accomplish those goals. Moreover, the various trends in jihadi thinking are abundantly presented in books, on the Internet, and in the media—Muslim or not.[147]

For the purpose of this book an in-depth analysis of jihadi ideology is not necessary, and most of its followers in Europe, or elsewhere, may themselves be ignorant of its details. But there are a number of aspects that are relevant, especially as they relate to recruitment.

To begin with, to understand why a British-born citizen of Pakistani background blows himself up in Israel, or a French-born one of Moroccan background does the same in Iraq, one has to understand the term *jihad* in the context of its global strategy. Thus, as pointed out by Al-Qaeda's main ideologue, Ayman al-Zawahiri, in his book *Knights under the Banner of the Prophet*, focusing on the Israeli-Palestinian conflict is a way to gain the support of Muslims everywhere, since "it is a rallying point for all the Arabs, be they believers or non-believers, good or evil."[148] This idea is, in turn, the result of jihadists' perception of the world as generally hostile to Islam. Since Islam is everywhere under attack—from without by the infidels and from within by apostate regimes—resistance is necessary, (violent) jihad is its only realistic method, and it is the duty of every true Muslim is to participate. One may argue that this view is paranoid, but it cannot be denied that it is simple to understand and, if one is so minded, to agree with. For Muslims in Europe, the notion that Muslims are universal victims is made pervasive

by a combination of forces, ranging from establ:
organizations to non-Muslim academics, journalis
politicians—none of whom advocates jihad. The I:
tims of the Americans, as are the Afghans; Palestinians are persecuted by Israel, Chechens by Russia, Kashmiris by India, and
Thai, Filipino, and Chinese Muslims by their Buddhist, Catholic,
or Communist government. A Muslim in Britain does not have
to watch Al Jazeera or read Saudi-owned newspapers to obtain
that impression; it suffices to listen to the BBC or to London's
former mayor Ken Livingstone, or to read *The Guardian*, not to
mention statements by the Muslim Council of Britain. Once the
premise of universal victimhood is accepted—and it is widely accepted, from Scandinavia to Spain and from England to
Austria—the only issue remains the solution: which for many
means jihad.

Zawahiri's strategy, as excellently described by Faisal Devji,
is a reversal of traditional Islamic interpretations of jihad in
more than one way:

- Unlike traditional interpretations, Al-Qaeda's direction
  of jihad is centripetal, rather than centrifugal: It is not
  from the centers of Islam (e.g., Egypt or the Arabian
  Peninsula) that jihadist Islam would spread, but from
  the periphery (Afghanistan, Chechnya, Central Asia—
  to which one can add Europe) to the center.

- Instead of being authorized and led by the Muslim
  state, and thus a political matter, jihad is a moral issue
  and thus obligatory for all Muslims, regardless of their
  location and the immediate focus of a conflict between
  Islam and the world of the infidels.

- Instead of pursuing jihad locally (i.e., nationally, as in
  Egypt or Algeria), the Al-Qaeda approach adopts a global
  strategy—attack the enemy everywhere all the time.[149]

Once these aspects of the Islamist ideology are accepted, it becomes quite logical that a Muslim from Europe would feel compelled to participate in jihad wherever his privileged position—i.e., his possession of a passport that seldom requires entry visas, or of sufficient funds—allows him to travel. That is also a major reason Al-Qaeda is quite open in stating its interest in recruiting Western-based Muslims, and why it trained them separately and differently in Afghan camps prior to the fall of the Taliban at the end of 2001.

JIHADISM AND ETHNICITY

European national cultures and traditions are undergoing an identity crisis, often with political manifestations. Spain, Belgium, the United Kingdom, Italy, and France all face secessionist threats of various degrees, and significant numbers of citizens in virtually all EU states feel their cultural identity threatened by Brussels. All of this lowers even more the national cultures' ability—and sometimes willingness—to assimilate newcomers, and in some countries, such as Belgium, Germany, and England, that capacity was never very highly developed. It is thus not surprising, in an environment where the dominant group's ethnic or cultural identity is diluted or threatened, that Muslim immigrant groups experience such identity crises with even greater intensity.

Just as one can hardly talk about a generic "Muslim community" in Europe in terms of economic and educational success or social pathologies, the degree of re-Islamization and attraction to Islamism among the various ethnic groups also varies widely. Of the three largest Muslim groups in Europe—Turks, South Asians, and Arabs—the Turks are generally in a distinctly isolated, but self-chosen, position in terms of their involvement in fundamentalism. On the other hand, Asians (i.e., persons with roots in former British India) and Maghrebis are the main actors on the Islamic scene.

The present prominence of Algerians, Moroccans, and Tunisians on the jihadist scene could in part be explained by their countries' experience with colonial rule. That is not because of colonialism as such—India was under British rule much longer than the Maghreb was under French—but because the British seldom interfered with local customs or traditions, while the French sought to make Arabs or Berbers into Gauls— at least in theory. Hence in North Africa the threat to local customs and religious traditions was both more intense and more resented, even if of shorter duration. Superficially it was also more successful: Most Maghrebis in France, second- and first-generation, and many in North Africa as well, speak French, the former often at the expense of their Arabic (or Tamazight); while in England one can still find an elected city-council member who speaks only Urdu, and first-generation immigrants are more often than not monolingual.

True enough, some of these differences are due to present government policies: The French expect and require those who live in France to speak French; the English, at least until very recently, simply hoped that first-generation immigrants would learn the national language. Ultimately, however, Maghrebi communities in Europe have looser ties with North Africa than Asians in Britain have with their countries of origin. As for the Turks, they not only lack the historic baggage of colonialism, but many see themselves as already "Europeans"—not a common sentiment in the Rif, Kabylia, or Mirpur.

How are these differences manifested on the jihadi scene in Europe? The case of Moroccans and Algerians is perhaps the most representative of the peculiarities of Muslim communities in Europe, and of the importance of re-Islamization. On the one hand, Algeria and Morocco have almost gone to war repeatedly since each achieved independence, and have pursued distinctly different paths (socialism versus a monarchy legitimized by links to the Prophet himself). Rabat and Algiers still have very poor relations with and opinions of each other. Those realities are sometimes manifested in the diaspora as well—especially in those sectors of it still maintaining close ties with the country of origin. Thus in France the Rabat-controlled FNMF is perennially hostile to the Algiers-dominated Grand Mosque of Paris.[150]

The composition of jihadi groups in France and Spain, on the other hand, suggests that re-Islamization has resulted in the virtual disappearance of Algerian-Moroccan animosities among significant elements of the diaspora. The various jihadi cells in Spain have all been multi-ethnic, and GICM and GSPC members cooperated there long before joining to form the AQIM, whose creation in 2006 was expected to bring their members closer still. Considering the fundamental hostility of Salafism toward nationalism, and its absolute priority given to *ummah* solidarity, this phenomenon is not surprising.

As we have seen, many Maghrebi immigrants of the second generation in France and Italy do not speak Arabic any more. Nevertheless, those Arabs see themselves as the natural bearers of Islam's purest message and thus have a certain superiority complex *vis-à-vis* other Muslims. Furthermore, virtually all the freelance radical preachers in Europe, from the prominent figures of Londonistan (Abu Qatada, Abu Hamza, Omar Bakri, etc.) to the activists of the Viale Jenner mosque in Milan, are Arab and Arabic speakers—some monolingual. Salafism is not only an Arab-originated ideology, but it is often transmitted through Arabic, and thus an inadequate tool of recruitment for Balkan Muslims and Turks, whose opinion of Arabs, historically and at present, is very low.

Among the Turks, even those who are attracted by Islamism are more interested in events in Turkey than in global jihad. Although there are known ideological ties between the Kaplancis—a Turkish extremist organization of Khomeinist leanings—and the Muslim Brotherhood, at least in France, the largest Turkish diaspora organization, *Milli Görüs* is fundamentally nationalist.[151] For *Milli Görüs* the immediate goal is to maintain and strengthen the Turkish identity of immigrants—not to dilute it into a universal Islamist movement. That goal is furthered by the parochialism of Turks in Europe—among those in France in the 1990s, 85 percent of adults had trouble understanding the news in French on TV; while 50 percent of Algerian mothers in France could not speak French, 93 percent of the Turkish could not.[152] The number of those understanding Arabic is smaller still—another factor insulating Turks from Islamist propaganda. In addition, this author's interviews in 2000 with Turkish diplomats in Berlin, Paris, Madrid, and Lisbon, as well as with prominent Turkish diaspora members in some of those countries, suggest that Ankara's practice of sending officially approved imams to serve the Turkish diaspora works well in controlling Salafist infiltration.

While the Sarajevo and Tirana governments do not have the institutional and financial capabilities of Ankara in influencing their diasporas, those emigrant communities are decisively influenced by the nature of Islam at home. A popular joke in Sarajevo prior to the wars of the 1990s was that the difference between a Muslim, a Croat, and a Serb was that the first did not go to the mosque, the second to the Catholic Mass, and the third to the Orthodox liturgy. Add to this the impact of fifty years of ferocious anti-religion policies in Albania, the same number of years of official atheism in old Yugoslavia, and before that centuries of fairly moderate Ottoman Islam, and it is clear why Albanians and Bosniaks in Austria, Germany, or Switzerland are mostly uninterested in Salafi-motivated terrorism. All that, one may add, despite persistent and well-funded efforts by Saudi Arabia's government, its charities, and wealthy individuals to spread Wahhabism in Bosnia, Albania, and Kosovo and among Balkan Muslim diasporas in Europe.

Quite often there is a direct linkage between Third World terrorism and its implantation in the West. A terrorist organization takes root in, say, Algeria, Turkey, or Pakistan, creates massive internal disturbances, instability, and economic hardship, all of which result in massive emigration to richer and friendlier places—in the West. This process is made easier by the Western media, where popular sympathy for immigrants or even terrorists is created and pressure on politicians to "do something" develops—as in the cases of Chechnya or Bosnia. For instance, Abdelhamid Shaari, an Islamist from Milan, confirmed to Magdi Allam that when he and his friends, including imam Anwar Shaaban, an Egyptian jihad veteran of Afghanistan, were operating in Bosnia in 1995, they were doing so openly, "under sunlight."[153]

Another case is that of the Algerian "political asylum" seekers who have multiplied in Britain since the late 1990s.[154] The Algerian government has essentially defeated, at the cost of some 150,000 deaths, a murderous insurgency by Islamist groups there—the *Takfiri* GIA and Al-Qaeda–related GSPC—and the remnants had to flee for their lives. One may ask why they did not try France, the traditional Algerian emigration destination; the answer is that the French intelligence and counterterrorism agencies have close ties to Algiers, abundant information on fleeing terrorists, and no tolerance for their requests for "asylum." Hence, Britain is seen as a soft target, and the fleeing militants found it a friendly place for refuge.

Syrian Muslim Brotherhood activists, fleeing the Assad regime's violent crackdown of 1982, found refuge in large numbers in Spain under the pro-Arab Socialists and in Germany—again helped by lax asylum laws and, in the latter case, an undeserved sympathy as victims of an authoritarian regime. More recently, young Moroccans who have passed through Spain on their way to Iraq find it safer upon return to remain in Spain than go home.[155]

Islamist organizations in Pakistan—and there are many, with enormous local support—have what could only be called natural extensions in Britain's strong Pakistani, especially Kashmiri, community. Persons of Pakistani background have been involved in most terrorist activities in the United Kingdom. Moreover, in the past few years a significant Pakistani immigrant community has made its home in Spain's Catalonia and La Rioja and has brought with it close ties with Pakistani Islamist groups. Spanish authorities have discovered that those Pakistani groups have provided recruits for Iraq, Kashmir, and Lebanon, some of whom had gained experience in explosives in training camps like Razmak in Waziristan. The local immigrant communities in Catalonia also harbored jihadists fleeing the Islamabad government's crackdowns.

It is the omnipresent system of contacts across a European Union lacking border controls that explains the international impact of Islamist radicalism incubated in Europe—and the spread of its influence far beyond Western Europe. Many Muslim governments have long complained about Europe's tolerance for fundamentalists, who often re-export their radical ideology to their countries of origin.

Europe also plays the role of facilitator of meetings between various groups. For example, the meeting of the Egyptian Mohamed Atta and the German-based Yemeni Ramzi Binalshibh to plan 9/11 took place in Tarragona, Spain, because of the ease of travel within the European Union.

The Immigrant Networks

While conversion or re-Islamization forms the necessary background of Europe-based recruits to jihadi networks and creates a growing mass of supporters of Islamism, the presence of foreign members of terrorist groups is the key coalescing factor leading to specific action. These foreigners, in some cases numbering in the thousands—GIA "refugees" in England and Spain being good examples—are already indoctrinated and experienced; many have participated in terrorist activities in their own countries or in places like Bosnia, Chechnya, and Afghanistan. Such a record makes them role models and effective recruiters of young Muslims seeking adventure or a sense of identity and action. Moreover, such radical immigrants have the necessary connections abroad and often come to Europe in groups, as ready-made cells.

Many come unencumbered by family obligations with the intention of marrying in Europe, often as a means of obtaining legal status. The Spain-based Syrians involved in the Madrid train bombings of March 11, 2004, Imad Eddin Barakat Yarkas, Amer al-Azizi, and Mustafa Setmariam, had all married Spanish women. They were the organizers of a large network, "Soldiers of Allah," which included dozens of others—Moroccans, Tunisians, converts, Algerians. Meanwhile, a handful of Syrian Muslim Brotherhood refugees established a network reaching all the way to Indonesia, including at least 100 members in Spain itself, and active in Morocco, Iraq, and London.[156] What is important to note in this respect is that virtually the entire Spanish jihadi infrastructure is made up of immigrants.

While the Syrian refugees who came to Spain during the 1980s were not well known to European authorities, some terrorists who arrived later were associated with known terrorist groups like the Egyptian Islamic Jihad (EIJ) and the related *Gamaa Islamiya* (GI), famous for murdering Western tourists, and still found a haven. The following are a few particularly egregious examples:

- Fahmi Abdel Fattah, EIJ propaganda chief, fled Peshawar in 1990 or 1991 and took refuge in London. Arrested later in Jordan and extradited, he died in an Egyptian prison in 2004.

- Adel Abdel Majid, EIJ propagandist in Afghanistan, moved his operations to London, where he stayed from 1993 to 1998.

- Adel Abdel Quddus, founding member of EIJ, sentenced to death in Egypt for involvement in the murder of Prime Minister Atef Sidqi (1993), took refuge in Austria in the late 1990s and is still there.

- Ahmed Hussein Aguizeh, EIJ militant, fled to Sweden, where he was finally arrested and extradited to Egypt in December 2001, facing a life sentence.

- Ibrahim Hussein Eidarus, EIJ leadership member, sentenced to life in Egypt, fled to the UK in 1996.

- Ahmad Said Khudar was arrested and released in Pakistan, and received asylum in Canada in 1995 (and later citizenship). He founded an NGO, Human Concern International, accused of channeling funds to the EIJ. By 2001 he was in Afghanistan, and he was killed by the Pakistani military in Waziristan at the end of 2003.

Egyptian terrorists were far from the only ones finding refuge, succor, and often welfare payments in Western Europe, nor did they enjoy only personal safety—they were free to reorganize their propaganda, recruitment, and logistical infrastructure. That in turn made it possible for hundreds (or thousands) of Europe-based Muslims to be indoctrinated, recruited, and trained in Bosnia, Chechnya, and Pakistan, and in Al-Qaeda camps in Afghanistan. A similar number of "Arab Afghans" from various countries have found a home in Europe. Starting in France almost two decades ago, dozens of autonomous cells of Islamic terrorists have been uncovered, from the Algerian and Chechen cells in France and Germany, to al-Zawahiri's logistical and recruitment cells in Spain, Italy, Germany, Norway, and Britain. The EU's official list of terrorist organizations includes almost all significant Islamist groups, violent or not.

With the exception of the wave of GIA bombings in France in the mid-1990s, and until 9/11 and the 2003 intervention in Iraq, the jihadi infrastructure in Europe mostly served as the rear base for operations elsewhere. There is now a sense among intelligence agencies that groups like the Moroccan *Salafia Jihadia,* its smaller offshoot, the Right Path (*l-Sira al-Mustaqim*), and the larger GICM became more structured and organized in Europe than in Morocco proper. Considering that some of the most spectacular terrorist actions, including the Madrid bombings and the van Gogh murder in 2004, were done by mostly Moroccan Islamists, it is clear that Europe is now paying for years of neglect and tolerance. That is important to understand, because jihadi structures operate with a long period of incubation. That was demonstrated recently by a Moroccan GICM cell led by Abdelkader Belliraj, based in Belgium. It robbed a Brink's office in Luxembourg in 2000, stealing €17.5 million, and used the booty to buy weapons and plan attacks in Morocco. It was dismantled there only in February 2008.[57] Moreover, Belliraj was not unknown to the Belgians—since as early as 1999 he was a suspect in six murders, including those of two moderate imams and Joseph Wybran, the head of the major Jewish organization in the country.[58]

In December 2005, the Spanish authorities broke down a network in Lérida, Málaga, Sevilla, Granada, and Palma de Mallorca dedicated to the recruitment of terrorists for Iraq. The leader, Hiyag Maan, was Iraqi. Other leading members included Andrei Misura, a Belorusian convert previously active in Chechnya; Oussama Agharbi, a Moroccan, who had been trained by Misura; and the Ghanaian Mohamed Gazali, an imam linked to the same Al-Quds mosque in Hamburg that served as the center of the 9/11 cell. Other members were of Saudi, Egyptian, French, Algerian, and Spanish origins. In Belgium, where, on November 30, 2005, "Operation Asparagus 18" led to the arrest of 13 members of the GICM, it soon became clear that the cell had international links: A Tunisian member was arrested in Paris; at the same time, GICM figure Hassan al-Haski, who was linked to the Casablanca bombings of May 2003, was being interrogated by Moroccan prosecutors in Madrid.[59] These cases, involving individuals from three continents, clearly demonstrate the multi-national, multi-ethnic nature of Islamist cells in Europe, a phenomenon directly related to re-Islamization, whereby Islamic identity is the default position, trumping national, ethnic, or racial identity.

Although some Islamist cells deactivated in European countries in the past few years may have appeared to be basically local, a deeper look suggests that behind them there is the more threatening phenomenon of international networks, related to each other as well as to non-European networks. Often, it is precisely the combination of a core group of the same nationality, even the same region, and a larger, multinational membership that has obscured the size and nature of the Islamist terrorist presence, especially from the media. In fact, the mix of ethnicity and the global ideology of jihadism is far from contradictory, with re-Islamization providing the bridge between them.

Briefly, for the sake of simplicity, there are a few discrete major Europe-wide Islamist networks. Although they are all interrelated and willing to cooperate for specific actions toward a common goal, the existence of these separate networks, with different tactical goals and likely areas of operations, helps account for the decentralized nature of Islamism in Europe. In addition to their growing recent cooperation within the Al-Qaeda nebula, such networks often play specialized, complementary roles in the jihadi structures in Europe.

The Syrians

In February 1982 the underground Syrian Muslim Brotherhood initiated an insurrection centered in the city of Hama, against the Baath Party regime of then President Hafez al-Assad. Not only was the government ostensibly secular, and thus "apostate," but in reality it was a military dictatorship of the Alawi minority (12 percent of the country's population), considered heretical by the Sunnis. The revolt was defeated, Hama was largely destroyed, and between 20,000 (the Syrian government's figure) and 30,000 people (according to the Syrian Human Rights Committee) were killed or missing.[160] As usual in such circumstances, many of the leaders of the rebellion escaped and fled the country.

Despite the general picture created by the regime's opponents and human-rights groups, the events demonstrated that the Muslim Brotherhood was not a peaceful, democratic organization victimized by what was then, and remains today, an authoritarian dictatorship, but a group intending to replace it with its own dictatorship, a Sunni fundamentalist regime. Nevertheless, in Western Europe the Muslim Brotherhood managed to depict itself as a persecuted victim and to obtain asylum for many of its leaders and cadres, mostly in Spain and Germany—perhaps because those countries' governments knew or cared little about Syrian events, unlike, say, the French government. In time they formed a major network of Islamist ideologues, recruiters, and financiers of terrorism, with tentacles throughout Europe. Syrians have played a major role in the more recent networks of Islamists of assorted nationalities in Europe—almost always as the men behind the scene.

In all respects the following account by a London-based scholar is correct: "The decimation of the Syrian Muslim Brotherhood in 1982 had many long-term implications, the most pernicious of which was the emergence of a particularly extreme form of Syrian Salafism. At the center of this is Mustafa Setmariam Nasar, better known as Abu Musab al-Suri ('the Syrian'), who is widely believed to be among the most prolific al-Qaeda ideologues and trainers alive. Currently working closely with the Zarqawi network, and probably based in Iraq, Nasar also allegedly exercises operational control over several al-Qaeda linked networks in the West."[161]

It is hard to overstate the importance and relevance of Abu Musab al-Suri for the theory and practice of contemporary jihad. One may even say that the entire phenomenon is structured around bin Laden's charisma and business acumen, al-Zawahiri's ideological formulations, and al-Suri's practical and theoretical formulations. Despite being far less known in the West than the other two—his capture in Pakistan in November 2005 was barely noticed in the media—his is a familiar name among jihadis everywhere. He has written extensively, including such works as "The Syrian Memorandum," used in the Arab-Afghan camps in Afghanistan since 1989; the 900-page treatise *The Islamic Jihadi Revolution in Syria,* published in Peshawar in May 1991; and the even more influential 1,600-page treatise *The Call to Global Islamic Resistance.* Dozens of CDs with his videotaped lectures are still circulating throughout Europe and the Muslim world. These were originally used by him to train jihadis at his own pre-9/11 Afghan camp, called *Mu'askar Al-Ghurabaa* (the Strangers' Camp), in Karghah, near Kabul, which "graduated" a large number of Muslims from Europe.[162]

Al-Suri, now in U.S. custody at an undisclosed location, offers a unique combination of personal jihadi experience. He participated in the Hama insurrection as a member of *al-Talee'a al-Muqatelah* (the Fighting Vanguard), started as a follower and became a staunch enemy of the Muslim Brotherhood,[163] personally knew and advised Abdullah Azzam in Peshawar, later became close to bin Laden and served as his explosives instructor, and was active in Iraq. Most importantly for our purpose, he had extensive European experience.

Mustafa Setmariam Nasar was born in Aleppo, Syria, in 1958 and studied mechanical engineering at the university in that town for four years. By 1980 he was a member of the Fighting Vanguard; after its defeat he fled, first to Jordan, then to Iraq, then to France, ending up in Spain by 1985. Following a familiar pattern, he married (and converted to Islam) Elena Moreno, a Spanish citizen, had four children, and became a citizen himself. His passport allowed him to travel freely in Europe and elsewhere—especially Afghanistan. By 1994 he was back in Europe—in London, where, with Abu Qatada, he edited *Al-Ansar,* the most important jihadi magazine at the time, with ties to the GIA, until 1996. A year later he established a media company called the Islamic Conflict Studies Bureau with Mohamed Bahaiah, better known as Abu Khalid al-Suri, an Al-Qaeda courier. Through this company he facilitated two important media events for bin Laden in Afghanistan, in particular CNN's famous interview with him in March 1997.[164] From London, al-Suri returned to Afghanistan with his family and became close to Mullah Omar; his *Al-Ghurabaa* camp was formally under Taliban, not Al-Qaeda, control. In fact, he took the Taliban's side when its views diverged from bin Laden's.

While he never made a secret of his Al-Qaeda ties, al-Suri had extensive independent ties with a plethora of jihadi groups in Morocco, Algeria, Libya, Egypt, Syria, Lebanon, Iraqi Kurdistan, Saudi Arabia, Yemen, Uzbekistan, and elsewhere, which explains the widespread, though not confirmed, suspicions of his being behind the Madrid and London bombings—and even being behind 9/11 and al-Zarqawi's organization in Iraq. Peter Bergen was correct when he stated: "To the extent that al-Suri played a pretty important role in creating the ideological movement . . . he bears some responsibility for these attacks [in Europe]."[165]

The most influential of al-Suri's ideas, at least as applied to Europe, is that, as the Norwegian historian Brynjar Lia put it, "the *tanzim* model—the centralized hierarchical and regional secret jihadi organization—has outlived its role. Their Achilles' heel was their hierarchical structure, which meant that if one member was caught, the whole organization would be at peril."[166] Moreover, al-Suri considered that to be true everywhere:

> Nasar's goal is best described as a movement of autonomous jihadists constituting a global insurgency. Upon the successful establishment of these autonomous jihadists operating in both Dar al-Harb and Dar al-Islam, Nasar believes that this self-perpetuating global insurgency will sap the US and the West of their strength by forcing them to fight on hundreds of fronts. In so doing, Nasar is reliant upon awakening the

Muslim masses resident in both the Arab world and the West, a point he elaborates to great length throughout his teachings and writings. In this way, Nasar will be the ideological progenitor not just of a global insurgency, but of a generation of international Islamic resistance.[167]

Jihadi cells need not, indeed should not, be large, for security reasons, on the model of European Marxist terrorist cells:

Many European gang organizations were able through experience to develop very accurate and durable methods that helped them withstand the onslaught of very advanced and powerful security organizations (e.g. the red brigades of Italy, Badder Meinhoff [sic] of Germany and the Spanish separatist organization ETA). Our experience taught us that security and strength of an organization could be contradictory to its growth or ease of management.[168]

While the present forms of jihadism in Europe and elsewhere could not be attributed solely to al-Suri's concepts, they certainly confirm his diagnostic skill and demonstrate his wide experience and learning. Moreover, it is important to note that in Spain al-Suri had a circle of followers, mostly fellow Syrians and some from his native city, whom he took to Afghanistan in 1987. Those included Imad Eddin Yarkas, the head of Al-Qaeda's Madrid cell.

The following are among the most prominent Syrians in European jihadi networks:

Imad Eddin Yarkas, a.k.a. Abu Dahdah, comes from al-Suri's hometown of Aleppo. He was generally recognized as the major Al-Qaeda figure active in Spain, where he was arrested in November 2001 and later convicted and sentenced to 25 years for recruiting for Afghanistan and as an accomplice of the 9/11 hijackers. He met Atta in Tarragona in July 2001 and had contacts, in London, with Abu Qatada. Spanish intelligence, listening to his cell phone, overheard a conversation with Abu

Nabil, the present leader of the Syrian Fighting Vanguard.[169] It is widely believed that Abu Dahdah was the key figure linking the Al-Qaeda core leadership in Pakistan to the operatives in Madrid. The manner in which the Atocha bombings of March 11, 2004, were prepared and the perpetrators indoctrinated and recruited suggests that he had learned from al-Suri.[170]

Redouan al-Issar, a.k.a. Abu Khaled, was born in Syria in the late 1950s or early 1960s. He is by profession a geologist and thought by the Dutch to be the spiritual mentor of the Hofstad Group. Known as "the Syrian" and "the Sheikh" by Hofstad Group members, he used the name of Mohammed Basel al-Issa (a real Hama resident) when applying for Dutch asylum.[171] In 1995 he demanded and received asylum in Germany, claiming to have been in prison in Syria for 14 years, and to have been tortured. Al-Issar was arrested in the Netherlands as an illegal alien in October 2003 and deported to Germany.

Mohammed Haydar Zammar, a Syrian/German citizen, was trained in Afghanistan, fought in Bosnia, met bin Laden, and had close ties with known Moroccan terrorist Zakariya Essabar. According to a report in *Der Spiegel:*

> Zammar, nicknamed "Fratello Mohammed" in Italy and "Bruder Haydar" (Brother Haydar) in Germany, was a known entity in Islamist circles. He was an enormous man, weighing in at 145 kg (320 lbs.), with arms the size of small tree trunks. His appearance alone—he was thickly bearded and wore a flowing blue caftan and a Palestinian kaffiyeh—made him a dead ringer for a dedicated servant of Allah. . . . Zammar occasionally spent the night at the notorious apartment on Marienstrasse in Hamburg where some of the 9/11 terrorists lived, acting as a sort of surrogate father to the pilots surrounding Mohammed Atta. When they searched the apartment, Hamburg police found 94 copies of an appeal from Osama bin Laden. Zammar and his family were then living with his brother in low-income housing on Bilserstrasse in the north part of Hamburg—nine people in a two-room, ground-floor apartment.

When confronted with the bin Laden pamphlet, Zammar told authorities it was "a declaration of war on the USA. I photocopied it to distribute to Muslims." His friends say that Brother Haydar had always been a bit naïve, but the reality is that he was anything but an overgrown child. . . .

When he flew back to Afghanistan years later, on Emirates Airlines via Dubai, Zammar had already taken up a collection back home in Germany. Fellow Islamists in Germany had given him 12,000 deutsche marks for jihad, including a 2,000 deutsche mark donation from an imam in the northern German town of Minden and 5,000 deutsche marks from an Islamic charity. Zammar, by then a self-proclaimed source of funding to al-Qaida, delivered some of the money to a Palestinian named Abu Atta, who taught would-be terrorists how to use explosives in Kabul and had seven children to feed.[172]

Zammar's brother, Abdulfattah, was also connected with Mamoun Darkazanli (see below), driving him to a Madrid meeting with Abu Dahdah in January 2000. After being arrested in Morocco in 2001, Zammar was "rendered" by the U.S. to Syria, were he was tried and jailed for membership in the banned Muslim Brotherhood. It is interesting that, even in the light of his extensive jihadist connections, in some German media circles he became a "victim" simply because of the American rendition.

Mamoun Darkazanli, born in 1958, is a German citizen who, along with 9/11 hijackers Mohamed Atta, Marwan Al-Shehhi, and Ziad Jarrah, attended Hamburg's Al-Quds mosque. Although he had been on a German-intelligence watch list since 1998, Darkazanli was ignored by both the FBI and the CIA after 9/11. He acknowledged knowing the three pilots and sharing several common friends in Hamburg's insular Muslim community.[173] In January 2000 Darkazanli met in Madrid with Imad Eddin Barakat Yarkas. As with Yarkas and al-Suri, Darkazanli's hometown is Aleppo.

Yet another Syrian, **Basel Ghayoun**, a native of Homs, was also sentenced in connection with the Madrid bombings. He was a friend of the Moroccan-born cell leader Jamal Zougam, who, like the Syrian **Adnan Waki**, was one of the actual perpetrators. **Mohammed Almallah Dabas**, another Syrian with Spanish nationality, an appliance repairman who rented a room to Basel Ghayoun, fled and was arrested in Britain in 2005, accused of indoctrinating and providing logistical support to the actual bombers.

Dabas and his brother, **Moutaz Almallah Dabas**, who also held Spanish citizenship, had the same London and Al-Qaeda links as al-Suri and Abu Dahdah. Those included Mohamed Bahaiah, considered by the Spanish to be Osama bin Laden's personal representative in Europe, and Abu Qatada. Moutaz was a regular at Abu Hamza's Finsbury Park mosque, while Mohammed, in Madrid, hosted meetings of the group led by the Moroccan Mustafa al-Maymouni, another of the Madrid bombers.[174]

What characterized the Syrian connection was their origins (Aleppo and Homs), their shared experience with the jihadists of the Vanguard, their strong ideological coherence, which made them effective recruiters, and their close ties with the Londonistan nexus and Al-Qaeda's top leadership. While a few were involved in actual operations, they mostly served as recruiters and links with global jihad.

The Algerians

By contrast, the Algerian network in Europe was, from its start in the 1990s until today, operationally oriented and to some extent the extension of Islamist terrorism in Algeria proper. "To some extent" is a key qualification, because Algerian Islamists in Europe are now operating in conjunction with non-Algerians, especially Moroccans. Algerian terrorism in Europe always had close links with the two major Islamist groups back home, first the GIA and, since 1998, the GSPC, and it preceded all other jihadi groups in operating in Europe.

Already in June 1999 a GIA cell of 24 went on trial in France, some *in absentia*, accused of responsibility for the hijacking of an Air France plane in Algiers in 1994 and for the 1994–95 bombings in Paris, which killed 12 (including 10 at the Saint-Michel subway station on July 25, 1995) and wounded 200.[175] The cell leaders were identified as Rachid Ramda, finally extradited from England in 2005; Boualem Bensaid; Khaled Kelkal; and Ali Touchent, probably shot by police in Algeria in 1997. Included among the 24 were nine French, five French-Algerians, eight Algerians, and two Moroccans.

In 1998, bin Laden and al-Zawahiri had a meeting of their International Islamic Jihad Front in Peshawar that was attended by GIA members. In May of that year, bin Laden conditioned his support for Algerian jihad upon the GIA's renunciation of indiscriminate massacres of civilians. This resulted in a split of the GIA and the creation of the GSPC under Hassan Hattab.[176] To be sure, bin Laden's displeasure with the GIA should be considered as a tactical matter rather than the result of moral restraint, and the fact is that, while in Algeria itself the GSPC did concentrate on the murder of military, police, and secular intellectuals, rather than Muslim peasants, its members did not demonstrate similar discrimination in their European or Iraqi operations.

As long as Hassan Hattab ran the GSPC—he was removed in 2003 and surrendered to the authorities[177]—he was fairly successful in maintaining some control over the group's followers in Europe, as well as the GIA remnant there. Even so, already in 1998 some of his representatives in Germany, Belgium, Italy, the UK, and France were arrested. In December 2000 the Meliani

Commando group was captured in Germany, while planning to blow up the Strasbourg Cathedral across the Rhine in France. In February 2001 the British captured a senior former member of the GIA, Ammar Makhloufi, a.k.a. Abu Doha, linked to a number of attempted attacks, including the "millennium bombing" in Los Angeles. In May 2001 Mohamed Bensakhria was captured in Alicante, following the Milan capture of a GSPC cell made up of Tunisians preparing a chemical attack in France. The Beghal network, led by the Algerian Djamel Beghal, was also closely linked to the GSPC. In December 2001 the British dismantled an Algerian cell preparing an attack against the London Tube system—on the pattern of the 1995 bombings of the Paris Métro.[178]

Compared to other large Muslim groups in Europe, such as Moroccans or Pakistanis, the Algerians have better organizational skills, especially in regard to larger cells, and a larger number of cells. They developed these administration, communications, and logistics skills during operations in Algeria, then later applied them to their European operations. Add to these relative advantages the sheer number of Algerian immigrants in Europe—they are the largest Muslim group there—and the continuing influx of militants fleeing Algeria as GSPC is in its death throes there, plus the Algerian immigrants' established reputation for violent criminal activity (in Spain, according to this author's police sources, Algerians, accounting for perhaps 10 percent of Muslim immigrants, commit a large majority of crimes, especially violent ones), and one should expect further Algerian involvement in terrorism throughout Europe—and larger-scale attacks.

As Omar Nasiri testified in his book, *Inside the Jihad,* the GIA had a major operation in London, including the production of its magazine, *Al-Ansar.* It received the religious blessings of first Abu Qatada and then Abu Hamza—only to have both shift their support to the GSPC. Eventually, as the GIA was virtually destroyed by the Algerian military, its operations, both in Algeria and in Europe, merged with those of the GSPC.[179]

France remains the main target of the GSPC—a September 2005 statement of the group claimed that "the only way to discipline France is jihad and Islamic martyrdom," because "France is our enemy number one, the enemy of our religion, the enemy of our community."[180] In practice, however, mostly because France is a tougher environment for terrorists than most other European countries, GSPC remnants in Europe now operate primarily in Spain, Italy, and Britain, and support the al-Zarqawi network's Iraqi jihad recruitment efforts throughout the continent.

The GSPC, long associated with Al-Qaeda—in fact, as we have seen, created at the instigation of bin Laden as a breakaway faction of the GIA,[181] and since September 2006 publicly affiliated with Al-Qaeda under the label "Al-Qaeda Organization in the Islamic Maghreb" (AQIM) —has steadily absorbed the Moroccan GICM as well as Libyan and Tunisian violent Islamists.[182] Already in May 2005 Islamist sources announced the creation of a *Qa'idat Al Yihad fi Al-Jaza'ir* ("jihad base in Algeria"), and in June of that year six Yemeni "students" were arrested in Algeria and accused of forming a terrorist cell.

In September 2006 the French Unit for Coordination of Antiterrorist Combat (UCLAT) expressed its concern with the training by the GSPC of Tunisian, Libyan, Moroccan, and Mauritanian militants.[183] In Spain, quite a number of police operations during the past few years—"Tigris" in June 2005, "Gamo" and "Green" in November-December 2005, "Chacal" in January 2006—have involved Algerians linked to the GSPC and to al-Zarqawi's organization in Iraq. One of the Algerians in Iraq, Belkacem Bellil, killed 19 Italian carabinieri in a suicide bombing in Nasiriya in November 2005. GSPC militants were arrested in Italy and Switzerland in October 2006.

The links between the GSPC and GICM in Europe have been established for a long time—the Madrid cells included both, and members of both have repeatedly been arrested in Spain, France, and Belgium as part of the al-Zarqawi Iraq network. Given the size and distribution of the Moroccan diaspora in Europe, the GICM's cooperation with the GSPC, now strengthened with the formation of the AQIM, is the most threatening element in the continental jihadi infrastructure.

THE MOROCCANS

For a long time the Moroccan Islamist Fighting Group (GICM) was more active among the Moroccan diaspora than in Morocco itself. Part of the explanation lies in the Rabat government's harsh counter-terrorism measures, and part in the greater opportunities to recruit and operate in the tolerant European environment, including ease of travel and lax police surveillance.

In relative terms, Moroccans have played only a small role among the "Afghan Arabs" that formed the core of Al-Qaeda cadres throughout the world. Indeed, members of smaller populations, like Yemenis, Jordanians, and Palestinians, were involved in larger numbers, and before Moroccans became involved. The efficiency of the Moroccan intelligence force and police, and the high degree of Islamic legitimacy of the Alaoui dynasty, are among the likely explanations. Things began to change after the death of King Hassan II in 1999, in many respects owing to a new degree of liberalization, and thus tolerance for Islamists, under Hassan's successor, Mohammed VI. On the one hand, some of Mohammed's policies—such as increasing the minimum age of marriage from 14 to 18; forcing through Parliament a new and quite progressive family code, giving women a status of near-equality with men unusual in the Muslim world; continuing the traditional, if mostly discreet, good relations with Jews and Israel, as well as the United States—have all enraged the Islamists: including bin Laden, who specifically mentioned Morocco as a primary target (after Saudi Arabia and Jordan) for jihad against traitors to Islam.[184] On the other hand, the general political liberalization has opened the regime to strong pressures from European "human-rights" NGOs—with Islamists so far the main beneficiaries.

Geography has also played a major role in the growth of Moroccan Islamism, at home and in Europe. On the one hand, the proximity and relative ease of entering Spain (especially via the Spanish enclaves of Ceuta and Melilla), and hence the EU, has made a larger proportion of Moroccans than of other Arabs aware of the backwardness of their country; on the other hand it has created opportunities for operations on either side of the Strait of Gibraltar, opportunities made even greater by northern Morocco's dominant position as Europe's main provider of hashish and marijuana.

All these elements contributed to the relatively recent outburst of Moroccan Salafi activities, both at home and in Europe, most spectacularly the related bombings in Casablanca in 2003 and Madrid in 2004 (see below).[185] Since 2003, arrests of Moroccan Islamists have taken place in Spain, Italy, Belgium, Germany, the Netherlands, and the United Kingdom. According to Moroccan sources cited by the American analyst Stephen Ulph,[186] there is even a grand strategic plan, coordinated with Al-Qaeda, to train militants in camps in Morocco and Algeria and dispatch them to Europe and Iraq.

Ulph claims that the GICM network in Europe is led by the

Algerian Abdelkader Hakimi (now in prison), a Belgian citizen and an active traveler to Libya, Turkey, Saudi Arabia, and Malaysia, and that the group includes

> some few hundred committed radicals, supported by 1,000 to 2,000 sympathizers operating on both shores of the Mediterranean. Cells have operated in Italy, the United Kingdom, the Netherlands and Spain, the last of which announced on November 23 the arrest of 10 Moroccans and Algerians suspected of financing and giving logistical support to counterparts from the Algerian GSPC resident in Germany, the Netherlands, Britain, Belgium and Denmark.[187]

Whether that is true or not, all indications are that the GICM and associated groups, mostly based in Belgium, have an extensive reach in Europe and North Africa.

Belgium has long had some of the most lax laws against terrorism in Europe, and the most politically correct governments. Hence it is far from surprising that it has long served as a base for international terrorist groups—from the Kurdish PKK to the Basque ETA and more recently various jihadists, the latter supported by elements in the large Moroccan immigrant community. The Belgian town of Maaseik was found to be a center of the GICM, where meetings and planning for attacks took place, under the leadership of Hakimi and of Khalid Bouloudou.

Hakimi, born in 1966, is the prototype of the professional Salafi terrorist. Under a death sentence in Morocco, he has spent most of his life underground, living for ten years in Algeria, working with the GIA, and traveling to Libya, Turkey, Saudi Arabia, and Malaysia. He probably fought in Afghanistan and Bosnia. Bouloudou, born in 1974, is considered by the Belgians to be the co-coordinator of the GICM in Belgium. He trained in Afghanistan in 2000 and later studied Islam in Syria.[188] In November 2005 both Hakimi and Bouloudou received seven-year sentences in a Belgian court.[189]

The careers of Hakimi and Bouloudou are similar to that of another Moroccan international jihadist, Saad Houssaini. Houssaini, born in 1969, was allegedly the head of the GICM's "military commission." Suspected of being behind the Casablanca bombings of 2003, he topped Morocco's most-wanted list, along with Abdelkrim Medjati, another important GICM leader, who was killed by Saudi forces near Riyadh in 2005. Hussaini embraced the jihadist cause while studying chemistry in Spain and went on to Afghanistan and the Pakistani training camps. He is thought to have personal ties to the Madrid bombers of March 2004.[190]

Meanwhile, a Moroccan "Charter of the Jama'at al-Tawhid wal-Jihad bil-Maghrib" published in 2005 criticized the Rabat regime for its "government based on manmade infidel laws" and the "education of a new apostate generation that will tend the seedling of the infidel colonizers after their departure." King Mohammed VI and his government are seen as even more dangerous than the old French and Spanish colonizers, "since this group comes from among us, speaks our language, and most of the populace know little about them; the disbelief of apostasy is more injurious than original disbelief." This is a common Salafi theme. The "criminal tyrant," Mohammed VI, is to be fought "in the path of jihad in the land of Tariq bin Ziyad [the Berber conqueror of Spain in 711 CE] and Yusuf bin Tashufin" (leader of the fanatical Almoravid sect of the 11th and 12th centuries, who also invaded Spain).[191]

As the Geneva-based researcher Mathieu Guidère points out, Moroccans have been among the most committed volunteers to Iraq since the war began. A Moroccan, "Abu Ussama al-Maghribi," was the suicide bomber who killed Sergio Vieira de Mello, the United Nations' representative in Baghdad, in August 2003.[192] The records captured by U.S. forces in Sinjar, in northwestern Iraq, in October 2007 showed that during the period August 2006 to October 2007, 291 of the 595 foreign fighters listed came from North Africa, of whom 43 were Algerians and 36 Moroccans.[193]

THE NEW MAGHREBI NETWORKS AND AL-QAEDA

In a September 11, 2006, videotaped message, Ayman al-Zawahiri announced the union of the GSPC and Al-Qaeda:

> "Our Emir, the sheikh, the *mujahid*, the lion of Islam, Osama bin Laden, may Allah protect him, has assigned me to bring the good tidings to all Muslims, and to my brothers, the *mujahideen*, wherever they are: The Salafist Group for Preaching and Combat has joined the Al-Qaeda organization. Praise be to Allah for this blessed union. We ask Allah that it be a thorn in the throats of the American and French Crusaders and their allies, and that it be affliction, anxiety, and grief in the hearts of the apostates [i.e., the Algerian government], the traitorous sons of France." In the same video, Ayman Al-Zawahiri called for the liberation of "any land that was once Islamic—from Al-Andalus [i.e., Muslim Spain] to Iraq." . . .
>
> Never in the past has Al Qaeda had such a solid territorial base in such proximity to Western states, and it has threatened to employ this base to attack Europe. The unification of the North African jihad groups under the banner of Al Qaeda, the use of the Sahara for training and arms-smuggling, and the number of North African cells discovered in Europe in the past all indicate the magnitude of the threat.[194]

That process of unification was completed when the Libyan Islamic Fighting Group (LIFG) officially joined Al-Qaeda on November 3, 2007.

According to Moroccan Interior Minister Chakib Benmussa, in 2006 alone 30 inhabitants of Tetuán—a city of 300,000—left for Iraq, most of them passing through Spain.[195] The majority of the Moroccans involved in the March 2004 bombings in Spain were also from the Tetuán area. In January 2007, 90 would-be jihadis linked to the GSPC, all ready to go to Iraq, were arrested. Putting these facts together with a late-2006 cross-border attack in Tunisia, we can see that Al-Qaeda in Islamic Maghreb has indeed become a regional, rather than purely Algerian, organization. Its founder, Abu Musab Abdulwadud, could be seen as a clone of al-Zarqawi—formally loyal to bin Laden, but in fact an autonomous regional actor. That has direct implications for Europe, since the already-established GSPC and GICM infrastructure in Belgium, the United Kingdom, and Spain is now absorbing the smaller Libyan and Tunisian jihadist groups, active especially in Italy.

The structure of the Spanish jihadi cells has already demonstrated the North African militants' ability to work together, as they have involved Moroccans, Algerians, Egyptian, Tunisians, Mauritanians, and Libyans. The latter, now the largest North African contingent in Iraq, could be expected to become more active in Europe once the insurgent Islamic State of Iraq is defeated and the survivors return—probably to Europe rather than Libya. The same could be expected in the case of the other North Africans. Already in Morocco, whereas before one could speak of "Afghan Moroccans," now one hears mentions of "Iraqi Moroccans"—which suggests that the number of returning jihadis is growing.

It is clear now that jihadi cells implanted in a number of countries for more than a decade are increasingly being assimilated into the Al-Qaeda nebula, and many are now linked to it formally. That, however, does not mean that European cells operate according to a grand strategy decided and directed from the mountains of Pakistan. A common long-term goal does not contradict the existing pattern of highly autonomous cells, self-financed and pursuing their own immediate as well as some global causes. In this sense the debate over Al-Qaeda's direct presence in Europe—still going on in the media, if not among intelligence experts—is as misguided as it is fruitless. Ultimately the positions taken by the two sides on the issue depend on their understanding of what Al-Qaeda is—an organization with clear command-and-control structures, or a loose movement glued together by a few symbolic and charismatic figures, a general ideology, and personal ties among important actors. Because the situation, in Europe more than anywhere else, is in flux and influenced by so many disparate factors—ethnicity, different speeds of re-Islamization, and diverse country conditions—the term used by the French media, the Al-Qaeda "nebula," remains the best overall description of the jihadi universe there.

The fact is that the original core leadership of Al-Qaeda has reduced its direct, operational involvement in Islamist terrorist activities and replaced it with the role of ideological arbiters and motivators. The reasons for this are many, and well known. Some are logistical, since communication with the outside world from the Pakistani mountains is both difficult and dangerous; some are financial, since bin Laden's sources of funding have decreased.

These facts do not mean that Al-Qaeda has no distinct role or presence in Europe or the West in general, only that it has become more a "movement" than a hierarchical, structured organization. Hence, when Hamed Abderrahmane, a Spanish citizen from the Melilla enclave in North Africa, was captured by the U.S. in Afghanistan, sent to Guantanamo, and then back to Spain, where he was found guilty of membership in Al-Qaeda and sentenced to six years in jail,[196] that was the exception rather than the rule. Claims of authorship of the 2004 Madrid bombings by a so-called "Abu Hafs al-Masri/al-Qaida"[197] should also be viewed with skepticism. The Al-Qaeda core leadership has established a pattern of claiming responsibility for attacks conducted by autonomous groups, or even for events that proved to be unrelated to terrorism (such as the 2003 blackout on the East Coast of the United States).

THE "NATIVE" CELLS—ENTHUSIASTIC AMATEURS?

To these more or less ethnically based networks one must add the local freelance cells, whether in Britain, Italy, or the Netherlands, which appear spontaneously, usually led by an individual who has some ties with non-European Islamist groups in the Middle East or Pakistan. The London bombers of July 7, 2005, are a good example. On the other hand, their July 21 amateurish imitators, mostly of Somali/Ethiopian backgrounds, were, apparently, isolated from the global jihadist movements and networks. However, through ethnic ties, they had connections with the Somali community in Italy and, more likely than not, some help elsewhere, which explains how Osman Hussain, the presumed leader of the cell, managed to escape Britain, cross France, and end up in Italy, despite an intense manhunt for him.

Another example of a small jihadi network—and one of the very few involving Muslims from the Balkans—was the one centering on Mirsad Bektasevic, a.k.a. Maximus. Bektasevic, a 19-year-old Bosniak refugee with a Swedish passport, and his closest associate, Abdulkadir Cesur, a Turk with Danish resident status, were arrested in Sarajevo in October 2005. Both were involved in the Zarqawi recruiting network for Iraq, and they had contacts in Britain, where related arrests were made, and among young Danish radicals.[198]

When Bektasevic was a young boy, his father was killed in a traffic accident. A few years later his mother fled war-torn

Bosnia and took her two sons to Sweden. Bektasevic grew up as an assiduous worshipper at the Islamic Sunni Centre, better known as the Bellevue Mosque in Gothenburg, a well-known Salafi center subsidized by the Swedish government and linked with the Al-Haramein Foundation, an Al-Qaeda–related Saudi "charity" that has been dismantled since.

The rest is by now familiar. Maximus's mother claimed: "He was not religious before, but in the past two years he practiced more seriously. Some people frightened him and talked to him about hell, and told him he would be tortured in hell if he does not pray and does not believe."

The cell had a computer expert and hacker, Younis Tsouli, age 22, based in London; four of its members were based in Denmark and were worshippers at the Noebbro mosque of the late imam Abu Laban, of cartoon-controversy fame.[199]

Bosnia has for a number of years served as a focus of global jihad. After the end of the war, some 800 foreign Islamists settled there, and there was a degree of radicalization under their influence.[200] However, Bosniaks abroad are not a particularly radical group. In fact, the Bosniak members of the cell—and they were a minority—were radicalized in Denmark, Britain, and Sweden, not in the Balkans, and their goals were typically jihadist—i.e., unrelated to local causes but directed toward whatever the current focus of global jihad happens to be: in this case, Iraq and Afghanistan.

The Hofstad Group (Hofstadgroep) in the Netherlands first came to the attention of the authorities in 2002. In October of 2003 Samir Azzouz and fellow members Radwan al-Issa, Jason Walters, Ismail Akhnikh, and Zine Labedine Aouragha were arrested in the Netherlands under suspicion of planning terrorist attacks, suspicions based in part on the fact that both Jason Walters and Ismail Akhnikh had visited the Pakistani terrorist training camps of *Jaish-e-Mohammed*.[201] The same month, the group's Syrian mentor, Abu Khaled, was expelled to Germany after being found to reside illegally in the Netherlands.

In April 2004 Azzouz was again arrested, as a suspect in a bank robbery; when police searched his home they found floor plans of the Schiphol airport, the Dutch Parliament ("Hofstad"—hence the group's name), and a nuclear-power plant. A judge nonetheless released him, admitting that he "suspect[ed] that [Azzouz] was preparing a crime, but it is unclear what crime he intended to carry out." In June 2004 two other group members, Nouredine el-Fatmi and Mohammed el-Morabit, were arrested in Portugal under suspicion of planning the assassination of Prime Minister Manuel Baroso during the European soccer champonships. That same year Portuguese intelligence found that group members were meeting in Lisbon, and deported them to the Netherlands—where they were again released. Finally, in November 2004, Jason Walters and Ismail Akhnikh, surrounded by police in an apartment in The Hague, threw hand grenades at the police, injuring three. They were arrested and eventually convicted of terrorism.[202]

Another member of the group, Rachid Bousana (age 32) was arrested in London in June 2005 and extradited to the Netherlands. In October that year Azzouz and six other members were arrested, accused of acquiring weapons and explosives—and, once again, acquitted by the Hague Supreme Court for "inconclusive evidence." In November 30 Outman ben Amar, an interpreter for the AIVD (the Dutch General Intelligence and Security Service), was accused of deliberately passing on secret AIVD information to the Hofstad Group.[203]

The Netherlands is proud to be known as a politically dull country, where decisions are made on the basis of the largest possible consensus, sharp political debates are rare, and political assassinations were unknown since that of Willem van Oranje, the founder of the Netherlands, in 1584. This is also a country where gay marriage, drugs, and euthanasia are all legal, where prostitutes and the military are unionized, and which right-fully considers itself one of the most liberal in the world. For all these reasons the twin murders of Pim Fortuyn and Theo van Gogh had an extraordinary impact on the Netherlands—perhaps, proportionately speaking, more than 9/11 did on the United States.

Dr. Wilhelmus Simon Petrus Fortuijn, better known as Pim Fortuyn, was murdered on May 6, 2002, by Volkert van der Graaf, a fanatical "animal-rights" activist claiming that he was protecting Muslims against Fortuyn's attacks.

Fortuyn was a hard-to-define, reluctant politician. Wikipedia was forced to engage in verbal acrobatics to arrive at this "defi-nition" of his politics:

> Fortuyn could perhaps best be described as a liberal right-wing populist, or a reactionary liberal, although some of his ideas were rather leftist[!]; he was in favor of free public transportation and reducing the size of the Dutch military. This could be seen as a lack of political ideology and mere populism, saying whatever will appeal to voters, though some have described this as syncretic politics, combining ideas from the left and right into a new ideological synthesis.[204]

Fortuyn's celebrity came from his articulating what many Dutchmen felt but were reluctant to express: that Muslims in the Netherlands are increasingly intolerant of aspects of Dutch culture—especially gay rights and women's rights—and that, at any rate, "The Netherlands are full," as Fortuyn put it, refer-ring to the fact that the country is one of the most densely pop-ulated in the world. In *Against the Islamicisation of Our Culture* (1997) Fortuyn made it clear that Islam is incompatible with Dutch values. Later he said, "Look at the Netherlands. In what country could an electoral leader of such a large movement as mine be openly homosexual? How wonderful that that's possible. That's something that one can be proud of. And I'd like to keep it that way, thank you very much."[205] In a 2004 TV show, Fortuyn was chosen as "The Greatest Dutchman of all times," followed closely by Willem van Oranje.

Fortuyn's murder produced an immediate backlash against immigrants, and especially Muslims, with his political party, the Pim Fortuyn List (LPF), winning 17 percent of the vote in the 2002 elections and 26 seats out of 150 in the Parliament. Without its leader, the LPF soon collapsed into chaos; in the parliamentary elections of 2003 its members gained only eight seats. However, the votes it lost went to conservative parties, which adopted most of the late maverick's ideas—including a crackdown on immigration and asylum seekers.

While Fortuyn's murder seemed to awaken the Dutch public to the Islamic problem in their midst, that of Theo van Gogh in 2004 transformed what used to be the most multicultural country anywhere except Canada into one of the most serious about its cultural identity, security, and laws.

Indeed, the November 2004 murder of van Gogh, the bearer of a famous name (he was the grandnephew of Vincent van Gogh), truly changed Dutch political culture. Van Gogh's assassin, Mohammed Bouyeri (a leading member of the Hofstad Group), left a message at the scene that he would also kill Hirsi Ali, a Dutch MP of Somali origin, who had collaborated with van Gogh on his film *Submission*. At his trial, Bouyeri expressed no remorse and stated that he would do it again to defend his faith.

Generally speaking, the Dutch Islamist problem is a Moroccan one—not that the "Turks" (or, more accurately, the Turkish Kurds) in the country do not raise problems, but their activities, including PKK training camps, are directed against Ankara, not The Hague. The Moroccans, on the other hand, not only are resisting assimilation but are increasingly radicalized—including a growing support for the GICM. They also remain behind socially and economically, despite Dutch efforts to help through an oversized welfare state.

Islamist and other terrorist networks have been discovered in the Netherlands since the van Gogh murder—which strongly suggests that previously either the AIVD did not want to discover them or its political bosses did not want such discoveries made public.

In any case, the AIVD, as suggested by its director's statement, now realizes the depth and seriousness of the Islamist problem in the country:

> "The threat represented by Islamist terrorist groups is not only directly related to violence . . . Islamist fighters (mujahidin) resident in the Netherlands who are involved in recruitment threaten the democratic legal order by these activities also in another way. They purposefully influence members of the Muslim communities in the Netherlands in order to create a polarization in society and to alienate the Muslims from the rest of the population. The polarizing influence of the mujahidin reinforces purposeful efforts by radical Islamic persons and organizations within and outside the Netherlands to prevent the integration of citizens with a Muslim background and to create a religiously based antagonism between Muslims and their non-Islamic environment."[206]

Moreover, the global reach of Islamist jihadism has a presence in the Netherlands —as the AIVD now acknowledges:

> "Two young Dutchmen of Moroccan origin resident at Eindhoven were killed in the Indian province of Kashmir in January 2002. It turned out that the two young men had been recruited in the Netherlands by radical Muslims who mentally prepared them for participation in the violent jihad. This incident made painfully clear that also some Muslims raised

in the Netherlands are receptive to radical Islamic ideas. These
young people appear to be susceptible to indoctrination by
charismatic spiritual leaders. Meanwhile, on the instigation
of the AIVD, several members of an international network
of Islamist fighters have been arrested in the Netherlands.
Several of them are suspected of involvement in recruitment
of Muslims in the Netherlands for Islamist purposes."[207]

In all these cases, the pattern of cell formation and action is
similar. First an immigrant Islamist recruiter (Abu Laban, Abu
Khaled) transforms a group of friends, often co-nationals—
Maximus's group included other Bosniaks—into an ideological
unit. Second, one of the more promising members of the group
travels abroad and establishes links with some prominent jihadi figure—Maximus apparently met al-Zarqawi; Jason Walters
and Ismail Akhnikh went to Al-Qaeda camps in Pakistan—who
may suggest a selection of targets. Third, the now-structured
cell seeks financing, usually through crime, and finally the operation is on the way. It is important to note that cells in Europe
always include members with computer skills, the equivalent
of the communications expert in a military unit.

The most important common pattern is that European cells
always have some link, direct and personal, with established
global jihadi structures—the cells may be homegrown, but the
seeds are always imported. All of this raises the issue of how
Muslims in Europe take the path of jihad—the personal and
cultural motivations, and the mechanics of indoctrination.

The Roads to Jihad

For the Muslim of the French *banlieue* or the ethnic neighborhood of Leeds or Amsterdam, the road to action, whether
overseas or more recently at home, always passes through
contacts with the established recruitment and logistical networks that operate in most countries. There is no spontaneous,

independent way for most of them to travel to Syria, the main gateway to Iraq, or to Chechnya or Pakistan—especially given the fact that many of them are on welfare or in poorly paid occasional jobs. How, in the absence of organized networks, could one explain the extensive travels of perennially jobless individuals like Richard Reid (Israel, the United States) or Nizar Trabelsi (Pakistan, Afghanistan)? Even travel within Europe has costs that most of them could not cover from their known income. Moreover, while Iraq is now the main attraction for Europe-based Islamists, their interest in fighting for Islam abroad is much older than the Iraq war, and has shifted in location—at various times it has been Kashmir, Bosnia, Kosovo, Afghanistan, Chechnya.

It is hard to define a general profile of those involved, as is often pointed out in frustration by analysts and intelligence officials alike. Still, France offers a large and well-analyzed sample, and we can assume that the following profiles have some validity for other Europe-based jihadists.

Kamel Daoudi of the Beghal network was born in 1965 in Sedrata, Algeria. He arrived in France at age five, which practically makes him second-generation. His father, a hospital worker at Pitié-Salpêtrière, hoped that Kamel would become an engineer—and indeed he was a good student. However, having converted to Islamism in a radical mosque at Corbeil-Essonnes, the young man dropped out of his studies of informatics, worked for a while in a cybercafé, and moved to the United Kingdom, to Leicester, together with his close friend Djamel Beghal. Beghal was already a major terrorist figure, a veteran of Afghan camps and close to the Finsbury Park circle and Abu Qatada in England. In the spring of 2001, the two moved to an Al-Qaeda training camp at Jalalabad, in Afghanistan, while Daoudi applied for, and received, French citizenship (following in the tracks of many other immigrants, yet in his case and in hindsight, this fact does not fail to astonish). Back at Corbeil in August 2001, Daoudi learned that Beghal had been arrested; he fled to England, where he was arrested and sent back to France. There he was tried and jailed—and his citizenship was withdrawn.[208] As for Beghal, he had grown up in Algeria and later moved between France, Germany, and England, operating as a recruiter of importance in the Al-Qaeda networks, and was personally close to that organization's main recruiter and trainer—the Palestinian Abu Zubaida.

Here was a clear instance of an individual who appeared to be well integrated and indeed assimilated, with a good future ahead, who made a personal choice to join the jihad—and to take advantage of the laws of his country of adoption—all under the influence of an immigrant radical. One may conclude that one of the main obstacles—if not *the* main obstacle— to Muslim integration and a major cause of radicalization in Europe is the continuous immigration from Africa, the Middle East, and South Asia. These immigrants reinforce, or even create, Salafi centers in Europe.

Atef el O, the bachelor of Tunisian origin briefly discussed above, flew to Cairo one day in April 2005. At age 22, living in Aubervilliers, he was working in shabby pizzerias and temporary jobs while also involved in small thefts and various acts of violence. According to his friends, the trip to Egypt was intended for learning Arabic and the Quran, but one of his Aubervilliers buddies claimed that "the true goal of Atef was Iraq," and a policeman confirmed that he had indeed manifested such an intention before getting his ticket for Cairo. "Atef of Aubervilliers" then disappeared into Iraq and is presumed dead. Atef el O was in contact with one of the gangs of Seine-Saint-Denis that crisscrossed Aubervilliers, Bondy, and La Courneuve.

These Islamists, all between 21 and 25 years of age, alternating between unemployment and small jobs, tried to recruit others in the same circumstances. At one point the group merged with the better-known gang of Buttes-Chaumont, dismantled by the *Direction de la Surveillance du Territoire* (DST) in January 2005, after having sent half a dozen youths to Iraq. Badi B., alias "Abu Hamza," 25 years of age, the chief of the gang, founded a Quranic school in Egypt, where a dozen young Muslims from France have gone already. According to the French intelligence services, the two groups intended to send volunteers to Iraq via Egypt and Syria. Interrogated by the DST in September 2004, Badi B. and his comrades denied these accusations before being released. A month later, Atef el O reached Iraq via Egypt and Syria.

"Iraq is a propaganda tool for the Islamists," observed a *Renseignements Généraux* officer. He explained that recruiters exploit the sentiment of exclusion felt by the youths of difficult neighborhoods, their desire to return to mythical roots, and their hatred for Jews and the United States. A specialist of the DST adds that this is especially true if the neighborhood and the gang are ones "where youths from the Maghreb immigration mix with black and converted kids."

Compared to Atef el O, "**Tewfik**" appeared more stable and traditional. A truck driver, from a Moroccan family living in Val-d'Oise, he "sees the hand of God everywhere." Convinced of the superiority of Islam, he thought it necessary to fight the "ungrateful and treacherous" Jews and the "domineering" Christians. He intended to follow his brother Karim, who left for Iraq via Syria in 2003. Karim had sent news, saying he was living in a house with a hundred other French Muslims and they were trusted with "missions"—including the shooting of an American soldier soon after he surrendered. The figure is probably exaggerated, since French antiterrorist services believe that only some twenty youths from France have fought in Iraq. British authorities estimate the number of jihadis from the UK bound for Iraq at close to one hundred.[209]

The first instances of Muslims from Europe becoming engaged in jihad abroad did not raise many eyebrows among the public and media since the jihadists were involved in causes which, for different reasons, enjoyed widespread, including official, sympathy: Bosnia, Kosovo, and Chechnya.

Arab volunteers (from Europe and the Arab countries) in Bosnia and Kosovo during the 1990s largely failed to radicalize local Muslims. The jihadist cells in Bosnia were uncovered, and some foreign Islamist volunteers were arrested and deported or turned over to the United States. Relevant here are the cases of two men active in Bosnia: the Moroccan Karim Said Atmani, a GIA operative previously jailed in France for collusion with bin Laden, and Abu el Maali, an Egyptian accused in France of smuggling explosives for a *Jamaa Islamiya* attempt to blow up U.S. military installations in Germany. So are the activities of the Al-Haramain Islamic Foundation (AHF) in Sarajevo. In June 2002, AHF was linked by the U.S. Treasury Department with Ayman al-Zawahiri's own, *Al-Gama'at al-Islamiya* (the Egyptian Islamic Group), and placed on the list of terrorist groups.[210]

A somewhat peculiar case is that of Chechnya. It is also a good example of Europeans' unwitting encouragement of Islamist terrorism: "It's of no concern as long as it stays away from our shores." The problem, of course, is that jihadism is fungible—as the Afghanistan case should have demonstrated. Once engaged on that path, the terrorist will always find other battlefields in defense of the *ummah* and against its persecutors, wherever they may be found.

Chechnya's cause had enjoyed significant European public sympathy, the war having long been seen as pitting the Chechen underdogs against the Russian juggernaut. That the nature of the Chechnya war has changed dramatically since its inception in the 1990s is a fact still neglected or not understood in European capitals, where it is not recognized that Chechnya's leaders (such as the late Shamil Basayev) have fallen under the influence—in ideology and methods—of Al-Qaeda–style Salafism. This despite the Beslan massacre of September 1, 2004, for which Basayev accepted responsibility. As in the cases of Bosnia and Kosovo, many European countries turned a blind eye to those of their Muslim citizens or legal immigrants who decided to "volunteer" to go and fight there—not for freedom or independence, but for the sake of Salafi Islam. After the well-known example of Afghanistan, it should not have been surprising that jihadists returning from the Balkans, Chechnya, or Kashmir have used their newly acquired combat experience and ideological convictions against their European countries of residence. Moreover, Chechnya was the first instance of suicide bombings on the European continent—albeit mostly by Chechens rather than outsiders.

One of the indirect results of the flow of jihadis to Bosnia and Chechnya was the establishment of a logistical network, which was later used for operations in Europe itself and further away, in Iraq and elsewhere. In addition, a fraternity of veterans was established, all to some extent due to the tolerance of European authorities. However, many of the volunteers who went to Bosnia or Chechnya were not just idealists who took the first plane to Sarajevo or Tbilisi, but already members of established networks.

Thus, under the spiritual and religious patronage of Abu Qatada from London, Abu Dahdah and al-Suri—together with the Palestinian Anwar Adnan Mohamed Saleh, who worked directly with bin Laden in Afghanistan as early as 1995—formed the Islamic Alliance in Spain, largely unhindered by the authorities. The Islamic Alliance's spinoff, "The Soldiers of Allah," recruited *mujahedin* for Bosnia, Chechnya, and Afghanistan. Members of the group included Abdalrahman Alarnaot Abu Aljer and Mohamed Zaher Asade, a.k.a. "Zaher," both recruited by Abu Dahdah and sent to Bosnia, where they received training at Zenica; Mohamed Needl Acaid ("Nidal"); Jasem Mahboule ("Abu Mohamad"), who fought in Bosnia and was twice in Afghanistan; and Osama Darra ("Abu Thabet"). All of these men had already been indicted in 2003 by Judge Garzón in Madrid.[211] Upon returning from the Balkans or the Caucasus, these veterans, with their prestige enhanced, continued their activities in Spain. The Abu Dahdah network led directly to the Madrid bombings and Leganés.

By the same token, Nouredine Merabet, an Algerian colleague of Menad Benchellali in the Chechen camps of the Pankisi Gorge, was later linked with a group of Algerian "refugees" allegedly plotting to attack the London Underground with poison gas. In March 2007 he was on trial for plotting attacks in France, against the Russian embassy and French targets.[212]

CHAPTER SIX

Perpetrators and Patterns

"The future generation of international jihadists will form a fluid, non-hierarchical movement of autonomous armed groups instigating simultaneous armed struggle."

—Shane Drennan and Andrew Black,
referring to Abu Musab al-Suri[1]

Europe is now the front line between radical Islamism and the rest of the world. Importantly, some of the ideological and recruitment centers of global Salafism have steadily moved from their traditional locations in Saudi Arabia, Egypt, and Pakistan to Europe. When London-based imams provide religious cover to Salafi groups in Yemen or Algeria, and recruit members for operational cells involved in attacks in the United States, Iraq, Yemen, Tunisia, and Europe itself; when Maghreb-originated terrorist organizations like the GIA, GSPC, and GICM have a better infrastructure in Europe than at home, it is clear that Europe's role has changed dramatically.

There are many political and cultural reasons for this phenomenon, but there are also tactical and strategic ones, having to do with European Salafists' new role as major contributors to the global activities of radical Islam. If there is indeed a struggle inside Islam in Europe between the followers, usually called "moderates," of a "European" Islam, and the radicals seeking a thorough re-Islamization of Muslims in Europe, so far the latter are way ahead.

What are the roots and manifestations of the present Salafist and terrorist infrastructure in Europe? Who belongs to it, and what are the goals of the Islamist micro-culture? Are they nationally based or are they re-creating an international or pan-European scene? And how are they linked with non-European Islamist structures, including elements of the Al-Qaeda nebula elsewhere in the world? Finally, is there something specific to the actions of Europe-based groups or individuals, or are they following more general jihadi patterns?

We can take as an example the Moroccan and Algerian networks we looked at in Chapter 5. Chased from their countries, they found refuge in Spain, France, Belgium, and the United Kingdom, both among immigrant communities from the Maghreb and beyond. Once established there, they spread and established ties with each other and ultimately with Al-Qaeda elements already in Europe or, like al-Zarqawi's Iraqi network, seeking support there. That implies ideological homogenization[2] and involvement in new geographic areas—including Europe itself. Are such groups and their European activities primarily directed at continental targets, or extensions of their North African logistical and tactical operations? To examine these issues one has to consider specific cases of jihadis, their cells and operations in Europe, and their links with the larger Islamist world.

A preliminary view suggests a sort of concentrated neo-Salafi ideology formed around a few basic ideas: hatred for a vaguely defined "West," the legitimacy of violence against "apostate" governments in the Muslim world and "infidel" powers alike, and a desire to establish an equally vaguely defined "Caliphate" and to apply the Sharia on a global basis. This general and simple view of the world explains the cooperation between Islamist groups initially oriented toward national goals and the supranational Al-Qaeda. Specific causes like Afghanistan, Iraq, Palestine, and Chechnya serve as pretexts for action, which can, and indeed do, change over time and according to circumstances, without any of them being the sole, motivating cause for specific acts. Inevitably, ideological homogenization leads to common tactics, often facilitated by similar training— suicide bombing being a good example.

Whereas one cannot state with any confidence that European Salafist terror is inspired, manipulated, or directed from the caves of Waziristan or the Sunni Triangle of Iraq, it should not be interpreted as being a completely separate phenomenon, somehow due to specific "root causes" local to Spain, or Britain, or the Netherlands. Indeed, *if* there is such a thing as "root causes," then they are to be found, first and foremost, in the general cultural malaise of Islam everywhere, especially the widespread sense of victimhood among Muslims, and, second, in the influence of the situation in non-European countries like Morocco, Algeria, or Pakistan.

An examination of Islamist terrorism, and terrorist profiles, in or from Europe reveals some basic patterns, at least since the mid-1990s:

- The migration to Europe of radical Salafist ideologues and activists, many via phony asylum applications. Some of those individuals had and still have direct personal and ideological ties to the Al-Qaeda core leadership, including bin Laden and al-Zawahiri, and some were involved in terrorism even before Al-Qaeda was formed.

- The more recent wholesale migration of cells and even larger structures of outside (mostly Maghrebi) Islamist terrorist organizations to Europe, via immigration, legal or otherwise.

- The active recruitment by both of the above among resident Muslims and, in disproportionately large numbers, native converts.

- Occasional visits, for purposes of targeting and technical help, by core Al-Qaeda experts, helping immigrant or local cells.

- Spontaneous formation of cells by personally disgruntled individuals and engagement in "copycat" terrorism, the failed London bombings of July 21, 2005, being an example.

Characteristics of Jihadis

While national variations could be significant, as the following case studies demonstrate, the general trend is toward increased similarity of European jihadi profiles as well as growing ideological unity.

In terms of ethnicity, while the largest single group of Muslims in Western Europe is the Turks (there is also a significant number of Bosniaks and Albanian Muslims in Europe), the overwhelming majority of *Islamists* come from Maghrebi and Pakistani backgrounds. This phenomenon contradicts many of the standard explanations of Muslim radicalization in Europe, such as underprivileged status, since there is no significant difference between the socioeconomic status of Turks, Bosniaks, and Albanians on the one hand, and Arabs and Pakistanis on the other. The causes of radicalism and Islamization are to be found elsewhere—specifically in (1) the culture and nature of

Islam in the country of origin, and (2) the dominant discourse in the Muslim world in general.

That the first is true even among second- or indeed third-generation Muslims in Europe, whose language and ties to the country of origin of their immigrant parents (or grandparents) are often limited, may appear surprising, but, given the re-Islamization process and search for a new identity, it is only superficially so.

As we saw so strikingly in the case of the London Transport bombers, there is a tendency in the European media and academia to assume that terrorists operating in Europe are somehow "homemade" and acting spontaneously. In England, until Al-Qaeda–made videotapes of two of the July 2005 terrorists were seen, they were considered isolated cases with no outside links. When Lebanese students Youssef El-Hajdib (age 21) and Jihad Hamad (age 20) were found planting explosive devices on German trains on July 31, 2006,

> . . . it had looked like an isolated plot because they declared they had been radicalized by the row over the publication of cartoons of the Prophet Muhammad in European newspapers. But eight months on, after analyzing computer hard drives, mobile phone data, DNA traces and interrogation records, German authorities have reached a different conclusion—that the attacks were commissioned by a man with links to al-Qaida as a test of courage to qualify them for attacks on US-led forces in Iraq.[3]

Similarly, Mohammed Bouyeri's murder of Theo van Gogh was initially seen as an isolated case, until his links with the Hofstad Group and the group's own extensive connections with jihadi circles in Spain and Germany became public. The answer to the cries of the British tabloids after the 7/7 bombings, "Why are they turning against their own country?" is obvious: England was not "their" country and British commuters were not "their" fellow citizens. England was the proximate location of *Dar al Harb* (the "abode of war").

Indeed, the 7/7 cell had close links with Pakistan, which is, with Saudi Arabia, the main source of Salafist ideology and jihadi recruitment in the world. Consider that in Britain, some 600,000 of the c. 2 million Muslims of Indian-subcontinent origin came from the region of Mirpur, in the Pakistani part of Kashmir.[4] Within deeply Islamist Pakistan, the Kashmiris are the most radicalized, with terrorist groups like *Lashkar-e-Toiba* and *Jaish-e-Mohammed* supported by large segments of the population—and linked to the popular Al-Qaeda as well.[5]

A more general, and very accurate, description of the Islamists' view of Al-Qaeda is provided by "Rashid," an Algerian radical living illegally in London in 2003:

> Al-Qaeda is a cloak patched from different sources of discontent. Certain views are shared, but we Algerian rebels have our own agenda and our own scores to settle with the oppressors of our country. . . . The police and gendarmes who burst into our homes and kill our friends and family have wounded us far more than American decadence. They are the immediate source of our rage. Bin Laden's skill as an ideologue is to transform particular grievances into a universal struggle.[6]

As this suggests, many join the jihad for personal reasons. How did a Sidique Khan or a Mohammed Bouyeri, both apparently well integrated, and a petty criminal like Khaled Kelkal all reach the same degree of alienation, the same level of re-Islamization, to the point of acting violently against their own countries of residence (and even birth)? The answers are incomplete, but some aspects seem decisive: the influence of personal alienation, which brings us into the slippery field of psychology, and outside influences—from more recent Muslim immigrants and, especially, from itinerant recruiters/imams.

In a somewhat different category, since unlike Sidique Khan he did not have the culture and family ties of the country of origin to influence him, is Xavier Djaffo, the son of a French mother and a Beninois father, who in 2000 went to fight jihad in the Caucasus. A big man with green eyes, the father of a child left behind in France, he was a friend of Zacarias Moussaoui, whom he had met while they were both at high school in Perpignan, in southern France. Installed in London after obtaining an M.A. in economics, Djaffo converted to Islam. Becoming "Massoud al-Benini," he learned Arabic and frequented fundamentalist mosques, before going to fight in Chechnya with the "battalion of martyrs Abdus Samad." He was first wounded by a mortar round that smashed his foot, then killed by Russian soldiers.[7]

Like Djaffo, many terrorists based or born in Europe are above average in terms of education—even when compared to the natives, and especially when compared to people in their countries of origin. Even when, like Sidique Khan, they have close ties to the country of origin, most do not associate themselves with those ethnic groups or their specific grievances, but rather just with "Islam." The younger they are, the less they identify with their parents' country of origin. Nor, as we saw in Chapter 5, do the main factors explaining the rise of jihadism in Europe have to do with specific national, social, or economic conditions in the country of residence.

METHODS AND STRUCTURE

The structure of jihadist cells in Europe has been best examined by the Norwegian researcher Petter Nesser, who linked it to the process of recruitment in general. His conclusion is that there are four general types of cell members: the *entrepreneur*, the *protégé*, the *misfit*, and the *drifter*:

The entrepreneur and the protégé are often religiously devout idealists who appear to join through intellectual processes and appear to be driven mainly by political grievances and a call for social justice. Misfits appear to join cells mainly to deal with personal problems or out of loyalty to other cell members, whereas the drifters join a cell more unconsciously, through their social networks.[8]

As general categories, these are useful, but there are three questions they don't answer:

1. Are there differences between this pattern, common in Europe, and the patterns in jihadist cells in the Islamic world?

2. What makes a misfit or a drifter—presumably the least ideologically or religiously committed member of a cell, at least initially—ready to become a suicide bomber, as Germaine Lindsay did in London and Jamal Ahmidan did in Leganés, and as Nizar Trabelsi was ready to do in Belgium? Murder through suicide is hardly a way to deal with personal problems—much higher motivation is needed.

3. What is the glue that brings such socially, ideologically, and psychologically disparate types together?

The answer to these questions seems to lie in (1) adherence to a certain version of Islam that gives unity to a combination of personal, political, and social grievances, and (2) the strong conviction that only action/violence offers a solution.

Analyzing two major jihadist networks in Spain, Javier Jordán and Robert Wesley noted that

one of them, led by Imad Eddin Barakat a.k.a. Abu Dahdah, started with a nucleus of Syrians, former Muslim Brotherhood militants, long established in Spain. Brothers Moutaz and

Mohannad Almallah Dabas, both Spanish citizens, were essential in the process of indoctrination and organization. Moutaz, who lived in London and was close to Abu Qatada, the Finsbury Park mosque and Abu Hamza, was an ideologue, together with Abu Dahdah, while Mohannad used his Madrid house for meetings of al-Maymouni's group. The latter was himself recruited by fellow Moroccan Amer al-Azizi, who also maintained relations with the Libyan Islamic Fighting Group and with the Moroccan Islamic Combatants Group (GICM), both associated with al-Qaeda. Mustapha al-Maymouni in turn established cells in Madrid and in Kenitra and Larache in Morocco.[9]

Following al-Maymouni's 2003 arrest in Morocco in connection with the Casablanca bombings, the cell's leadership was taken over by his brother-in-law, the Tunisian Serhane ben Abdelmajid Fakhet ("El Tunecino"), and the remnants of the Abu Dahdah network became the March 11 network. With Fakhet also came the Algerian Allekema Lamari, an old GIA hand, and Jamal Ahmidan, a Moroccan thief and drug trafficker—all three among the suicide group of Leganés.

> Abu Dahdah had extensive international links—in fact two Spanish judges, Juan del Olmo and Baltasar Garzón, considered him Al Qaeda's representative in Spain. He offered to send al-Maymouni to a training camp in Indonesia and, as head of a jihadist group, "Soldiers of Allah," active around the Abu Baker mosque in Madrid, was sending volunteers to Bosnia, Chechnya and Afghanistan.[10]

On the other hand, according to Jordán and Wesley, "Communication channels existed between Fakhet's group, Al-Qaeda, and two important members of the GICM in Europe, Youssef Belhadj and Hassan al-Haski [both on trial in Madrid by February 2007] who had previous knowledge of the attacks."[11] In addition, al-Azizi, al-Maymouni, and Fakhet were all involved with *Jamaat al-Tabligh Wal-Dawa* in Madrid.[12]

What patterns can we see here? First, most of the important members had **prior ties with jihadi circles**—global in the case of Abu Dahdah and Amer Azizi, North African in those of Azizi, al-Maymouni, and Lamari. Whether **involvement with *Tabligh*** radicalized them, provided the occasion of meeting one another, or both, is not clear, but it certainly demonstrated fundamentalist convictions. **Family connections** also contributed to the recruitment process, although in the case of al-Maymouni and Fakhet, their marriages to sisters were probably the result of moving in the same circles, rather than a factor in radicalization.

Perhaps the most important element in the origins and structures of the Spanish jihadists' networks is their international nature—these men were not "homegrown radicals" upset by Madrid's policy in Iraq. At most, considering the chronology of events, the time needed for planning, and indeed the statements of the Leganés suicides, Iraq provided the immediate pretext for the March 2004 attack; it certainly had nothing to do with Abu Dahdah or the Syrian Muslim Brotherhood exiles.

Nor is the Spanish case unique. The same seamless tissue of local and global ideological and personal jihadi linkages (most of them ultimately leading to London), criminality, and fanaticism exists elsewhere. Such is the case with the cell dismantled in London in February 2008, accused of supplying terrorist materials to Pakistani groups and planning attacks in the United Kingdom. The "brain" of the cell was Mohammed Hamid, a drug addict with a long criminal record, who became a disciple of the radical preachers Abdullah el-Faisal and Abu Hamza and went to Pakistan and Afghanistan. All four of the failed suicide bombers of July 21 attended meetings in his house, and Hamid ran an Islamic bookstall on Oxford Street with Muktar Ibrahim, the leader of the July 21 gang.[13] The "emir" of the group, Atilla

Ahmet, a Turkish Cypriot, was Abu Hamza's main aide and his successor as leader of the Supporters of Shariah. The Hamid cell's connections abroad are familiar: an East African criminal in London with links to Pakistan and the Taliban, in association with a Turkish follower of Abu Hamza, the Egyptian freelance imam of Finsbury Park, himself involved in plots in Oregon and Yemen, indoctrinating Somali would-be suicide bombers in England. The membership of Hamid's cell was also typical: Kader Ahmed, age 20, a Somali, who saw in Hamid a father figure; Kibley da Costa, 24, a Jamaican former bus driver and convert; Mohammad al-Figari, 44, born Roger Michael Figari in Trinidad, a convicted drug smuggler and convert to Islam, brought up by "very religious" grandmothers—one Catholic, one Hindu.[14]

Within the jihadist context in Europe a few prototypes can be detected, who stand out from the others in terms of their relative importance, ability, personal motivations, and range of activities.

TYPES AND NETWORKS

The Globetrotting Recruiter:

Luai Sakra, a.k.a. **Loa'i Mohammad Haj Bakr al-Saqa**, was arrested in Antalya, Turkey, while preparing a major attack against Israeli cruise ships—as he admitted and as the 750 kilograms of hydrogen peroxide found in his possession supported.

Born in Aleppo, Syria, in 1974, into a wealthy family, Sakra went to Germany in 2000 with his 18-year-old wife and two sons, applied for asylum, and, while waiting for resolution of his case, was already closely associated with Abu Musab al-Zarqawi. Before coming to Germany he had traveled extensively, to Turkey, Jordan, and especially Afghanistan, where he became one of the first trainees in Zarqawi's camp near Herat. During those travels he met a couple of German converts (one of whom was working for the Bundeswehr), who each later married one of his sisters and who served as his translators during his stay in Germany. Following the Istanbul bombings of November 15 and 23, 2003, captured Turkish terrorists told the police that a certain "Aladdin," also known as "Dr. Alaa" (later identified as Sakra), had financed the attacks.[15]

By then he was well known—the Syrians wanted him for involvement in a 1999 uprising in a refugee camp in Lebanon, and in February 2002 a court in Jordan convicted him to 15 years *in absentia*, together with Zarqawi, for participation in the failed millennium attack on the Marriott Hotel in Amman.

Even before that, Sakra had become close to Abu Zubaida, a major Al-Qaeda figure (now in U.S. custody), when the latter was recruiting *mujahedin* in Peshawar in the mid-1990s. In 1997 he attended the Khalden military training camp, specializing in explosives. After the Herat training camp was set up in 1999, Sakra was one of the five Arabs in charge; another was Zarqawi. At the time of his arrest, Sakra also claimed to have fought with Zarqawi in Fallujah, Iraq, and to have personally murdered a kidnapped Turkish truck driver. In Fallujah he even faked his own death, which explains his ability to remain undetected much longer than his fame would otherwise have allowed.[16]

Upon his arrest in July 2005 at the airport of Diyarbakir, in eastern Turkey, he was carrying $120,000 in cash (as well as psychiatric medications and antidepressants). He later claimed that not only did he know one of the 9/11 pilots and know of their plans, but he gave them money and passports.[17] Whether this is true or not, the fact is that Sakra was (mostly) in Germany until July 2001, as were three of the 9/11 pilots.

His psychological profile is complex but far from unique. On the one hand, when offered by the Turkish investigators the opportunity to pray, he refused, stating, "I don't pray . . . and I like alcohol. . . . Especially whiskey and wine." On the other, he confessed to ordering the attacks in Istanbul and to taking part in the execution of a Turkish truck driver in Iraq and shouted "I have no regrets!"[18]

Considering Sakra's unstable personality and his use of antidepressants and alcohol, his claims have to be taken with a large grain of salt. Nevertheless, his known personal trajectory, closeness to major terrorist figures like Abu Zubaida and al-Zarqawi, and involvement in recruiting and financing Islamists in Europe and training them in Afghanistan, make him perhaps the best case study of a recruiter and "visitor" for the Al-Qaeda core group. It is individuals like Sakra that give operational substance to Al-Qaeda as the jihadi organization with the most extensive international reach.

The Islamist Thug and Foot Soldier:

Khaled Kelkal, born in Alegria in 1971, was killed in a shootout with police near Lyon in September 1995. Coming from a large family (four sisters and three brothers), he was brought to France as an infant by his mother, joining his immigrant father in Vaulx-en-Velin, a suburb of Lyon. He studied at the reputable La Martinière Monplaisir *lycée* in Lyon, where he had good grades until he dropped out—because, he said, he could not "tolerate being marginal and rejected by the others." Following in the steps of his older brother, Nouredine (sentenced to nine years in prison for armed robbery), he became engaged in delinquency. In 1990 he was first sentenced to four months' probation for traffic in stolen cars, and then, for car theft and violence, to four years in prison, of which he served two. While in jail he came under the influence of a certain "Khelif B.," an Islamist and GIA member, then serving a seven-year sentence and actively recruiting among inmates.

Upon release, Kelkal studied Arabic and became a regular at the Vaulx-en-Velin Bilal mosque, whose Malian imam, Mohamed Minta, was a *Tablighi*.[19] In 1993, during a visit to his family in Mostaganem, Algeria, he was contacted and recruited by Safé Bourada, of the GIA *takfiri* faction of Dijamel Zitouni, who, a year later, became the supreme leader of the organization. It should be pointed out that even within the GIA, probably the bloodiest of all Islamist groups of recent decades, Zitouni was the most bloodthirsty and anti-French.[20] Bourada, meanwhile, after spending five years in jail, and later joining the GSPC, was arrested again in September 2005, this time for suspected links with the Zarqawi network.[21]

On July 11, 1995, Kelkal began his brief terrorist career, under the influence of another prominent Algerian terrorist, Ali Touchent. He was involved in the murder of Algerian FIS founder and head of the Khaled ibn Walid mosque of rue Myrha in Paris, Salafist Sheikh Abdel Baki Sahraoui—found too moderate by the GIA—and became an active, though not particularly high-ranking, member of the GIA terror network in France, under the leadership of Boualem Bensaïd. He was involved in a series of bombings targeting French civilians, including the bombings of the Parisian Métro stations at Saint-Michel and Blanche—both claimed by the GIA. Then, on August 1995, a device with his fingerprints—similar to the one used at Saint-Michel—failed to explode near the line of the Paris-Lyon high-speed train. Finally, in September 1995, he was shot down by the gendarmes after resisting arrest—on live TV. Only a few days before, he had placed a car bomb in front of a Jewish school in Villeurbanne, near Lyon.

Speaking in 1995, a policeman from the Lyon area stated:

> For four or five years we have seen being set in place a perfectly structured system, with some very educated gurus at the top—doctors, professors, researchers, and a small battalion of recruiters at the exits of high schools. By now there are all sorts of networks in the neighborhoods, pro-Pakistanis, pro-Iranians, pro-Shiites, but the authorities have chosen to close their eyes when faced with their activism, in exchange for an illusory social peace. All these people have been received by the *préfet*. They are an arch-minority in the community, but it is they who could instrumentalize the kids.[22]

Unlike most jihadi foot soldiers, Kelkal became a folk hero in the French *banlieues* and the pretext of a flurry of "progressive" academic studies—an image reinforced by French rapper Rohff in *"Rohff Vs. l'État"* (1999). There are still Muslims who accuse the police of "excessive force" in his death. In 1998 leftist film and theater director Bernard Bloch presented a play comparing Kelkal with the mad Marxist philosopher Louis Althusser (who killed his wife)—"Two passion murders, one political/religious and the other for love."[23]

There are reasons for Kelkal's popularity among young Muslims—and not just in France. He was quoted as stating, "I am neither French nor Algerian, I am Muslim,"[24] a sentiment widely and increasingly shared by young Muslims in Europe. In fact, according to author Abdallah-Thomas Milcent, who interviewed Kelkal's family, he "didn't know anything about Islam" but was indoctrinated by small groups, themselves "manipulated" by governments.[25] Conspiracy theories aside, Kelkal's ignorance of Islam and his personal identity crisis, with Muslim as the default self-identification, is by now common in Europe. Also quite common are his criminal background, entry on the path of Salafism through the door of *Tabligh*, indoctrination in prison and in his parents' country, and recruitment by members of an established foreign terrorist group. Ultimately, "Khaled Kelkal has paid with his life for his role in the network established in France by fundamentalists who sought precisely to use this type of recruit, at the limit between revolt, banditry and fanaticism."[26]

The Organizer and His Network:

Djamel Beghal, a.k.a. "**Abu Hamza Lokmane**," is not just one of the most important Islamist terrorists ever captured in Europe; he was considered by the French authorities to be one of the leading Al-Qaeda operatives in the country and perhaps the continent.[27]

Born in 1965 into a family with ten children, in the small Algerian town of Bordj Bou Arreridj, he studied accounting at Setif. At age 21, he came to France, where he intermittently studied computer science. In 1990 Beghal married Sylvie Gueguen, a Frenchwoman, with whom he had three children; he became a French citizen three years later—a common pattern among Salafis in Europe; Abu Hamza and al-Suri, among many others, married European (Christian) women to obtain citizenship.

Described as smooth and charming, Beghal was tall and big-jawed, with striking green eyes. He lived with his family in Corbeil-Essonnes, a suburb south of Paris, in a government-subsidized, but well-kept, building complex. Corbeil had a well-established Islamist presence, and Beghal had joined *Tabligh* by 1994. Interestingly, at his trial Beghal claimed that not only did he meet the influential and controversial Swiss Islamist intellectual Tariq Ramadan but even "prepared his speeches" in 1994.[28]

Although unemployed and never having had a regular job, in 1990 Beghal began a series of travels to Germany, England, Belgium, Pakistan, and Afghanistan. He was jailed briefly in 1997 for his support of the GIA's terrorist network in France, and was again under police surveillance by February 1999, when he was a frequent traveler between England's radical mosques, Germany, and France.

He has admitted that he met Abu Qatada in 1997 in Germany, and the following year he moved to England (Leicester and London). However, at the trial he claimed not to share Abu Qatada's ideas, and he said that his departure to Afghanistan in 2000 was an attempt to avoid British police. In fact, he was a *Takfir-wal-Hijra* member and became Abu Qatada's emissary in continental Europe, distributing his inflammatory sermons.[29] The British were looking for him both because of his Islamist activities and in relation to a case of kidnapping of children. As for Afghanistan under the Taliban, he described it as "an Islamic country where most answers and facilities for my needs at the time were to be found."[30]

In a common pattern, after moving to Britain, he became a close associate of Abu Hamza al-Masri at Finsbury Park as well as of Abu Qatada.[31] According to Reda Hassaine, an Algerian working for British (and French) intelligence, Beghal was recruited for Al-Qaeda at Finsbury Park (as was convert Jérôme Courtailler).[32]

At Finsbury Park, Beghal was a feared figure, even in the context of *Takfir-wal-Hijra*'s fearful reputation.

> Members of the Algerian community in north London have told *The Observer* that Beghal was a feared figure around the mosque. "It is always the ones without beards who are the most dangerous," said one moderate Algerian who met him. "Members of this group would kill their own fathers if they caught them smoking or drinking." Indeed, one video doing the rounds at London mosques is a Takfir-wal-Hijra "snuff movie," showing the execution of a member of the organisation judged to have committed a sin.... One man who knew Beghal during his time in London said: "This is the most terrifying group of extremists you are ever likely to meet. If you don't agree with them you are an enemy to Islam, and they believe it is legitimate to kill you."[33]

From England, via Paris, Beghal moved with his wife and children to Pakistan and then, in March 2001, to the Taliban capital in Kandahar, where he met Abu Zubaida, through whom, he claimed, he received a few symbolic gifts from bin Laden himself, and was given the order to return to Europe and organize an attack against the U.S. Embassy and Cultural Center in Paris.[34] While in Afghanistan, he trained at the Khowst and Darunta camps. However, on his way back to France, Beghal was arrested in Dubai in July 2001 for carrying a false passport. Upon interrogation, with the help of an Islamic scholar, he spilled the beans: his meeting with Abu Zubaida, the plots in Paris, and the names of his cell members in the Netherlands, Belgium, France, and Spain. After 9/11, he was promptly extradited to France.

After Beghal's capture, French, Dutch, and Belgian authorities began arresting members of his cell—Nizar Trabelsi in Brussels and Jérôme Courtailler in Rotterdam; Kamel Daoudi, who had fled to Leicester, was also arrested and promptly extradited to France by the British.[35]

At his trial in January 2005, Djamel Beghal, with a long beard and gold-framed eyeglasses, speaking correct French and referring to himself in the third person, was arrogant and slippery—an attending journalist claimed that "he spoke but said nothing." "There is no secret that Beghal Djamel is a practicing Muslim," he said, denouncing the "Inquisition tribunal." He avoided questions about his beliefs: "It is not for me to explain Islam, Islam is enormous and all is mine." He refused to say anything about international jihadism because "first one has to agree over its definition," and he denied links to extremist groups: "I am one of those in permanent search of religious knowledge. If that makes a new sect, go ahead." Asked to define his concept of Islam, or to confirm membership in *Takfir*, he refused because "It is dangerous for my defense."[36] As for his return to Europe in June 2001, it was only because his Jalalabad roommate asked him to accompany his wife and three children to Morocco—a lie demolished by the joint testimonies of his and Trabelsi's wives. In what was a by-now common tactic recommended by Al-Qaeda's manuals, he recanted his previous confession, claiming that he was tortured in Dubai, but he was nevertheless sentenced to ten years in prison, the maximum under the law.

Beghal's ability to recruit and indoctrinate is demonstrated by the diverse backgrounds of his closest associates:

Kamel Daoudi, born in Algeria in 1975, was brought to France when he was five years old. Daoudi's father, Tahar Daoudi, said that his "brilliant boy" enjoyed a good life in Paris's fashionable 5th arrondissement until financial problems forced the family to move to the suburb of Corbeil-Essonnes: "When we moved he changed all his friends. He was very generous and they got a lot of money out of him—all the money that was supposed to pay for his studies. We were furious with him and threw him out of the house. I was furious with him for hanging around with kids who filled his head full of nonsense."[37]

Kamel had wanted to become an engineer, and indeed he was very bright. "He was a good student, without troubles, very quiet, shy; he worked well," according to his high-school principal. "He never expressed hatred against anyone or anything in particular. He was the very model of integration."[38] He was handy enough with a computer keyboard that the Athis-Mons City Hall put him in charge of a special program of computer training for young "*beurs*" (French citizens of Algerian origin). In 1998 he was hired by the Corbeil-Essonnes City Hall to work at the municipal cybercafé, a job he eventually lost because of spotty attendance.[39]

He had become such close friends with Djamel Beghal that after Beghal left for England, Daoudi was using his apartment in Corbeil. Converted to Islamism in a *Tablighi* mosque at Corbeil, Daoudi dropped out of his studies of informatics and moved to Leicester, where he joined Beghal. Soon thereafter, Daoudi broke with his family. "I saw him for his civil marriage in 1999, but that was pretty much it," said Tahar. This is a nearly universal pattern in the trajectory of Salafist converts in the West: sudden behavioral changes following the decision to join a radical organization—including a break with family, friends, and previous social ambitions.

Within the network, Daoudi was the electronic communications expert[40] and logistics man, but also, it seems, the network's main bomb-maker. His role also included keeping contact with other cells and transmitting orders in encrypted e-mail messages. Following his capture in Leicester, police found a book of codes and encrypted messages and speculated that those may have been used to prepare the 9/11 attacks. The dismantled cell phones and alarm clocks found in Daoudi's apartment at the time of his arrest could have been bomb-making components.

At the time of his trial, he wore fashionable eyeglasses and a suit and tie, and was well shaved. On the other hand, he imposed the *hijab* on his wife and had twice attended Al-Qaeda training camps in Afghanistan. At his trial, Daoudi claimed that his training in Afghanistan was "hell." He "suffered enormously" and decided to leave in June 2001, at the same time as Beghal, because his children "were sick and without a future."[41]

At the beginning of 2002 Daoudi's French citizenship was withdrawn, and in March 2005, he was tried along with Beghal and was sentenced by a French court to nine years in jail.

Jérôme Courtailler and his brother, **David**, are converts to Islam, the sons of a local butcher in Bonneville, in the Savoie.

Born in 1975 and 1976, respectively, they had a perfectly normal childhood, including soccer and judo lessons. Jérôme worked briefly as a butcher himself and David studied accounting in a Catholic school and, while in the army, served in an elite mountain unit. All this changed when their father went bankrupt and left their mother, after which both brothers started drinking and using drugs.

How their path to Islam opened remains unclear. David mentioned "friends" who helped convince him, and Jérôme was told that conversion to Islam would help him shake his drug addiction. In order to learn more, the brothers went to England together, where Jérôme converted to Salafism at Finsbury Park and David at Leicester, under Beghal's direct influence.

While David Courtailler was in London, where he is said to have been Zacarias Moussaoui's roommate (Jérôme also knew Moussaoui), he was offered $2,000, a visa to Pakistan, and the phone number of a contact in Peshawar by "a man at the prayer center on Baker Street."[42]

By 1997 both brothers were in Pakistan and then Afghanistan. From Peshawar, David Courtailler was taken to Khowst, Afghanistan, where he admitted spending several months at a training camp, together with Algerians, Yemenis, and two Californians. While in training in Afghanistan, he told his father that he was in London.

Upon his return to France in 1998, David was arrested and spent six months in jail for theft. By then even the old policeman from Bonneville barely recognized him, with his beard, long robe, and friendship with local North African immigrants. Jérôme, by then known as "Salman," had never returned to Bonneville since 1997. Based in Rotterdam, he was linked to the conspiracy to murder Ahmed Shah Massoud, and he supplied Nizar Trabelsi with false passports[43]—actions demonstrating his commitment to the Al-Qaeda network in Europe. Indeed, Massoud's assassination on September 9, 2001, was a strategic Al-Qaeda decision, proving that, already at that time, the organization had a functioning network in Europe.

Jérôme was arrested in Rotterdam on September 13, 2001, together with two other French converts, Johann Bonté and Jean-Marc Grandvisir. They were in possession of fake documents and a machine for printing bogus credit cards. In 2002, a Dutch judge dismissed the charges against Courtailler because the evidence consisted mostly of information from illegally obtained wiretaps. The prosecution appealed, and in July 2004 Jérôme was sentenced by a Rotterdam court to the maximum six years in jail.

Nizar Trabelsi, a Tunisian born in 1970, was arrested in Belgium on September 13, 2001, and admitted to plans to drive a car bomb into the Kleine Brogel NATO air base, where U.S. nuclear weapons are believed to be stored. Tried and convicted two years later, he was sentenced in September 2003 to the maximum ten years in prison.[44] The light sentence was due to the lack of an anti-terrorism law: Trabelsi was charged only with attempting to destroy public property, illegal arms possession, and membership in a private militia.[45]

Physically fit at 6'4" and about 190 pounds, by age 20 Trabelsi was a professional soccer player with a third-division German team in Düsseldorf. Dreadlocked and pleasant, as a rookie Trabelsi demonstrated no particular religious interest and, the father of a young daughter, seemed quite satisfied with his life. However, he was not interested in socializing with his teammates and, according to his coach, was lazy and often missed training. In 1992, he changed teams, only to be fired after a few months for laziness. He went to an even lower league, and by 1995 his soccer career was over. He divorced his wife and got involved with alcohol and drugs—both as a user and as a trafficker. In 1994 he was sentenced in Düsseldorf to 18 months' probation for importing cocaine. By 2000, Trabelsi had a long criminal record, including theft, unauthorized use of a car, illegal gun possession, and cashing two forged bank checks.

After a first visit to Saudi Arabia in 1996, in October 2000 Trabelsi went to Afghanistan and underwent training in an Al-Qaeda camp. Upon his return, somehow he had enough money to move into a well-off suburb of Brussels, and in the summer of 2001 he traveled to Spain.

Besides the Kleine Brogel operation, Trabelsi was also involved in a plot against the U.S. embassy in Paris and other multinational conspiracies. He was accused of planning to strap a bomb onto himself before walking into the embassy, wearing a business suit to conceal the bomb. All indications are that Trabelsi was the "designated suicide bomber" of the Beghal network—the most desperate and expendable member of the cell, precisely his personal characteristics.[46] That may also explain why, according to Trabelsi himself, he was twice hosted in bin Laden's house in Jalalabad, and that "Ossama ben Laden told me that I could consider him my father. That is the reason I love him so much."[47] Obviously, for bin Laden, spending time with an obscure thief and drug addict from France was not a common occurrence, but it was worth the effort to strengthen the convictions and willingness of a would-be suicide bomber in a major operation at a time when Trabelsi was at his most vulnerable. Moreover, at that time would-be suicide bombers in Europe were quite rare. It also appears that, considering the timing of Trabelsi's Kleine Brogel plan, bin Laden intended a European operation simultaneous with 9/11.

At the time of his arrest, police found in his apartment an Uzi submachine gun and a notebook with scribbled references to acetone and sulfur; and in the basement of an Egyptian bar in Brussels owned by the family of a man arrested with Trabelsi, investigators learned about 220 pounds of sulfur and 16 gallons of acetone—all bomb-making material. After his arrest Trabelsi claimed that the suicide operation was meant to cleanse him of his sins.[48]

Network links: There is a consensus among intelligence officials and experts on terrorism that the Beghal network's planned attack on symbolic American targets in Paris was the result of an initiative of bin Laden's chief training-camp operative in Afghanistan, Abu Zubaida, and that bin Laden himself was well informed about it. Beghal even talked with Zubaida about the cost of the operation, which they assessed at €53,300.[49] Beghal himself indirectly admitted his link with bin Laden when he stated that, in May 2001, his training camp at Khowst was transferred by the Taliban to Al-Qaeda.

L'Express claimed that Daoudi communicated via e-mail with Zou Bejod and Abu Zubair al-Haili, described as bin Laden's main Afghan agents in Europe.[50] Trabelsi was known to be in touch with Sajid Badat and Richard Reid,[51] and suspected of having had contact in Tarragona, in the summer of 2001, with Mohamed Atta.[52]

The Libyan Omar Deghayes, a former Guantanamo prisoner now back in the United Kingdom, provided David Courtailler, then in London, with phone numbers for militants in Spain and Morocco, including one later arrested in connection with the Madrid bombings, and another now serving a 19-year sentence for his role in the suicide bombings of 2003 in Casablanca. Courtailler actually stayed with the latter while visiting Tangiers.[53]

Another member of the Beghal network, Khaled Ben Mustapha, was born in Lyon in 1972, studied in a Catholic high school, failed to obtain a degree in management, and moved to Paris in 1995. There he married a Catholic and worked for a satellite antenna company until 2001, when he moved to London and started frequenting Abu Hamza's Finsbury Park circle. From there he went to a training camp in Afghanistan, fled from Tora Bora to Pakistan at the end of 2001, was captured and sent to Guantanamo,[54] and subsequently returned to France. His close ties to Al-Qaeda and training in its Afghan camps reinforce the image of the Beghal network as one of the earliest jihadi structures in Europe clearly linked to and directed by bin Laden's intimate circle.

The Beghal network, involving Algerians and Tunisians, French converts, a black (Jean-Marc Grandvisir), and a Dutch-Ethiopian (Saad Ibrahim), confirms the observation of former Milan anti-terrorism prosecutor and judge Armando Spataro that by the end of the 1990s there was a clear change in the composition of Islamist terrorist cells in Europe, from nationally homogeneous and linked to nationally identified groups, such as the Algerian ones, to multi-ethnic, ideologically motivated, and globally active.[55]

The prosecutor at the Beghal/Daoudi trial in France concluded that the entire affair was "revealing of a Europeanization of terrorist groups," citing ties the accused had to Islamists already sentenced elsewhere in Europe, such as the Frankfurt group and cells in Spain.[56] Another author talks of "glocalisation": Some of the attackers' bonds of solidarity are local and gang-like, often deriving from the same neighborhood or town; while linkmen such as Beghal are global and cross many borders to cover their tracks. One may quibble with those who say that "the group seemed to have its head in Paris, its soul in London and its heart in Afghanistan,"[57] in the sense that the brain, in this case, was in Afghanistan as well; but the pattern has since been repeated elsewhere, although seldom with such clarity.

The membership structure of the Beghal network also evidenced a pattern found later in England and Spain. Family and personal ties, rather than ethnicity, played the main role in recruiting. Beghal and Daoudi were close friends, Beghal and Johann Bonté were related, the Cortaillers were brothers. Finally, all were pupils of Abu Qatada in London.

Socially, the network's members were a mixed group. Beghal was a professional terrorist, but there were also the educated computer nerd Daoudi, social workers, and a professional soccer player. Many members seemed well integrated in society and relatively successful—at least up to a point—and, Beghal aside, not particularly religious prior to their joining *Tabligh* and then *Takfir-wal-Hijra* in England.

Their family relationships were also to become a common pattern among jihadis in Europe. Many married Christian women (Beghal most likely in order to get French citizenship), who always converted, and most had children, but none seems to have been particularly worried about the fate of his wife and children after the mission was accomplished. Amal Halim, Trabelsi's wife, 26 years old, met him in Düsseldorf in 1999 and often met there with Beghal and his French convert wife, Sylvie Gueguen. In 2000, with false visas, the four went to Jalalabad via Pakistan. Beghal had an important role in opening training camps in Afghanistan—especially the "French" camp at Khowst, where Maghrebis and converts were concentrated.[58] When, after discovering her husband's "martyrdom" ambitions, Amal Halim contacted Beghal, he was upset with her knowing of the plans, demanded that she forget everything, claimed that "it is the duty of every Muslim to rejoin Paradise," and counseled that she should already do her mourning rituals and find another husband in the camp.[59] She refused to do so, and she later returned to Belgium and her husband. Meanwhile Trabelsi cut off communications with his in-laws, developed an interest in chemistry and explosives, and always kept an Uzi at hand.

Also left behind in Jalalabad by her husband after the beginning of the American campaign, Sylvie Gueguen was stopped by the Iranians while trying to flee Afghanistan and sent home. As for Kamel Daoudi's wife, Juliana, a computer analyst of Hungarian background who met him via the Internet, she was left behind in France. Before leaving for Afghanistan Daoudi wrote her a letter "between goodbye and repudiation."

The Amateurs: From Buddies to Jihadis:

The assassination of Theo van Gogh in Amsterdam on November 2, 2004, led to a wide realignment of European attitudes toward Muslims in general and Islamists in particular. At least the Netherlands, Germany, and Denmark—the latter also pushed by the global uproar following the publication of the Muhammad cartoons in 2005—have began a serious reassessment of policies *vis-à-vis* Muslims' integration, their customs, and the compatibility of their faith with European traditions.

The impact on Dutch culture of the successive murders of Pim Fortuyn and Theo van Gogh was compared to the impact of 9/11 on Americans, but despite the difference in the number of casualties, the van Gogh murder actually had a more profound effect on the formerly bland political culture of the Dutch.

The individual who actually committed the murder, Mohammed Bouyeri, supposedly acted alone, according to initial official statements. In fact, as we have seen, he proved to be the leader the Hofstad Group (De Hofstadgroep or Hofstadnetwerk), whose members were Salafis and, both before and after the van Gogh assassination, were involved in various terrorist activities. On the Islamist spectrum of Europe, Bouyeri and the Hofstad Group were distinct in that they were largely self-recruited, unlike the Beghal network; were directly tied to the Al-Qaeda core; and did not have foreign roots like the "Martyrs for Morocco" in Spain (see below). As the cell leader and the oldest member of the network, Mohammed Bouyeri's trajectory and beliefs are instructive.

Mohammed Bouyeri was born in Al Hoceima, Morocco, in 1978 and lived in Amsterdam's Slotervaart neighborhood after coming to the Netherlands as a child.[60] His immigrant father, an unskilled worker who spoke Dutch poorly, married again after Bouyeri's mother died. The fact that Bouyeri assassinated van Gogh only months after his mother died led both his sister and some psychologically inclined analysts to attribute his act to personal and emotional motivations—an interpretation contradicted by his already well-established links with Islamist groups, and by the manifestations of his radicalism long before that act. His mother's death may have had an effect on the timing of his act—which, characteristically for a *Takfir* follower, took place during Ramadan—but not on his beliefs and ultimate intentions. In fact, by 2002 Dutch intelligence was already checking on Bouyeri, after he published some Salafist texts on the Internet under the pseudonym "Abu Zubair." In 2003 another suspect warned of his dangerousness.[61]

> At the Mondriaan High School he graduated from, Bouyeri was described by his former teachers as "articulate, honest, sympathetic" but, apparently feeling excluded, he began to frequent the "Al-Tawhid" mosque. The imam of that mosque, Mahmoud El-Shershaby, was known enough for his rhetorical assaults against homosexuals and "fornicators" that some legislators demanded the closing of the mosque. As could be

expected, after the Van Gogh murder, Al-Tawhid, a typical Tablighi center preaching separation from the infidels, claims never having heard of Bouyeri, condemns violence and deplores the fact that "the entire community is a victim of an unhinged individual."[62]

Thus, we see again the denial of responsibility and diversion of attention to the notion of Muslims as "victims."

Bouyeri grew up in the Amsterdam area known as Satellite City because of the omnipresent antennae catching Al Jazeera and, before, Arab and other Muslim media. In many ways Bouyeri's trajectory is typical—as is the "mainstream" Muslim reaction to his crime. He attended the Tablighi El Tawheed mosque, whose Moroccan spokesman, Farid Zaari, "explained": "He [Bouyeri] is not accepted by society, and he is not accepted at home, either. . . . Everyone is pushing him, and no one understands him. And he becomes an easy target for the extremist who uses religion as bait."

In fact, however, Bouyeri enjoyed all the benefits of the overgrown Dutch welfare state. For five years, he attended one of the best high schools in the area, Mondriaan College, where he was known as "a B-level student . . . He did well and passed in five years and went on to a polytechnic. This was a very gentle and cooperative guy. When we talked to our teachers, the big question we asked is, did we miss something? And the answer is no."[63]

Did he have some family problems? Yes, a sister refused to behave like a "good Muslim girl," his parents divorced, his mother died of cancer. On the other hand, he did go to prison, briefly, for acts of violence, and it is believed that that is where he became attracted to radical Islam. That did not prevent him from going back to school to study "social work" so that he could work as a volunteer in a community center, and to publish locally—under the alias of "Abu Zubair" (after the al-Qaeda in the Arabian Peninsula late commander Abu Zubair al-Haili). There, he organized soccer games, petitioned the city of Amsterdam for funds, while wearing Islamist garb and protesting the serving of beer and the presence of women—for which he had to leave and go on welfare.

Van Gogh's mother, Anneke, was probably right when she commented in court that "He had the time to plan this, because for three years he was on unemployment benefits."

Again, in a pattern later repeated with most Hofstad Group members, he was briefly picked up—in connection with a suspected attempt to bomb a target during the 2004 European soccer championship in Portugal (his car was used by suspects arrested in Lisbon)—and released.

> After September 11th he seemed shattered, and engaged in discussion groups with local Moroccan youths, mostly about the rising star of Dutch politics, the anti-Islamic Pim Fortuyn, opposed the renovation of the area, and then, abruptly, broke ties with those previously close, grew a beard and started wearing a djellaba[64]—all clear and common symptoms of conversion to Takfir. By 2002 Bouyeri's apartment was known locally as a meeting place for young radicals under the mentorship of Syrian imam Redouan al-Issar, a.k.a. "Abu Khaled."[65]

> Later he confessed that the Iraq war forced him to "occupy himself with other things," and moved to the fundamentalist influenced De Baarsjes district, where Islamist recruiters were busy isolating their followers from family and friends. Obviously, that environment had an immediate impact on him, since his new associates were Algerians, as well as Moroccans.[66]

This was yet another step from re-Islamization into Salafism, one of whose characteristics is precisely the disappearance of traditional national/ethnic distinctions in favor of the default Islamist identity and commitment to jihad. As usual, widely available taped lectures and videos describing the "oppression" of Muslims worldwide were the instruments creating the Amsterdam microclimate of which Bouyeri was to become the most infamous product. In turn, he contributed to that environment by translating into Dutch some works of Sayyid Qutb, the Egyptian Muslim Brotherhood jihadi apologist and the most influential ideologue of contemporary Salafism.

Bouyeri's motivations and beliefs are quite typical of Islamists in Europe and thus deserve a closer look, especially as he is better educated than many and, some incoherence (and, apparently, a loose grasp of the Dutch language) aside, more articulate and thorough than most.

Prior to his act, Bouyeri was telling people that he was following the Prophet, and that he submitted himself "to that one power who is the creator of the greater whole."[67] *"Migrants' children do not choose orthodox Islam on the basis of conviction, but out of frustration."* He knows young people of Moroccan descent who do not feel accepted in Dutch society and who try to set themselves apart with radical religious views: "They are lost, because when you are teenager you are looking for your roots and identity."

When Bouyeri stabbed Theo van Gogh to death, he left an "Open Letter to Hirsi Ali" pinned with a knife to his victim's chest, and a personal last will was found on Bouyeri upon his arrest. The open letter to the "infidel fundamentalist" Hirsi Ali states that *"There is no aggression* except against the *aggressors*. . . . Since your appearance in the political arena of the Netherlands you are constantly engaging in *terrorizing* Muslims and Islam with your remarks. You are not the first at this and will also not be the last who has joined the *crusade* against Islam." (Emphasis added.)[68]

In language typical of Salafi ideologues, the meaning of words is reversed: Hence the threatened Hirsi Ali is the "aggressor," a "fundamentalist" "terrorizing" Muslims by joining "the crusade"—another Salafi obsession. Terrorism is what the enemies, rather than the followers, of Islam do: "Your *intellectual terrorism* will not stop this, on the contrary you will only hasten it." Indeed, this perverted use of the term is theologically absolutely necessary to justify terrorism, since the Quran allows jihad only in defense of the faith.

There should and could, he said, be no Muslim obedience to infidel laws. He stated: "I was motivated by the law that commands me to cut off the head of anyone who insults Allah and His Prophet."[69] He remained unrepentant throughout: at his trial he told van Gogh's mother, "I do not feel your pain."

A typical Islamist cult of death permeates Bouyeri's view of the world:

> There is one certainty in the whole of existence; and that is that everything comes to an end. . . . Death, Miss Hirshi Ali, is the common theme of all that exists. You, me and the rest of creation can not disconnect from this truth. . . . You, as unbelieving fundamentalist, of course do not believe that a Supreme being controls the entire universe. . . . You do not believe that your heart, with which you cast away truth, has to ask permission from the Supreme being for every beat. You do not believe that your tongue with which you deny the Guidance from the Supreme being is subject to his Laws. . . . You do not believe that life and death has been given you by this Supreme being.

But ultimately,

> Islam will conquer by the blood of the martyrs. It will spread its light to every corner of this Earth and it will, if necessary, drive evil to its dark hole by the sword. . . . This unleashed battle is different from previous battles. *The unbelieving fundamentalists have started* it and Insha Allah the true believers will end it. *There shall be no mercy for the unjust, only the sword raised at them. No discussion, no demonstrations, no parades, no petitions; merely DEATH shall separate the Truth from the LIE.* [Emphasis added.]

Bouyeri acts in what he considers to be a universal, indeed apocalyptic conflict, in which Hirsi Ali (or Theo van Gogh, or others on Bouyeri's list of targets, such as Dutch MP Geert Wilders, Amsterdam mayor Job Cohen, and Cohen's second in command, Ahmed Aboutaleb, the latter a Muslim of Moroccan origin) is of much lesser importance than the greater enemies: the United States, Europe, the Netherlands, in this order. Hence, his act will be heard throughout the universe: "so that the heavens and the stars will gather this news and spread it over the corners of the universe like a tidal wave."

Of course, the greater the enemy and the more important the nature of the war against him, the greater the sense of self-importance of the would-be "martyr," a psychological mechanism that may explain the attraction of "martyrdom" for criminals, petty thieves, and other failed individuals, such as Nizar Trabelsi or Bouyeri himself.

Some observers blame the Internet for the wide and rapid spread of Islamism:

> He is not so much a product of zealous imams from rural Morocco as of the West's information society and the *Tablighi* and *Takfiri* imams of the Netherlands. The gospel of Muslim extremism has found a global market through the Internet. Something similar is happening on the extreme right, with "white power" offering an apparent certainty to youngsters who are adrift.[70]

The Internet may provide some reinforcement to existing beliefs, but it remains only an instrument. Far more important are one's own life experience, psychological dynamics such as those analyzed above, the very nature of simplistic and archaic interpretations of Islam, and, most important of all, the personal and immediate influence of an imam—Redouan al-Issar in the case of Bouyeri and his associates in the Hofstad Group.

That circle of individuals—some brought up as Muslims, others converts—were mostly not recruited, the way the members of the Beghal group were. They decided, largely on their own, to join and act in the name of jihad. They called themselves *polder* ("lowlands") *mujahedin*. The Hofstad Group had no clear, or at least permanent, hierarchy, unlike the otherwise similar London cell of suicide bombers, but it did have links with jihadist elements outside the Netherlands. Samir Azzouz was first arrested in Ukraine while on his way to Chechnya, and both Jason Walters and Ismail Akhnikh visited the Pakistani terrorist training camps of *Jaish-e-Mohammed* and probably even received training in a JeM camp.[71]

The group's most active member, Samir Azzouz, was born in 1986; its most famous, Bouyeri, was born in 1978. The group's Syrian mentor, Redouan al-Issar, a.k.a. "Abu Khaled," born in the late 1950s or early 1960s, was older than all the others, and, with Dutch-American converts Jason and Jermaine Walters, the only non-Moroccan.[72]

The Hofstad Group was willing to operate mostly on its own, certainly without direct orders from Al-Qaeda or anyone else. That it managed to murder van Gogh and go far in its plot to attack the European soccer championship in Portugal is due to the weakness of the AIVD and the Dutch legal system but, especially, the irresponsible behavior of Dutch courts. For a judge to openly admit, in court, that the suspect (Samir Azzouz) was probably guilty but there was insufficient proof to condemn him was tantamount to saying that the lives of probable victims are less important than the "rights" of the obvious terrorist—an opinion shared by judges in British courts and the European Court of Human Rights.

Among the Hofstad Group's members, convert Jason Walters and Moroccan Ismail Akhnikh were Bouyeri's most dedicated followers. At the time of their arrest on November 9, 2004, they threw grenades at the police and—again the obsession with Iraqi-style beheadings—threatened to "decapitate you. . . . We go to paradise, you go to hell."[73]

This young group, linked to each other through personal ties, the Internet, and a much older common mentor and ideologue, kept in touch and strengthened their group identity through frequent meetings, usually in Bouyeri's apartment.

The Ideologue/Mentor:

Redouan al-Issar, "Abu Khaled," who has also assumed many other names, is by profession a geologist, a native of Qamischli, Syria. His birthdate is unknown, but he was probably around 35 in 1995, when he went to Germany and asked for political asylum, claiming that he was tortured back home. His asylum application was denied, but he did receive monthly welfare payments of €225. He illegally entered the Netherlands, only to be deported back to Germany in 2003. The AIVD claims that he returned to the Netherlands, stayed in Bouyeri's apartment, and the day of van Gogh's murder fled to Syria, where, his relatives claim, he was arrested in Hama on his wedding day.[74] (As an aside, this raises once again the issue of political asylum in Europe. How is it that an alleged victim of Syrian torture returns to Syria and starts wedding preparations?)

In the first known such case, Abu Khaled managed to recruit an AIVD Muslim translator, Outman ben Amar, who was later arrested for providing intelligence to the Hofstad Group.[75] The Dutch believe, quite plausibly, that Abu Khaled was a *Takfir-wal-Hijra* recruiter and ideologue—part of the Syrian network specializing in these tasks, and active in Spain, Germany, and elsewhere. In fact, the Moroccan government wants him in connection with the Casablanca bombings of May 16, 2003.

The Members:

The members of the Hofstad Group, in majority Moroccan, managed to establish some connections with established North African networks, such as the GICM, demonstrating once again the facility of even self-recruited European cells for inserting themselves into the larger, global structures of jihad.

Nouredine el-Fatmi, born in 1982, an old friend and Amsterdam roommate of Bouyeri (with whom he grew up in Al Hoceima), was a prominent member. Upon an initial brief detention, he told police that Bouyeri was a *Takfir-wal-Hijra* member. When he was eventually arrested again, he was found to be in possession of a loaded machine gun, ammunition, and a silencer. A martyr's testament signed by him was found in his apartment. El-Fatmi was more experienced than most of the others, and managed to stay on the run longer, in Morocco and Europe. He was also adept at recruiting young Muslim women, often first seducing them and later converting them to *Takfiri* beliefs:

> Nouredine el-Fathmi was also building a new network, while he was on the run from the police after most of the group's members were arrested in November 2004. It appears that Fathmi had been giving Quran lessons at the house of a Dutch friend in The Hague. Three girls and a boy were present at three sessions or more. One of them was a young Muslim girl with whom he had got married under Islamic law; another was a former girlfriend of Mohammed Bouyeri. *As his knowledge of the Quran was negligible, Fathmi used his laptop to read aloud Quranic verses and other details about what he called "pure Islam."* [Emphasis added.] The girls were also shown videos of decapitations.[76]

In 2005 el-Fatmi was sentenced to five years in prison.

Jason Walters, a.k.a. "**Jamal**," born in 1985, is the son of a black American Muslim father and Dutch Christian mother.

He is a convert to Islam, together with his younger brother **Jermaine**. Upon their conversion, their behavior forced their mother to flee her home because she was "mentally abused" by her sons.[77] At his trial in December 2005, before receiving a 15-year jail sentence, Jason stated, "People have a romantic idea about jihad fighters . . . I didn't have a job at the time. So I looked for things to make life a little more exciting."[78] Perhaps the search for "excitement" may have played a part at the beginning of his path to terror—but unemployment or a search for adventure as explanations for training in Pakistani terror camps is a stretch.

Ahmed Hamdi, the computer expert of the group and also responsible for its finances, was 27 years old at the time of their trial in 2005; **Zakaria Taybi**, a colleague of Jason Walters in the Pakistani training camp, was 21; **Mohammed el-Morabit**, age 24, was, with el-Fatmi, one of the pair arrested in Portugal, extradited to the Netherlands, and released.

The most significant figure in the group, after Bouyeri, was one of the youngest, **Samir Azzouz**, a.k.a. **"Yassine,"** whose ability to avoid justice repeatedly made him something of a "Teflon terrorist." Azzouz was born in Amsterdam in 1986 and grew up in a poor immigrant family from Morocco. His father was a laborer; his mother was so ill that the child was sent to live with his grandmother. Later, Azzouz's father married another woman, a Palestinian.[79]

The father was very religious. It was he who introduced Samir to the Al-Tawheed *Tabligh* mosque. By age 15 Samir was a radical, and in 2003, at age 17, he tried to go and fight for Islam in Chechnya. This is, to some extent, a departure from the general pattern of Europe-born Islamists, who tend to come from non- or only moderately religious families.

In school, at the Catholic College of Amsterdam, he was known for modest clothes and avoidance of alcohol, as a loner and quiet individual. From the testimony of his former schoolmates, it appears that the aftermath of 9/11, which he interpreted as an assault on Islam, pushed him into active militantism. He suddenly developed an interest in Arab literature and radicalism but, as in so many other cases, his teachers could only say, "It is terrible that we did not understand what was happening to him and others."

Azzouz was a frequent visitor to the Al-Tawheed mosque, where he met Bouyeri—another good student, intelligent, who suddenly turned toward fundamentalism.[80] By 2003 Azzouz was in action—he was arrested in Ukraine while trying to get into Chechnya, and returned to the Netherlands where, despite his teachers' efforts, he refused to take his final high-school exams. By this time, age 17, he already had an illegal gun and had tried to make bombs, and by the time he was 18 he was on trial for the first time, on charges of armed robbery, planning a bomb attack, and possession of bomb-making materials. He had also robbed his grocer employer of $400—most likely in order to pay for his activities rather than out of Kelkal-type criminal inclinations. His wife, Abida, seven years his senior and herself the daughter of a Dutch convert mother, seems to have had an important role in his radicalization.[81]

By the spring of 2003 Azzouz was known to the Spanish police as well, owing to intercepts of his calls to a Moroccan involved in the Casablanca bombings. The Dutch police were informed of this connection, arrested him, and found bomb-making materials, maps, and photos of potential targets in his possession. However, as we saw in Chapter 5, a judge released him after ten days because "it is unclear what crime he intended to carry out."

When he was rearrested in 2005, police found a handwritten letter by Azzouz to his yet-unborn child, expressing the hope that, if a boy, by age 15 he would be a jihadist and go to training camp. However, on April 2005 Azzouz was able to leave the court smiling after another judge acquitted him. Why? Because although Azzouz had "terrorist intentions," his preparations were "in such an early stage and so clumsy and primitive that there was no concrete threat." [82] In other words, a terrorist's incompetence was proof of absence of guilt.

At the end of 2005, for at least the third time, Azzouz was detained and put on trial, this time with six other cell members, accused of trying to blow up the Parliament and AIVD headquarters in a massive suicide attack. At that trial, an Azzouz video was shown. Wearing black and a black bandana, he was telling his family that his was "the right path," that the Dutch government was responsible for American crimes, and that all Dutch are "considered soldiers (hence targets) because you elected this government"[83]—precisely the same arguments in favor of murdering civilians used by bin Laden himself in his "Letter to America." Only after another arrest in December 2006 was Azzouz finally convicted and sentenced to eight years' imprisonment.

The performance of the Dutch legal system vs. the Islamists of the Hofstad Group is representative of European legal systems in general. This is part of the explanation of the proliferation of jihadi groups. Helped by skilled lawyers from the ranks of the radical Left, time after time Azzouz and his colleagues avoided convictions, despite repeated arrests and abundant intelligence on their activities and intentions.

> His telephone was tapped, his apartment—where Abu Khaled was showing videos of the decapitations in Iraq and Chechnya—was watched, and many of his friends were already

behind bars, so the Dutch authorities were not surprised by evidence that it was Mohamed Bouyeri, a Dutchman of Moroccan descent, who murdered the filmmaker Theo van Gogh in broad daylight one morning this month. Yet they had been powerless to stop the crime.[84]

Although Bouyeri did receive a rare life sentence, the maximum possible under Dutch law, his "rights" were still protected to the extent that, despite his conviction, his citizenship was never revoked. Like many Islamist terrorists in Europe, Bouyeri knew how to game the system he claimed to reject. He chose the Amsterdam law firm Boehler, Franken, Koppe and Wijngaarden, all far-left lawyers who specialized in defending terrorists.[85] That said, throughout his two trials (he was also tried with the Hofstad Group), Bouyeri was contemptuous of the judges, prosecutors, psychologists, and police. He repeatedly yawned, stroked his beard, prodded his face with a pen, and played an imaginary piano on his thighs.

The next time Azzouz was on trial he too was represented by Victor Koppe and colleagues. Koppe challenged the use of intelligence information at the trial and claimed that while his client may have extreme views, "intentions are not crimes." In a newspaper interview he went further, and publicly claimed that "For what is going on at this trial there is only one explanation . . . They are on trial because they are Muslims . . . This is a variation of the classical witch hunt." His colleague Britta Boehler (the defender of Zakaria Taybi, Jason Walters, and Ismail Akhnikh)—a known admirer of Germany's Marxist terrorists and of Abdullah Ocalan, the convicted mass murderer and founder of the PKK—added: "This is a religious trial." All of this seems outrageous, but a good part of the Dutch media sympathized with the lawyers' arguments.[86]

As for Azzouz, despite his lawyers' efforts, he, like Bouyeri, was defiant: "We reject you. We reject your system. We hate you. I guess that about sums it up."

The other group members were more circumspect in their trials and followed the advice of Internet manuals for captured jihadis:

> In keeping with al-Qaeda's instructions—deny, deny, deny—an altogether different Walters has emerged during his trial. Of his assault on police, Walters has claimed that he had been overcome by emotions—it had never been his intention to kill or wound anyone. Indeed, Walters now claims to disavow the legitimacy of murder. In court, Walters has said that it is not right to kill people, though he insists that is allowed in "countries under occupation, like Iraq, Afghanistan and Chechnya." Moreover, some of them did possess a manual entitled, "What to do after being arrested by intelligence services." The manual presents an overview of interrogation techniques and offers lessons in the strategy of denial.[87]

For instance, with respect to the killing of van Gogh—an act expressly praised by Walters in taped conversations in his apartment—in court he maintained that he would never have contemplated such a measure. "I myself would not have done it, I was not allowed to do it. The fact that I was happy about the killing of Theo van Gogh does not mean I condoned it." Incredibly, he further claimed that the menacing open letter Bouyeri left on van Gogh's body had not been intended as a threat to Ayaan Hirsi Ali.

Perhaps the Dutch courts' leniency is more understandable given the misconceptions presented to them by both experts and "experts." The AIVD had for a long time insisted that the Hofstad Group was strictly local, although it did admit that there were some 150 "extremists" in the country, and that they had outside connections. In fairness, after the events, the AIVD produced some realistic and politically incorrect reports on Islamism in the Netherlands.

So-called academic experts, like Islamic-law professor Ruud Peters of the University of Amsterdam, told the court that "They [the Hofstad cell] were amateurs because they were not part of a well-organized group of terrorists and their skills in military things were mainly collected through the Internet."[88]

In fact, young as they were, the members of the Hofstad Group were experienced enough to keep in touch with like-minded groups and individuals in Spain, Germany, Morocco, Italy, and Belgium. They also had enough contacts for two of them, Jason Walters and Ismail Akhnikh, to train in Pakistani jihadist camps. (At his trial Walters admitted to having gone to Pakistan twice, but he claimed that he "just visited madrassas.") Walters also had a connection to Maulana Masood Azhar, the founder and leader of JeM. And the group was ambitious enough to plan bombings of the Hague Parliament, the Amsterdam Schiphol airport, and the nuclear plant in Borssele, and the murder of the president of the European Commission.[89]

In fact, the AIVD itself later described the group as follows:

> The local character of the Hofstad group is underlined by the lack of specific indications for international control. It is true that in October 2003 the AIVD saw contacts between the Hofstad group and a Moroccan jihad veteran who was allegedly involved in the Casablanca attacks, but since his arrest no such contacts have been established. Even the role of the group's Syrian spiritual leader is no indication of external control. Although this Syrian played an important role in the ideological and religious development of the Hofstad group, he was not the only driving force behind their radicalization. The Internet also played a very important role in this process.[90]

All subsequent information, however, strongly suggests that the network's links abroad were far more extensive than the

AIVD admitted, or perhaps knew. The fact that all but the Walters brothers were of Moroccan background played a role in their international links. As already said, there is a widespread Moroccan terror infrastructure throughout Europe, often working with the remnants of the Algerian GIA and GSPC. In addition, Bouyeri had telephone contacts with the UAE-born Algerian Mohammed Achraf, now jailed in Spain after extradition from Switzerland, accused of involvement with the Spanish cell behind the planned attack against the Madrid *Audiencia Nacional* (see below).[91]

When he was 16 or 17, Azzouz met at Al-Tawheed and befriended one Abdelaziz Benyaïch, and it was with Benyaïch that he made the already-mentioned attempt to go to Chechnya. Benyaïch, however, was no ordinary militant: Arrested in Spain in June 2003, in September 2005 he was sentenced to eight years' imprisonment for being in charge of propaganda for the *"Soldados de Alá"* ("Soldiers of Allah") group at the Abu Baker mosque in Madrid. Meanwhile, Morocco linked him to the 2003 Casablanca attacks.[92]

Equally important or, in the opinion of Spanish judge Baltasar Garzón, even more so were the connections between Bouyeri and Azzouz and GICM militant Abdeladim Akoudad, a planner of the Casablanca bombings.

Akoudad, a.k.a. "Naoufel," born in 1968 in Nador, Morocco, was accused by Judge Garzón of involvement in "at least the coordination and structuring of various Islamist terrorist groups in Holland, Belgium and Spain," including association with Abu Khaled, guru of the Hofstad Group. The links go further, since Garzón also accused Akoudad of ties with GICM elements in Belgium and with Mouhsen Khaybar, the leader in Syria of the Iraqi terrorist group Ansar al-Islam and a recruiter of European *mujahidin* for Iraq, as well as with al-Zarqawi himself.[93] Hofstad member Ismail Akhnikh's name was found on a document in Akoudad's possession at the time of his arrest.[94] At least one well-informed source claimed that there was a Moroccan group in the Netherlands, led by an Iraqi, planning to blow up the AIVD headquarters—a reference to Hofstad.[95]

How dangerous the Hofstad Group was remains a matter of some debate. Dutch investigative reporter Emerson Vermaat compares it with the al-Zarqawi network and Redouan al-Issar's role with that of Abu Mohammed al-Maqdisi, Zarqawi's longtime ideological mentor,[96] but that is an exaggeration. On the other hand, the ideological attraction of Al-Qaeda for the group is not in doubt. As Vermaat pointed out,

> Prominent members of the Hofstad group such as Bouyeri and Samir Azzouz strongly sympathize with Al-Qaeda, Osama bin Laden and Musab Al-Zarqawi; Bouyeri had a book on *The Experiences of Zarqawi* in his possession; Samir Azzouz said that "Bin Laden is fighting the Americans just as he was fighting the Russians . . . We love Bin Laden so much that he is in our soul."[97]

This demonstrates that, with just a little help (through its allies in Pakistan), the Al-Qaeda core could transform ideological sympathizers into operational cells for "the cause."

Blindness and Misunderstanding: The United Kingdom and "Our Own Boys"

After the London bombings of July 7, 2005, the English media expressed shock. Yet by then Londonistan was a known reality, and the British government was widely seen, in Europe and the Muslim world, as America's closest ally. However, as Abu Hamza and Omar Bakri stated, it may have been precisely because Londonistan was allowed to exist for so long that local attacks were unexpected.

The Islamist microclimate of Londonistan and the inevita-
bility of its leading to to an attack in Britain could have been
reasonably predicted, as one can see from the materials already
discussed above. As for the surprise, Olivier Roy was partially
correct in stating:

> The British and Dutch were stupefied to discover that the
> authors of the attacks which touched them were among the
> Muslims best integrated, even Westernized (they studied, even
> married Europeans . . .). Which means that they should not
> have been surprised that "traditional" Muslims switched to
> violence. Or, it is precisely because these youths have lost the
> culture of their parents or grandparents that they drifted?[98]

In fact, apparent integration by jihadis is just that—apparent.
And Islamist jihadis are anything but "traditional Muslims." It
is precisely because of the Londonistan circumstances that the
British cells—not just the 7/7 one—are important.

At 8:49 A.M. on July 7, 2005, an explosion on the Circle Line
near Liverpool Street was reported, followed within minutes
by one at Edgware Road and another at King's Cross. An hour
later, as the Underground system was being shut down, there
was a final explosion on a bus at Tavistock Square. Fifty-two
people died and over 700 were wounded—the third deadliest
Islamist terror attack in the West, after 9/11 and Madrid's 3/11.
On the face of it, and according to most Western media, left-of-
center academics, and even the British public at large, the July
7 bombings were the result of Britain's participation in the Iraq
operation and general closeness to George W. Bush's America.

Thus, Azzam Tamimi, Director of the Institute of Islamic
Thought in London (and former Muslim Brotherhood spokesman in Jordan), was expressing a widespread opinion when
he stated that Britain's role in Iraq and Afghanistan, the
"abuse" of Muslim detainees in Belmarsh prison in London and

Guantanamo Bay in Cuba, and even recent comments by Prime Minister Blair against "extremists" all contributed to the blasts: "This blow was expected any time."[99] But popular as they have been, such views missed some important questions.

To begin with, why would Al-Qaeda, which (falsely) claimed authorship of the attacks, target Londonistan, its main ideological, recruitment, and communications center in the West, thus endangering networks it had taken more than a decade to establish? Why, considering the deep roots of those networks in British soil, did it take more than two years after the fall of Baghdad for them to react? And why, if the ultimate goal was to repeat the Spanish scenario—i.e., produce a change of government—did the attacks come soon *after*, rather than before, the British general elections? Among the alternative answers, which are not necessarily incompatible, are that the attacks were the work of an autonomous, self-selected cell with its own particular motivations, or that, if Al-Qaeda was indeed responsible, something had changed in its assessment of England's importance for its strategy.

Despite the initial official claims that the July 7 bombings were the work of "homegrown" terrorists, unconnected to Al-Qaeda or any other foreign group, subsequent developments suggested precisely the opposite. Not only were the two main perpetrators, Sidique Khan and Shehzad Tanweer, found to have been in Pakistan—where they had undergone training, and where Khan even prepared, with the participation of al-Zawahiri himself, a suicide video—but the second group, the failed bombers of July 21, largely considered "copycats," also had a direct Pakistani link.

Unlike Khan and Tanweer, the leader of the July 21 group, Muktar Said Ibrahim, was not of Pakistani but of Somali origin. Although there are no indications of any direct contact between the two groups in Britain, there was a common link via Pakistan, to which Ibrahim had also traveled. In addition, Al-Qaeda has by now established a pattern of planning attacks in multiples—one may even call them campaigns—rather than as isolated, single operations, as demonstrated by the East Africa embassy bombings of 1998, the 1993 bombings in New York, the 9/11 attacks, and the failed August 2006 multiple plane attacks over the Atlantic. While much information is still missing or incomplete, such elements combine to suggest strongly that Britain had become the target of an international jihadi campaign.

Whether the decision to transform England from an R&R area of global jihad into a target was taken abroad (the likeliest scenario) or "at home," the attractiveness of the target was obvious. Not only is London a major "infidel" financial and media center, but in the jihadi view it was by then committed to the "crusader" assault on Islam. While this has to be speculation, it was also likely that by 2005 U.S. post-9/11 pressures, combined with the increasingly open jihadi activities in Londonistan, were bound to provoke some crackdown—as they did. At that point, it may be that some freelance elements of the Al-Qaeda nebula decided to take an easy opportunity.

Incomplete (or, depending on the harshness of Britain's critics, insincere or half-hearted) as the post-9/11 efforts to dismantle Londonistan were, they did exist and were accelerating prior to the London bombings. New counter-terrorism legislation making it punishable to plan attacks abroad had already been passed following the 1998 bombings of the U.S. embassies in Kenya and Tanzania and, "when it became law ... in 2000, effectively ended the '[British] compact' with Islamic radicals."[100] Judging by their subsequent claims in court, prominent activists of Londonistan may have overestimated the degree of protection the "human-rights" lobbies in England, or Europe, could provide. Moreover, when in May 2003 it turned out that two British-based Muslims had committed suicide attacks in Israel, some orders restricting movement of terrorism suspects were also introduced. The brief detentions of Abu Hamza in 2004 and Abu Qatada in 2002 were also part of a slow trend toward some seriousness regarding the Islamist threat.

Nevertheless, the bombings did put at risk the comfort of many Islamists who had been safely ensconced in Britain, and some were both surprised and inconvenienced. This explains why some Islamist terror groups, not usually known for their squeamishness regarding the murder of innocent civilians but with an established presence in England, declared themselves upset by the attacks. Mussa Abu Marzouk, then deputy chief of Hamas's political bureau (whose newspaper was still published in London at the time), claimed from Damascus that "targeting civilians in their transport means and lives is denounced and rejected,"[101] and *Hizbollah*'s "spiritual leader," Mohammad Hussein Fadlallah, stated: "These crimes are not accepted by any religion. It is a barbarism wholly rejected by Islam."[102]

As for the reaction of moderate Arabs, the chief of the Saudi-owned Al Arabiyya TV network, known for his blunt realism, was as critical as he was descriptive:

> For over 10 years now, I myself and other Arab writers have warned against the dangers of the reckless handling of the extremism that is now spreading like a plague within the British community. It was never understood why British authorities gave refuge to suspicious characters previously involved in terrorist activities. Why would Britain grant asylum to Arabs who have been convicted of political crimes or religious extremism, or even sentenced to death? Not only were they admitted to this country, but they were also provided with accommodation, a monthly salary, and free legal advice

for those who want to prosecute the British government. The answer, I believe, is what . . . I call "blind generosity."

> The battle we face is against the ideology, as opposed to against the terrorists themselves. The terrorist groups make the most of the concept of freedom of speech, as well as of the ability to promote such ideas to gain support. . . . So why has this happened? Until recently, London held the delusion that extremists would not target Britain, but only use it as a base, protecting their freedom as they worked against Arab and Islamic governments. For this reason, Britain was full of convicted [extremists] known for propagating their extremist ideologies. The time has come for British authorities to deal harshly with extremism, before complete chaos is unleashed onto British society. In the past, we talked about stopping them. Now, it is time to expel.[103]

This should have been obvious to anyone outside London's upper classes. It is this context that makes the initial almost universal public and official surprise that "our boys" could do such thing against "their own people" so difficult to understand. The profiles of the four 7/7 bombers, their international links, and the cultural microclimate they lived in at home should have made their actions as predictable as they were intelligible. Ultimately, the London bombers of 7/7 were as representative of jihadis in Europe as the Dutch and French cases considered above, but, coming from a truly multiculturalist society, they magnified the problems of that socio-political approach.

To begin with the **members of the initial cell** (on the assumption that the bombing was part of an intended serial assault on London), there is little new.

Mohammad Sidique Khan, born in 1975, was the eldest, and the dominant member of the cell. He was instrumental in recruiting the other three attackers, and he provided the cell's links with jihadi elements abroad,[104] as Bouyeri did for the Hofstad Group. Khan had studied at Leeds University; he was married and had an 18-month-old girl and another child on the way at the time of his death. After briefly working as a taxi driver, Khan was employed from 2001 to 2004 as a "learning mentor" at a primary school in Beeston, near Nottingham,[105] but by 2003 he had become critical of the government's social spending in the area. Meanwhile, in 2000, with local government funds, he had established the "Kashmiri Welfare Association," in fact a gym, associated with the Hardy Street mosque in Beeston. However, he was expelled from the mosque in 2003 because of his fundamentalist leanings.

In 2004 he established another gym, also in Beeston (although he was not living there any more), and it was there that the planning for the attacks took place—in fact, although the building was closed for repairs, neighbors noticed that youths were still meeting in it. Khan's case, like those of Bouyeri, Daoudi, and others, suggests that the European welfare system offers abundant recruitment opportunities to Islamists disguised as "community" organizers, sports coaches, or other publicly subsidized roles. In practice, Khan was a product of the British welfare system, which made his activities possible and paid for them. It also paid for his recruitment operations and travels. It is significant that in a Muslim-majority country such travel expenses would attract the attention of intelligence services—the very ones "human-rights" fundamentalists in Europe accuse of "torture" and other alleged abuses.

Shehzad Tanweer, 22 years old at the time of the bombing and British-born, came from a middle-class Pakistani family in Britain. The family was a classic immigrant success story, "proof" of the rightness of Britain's multiculturalist policies.[106] Mumtaz Tanweer, Shehzad's father, had arrived in 1961 from the Pakistani city of Faisalabad, to study for a degree in textile manufacturing. Upon graduation, he became a Yorkshire police officer, and in a few years he saved enough to open a corner shop. Slowly, he built it into a thriving business that today includes a halal slaughterhouse and a fish-and-chips shop. Along the way, he returned to Pakistan to marry his wife, Parveen.

The Tanweers settled in Bradford, about 10 miles from Beeston. Mumtaz "always worked hard because he never wanted his kids to struggle like he did." When the family later moved to Beeston, Mumtaz became a pillar of the local Pakistani community. He gave legal and business advice to friends and neighbors and helped fill out forms for those who could not read or write English. The Tanweers had three other children and lived in a large, two-story house—one of the largest in the neighborhood. Each parent drove a Mercedes.

According to friends and neighbors, the family was not known for being particularly religious. They typically attended Friday prayers at a mosque on Hardy Street, but they seldom prayed five times a day, as some Beeston Muslims do. Shehzad's mother and sisters wore fashionable traditional outfits of the type favored by many Westernized urban Pakistani women.

At Wortley High School, and then at Leeds Metropolitan University, where he studied sports science, Shehzad was popular and never experienced the racism that older Asians felt. "He felt completely integrated and never showed any signs of disaffection." And yet, as a friend of his stated, "We're not English, and we're not Pakistani. In the last few years, we had to find our identity. A lot of people here have gone back towards their religion to find out where they come from."[107] Shehzad was sent by his family to Pakistan for a year to study the Quran and Arabic, but he returned after only three months, complaining of the weather, the food, and Pakistani attitudes toward the British.[108]

The day before he blew himself up, Shehzad took part in a pickup soccer match, a ritual he carried out most days, if he wasn't playing cricket. "He was laughing and joking like normal," said a friend. In a pattern that is quite common in European terrorist cases, immediately after the bombings "many friends, relatives and elders in Tanweer's community still dwell in a realm of denial. 'I think there was somebody else behind it . . . If you saw Shehzad on the street, he wouldn't even say boo to you,' said a friend."[109]

If such reactions are sincere, they suggest that *Takfir* followers are very good practitioners of *taqiyya* (dissimulation of one's religious beliefs), and that their family and friends are not very close to them—or not as close as they may think. Nevertheless, both Mohammad Sidique Khan and Shehzad Tanweer were briefly under MI5 surveillance as early as one year before their actions, though they were not seen as serious threats.[110]

Hasib Mir Hussain, aged 18, was born in 1986 in Leeds into a family of Pakistani background and lived in the rather poor area of Holbeck. He was the Tavistock Square bus bomber, killing 13 people. The youngest of four siblings, a mediocre student in school, he had the interest and physical traits to become an athlete, and wanted to be a professional cricketer. In 2003, however, he dropped out of school, "went a bit wild," was caught shoplifting, and started drinking and swearing.[111] However, he did not seem uninterested in studies, and was admitted to the University of Leeds for a business course. Meanwhile, an arranged marriage with a woman in Pakistan was on the way— his brother had had a similar wedding there in 2002, which Hasib attended. He visited Pakistan again in July 2004.

Despite his young age, Hasib had already made the pilgrimage to Mecca, after which he stopped drinking and smoking and exchanged jeans for traditional Kashmiri Muslim garb. However, just prior to the bombings, he shaved—a common Salafi signal that death is coming.

Hasib's father, Mahmood, was a devout Muslim and an occasional factory worker, often in ill health; his brother Imran was an administrator in Leeds, was a friend of Sidique Khan's, and played cricket with Shehzad Tanweer.[112] In the now-familiar pattern, the family did not notice Hasib's radicalization, and the day of the bombings they were frantically looking for him—it was Imran's hunting in his brother's computer for clues to his whereabouts that directed police to the group's bomb factory in Leeds. In hindsight, the family realized that Tanweer and Khan had been meeting with Hasib in the Hussain home; a relative claimed, "Perhaps [Khan] was doing all that brainwashing and not uttering a word about it. That was a big betrayal."[113]

The Jamaican-born 19-year-old carpet fitter **Germaine** (**"Jamal"**) **Lindsay** had recently relocated to his English wife's hometown of Aylesbury in the south of England. He had grown up in the small working-class town of Huddersfield, close to Leeds. Lindsay lacked a father figure and converted to Islam following his mother's relationship with a Muslim. School friends portray him as an intelligent young man "fascinated by world affairs, religion and politics" who changed markedly after his conversion during the summer of his final year at school. Lindsay's deepening religiosity became increasingly obvious: He studied Urdu, wanted to be known as Jamal, and condemned those who drank alcohol. Moreover, his best friend revealed that he "had been going to a mosque in London and spoke of the teachings of someone down there"—most likely a reference to Abu Hamza. Lindsay's wife, Samantha Lewthwaite (a.k.a. Asmantara) was two years older, had converted to Islam prior to the marriage, and met Lindsay through her Muslim girlfriends. She was eight months pregnant with their second child at the time of the attacks. After the attacks, Lindsay's sister said that "he was not my brother any more." [114]

An acquaintance describes Lindsay as a

> nice quiet guy, a proper Muslim who didn't drink or smoke. I used to meet him at a friend's house with a group of others and we would all weight-train together. He was quite a fit guy and a wrestling fanatic and used to watch it on the television all the time. I'm really surprised they are saying this about him. [115]

According to a friend's declaration after the attacks, Jamal wanted to become a human-rights lawyer and was a member of Amnesty International while in high school. He left school because he wanted to go and "learn more in an Islamic state, like Saudi Arabia," but, after moving to north London and frequenting the mosques there, he slowly changed. "They [the imams there] have poisoned his spirit," a friend said, and by 2004 he was a changed man, sometimes disappearing for days in a row. The morning of the bombings, after heavily perfuming himself—again, a jihadi ritual prior to death—he left for central London, from where he sent his wife a message on his cellular phone: "I will always love you. We will be together forever, God willing." [116]

Lindsay may have seemed the odd man out in the Pakistani group, but his role is reminiscent of Richard Reid's and of a number of French and Dutch black converts, such as Willie Brigitte and the Walters brothers. In all those cases the black converts played a secondary role in their respective networks.

The only (indirect) endorsements of the London bombings came from Anjem Choudary, former UK secretary of the now defunct *Al-Muhajiroun* (whose "spiritual leader," Omar Bakri, claimed that the "covenant of security" between Islamists and the British state had expired when he refused to condemn the attacks), and from Hani al-Siba'i, director of the Al-Maqrizi Centre for Historical Studies. Al-Siba'i stated that if Al-Qaeda were responsible for the attacks, which he did not believe it was, then "it would be a great victory" and—referring to the G-8 summit taking place in Gleneagles, Scotland—would have "rubbed the noses of the world's eight most powerful countries in the mud."[117]

The **structure of the cell** itself was relatively simple. The meetings at Sidique Khan's Hamara youth access center in Lodge Lane, Beeston, a derelict building since closed, involved indoctrination as well as planning. Interestingly, and confirming the pattern already seen in the case of the Hofstad Group, there was a still-mysterious "Mr. Khan" (not Sidique Khan), a Pakistani preacher, mentioned by former attendees at those meetings, serving as the recruiter and ideologue. Apparently he came from France and left Britain just before the attacks—a pattern found in the case of other "Al-Qaeda visitors." Mahmood Hussain accused "Mr. Khan" of having brainwashed his son, and claimed that Hasib "had developed two religions . . . Muslim and another kind of Muslim"—presumably Salafi jihadism. In addition, the Leeds metropolitan area, including Beeston, was a known area of intense *Al-Muhajiroun* activities,[118] and three of the four bombers were known admirers of Abu Hamza (Hussain was the exception).[119] It is important to note that the bombers were relatively well trained: They cased the area and rehearsed the operation and, unlike their Somali imitators two weeks later, prepared functioning devices.

The **links of the cell** with international networks, albeit initially dismissed by police and the media, were extensive, probably more so than we know even now, and led directly to the Pakistani terrorist universe. In fact, considering the public involvement of al-Zawahiri himself, the London bombers—unlike the Hofstad Group—had contact with and likely received direct instructions from the Al-Qaeda core leadership.

It is well established that Sidique Khan and Shehzad Tanweer had close connections with Islamists in Pakistan, and Hasib Hussain also had some links.[120] Some Pakistani sources go further and claim that it is possible they had contacts there with Mustafa al-'Uzayti, better known as Abu Faraj al-Libbi, a major Al-Qaeda figure, in U.S. custody since May 2005.[121] Of other facts there is direct proof. By 2004 MI5 was aware of Khan's and Tanweer's trips to Pakistan, and knew from phone intercepts of their conversations about using crime to raise funds for other Islamists. However, MI5 decided that they were not an "immediate risk" or "direct threat" to national security, and surveillance was stopped. In fact, it turned out that Khan had visited, and was trained in bomb-making at, a terror camp in the tribal areas of Pakistan's chaotic Northwestern Province as early as 2003. By 2004 he and Tanweer were traveling throughout Britain looking for recruits.[122] In an unconfirmed report, two veteran *JeM* militants in Pakistan claimed that Tanweer expressed the wish to murder President Pervez Musharraf and that he trained in an organization camp north of Islamabad.[123]

At the end of July 2005, at a ritual funeral ceremony in the Tanweer family's home village of Kottan in southern Punjab, the local imam, Molvi Abdul Rehman, hailed the bomber as a "hero of Islam." Rehman was arrested, together with Mawlana Abdul Aziz Faridi, the leader of the local madrassa, Jamia Masjid Ahle-Sunnah Wal-Jammat, which Tanweer apparently attended.[124] Both men were closely linked to the *Jaish-e-Mohammed* organization.

Following the London bombings, something called "The Secret Group of Al-Qaeda of Jihad Organization in Europe," previously unknown and never heard of since, claimed credit, as did a certain "Kataëb Abu Hafs al-Masri–Qaïdat Al-Jihad–Liwa Europa."[125] However, Yasser al-Sirri of the Islamic Observation Centre in London, himself suspected of links with international jihadi networks, claimed that the statement "contradicts the language and literature of al-Qaeda."[126]

On the other hand, the *modus operandi* of the London attacks bears similarities to known Al-Qaeda operations: synchronization of detonations, choice of date (the day of the opening of the G-8 summit), timing (morning rush hour, guaranteeing a large number of fatalities), and location (in London itself).[127] Furthermore, Tanweer's uncle in Pakistan, Tahir Pervaiz, was quoted in the Pakistani newspaper *Dawn* as saying: "Bin Laden was Shehzad's ideal and he used to discuss the man with his cousins and friends in the village."[128] While none of this is absolute proof of direct Al-Qaeda planning and control of the operation, all the circumstantial evidence suggests such links.

As noted above, after the bombings the British government did try to strengthen the anti-terror laws, but judging by the reception of such proposals by Parliament, the courts, and the elite culture—media and academia—Londonistan is still very much alive.

Suicide Jihadis from Europe

The phenomenon of suicide terrorism in Europe is relatively new, but it was probably inevitable, considering the evolution of continental jihadi culture. As early as 2000, *Jane's Intelligence Review* noted that virtually all terrorist groups known to practice suicide operations had a presence in Europe, and British intelligence had expected it since 1999, given that some 3,000 Muslims from Britain had been trained in Afghanistan by that time.[129]

Failed attempts occurred in Europe in the 1990s, but the first successful ones were in Italy, where the Palestinian Muhammad al-Khatib Shafiq blew himself up in front of a synagogue in Modena in December 2003, followed by the Moroccan Mustafa Chaouki doing the same at a McDonald's in Brescia in March 2004, both isolated cases of individual action. Before that, Europe-based jihadis had committed suicide abroad, the first known case being that of Mohammed Bilal, a British citizen of Pakistani origin from Birmingham, who, on December 25, 2000, drove a car bomb against the 15th Indian Army Corps headquarters in Srinagar, Kashmir. Since then the number of Europe-based suicide terrorists has increased, both inside and outside the continent. A brief examination of some of those cases suggests the motivations for suicide attacks—and the mistaken interpretations of the phenomenon.

Wail al-Dhaleai was born in Yemen in 1981 and arrived in the UK in 2000, claiming and receiving political asylum on the grounds that, after writing newspaper articles critical of the government, he was "persecuted." In 2001 he married a British woman; they had a son and, at the time of his death, were expecting another child. Established in Sheffield, he was a *Tae Kwon Do* enthusiast, described as "a very jolly person, a very sociable person." He was teaching martial arts, trained with the UK Olympic team, and "couldn't wait to get his British passport so that he could try for selection for Britain." Until September 2003 he was receiving welfare and allegedly studying computer science. At that point he told his family in Yemen that he was going to a martial-arts competition in Amsterdam and from there to a "country bordering Iraq"; he told those in Sheffield that he was going to the UAE, where he had been offered a job as a security guard and martial-arts trainer, and where he would earn £250 a week and be given a house for his family.

In fact, in November 2003 he drove a car filled with explosives into a U.S. army patrol in Iraq.[130]

The Dhaleai case is quite characteristic of Europe-based jihadis, and raises some important general questions:

> First, he obtained political asylum claiming he was persecuted in Yemen for his opinions. What, then, explains his apparent lack of interest in religion or politics while in Sheffield? Second, he formed a family but never managed to find a job, living instead on welfare while increasing that family—a demonstration either of irresponsible behavior or of contempt for the "infidel" society in which he lived. Third, he never demonstrated particularly strong religious beliefs in public but was interested in violence, through sports—probably an indication of *taqiyya* at work, but also similar to the physical-training regimens of the London bombing cell. Finally, he came from Yemen, a country with a particularly strong fundamentalist presence; it is the bin Ladens' native country and has an extensive network of Al-Qaeda supporters, a network with strong ties in Britain, via Abu Hamza.

The flow of volunteers to Iraq started in 2003; by the end of that year some 150 jihadis had already gone there from Britain alone, and by 2006 the figure was in the thousands. This was possible because of the existence of a well-oiled network of recruitment present throughout Europe, run by al-Zarqawi. While little is still known about it, there are some indices as to its *modus operandi*. In 2003, a certain Abderrazak M., a 30-year-old Algerian based in Hamburg and, like Mohamed Atta, close to the Al-Quds mosque, allegedly a Chechnya veteran, was caught in Syria and returned to Germany; he was arrested later in Italy for recruiting for Iraq as part of the Al-Ansar organization. The Hamburg authorities accused him of recruiting in Spain's Costa del Sol as well.[131] Such activities are possible in Europe because, as Manfred Murck of Hamburg's Office for Protection of the Constitution stated, "One cannot legally prevent someone from going to Iraq on the chance that they might shoot American soldiers there.... The Jihadis would have to boast about it publicly beforehand."[132]

In a 2006 report, French intelligence listed Iraq, Afghanistan, Kashmir, Lebanon, Somalia, Algeria, and Morocco among the motivations of jihadists in Europe,[133] and those are indeed the immediate motivations of most Europe-based jihadis, but they do not explain why suicide bombers from Europe appeared when they did and not earlier.

Magdi Allam observes that

> This is the tragic truth of the ideology of hate which binds together all Muslims obsessed by anti-Americanism, anti-Westernism and by the prejudicial denial of Israel's right to exist. They are able to find many pretexts to fly into a rage, from Israeli occupation to the American war, from the cartoons about Muhammed to the Pope's words. Nevertheless the problem is inside Islam itself, an Islam that extremists turned from a faith in God into an ideology aiming at the imposition of a theocratic and totalitarian power on everyone who is not like them.[134]

But this still cannot explain it, since that ideology predated suicide terrorism. As with other elements in the jihadi picture in Europe, the roots are to be found in the maturation of an existing radical environment, bursting into action in response to outside impulses and events. To this one may add the obviously inadequate European laws regarding asylum and terrorist conspiracies, and one arrives at a truer picture.

All this raises serious questions as to the accuracy, indeed relevance, of various popular explanations of suicide terrorism. The American researcher Robert Pape, for instance, insists that

> Suicide terrorism is a strategy for national liberation. Although isolated incidents do occur, the overwhelming majority of suicide attacks take place as part of organized, coherent campaigns in which individual after individual, or

team after team, voluntarily kill themselves as a means to kill
the maximum number of people in the target society in order
to compel the state to desist from participating in the foreign
occupation of their homeland.[135]

Is this explanation valid in the growing number of cases of
suicide terrorism by Muslims based in Europe? Since 2000, we
have seen a progressive shift in targets of suicide attacks by
Muslims in Europe: first they were against "outsiders" (Jews
in Modena, Americans in Brescia); then against foreigners
abroad (Iraq, Israel, India); and finally against local populations (Madrid, London). In terms of techniques, first there were
bombs in transportation systems (Madrid, London), then attempted use of hijacked planes against highly symbolic targets
(the Eiffel Tower in Paris, Atatürk's tomb in Ankara), then car
bombs against targets outside Europe (Kashmir, Israel, Iraq).
Finally, how does that theory explain Dhaleai, a Yemeni refugee in Britain, detonating himself in Iraq?

With the possible exception of Pakistanis of Kashmiri extraction living in Britain who went to Kashmir to kill Indian occupiers, it is difficult or impossible to find any link between the
actions of Muslim suicide terrorists from Europe and the "liberation" of their "homeland." The Tunisian Nizar Ben Mohammed
Nawwar, a drifter moving between Germany and Canada, did
commit suicide on Djerba Island, off the coast of Tunisia, but
where was the "foreign occupation" of Tunisia? Were the mostly German tourists he murdered "occupiers"? Furthermore, no
person of Iraqi origin based in Europe is known to have gone
to Iraq to fight the American "occupiers."

These examples are enough to make Pape's explanation of
suicide terrorism untenable as a general theory. The exceptions
are not, as he says, "isolated incidents;" there are just too many
of them to give his theory any explanatory value in the case of

Muslims from Europe. If the bulk of actual examples lie outside a theory, it ceases to be a theory.

Others have tried to find emotional explanations for suicide terrorism, including "humiliation."[136] The virtue of that argument is that it does reflect an element common to suicide terrorists in general, and, like Pape's, it at least avoids the prevailing academic temptation—a remnant of the days of Marxist domination—to find economic explanations for everything. The problem is that "humiliation," even "collective humiliation," is too vague and limited as a cause of a complex phenomenon that is part of a more complicated and larger sphere. A feeling of "humiliation" that would lead a Yemeni refugee enjoying a good life in England to kill himself in Iraq has to be part of something bigger and collective indeed—e.g., religious hatred or defense of the *ummah*—included in a more complex ideology with global goals that go beyond emotions. In the absence of such an all-encompassing ideology reinforced by religious faith, why did not similar, or even greater and more recent, "humiliations" push hundreds of Serbs, until recently the dominant people of the Balkans' largest country, or Russians, the masters of the world's largest empire until less than two decades ago, to global terrorist activities? Humiliation, then, or, better put, cultural humiliation, is a facilitating and perhaps necessary factor in explaining jihadist terrorism, but it is not a primary one. Where it does play a key role is in explaining the sympathy, if not support, for Islamist terrorism on the part of otherwise peaceful Muslims, in the West and elsewhere.

If there is a case clearly contradicting theories such as Pape's, it is that of **Muriel Degauque**, a Belgian convert from near Charleroi, who became the first known European female suicide bomber when, at age 38, she blew herself up in Bakuba, Iraq, on November 9, 2005, killing only herself but wounding six. Gender aside, her profile has many common traits with other European converts to jihad.[137]

As in so many cases, Muriel's parents, a crane driver and a hospital secretary, had known nothing of her violent mission. Andrea Dorange, who had known Muriel from the age of five, described her as "an adorable little girl, smiling all the time. But then, later, everything became . . . different. She was really weak and very easily influenced." By the time she had left school at 16, Muriel was experimenting with drugs and often running away from home. She had a turbulent and distant relationship with her parents, who found her difficult to control. She was pretty, her mother says, and so popular with boys she wasn't even sure how many boyfriends she'd had.

Those who knew Muriel best believe a defining moment was the death of her brother in a motorbike accident in 1989. A downward spiral began. She worked for a short while in a bakery, where she was remembered mostly for her frequent absences and drug abuse. Later she briefly had a job in a café; her mother said she had an irregular work history and was claiming state benefits.

Her childhood friends seemed to lose track of her when, in her early twenties, she moved to Brussels, where she married a not very religious Turk and converted to Islam. Friends said she was more religious than her husband, and soon she left him, struck up a new relationship with an Algerian man, and later married a Moroccan Salafist, Issam Goris, seven years her junior. She changed her name to Myriam, and her parents began to worry about the radical turn her Muslim faith had taken, fearing she had been brainwashed.

A three-year stay in Morocco increased her religious zeal, so much so that she even began wearing a *hijab* in the presence of her father. Goris tried to impose his own rules when visiting her parents, insisting the women and men ate separately, and banning beer and television. "The last time we saw them we told them that we had had enough of them trying to indoctrinate us," said Liliane Degauque. Her stand-out memory of her daughter's increasing remoteness was when she spent two weeks in a hospital just a few hundred yards from where Muriel was working. "She did not come to see me once," said Liliane.

In Brussels the couple kept a low profile in their rundown apartment block on Rue de Mérode in the heart of an immigrant quarter. Muriel cloaked herself in a *burqa*. After her mission, her neighbors were astonished to learn she had been the suicide bomber. Most had not even realized she was a white Belgian.

Neighbors of Muriel's parents rarely saw the young couple, but were taken aback when they did: On a couple of occasions they arrived at the family home in a luxurious white Mercedes.

In Brussels, Muriel lived an isolated life in the home, while her husband was already under surveillance by the anti-terrorism police. By July 2005 the couple was in touch with an Iraqi recruitment network and left for Syria.

Interviewed a month after her death, Claude Moniquet, of the Brussels-based European Strategic Intelligence and Security Centre, expressed concern that Muriel could become a "model" for other fanatical young women to follow.

> She had a classic profile for a convert to radical Islam. . . . She had a drug problem when she was younger, she had no real job, and was not very close to her family. Maybe she thought that she had no future and she was clearly under the influence of her husband who was a radical. What is surprising is that she was a young European woman, but we could maybe expect more cases.[138]

The Madrid-Leganés Group

While Degauque was the first known native European to complete the road from conversion to suicidal murder, the jihadi group of Madrid was an almost complete North African transplant, and thus more typical of jihadis on the continent. In addition, its multi-ethnic composition and foreign ties are closer to the patterns noted among other cells, and more likely to be repeated.

On the morning of March 11, 2004, the Islamist cell placed bombs at Atocha, the main train station in Madrid, killing 191 and wounding some 3,000 persons. The attack, only three days before national elections, which the then-ruling Partido Popular was expected to win, changed the electoral dynamics and, to everyone's surprise, resulted in the narrow victory of the opposition Socialist Workers Party of Spain. Prompt police work led to the discovery of most of the perpetrators in the suburb of Leganés on April 3. With police and special forces surrounding the building, and after a commando was killed in an exchange of fire, all seven terrorists inside the building committed suicide by blowing up themselves, and most of the building.

The suicides, and their numerous accomplices who were not there at the time, were a multinational, mostly Moroccan cell, with extensive connections on four continents. They included the following:

The Algerian **Allekema Lamari**, a.k.a. "**Yasin**," was the "emir," the religious and overall leader of the group. Arrested in 1997 for membership in the GIA and sentenced in 2001 to 14 years in prison, he was released in 2002 on a technicality and went underground. Upon his release, Lamari associated himself with the GICM, in another example of what amounts to a group of professional Salafis present in a number of European countries, who join other groups, regardless of ethnicity, if their own is defeated.[139] His commitment was already well known in Islamist circles long before he died. Safwan Sabagh, a Valencia restaurant owner of Syrian origin and an associate of Lamari, told interrogators that, after the Bali bombings of October 12, 2002 (202 fatalities), Lamari commented how very easy it was to do much damage. A week before the events of Leganés, he stated, "They will never catch me alive."[140]

The Tunisian **Serhane ben Abdelmajid Fakhet**, a.k.a. "**El Tunecino**" (age 35), was the main recruiter and the coordinator of the Atocha bombings. Married to the 17-year-old sister of Mustafa al-Maymouni, a leader of the Casablanca bombers of 2003, and close to Abu Dahdah, he was, together with Jamal Zougam, in charge of the Leganés group. Fakhet was the recipient of the equivalent of a €30,000 Spanish-government scholarship to study economics at the Autonomous University of Madrid from 1994 to 1998, where he was pursuing a doctorate while working illegally as a very successful real-estate salesman, both in Spain and in Tetuán.[141] He was openly and aggressively Salafi in his beliefs, so much so that he was even confronted by imam Moneir Mahmood Ali al-Messerey of the M-30 mosque in Madrid, himself a Wahhabi. [142]

Fakhet recruited Jamal Ahmidan, who at the time was out of prison and becoming more religious. Together, and under the supervision of Abu Dahdah, they recruited more followers at Alhambra, an obscure restaurant in Madrid known for being a recruitment location for volunteers to Afghanistan.[143] All of this was known to the police, who kept Fakhet under surveillance between 1996 and 2001, and again starting in 2003—only to lose him just before the attacks.

Basel Ghalyoun, another Syrian arrested in connection with the March attacks, claimed that already in August 2003 Fakhet told him that he, Fakhet, was a better Muslim than others and that there would be an attack in Spain; he reiterated that intention in February 2004 and told similar things to many others, justifying his intentions with the assertion that "Spain is against Muslims," citing the fact that it was involved in the war in Iraq. Ghalyoun's statements were confirmed by yet another Syrian living in Spain, Mohammed Almallah Dabas, who also told police that "Sirhane was talking about bank and jewelry shop robberies to fund the murder of policemen" and that "something important had to be done."[144] El Tunecino had close contacts with "Muhammad the Egyptian" (see below), the likely successor of Abu Dahdah as supervisor of the cell.

Jamal Ahmidan, a.k.a. **"El Chino"** and **"Mowgli,"** a 33-year-old Moroccan, had an extensive police record for drug trafficking, in Morocco as well as Spain. The cell's operational leader, he had his own small group of associates, mostly common criminals, who joined Fakhet's cell in 2003. Ahmidan was jailed in Tetuán, Morocco, in the late 1990s, for drug trafficking and murder, and it seems that it was there that he became a fanatical Islamist. A fellow trafficker testified in the Spanish court that "while in jail in Tetuán he had numerous privileges, including a cell by himself, where he had photos of Ossama bin Laden, a TV and a cell phone, with which he maintained contacts with 'Al Qaeda people'."[145] Those privileges suggest that he was far from a petty criminal, and indeed the Spanish police now believe that it was precisely his financial ability and importance in the criminal underground that attracted Fakhet's attention and led to the merger of the two groups.[146] Ahmidan, whose family owned a clothes shop in a middle-class neighborhood of Madrid, like other members of the network (Fakhet excepted), had shown few apparent signs of radicalism. In Spain he was not known for religiosity—to the contrary, his friends included women who sported crop tops, tattoos, and piercings. "Many of them [the Madrid cell members] appeared westernized and integrated into the Spanish community, with a liking for football, fashion, drinking and Spanish girlfriends, say Spanish press reports. Neighbors said they were always polite, although sometimes hid their faces."[147]

On December 5, 2003, Ahmidan was stopped, fined, and released by traffic police on a highway north of Madrid. They reported that he looked nervous and had in his possession a false Belgian passport, two suitcases full of clothes stolen from a supermarket, and three large knives. Moreover, after being fined, he accused police of "racism" and threatened to "bury" them.[148] While this could have been just standard behavior on the part of a habitual criminal with experience in Europe's liberal courts, it does demonstrate how easily early signs of radicalism can escape detection.

Through his contacts in the criminal underworld, Ahmidan approached an unemployed Spanish miner, José Emilio Suárez Trashorras, and bought 200 kilograms of explosives, paid for with Moroccan hashish and €7,000 in cash. According to Mostafa Ahmidan, brother of Jamal, the latter changed suddenly upon his return from a trip to Morocco. "He did not drink and smoke anymore, and was giving much advice," though, like his cousins, he was involved in drug trafficking. Moreover, he considered "unjust" the initial arrests of some of the Atocha perpetrators because of "your brothers who are dying in Iraq."[149] As in other cases mentioned, the conversion to Salafism changed personal behavior, but did not prevent continued participation in criminal, and un-Islamic, activities when they helped the cause. Clearly, by then Ahmidan had accepted the standard jihadi justification of indiscriminate murder of "infidels": the fact that Muslims died in Iraq, Afghanistan, or elsewhere, no matter why or how, made the killing of commuters in Madrid legitimate revenge.

Abdennabi (Abdallah) Kounjaa was a known member of the GICM. Two years after the Atocha events, Spanish police concluded that that group was instrumental both in planning the bombings and, using its extensive European networks, in providing safe refuge to the surviving cell members.[150]

Less than two hours before blowing himself up at Leganés, Kounjaa called his brother, Abdelkader, to tell him: "Now I am going. I am going to meet God. We are surrounded in a house and we'll blow up with them. Listen! Did you give the money to that gentleman?"[151] The desire, indeed the expectation of going to Paradise, the worry of leaving debts behind—these are typical last words of Islamist suicide bombers, common among Palestinians and similar to the tape left behind by Sidique Khan and Mohamed Atta's letter.

Asri Rifaat Anouar, although a suspected GICM member, was not in police files in Spain or Morocco.

Rachid Oulad Akcha, age 33, and **Mohammed Oulad Akcha**, age 28, were both Moroccans. Their brother Khalid is in jail in Spain for common crimes, and their sister Naima was the only woman arrested in connection with the bombings. According to Judge del Olmo, the brothers had helped obtain the explosives, and the attacks were planned, and bombs made, in the house they had rented at Morata de Tajuña, near Madrid.[152]

Abdelmajid Bouchar, a 22-year-old Moroccan, was the only Leganés terrorist to escape the day of the event—mostly because he was an accomplished distance runner. He was taking out the garbage when he noticed the police surrounding the apartment block. He warned his confederates via his cell phone and then ran away. He was arrested in Serbia in August 2005 and extradited to Spain.

The Leganés group was described in a study for the U.S. National Security Council as follows:

> 5 of the 7 Madrid Train Bombers who blew themselves up when cornered by Spanish police grew up in one section of the Jamaa Mezuak neighborhood of Tetuan. 3 had reputations as being religious (brothers Rachid and Mohamed Oulad Akcha and Abdennabi Kounjaa), one was a notorious drug smuggler (Jamal Ahmidan, who became the operational chief of the Madrid bombing) and one (Asri Rifaat Anouar) was a non religious a seller of candies who looked up to the others (especially to Ahmidan, according to his own father and others).[153]

This description is both correct and misleading. On the one hand, the fact that all the Moroccans came from the same area of Tetuán helps explain why they were close to one another. On the other hand, the two leaders were not Moroccan, and the fact that Ahmidan was a drug smuggler does not mean he was not religious, nor was Anouar's view of Ahmidan as a father figure (not uncommon among jihadi cells in Europe) unrelated to the latter's Salafi beliefs. As for the drug connection, far from demonstrating lack of strong religious beliefs, it was a necessary tool in the jihadi operation—and thus religiously acceptable. According to the Spanish authorities, "using common drug traffickers as intermediaries, the bombers swapped ecstasy and hashish for the 440 pounds of dynamite used in the blasts that killed 191 people and wounded more than 1,400 others in the Spanish capital. Money from the drug trafficking paid for an apartment hideout, a car and the cell phones that were used to detonate the bombs, an Interior Ministry spokesman said."[154]

The Leganés suicides were only the spectacular end of a much larger conspiracy, with only Lamari and Fakhet being more than foot soldiers. Behind them were the more important **ideological leaders and recruiters** of a network with wide international ramifications.

Jamal Zougam, born in 1973 in Tangiers, was the main planner and ideologue of the cell behind the Atocha bombings. Tangiers and nearby Tetuán are close to the Strait of Gibraltar—hence to Spain—and the center of Morocco's cannabis production and trafficking. Furthermore, on the basis of a 1956 Moroccan-Spanish accord, Moroccan residents of these two areas are allowed to enter the Spanish North African enclaves of Ceuta and Melilla without visas.

Zougam came to Spain at age 10, with his mother and older half-brother, Mohamed Chaoui, also implicated in the attacks. In 2000 the half-brothers opened a cell-phone repair shop, from which the phones used to detonate the Atocha bombs came. They were assisted by Mohammed Bekkali, another Tangiers native and a graduate in physics from the University of Tetuán. The Moroccan police claim that Zougam had entered fundamentalist ranks by 1993 and had joined a group associated with Al-Qaeda by 1997, recruited by the Franco-Moroccan Abdelaziz Benyaïch,[155] a major player in the Casablanca attacks. Benyaïch was an old Islamist militant, from a radical family—one of his brothers, Salaheddin, was charged in the Casablanca affair, and another, Abdallah, was killed in November 2001 at Tora Bora, suggesting the group's direct ties to Al-Qaeda.

For a number of years, Zougam had frequent meetings at the Alhambra restaurant and phone conversations with Abu Dahdah, who also visited his phone shop. How important Zougam was in the Islamist networks in Spain may never be completely known, but he certainly had widespread connections. Thus, on September 5, 2001, he called Abu Dahdah to announce that he was fleeing Spain for Morocco—probably in expectation of likely police reactions to the New York attacks to come.[156]

Abu Dahdah (Imad Eddin Barakat Yarkas) was the link between the older Syrian network, Al-Qaeda, and the Madrid bombers. When detained in November 2001, he was ostensibly a used-car dealer, married to a Spanish woman and the father of five children. He was also, as has been mentioned, the leader of "Soldiers of Allah," a radical Islamist group centered on the Abu Baker mosque in Madrid, and involved in sending fighters to Bosnia, Chechnya, and Afghanistan, as well as financing Al-Qaeda through various Islamic NGOs.

Amer al-Azizi, Moroccan, born in 1968, was co-leader, with Abu Dahdah, of the Spanish Al-Qaeda cell broken up in November 2001. Associated with al-Zarqawi and a friend of Fakhet, al-Azizi is a veteran of jihad in Bosnia and Afghanistan, and one of the leaders of the GICM. He had been indicted in Spain *in absentia* for helping to plan the 9/11 attacks. With the Moroccan Driss Chebli he was accused of setting up the July 2001 meeting of Mohamed Atta and other 9/11 conspirators in Tarragona. According to uncorroborated Spanish media reports, in February 2002 he participated in an Istanbul meeting with leaders of assorted Maghrebi groups, including the Libyan, Tunisian, and Moroccan Islamic Fighting Groups.[157]

Like other jihadis, al-Azizi was a somewhat contradictory figure. On the one hand, he was known to be a drug addict; on the other, he was attending some basic classes on Islam—and made no secret of his convictions: "In June, 2000, when the Arab countries' ambassadors to Spain came to the mosque to mourn the death of the Syrian dictator Hafez al-Assad, al-Azizi insulted them, yelling, 'Why do you come to pray for an infidel?' "[158]

Mustafa al-Maymouni, a Moroccan and brother-in-law of El Tunecino, is generally considered the leader of *Salafia Jihadia* in

Spain. The group is part of the same collection of violent Salafist groups associated with Al-Qaeda as the GICM; in fact it is considered to be the ideological source of the GICM, and subscribing to the *Takfir-wal-Hijra* ideology. Like Fakhet and al-Azizi, Maymouni began his Islamist career as a *Tablighi* member. Abu Dahdah offered him training in an Indonesian camp of *Jamaa Islamiya*, Al-Qaeda's Southeast Asian associate (he declined because of the imminent birth of his child). He recruited terrorists for Bosnia and Chechnya, and was in contact with Zougam's group. Arrested in Morocco, he was tried and jailed for participation in the Casablanca bombings.[159]

A year after Atocha, Spanish police confirmed that Youssef Belhadj, "Al-Qaeda spokesman in Europe," arrested in Belgium, had given the green light for the attack during a trip to Madrid—where he stayed at his sister's house—at the end of 2003. Although the predominantly Moroccan cell was established, financed, and operated tactically as an autonomous entity, its ideological and religious leadership, absolutely necessary for action, was provided by two Syrians: Abu Dahdah and Abu Musab al-Suri. Al-Suri's excellent knowledge of the Spanish scene, and of the likely reaction of the electorate, may explain the timing of the attacks.[160]

Rabei Osman Ahmed, a.k.a. **"Muhammad the Egyptian,"** born in 1967, was arrested in June 2004 in Rome on an international warrant issued by Spanish authorities. He is considered "probably among the principal authors" of the Madrid attacks; arrested with him was a 21-year-old Palestinian, Yahia Payumi, an alleged accomplice. On intercepted phone calls, Ahmed claimed that "The Madrid attack is my project," and "The project has cost me a lot of study, it took me 2½ years." Referring to the Leganés seven, he declared: "Some have died like martyrs, eight others have been arrested. They are my best friends."[161]

A former Egyptian-army explosives expert, Ahmed arrived in Germany in 1998 and, although briefly detained for being illegally in the country, managed to preach for a year in a German mosque. In 2001 he left for Spain—but not before, apparently, undergoing some training in Afghan camps, where he was associated with Abu Dahdah.[162] In 2003, he recruited Serhane Fakhet in Madrid.

That same year he was illegally in France, working on building sites. Telephone intercepts clearly linked him with both the Madrid/Leganés group (he admitted as much), and with recruitment of would be "martyrs" for Iraq. Although he was tried and sentenced to ten years in Italy, a Madrid court could not find enough proof of his involvement in the Madrid bombings to convict him in 2006.

The **international links** of the Madrid/Leganés group were truly global, reaching from Europe to Asia, North Africa, and the United States. Equally important, the size and organization of jihadi structures in Spain were such that they could afford to wait for the best moment to strike—a few days before the general elections.

The March 11 bombings were the joint operation of three distinct groups: one, led by Zougam, was based in the Madrid neighborhood of Lavapiés; another, under Ahmidan, was made up mostly of common criminals who worshipped at the Villaverde mosque; and the third, under Fakhet, was directly linked to the GICM and involved in the Casablanca bombings of 2003. It was Fakhet, El Tunecino, who brought them together— he was a friend of Ahmidan, the brother-in-law of Maymouni, and well known to Zougam. The common trait, in addition to the mostly Moroccan origin, was ideology—hatred for the West and for moderate Muslims. The police found a videotaped message in the ruins of the Leganés building:

After finding that the situation did not change [after the March 11 attacks] and after the new government has announced its new mandate with more fight against Muslims and the sending of more crusader troops to Afghanistan, the Companies of Death and Ansar al Qaeda have taken the decision to continue on the path of blessed jihad and resistance.... For this reason it has been decided that the brigade located in Al-Andalus will not leave here until [the government] troops leave the Muslims' lands immediately and without conditions.... If they do not do this within a week, we will continue our jihad until martyrdom in the land of Tarek Ben Ziyad....* We will kill you anywhere and at any moment.... There is no difference between civilians and militaries: our innocents die by the thousands in Afghanistan and Iraq. Perhaps your blood is more valuable than ours?... I'll direct some words to all those who suffered injustices and aggression under the accusation of participating in the March 11th operations. You have followed the hadith of Mohammed (Allah bless and save him) who parted from Muslims who live with the polytheists. Do you know of the Spanish crusade against Muslims, and not long ago of the expulsion from Al-Andalus and the tribunals of the Inquisition? We feel for your injustice but our jihad is above all, because our brothers are assassinated and decapitated throughout the world. Blood for blood! Destruction for destruction! Allahu Akbar![163]

The terrorists' mentions of the past Muslim occupation of the Iberian peninsula, references to which are found often in texts of bin Laden and al-Zawahiri; of the leader of the invasion of 711 CE, Tarik ibn Ziyad; and of contemporary Spain as "Al-Andalus" demonstrate that the Islamists' hostility to Spain has profound historic and religious roots, a hostility that is especially strong among Moroccans. The suicide communiqué's threat to continue attacks in Spain even after the announced post–March 11 withdrawal of troops from Iraq, because of the

---

* Some similarities are interesting and symbolic. Tarik ibn Ziyad, a Berber like Ahmidan, was the leader of the Muslim invasion of Visigothic Spain in 711, as deputy of the Tunisian (like Fakhet) governor of Ifriqqiya, Musa Ben Ibn Nusayr. Most of the terrorists came from the Tangiers/Tetuán area, like the bulk of Tarik's detachment of 711.

continued presence of Spanish forces in Afghanistan, also demonstrates that—contrary to the widespread Spanish popular and "progressive" opinion, found especially in the pro-socialist newspaper *El País*[164]—the issue of Iraq was only a circumstantial pretext, important as it may have been, and, absent that pretext, another would have been found. In fact, jihadi websites today continue to describe Spain as an important enemy, because of its historic defeat of Islam as well as because of the presence of Spanish troops among the allied forces in Afghanistan and Lebanon.

In addition to their role in both the Madrid bombings and the Leganés collective suicide, members of the group had prior ties with Mohamed Atta and other members of his Hamburg cell; this was true not just of Abu Dahdah,[165] but also of al-Maymouni, as well as Zougam.[166] The former had contacts with Australian Islamist Belal Khazaal, a militant of the Islamic Youth Movement and editor of the Islamist periodical *Nida'ul Islam* (copies of which were found in Abu Dahdah's home in Madrid), and with Mohamed Jamal Omran, a.k.a. Abu Ayman, a Khazaal collaborator and, according to Judge Garzón, a recruiter of *mujahedin* for Iraq and a follower of Abu Qatada. In recorded tapes between December 2000 and July 2001, Khazaal informed Abu Dahdah that a "brother" would be passing through Spain—apparently al-Suri.[167] Also according to Garzón, Abu Dahdah visited Abu Qatada 17 times in the UK between 1995 and 2000 and on one occasion gave him $11,000 for Abu Mohammed al-Maqdari, a terrorist arrested in Jordan for his links with Al-Qaeda.[168] Luis José Galán, a.k.a. "Yusuf Galán," a Spanish convert to Islam who was sentenced to nine years at the 2005 Al-Qaeda trial in Madrid, was trained in an Indonesian terrorist camp by Abu Dahdah.

Said Berraj, another suspect in the Madrid bombings, was arrested in Istanbul in 2000 along with Amer al-Azizi and expelled. The fact that Berraj, known to be close to Fakhet, was in Istanbul in the company of al-Azizi, an important Al-Qaeda "military" leader in Europe, further clarifies the links between Al-Qaeda and the Madrid cell—just as the ideological and financial links among al-Suri, Abu Dahdah, and Abu Qatada clarify the logistics and the connection to Londonistan. What's more, one of the men on trial in Spain for involvement in the Atocha bombings linked them with two individuals who escaped, only to be killed in Iraq: Mohamed Afalah and Daoud Ouhnane, both killed in 2005.[169] Although uncorroborated, that testimony is plausible, considering the known links between the GICM (deeply involved in the Madrid events), the al-Zarqawi Iraq recruitment network in Europe, and the prominent role of Moroccans in Iraq, who usually went there via Spain and Turkey.

In fact, the role of the GICM in the Madrid attack is well documented—and not only because most members of the cell who planned and executed it were Moroccans.

Youssef Belhadj—the grandly described "Al-Qaeda spokesman in Europe," who gave the green light for the attack—is a known GICM militant. He is also suspected of being the same "Abu Dujanah al Afghani" who signed the communiqué claiming credit for the attacks.

The usually well informed Madrid newspaper *ABC* has linked the Atocha bombings to the previously mentioned February 2002 Istanbul meeting of Maghrebi jihadist groups. At that meeting the four groups involved—from Morocco, Algeria, Tunisia, and Libya—decided to associate formally with Al-Qaeda and to concentrate their operations in those areas where they had a presence—i.e., Europe and North Africa—rather than faraway places like Afghanistan, Chechnya, or Kashmir. The details of the Istanbul meeting and its decisions are yet to be completely revealed, but the involvement of Tunisians and Algerians in the Spanish cell suggests, at the very least, better cooperation than had been previously suspected between ethnic groups not known for their friendly relations. To that one may add bin Laden's own intention, made public in October 2003, to concentrate on Spain and Poland, as the "weakest links" in the pro-U.S. coalition in Iraq.[170]

How extensive and complex the jihadi networks in Europe are is exemplified by the false documents in possession of the Benyaïch brothers. Those included a British passport in the name of Ian Gerald Frost of Brighton, used by Abdelaziz Benyaïch; a Spanish passport for José Cristian Rodríguez Cuenca from Ceuta, used by his brother Abdallah, already in prison in Spain under that name; and another British document for David Charles Burgess, also of Brighton, used by Salaheddin Benyaïch.[171] The link with Brighton—a known center of *Hizb ut-Tahrir* activities, the place of conversion to Salafism of Jérôme Courtailler, and a base of support for Osman Hussain of the failed London bombings of 2005—is not a coincidence, and it is likely that the false passports were produced there. Following the Madrid attacks, Belgian police, acting on information from Italy, arrested 15 people suspected of preparing another attack in Spain. Further raids took place in France, while the Moroccan Abdelmajid Bouchar was arrested in Belgrade.

So the evidence seems to confirm that the Madrid attacks were organized over a period of at least two and a half years, as stated by Rabei Ahmed, by a network spread over five continents—Europe, Africa, North America, Asia, and Australia— and a dozen countries.

The reactions of Muslims in Spain to the Atocha and Leganés events was mixed. Kamal Rahmouni, vice president of an association of Moroccan immigrant workers in Spain, told the press that he did not think it appropriate to talk about "Islamic terrorists," just as one should not say "Basque terrorism" or "Catholic terrorism." "Islam forbids killing," he stressed. Another Muslim, Mohamed Afifi, spokesman for the Islamic Centre of Madrid, also said in an interview that terrorist acts should not be perpetrated in the name of his faith, and complained that these are often referred to as "Islamic attacks." "Can it be that no one in the United States commits attacks on the Christian Sabbath?" he asked. "Of course there are, but nobody talks about, or should talk about, Christian terrorism." Organizations representing the Muslim community in Spain tried to take advantage of the events to increase their reach and capabilities. Thus, for FEERI's Mansur Escudero, implementation of the provision is a 1996 treaty with Morocco for Islamic religion classes in local schools is a way to combat Islamism, because "it would be an opportunity to impart knowledge about what Islam really is, placing emphasis on values like tolerance and democracy."[172]

Jihadi Profiles?

As Marc Sageman, perhaps the most non-ideological analyst of the problem, has consistently noted, it is virtually impossible to establish a "profile" of the international jihadi, and especially futile if the starting assumptions are based, as they often are among the media and academia, on some quasi-Marxist economic or social determinism. To that one may add Pape's equally fallacious "nationalist" explanations. If one eliminates both of these, one is left with very little if the sample is global—i.e., if it involves jihadis from both Muslim-majority and European contexts. However, if the attempt is directed at Europe-based jihadis, it will be more successful, even if a perfect profile remains illusory.

Is it possible to construct a "profile" of Europe-based jihadis? Are they different from their colleagues in the Muslim world? There is probably no complete answer to these questions, but a few elements stand out. They are generally young (between 18 and 33), and almost all male. Many are single; some are married with families. Some were born abroad and were brought to Europe as children; some were born in Europe; all were recruited and indoctrinated there, either by established Europe-based jihadis or by transient operatives of outside Islamist groups. Their ethnic backgrounds are mostly Pakistani, Palestinian, Egyptian, or Maghrebi. Kashmir aside, most do not associate themselves directly with events in their countries of origin; rather, they are interested in "Islam." The growing number of converts remains a case apart, and operationally the most dangerous.

While none of this makes a profile, what is essential is that most were indoctrinated and recruited in Europe, mostly under the influence of Londonistan, which raises the issue of Europe's own cultural environment.

What distinguishes Europe-based jihadis from most others is their ability to plan, recruit, and indoctrinate freely among a Muslim population largely devoid of the theological and traditional factors countering Salafism/jihadism in the Muslim world. What is more important still, re-Islamization and the related *ummah* solidarity as manifested in Europe prepared a mass of potential recruits to jihad, a process facilitated by specific European cultural fashions. Moreover, the very social and economic circumstances of Europe give locally bred jihadis certain advantages. The most important are the following:

- Europe-based jihadis are far better educated that their counterparts in the Muslim world.

- They have a safer economic base—whether through welfare payments or higher salaries or crime-derived income—than their associates elsewhere. That translates into greater travel opportunities and wider tactical and ideological contacts throughout the Muslim world.

- They have better links with *ummah* developments and reactions than their often illiterate fellows in Pakistan or Indonesia, Morocco or Egypt.

Ultimately, just by being inherently privileged as they are (contrary to the common pretensions of the Left), Europe-based Muslim recruits to jihad form an elite—in technical, ideological, and cultural terms—and thus have a disproportionate role in international activities. A few examples are interesting.

The *Mártires por Marruecos* cell, dismantled by the Spanish at the end of 2004 during *Operación Nova*, was planning to ram an explosive-filled truck into the building of the *Audiencia Nacional*—presumably with the goal of killing the Islamists' nemeses, prosecuting judges Juan del Olmo and Baltasar Garzón, and destroying the files on terrorist networks. Despite its name, the cell included more Algerians than Moroccans, and it had extensive links abroad—in Morocco and elsewhere.[173]

Its leader, Mohammed Achraf, was born in 1973 in Figuig, Morocco; the majority of its members were born between 1959 and 1978, most before 1970, making it an unusually old group. It is also unusual that the leader was younger than many of the cell members; in most previous cases, the leader (emir) has been, in accordance with jihadi Internet sites, "the most educated, wise and oldest" cell member.[174] The *Mártires* comprised 20 Algerians, 12 Moroccans, a Palestinian from Lebanon, an Afghan, a Mauritanian, and one Spaniard, Baldomero Lara Sánchez, a gypsy convert, probably involved simply for money (his police record included 99 crimes against property). Six members had convictions for theft and robbery, two for falsification of documents, four for violent crimes, one for drug trafficking, one for illegal entry, and three for involvement in terrorist groups; one had 14 different false identities, one had 10, and another had three.[175] As already mentioned, a criminal background is common for logistical, psychological, and recruitment reasons.

Achraf was the planner and recruiter for the *Mártires*. Three or four of the members were tasked with the preparation of false documents; a few, who had a record of violence (such as the Algerian Brahim Amman, nicknamed "the beheader"), provided the muscle; and most contributed to the financing of the operation through criminal activities. Samir Ben Abdellah, a 36-year-old Moroccan and former imam in the Madrid mosque of Alcorcón and later at a mosque in Barcelona, provided religious preparation and legitimacy for the group's activities. In many ways, the MpM cell was self-sufficient, a characteristic of most Islamist terrorist cells in Europe today, although it had an international membership and ideological links with the global Salafi networks.

The cell's planning and intended date for the attack were both after the March 2004 Madrid bombings and the new government's withdrawal of Spanish troops from Iraq—which strongly suggests that the Madrid attack was part of a larger campaign against Spain, whose goals went beyond the issue of the Iraq deployment.

Most of the above are recurring themes. The London group plotting a mass attack on transatlantic flights in August 2006 also had most of the usual characteristics of Islamist groups in Europe.[176] They were not seen as particularly different from the other members of their community:

> "They were ordinary British boys. They liked football, they were practicing Muslims and they wore traditional dress. They were good boys; this would be totally out of character," said Imtiaz Qadir, spokesman for the Waltham Forest Islamic Association. . . . [As teenagers] their interests were those of most young men: Premiership football, girls, clothes and music; and as young adults they grew devout together.

That last point is important, because the area was also known to be one of activity by Omar Bakri's *Al-Muhajiroun* Islamist radicals.

- The members of the cell lived in the same small area: 13 of the 19 had addresses in east London, most of them clustered within a 500-meter radius.

- The social and professional background of the group was fairly representative of the Muslim community in general. "One terror suspect made cakes; two were wheeler-dealing brothers from the East End of London; there was a bookkeeper and an expectant father, a secretary for a trendy East London music company, a computer salesman, two company directors and a security guard who worked at Heathrow."[177]

- Some were closely related—there were two sets of brothers, the Hussains (Nabeel, 21, Tanvir, 25, and Umair, 24) and the Khans (Assan Abdullah, 21, and Waheed "Arafat," 25, whose young wife and baby were also arrested in the raids).

- At least one, Muhammed Usman Saddique, had a criminal record, mostly petty crimes.

- Ties with Islamist groups and better education explain the leadership of the group. A popular young biochemistry and medical student, Waheed Zaman, 22 years old, was a known activist and leader at the Islamic society of the London Metropolitan University—and he was also known to be associated with *Tabligh*.

- The group included at least three computer experts (the Hussain brothers).

- Three of those arrested were converts.

- The leaders of the group had extensive ties to radicals in Pakistan. The converts aside, all were of Pakistani background and had British citizenship.

The Nature of Al-Qaeda in Europe

All the above makes clear that Al-Qaeda is a *de facto* presence in Europe that can be denied only by those who do not want to examine the growing problem of radical Islamism in Europe. Terms such as "homegrown" terrorists, applied particularly to jihadis in England, are misleading. While all of those in England were born or grew up there, those in Spain and Germany were mostly immigrants, with the French cells a mixture of both. A deeper analysis demonstrates that all the jihadi cells have been linked to certain networks, and ultimately to the core Al-Qaeda leadership in Pakistan. If "homegrown" means strictly locally recruited, indoctrinated, trained, and motivated, few, if any, of the known jihadi cells in Europe fit the description. Whether all the members of a cell or just the leaders were trained in Pakistan, Afghanistan, or the Maghreb, their links with the centers of Salafist operations in the Islamic world are a con-

stant feature. Nor is their motivation related to any single instance of perceived threat to Islam—most were active prior to
9/11, certainly prior to the Iraq war, and most of their known
grievances were general, or varied from Bosnia to the retaking
of "Al-Andalus," passing through Iraq, Palestine, Chechnya, or
Kashmir.

At least since 9/11, it has become clear to many, although not
to all, European governments that Islamism, including its terrorist versions, does not simply have a presence in all European
countries but is a truly Europe-wide phenomenon. It may have
been, and far too often still is, convenient for politicians playing the politically correct cards to talk about "a minority," usually described as "unrepresentative" of Muslims in general, or
of "home-bred" Muslims versus the "imported" radical minority, when in fact the phenomenon is increasingly integral and
well rooted inside all European Muslim communities.

The various aspects of Salafism/Islamism/terrorism in
Europe developed at various speeds. In indoctrination and propaganda, Europe, and especially Londonistan, played and to an
extent still plays a crucial role. In recruiting it has a still-limit-
ed but rapidly growing role, and has become a main object of
global Islamist networks' efforts. In financing it is still behind
the Gulf and Iran—a factor in the trend toward self-financing
by terror cells.

While not all, or even very many, Muslims in Europe adhere to Islamism, the trend is toward radicalization in larger
numbers. The reality is that there is a self-sustaining Islamist
microculture alive in Europe, one that is continuously being
replenished by illegal immigration and misguided official policies—on immigration, multiculturalism, "tolerance," etc.

It is important to examine how Europe's Islamist networks
sustain themselves and how they operate. That implies an un-

derstanding of the processes of recruitment and indoctrination, as well as financing and, ultimately, strategies.

The issue of Al-Qaeda's direct presence in Europe is, as we have seen, still debated, but, in fact, direct links between European elements and the Al-Qaeda core leadership do exist, and have even been proved in court.

A shadowy entity known as "Al-Qaeda in Europe," a media nickname for the Abu Hafs al-Masri Brigade, claimed responsibility for the attacks in Madrid, London, Jakarta, and Istanbul, and even the 2003 blackout in the northeastern United States, claims that have tended to be dismissed. However, when the late Musab al-Zarqawi's Iraq-based organization, which has pledged formal allegiance to bin Laden and operated under that name, did the same, it was also dismissed—only to prove active in multiple countries.[178] Al-Qaeda in Europe's claim of responsibility for the attacks in Madrid is highly doubtful,[179] that does not prove that there is no Al-Qaeda operational presence in Spain or elsewhere in Europe.

French analyst Mathieu Guidère[180] believes that following the establishment of the Al-Qaeda Organization in the Islamic Maghreb (AQIM) in 2006, significant changes took place in Al-Qaeda's European activities. Whereas before his death the leadership of those activities was in the hands of the Moroccan Abdelkrim Medjati of the Decentralized Al-Qaeda Emirate for Europe and the Maghreb—who Guidère believes was behind the Casablanca, Madrid, and London attacks—since then the strategic control of terrorist actions in Europe has passed to the AQIM leaders. One likely result, Guidère claims, is that France, AQIM's main Western enemy, will become a more frequent target.

The new and still-evolving Al-Qaeda Organization in the Islamic Maghreb has direct links to the leadership in Pakistan, and from various indications—ranging from its language, to the sending of volunteers to Iraq, to the use of suicide belts and car bombs, to suicide rather than surrender—follows known al-Zawahiri orders and methods.[181]

Far more direct is the link between al-Zarqawi's "Al-Qaeda in the Land of the Two Rivers" and bin Laden, although, once again, al-Zarqawi was not directly dependent on bin Laden or under his authority; rather, he was an autonomous actor in need of the radical legitimacy his swearing "obedience" to the latter could provide.[182] In fact, as demonstrated by al-Zawahiri's July 9, 2005, letter to al-Zarqawi, there are significant tactical and even doctrinal differences between the two, and the latter certainly did not behave as a subordinate to the bin Laden–al-Zawahiri core leadership of Al-Qaeda. With these caveats in mind, the reality is that, in the name of Al-Qaeda, al-Zarqawi managed to establish an extensive network in Europe—so far mostly dedicated to financing and recruiting for Islamist operations in Iraq.

Another example is the Madrid cell responsible for the March 2004 attacks. On the one hand, it was in no way "controlled" from Pakistan or formally "part of Al-Qaeda," or even of the GICM or GSPC—but that does not make it "homegrown" either. As we have seen, it had direct ties with the Abu Dahdah network, itself made up largely of Muslim Brotherhood Syrian refugees.[183] Al-Maymouni, a member of Abu Dahdah's network, directly recruited Serhane ben Abdelmajid Fakhet, "El Tunecino," the leader of the Madrid-Leganés cell, while another leader of that group, Allekema Lamari, was an old GIA member. On the other hand, Fakhet had close ties to Youssef Belhadj, the GICM's main leader in Europe, based in Belgium and involved in the al-Zarqawi network's recruitment of volunteers for Iraq—one of whom, Mohamed Afallah, actually blew himself up there in May 2005.

Thus, one may conclude that the Madrid cell was international and directly linked through personnel, and not just ideology, to Al-Qaeda and to North African jihadist groups that are themselves linked to Al-Qaeda. In this sense, the question of "control" is misplaced: The cell was an autonomous but not separate part of the global jihadist movement, at whose apex is the Al-Qaeda core group.

On the other hand, one of the unusual characteristics of the Leganés episode was the group's willingness to die rather than surrender—a pattern that has become increasingly common among Maghreb jihadis, repeatedly demonstrated later in Algeria and Morocco, but also demonstrated by the Moroccans' preference for suicide rather than combat among jihadis in Iraq. It is a pattern related to a letter from al-Zawahiri to all jihadis, ordering suicide rather than surrender.[184] Far too often, judging by media reactions, Spanish judges' statements were disregarded in the other European countries.[185]

How Europe-based jihadis create security problems elsewhere was demonstrated in March 2007, when a Moroccan court sentenced eight members of a cell whose membership and activities are an example of the developing pattern in Europe. The leader, Muhammad Benhedi Msahel, is a Tunisian who used to run a GSPC cell in Milan, and most of the members were Moroccans. The group was involved in planning attacks against the Paris Métro, Orly Airport, the headquarters of France's domestic intelligence service (DST), Milan's police headquarters, and the Basilica of San Petronio in Bologna.[186] Just as with the cells in Spain, it is meaningless to ask whether "Al-Qaeda" was behind this group, since the answer is so complex. However, since the GSPC has now become part of the

Al-Qaeda Organization in the Islamic Maghreb, pledging allegiance to bin Laden, the technical answer is affirmative.

Just as the North African jihadi networks are active in Europe and linked to Al-Qaeda without being an integral part of it, so are Pakistani terrorist organizations—especially the two most lethal and closest to Al-Qaeda, *Lashkar-e-Toiba* and *Jaish-e-Mohammed*.[187]

Although the existence of *Lashkar-e-Toiba* only became apparent to the general public following the spectacular bombings in London in 2005, the Pakistani network has a significant concentration in the United Kingdom, and is also increasingly active in Spain, especially Catalonia, and in Italy.

As an Indian press report puts it, *Lashkar-e-Toiba* "declares the U.S., Israel and India as existential enemies of Islam and lists eight reasons for global Jihad. These include the restoration of Islamic sovereignty to all lands where Muslims were once ascendant, including Spain, Bulgaria, Hungary, Cyprus, Sicily, Ethiopia, Russian Turkistan and Chinese Turkistan, and even parts of France."[188] That is precisely the same language as Al-Qaeda's and an indication that the Pakistani groups' ambitions, rhetorically at least, go far beyond Kashmir.

For instance, Rashid Rauf, an English Muslim of Pakistani origin, was associated with the 2006 plot to blow up transatlantic flights and arrested in Pakistan. His wife is the sister-in-law of Maulana Tahir Masood, brother of *Jaish-e-Mohammed* chief Maulana Azhar Masood.[189] Son of a bakery owner in Birmingham, Rauf was suspected in the murder of an uncle and fled to Pakistan in 2002. His father was the founder of Crescent Relief, a Kashmir charity with links to jihadi groups there. Pakistani officials suspect that behind the transatlantic plot, as well as the 2005 London bombings, was a shadowy group called

Al-Jihad. It runs a training facility in the Khowst province of Afghanistan, where the British-born militants were mainly trained and supervised by Abu Nasir, an Al-Qaeda expert in explosives. Its main Pakistani link is *Jamaat-ul-Furqan*, a dissident faction of *Jaish-e-Mohammed*, led by Mati-ur-Rehman, himself linked directly to Al-Qaeda and suspected of involvement in assassination attempts against President Musharraf.[190] How intense the contacts between England and Pakistan are is demonstrated simply by the fact that some 400,000 persons fly between the two each year—making these flights impossible to check, even if there were a will to do so. And London is not the only link between Europe-based jihadis and Pakistan's networks.

Mati-ur-Rehman had contacts with the Pakistani jihadi cell dismantled in Barcelona in 2004.[191] In fact, *El Periódico* of Barcelona claimed that Spain in general and Barcelona in particular have become JeM's main European base, recruiting among resident Pakistani immigrants and sending them to the Al-Qaeda camps in Pakistan's uncontrolled tribal areas—the same camps where the leaders of the London cell of 2005, Shehzad Tanweer and Mohammad Sidique Khan, underwent training.

Lashkar-e-Toiba also went beyond its natural recruiting pool among Pakistani immigrants in Britain and recruited a black Frenchman, Willie Brigitte, sending him to conduct operations in Australia after training him in Pakistan.[192] *The Observer* of London claimed that British citizens have been trained in Pakistan by Afghan, Arab, and local veterans, and sent to fight in Afghanistan against, among others, British forces. The estimated number is "between 20 and 30," and they are all believed to have strong family ties in Pakistan.[193]

Yet another example of foreign groups—in this case Egyptian—operating in Europe is that of Islamic Jihad, long led by al-Zawahiri himself. The above-mentioned Rabei Osman Ahmed, a.k.a. *"Mohamed el Egipcio,"* admitted his role in the Madrid bombings and boasted to friends in Spain that two more groups organized by him were ready for operations, including one on its way to Iraq via Syria in June 2004.[194]

Jordán and Wesley, in a study of Islamist groups in Ceuta, concluded that they represent an example of "the emergence of grassroots jihadi networks in European countries. 'Grassroots jihadis' refers to groups that sympathize with and relate to the global jihadi movement, sharing common strategic objectives, but have little or no formal connections to al-Qaeda or any other associated organizations. They could, however, eventually secure relationships with some established operatives."[195] The Ceuta Islamist cell, dismantled in December 2006, included at least 11 individuals, and was centered in the small Darkawia mosque, led by a Salafi imam and located in the poorest and most lawless area of the city. The cell had made it known that it intended to begin attacks—it planned to destroy a *morabito* (tomb of a Sufi "saint"), and it had plans for bombing a shopping mall and a fuel depot.

The cell leader, Karin Abdelselam Mohamed, was a petty criminal radicalized while in prison, with known ties to Tarik Hamed, an Islamist imprisoned in Spain for membership in a recruiting network for Iraq. Although the authors minimize this connection, the Ceuta cell was linked ideologically to the jihadi concept of "liberation" of formerly Islamic lands.

Is this a case of "spontaneous" self-recruitment, a radicalization of local grievances, or is it part of a process found elsewhere (in France with Beghal, in Spain with Abu Dahdah), suggesting the paradigm of internationally connected veteran

Salafis attracting followers who are later sent forth to multiply and create new cells? Is there a clear distinction between these possibilities? One may raise an even more basic question: Why was a significant part of British opinion denying the evidence of international connections of Islamist terrorists?

Even attempts to understand European jihadist cells as a combination of local and international elements can be less than convincing—or can require additional explanations. Thus Rik Coolsaet asserts:

> Jihadi terrorism today is a "glocal" phenomenon: its core is essentially local, but its appearances are global. Even if remnants of the old structured al-Qaeda network probably still remain at large, al-Qaeda has failed to gain significant traction for actions in Europe and the United States. Jihadi terrorism now basically is a cloak patched from different sources of local discontent, real and perceived, stitched together by a puritanical and radical interpretation of Islam, and thriving on an enabling global momentum. . . . The main global root cause is an enabling global environment, characterized by an astonishing degree of solidarity amongst Muslim communities worldwide, build upon shared feelings of humiliation, bitterness and besiegement.[196]

In fact, the data suggest that Coolsaet has it upside down: Appearances may be local, but the indications are that the phenomenon is global. What, other than the country of residence—which is often a recent one—is "local" in any of the cells described so far? What is apparent in the existence and activities of Maghrebi, Egyptian, Syrian, and Pakistani jihadi organizations on European soil is an international ideology with "local" followers, or foreign transplants, acting in the name of that ideology and taking advantage of favorable cultural, legal, and political conditions.

All the above cases taken together confirm that Al-Qaeda, both as an ideology and as a group, is in Europe and is growing. Nonetheless, following the release of official reports on the London bombings, *The Washington Post's* Kevin Sullivan found no proof that Al-Qaeda had any direct connection with the attack.[197] This suggests a predisposition to find no connection. It also suggests a simplistic understanding of what jihadi connections in the post-9/11 era mean. Hence the repeated claim that bin Laden provided "no aid" to European terrorists, which is given as "proof" that there is no real connection. In fact, the very common link between crime and Islamist terror in Europe should suffice to demonstrate that financial links between the Al-Qaeda core and its distant allies are not just unnecessary, they are discouraged.

Far too often, the media and some academics focus on the lack of direct, hierarchical links of command and control between Waziristan and Islamist cells and networks in Europe and ignore the latter's allegiance to the ideological movement led by bin Laden. Although bin Laden has long ago stopped writing checks for jihadi groups, and although his organization was obviously weakened after 9/11,[198] the reality is complex and changing. In fact, as of 2007–2008, one could argue, as Daveed Gartenstein-Ross and Peter Bergen did,[199] that the core of Al-Qaeda has not only recovered and re-created its training-camp system in Pakistan, but has reasserted some operational control over farflung cells. While that still does not mean that orders to blow up targets in London, Paris, or Madrid come from the tribal areas of Pakistan, it does mean that, as abundantly demonstrated above, Al-Qaeda, if properly defined, is a well-rooted presence in most of Europe today. In the 13th century, St. Bonaventure defined God as a circle whose center is everywhere and circumference nowhere, and that is a good analogy for Al-Qaeda today.

By becoming fundamentally synonymous with Islamism, at least as a symbol if not as the only theological current, Al-Qaeda has established a "presence" in all countries with significant Muslim communities. There are national Islamist terror groups everywhere, from Indonesia and the Philippines to Morocco and the United Kingdom. These groups were not invented by someone hiding in the mountains on the Afghanistan/Pakistan border. However, they are the products of a global Islamist revival that is increasingly defined by Al-Qaeda's way of thinking.

Nor is the organization's influence limited to past personal ties or ideology. To the contrary, it appears that Al Qaeda "visitors"—high-level operatives sent from the core leadership to advise on important operations—appear prior to many attacks. They leave before the attacks themselves and are seldom caught, the arrest of Eisa al-Hindi in Britain being a possible exception.

Al-Hindi, a convert from Hinduism, was arrested in August 2004 in London. He had done surveillance of New York targets in 2001 and was suspected of planning additional operations in Britain or the United States. He was directly linked to the top Al-Qaeda operatives Khaled Sheik Mohammed and Ramzi Yousef.[200] Similarly, there were unconfirmed reports that prior to the attacks in Casablanca in May 2003, Istanbul in November 2003, Madrid in March 2004, and probably Bali in October 2002, a close associate of Osama bin Laden traveled to the target cities beforehand to provide advice to the local activists who would actually perpetrate the attacks. The visitor was usually based in Pakistan or in Saudi Arabia.

While for counter-terrorism organizations, catching the Al-Qaeda visitor is tantamount to preventing an attack, he is not an essential ingredient in a successful terror attack. The fact that virtually all Europe-based jihadi cells include computer experts—Kamel Daoudi being an obvious example—is no coincidence; it is a necessity for communications across international boundaries. Nor does the visitor have to be physically present. Jamal Ahmidan, the operational leader of the cell behind the Madrid bombings, continued to receive instructions for future attacks, accessing them via a secret code (the intended targets being trains, a synagogue, and the British high school in Madrid) from the "Al-Battar Training Camp," a virtual magazine published by the Military Committee of the Mujahidin in the Arabian Peninsula, the local Al-Qaeda branch in Saudi Arabia.[201] As an example of the complexity of the links between the Madrid cell and Islamist structures abroad, Al-Battar (named after the nom de guerre of Sheikh Yousef al-Ayyiri, bin Laden's personal bodyguard, killed in 2003) mentioned concern over Ahmidan's "unauthorized use" of the Al-Qaeda flag on a video taking credit for the March 11 bombings.[202]

It is often claimed that the Internet is now the major recruitment tool of terrorists: "It is no longer necessary for young men to physically attend the camps. A pattern seems to be emerging of groups of like-minded youths forming a 'cell' locally, procuring weapons and explosives and training themselves using al Qaeda manuals."[203] In fact, while there is no doubt that the Internet does facilitate terrorist communications and greatly expands the pool of potential recruits for jihad,[204] some caveats and clarifications are needed.

First, access to the Internet, while spreading, is often censored in the Muslim world and remains limited there to the literate, young, urban population. It does play a much larger role in the West,[205] especially because of the attraction computer science and related fields have for Muslim students in the West.

That said, however, one should not exaggerate the practical role of the Internet[206] in recruitment and training, or in the execution of terrorist attacks. To begin with, while Islamist sites on the Web may attract the interest of young Muslims in Europe,[207] the fact that virtually all known cells have a direct and personal link with an imam, Islamic scholar, or structured organization (*Tabligh*, HuT) is not a simple coincidence—it is a necessity. It is a necessity at the personal level, because commitment to jihad is a personal and indeed emotional matter. Furthermore, not only does recruitment imply personal contact and help in clarifying and justifying points of doctrine and ideology—simply reading Qutb or al-Zawahiri is not enough—it also needs personal, physical contact between cell members, and this cannot be done by e-mail, even setting aside the security issue.[208] All of this is even more essential in the case of suicide terrorism—where the deep indoctrination that is absolutely necessary simply cannot be provided by an impersonal website.

As for training, while some things could be learned from the Internet, others cannot—hence the reality that Islamist cells in Europe often, though not always, include at least some members who have undergone training in a camp, usually in Pakistan/Afghanistan, Bosnia, Chechnya, Kashmir, or now Iraq, but sometimes in Europe itself. As mentioned earlier, some of Abu Hamza's disciples underwent physical training in remote areas of Wales, French cells found some training areas in the Alps, and such exist even in the Netherlands. More often than not, however, the training takes place abroad—and many of the major recruiters in Europe already had training or even combat experience in Algeria.

Nor can the Internet offer the contacts necessary for terrorist operations—it can explain how to make a device and plant it in a train or bus, but not how to establish the contacts with providers of weapons or explosives. All of this without mentioning the necessity for travel arrangements and false passports and visas.

More often than not the Internet is an addition to other recruitment and indoctrination tools. Thus Abu Hamza al Masri's "Supporters of Sharia" site claimed that "Muslims and non-Muslims are being oppressed throughout the world. SOS is one of the organizations struggling to remove this oppression created by manmade laws."[209] This played well with young Muslims from Europe seeking confirmation of their personal feelings of victimization. The result was their flocking to Abu Hamza's Finsbury Park mosque, where they met GIA veterans of the Algerian war in an environment obsessed with jihad—an environment described capably by Omar Nasiri, who was briefly immersed in it.[210] Abu Hamza was able to send at least eight Muslims from Britain (including his own son) to Yemen to carry out attacks against Western targets.

Meanwhile, it is true that ideological, religious, and even military training can be provided online, as Al-Battar's first issue pointed out:

> "Oh Mujahid brother, in order to join the great training camps you don't have to travel to other lands. Alone, in your home or with a group of your brothers, you too can begin to execute the training program. You can all join the Al-Battar Training Camp. . . ." and in the same issue Abu Thabit Al-Najdi wrote: ". . . The Al-Battar Training Camp is a new magazine (and 'virtual training camp') of the military committee of the Al-Qa'ida organization in the Saudi peninsula . . . and it is given as a gift to the youth of Islam whose hearts burn in support of the religion by means of Jihad for the sake of Allah."[211]

The analogy with Marxism-Leninism is again useful, if limited. The Marxist terrorists of the Italian *Brigate Rosse*, German *Rote Armee Fraktion*, and French *Action Directe* of the 1970s did not receive orders from Moscow, nor did they receive (many) checks from the Kremlin—indeed, some saw Leonid Brezhnev as a decrepit traitor to the working class. But that did not stop them from getting training in East Germany, joining the Soviet line in regard to Palestine or Cuba, etc. Ultimately, they shared the ostensible goal of the Kremlin's ideologues—a socialist world—even when expressing contempt for them.

Ultimately, the debates over Al-Qaeda's responsibility for Madrid or London are meaningless. What is important, indeed crucial, is Europe's role as a major center of Islamist radicalism throughout the world. This is not just a matter of Europe-based Islamists using their French, British, or Belgian passports to gain access to targets outside of Europe. More important is that radical, indeed virulently violent, Islamist ideologues, financiers, and recruiters have found tolerant Europe to be a more friendly environment for their activities than the Islamic world itself. Thus people openly advocating the replacement of moderate (Jordan, Morocco), more or less secular (Turkey, Egypt, Pakistan), even Islamist (Saudi Arabia) governments with Sharia-based regimes are welcome in London (and in Brussels, Berlin, Madrid, and Rome), despite having been tried *in absentia,* convicted, and sentenced to long jail terms (or death) at home. It is this European application of "tolerance" that has made the above-mentioned capitals centers of Islamist terrorism. It is also the interpretation of "human rights" according to the definition of Amnesty International and the European Court of Human Rights that makes international anti-terrorist cooperation so difficult.

Patterns

The general environment of Europe is too different from that in Muslim countries for jihadi operations to follow the same patterns. However, to a large extent they adapted well to local conditions and selected their targets accordingly. Jihadis have understood that democracies will continue to operate even if a particular individual is eliminated—hence there have been no known assassination attempts against major leaders in the West, unlike, for example, the repeated attempts to kill Pervez Musharraf or Hosni Mubarak. On the other hand, in the relatively crowded cities of Europe, transportation systems are an obvious vulnerability.

It is often not understood, in Europe and the United States, that terrorism, Islamist or not, is primarily a media event, and that important as they may be, strictly economic or industrial targets are less valuable than targets in urban areas with immediate media access. Thus, a railroad connection or key factory may be economically more important than a subway station but is less likely to be a target simply because its destruction would not be as dramatic.

While an argument could be made that the Paris Métro bombings of 1995 were a peculiar case, inasmuch as they long preceded the Al-Qaeda–inspired attacks and could be seen as a European extension of the Algerian civil war, they, and the related December 1994 attempt to use a hijacked aircraft in a suicide attack against the Eiffel Tower, certainly established a pattern. Similarly, the planned 1998 attack by the German-based Turkish fundamentalist Metin Kaplan against Kemal Atatürk's tomb in Ankara, again using aircraft, should have been seen as part of the pattern that led to 9/11 and was to be attempted again, though without success, in London in August 2006.

If targeting mass-transportation systems was a pattern established in Europe, individual suicide attacks were a method borrowed by Europe's Islamists from the Middle East and the Indian subcontinent. Hence such cases as the suicide bombings in Modena and Brescia in 2003-2004 and the combination of individual suicide and aircraft attacks represented by the English-born "shoe bomber," Richard Reid. Dhiren Barot, a Britain-based Hindu convert to Islam, who pleaded guilty to planning major attacks in England and the United States, wanted to emulate the Madrid train bombings. The court heard him describe the blasts as a "respectable project" that deserved to be "emulated more than any other."[212] Both Reid and Barot, the latter described as a "member or close associate of al-Qaeda," had direct links with people in Pakistan and traveled there.[213] In retrospect, one may speculate that Reid's attempt was part of another Al-Qaeda pattern—simultaneous attacks on related targets (in this case, U.S. air transportation).

The different types of attacks are a reflection of the distinct natures of the perpetrators—isolated immigrants in the cases of individual, sometimes copycat, attacks; large networks with complex membership and international connections in the case of major operations directed against mass-transportation systems. But they are not always neatly separated. In some instances, largely self-selected groups, such as the Hofstad Group, seek and obtain contacts with established networks or with individuals, generally imams, who have international links, while members of the group may also engage in individual actions— Bouyeri's murder of Theo van Gogh being a prime example.

The issue of converts has been examined, but in tactical terms it is important to note their presence in virtually all major Islamist operations known in Europe. There is also the unpleasant, for many Europeans, question of why there are so many converts and why so many of them become suicidal jihadis. In both the 7/7 bombings and the failed plot to blow up transatlantic flights, some, though not all, of the converts involved were of black (Caribbean) origin.

Race is a problem for multiculturalists. Given that racial conflicts in Britain, from Brixton to Beeston to Manchester to Birmingham, often oppose blacks from the Caribbean against Asians, multiculturalists have a difficult choice to make among the "racially oppressed." This is even more true in France, where most blacks are not Muslim and have been known to establish their own racist groups; the Tribu Ka in France—founded in December 2004 by black radical Kémi Séba, and now banned— was both anti-white and anti-Muslim. The obvious point is that blacks can escape multicultural assumptions and be as "racist" as anybody else.

Another important element in transforming Europe into a major center for global Islamist terrorist activities is the encouragement, or at least tolerance, of close ties between immigrant Muslim communities and their countries of origin. This is not a matter of controlling travel or attempting to break cultural ties, which is naturally rejected by democratic countries, but rather of toleration of transnational, openly Islamist groups advocating a Caliphate, separation from the *kuffar*, etc. It's true that Britain stands alone among EU countries in its toleration of groups like *Hizb ut-Tahrir* and the *Tablighi*, which are banned in the rest of Europe, but the EU's "human-rights" rules make it easy for those elements to live and even flourish within and across Europe.

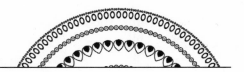

CHAPTER SEVEN

Eurojihad—
The Cultural Environment

"Islam will return to Europe. Islam entered Europe twice and left it. . . . Perhaps the next conquest, Allah willing, will be by means of preaching and ideology. The conquest need not necessarily be by the sword. . . . [The conquest of Mecca] was not by the sword or by war, but by a [Hudabiyya] treaty, and by peace. . . . Perhaps we will conquer these lands without armies."

—Sheikh Yusuf al-Qaradawi[1]

For years, European culture has facilitated the growth of Islamism and, ultimately, of Islamist terrorism. While the security threat posed by Islamism to Europe is now recognized by virtually everyone, its European causes and dimensions, as well as the best means of responding, are still debated—though both the intensity and the seriousness of the debate vary significantly from country to country. At this point one must examine the *cultural* aspects of that debate—much more important in Europe than in the United States, where the Islamist problem is seen more in security terms.

With anywhere from 15 to 20 million Muslims living in Europe, it is only natural that there would be a deep pool of potential recruits for radical Islam—an ideology with a large, potentially supportive population in the regions of origin of most immigrants: the Indian subcontinent, North Africa, and the Middle East.

This chapter will explore a number of specific reasons why Muslim communities in Europe provide a growing supply of jihadists. These include:

- The growing alienation of young, European-born Muslims, regardless of their parents' country of origin.

- The continuous supply of newly arrivaling radicals, especially ideologues and recruiters, from Muslim countries, especially the Maghreb, Pakistan, and the Middle East. This is permitted by an immigration policy dominated by emotion and multiculturalism rather than reason.

- European Union legislation on asylum and refugees, as encoded in the European Convention on Human Rights and enforced by the European Court of Human Rights in Strasbourg, which provides extraordinary advantages for Islamist operatives, especially protection against extradition or expulsion.

- European criminal laws, which, as enforced by the courts, provide for limited penalties for terrorism, maximum liberties for those on trial, restrictive rules of evidence, and much support from NGOs. Even when caught, tried, and convicted, jihadis can still operate or, at the very least, hope for another chance. The case of Safé Bourada is far from unique: He was involved in the 1995 GIA bombings in Paris, sentenced in 1998 to 10 years, out of jail after five, only to be arrested for even more serious plots in 2005—and French legislation is stricter than most.

- The structure of the EU, which allows for only limited legal coordination among member states (see Chapter 8), although that is beginning to change. Thus, jihadists can choose their countries of operations accordingly.

- The prevalence of multiculturalism in the European elite mentality—the major obstacle to understanding, let alone dealing with, Islamist radicalism and its associated terrorism.

- Rampant anti-Americanism in Europe, at least at elite levels, reinforcing Islamist propaganda themes. Anti-Semitism, now often a by-product of anti-Americanism, is also growing among Muslims in Europe—as it is among white Europeans on the Left and the remaining Far Right. What's new is that Muslims, especially young ones, do not feel they must hide hatred for the United States or anti-Semitic views, or that such views are outside the mainstream.

- The practical legal advantages that the relatively liberal European security environment provides Islamist radicals, which allow them to travel relatively freely, as opposed to in their countries of origin.

The Cultural Context

Before examining the views of the European elites on the issue of Islam, Islamism, and the relationship between them, one has to make a few preliminary observations. First, Europeans, unlike Americans, are typically not prepared to discuss religion—any religion—either because they are thoroughly secular and indifferent or hostile to it, or, for the minority that still has a faith, because it has become a strictly private matter. Naturally, that observation does not apply to intellectual elites, who, especially in France, have a tendency to over-examine religion—and everything else.

While there is by now little argument about Europe being a theater, a target, and an exporter of Islamist terrorism, the fact remains that there is still a debate about why and whose fault it is—and even about the language of the debate itself. However, that by itself is a change, since for almost two decades the cultural and political environment in Europe was so thoroughly dominated by multiculturalism and the associated political correctness that even the mention of an Islamist problem, let alone terrorism, was impossible outside the farthest reaches of the extreme Right.

One of the reasons for this change is some dramatic changes in electoral behavior, which forced the elites to adapt their discourse. Denmark, France, Sweden, and Germany have all seen right-of-center parties come to power and engage the debate on Islam and the status of Muslims. Islamist terrorism and the increasing assertiveness of Muslim organizations further increased the public demand for a reassessment of those issues.

While dramatic events made a difference in some cases, they did not create the present debate but merely pushed it onto the front pages. They added to existing problems, symbolized by what elites preferred to see as isolated cases, such as those of Salman Rushdie, Michel Houellebecq, Oriana Fallaci, and Robert Redeker, to fuel debate over the place, role, and acceptability of Islam, Muslims, and Islamism in Europe.

Forests have been felled for the paper used to examine the links between Islam and Islamism. Far too often this subject is discussed in strictly historical and religious terms rather than the equally applicable political and ideological ones. Entire chapters in volumes on Islamism and terrorism are still dedicated to seventh-century Islam or 14th-century Sunni thought, on the false premise that 20th- and 21st-century ideologues of Salafism are their direct and legitimate descendants or, indeed, that the latter's followers in Leeds, Kandahar, or Madrid know much about them. Even in purely analytical terms one may doubt the usefulness of studying Ibn Taymiyya in order to understand the thinking of an al-Zawahiri, let alone an al-Zarqawi. That is like studying Heraclitus of Ephesus in order to understand the thinking of Marx, let alone Lenin.

Second, discussing Islam as a "natural" source of terrorism, or, conversely, as totally innocent of any link to it, is far from enlightening—but frequently indulged in. It does not help, either, to claim that Christianity had its Inquisition or, more absurdly still, the 12th- and 13th-century Crusades (which had nothing to do with terrorism), and thus today's Islamist terrorism is just another example of religion being used for violence.[2] Indeed, since terrorism in the name of Jesus Christ has been extremely rare if not nonexistent for a few centuries now, such claims are more often than not excuses, Western cultural masochism, or forms of denial.

The fact that Islamist terrorism takes place today in the name of Islam and by Muslims from Indonesia to England and from Tanzania to Amsterdam makes it impossible to avoid a contemporary link between aspects of that religion and terror—as does the equally important fact that not only do the terrorists proclaim their Islamic faith, but no widely recognized Islamic authorities, such as there are, deny them that quality.

There are a number of European cultural traits that help explain the formation of a favorable environment for the development of Islamic militantism, whether openly violent or not, throughout Britain and the continent.

First and foremost is the importance of the Left in European culture and politics, which is reflected in anti-assimilationist policies and overly tolerant immigration and asylum policies, and in the obsession with "human rights."

Second, as mentioned above, is a virulent form of anti-Americanism, often closely associated with anti-Semitism. These are often rather poorly disguised as being "anti-Zionist" or (during the past decade) "anti-Bush," but one should be clear that anti-Americanism among European elites is not limited to opposition to a given administration. It extends to wider phenomena in American social and political life, mostly the deeper religiosity and the widespread support for free markets and individualism—all the opposite of the dominant European secularism and collectivism.

Third, a pernicious sense of historical guilt, often verging on masochism, over the real or imaginary faults of the West—colonialism; its very wealth, assumed to be obtained at the Third World's expense; and capitalism itself. That sense leads very often to historic revisionism, including the idealization of Muslim-Christian relations in the past as a model for the present.

Fourth, an inability or unwillingness to distinguish between being tolerant and being oblivious to enemies in the society. Some countries, Britain being the best example, have long tolerated the development of a deadly microclimate of fundamentalism, leading directly to jihadism. That attitude has shocked even Muslim observers, like Abd al-Rahman al-Rashed, director of the Saudi-owned Al-Arabiyya TV network. It is worth quoting again his acute observation:

> [The extremists] are enjoying all the benefits of the regime they despise. What makes Omar Bakri, who enjoys liberty in Britain, spread hatred [against Britain], fight its culture, and

say obscenely that [Britain] is a toilet in which he lives in order to defecate there? Does it make sense for someone like him to express a desire to return to Britain after everything he has said and done? As for Abu Qatada, he prefers to remain in prison and not to return to his homeland Jordan, just like [Osama Nasser], the imam from Milan, who is protesting about being taken to Egypt and about being imprisoned there. Not only is he protesting his abduction; he has also decided to sue for €20 million in damages. . . . It is blatantly obvious that all three are enjoying all the benefits of the [government] they despise: They want the financial aid, the security, the [rule of] law, the justice and the freedom of expression afforded by this government. Is this not the epitome of hypocrisy? When they preach, aren't they greatly deceiving their followers— [considering this discrepancy] between what they say and what they do?[3]

The answer to this question is simple: They do it because they can get away with it, which they could not do at home. Nor are those major ideologues the only beneficiaries of such largesse—even the four perpetrators of the London bombings of July 2005 received a combined total of $1 million in welfare benefits before murdering dozens of commuters.[4] These are not isolated but common cases, and not just in Britain.

Even when subsidized enemies act against the national interest, such as the radical imams from Denmark who provoked the global Islamic reaction to the cartoons in a Danish newspaper,[5] there are no penalties. True enough, Ahmad Abu Laban, Ahmed Akkari, and their "European Committee for Honoring the Prophet" would not have been able to produce a global confrontation if the ground had not been prepared by their colleagues in the Muslim world, but the relevant point is that the originators were people living (generally on public welfare) in Europe. More importantly still, several of the most virulent ideologues—such as Laban in Copenhagen; Abu Hamza, Omar Bakri, and Abu Qatada in England; and Mullah Krekar in

Norway—were expelled from Arab countries (in Laban's case the UAE, in Bakri's case Saudi Arabia) for radicalism seen as incompatible with orthodox Islam.

The latter phenomenon—European acceptance of radical Islamists rejected by or even sentenced for terrorism in their home countries, all under the cover of giving asylum to those who were "persecuted" for their ideas—is one of the main roots of the Islamist problem in Europe. That is ultimately a political and ideological choice on the part of European governments— it is not a matter of law, since laws can always be modified. One can only imagine what would happen if Nazis from South America, "persecuted" for their genocidal anti-Semitism there, asked for asylum in Europe. And yet those old followers of the Führer only did what the likes of Abu Hamza or Omar Bakri seek to do under a different, politically correct label.

Political expediency is always a dangerous thing. What is useful now could become a threat tomorrow. The development and growth of Islamism in Europe has not always been in opposition to European public opinion, certainly not the dominant left-of-center opinion. Indeed, it has been pointed out that in the case of Iraq, "Popular opposition to the war was widespread in Europe during 2003 and this also influenced the sentiments in Muslim communities."[6] And Iraq was not the first such instance. Bosnia, Kosovo, Chechnya, even Palestine were, and the latter two remain, conflicts in which European opinion and Islamist interests coincided—with the result that intelligence and police attention was less focused than it should have been, and many Muslims in Europe were implicitly encouraged to feel that engaging in jihad in Grozny or Banja Luka was not just an Islamic religious duty but had support beyond their communities—in other words, that it had universal moral legitimacy.

It is often said that ordinary Muslims, and, even more so, reformist and progressive intellectuals, are disregarded and unprotected by European society. That is often true, but the painful reality remains that if reformist Muslims need the help of the infidel regimes, that only disqualifies them in the eyes of most of their co-religionists. Indeed, it is counterintuitive to expect a Pakistani, Algerian, or Egyptian immigrant in Europe, long used to government manipulation and control of mosques in his country of origin, to accept help from a non-Muslim government in Europe.

However, the main and most persistent reason Europe has became, first, a permissive environment for and later an exporter and target of jihadis remains the cultural atmosphere in Europe itself. There are important areas of agreement, though they are seldom admitted, between mainstream, which is to say left-of-center, European intellectuals and the ideologues of Salafism—and the latter know it and have learned to manipulate those areas of agreement.

Ideological Convergence

The European Left, whether political, academic, in the media, or in NGOs, bears a heavy responsibility for the growth of Islamism in Europe. In part, that is due to its devotion to multiculturalism, which has encouraged the development of ethnic and religious separatism—and the growth of the very *ummah* solidarity that allows Islamism to grow. This is connected to the Left's persistent self-flagellation, as well as its continual discovery of "Muslim persecution," "Islamophobia," and "disfranchisement," all of which encourages the sense of victimhood upon which jihadism depends for recruitment and justification of its acts.

The more radical a European leftist group, the more likely it is to support unlimited immigration and Muslim "rights" and even, in the fringes of the fringes, to express "solidarity" with jihadis. Socialist parties, on the other hand, often currently in the government or recently part of it, are somewhat more restrained, and must pay more attention to the growing anti-immigration and anti-Islamist sentiments of the voters. Nevertheless, there are some ideological reasons explaining the Left's general tolerance for Islamist demands.

For instance, the two main Salafi ideas, held by the Muslim Brotherhood as well as by jihadis—anti-nationalism and a paranoid view of the world—are also shared by the European Left. True enough, the Islamists' hostility to the nation-state is based on the notion that it creates division within the *ummah*, while for the European Left it is to blame for centuries of wars and for the rise of fascism. As for the perceived threat to Islam, for the Left that is a natural result of the predatory and aggressive nature of capitalism in general and of its American version in particular.

Some in Europe have expressed surprise that prominent leftists such as London's former mayor "Red Ken" Livingstone and George Galloway of the Respect Party—widely described as the first extreme leftist elected to Parliament in half a century—are supporters of Islamists ranging from Qaradawi to *Hizbollah*. In fact, the ideological similarities are such that a *de facto* alliance between the Left and Islamists in Europe is almost inevitable. These similarities include anti-Americanism, anti-Semitism or indiscriminate anti-Israel stands, anti-capitalism, anti-globalization, anti-nationalism, and Third Worldism. The two also share a less defined hatred for "the system" they both believe is a Western creation.

Thus Jack Lang, the Socialist former culture minister of France, in a visit to Algiers in February 2007, demanded that France "recognize the reality of crimes committed by colonization" between 1830 and 1962 and claimed a need for "historical reparations" from his country.[7] The fact that Algerian Islamists alone have murdered many more Algerians since 1990 than the French did in 130 years seemed to have escaped the former minister, who was serving as an advisor to Socialist presidential candidate Ségolène Royal.

Meanwhile, Oskar Lafontaine, formerly of the Social Democratic Party in Germany, and now the leader of the Left Party, sees "commonalities between leftist policies and the Islamic religion." In an interview with *Neues Deutschland*, he said: "Islam depends on community, which places it in opposition to extreme individualism, which threatens to fail in the West. The second similarity is that the devout Muslim is required to share his wealth with others. The leftist also wants to see the strong help the weak. Finally, the prohibition of interest still plays a role in Islam, much as it once did in Christianity. At a time when entire economies are plunging into crisis because their expectations of returns on investment have become totally absurd, there is a basis for a dialogue to be conducted between the left and the Islamic world." He also claimed that Westerners "must constantly ask ourselves through which eyes the Muslims see us . . . people in Muslim countries have experienced many indignities, one of the most recent being the Iraq war. What we are seeing here is resource imperialism."[8]

This is identical to bin Laden's persistent claim that the "infidels" are stealing Muslims' oil and other resources. In England, Ken Livingstone, who was heavily dependent on the Muslim vote, is a vocal exponent of similar notions, and he is only the most prominent example. Indeed, in 2006 a "high-powered coalition, involving MPs, Muslim groups, trade unions and the campaign group Liberty, [was formed] to confront Islamophobia"—i.e., to oppose attempts to strengthen anti-terror laws. The coalition was supported by figures from the three major British parties, Sikhs, black-led organizations, and human-rights groups. "Many leading figures are concerned about issues such as Jack Straw's observations on Muslim women who wear the veil and criticisms from ministers who say Islamic communities should do more to root out extremists."[9] Jack Straw's unsuitability for the post of foreign secretary, according to the group, was demonstrated by his being upset and confused when meeting a *burqa*-wearing constituent.

That the Muslim world is highly vulnerable to conspiracy theories is a fact well known to any reader of the English-language Arab newspapers published in . . . London. When a former cabinet minister subscribes to those conspiracy theories—such as the CIA-Mossad plot behind 9/11, or the Bush conspiracy to obtain oil behind the attacks on Afghanistan and Iraq—[10]that only "proves" their point.

Reacting in 2006 to the conservative Dutch government's proposal to ban the *niqab* and *burqa* in public places, Jeroen Dijsselbloem, a Labour MP, had this to say: "There are hardly any *burqas* in the Netherlands at all. This is a right-wing move to say our norms and values are of a higher order and Muslims have to behave the way we do."[11] In translation, Dutch mores and customs, in the Netherlands, are no more legitimate than Moroccan or Turkish mores in the Netherlands, and to demand that the latter respect the former is "a right-wing move." Wasif Shadid, a Muslim professor of Intercultural Communication at Tilburg University in the Netherlands, was not engaging in the public debate on Islam but talking about how to avoid it when he claimed that "Everything in Islam is criminalized the last ten years. Everything concerning Islam is discussed daily in the newspapers and in the parliament. 150 MPs are spending days discussing banning the burka, which is worn by a maximum of 50 persons of Islamic background."[12]

The problem, as he knew well, was not the number of *burqa*-wearing Muslim women, but what their existence meant: the open rejection of belonging in the Netherlands. Not surprisingly, the Dutch Left's position mirrored that of Muslim "leaders." Ayhan Tonca, spokesman for the one of the principal Islamic bodies in the Netherlands, the CMO, called this a "big law for a small problem," while Mohamed Hamidi, spokesman for Rotterdam's Moroccan community, claimed that "The way of dressing is a question of personal freedom. There are not many people who wear burqas: maybe 10 in Rotterdam and 10 in Amsterdam. But there are lots of people without work. *Burqas* are not a problem. This is populism, playing with the feelings of the people."[13]

Going much further, former justice minister Piet Hein Donner, although a Christian Democrat, reflected prevalent leftist opinion when he objected to growing demands for Muslim integration:

> A tone that I do not like has crept into the political debate. A tone of: "Thou shalt assimilate. Thou shalt adopt our values in public. Be reasonable, do it our way." That is not my approach. . . . For me it is clear: if two-thirds of the Dutch population should want to introduce the Sharia tomorrow, then the possibility should exist. . . . It would be a disgrace to say: "That is not allowed!"[14]

In translation, that means that present popular objections to Muslim demands for special privileges—such as permission to wear the *burqa* in public—are condemnable, but a potential future popular demand for imposition of the Sharia would be justifiable. Such attitudes have led to strong opposition from some quarters—hence the appearance and growth of the Freedom Party of Geert Wilders, which went from its founding in 2004 to becoming the country's fifth-largest party three years later, mostly by combining free-market ideology with rejection of Islamist demands, Muslim immigration in general, and asylum abuses. True enough, by March 2008 Wilders was intentionally provoking a conflict with the Muslim world with a short film attacking Islam as such. This forced The Hague to make a choice between free speech and Muslim claims for special treatment—precisely Wilders's (and before him Fortuyn's) intention.

Admittedly, the cases of the Netherlands and Denmark, both previously known as peculiarly tolerant even in the European context, are extreme. That is precisely why they are relevant. If these two small and longtime "liberal" democracies reach a point where there can be open debate on restricting Muslim "rights," then the Islamist problem has indeed come to a head.

In Denmark the change came quickly, with the cartoon controversy provoking it to become the most restrictive among Western countries regarding Muslim immigration and asylum. In the Netherlands, even after the shock of two spectacular assassinations, polls prior to the November 2006 elections suggested that Muslim integration was a somewhat important issue for just 24 percent of the voters. Only 4 percent considered it the main election theme.[15] In other words, even after the Fortuyn and van Gogh murders Dutch public debate largely returned to its historic search for consensus across ideological lines.

The headscarf issue is dividing not only European secular culture but also relatively integrated Muslims from Islamists. An October 2006 dispute in Italy was illuminating. First, in a TV debate, a conservative National Alliance MP, Daniela Santanchè, stated that the headscarf is not even mentioned in the Quran, and is even less a religious requirement. At this, Ali Abu Shwaima, described by Magdi Allam as the self-appointed imam of the Segrate mosque near Milan and "emir of the Islamic Center of Milan and Lombardy," accused her of ignorance and lack of qualifications to comment on the Quran.[16] Some interpreted that as a threat, and Santanchè received police protection. The debate continued, and became an issue among Muslim women themselves. Asmae Dachan, spokeswoman of the Association of Muslim Women in Italy, claimed that the headscarf is "an act of faith, like prayer," while Dunia Ettaib, representative of the Union of Moroccan Women in Italy, denied that the headscarf is obligatory or required by the Quran.[17]

As mentioned earlier, for other prominent Muslim leaders, such as Daud Abdullah of the Muslim Council of Britain, the debate over the *niqab,* a much more controversial garment than the *hijab,* is "opportunism" and "incitement to violence," when not a diversion from the "real" problem: "The government's refusal for so long to recognize the link between its own disastrous foreign policy in the Muslim world and the extremism it was fomenting is now fuelling the flames of Islamophobia."[18]

Also in Britain, the Islamic Human Rights Commission reacted hysterically to the Education Ministry's proposal to ban the *niqab*: "To now proceed to issue guidance against Muslim communities is simply shocking. Although these guidelines affect a small section of the Muslim community, they could force Muslims to withdraw their children from schools enforcing the ban and teach them at home or enroll them in Muslim-only schools."[19]

If the issue only affects a "small section" of the Muslim community, how is it that simple guidance is "against Muslim communities"? Even Inayat Bunglawala of the MCB admitted that "there are fewer than a dozen schoolgirls who actually wear the niqab out of half a million state school pupils." Once again, the label of "human rights" is used to cover extremism and support for radicals.[20]

MUSLIMS AND THE LEFT

Muslim communities in Europe may have limited political participation, mostly due to the high incidence of lack of citizenship, but they do have clear political preferences, and those are invariably to the left. That is quite natural, and it goes beyond ideology, since left-wing parties and NGOs are generally supportive of the rights, real or imagined, of immigrants, of multiculturalism, and of the welfare state, among whose beneficiaries Muslims are overrepresented. A good example can be found in France, in some suburbs of Paris and Lyon that used to be working-class bastions of the Communist Party. During recent decades the party has retained its influence because of the heavy influx of Muslim immigrants. There are some exceptions and nuances. The immediate goal of the network of Muslim Brotherhood recruiters discovered in France in 2002 was to support candidates in close races, thus making them as dependent as possible on even the smallest Muslim voting bloc. Thus, the group will sometimes even attack the socialist Left for being too influenced by the Jewish lobby, while it may praise politicians of the Center-Right for being more "balanced" vis-à-vis Jews and Israel. The best places for cooperation with the Center-Right were Bordeaux, the Languedoc, and Marseille.[21]

In the aftermath of the 2005 riots in France, opinion polls made it quite clear that the French public supported a hard line.[22] As it turned out, in the first round of the French presidential elections of 2007, the front-runner and ultimate winner, the relatively conservative, law-and-order Nicolas Sarkozy, re-

ceived 1 percent of the Muslim vote (vs. 31 percent of the overall vote), compared with 64 percent for the Socialist Ségolène
Royal (vs. 26 percent overall), 19 percent (vs. 18 percent overall)
for the centrist François Bayrou, and 8 percent (vs. 4.5 percent
overall) for the Trotskyite Olivier Besancenot.[23]

In England, nearly all regions with large Muslim populations
are represented by Labour MPs, and it was the Muslim vote that
led to the election and re-election of Ken Livingstone as mayor
of London. Many Islamist militants have joined the Respect
Party of George Galloway, whose ideology includes anti-Semitism, socialism, and anti-Americanism in equally large doses.
In 2005, Galloway, albeit a Scottish carpetbagger, won a seat in
Parliament from London's heavily Muslim Bethnal Green district, precisely because he made the most of incumbent Labour
MP Oona King's partly Jewish origin. One of the party's leading
figures, Dr. Mohammad Naseem, chairman of the Birmingham
Central Mosque, became famous for his July 27, 2005, claim that
"Muslims all over the world have never heard of an organiza-
tion called al-Qa'eda."[24]

In the September 2002 general elections in Germany, the
narrow victory of Social Democrat Gerhard Schroeder was as-
sured by the overwhelming support he received from the c.
700,000 Turkish-German voters.[25] According to the Institute for
Migration and Ethnic Studies of the University of Amsterdam, in
2006, 84 percent of the Turkish immigrants in the Netherlands
who are registered to vote voted for the Left, as did 90 percent of the Moroccans. In Antwerp, Belgium's largest port, the
anti-Islamist *Vlaams Belang* party took 33.5 percent of the vote
in the October 2006 local elections. Sociologist Jan Hertogen
calculated that without the immigrant vote the VB would have
polled 40.4 percent and would have beaten the Socialists.[26]

Tolerance and Multiculturalism

In the West, multiculturalism is a barely disguised form of Third Worldism—i.e., admiration for the "noble savage," an anti-industrial, anti-modern "pure" human being, devoid of pernicious Western influences. Jean-François Revel and, before him, the late Venezuelan writer Carlos Rangel[27] were referring to the West's responses to Communism when they described democracy as "the first system in history which, confronted by a power that wants to destroy it, accuses itself," but, *mutatis mutandis*, the same applies today to the Left's responses to Islamism.

In the immigration context, multiculturalism assumes that immigrants have a right not to integrate in the culture of the country they have chosen to live in, with the implication that the country's culture does not deserve to be preserved or respected. Not surprisingly, multiculturalists are almost always highly critical of Western culture and highly tolerant, when not downright approving, of non-Western cultures.

However, two points have eluded elites in the West: (1) there must be good reasons why millions of Western Europeans and Americans do not assault the borders of Morocco, Saudi Arabia, or Mexico, but vice versa; and (2) the "rights" of the immigrants that multiculturalists are so eager to support, and even expand, must be balanced by at least some obligations, such as respect for the local culture and laws. That may appear logical enough, but not to such as the Dutch former cabinet minister quoted above, who, even after the murder of Theo van Gogh, wrote: "A tone that I do not like has crept into the political debate. A tone of: 'Thou shalt assimilate. Thou shalt adopt our values in public. Be reasonable, do it our way'."[28] For a moderate Muslim who came to Europe precisely because its freedoms and laws are better than those of his native country, such statements, from high officials, are disheartening; for Islamists, they are encouraging.[29]

In the UK a recent Royal United Services Institute report offered what could be the best explanation for the existence of Londonistan: "The United Kingdom presents itself as a target, as a fragmenting, post-Christian society, increasingly divided about interpretations of its history, about its national aims, its values and its political identity. . . . The country's lack of self-confidence is in stark contrast to the implacability of its Islamist terrorist enemy."[30] Considering that the RUSI is part of the Defense Ministry, that is a disturbing admission.

ANTI-AMERICANISM

Anti-Americanism and its twin, anti-Israeli/pro-Palestinian sentiment, are omnipresent among the cultural elites. Indeed, they are quasi-official policies in education, at all levels, reinforced on a daily basis by mass media, political discourse, and culture, from movies and plays, all the way to Nobel Peace and Literature prizes and major film awards at Cannes and Venice.

Anti-Americanism and anti-Semitism and/or anti-Israeli attitudes (not the same, but the lines are far too often blurred) are the strongest common denominator between the European Left and Islamists of all hues. For the former, Israel is disliked because it is seen as an American ally or puppet; for the latter, America is hated because it supports Israel. In those circumstances, the Islamists' "Crusaders" and "Great Satan" and the Left's "American imperialism" (a.k.a. "unilateralism") are quite close in substance, and the pro-Palestinian/anti-Israeli sentiments of the progressives meet Islamist anti-Semitism more than halfway. In this case, unlike in Kipling's, "the twain" do meet.

Thus the famous (and fame-seeking) Spanish judge Baltasar Garzón—a former Socialist MP, long in charge of investigating terrorism in Spain and the author of an impressive study of Islamism in his country in the wake of 9/11—still believes Islamist terrorism is the result of despair, poverty, and "humiliation," as well as American support of "state terrorism."[31]

Even when not fully integrated, Muslims in Europe do not generally live in a strictly isolated cultural environment. Through education and the media, especially television, they are inevitably influenced by the general cultural and political trends in their countries of residence. When anti-Americanism is rampant in a culture—say, in France or Spain—it is natural that Muslim anti-Americanism is reinforced. A German Marshall Fund poll found the following:[32]

FAVORABLE ATTITUDES TOWARD U.S. (PERCENT)

	2005	2004
UK	57	62
Italy	57	61
Poland	56	56
Slovakia	55	50
Netherlands	54	55
Germany	51	55
Portugal	51	50
France	50	51
Spain	42	42
Turkey	28	28
Europe 10	50	55

Source: German Marshall Fund, "Transatlantic Trends," 2005

It is significant that in most countries with sizable Muslim populations, sympathy for the United States declined, with the largest drop in the United Kingdom, while Turkey, with probably the largest diaspora in Europe, is at the bottom of the ranking.

A similar trend was found in major Arab countries:

FAVORABLE ATTITUDES TOWARD U.S. (PERCENT)

Egypt

	2005	2004	2002
Favorable	14	n/a	15
Unfavorable	85	n/a	76

Saudi Arabia

	2005	2004	2002
Favorable	14	n/a	15
Unfavorable	85	n/a	76

Morocco

	2005	2004	2002
Favorable	14	n/a	15
Unfavorable	85	n/a	76

Source: James Zogby, 2005, "Arab Attitudes toward U.S.: Good News and Bad News"[33]

Opinions like the following in a major weekly, *Le Nouvel Observateur*, are common:

> In the name of the fight against terrorism and "national security" the American Army and the CIA do not even avoid "extreme interrogation measures." ... A question, the question,

nibbles the messianic regime of George Bush. America, which sees itself as the beacon of freedom and human rights in the world, which pretends to democratize the Arab world and the ex-Soviet space, America practiced torture?[34]

And a 2005 Pew poll found that

The polling in Western Europe, conducted in the weeks leading up to the decisive rejection of the European Union constitution by voters in France and the Netherlands, finds pockets of deep public dissatisfaction with national conditions and concern in several countries over immigration from the Middle East, North Africa and Eastern Europe. . . . Indeed, opinion of the U.S. continues to be mostly unfavorable among the publics of America's traditional allies, except Great Britain and Canada. . . . Moreover, support for the U.S.-led war on terror has plummeted in Spain and eroded elsewhere in Europe. . . . Japan, France and Germany are all more highly regarded than the United States among the countries of Europe; even the British and Canadians have a more favorable view of these three nations than they do of America. Strikingly, China now has a better image than the U.S. in most of the European nations surveyed. . . . The biggest gap between the way Americans are seen by other Western countries, and the way they see themselves, is with respect to religion. Majorities in France and the Netherlands and pluralities in Great Britain and Germany see the U.S. as too religious. By contrast, a 58 percent majority of Americans say their country is not religious enough. On this point, Muslims find themselves in rare agreement with the American public; majorities in Indonesia, Pakistan, Lebanon and Turkey all believe the U.S. is not religious enough.[35]

Even the respected and respectable *Economist* has run headlines like "Americans: Still not loved. Now not envied."[36] As for the Germans, they "regard U.S. attempts to enrapture the world with democracy as naïve at best, while Americans take a cynical view of Germany's willingness to cooperate even with rivals. So there we are again: with that century-old clash between the American idealism of a president like Woodrow Wilson and a pragmatic European political rationale."[37]

Things are no better in the most Westernized Muslim country, Turkey—a candidate for EU membership. Indeed, a February
2005 survey by the private Metropoll organization found that
four in 10 Turks regard the United States as their country's biggest enemy. That is more than double the number who named
Greece, the ancient rival Turkey has come to the brink of war
with three times in the last half-century.[38]

An example of this is the reaction of many—actually a decisive number of—Spaniards to the Madrid bombings of March
2004. Spaniards blamed the attacks on the U.S. invasion of Iraq
more than on the international Islamist network that actually
perpetrated them.

JEWS AND ANTI-SEMITISM

During the February 2007 Paris trial of the satirical weekly
Charlie Hebdo—accused of "blasphemy" and "racism" by the
Grand Mosque of Paris, the UOIF, and the Saudi-controlled
World Muslim League for publishing the Danish cartoons—
the only witness for the accusers was a notorious anti-Semite,
the renegade Catholic priest Michel Lelong, previously known
for his support for Holocaust-denier Roger Garaudy and for
Hizbollah's anti-Semitic TV station Al-Manar. On the other side,
defending the journal, was what amounted to the whole of mainstream French society: Nicolas Sarkozy and François Bayrou of
the Center-Right, the feminist Elisabeth Badinter and Socialist
Party leader François Hollande of the Left. Equally significant
were the pro-defense testimonies of two prominent Muslims:
French Tunisian philosopher Abdelwahab Meddeb, who asked
the accusers whether they would sue Dante for his well-known
Islamophobia, and exiled Algerian journalist Mohamed Sifaoui.
The latter presented the flag of Saudi Arabia, with its profession of faith and its scimitar, and a poster of the Algerian ter-

rorist GSPC, with a religious verse and a Kalashnikov. Sifaoui stated: "This association between violence and the Quranic text is not made by the Danes but by fundamentalists. The ... mixing of terrorism and Islam we are talking about, and because of which I suffer daily, was made by Muslims."[39] The prosecution dropped the case.

The French *Commission Nationale Consultative des Droits de l'Homme* in its 2005 report on racism, found that there was a general decline in anti-Semitic and racist acts and threats compared to 2004, from 1,574 to 974, or 38 percent, and congratulated itself for the decline. Behind these figures, however, there is an alarming signal. While "not anti-Semitic" attacks (i.e., "racist" attacks, or, in translation, attacks against Muslims or blacks) also declined, in this case by 28 percent, in total numbers there were more anti-Semitic violent acts (504) than "racist" ones (470).[40] Considering that France's Jewish population is c. 600,000 and that of Muslims and blacks in the neighborhood of six million, this is not encouraging.

Former mayor Livingstone is very popular among Muslims and a friend of al-Qaradawi, whom he invited to the city and has defended repeatedly against accusations of anti-Semitism and legitimization of suicide murderers. Livingstone is also a prominent representative of the radical Left inside the Labour Party, and thus the motivations behind his anti-Israel pronouncements and sympathy for Islamism deserve an analysis— offered by British journalist Charles Moore of *The Telegraph*.

> I know of no evidence that Mr Livingstone is personally anti-Semitic, but this whole saga shows that he is not politically averse to being seen to be rude to Jews. Why would that be? Two related reasons suggest themselves. The first is that roughly 15 percent of the London electorate (and a much larger percentage of his own vote) is Muslim, and standing up to

"the Zionists" may commend itself to some of the more vocal Muslim leaders. The second is the project of the Livingstone Left, worked out even before he first came to power in the Greater London Council in 1981. This is to subvert the dominant values of traditional Britain by ascribing them all to colonialist, racist oppression, and to build up a coalition of their supposed victims. Hence the obsession with gay liberation, the support for West Indian rioters against the police in the 1980s, the pioneering invitations to IRA terrorists. And hence, today, an obsession with the question of Palestine. Palestine can combine all those who hate Britain and America and Israel, even if some of them are as "reactionary" (to use a Ken word) as you could find. One of the Mayor of London's most honored visitors has been Sheikh Yusuf al-Qaradawi . . . Qaradawi says: "O God, destroy the vile usurper Jews, the vile Crusaders, and infidels." He supports suicide bombings in the Middle East and he calls on Muslims to kill Jews, quoting the sacred text: "There is a Jew behind me. Come and kill him." Yet the Ken who spoke of an ideology that makes one human being inferior to another leading to Auschwitz makes no complaint.[41]

Other politicians go at least as far toward "understanding" jihad. A March 2004 ICM poll of Muslim opinion in Britain posed the following question: "Jenny Tonge, a Liberal Democrat MP, said she condemned all forms of terrorism, but if she had to live in the same situation as a Palestinian she might consider becoming a suicide bomber herself. Do you agree or disagree with her?" Of Muslims polled, 47 percent agreed, while 43 percent disagreed.[42] Even less surprising, Tonge's statement was used by Muslim groups, the MCB included, to justify their claim that jihadis have understandable and legitimate grievances.

DISSONANCE BETWEEN ISLAMISTS AND THE LEFT

While Islamists and the Western Left have much in common, there have always been differences between the two on social and cultural issues. The first and most spectacular sign that the progressives and the Islamists sometimes seek different, con-tradictory goals came from the Netherlands, that most progres-sive of all countries, the land of legal drugs, legally sanctioned euthanasia, gay marriages, and unionized prostitutes. And that sign had a face: Pim Fortuyn.

Islamists decried Fortuyn's public criticism of Islam as blas-phemous, and the Far Left called him "racist," but the charge of racism was spurious: He was a libertarian, *bon vivant*, and ho-mosexual. In 2002, shortly after Fortuyn's assassination by a radical Dutch environmentalist claiming to "protect" Muslims, his party came out of nowhere to place second in that year's general elections. While the party soon collapsed without his leadership, its radical (by European standards) anti-immigra-tion program was largely adopted by the government in The Hague.

Meanwhile, the same year, the gay Socialist mayor of Paris, Bertrand Delanoë, was almost killed by a Muslim who did not like gays. No matter how multiculturalists may tie themselves in knots over the issue, Islam and homosexuality are irrevoca-bly incompatible. Muslims condemn homosexuality as fervent-ly as fundamentalist Christians do, but unlike fundamentalist Christians, they are willing and ready to kill over it. American journalist Bruce Bawer, who moved to Europe because he thought American Christians are anti-gay, became one of the most articulate critics of Islam and prophets of "Eurabia" as a result of his first-hand experiences with Muslims in Oslo, Copenhagen, and Amsterdam.[43]

If homosexuality is a major point of contention between the European Left and Islamists, Islam's problem with feminism, and with women in general, is more complex. As pointed out elsewhere, polygamy, which is illegal everywhere in the West, when practiced by Muslims is in fact widely tolerated, indeed subsidized in a number of countries, including Britain and France. There is also the practice of FGM and the general and theologically orthodox Islamic denial of the most basic rights to women. Put polygamy, genital mutilation, anti-abortion attitudes, and the *burqa* together, and one is likely to drive feminists wild indeed. It is also a combination that makes Western women—and most decent men, for that matter—question the realism of accepting Islam as just another religion to be respected and tolerated in our midst.

Muslim moderates themselves complain that the more left-wing media, NGOs, and academia implicitly help the radicals and prevent reform of Islam. Thus Dr. Tawfik Hamid, former *Jamaa Islamiya* member:

> Yet it is ironic and discouraging that many non-Muslim, Western intellectuals—who unceasingly claim to support human rights—have become obstacles to reforming Islam. Political correctness among Westerners obstructs unambiguous criticism of Shariah's inhumanity. They find socioeconomic or political excuses for Islamist terrorism such as poverty, colonialism, discrimination or the existence of Israel. What incentive is there for Muslims to demand reform when Western "progressives" pave the way for Islamist barbarity? Indeed, if the problem is not one of religious beliefs, it leaves one to wonder why Christians who live among Muslims under identical circumstances refrain from contributing to wide-scale, systematic campaigns of terror.[44]

In a 2006 debate in the left-of-center French weekly *L'Express*, Caroline Fourest, a self-described left-winger, noted,

> Under the pretext of resisting Western imperialism, Israeli colonialism or the dictatorship of certain Maghreb regimes, people who advocate ideas close to mine consider the Muslim fundamentalists, particularly the Muslim Brothers, as a movement for democratization, even of liberation, to the extent of excommunicating those who criticize fundamentalism, treating them as Islamophobes, even as sellouts to the "Bushist" or "Sharonist" thinking.[45]

Fourest's adversary, François Burgat, also a self-described leftist and an "intellectual colleague of Tariq Ramadan," manages even to make a sharp distinction between Islamists and Salafis. Salafis are to be condemned for "rejecting the baby of modernization with the bathwater of deculturalization," while Islamists, "behind the identity veil of religious rhetoric, demand perfectly universal rights, in economics or politics, locally and globally."[46] All in all, Burgat is one of the few remaining French Arabists who either deny the influence of Salafism and Islamist terrorism, or consider Islamism, whether in Algeria, Tunisia, or Egypt, to be a modernizing factor simply using "the language of religion"— and if there are deviations into violence, they are explained away by government suppression, past colonialism, etc.[47]

Fourest's arguments are espoused by a growing minority of intellectuals of the Left. Among recent example are the Danes Karen Jespersen and Ralf Pittelkow, authors of *Islamists and Naïvists: A Bill of Indictment*, published in Denmark in September 2006. The authors are described as

> establishment figures previously known for their progressive attitudes toward Islam and integration. . . . The authors' backgrounds could hardly be more mainstream. Pittelkow, a former literature professor and prominent Social Democrat, advised former (social democratic) Prime Minister Poul Nyrup Rasmussen before becoming a commentator for *Jyllands-Posten*, the newspaper that published the Muhammad cartoons. Jespersen, Pittelkow's wife, is a former interior minister and social-affairs minister who belonged to a leftist revolutionary party in her youth. . . . Indeed, Jespersen claimed, "If anyone is identified with the values of freedom and human rights, it is us, social-democrats."[48]

Nevertheless, as Pittelkow said at the time,

> "The threat is that the Islamists and their values are gaining ground in Europe, especially among the younger generation. . . . They try to interfere in people's lives, telling them what

to wear, what to eat, what to think and what to believe. They warn Muslims to create their own societies within Europe or risk disappearing like salt in water."[49]

The reaction of "progressives" in Denmark was interesting. Jakob Nielsen, a commentator for the left-leaning newspaper *Politiken*, said that the book "is significant because it shows how attacks against Islam are no longer limited to people on the right, but have become acceptable, even fashionable, among people close to the establishment."

Muslim reaction was equally interesting: "Pittelkow and Jespersen are Islam-bashers who show how acceptable it has become to attack Islam. . . . They are dangerous because by pushing the debate to the edges, they are making it harder for moderate Muslims in this country to find a middle ground," said Imam Wahid Pedersen,[50] without noticing the irony of a self-described "moderate" accusing two leftists who oppose Islamists—not Muslims, as they have repeatedly made clear— of being "Islam-bashers."

Pittelkow and Jespersen may have touched some sensitive nerves by suggesting that "Denmark and the rest of Europe need to integrate their existing Muslim communities," and by mentioning then PM Blair among the "naïvists," as well as by mentioning the similarities between Islamism, Nazism, and Communism. But the popularity of their book suggests that their worries are widely shared even in such a tolerant society as Denmark.

MULTICULTURALISM ON THE DEFENSIVE?

In the opinion of Christopher Hitchens, the Anglo-American militant atheist and intellectual stalwart of progressivism,

For the British mainstream, multiculturalism has been the official civic religion for so long that any criticism of any minority group has become the equivalent of profanity. And Islamic extremists have long understood that they need only suggest a racial bias—or a hint of the newly invented and meaningless term "Islamophobia"—in order to make the British cough and shuffle with embarrassment.[51]

Those observations, from a lifelong leftist, apply equally to continental Europe, Canada, and the United States.[52]

The problem with multiculturalism is its fundamental premise: that all cultures are worthy of equal respect in all their social, cultural, and political forms, everywhere. Any contrary analysis is instantly labeled "racism" or "Eurocentrism" and dismissed from the spectrum of rational discourse.

When non-Western cultures are known to follow, or to have followed, practices completely alien to "human rights," the Left's answers are either absurd denials or the blaming of Western interference and impact. A perfect example of the former is William Arens, author of *The Man-Eating Myth: Anthropology and Anthropophagy* (1979), who simply rejected all historical and archaeological proofs of cannibalism as expressions of Western racism. As for blaming the West, there is the entire ideology of Third Worldism, still influential in the corridors of the United Nations. This was notable in the activities of Swiss socialist Jean Ziegler, UN Special Rapporteur on the Right to Food, who in 2005 likened Israelis to Nazis and called world undernourishment a "capitalist crime."

More directly related to the topic at hand, one has only to look at the obsession of the influential French philosopher Jean-Paul Sartre with anti-Western ideologues "of color," such as Frantz Fanon, a Martinican whose *Black Skin, White Masks* (1952) and especially *The Wretched of the Earth* (1962) advocated and justified "anti-colonial" violence on behalf of Algeria and, indeed, the whole Third World. It is in this context and tradition within mainstream French culture—which, even if in steep decline, still remains the most influential in Europe—that one can find some explanations for the European elites' widespread tolerance of Islamism and "understanding" of its use of violence.

The double standard applied to the way Muslims are treated in the West as compared to the way non-Muslims are treated in the Islamic world is taken as a natural given. There is little opposition (and none from the Left) to the practice of allowing the Gulf States and Saudi Arabia to pay for the building of mosques throughout Europe, from Sarajevo to Rome to Granada, while virtually no one even asks how many churches are allowed to exist in those states (answer: none). One may argue about the cultural or historical reasons for this reality, but, *pace* many on the Left, noticing it does not make one a "racist." As the liberal Cardinal Walter Kasper, president of the Pontifical Council for Promoting Christian Unity, observed in an interview with *Der Spiegel*,

> One unanswered question is whether a Euro-Islam that combines Islam with democracy will be possible in the future. We mustn't confuse desire with reality. How should Europe behave? Europe sees itself as a liberal-minded society. It has no desire to be, nor can it be, a "Christian club." But Europe's experiment with multiculturalism, or the side-by-side existence of different cultures, has failed throughout the continent. Integration requires a minimum basis of shared values, that is, a culture of mutual tolerance and respect—in other words, what constitutes the heart of European culture. This is why integration is not possible without excluding those who do not recognize this culture. Those who are unprepared to demonstrate tolerance cannot expect or even demand tolerance for themselves.[53]

Even when events such as the Atocha or London bombings make it indefensible to deny the existence of Islamist terrorism, the multiculturalists, and many others, tend to minimize its religious significance with the claim that jihadis are just a deviant minority, "unrepresentative" of the mass of Muslims. Indeed, if there is one consistent theme in the European cultural approach to Islam, from Stockholm to Seville, it is the persistent drive to divide Muslims into "moderates," usually described as the overwhelming majority, and radicals, usually described as a small minority.

On the face of it there is nothing wrong with this distinction, except that, moderate or radical, Muslims perceive themselves as part of the universal *ummah*, the community of believers in the only true faith, and that simple fact is systematically missed by outsiders. No poll taken of Muslims ever asks: Are the perpetrators of Atocha, London, or 9/11 "true Muslims"? If such a question ever were asked, the answer might surprise many of those proclaiming the difference between moderates and radicals. And that is the problem: As long as *ummah* solidarity, more often than not encouraged by official policies of multiculturalism, trumps everything else, including loyalty to the country of one's birth, integration is simply a pipe dream.

How relevant is Muslim denial of association between Islam and terrorism, as long as Muslims oppose each and every Western action (always seen as an assault on Islam) against any Muslim government or organization, including the Taliban, *Hizbollah*, Hamas, or Al-Qaeda? The persistent mention of the anti-Taliban campaign in Afghanistan as an example of the West's "anti-Islamic" policies is perhaps the best illustration. When the removal of a regime that was recognized by only three Muslim countries, and condemned by most for its policies, is itself condemned, the only conclusion to be drawn is that, for most Muslims, Mullah Omar's Islamic faith trumps everything else. Never mind that the Taliban has long and openly supported Al-Qaeda and was responsible for killing thousands of Muslims in Afghanistan—Sunni Tajiks and Shia Hazaras alike. It looks as if *any* Islamic entity under attack by the West is worthy of sympathy—and that only Muslims are entitled to use violence against other Muslims, no matter the reasons or circumstances.

While it is said far too often by politicians and academics, it is nonetheless true that *ummah* solidarity does not mean that all or even most Muslims are terrorist sympathizers, or that Islam is naturally associated with terrorism. However, the question in practical terms remains whether this is not, more frequently than anyone would like to admit, a distinction without a difference.

Ndeye Andújar, vice president of the Islamic Council of Catalonia, has gone so far as to accuse the French Muslim group *Ni Putes ni Soumises* (NPNS), led by Fadela (Fatiha) Amara, of "Islamophobia" because its activities in favor of Muslim women and against their mistreatment by men "in reality are not about progress towards the rights of Muslim women but about the stigmatization of the Arab-Muslim man of the suburbs, as a scoundrel who lives between the fundamentalist mosque and the garbage can, where he rapes."[54]

Not surprisingly, Andújar was able to find a number of radical French sociologists and psychologists who also believe that any criticism of Muslim men, even by socialist-minded Muslim women, is a bourgeois diversion from the reality of French racism, oppression, etc. Indeed, one of Andújar's main problems with NPNS is its consistent rejection of anti-Semitism. For her, covering up for Muslim rapists and being "anti-Zionist" is more important than the fate of Muslim women.

When, as is often the case in Britain, the U.S., and elsewhere, non-Islamist Muslim organizations explain Islamist terrorism as caused by Western policies of the past and present, they impede both the general public and Muslims in the West from understanding the very nature of the threat. And when the very same organizations, like the MCB, oppose common-sense counter-terrorism legislation and persist in denying the very problem of Salafi terrorism in their midst, they play a role analogous to that of the anti-anti-communists of the Cold War, with the same practical result: their negation of a negation equals affirmation.

It is precisely the Muslim majority's denial of the Islamist and jihadi problem, and its *de facto* rejection of integration, that led British Communities Secretary Ruth Kelly to call for a "new and honest debate" on the value of a multicultural society in Britain. Launching the Blair government's Commission on Integration and Cohesion, she warned that there was a danger that communities were becoming increasingly isolated from one another.

> "We have moved from a period of uniform consensus on the value of multiculturalism to one where we can encourage that debate by questioning whether it is encouraging separateness . . . They are difficult questions and it is important that we don't shy away from them. . . . *In our attempt to avoid imposing a single British identity and culture, have we ended up with some communities living in isolation from each other with no common bonds between them?*"[55] [Emphasis added.]

That, in fact, was an implicit recognition that multiculturalism does not work. The Indian-born British scientist Kenan Malik has put it better still: "The problem is not that ethnic minorities are alienated from a concept of Britishness but that there is today no source of Britishness from which anyone—black or white—can draw inspiration."[56]

Commenting on a number of recent opinion polls and statements by government and police officials suggesting that

Muslims in Britain are much more alienated than their co-religionists in France (or elsewhere in Europe), Timothy Garton Ash[57] found that one explanation is place of origin (typically North Africa for France, Indian subcontinent for Britain), combined with the distinct nature of French and British colonial policies—ostensibly assimilationist in the former case, indirect rule in the latter.

A second explanation Garton Ash offers is Britain's close alliance with the United States, as demonstrated by Iraq, contrasting it with France's opposition to the Iraq operation and closer ties to the Arab world. The problems with this common argument are many—but to mention only two, British-based Islamist terrorists were involved in suicide bombings before the Iraq invasion, and France was the earliest target of Islamist terrorism in Europe. Equally important, such views serve to reinforce the frequent attempts by Muslims to explain jihadism away by blaming Western policies rather than causes indigenous to the Muslim world. And that, even though—his obsessive hostility to the "neocons" in Washington aside—Garton Ash is among the most balanced and lucid European political observers. He even goes so far as to suspect that the French assimilationist approach may work better than the British laissez-faire—a very un-British thought—but his solutions are, at best unclear. In fact, he seems to believe that if we avoid the obvious links between Islam and Islamism they will somehow disappear. That is not a solution; it is denial.

How far the diehards of multiculturalism can go is demonstrated by this letter to *The Guardian* by Kevin Courtney, executive member of the UK's National Union of Teachers:

> The claim that the tiny number of girls who wear the *niqab* are a security risk would be laughable if it did not demonise a vulnerable group of students. . . . As teachers we are committed to building inclusive, multicultural and tolerant school

> communities. At a time of increased Islamophobia, talking
> about bans on the very few young women who wear the veil
> can only help to sow discord in our schools.[58]

Not only does a leader of the teaching profession accept the
standard Islamist claims of "increased Islamophobia" and "de-
monization," but Courtney becomes positively Orwellian when
he pretends that the *niqab*, by definition a symbol of separation—of women from men, of Muslims from non-Muslims—is
compatible with the alleged commitment to "building inclusive,
multicultural and tolerant school communities."

There are British observers who offer a better diagnosis of
the problems of multiculturalism. Thus Conservative analyst
Rupert Darwall noted that

> The Blair government's multicultural agenda, which
> deconstructs the idea of Britain as a nation into a "community
> of communities," has ended up playing into the hands of the
> extremists. It rewards separateness and feeds the victim/
> grievance culture of Muslim activists and community
> representatives. It is dangerous because it delegitimizes social
> pressure on British Muslims to join the mainstream and
> supports a continuum of Muslim attitudes toward Britain—
> from neutrality through resentment and suspicion to hatred
> and hostility.[59]

To this one might add that Blair's support for the devolution of constituent parts of the United Kingdom did nothing
to strengthen a sense of Britishness. It is hard to see how one
could accept the devolution of Scotland and, at the same time,
hope to integrate millions of Pakistanis or Bangladeshis into a
"United" Kingdom.

British journalist Matthew d'Ancona has argued that multiculturalism, so far from being a sinister left-wing conspiracy, is
in fact, as the philosopher John Gray has written, "an historical
fate," a purely empirical description of the modern condition.

The challenge for a multicultural society like Britain, therefore, is not to identify the areas of differences among its component communities, but to have the courage to identify, and insist upon, the points of non-negotiable conformity. Furthermore,

> Muslims, in my view, have as much a right to their own schools as Anglicans, Catholics and Jews. But they have a corresponding duty to treat their female pupils in a fashion consistent with British social practice. It is absolutely right that a basic command of English should now be a condition of British citizenship. It is sensible of Charles Clarke, the Home Secretary, to propose clear boundaries within which the imams may operate, and to suggest that Muslim clerics should be accredited in some fashion, rather than unrestrained, globe-trotting firebrands . . . Religious freedom does not equate to the right to call for jihad on British soil. Diversity is not the same as moral relativism.[60]

There is much to what d'Ancona says. However, he avoids the fact that no proponent of multiculturalism believes that it means simply allowing Muslims in Leeds to eat curry at home and quietly pray on Fridays. To the contrary, in its intended sense, multiculturalism means the equality of free and public expression of every culture, as a matter of law.

The main problem and danger with multiculturalism is its failure to *discriminate*—in the correct sense of the term, which is to think critically. For instance, after repeated cases of British universities being targeted by Islamist groups for recruitment and propaganda, and despite warnings from both the government and moderate imams, university ad-ministrations still refuse to check on what is going on, be-cause to do so would "target a particular group within our diverse communities."[61] Ironically, by refusing to target the Islamists' activities, the universities make no distinction be-tween Muslims who want to study and HuT recruiters who want to destroy the infidel "system."

Such attitudes, unfailingly multicultural, only help along a process that began during the late 1970s and is now growing at an ever faster pace in more and more European countries: Islam and Muslims are involved in a conflict with their host societies. The process did not begin with 9/11—although it has become more visible since then—but that event and the bombings in Madrid and London, the Danish cartoon affair, and the murders of Fortuyn and van Gogh intensified the debate and pushed it at the national level.

Despite strenuous efforts by mainstream media and political parties and Muslim organizations to separate terrorism from Islam, and although they are in fact different (albeit related) issues, the debate now inevitably involves both. Indeed, when Islamists physically assault male gynecologists treating their wives in France, or claim a right for their daughters to wear the *niqab* in schools, or practice polygamy, FGM, or "honor killings," the issue is not terrorism but cultural aspects of Islam— or at least practices associated with Islam, rightly or wrongly.

Discussing the proliferation of Muslim demands for such "rights," French Muslim philosopher Abdennour Bidar correctly noted:

> Two trends are actively promoting these rights. First, the multiculturalist school, according to which the French Republic treats unequally its citizens, persistently denying cultural differences in the name of a formal understanding of [the meaning of] equality and of an extremist understanding of [the meaning of] secularism. [The second trend] is [composed of] conservative Muslims, followers of Tariq Ramadan: their strategy is to ask for these special rights in the name of "religious freedom," which is a component of the freedom of conscience. This is a repetition of the worn-out tactic of the Muslim Brotherhood, which directs against the West its own weapons: "freedom of conscience" is used against true freedom, since it is a means to maintain the domination of an intolerant kind of Islam.[62]

Rowan Williams, the Archbishop of Canterbury, is representative of British elites' attitude toward multiculturalism in general and Muslims in particular—a combination of fatalism and accommodation. In a February 2008 speech he created a stir, and opened a national debate, by stating that a "constructive accommodation" with Islam is both desirable and unavoidable, including acceptance of aspects of Sharia, especially as "certain conditions of Sharia are already recognized in our society and under our law, so it is not as if we are bringing in an alien and rival system." Among aspects of Sharia he deems acceptable are its methods of resolving marital disputes, where it provides "an alternative to the divorce courts as we understand them. In some cultural and religious settings they would seem more appropriate."[63]

The premises of Williams's arguments, some lifted from Tariq Ramadan's writings, include a claim that "the Muslim, even in a predominantly Muslim state, has something of a dual identity, as citizen and as believer within the community of the faithful."[64] While this view echoes that of the MCB, which claims that "Muslims balance a sense of allegiance to the global Muslim community with responsibilities of citizenship to their nation state—the *ummah* and *qawm* respectively in Islamic terminology,"[65] it is hard to confirm this in practice, particularly in the case of Pakistan, the foremost example offered by Williams. Moreover, the prelate assumes, without a serious basis in practice (or theory), that Sharia is not a coherent legal body inextricably related to faith, but a collection of disparate rules, some of which could be adapted to Britain and some of which must be rejected. There is also a profound lack of logic in Williams's musings about existing legal concessions to some Muslim practices, as the *Wall Street Journal* pointed out:

> There is a critical difference between permitting some
> flexibility for religious practices within the larger society
> and encouraging separate, and potentially inconsistent, legal
> systems for different parts of the population. Toleration
> suggests an exception to the norm. Interposing alternative legal
> rules, and institutions to administer them, creates competing
> norms. In effect, one part of the body politic secedes from the
> other parts with regard to certain aspects of national life.[66]

Leaving aside the issue of foreign legal principles being applied in Britain, Williams's position was characteristic of the multiculturalist approach—and its logical contradictions:

> If what we want socially is a pattern of relations in which
> a plurality of diverse and overlapping affiliations work
> for a common good, and in which groups of serious and
> profound conviction are not systematically faced with
> the stark alternatives of cultural loyalty or state loyalty, it
> seems unavoidable.[67]

It is far from clear how Sharia and British law work for the common good, or why the application of British laws in Britain is a "stark alternative" between cultural (in fact religious) and state loyalty rather than common sense. In another non-sequitur, Williams considers that Sharia is not "alien" to Britain because . . . it is already there.[68]

Reactions to Rowan Williams's speech were predictable, with some Muslims approving (HuT is an example) and others, such as the Conservative baroness Sayeeda Warsi, the shadow minister for community cohesion and social action, bluntly stating: "Let's be absolutely clear: all British citizens must be subject to British laws developed through Parliament and the courts."[69] Another moderate, Khalid Mahmood, the Labour MP for the Perry Barr section of Birmingham, asked: "What part of sharia does he want? The sort that is practised in Saudi Arabia which they are struggling to get away from?"[70]

In the intellectual center of Anglicanism, Oxford, the imam of the Central Oxford mosque, Mohammed Chisti, stated: "Britain is a Christian country, which allows religious freedom. We are grateful for that and don't want it to change"—except for "practical changes," including recognition of mosque marriages and permission for weekend burials and Islamic interest-free mortgages.[71]

That position is indicative of the sorts of problems raised by Sharia—and ignored by Williams. Indeed, Sharia courts already exist in England—and present difficulties. An example is the Islamic Sharia Council established in 1982 in Leyton, a suburb of east London, which handles personal disputes between Muslims. Its general secretary, Suhaib Hasan, asks: "If people can have mistresses in this country and have homosexual relationships, then why can't a Muslim have a second wife?"—no matter that polygamy is illegal under British law.[72]

The Catholic Primate of England and Wales, Cardinal Cormac Murphy-O'Connor, was straightforward: "I don't believe in a multicultural society. When people come into this country they have to obey the laws of the land."[73] Meanwhile, Lord Carey, the former Archbishop of Canterbury, said of his successor: "His acceptance of some Muslim laws within British law would be disastrous for the nation. . . . There can be no exceptions to the laws of our land which have been so painfully honed by the struggle for democracy and human rights." Multiculturalism is "disastrous," creating Muslim ghettos, and Williams's support for Sharia will "inevitably lead to further demands from the Muslim community."[74]

David Blunkett, home secretary in the Blair government, stated:

> This is very dangerous because the archbishop used the term "affiliations." . . . We have affiliations to football clubs, to

cricket teams, to all sorts of things that aren't central to our citizenship and the acceptance of that in terms of a common society. . . . We don't have affiliations when it comes to the question of the law. And when it comes to equality under the law, we have to be rigorous in terms of making sure people do not find themselves excluded from it because of cultural or faith reasons. . . . Formalising Sharia law . . . would be wrong democratically and philosophically, but it would be catastrophic in terms of social cohesion.[75]

Tariq Ramadan, on the other hand, was ambiguous as ever, saying, "These kinds of statements just feed the fears of fellow citizens and I really think we, as Muslims, need to come with something that we abide by the common law and within these latitudes there are possibilities for us to be faithful to Islamic principles."

The MCB's Ibrahim Mogra agreed with Williams:

We're looking at a very small aspect of Sharia for Muslim families when they choose to be governed with regards to their marriage, divorce, inheritance, custody of children and so forth. . . . Let's debate this issue. It is very complex. It is not as straightforward as saying that we will have a system here.[76]

The politics of the debate are also interesting, with the Labour government, traditionally sympathetic to multiculturalism, now taking a hostile line, as did both opposition parties and even some Muslims, while the MCB pretends that marriage, divorce, and custody of children are "a very small aspect" of Sharia, despite their direct link to major social pathologies like polygamy and "honor" killings, and to the education of future generations.

Ultimately, in a larger cultural sense, Dr. Williams does not believe in the justice, or realism, of British law because he does not believe in the existence or necessity of Britishness. Indeed, as Lambeth Palace explained, the archbishop "sought carefully to explore the limits of a unitary and secular legal system in the presence of an increasingly plural (including religiously plural) society and to see how such a unitary system might be able to accommodate religious claims."[77] Perhaps the best answer came from across the English Channel, where President Sarkozy, in a January 2008 speech, bluntly declared: "There is no place in France for polygamy, FGM, forced marriage, the scarf in schools, nor for hatred against France. Because behind all of these is tribal law. And if one lives in France, I want France to be respected."[78]

While it is clear that Williams and Sarkozy represent opposite sides in the debate over the nature and role of Islam in Europe, it is far from clear which side is gaining. Judging by the still-dominant views of the cultural elites, in France as well as Britain, the outcome is still pending.

ISLAM AND WESTERN CULTURE: THE MYTHS

Muslims in the West (radical or not) and their multiculturalist academic and political fans often complain that Westerners do not know or understand Islam. By that, they usually mean that the peaceful, progressive, and glorious past of Islam is not known or appreciated. That may or may not be true, although a pertinent point could be made that present-day Europeans do not have a very good understanding of Christianity either, or any religion, for that matter. But by far the main reason Europeans do not appreciate Islam as much as its followers would like lies with the persistent efforts by Muslims and multiculturalists to whitewash Islamic history and culture.

It has been said that those who control the past control the present, and Islamists and their Western sympathizers are engaged in an intense campaign of rewriting history, aiming to "demonstrate" the Islamic world's cultural superiority *vis-à-vis* the West. For the multiculturalists, the apology for the Islamic past serves as proof that the arrogance of which they accuse the West has no historical basis. For the Islamists, it is yet another tool for uniting the *ummah* and giving it a sense of superiority over the nonbelievers. Attempts to treat the past objectively, let alone critically, are seen as additional examples of victimization of Muslims or, worse still, "racism." Considering that the central pillars of the Islamists' approach to politics today are the notions that Muslims and Islam are under assault and that whatever means they use in response are only defensive—in short, victimization, with jihad as the answer to it— the manipulation of history serves as a powerful instrument. It is in this context that Western multiculturalists and historical revisionists are useful to the Islamist cause.

As an instrument of current cultural conflict, historical revisionism has two related aspects: It claims a millennium-old unjustified Western hatred for Islam and presents a romantic idealization of the Islamic past. Ultimately, it repeats from the halls of academia a recurrent theme of jihadis, bin Laden and al-Zawahiri included: the claim that the medieval Crusades opened the era of Western aggression against Muslims, an era that continues today.

Thus Graham Fuller, a former CIA and Rand Corporation analyst, cavalierly asks: "After all, what were the Crusades if not a Western adventure driven primarily by political, social, and economic needs? The banner of Christianity was little more than a potent symbol, a rallying cry to bless the more secular urges of powerful Europeans."[79] Actually, the Crusades were complex events, with a deep religious motivation, as a basic reading of participants like William of Tyre, or of respected modern historians like Steven Runciman or Christopher Tyerman, abundantly demonstrates.[80]

The British author Karen Armstrong, a regular apologist for Islam, goes even further along the path blazed by jihadi ideologues:

> Ever since the Crusades, the people of Western Christendom developed a stereotypical and distorted vision of Islam, which they regarded as the enemy of decent civilization. . . . It was, for example, during the Crusades, when it was Christians who had instigated a series of brutal holy wars against the Muslim world, that Islam was described by the learned scholar-monks of Europe as an inherently violent and intolerant faith, which had only been able to establish itself by the sword. The myth of the supposed fanatical intolerance of Islam has become one of the received ideas of the West.[81]

Elsewhere, Armstrong claimed that "Islam was everything that the West thought it was not, and it was at the time of the Crusades that the idea that Islam was essentially a violent religion took hold in the West . . . Europe was projecting anxiety about its own behaviour onto Islam, and it did the same thing too with the Jewish people."[82]

This is worse than bad history and psychoanalysis. It is history *à la carte* with a transparent political aim. In fact, the Crusades were a (delayed) reaction to protracted Muslim aggression justified by religion and implied in the very term *jihad*. Considering the religious background of the Arab conquests of North Africa, the Middle East, and Iberia, almost half a millennium before the First Crusade, one may wonder if Armstrong can distinguish between cause and effect—or wants to. Indeed, ever since the period of the first Umayyad emir of Al-Andalus, Abd-ar-Rahman I (756–788) Arab writers have praised his virtues as a *mujahid*, a holy warrior of Islam defeating the infidel.[83] Arab attacks against Constantinople or raids into central France during the first century of Islam were motivated as much by religious zeal as by the desire for booty—just as the Crusades were, a few centuries later. These are all simple historical facts and say nothing about the morality of 21st-century Muslims and Christians—except that for revisionists anachronism is a favored tool. To observe that Islam had periods of religious zeal and expansion promoted by war, just as Christianity did later, is not good enough. For those who see the West as today's aggressor, they need to find the roots of that behavior in history, and if the facts do not fit, too bad for the facts.

Likewise for the ubiquitous claim that Islam is a "religion of peace." This idea is absurd on its face. To begin with, each of the three Abrahamic religions includes violent passages in its holy book—hence none is essentially "peaceful," as Islam's apologists claim for it. Furthermore, the history of Islam itself proves the fallacious nature of the claim. Indeed, even a cursory study of Islamic expansion in the Middle East, Europe, and North Africa clearly demonstrates that Islamization followed the Arab or Ottoman armies and administrations. Conversely, where those armies did not or could not reach, such as Southeast Asia and parts of sub-Saharan Africa, Islam was propagated by missionaries, and became more tolerant or syncretic and to some extent remains so today. All these known facts suggest that, at the very least, Islam is no more a "religion of peace" than Christianity or Judaism. The fact that Muslim apologists consistently bring up historic cases of Christianity's use of violence to expand, such as the Crusades, only makes the point that these were historic cases, the most recent having occurred centuries ago. By contrast, the Nuristanis of northeastern Afghanistan were forcibly converted to Islam only in 1896.

Not only have Muslims and Islam been victimized by the West since the Crusades, they were in fact punished for their tolerance and cultural superiority—or so we are told. The history of Islamic Iberia is manipulated to support a present-day political grievance. In this view, Islam has been a model of inter-religious tolerance, in Spain and in the Ottoman Empire, among other places. The implication is that Europeans should be at least as accommodating of minorities as Islam allegedly was.

The old image of *convergencia,* the harmonious coexistence of Islam, Christianity, and Judaism in Islamic Iberia, has its roots in Romanticism, but it is revived today for specific political purposes. That requires redrawing history with a very broad brush indeed, and there are a lot of revisionist Western academics prepared to do so, María Rosa Menocal's *The Ornament of the World* (2003) being only one notable example.

To begin with, if allowing Christians and Jews to practice their religion under very restrictive conditions, as second-class subjects—*dhimmis*—passes for tolerance, then Islam was tolerant. So tolerant, in fact, that in a few centuries what used to be an overwhelming majority of Christians in Iberia became a minority. More recently, the Jewish population of the Arab countries has shrunk from hundreds of thousands to, literally, hundreds. The very existence of synagogues and churches is still banned in places like Saudi Arabia, and churches are still being burned by Muslims in Indonesia. One may also mention that during the first century of Islam, conversions were discouraged for economic reasons: *Dhimmis* paid taxes essential to the empire's coffers.

The key argument made in support of the supposed Islamic tolerance in Iberia is the cultural flourishing of the area (ironically, more obvious after the collapse of the Córdoba Caliphate in 1031). This is again history *à la carte.*[84] As a recent and very competent Spanish Islamic expert, Serafín Fanjul García, has pointed out, the myth of Al-Andalus as a heaven of intellectual and cultural "multiculturalism" *avant la lettre* is just that—a myth.[85]

Furthermore, it greatly exaggerates the medieval Muslim contribution to Western culture. To begin with, most of that contribution, coming through Islamic Iberia, was in the form of ancient Greek—hence initially European—culture being brought back to Europe, and mostly by Jewish and Christian translators.

Another problem with the myth of Al-Andalus is that when major thinkers did appear in Islamic Iberia, their treatment by religious authorities suggests anything but tolerance. Ibn Roshd (commonly known as Averrhoes, 1149–1206), a great interpreter of Aristotle, was condemned for heresy and forced to recant. His Jewish contemporary and fellow Córdoban, Moses Maimonides (1135–1204), was forced to convert (temporarily); he ultimately fled. And, unmentioned by apologists of medieval Islam in Al-Andalus, the Almohad fundamentalists in the 12th century offered the Jews a choice between conversion, exile, and death, and their Almoravid predecessors were no more tolerant.[86]

Notwithstanding the claims by Muslim apologists and secular revisionists in Europe, Islamic culture had a very limited impact on the continent's culture, and Islam *as a religion* had even less. Yes, perhaps Spanish Moorish poetry had some influence on the Provençal troubadours of the 12th and 13th centuries; and yes, some classical Greek texts were translated into Latin in Islamic Spain (usually by Jewish or Mozarabic scholars). But historically speaking Europe's relationship with Islam has been one of conflict far more than of influence. Nor, warfare aside, has Europe's contact with the world of Islam been close, if one considers the colonial ventures of France in North Africa and England in the Middle East as separate and qualitatively distinct forms of contact. One may even make the case that, for most Europeans between the 15th and 18th centuries, the most likely contact with Islam was as slaves in Algiers, Tunis, or Tripoli.

In summary, the much-trumpeted Muslim role in transmitting the Graeco-Roman cultural legacy to "Europe" was almost totally the work of Christian and Jewish intellectuals, oppressed albeit tolerated by Muslims, rather than some inherent Islamic respect for Aristotle or Plato. And, to justify the glorifying of Islam's cultural impact on Europe for contemporary political purposes, one has to redefine medieval Europe by reducing it to the Western part. Hence Byzantium (Constantinople), the successor of the Greek and Roman civilization, somewhat conveniently disappears from such anachronistic comparisons.

It is true that in Western Europe from about the sixth to the 11th century, culture, in the sense of literacy, was a monopoly of the clergy, and even they seldom knew Greek (hence the origin of the phrase, "It's Greek to me"). Meanwhile, in Córdoba Jews and Muslims and in Baghdad Muslim Persian intellectuals adopted and occasionally improved on classical Greek, Roman, and Persian, as well as Indian and occasionally Chinese, scientific and technological accomplishments (the concept of zero and the "Arabic" numerals were originally Indian). On the other hand, Constantinople never had any reason to feel "inferior" to the Islamic world. Literacy was widespread, emperors wrote important books on history and diplomacy, women occupied the throne, and as early as the 830s the Emperor Theophilos impressed Arab ambassadors with his court's mechanical gadgets and its luxury.

Nonetheless, virtually all Arabs today claim that theirs was the superior civilization in the past and blame Western "imperialism" and colonialism for ending that period of glory. The differences today are on how to recover that alleged superiority, with the Islamists pretending that a return to "pure" Islam, as they define it, is the only way, while others advocate the importation, or imitation, of Western ways to reach the same goal.

As to what we mean by Arab or "Islamic" civilization, the answer starts with the primitive tribes of Arabia, which were the main military force behind the expansion of Islam during its first century. But they were just that: primitive tribes, certainly when compared to the Persian Sassanid Empire they destroyed or, more importantly for the topic at hand, the Byzantine Empire they reduced by half. On the other hand, once permanent contact was established with Christian areas of the Middle East and North Africa that once belonged to Byzantium, including Damascus, Antioch, Alexandria, and Carthage, the Arabs learned fast and well—but at the cost of becoming less and less "Arab." Same story in the Iberian peninsula, where the initial conquerors of 711 were not even Arabs for the most part but Berbers from North Africa, recently and incompletely Islamized and treated as inferior. It was only after the establishment of a refugee Umayyad from Damascus in Córdoba that the city became a beacon of high culture—in very large part, as mentioned earlier, due to the large Jewish community.

By the 13th century, when the West was producing Chartres, Giotto, and Dante, Islam produced the profoundly reactionary Ahmad bin Taymiyya, the theological and philosophical forerunner of Wahhabism and Al-Qaeda. By then, in Al-Andalus, two successive waves of Moroccan Islamic fundamentalism, the Almoravids and Almohads, had already managed to destroy the local high culture—and Islam's military power in Iberia with it. Much more than in the West, there were always powerful forces within Islam opposing high culture and intellectual debate. Islam's greatest philosopher, the Córdoban Ibn Roshd (Averrhoes), died in disgrace and under a ban in Morocco—

while little more than a century later Aquinas, whom he heavily influenced, was canonized.

One reaches a few conclusions from all this. First, that the claim popularized in the media that Islam was, centuries ago, the bearer of a culture superior to Europe's is simply and factually false. The point here is not to deny Islam's past cultural contributions but to note a trend in present-day analysis, a trend toward the politically correct and politicized. Ultimately, Islam is not unknown or misunderstood, but its history is being manipulated and indeed falsified—not by the heirs of the Crusaders, but by its own followers and apologists.

ISLAM AND WESTERN CULTURE: THE PRESENT

After successfully keeping any mention of Christianity out of the preamble of his ill-fated EU Constitution, Valéry Giscard d'Estaing became quite vocal in opposing Turkey's application for EU membership because . . . Turkey's Islamic roots made it non-European—an obvious admission that Christian roots are at least part of what makes a European a European. It is precisely these sorts of intellectual contradictions and opportunistic confusions that make Europe, as a cultural entity, vulnerable when faced with an increasingly militant and revivalist Islam. Simply put, when one has trouble defining one's own identity, it is hard to defend it against those who assault it—and that is precisely where Europe finds itself: beginning to fight something with . . . nothing much.

The main reason for this situation is Europe's unique position among the world's major cultures, in that instead of claiming and being proud of its history—which it has so many reasons to be—it has for decades seen itself as historically guilty. It has abased itself and decided—or at least its elites decided—that

European culture, its roots, its values cannot and should not be defended. Instead those elites have pumped huge amounts of taxpayers' money and rivers of rhetorical nonsense into a vacuous "human-rights" ideology, based on limitless tolerance for the intolerant. As usual, it all started in France, but it has spread everywhere.

This process began decades ago, with the massive influx of Third World, mostly Muslim immigrants. The very idea that obligations and rights go hand in hand was not applied to them—they, after all, came from the oppressed Third World, and thus had special "historic entitlements" to the riches of the First World. That was taken for granted by elites from Paris to Berlin to London to Brussels to Amsterdam, all "guilty" for their colonial past. Is has since been picked up by the new elites in places like Martinique and Guadeloupe, now perfectly equal parts of France, but whose elites opposed a visit from then Interior Minister Nicolas Sarkozy because they did not like his party's courageous vote for a reassessment of the politically correct condemnation of everything France did in its former colonies. Needless to say, those elites, including the wealthy left-wing poet Aimé Césaire, have no problem with the taxpayers of Corrèze, Ile de France, or Normandy subsidizing them and their ideas. That, one assumes, is somehow their "right."

Not surprisingly, Muslims have taken advantage of this self-imposed weakness. A brief overview of Muslim efforts to limit Europeans' freedom of expression and pose challenges to European values is illuminating. It all started in a dramatic fashion with the Rushdie affair, when Iran's Ayatollah Ruhollah Khomeini stated on Radio Tehran, on February 14, 1989, that: "I inform proud Muslims all over the world that the author of *The Satanic Verses*, which is inclined against Islam, the Prophet and the Quran, and everybody connected knowingly with the book's publication, is hereby condemned to death. I challenge all Muslims to execute these persons wherever they may be found."

By then, Rushdie's book had already been banned in Saudi Arabia, South Africa, India, Indonesia, and Pakistan. Before the ban, Islamic fundamentalists had assailed the United States' Cultural Institute in Pakistan. Even Pakistan's government, led by the late Benazir Bhutto (who in the summer of 1989 was President George H. W. Bush's guest at the White House), stated that blasphemy was an offence against the state. The highest-ranking Islamic official in India, Syed Abdullah Bukhari, supported the *fatwa* in a sermon, and something called "the Lebanese Revolutionary Front of Justice" agreed, as did the Islamic World Conference, which judged Rushdie to be "blasphemous" and a "heretic."

The reaction in the non-Muslim world was confused and, ultimately, accommodating. Most Japanese publishers refused to produce the book, and a person who translated it was murdered—as was a Belgian Muslim leader who did not support Khomeini's call. In Italy, on the other hand, the Mondadori publishing house did come out with an Italian version of the book—and its Padua bookstore was burnt down, and stores in Venice, Trieste, Verona, and Bolzano were attacked.

France's government, and most of its elites, protested and condemned Iran's call to murder, and EU member states recalled their ambassadors from Tehran—but sent them back after a while.

The most striking alarm signal, ignored at the time, was in Britain, where Muslim immigrants in Bradford publicly burned the book amidst riots. Among those involved was Yusuf Islam—formerly a pop idol known as Cat Stevens.

The general problem of Islam's incompatibility with the values of postmodern Europe has thus been apparent for two decades, but it has finally been made visible even to some members of the elites by more recent developments. At the time, the Rushdie affair was viewed as an aberration. It has since become a pattern, with the Houellebecq trial and the Redeker and Finkielkraut affairs in France, the Fallaci trial in Italy, and the diplomatic and political crisis over the cartoons in *Jyllands-Posten* in Denmark.

Michel Houellebecq, a highly regarded French novelist, was sued, unsuccessfully, for saying that Islam is "stupid," although he denied being hostile to Muslims.

In September 2006 a philosophy professor at a French provincial high school, Robert Redeker, published an article in *Le Figaro*, "Faced with Islamist intimidations, what should the Free World do?" in which he described the Prophet Muhammad as a "pitiless warlord, killer of Jews and polygamist." Following the publication, Redeker received so many death threats that he had to give up his job and live under police protection. One of the authors of the threats posted on the Internet was arrested in Morocco, while on his way to fight in Iraq.[87]

Alain Finkielkraut is one of France's "new philosophers," most of them Jewish and recovered leftists of the 1968 generation. In an interview in Israel, following the 2005 riots in the French suburbs, he observed, "When an Arab torches a school, it's rebellion. When a white guy does it, it's fascism. I'm 'color blind.' Evil is evil, no matter what color it is. And this evil, for the Jew that I am, is completely intolerable."[88] For that, he was accused of "racism" and sued by the MRAP (Movement against Racism and for Friendship among Peoples), an NGO close to the Socialist Party. Although he apologized for his initial remarks, he remains a critic of Islamism and its opposition to integration:

"Why have parts of the Muslim-Arab world declared war on the West? . . . They, and those who justify them, say that it derives from the colonial breakdown. Okay, but one mustn't forget that the integration of the Arab workers in France during the time of colonial rule was much easier. In other words, this is belated hatred. Retrospective hatred . . . We are witness to an Islamic radicalization that must be explained in its entirety before we get to the French case, to a culture that, instead of dealing with its problems, searches for an external guilty party. It's easier to find an external guilty party. It's tempting to tell yourself that in France you're neglected, and to say, 'Gimme, gimme.' It hasn't worked like that for anyone. It can't work."[89]

Oriana Fallaci (1929–2006) was, like Finkielkraut, a former leftist who, following 9/11, turned against Islam—with particular virulence in her best-selling books *The Strength of Reason* and *The Rage and the Pride*. Both as a leftist who initially supported and interviewed Khomeini, and as an avid defender of European values at the end of her life, she was always something of a provocateur. Indeed, even Finkielkraut and Bernard-Henri Lévy, who shared her views on many issues, thought she went too far in her diatribes against all Muslims.[90] In her native Italy she was both decorated and sued. The lawsuit, for "blasphemy," was brought by Adel Smith, a convert and head of the Italian Muslim Union. Smith also called for Fallaci's murder.

In Switzerland, the Islamic Center and the Somali Association of Geneva and SOS Racisme of Lausanne sued her for the supposedly racist content of *The Rage and the Pride*, and in November 2002 they even found a judge to issue an arrest warrant against her and requested the Italian government to either try her or extradite her—a request promptly denied in the name of freedom of expression.

The excessive sensitivity to even potential negative Muslim reactions reached quasi-comical levels when, in September 2006,

Kirsten Harms, artistic director of the renowned Deutsche Oper in Berlin, cancelled several performances of Mozart's opera *Idomeneo*. The reason, according to the Berlin police, was that the new production featured the severed heads of Muhammad, Jesus, and Buddha, and could have been the target of a violent Muslim attack.[91]

Most German media and politicians criticized Harms's decision—but the fear of attack was not groundless. There were the Rushdie affair and the Fortuyn and van Gogh murders. Earlier in 2006, Muslim extremists had planned to blow up the Basilica of San Petronio in Bologna, Italy, because a fresco there, painted by Giovanni da Modena (active 1409– 1456), represented Muhammad in Hell—as described by Dante in the *Divine Comedy*.[92] However, far more important than any rational fear was the effect of self-censoring, politically correct European opinion, which allows radical Islamists to raise such "issues." The head of Germany's Islamic Council, Ali Kizilkaya, welcomed the Deutsche Oper's decision, saying it was taking account of "Muslim sensitivities."[93] However, Kenan Kolat, a leader of Germany's Turkish community, told the online *Netzeitung* newspaper, "I would recommend Muslims learn to accept certain things. . . . Art must remain free."[94] This incident is thus a clear example of how political correctness actually encourages radicals and undercuts moderate Muslims.

The common link among the incidents described above, involving at least five European countries over almost two decades, is the open conflict between Muslim beliefs and European beliefs. The most important fact is that these are conflicts that pit fundamental European beliefs and customs against general (not just radical or Salafi) Muslim beliefs. Equally important, these cultural conflicts, because that is what they ultimately are, raise the key question of how far some Europeans are able, willing, and likely to go in support of multiculturalism and "tolerance." Finally, in many of these cases. Muslims attacking freedom of expression in Europe found, at least temporarily, support in European courts—the same courts that have long protected Abu Qatada, Mullah Krekar, and many other promoters or practitioners of jihad.

Spain offers perhaps the best current example of cultural confusion. Prime Minister José Luis Zapatero is a fervent adherent of an ill-defined "Alliance of Civilizations" with Islam—a passion shared by only one other European head of government, Turkey's Islamist Prime Minister Recep Tayyip Erdogan. Among other things, that means that Madrid has decided, for the first time ever, to extend public subsidies to Islamic organizations and institutions. Moreover, Zapatero's PSOE (Socialist Workers' Party) government is engaged in the most strident clash with the Catholic Church since the Civil War. The PSOE is seeking to establish the Left's interpretation of the Civil War—for instance, in its legislation about "historical memory" (*Ley de Memoria Histórica*). In this atmosphere of historical revisionism, revisionism of all kinds finds a friendly environment—and the Islamists were prompt in taking advantage.

As mentioned earlier, Islamists have been attempting to gain equal rights with Catholics to the Cathedral of Córdoba. In February 2006 Mansur Abdussalam Escudero of the *Junta Islámica* proposed to transform the cathedral into an "ecumenical temple" where faithful of the Christian, Muslim, and other religions "could pray together and strengthen spiritual and affective ties . . . to bury past confrontations." He later made this proposal to Pope Benedict XVI himself.[95] The Bishop of Córdoba, Juan José Asenjo, rejected the request on the grounds that it would create confusion among the faithful and lead to religious indifference. He also pointed out that before being transformed into the Grand Mosque of the Umayyads in the eighth century, the building was the Visigothic Church of San Vicente, and that Christians are not permitted to pray in a mosque anywhere in the world, including the Hagia Sophia in Istanbul (even though it was originally a church, and it is now a museum and not a working mosque). The *Junta Islámica* has laid similar claims to the Catedral de Santa María de Ciudadella in Menorca, built after the 1287 *reconquista* of the island on top of the Muslim Medina Menurka.[96]

Not surprisingly, conservative opinion in Spain interpreted the Muslim demands regarding Córdoba as provocations,[97] and the political polarization that began after March 11, 2004, is now being slowly translated into religious cleavages and, most importantly, into issues of Spanish cultural identity.[98]

The *Junta Islámica* and Escudero are viewed by some as "moderate," but that is relative. For Escudero the cathedral was "closed to light and decorated according to the taste of inquisitors," and the bishop who refused Muslims the "right" to pray inside is "fortified in titles obtained by the right of conquest."[99]

As quoted earlier, in Chapter 3, the Muslims pushing this agenda are being somewhat careful in their wording. "In no way is this request about reclaiming our rights—far less any kind of reconquest," Isabel Romero, a member of the Islamic Council of Spain, told a local newspaper. "Instead, we want to give our support to the universal character of this building."[100] Escudero tried again in December 2006, claiming that "What we wanted was not to take over that holy place, but to create in it, together with you and other faiths, an ecumenical space unique in the world which would have been of great significance in bringing peace to humanity." Escudero complained that security guards often stop Muslim worshipers from praying in the former mosque—as they should, since that is against

Catholic rules—and went further, claiming that "There are re-actionary elements within the Catholic Church, and when they hear about the construction of a mosque, or Muslim teachings in state schools, or about veils, they see it as a sign we are growing and they oppose it."[101] This language is clearly intend-ed to please the openly anti-Catholic Socialists in power in both Madrid and Córdoba.

On the one hand, if this is not "reclaiming the rights" of Muslims, it would have been helpful if the largest mosque in present-day Spain had not been built in Granada, the loca-tion of the last Islamic state in the peninsula. Nor is it clear why the Córdoba Cathedral has a "universal character" but the thousands of churches transformed into mosques, from Iran to Morocco to Turkey, do not. What makes Córdoba differ-ent from the Hagia Sophia in Istanbul, for a thousand years Christendom's largest church?

The Muslims' request, while rejected by the Vatican, was supported by the Socialist mayor of Córdoba, and the Granada project was also supported by the Socialist mayor there, against local opposition.

Not to be outdone by the *Junta*, the FEERI (of which Escudero is also president) asked for "a dialogue with the Church for the recuperation of the Muslim patrimony" of the "Mezquita [mosque] de Córdoba," but went further, demanding the "recu-peration of Muslim patrimony in Spanish territory that belongs to the Vatican" in exchange for the "Catholic patrimony which could be in Muslim hands in Spain." Revealingly, FEERI spokes-man Javier Isla underlined that the proposal is "in line with the demand of the trade unions to the Spanish Government for the devolution of trade union patrimony taken over by Francoism and that it desires to limit the petition to Spanish territory only."[102]

As for the Córdoba Cathedral, for the time being the FEERI demanded that a room inside be prepared for Muslim prayers, with a view toward transforming the building in the future into a "common patrimony" of two, even three ("the Jews also had a synagogue there") religions. And, to look moderate, the FEERI said it "sincerely advocates an inter-religious dialogue in a Spanish society where we have a percentage of Muslims, a Catholic majority and others who are secular, and we do not want to bring here the problems that exist today in other places, like Morocco or Saudi Arabia."[103]

The trouble is that those problems have already come to Spain. The FEERI is controlled by a group of Spanish converts and pro-Moroccan and Saudi imams (from the Saudi-funded mosques of Madrid and Fuengirola), and it reflects views coming from those countries.[104] Thus a Saudi daily on the descendants of the Moriscos (Muslims living in Spain after the *reconquista*):

> After more than five centuries, Muslims of Al-Andalus (now Spain) still mark every year in anguish the mass exodus of their ancestors [driven] by Spanish authorities to North Africa. . . . Today, up to four million grandsons of the Moriscos are living in North African countries like Morocco, Algeria and Tunisia.[105]

Going further—and again seeking to take advantage of the Western fashion of apologizing for historical events, in 2002 Bin Azouz Hakim, a Moroccan specialist in the history of the Moriscos, "sent a message, inked by an elite of Moriscos, to Spanish King Juan Carlos asking for a public apology to the descendants [of Moriscos]." When no answer came,

> [Hakim] sent another message to the king, asking him to explain why he rejected his call while he apologized to the Jews in a visit to Israel in 1992 for the mass exodus from Al-Andalus—and provided his own answer: "I think because we don't have a powerful lobby like the Jews, who make the best

use of the past to get financial gains. . . . But the Muslims only
want a moral compensation. . . . It is an inalienable right of
the Moriscos. It makes no sense that the Spanish king had
apologized to the Jews of what is now Israel, who have nothing
to do with the Sephardim (the Jews of Al-Andalus), while he is
reluctant to say sorry to the Moriscos' descendants."[106]

Historically, all of this is highly dubious. As Serafín Fanjul,
professor of Islamic Studies in Madrid, has pointed out, both in
Muslim Al-Andalus and in the Maghreb there was, and in the
latter still is, an "inexhaustible hotbed of invented lineages because it was fashionable and gained social status—all [wanted]
to be from the East and, even better, Quraish (Banu Quraish
is Mohammed's Mecca tribe)." Now "all want to be Andalus."[107]
This is not only because of what Fanjul calls the "lachrymose"
motivation, and Bin Azouz Hakim calls "moral compensation."
There is also an opportunistic reason: There are demands for
Spanish citizenship—and thus free entry to Spain—for Morisco
descendants.

The recent and growing Islamic, or at least Arab, nostalgia
for Al-Andalus is manifested by the concentration of efforts
around the cities that were the three major centers of Islamic
Spain: Córdoba, Seville, and Granada.[108] Granada has had a
very large and influential population of Spanish converts to
Islam since the 1960s. As for Córdoba, besides the battle over
the cathedral, a half-size replica of the former Great Mosque
is planned with funding from the governments of the United
Arab Emirates, Saudi Arabia, and Kuwait, and from Muslim organizations in Morocco and Egypt.

The other manifestation, however, is more immediately
threatening: Islamist terrorism. As *Junta Islámica*'s Abdelkarim
Carrasco himself complained, the existing "romantic and symbolic" idea of Granada is not just unrealistic ("Is like we would

like to reproduce the Roman Empire"), but it could also bring cells of Islamists to the city. Indeed, the suicidal terrorists of Leganés, who prior to the bombings had hidden in the Granada region, left behind a tape full of revisionist nostalgia, complaining about "the Spanish crusade against Muslims and the expulsion from Al-Andalus and tribunals of the Inquisition."[109] And, of course, bin Laden has consistently mentioned Al-Andalus as a land to be recovered for Islam—just like Israel.[110]

Centuries ago, the Arab historian Ibn Idari al-Marrakushi, in his *History of the Kings of al-Andalus and Morocco* (c. 1306), was already writing about the Muslim hope of reconquest (*is-tirya*) of all the territories of Al-Andalus lost after the battle of Las Navas de Tolosa (1212), which broke the back of Muslim power in Spain.[111] In our own time, Muslims in Spain have talked about "The tragedy of Al-Andalus, the genocide of Muslims and their expulsion from Spain, the natural mother country of them all, to be judged by God alone; and to the servant, to accept the Divine Decree and be thankful."[112] One may note, again, the manipulation of present-day "human-rights" language—"genocide" in the 15th century?

For jihadis, however, the issue of Al-Andalus is of immediate importance. On the tape left behind by the Leganés suicides, they claimed that "we will continue our jihad until martyrdom in the land of Tariq bin Ziyad."[113] Also, the 14 suspected Pakistani terrorists arrested in Barcelona on January 18, 2008, were associated with the Tariq bin Ziyad *Tablighi* mosque.[114]

By itself, each such episode may be and has been seen as unique. The problem is that these episodes have accumulated in direct relationship with the numbers of Muslims in Europe, the growing radicalization of Islam everywhere, and, the other side of the coin, Europe's headlong movement into postmodern cultural customs—including secularism, acceptance of homosexuality, the weakening of family (including rising rates of illegitimacy), radical feminism, and rampant individualism—all perceived by Muslims, including moderates, as both threatening and alien, and by most Europeans as natural and "progressive."

When Sayyid Qutb, the Karl Marx of contemporary Salafism, visited Middle America in the late 1940s, he was upset and shocked by the "immorality" he saw—and Greeley, Colorado, in 1949 was a place present-day "progressives" would consider conservative, restraining, and flat-out reactionary. Now imagine a newly arrived Muslim bride from Pakistan's Northwest Frontier Province meeting her British-born husband in today's Manchester or Leeds—not to mention a Moroccan bride from the Rif meeting Dutch culture in Amsterdam (say, the Neuwe Kerk neighborhood, Europe's pornography capital). Revulsion, repulsion, and indeed fear would hardly describe their feelings, and separation, isolation, and, ultimately, hatred would almost naturally result—and be transmitted to the children.

Thus, tolerance aside, present European and Islamic—not just Islamist—values are on a collision course. This is without even mentioning the previously examined cultural and legal provocations the customs of certain Muslim groups—whether truly Islamic or not—present to Europeans: polygamy, arranged and under-age marriages, honor killings, female genital mutilation.

It is quite fashionable, and widespread along the Western political spectrum, to deny that there is a "clash of civilizations" between Islam and the West, as described by Harvard scholar Samuel Huntington. In theory, one can always argue about this. One may bring up real or not so real examples of harmonious coexistence among Islam, Christianity, and Judaism, whether in Umayyad Córdoba and the Ottoman Empire or in

Tito's Bosnia, and there are many Westerners, from conservatives like President Bush to European Socialists, who engage in strenuous efforts to believe this.

As usual, reality has a way of interfering with the most well-intended of theories. When bin Laden and al-Zawahiri consistently proclaim war against the West and, most importantly, behave as if they are at war, it becomes very difficult, intellectually or practically, to persist in denying that a war with Islamism is going on. That is clearly the most important problem confronting multiculturalists in the West, and even more so when Muslim masses and many of their leaders, in the Muslim world as well as in the West, not only refuse to declare the Islamists out of bounds but, at least occasionally, act in ways that are in open and direct conflict with Western values. When in Britain, or elsewhere in Europe, Muslims engage in violent demonstrations against Rushdie's *Satanic Verses* or the Danish cartoons, or practice FGM, polygamy, anti-Semitism, or gay bashing, or are unwilling to condemn suicide terrorism, the very idea of peaceful coexistence within the boundaries of Western law is less than tenable.

The problem, then, is not what one may think about Huntington's theories but, as this author has discovered repeatedly during his travels to Europe and elsewhere, one of true and growing cultural disconnect. Whether one calls this reality a "conflict of civilizations" or not, there is a deadly conflict between Islamists, whose influence is growing everywhere, and the West. One side in that conflict is quite open about it—bin Laden's—and to have a war one side is enough.

The United States is in a different position from Europe on this issue, inasmuch as among Americans there is a wide consensus that there is indeed a war going on. Hence in both policy impact and motivations the debate here is different from that in Europe; even if, over the last few years, opposition to President Bush's specific policies on Iraq (though less so Afghanistan) was fierce, at issue were the means and method of fighting the war, not its existence. By contrast, until recently in a few countries, and still in most, European elite as well as popular opinion has rejected the reality of war with Islamism and has behaved accordingly—with obvious consequences in the political, military, and legal realms.

However, one has to notice that European perceptions, and behavior, are dynamic, both between and within countries. Denmark and the Netherlands are not Sweden, Belgium, or the UK, just as the Netherlands today is different from the Netherlands prior to the assassinations of Fortuyn and van Gogh, and Denmark today is different from the Denmark prior to the cartoon controversy. On the other hand, even such highly traumatic events seem to have less of an impact on other countries. One also has to note that there is an increasingly clear gap between popular and elite perceptions of the Islamist threat, indeed of Islam itself as a threat, made evident by the relative electoral success of anti-immigration (i.e., anti-Muslim-immigration) political parties and personalities.

In France especially, but in some other countries as well, the cultural and intellectual debates go beyond what Americans would call "culture wars"—they are openly political and have limits imposed by law. A philosopher who has strong opinions about the racial, ethnic, or religious components of the riots of 2005, a comic making fun of Jews, an author writing a textbook that discusses slavery or colonial history—all may run up against the law.

There is a certain confusion when intellectuals of the Left, even when full of good intentions and aware of the Islamist problem, look for solutions. Caroline Fourest, essayist and editor of the journal *ProChoix*, former minister Corinne Lepage, and Pierre Cassen of *les Amis de Respublica*, all three of them progressives, were a case in point, when they published this *cri de cœur*:

> Citizens opposed at the same time to racism and fundamentalism, we raise a cry! Since September 11th, 2001, public debate seems to have lost all bearings. While a populist and racist Right surfs on the fear of the Other and of Islam (by mixing together Arabs with Muslims, Muslims with fundamentalists, and fundamentalists with terrorists), a certain Left has abdicated all critical spirit in the face of obscurantism, and treats as "Islamophobic" all those having the audacity to say no to reactionary political Islam. Even when this resistance is made in the name of secularism, the equality between men and women, because of the rejection of incitement to sexist, homophobic or anti-Semitic hatred. One has to rapidly get out of this double trap. And say again, loudly and strongly, that we want to combat at the same time racism and fundamentalism, all racisms (anti-Arab as much as anti-Jewish, as anti-woman or anti-homosexual), and all fundamentalisms (of all religions).[115]

First, the authors cannot refrain from calling the populist Right "racist," as if Muslims were a "race" and fear of Islam were somehow irrational. They are guilty of what they accuse the Right of—amalgamation of different and unrelated issues. Second, they correctly point out the Left's abdication of its own principles and of critical spirit. But then they themselves claim to oppose "all fundamentalisms (of all religions)," obviously in the name of the same political correctness they otherwise reject. Indeed, what religious fundamentalisms other than Islamic are there in today's Europe? Are there Lutheran, Anglican, Catholic, Jewish fundamentalisms?

In an essay in the Italian Catholic journal *Studium*, "The Islamic Question" (April 2006), Jesuits Vincenzo Cappelletti and

Francesco Paolo Casavola offer a realistic analysis of the problem of Islam, and especially of its European followers, when confronted with modernity—or, perhaps better put, with the postmodern culture of Europe:

> The Islamization of the West is neither a phantasm nor merely something feared: it is an intention and a fact that emerges from an objective examination of the evidence. Moderate Islam, properly so called, does not exist because there is no institutional and moderate form of Islamic theology. There are moderate Muslims, and some of them see things with a clear and long-term perspective. But Islam itself, or rather the institutional religious culture of the Muslims, has reacted in its encounter with modernity by entrenching itself in fundamentalist positions. . . . There is, therefore, an objective convergence between the trend in Islamic theology and the ideology of the terrorists. . . . This is why it would not only be prudent, as Cardinal Giacomo Biffi has suggested, to discourage Islamic immigration in Europe, it would be masochistic to encourage it without demanding reciprocation in terms of integration. Islam is not compatible with liberal democracies. . . . Unfortunately, open and liberal society becomes paralyzed when it encounters a closed and incompatible civilization. . . . in Islam, there is no foundation for tolerance in the broad sense that characterizes our secular societies.[116]

Democracy, Tolerance, and Debate

Cardinal Biffi touched a neuralgic point, often avoided or obscured. Islam, whether in its Salafi, Sufi, or "mainstream" Sunni or Shia incarnations, does not and cannot distinguish between faith, law, and politics. The very idea of separation of "Church" and State is profoundly alien to Muslims. But how about Turkey? one may ask. The answer is found in the background of Mustafa Kemal Atatürk himself, the founder of the Turkish Republic. Atatürk was not just a secularist, modernizer, and Westernizer, but also a Freemason and, especially, a nationalist. For that reason he, and his followers ever since, are seen by other Muslims, and with some reason, as less than "good Muslims." To a large extent, Republican Turkey's secular elites have pursued a policy based on the implicit assumption that some Islamic beliefs and practices have to be controlled, if not eliminated, if their modernizing and Westernizing goals are to be reached. It is important to note that the Salafis make precisely the same point—hence the special place Atatürk has in their list of eternal enemies of Islam.

As we have seen, Islam, in principle if not always in practice, is hostile to the very idea of nationalism and indeed of nation, as defined in the West. If the Western concept of nation is that of a distinct human community based on common traditions, history, ethnicity, and language, in Islam the absolute allegiance of the believers is to the *ummah*, the universal community of the faithful, not to their country, its government, or its local historical traditions. Obviously, considering the reality of intra-Muslim conflicts almost from the beginnings of Islam, and of present conflicts among Muslim states, a case could be made that this principle is respected more in the breach than in the observance. However, in the peculiar situation of Muslims in the West, that principle is being reinvigorated and indeed is far more powerful than in the Muslim world itself. One need remark only two phenomena present among Muslim communities in Europe: the reluctance to condemn and act against Islamists (implicit feeling of solidarity masquerading as pretended victimhood), and, within the ranks of the latter, the close cooperation across ethnic lines (e.g., Algerians and Moroccans in Spain and France). It is important again to note that the Salafis make precisely the same point: All Muslims, indeed Islam itself, are under attack, and thus the solidarity of the *ummah* should be

strengthened and, in the future, instrumentalized via the revival of the (ideal and utopian) Caliphate.

Conservatives in the West may agree with Muslims that the
culture of modern Western nations is decadent and self-indulgent, but, especially in some European countries, that culture is
supported, democratically, by the majority. Ultimately, the key
issue is whether Muslims believe in, or are at least prepared to
live under, democratic rule as a minority.

For the Islamists democracy is itself anti-Islamic, because
it presumes that laws passed by people can take precedence
over the laws of God. It has become fashionable in the West to
call "racists" those who express doubts over Islam's compatibility with democracy. But that epithet is just that—an epithet,
not an argument. The reality is that, Turkey aside (most of the
time and with some caveats), there is not and never has been
a lasting democratic system in a Muslim-majority country.
There were, and are, freely elected governments, as in Pakistan,
Bangladesh, Malaysia, and Indonesia, but their democratic credentials remain dubious (Malaysia has never had a government
change, and in all the others the governments have been weak,
vulnerable, incompetent, or all of the above). Naturally, one
may hope that in the future things will be different, but the
historical record is simply not encouraging, especially when
even the few officially secular Arab countries (the former
People's Democratic Republic of Yemen, Somalia under Siad
Barre, Burguiba's Tunisia) have been far from democratic.

When that is the case in Muslim countries, why should one
expect Muslim minorities in the West to be strong defenders
of democracy, with its implication of majority rule? Unless,
of course, those minorities are integrated in ·the political
culture of the West—which is hardly the case today in
Western Europe.

Islamic tradition and experience is and always has been extremely leery of the idea of large numbers of Muslims leaving for *Dar al Harb*, "the abode of war," as opposed to the Muslim-controlled *Dar al Islam*, "the abode of Islam"—let alone the recent reality of *millions* of Muslims choosing to move to non-Muslim countries. Only a few times in the long history of Islam have large numbers of Muslims been forced to live under non-Muslim rule: in Spain at the end of the *reconquista*, between the 13th and 16th centuries, as Moriscos (Muslims under Christian rule), mostly in Valencia and Granada; and in the 20th century in the lost Balkan territories of the Ottomans (Bosnia, Albania), in Israel, and in India. In all those cases, the Muslims were forced by military defeat to live under non-Muslim rule. Thus, under usual interpretations of Islamic law, they were allowed a choice between (temporary) submission and emigration. In Spain, most chose, or were "encouraged" to choose, emigration, as was the case in parts of the Balkans after World War I, which is why so many Turks today trace their origins to Albania, Bosnia, Macedonia, or the Caucasus (Atatürk himself was born in Thessalonica, in what today is Greece's second-largest city, with zero Muslim population). When the British Raj came to an end in India, the eventual result was the creation of Pakistan. But all that was because Muslims were militarily defeated—which is not the case with what, for most Islamists and certainly all Salafis, is today's humiliating, indeed apostate habit of Muslims emigrating to *Dar al Harb* of their own free will.

Salafis aside, however, Islam has to deal with the reality of some 20 million technically Muslim people living in the West. It is in this context that an important debate has been taking place within "mainstream Islam," between the Swiss-based moderate Tariq Ramadan, strengthened by his genealogy (he is the grandson of Hassan al-Banna, the founder of the Muslim

Brotherhood), and the Qatar-based Islamist Yusuf al-Qaradawi, a Muslim Brother himself, and, as we have seen, very influential among Muslim leaders in Europe and European leftists. In fact the case of Tariq Ramadan is very important, since he is one of the most influential Muslim intellectuals in the West. As the American scholar Jonathan Laurence puts it, Ramadan "seeks the suspension of certain rules for all Muslims. . . . He wants thereby to preserve Islam's universality while allowing for the specificities of time and place."[117]

The main way to do that is by drawing a neat line—far too conveniently neat, one may add—between the universal principles of the Islamic faith and variations in culture:

> to define our Islamic identity by distinguishing it from the culture in which it is clothed in particular parts of the world. . . . Depending on where they live, Muslims of immigrant background will be by culture French, Belgian, British, Spanish or American. . . . More broadly, this process will give birth to what we have called a European or American Islamic culture.[118]

However, while religion and culture are indeed not coterminous, they are far more so in the case of Islam than in that of any other major religion. By nature, considering its direct and indeed revealed legal, moral, and political aspects, Islam is to a decisive extent a social and legal system—and separation of its various aspects is impossible in practice. This reality explains the criticism of Ramadan by orthodox Islamic scholars, not to mention the Salafis, who simply consider him an apostate.

The Anglo-Dutch scholar Ian Buruma notes: "Tariq Ramadan, Muslim, scholar, activist, Swiss citizen, resident of Britain, active on several continents, is a hard man to pin down. People call him 'slippery,' 'double-faced,' 'dangerous,' but also 'brilliant,' a 'bridge-builder,' a 'Muslim Martin Luther'."[119]

Indeed, precisely because of the theological and practical difficulties implicit in his reformist views, Ramadan is persistently accused of duplicity, of having a hidden agenda closer to the Muslim Brotherhood than he cares to admit.[120] On the other hand, precisely because he tries to understand the dilemmas facing second-generation Muslims in the West—like himself— and to solve them from an Islamic perspective, he has a huge following among educated Muslims in Europe.

The debate is between extremes—the Salafis, gaining ground among the alienated "Muslim" second-generation youth in Europe, and moderate, integrated Muslims with no voice and few ideologists, like Ramadan and Bassam Tibi.[121] Considering the growth of Islamist terrorism based in Europe, it appears that the former are winning hearts and minds everywhere.

One thing that makes Salafi recruitment in Europe easier is extraordinary Muslim resistance to unpleasant facts. The most spectacular case is the refusal of Muslims around the world to admit, even now—bin Laden's own public statements notwithstanding—that Arabs were the perpetrators of the 9/11 attacks.

Clearly, this is not a matter of lack of information, when 56 percent of British Muslims, presumably well informed in their homes in Leeds or London, deny an Arab role, whereas the often-illiterate Pakistanis and Nigerians do so by only 41 and 47 percent respectively. One can only conclude that, especially in the case of Muslims in the United Kingdom, the denial of the obvious is conscious—a form of "protecting" the image of Islam and, thus, of their own community.

One must add that 38 percent of young Muslims in the United States also reject the idea that Arabs had anything to do with 9/11.[122]

DID ARABS CARRY OUT 9/11 ATTACKS?

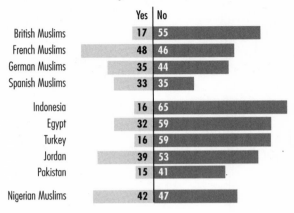

	Yes	No
British Muslims	17	55
French Muslims	48	46
German Muslims	35	44
Spanish Muslims	33	35
Indonesia	16	65
Egypt	32	59
Turkey	16	59
Jordan	39	53
Pakistan	15	41
Nigerian Muslims	42	47

Source: Pew, June 22, 2006.

"RACISM"

Europe today finds itself trapped in a posture of moral relativism that is undermining its liberal values. An unholy three-cornered alliance among Middle East dictators, radical imams based in Europe, and Europe's traditional left wing is enabling a politics of victimology. This politics drives a culture that resists integration and adaptation, and aggravates such debilitating social ills as high immigrant crime rates and entrenched unemployment.[123]

Nothing helps Islamists in their efforts to recruit Muslims in Europe more than the Left's efforts to describe Muslims as permanent victims—of something or another. A leading exemplar is the former mayor of London, Ken Livingstone, who said, with regard to the headscarf issue,

> "It is quite clear that the problems we have in Britain are not because Muslims wish to be separate...I think the entire debate has been totally lopsided as though Muslims were somehow

at fault for this. . . . That echoes very much the demonology of Nazi Germany when Hitler said it was the Jews' fault and the problems were brought upon themselves. There is a faint echo of that in a lot of the rubbish we have been seeing in the media recently."[124]

How far the Left will go, in the hope of stopping debate on the Islamist problem, by accusing those worried about it of "racism" is demonstrated by this pearl from A. Sivanandan, director of England's Institute of Race Relations. He even manages to include white immigrants among the victims of something called "xeno-racism":

"It is a racism that is not just directed at those with darker skins, from the former colonial territories, but at the newer categories of the displaced, the dispossessed and the uprooted, who are beating at western Europe's doors, the Europe that helped to displace them in the first place. It is a racism, that is, that cannot be color-coded, directed as it is at poor whites as well, and is therefore passed off as xenophobia, a 'natural' fear of strangers. But in the way it denigrates and reifies people before segregating and/or expelling them, it is a xenophobia that bears all the marks of the old racism. It is racism in substance, but 'xeno' in form. It is a racism that is meted out to impoverished strangers even if they are white. It is xeno-racism."[125]

Bassam Tibi has eloquently rejected loose accusations of racism.

The persistent attempt to divert the debate on Islam vs. Islamism by introducing abusively the label of "racism" is so pervasive that even prominent Muslim intellectuals fall victim to it—as Bassam Tibi has personally experienced: "Even the comparatively moderate Turkish organization DITIB says there are no Islamists, only Islam and Muslims—anything else is racism. That means that you can no longer criticize the religion. Accusing somebody of racism is a very effective weapon in Germany. Islamists know this: As soon as you accuse someone of demonizing Islam, then the European side backs down. I have also been accused of such nonsense, even though my family can trace its roots right back to Muhammad and I myself know the Koran by heart."[126]

Perhaps Tibi was referring to people like Soumaya Ghannoushi, a researcher at the School of Oriental and African Studies, University of London, and a frequent contributor to *The Guardian*. Ghannoushi is a perfect example of the "criticism of Islam is racism" school of "thought":

> When we speak of Islam, for instance, we speak of a religion, the bulk of whose followers are not white.... This also applies to the Muslim communities of Western Europe, whose origins are found outside Europe's imaginary frontiers. The majority are former colonials who have made the metropolis their home. The relationship with these minorities incorporates a multiplicity of dichotomies: between the colonial and the colonizer, the black/brown and the white, the Christian and the Muslim. To reduce the terms of this relationship to race alone is a crude simplification. . . . We are witnessing the emergence of a new type of hatred, where religion and culture overlap with race and ethnicity. The climate generated by the war on terror . . . has allowed the far-right to redirect its poison of exclusionism from specific racial minorities to specific religio-racial minorities: from the black and Asian, to the Muslim black and Asian.[127]

Leaving aside the fact that the Turks in Germany and the North Africans in the Netherlands or Italy are not "former colonials who have made the metropolis their home," this is a theme of the European Left as well, consistently manipulated by Islamists: Attacks against Islamist terrorism are attacks against Islam itself, and "racist" to boot.

To be sure, not all Muslim intellectuals in Europe share such opinions, with some going precisely the opposite way. For example, there is Abdennour Bidar, a French Muslim author, for whom there is no such thing as a Muslim "community" in France or elsewhere on the continent:

> This caricature, which is unfortunately very strongly rooted in our minds, should be left behind, and it is time we began to perceive the Muslims as they really are. Their predominant characteristic is what I have called "individual Islam": a culture of autonomy and personal choice, and therefore a culture of diversity and differentiated identities—an Islam composed of individuals rather than a community. Today in Europe nobody is so dissimilar from a Muslim as his fellow Muslim. There are those who consider themselves Muslims based on their religion, which may for some take the form of a simple creed or hope, and for others the form of active observance, which may itself be more or less regular, depending on the individual. But others—in great numbers—feel themselves to be Muslim on the basis of a cultural heritage in the widest possible sense of the word, and not at all in a religious sense. Islam is important to them not only as faith or prayer, but also as an ethical system (traditional values of togetherness and family), as [a set of] customs (diet, cuisine, holidays), and also as their own way of taking part in Western consumer culture (choosing products with an "Islamic" label, halal meat, Mecca Cola, etc.). There is no such thing as a typical Muslim. We have all become atypical Muslims.[128]

Considering the fact that Shia terrorism, paid for and organized by Khomeini's Iran, started in Europe as early as 1980, and that Sunni terrorism spilling from Algeria had arrived in Paris by the mid 1990s, one may be surprised that a serious debate over the entire issue of Islamism, Islam, and terrorism is only now beginning to be engaged throughout the continent. But the reasons are clear, and they are political and ideological—and fundamentally related to the influence of the Left.

It was the Left's control over the vocabulary of the discussion, mostly via the media, that prevented any serious debate.

Any criticism of Islam was described as "racist" or "far right" (implicitly fascist), or more recently "Islamophobic"—and that was that. Few politicians would risk being accused of all those sins—and not many do even today. However, much of the public did have clear and very politically incorrect opinions, and was looking for channels to express them—and found them in Austria, France, Belgium, and later Denmark, Germany, and Italy, even if not yet in any meaningful way in England or Spain.

"Islamophobia"

"Islamophobia" is nothing but a change of subject in order to avoid the key issues of integration and Islamist terrorism. Indeed, it is a dangerous avoidance of the issue, because when mainstream Muslims, or at least their self-appointed leaders, change the subject, it suggests, correctly or not, that they are implicitly supporting the radicals in their midst. This can take on an almost comic aspect, as when the chairman of the Islamic Human Rights Commission claimed that the British refusal to bring charges against police officers involved in the accidental fatal shooting of Jean Charles de Menezes in the aftermath of July 21, 2005, "showed 'the level of Islamophobia in Britain today'. Massoud Shadjareh based this on the fact that police mistook Mr Menezes, a Catholic, for one of four Muslim terrorists who had tried the day before to blow up London's transport system."[129]

Indeed, when a journalist or politician raises the question of Islamist radicalism and terrorism, and "mainstream" Muslim organizations reply by screaming "Islamophobia," one is forced to believe that political correctness and *ummah* solidarity are more important than condemnation of, let alone action against, terrorists amidst the Muslim communities—in Europe, the U.S.A., or elsewhere. The very definition of "Islamophobia," as implicitly or explicitly accepted by Western apologists for Islamism and by "human-rights" NGOs, is, in itself, incompatible with any serious discussion of the problem of Muslim integration in Europe.

The Runnymede Trust, a British (Home Office–subsidized) charity dedicated to (or obsessed by) ethnic and cultural "diversity," introduced the term "Islamophobia" into government policy with its 1997 document "Islamophobia: A Challenge for Us All."[130] Its definition of the term, approvingly quoted by the Islamophobia-watch.com website, is now widely accepted, including by the European Monitoring Centre on Racism and Xenophobia and by U.S. groups like the Council on American-Islamic Relations (CAIR) and the ACLU. The eight components of that pernicious attitude are supposed to be:

1) Islam is seen as a monolithic bloc, static and unresponsive to change.

2) Islam is seen as separate and "other." It does not have values in common with other cultures, is not affected by them, and does not influence them.

3) Islam is seen as inferior to the West. It is seen as barbaric, irrational, primitive, and sexist.

4) Islam is seen as violent, aggressive, threatening, supportive of terrorism, and engaged in a "clash of civilizations."

5) Islam is seen as a political ideology and is used for political or military advantage.

6) Criticisms made of the West by Muslims are rejected out of hand.

7) Hostility toward Islam is used to justify discriminatory practices toward Muslims and exclusion of Muslims from mainstream society.

8) Anti-Muslim hostility is seen as natural or normal.

Each and every one of these elements is mistaken, misleading, or intended to prevent rational debate.

It is unclear who sins by seeing Islam as monolithic and static—certainly not European governments, which treat Iran and Turkey quite differently, nor most of the public, who do not see Turks, Albanians, and Moroccans as similar. Islam is indeed perceived as "other" in the European context, by Muslims and non-Muslims alike, and while, for some, "other" may mean opposite, by itself it is simply a fact that Islam is not a European religion. To consider elements of the Sharia (especially the inferior position of women) and practices such as arranged marriages, polygamy, honor killings, and FGM as strictly related to Islam is inaccurate, but there can be no argument that they are unacceptable in the West.

When Islamists claim that they act in the name of Islam, and major Islamic scholars like Qaradawi refuse to declare them out of the faith's bounds, it is unclear why pointing that out is "Islamophobic"—but it is clear that those who use that label intend to avoid discussing the links between Islam and terrorism. That Islamism is political and an ideology is self-evident, as anyone who has studied the Salafi literature knows. To claim that by not accepting Muslim criticism, often grounded in conspiracy theories, misinformation, and a false sense of victimhood, one engages in "Islamophobia" is to say that only a penitent West is not "Islamophobic." The very mention of "exclusion of Muslims from mainstream society" turns problems such as self-segregation and rejection of mainstream values on their head. Where or by whom, outside the outer fringes of politics, "anti-Muslim hostility"—as distinct from anti-Islamist hostility—is seen as "natural or normal" rather than combatted and condemned is not told.

Despite all of this shaky conceptual ground, "Islamophobia" is a label routinely thrown at critics of Islamism, and in some countries it is in fact a violation of law—a "hate crime." More often than not, "Islamophobia" is also associated with "racism," which is against the law throughout Europe.

The very term "Islamophobia," its association with "racism," and its criminalization are European concessions to a Muslim obsession with "discrimination" and irrational sense of victimhood—and further feed both.

Hence, one routinely sees claims like this on Muslim websites:

> The mass media, popular culture and the leading forces in world politics are all mostly hostile to and in their representations of Islam and Muslims. The evidence for this is ample and can be demonstrated by reference to reportage on Islam in the British press for instance.... A more accurate expression [than Islamophobia] would be 'anti-Islamic racism' for it combines the elements of dislike of a religion and active discrimination against the people belonging to that religion. The discrimination is racist because it is based on the belief that no matter what such a person does s/he will never be an acceptable to or in the West.[131]

To claim as self-evident that "mass media, popular culture and the leading forces in world politics" are hostile to Islam and Muslims is patently false. It would certainly be news to *The Guardian*, *Le Monde*, *El País*, *Der Speigel*, and the *New York Times*, and indeed to Tony Blair, Gordon Brown, and George W. Bush, all of whom have been at great pains to distinguish between Islam as a "religion of peace" and those who do not fairly represent it (e.g., Al-Qaeda). Nor is it possible to find any legal discrimination against Muslims anywhere in the West; and to describe Muslims as a "race" is simple fiction.

As to what such a definition of "Islamophobia" leads to, here is a case:

> "We have more religious freedom in Britain than in any Muslim country," says even Aazam Tamimi, a pro-Hamas British Islamist. "Our grievances against Britain are not religious but political." And that is the heart of the problem. Convinced that they can never agree on a common understanding of Islam, Muslim sects in Britain have sought unity based on a political program: Islam, in its broadest expression in Britain, is a political movement. It has adopted part of the anti-capitalist discourse of communism, adding to it some anti-Semitic and anti-Christian themes of Nazism, and completing the mix with third-worldist lamentations against racism and imperialism. *This Islam is an ideology masquerading as a religious faith.* [Emphasis added.][132]

Here is a clearly "Islamophobic" accusation that Islamism is political and ideological. The author dislikes it and thus qualifies as "Islamophobic." The problem? He is Amir Taheri, a Shia based in London and Paris.

Hence, the authors of an important essay in *L'Express*—not exactly a right-wing newspaper—were accurate when they wrote:

> Islamism, like communism yesterday, has its blind people and "useful idiots" among European elites. Their instrument of war is "Islamophobia," the term with which the Iranian mullahs denounce women who refuse to wear the veil, introduced in Europe by Tariq Ramadan in 1998. Intended to shield Islam from the criticism to which other religions have been subject for centuries, the word serves first of all to penalize all those who want to reform Islam or to emancipate themselves. Thus, in France, Soheib Bencheikh, Abdelwahab Meddeb and Malek

Boutih have been denounced as "facilitators of Islamophobia" or "Islamophobic Muslims." The paradox is to notice the embarrassment provoked in Europe by personalities such as Ayaan Hirsi Ali ... or Magdi Allam, columnist of *Corriere della Sera*, who adhere without reservations to European values.[133]

Perhaps the clearest insight into what Islamophobia is and what the term is used for comes from Frank Furedi, formerly of the Revolutionary Communist Party, UK:

When someone is diagnosed as phobic, then they are seen as being beyond the reach of reason or open debate. As the British writer Kenan Malik has argued, in relation to what he calls the "Islamophobia myth", the word Islamophobia "has become not just a description of anti-Muslim prejudice but also a prescription for what may or may not be said about Islam." In recent years the term Islamophobia has been frequently invoked to silence criticism of Islam. Criticisms of any aspect of Islam are looked upon as expressions of a new form of racism. In reality, critics of Islam are questioning the values associated with the religion rather than the racial status of Muslim people. Today, promoting the concept of *Islamophobia is about setting up Islam as a criticism-free zone.* [Emphasis added.][134]

As with "Islamophobia," the "racist" charge flies every time phrases like "national identity" or "immigration control" are uttered. When Sarkozy expressed the intention of creating a Ministry of Immigration and National Identity, the *Ligue des droits de l'homme* declared itself "scandalized" and the MRAP condemned a "racist ideology."[135]

TERRORISTS, MUSLIMS AND HUMAN RIGHTS

As we have seen in earlier chapters, a large part of the Islamist problem in Europe has been caused by an unthinking devotion to the concepts of asylum and refugee status. At some point most EU member states apparently decided to apply literally the definition of the term "refugee" in the 1951 Refugee Convention. According to that definition, a "refugee" is a person who,

> owing to well-founded fear of being persecuted for reasons of race, religion, nationality, membership of a particular social group or political opinion, is outside the country of his nationality and is unable or, owing to such fear, is unwilling to avail himself of the protection of that country; or who, not having a nationality and being outside the country of his former habitual residence as a result of such events, is unable or, owing to such fear, is unwilling to return to it.[136]

Note that the substantive reason for persecution for "political opinion" is not supposed, in theory, even to be considered. We know that, in practice, this is not always the case. Thus, quite reasonably, former Nazis are not accepted as legitimate asylum seekers or refugees. On the other hand, Algerian Islamists, responsible for some 150,000 deaths since 1991, are, or were until recently, routinely considered as eligible for "refugee" status in most European countries, as are Kurdish sympathizers of the PKK.

A related phenomenon is the "torture" excuse. It is by now a standard lawyers' position that Islamists who have been tried *in absentia* and sentenced in countries like Egypt, Jordan, Morocco, and Algeria cannot be extradited to those countries because they may be subjected to "torture." The legal basis of such claims is international law—specifically, the 1975 Convention on Torture, whose Part I states:

> 1. For the purposes of this Convention, torture means any act by which severe pain or suffering, whether physical or mental, is intentionally inflicted on a person for such purposes as obtaining from him or a third person information or a confession, punishing him for an act he or a third person has committed or is suspected of having committed, or intimidating or coercing him or a third person, or for any reason based on discrimination of any kind, when such pain or suffering

is inflicted by or at the instigation of or with the consent or acquiescence of a public official or other person acting in an official capacity. It does not include pain or suffering arising only from, inherent in or incidental to lawful sanctions.[137]

Applying this provision necessarily requires making a subjective analysis based upon perceptions—precisely what the "human-rights" NGOs are so good at abusing and taking advantage of. Thus, what does severe mental suffering mean for a captured Islamist terrorist? The presence of a woman interrogator? The sound of a pig or dog in the background? Accidental damage to a single copy (among the billion in circulation) of the Quran? And who gets to decide what is "torture"? Good and unanswered question—or, rather, answered in the captives' favor by the NGOs, especially as regards Guantanamo—or what they have labeled its British equivalent, Belmarsh Prison in London.

The NGOs' circular argument against the deportation of Abu Qatada to Jordan is a good example of their stubborn refusal to understand that public safety is more important than the chances of mistreatment of a terrorist in his country of origin. For example, the international organization Human Rights Watch (HRW) claims that "The essential argument against diplomatic assurances contained in bilateral agreements such as 'memoranda of understanding' is that the perceived need for such guarantees in itself is an acknowledgement that a risk of torture and other ill-treatment exists in the receiving country."[138] This hides the fact that it was precisely the claims of groups like the HRW itself that forced the British government to seek assurances from Amman—those assurances were intended for Amnesty International and HRW more than anything else. Moreover, such high-minded groups offer no solution to the basic dilemma: Is the British government expected to allow an Abu Qatada to stay in London and continue his in-doctrination and recruiting activities on behalf of Islamist terrorism, including attacks within the UK? If so, as the implication of this position suggests, HRW (and Amnesty) should state clearly that for them the simple chance that a prominent figure of global terrorism could be mistreated in his home country is more important than the safety of British citizens.

EUROPEAN REACTIONS

When Kingsgate Primary School in West Hampstead, London, where three-quarters of the pupils are Muslim, decided to serve only *halal* meat in its cafeteria, a group of angry parents demonstrated outside. One of the protesters stated: "We allow people to come into this country and we end up being in a minority. We accommodate other cultures at the expense of ours." Instantly, accusations of "racism" started to fly, with a Muslim parent claiming, "This is just naked racism, it's got nothing to do with choice. They talk about keeping up English values but the most important value we have is democracy. It's about time that was upheld." By "democracy" he meant that there was a poll on the issue among parents. Less than six out of ten responded, but among those who did the decision was supported by three-quarters.[139]

This is precisely the kind of situation that alienates majorities from the Muslim community—and not only in Britain. If a school with a non-Muslim majority had decided to serve only non-*halal* meat, the charges of "racism" would have been even louder. In any case, accusations of "racism" rather than compromise—for instance, the school's offering pupils a choice—suggest that the Muslim parents want to prevent debate and discussion. And such attitudes are a far bigger problem than the issue of *halal* meat in one primary school.

In May 2006, a white Flemish self-declared racist shot a native Belgian infant and her Malian nurse—and the politically correct establishment, especially the Francophone one, went into a frenzy, accusing the Flemish nationalist *Vlaams Belang* party, in which some of the murderer's relatives were active, of responsibility.[140] The credibility of the accusers would have been greater if VB had advocated, or even implied, violence against immigrants, which it did not, or if it had supported the criminal, which it did not, or if that same establishment had been less threatened by VB's electoral advances in Flanders.

In April 2006, Philip Davies, a Tory MP, complained to his party's new leader, David Cameron, that political correctness, now also coming from the Conservatives, is driving people into the arms of the extreme Right, the British National Party (BNP):

> "People feel nobody is standing up and talking about [asylum and immigration] issues. This whole thing about political correctness is a key driver of that. They feel the only way they've got now to express their opinions is to put a cross in a secret ballot for the BNP. . . . The fear is if you are white and you say something that may be considered derogatory by somebody about an ethnic minority, you are going to be sacked or locked up." Labour MPs demanded the Tories disown Davies's views: "If David Cameron wants to show that his party has genuinely changed, then he needs to take action against the extreme right wing in his own party," said Martin Salter, the Labour MP for Reading West.[141]

From the Left, former Labour Minister of Welfare Reform Frank Field complained that by "playing the race card" and avoiding a serious discussion on immigration, politicians have created a situation in which "It is only because the BNP are so inept that the debate has not taken off." Mainstream politicians were "living on borrowed time" and needed to address the subject "before the BNP stumbles on somebody with talent."[142]

In fact, Davies and Field were only stating what should be obvious to any observer of the European scene during the past decade: The political mainstream's long refusal to even acknowledge, let alone deal with, the problems, economic, social, and cultural, of mass immigration, especially Muslim immigration, has created a vacuum inevitably filled by nationalist, populist, or even quasi-fascist groups and parties. In reaction, the establishment has generally taken one of two directions: either, as demonstrated by Salter (but not, one may add, by Blair), continuous and aggressive denial of reality (the call to "take action against the extreme right wing") and false accusations of "extremism" and "racism" against growing sectors of the public; or admission that there are indeed legitimate social, cultural, and security problems to be addressed. In some cases (the Netherlands, Denmark, partially France) the governing party has even taken measures to do so—generally at little or no political cost, or even to its own electoral benefit.

Philippe de Villiers, leader of the anti-EU Movement for France party and a presidential candidate in the 2007 elections, stated, in a voice close to that of Wilders or the late Fortuyn:

> "I believe that there are moderate Muslims, even an immense majority. I do not believe that there is a moderate Islam. . . . I believe . . . that Islam is incompatible with the Republic," because of "three principles [of Islam]: ummah, Sharia and, finally, jihad." Claiming to speak for the "silent French," he added that the "Islamization of the country is taboo" and suggested a moratorium on the construction of mosques.[143]

The same day, Sarkozy chimed in: "One has more than enough to have to apologize all the time for being French. One cannot change its laws, its customs because they do not please a minuscule minority . . . If some do not like France, they should not feel embarrassed to leave it." *Le Monde* and *Le Nouvel Observateur* did not lose a moment comparing that last sentence to de Villiers's "France—you love it or leave it," in a transparent attempt to depict Sarkozy as an "extremist," an attempt immediately copied by the Socialist Party leader.[144]

It is precisely that method of preventing debate—insults replacing arguments—that prompted Sarkozy to say that "Until a few years ago you only had to say the word[s] [chosen immigration] and you were immediately a 'racist.' I do not accept this unique idea that prevents talking about problems . . . Not to have the courage to talk makes the extremists' bed."[145]

Sarkozy may have been referring to Jack Lang, who criticized Sarkozy's concept of "chosen immigration" as "xenophobic drift." Lang pontificated that "When one pretends to accede to the highest state office one cannot dredge on the grounds of the National Front,"[146] as if the idea that regulating immigration and selecting immigrants according to national needs rather than tolerating a vast, unregulated, and often illegal influx of unskilled migrants at a time of huge unemployment is extremist and xenophobic.

The same tone and method characterizes the public debate in general. Even a highly respected and respectable Turkish analyst and former diplomat cannot refrain from labeling European reluctance to admit Turkey to the EU as "racist":

> A racist attitude that has surfaced in Europe all too often throughout its history—for hitherto obscure reasons and in not yet fully explained ways—is now gaining ground and taking root once again in various parts of the continent, especially in Germany, Austria, Switzerland, the Netherlands, Denmark and France. Meanwhile, Poland too is rapidly sliding towards racism.[147]

The French Human Rights Commission survey cited earlier, which found a decline in racist acts from 2004 to 2005, also found an "alarmingly" strong rise in the number of self-confessed "racists" and a radicalization of xenophobic opinions. One-third of respondents declared themselves "racist," 63 percent believed that certain types of behavior could justify racist reactions, and only 32 percent would alert police about racist behavior. There is also a "tendency to turn toward oneself, a growing indifference toward racist manifestations, combined with fears of communitarism" as well as a doubling of the number of people citing the "French" as victims of racism. Furthermore, 56 percent of respondents (an increase of 18 percentage points from 2004) thought that the number of foreigners was too large, and a similar number had the same opinion about the number of immigrants (+9 percent age points). Moreover, there was a decline of 11 percentage points in the number of those who considered that immigrant workers contributed to the French economy, and only half considered the presence of immigrants necessary in some professions. In a stunning reversal, whereas earlier the general attitude toward racist and anti-Semitic acts was indignation, support for victims, and demands for harsher sanctions, in 2005 it was the immigrants who were perceived as a threat.[148]

The authors of the poll found that

> Racism and xenophobia are linked, if not confused. The foreigner is clearly assimilated to the immigrant, the Arab, the Maghrebi, or the African ... and those who think that Muslims are a separate group (63 percent, +6) are more numerous, while those who believe that French Muslims "are French like everyone else" went down clearly (66 percent, –11).[149]

Interestingly, despite the fact that the poll was taken at the time of the 2005 urban riots, only 14 percent of respondents thought that immigrants are a security problem—compared to the 66 percent (+14) who see them as an economic problem in the light of the high unemployment rate.

But the elites also, for their own reasons, are loose in their thinking about race. Indeed, some "human-rights" NGOs, such as France's MRAP, have made it their *raison d'être* to confuse any debate over Islam and Islamism with "racism"—as if Muslims were a race. Thus Muslim converts Jérôme Courtailler, who was a Norman, and Muriel Degauque, a Belgian born in Charleroi, are somehow part of a "racial" victimhood community, along with Khaled Kelkal, an Algerian born in France, and Xavier Djaffo, a mulatto who was "martyred" by the Russians in Chechnya.

The notion that every conflict with Muslims or Islam, at any time, is clear proof of European "racism" can reach summits of the absurd, as in Alain Ruscio's claim, in the leftist *Le Monde Diplomatique*, that "anti-Arab racism" goes all the way back to the battle of Poitiers (732 CE), the semi-mythical battle of Roncevalles, and Saint Louis's crusades.[150]

Characteristically, Michel Tubiana, vice president of the Human Rights League (LDH), claimed that a principal reason for the increase in "ethnocentric attitudes" was "provocative" government statements *vis-à-vis* foreigners.[151] Nor is such denial limited to the French Left—indeed, it is shared at the higher levels of the European Union, as in this comment about the murder of Theo van Gogh: "The EU counterterrorism coordinator, the Dutchman Gijs de Vries, has refused to speculate over the motivations for the assassination, limiting himself to saying that 'violence is incompatible with democracy. The EU does not believe in a clash of civilizations'."[152] In fact, there was no need for de Vries to "speculate" at all about the motivation for the assassination, since Bouyeri made it quite clear, both in the note he pinned to the chest of his victim and later at his trial. But that is a good example of the major cultural impediment the European elites have burdened themselves with.

So, here we are. Islamists, including those operating in Europe, declare war on Western civilization as such, and on one of the basic characteristics of its modern manifestations: democracy. One wonders whether Tubiana or de Vries has ever read texts such as al-Zarqawi's "Democracy Is the Very Essence of Heresy, Polytheism, and Error."[153]

In the nations of Western Europe, what is the ordinary voter to think when he witnesses *burqa*-clad women in his neighborhood, hears of polygamy and "honor" killings, and reads of terrorist cells being uncovered? What is he to think when he hears from intellectual elites and most of the media that he is a "racist" for asking questions, and for being anxious? In such an environment, it is hard to expect any meaningful form of intra-EU cooperation on counter-terrorism.

The still-dominant mentality in the British legal and cultural elites is that terrorism is a criminal matter, and that even to talk of "war on terror" is wrong, dangerous, and threatening to "our values." Thus Sir Ken Macdonald, then director of public prosecutions, claimed that "The fight against terrorism on the streets of Britain is not a war. It is the prevention of crime, the enforcement of our laws and the winning of justice for those damaged by their infringement." The July 7 bombers "were deluded, narcissistic inadequates. They were criminals. They were fantasists. We need to be very clear about this. On the streets of London, there is no such thing as a 'war on terror,' just as there can be no such thing as a 'war on drugs'."[154]

A 2006 study by a group of academics went further along this logic, concluding that

> The key to successfully combating terrorism lies in winning the trust and cooperation of the Muslim communities in the UK. However, the government's counter-terrorism legislation and rhetorical stance are between them creating serious losses

in human rights and criminal justice protections; loosening the fabric of justice and civil liberties in the UK; and harming community relations and multiculturalism. Moreover, they are having a disproportionate effect on the Muslim communities in the UK and so are prejudicing the ability of the government and security forces to gain the very trust and cooperation from individuals in those communities that they require to combat terrorism.[155]

Of course, if the terrorists had been Lutherans or Hare Khrishnas, counter-terror legislation would have had a "disproportionate effect" on those communities—and that proves what? The report's argument, common in progressive circles, is that by making the public aware of the nature and magnitude of the threat, which is one of its obligations, the government makes the problem worse, by alienating the Muslim "community." The implication is that by simply calling Islamist terrorism by its name the government makes matters worse. This so-called analysis is similar to that offered by the self-appointed leaders of Islam in Britain, such as the MCB and MAB, interested in avoiding debate more than in helping to isolate and defeat the extremists.

The nature of the Europeans' problem, in dealing with the challenges posed by the growing presence of Islam, is best symbolized by the most fundamental of all issues: language. If a problem cannot be accurately described, it is unlikely that it could be analyzed or dealt with. Efforts to describe the Islamist terrorist threat at EU and national levels have been consistently derailed by political correctness. Thus, the official British-government report on the July 7, 2005, bombings carefully tiptoes around the definition of the ideology of the perpetrators:

"9. The Report refers in the main to 'Islamist terrorism'. This is the term used by the Security Service and the police to describe the current threat from individuals who claim a religious justification for terrorism, a claim which is rejected by most British Muslims, whose leaders point out that Islam is not a violent religion. Across the wider Government counterterrorism community the threat is also referred to as 'international terrorism' or 'AQ-related' terrorism."[56]

The following claim by Hilary Benn, Britain's international-development secretary (and son of Tony Benn), is a perfect example of incoherence and confusion:

> "In the UK, we do not use the phrase 'war on terror' because we can't win by military means alone, and because this isn't us against one organized enemy with a clear identity and a coherent set of objectives . . . It is the vast majority of the people in the world—of all nationalities and faiths—against a small number of loose, shifting and disparate groups who have relatively little in common apart from their identification with others who share their distorted view of the world and their idea of being part of something bigger. . . . by letting them feel part of something bigger, we give them strength."[57]

To describe jihadists as "shifting and disparate groups" who share nothing but a common ideology is incomprehensible; as for their motivation, it is not provided by the language of Washington but by that very ideology. The jihadists do not lack "a clear identity and a coherent set of objectives"—as anyone who studies the abundant Salafist literature and the statements of jihadi groups should know by now. While Secretary Benn represents the leftist wing of Labour, his statement is a good example of the sharp difference in perceptions between most of the European elites and the Washington of the Bush Administration—as demonstrated by Vice President Cheney's defense of the phrase "global war on terror":

> I'm left to wonder—which part of that phrase is the problem? Do they deny the struggle is global, after the enemy has declared the ambition of building a totalitarian empire that stretches from Europe around to Indonesia? Do they deny this is a war, in which one side will win and the other will lose? Do

they deny that it's terror that we're fighting, with unlawful combatants who wear no uniform, who reject the rules of warfare, and who target the innocent for indiscriminate slaughter? . . . That's the nature of the fight we're in. We can't wish it away, or define it away.[158]

For arguments such as Benn's to still be coming from a high British official after 9/11, 7/7, and the Madrid bombings only suggests how far many in London have to go to even begin understanding the nature of their enemies—and they are not alone.

In April 2006 it was announced that EU officials were discussing a "non-emotive lexicon" for public communication on terrorism and Islam.[159] A Brussels official explained that "The basic idea behind it is to avoid the use of improper words that would cause frustration among Muslims and increase the risk of radicalization."[160] While it was described as only a set of "guidelines" for Brussels officials—and presumably for national ones as well—it is highly indicative of the problems still faced by European elites in dealing with a spreading phenomenon that is at least a decade old. Thus, said an official, "Certainly 'Islamic terrorism' is something we will not use . . . we talk about 'terrorists who abusively invoke Islam', while 'Jihad' means something for you and me, it means something else for a Muslim. Jihad is a perfectly positive concept of trying to fight evil within yourself."

The EU's Gijs de Vries went further, claiming, against overwhelming evidence, that moderate Muslims "have been increasingly active in isolating the radicals who abuse Islam for political purposes, and they deserve everyone's support. And that includes the choice of language that makes clear that we are talking about a murderous fringe that is abusing a religion and does not represent it."[161]

A 2005 European Commission paper, presented by the Commission's vice president, Franco Frattini, claims:

> In an attempt to ensure that the vast majority of peaceful Muslims are not portrayed as terrorist sympathizers . . . The commission believes there is no such thing as "Islamic terrorism", nor "Catholic", nor "red" terrorism . . . The fact that some individuals unscrupulously attempt to justify their crimes in the name of a religion or ideology cannot be allowed in any way . . . to cast a shadow upon such a religion or ideology.[162]

This, after the very same Commission identified a "crisis of identity" among young people born to immigrant parents as a key danger. "The document . . . . describes radicalization as 'a modern kind of dictatorship', likens it to neo-Nazism or nationalism, and says the internet, university campuses and places of worship are tools of recruitment. It says second-generation immigrants often feel little connection to their parents' country or culture but may also encounter discrimination in European countries."[163]

Leaving aside the contradiction between Frattini's mention of an identity crisis among young Muslims in Europe as a "key danger" and his and de Vries's description of Salafis as "fringe," the arguments presented by these various officials are a glaring demonstration of denial and purposeful ignorance of reality. No serious Islamic scholar, non-Salafis included, describes jihad only as "a perfectly positive concept of trying to fight evil within yourself"; rather, all give it a dual meaning: as an individual, spiritual struggle to follow closely on the path of God—and in that sense not very different from the *Imitatio Christi* as described by the late-medieval Rhenish mystic Thomas à Kempis—*and* as physical/military action to propagate the faith. Thus, Ibn Taymiyya wrote: "Since lawful warfare is essentially jihad and since its aim is that the religion is God's entirely and God's word is uppermost, therefore according to all Muslims, those who stand in the way of this aim must be fought."

In this, he anticipated the German-based Bassam Tibi, one of the most prominent Islamic moderates in Europe today, who stated in 1996:

> Muslims believe that expansion through war is not aggression but a fulfillment of the Qur'anic command to spread Islam as a way to peace. The resort to force to disseminate Islam is not war (harb), a word that is used only to describe the use of force by non-Muslims. Islamic wars are not hurub (the plural of harb) but rather futuhat, acts of "opening" the world to Islam and expressing Islamic jihad.[64]

While the relationship between the two aspects of jihad is described very differently by Salafis and by orthodox Islamic scholars, none defines it the way the EU does. Which raises the question, Why do Messrs. de Vries and Frattini engage in Islamic theological arguments without a license? The obvious answer is that they purposefully confuse their legitimate, but so far unfulfilled, hope that most moderate Muslims will reject the militaristic interpretation of jihad in favor of the spiritual one, with the reality.

Where do de Vries, Frattini, and their colleagues get their information on Islam? The answer, other than the aforementioned Europe-based imams, is a particular set of European academic experts, who provide a degree of legitimacy to such reality-defying approaches to the issue. French scholars have produced an abundant, extremely intelligent, and diverse collection of studies of the issue of Islam in Europe (and in the world), some of which are examined elsewhere in this volume, but the Dutch case is perhaps more interesting, because it pits academics against public opinion and the politicians representing it.

National Debate: The Netherlands

The Netherlands has long had the reputation of being the most tolerant Western democracy in terms of minorities (religious, sexual, political), asylum requirements, and openness to immigrants from outside Europe. If there was a "Muslim" or "Islamic" problem in Europe, the Netherlands would be the last logical place to look for it. And yet, the Netherlands is precisely where one of the worst problems has surfaced.

Amsterdam mayor Job Cohen, as noted above, was on Mohammed Bouyeri's list of targets as a member of the Jewish cabal ruling the Netherlands. A member of the Dutch Labor Party, Cohen believes that Muslims in his country must be integrated through their religion, within the traditional Dutch system of confessional "pillars," which includes Catholics, Calvinists, and secularists. "The easiest way to integrate these new immigrants might be through their faith."[165] That assumes that Islam in the Netherlands is totally opposed to the Islamism of Bouyeri, and that it could behave like Christian denominations—in other words, that it could render unto Caesar what is Caesar's. This fits with Ian Buruma's assumption that, for instance, Europeans have to accept Islam's treatment of women as a fact of life that has to be lived with, because a frontal attack on Islam would not solve the problem.[166] That is precisely the inevitable trap of the multiculturalists: *Tolerance for "diversity" leads to tolerance of incompatible values and standards, and ultimately to tolerance of intolerance.*

Nor is this noted just by Western critics of Islamism. Thus when asked, "Is it therefore right to compromise in order to avoid antagonizing Muslims unnecessarily?" Bassam Tibi answered: "Quite the opposite. The Islamic officials who live here are very intelligent and view this as weakness. Muslims stand by their religion entirely. It is a sort of religious absolutism. While Europeans have stopped defending the values of their civilization, they confuse tolerance with relativism."[167]

The Netherlands, as we have seen, was deeply shocked by the murders of Pim Fortuyn and Theo van Gogh. However, as those murders receded in time, traditional approaches resurfaced, but with them, new reactions.

In the former category, *Dynamism in Islamic Activism*,[168] published in April 2006, is a fairly representative example of an academic study of Islam in the Netherlands. Its authors are not just subsidized by the Dutch government, but in fact are members of a think tank, the Scientific Council for Government Policy, supposed to give academic advice to the government. The other, *Declaration of Independence*, by Geert Wilders,[169] is the political program of a quite new political party, *Partij voor de Vrijheid* (Party for Freedom), formally established in March 2006 by Wilders, a member of Parliament and a defector from the ruling Liberal Party.[170] Two caveats are in order. The former is not completely representative of Western academic thinking on Islam, while the latter is not typical of the "xenophobic" or "racist" "Right" in Europe. Each, however, presents clear arguments common to its side of the debate throughout the region.

Dynamism in Islamic Activism starts by describing some terms of the debate, such as the notion of Islam's incompatibility with democracy and the "clash of civilizations," as "intemperate images and inflated words"—in other words, as emotions without substance. That, by itself, is not a serious analysis either of Huntington's approach, or of the growing number of politicians and parties reacting negatively to Muslim immigration and its impact. Next: "The Council intends to formulate a policy perspective that will contribute to reducing the tensions with and with-

in the Muslim world with regard to issues of Islamic activism"—
which, by definition, places in doubt any academic and objective
claim of the authors. Furthermore, the authors claim that "the
emphasis is on positive reference points for policy directed towards democratization and human rights in Muslim countries."
Which means trying to find something, anything, that contradicts the popular image of Islam as anti-democratic, anti-wom-
en's-rights, etc. Implicitly, the "proof" is in Morocco's decision
to grant women rights similar to those in Europe—never mind
that that was a royal decision forced through the Parliament
against, most of all, the Islamist parties.

The authors manage to find that "Islamic activism does indeed offer reference points for democratization and human
rights," and that "Even though these are tentative reference
points and much uncertainty still exists, it is inaccurate to assume that 'Islam' in a general sense is at odds with the acceptance of democracy and human rights." Simply put, the authors
give Islam all the benefit of the doubt, and then some. In fact,
most if not all prominent spokesmen for Islam in Europe, presumably those considered "moderate" by the authors, do indeed
exhibit anti-democratic and anti-Western tendencies, regardless of the opinions and behavior of ordinary Muslims. Once
again, one has to refer to the most influential and often-quoted
"moderate" authority on Islamic matters in Europe, Yusuf al-
Qaradawi, and his opinions on specific issues.

On children as suicide bombers in Israel: "The Israelis might
have nuclear bombs but we have the children bomb and there
human bombs must continue until liberation."

On killing Israeli civilians: "We must all realize that the
Israeli society is a military society—men and women. We cannot describe the society as civilian . . . they are not civilians
or innocent."

On suicide bombing in Israel: "It is not suicide; it is martyrdom in the name of God. I consider this type of martyrdom operation as an indication of the justice of Allah almighty. Allah is
just. Through his infinite wisdom, he has given the weak what
the strong do not possess, and that is the ability to turn their
bodies into bombs as Palestinians do."

On nonbelievers: "It has been determined by Islamic law that
the blood and property of people of Dar Al-Harb (non-Muslims)
is not protected. Because they fight against and are hostile towards the Muslims, they annulled the protection of his blood
and his property."[171]

The authors of *Dynamism* mysteriously refer to "so-called
Islamic activism"—are Salafis, Takfiris, Tahriris, and Muslim
Brothers not "Islamic activists"? They certainly claim to be, and
the authors offer no proof to the contrary. Instead they choose
to go around the issue: "The emphasis is on positive reference
points for policy directed towards democratization and human
rights in Muslim countries." In short, they avoid the issue of
Islamist radicalism in Europe—which is precisely the problem—and instead make the unwarranted assumption that what
happens (or might happen) in some Muslim countries is more
relevant to Europe that what actually happens in Europe.

The authors optimistically claim that

> There are increasingly more thinkers who strive for these
> same principles [democracy, human rights] precisely on
> Islamic grounds. They turn away from dogmatic approaches
> that claim that the precepts of the sacred sources should be
> followed to the letter. Rather, they are more concerned with
> the spirit and expressive power of these sources in relation to
> current circumstances. Thinkers holding such views can now
> be found in many Muslim countries—Indonesia, Malaysia, and
> Egypt, for example. This modernizing mode of thought can
> even be found in Iran, a country that has now had a quarter
> century of experience with Islamic theocracy.

Even assuming the existence of modernizing Islamic thinkers in Indonesia, Malaysia, and Egypt, it is hard to detect such
thinkers in Iran, without a strenuous effort to deny reality. But
the authors do make that effort, strenuous as it obviously is,
and also claim to detect a larger phenomenon:

> Moreover, Islamic political movements in many Muslim
> countries have abandoned their initially radical attitude in
> favor of a pragmatic political standpoint. The movements
> most strongly oriented towards the political arena, such as
> the Muslim Brotherhood in Egypt, have shifted the most in
> the direction of accepting democratic principles and norms. In
> doing so, they distance themselves from absolute truths and
> become familiar with the positive workings of democratic
> principles and human rights.

Evidently, the authors believe that participation in elections
makes the Muslim Brotherhood "democratic"—as if Hamas, a
Brotherhood branch, by participating in, and winning, elections in the Palestinian areas has become, *ipso facto*, "democratic." The authors seem unaware of the concept of "one man, one
vote, once," so widespread throughout the Third World, and
not just within Islam.

Contradicting themselves, the authors note that "In the last
few decades many Muslim countries have been exposed to the
pressure of introducing elements of Islamic law. The views on
what Sharia contains, however, are quite divergent, ranging
from very general guidelines to concrete codes of behavior."
They claim, however, again against empirical evidence, that,
except for Iran, Pakistan, and Sudan, there has not been a second wave of Islamization—in other words, that it did not get
worse. Furthermore, the report claims,

> Even when Sharia plays a formal role, it seems that this
> gradual modernization of the law is not excluded. Thus the
> reform of marriage laws has gone forward in most countries

despite activism. In reaction to universal human rights, ideas about Islamic human rights have been developed in the Islamic world. In addition to sharing similarities, these two concepts also demonstrate important fundamental differences. Nevertheless, here, too, there appears unmistakably a tendency towards gradual rapprochement.

In fact, "most countries" have not reformed marriage laws (a few, like Morocco, have). "Islamic human rights" are, simply, not similar to Western, or even UN, definitions of human rights. Thus, the Islamic Human Rights Commission in Britain claimed that the British government's anti-terrorism law is wrong because "The term extremism has no tangible legal meaning or definition and is therefore unhelpful and emotive." Really? Are the statements of Abu Hamza, Omar Bakri, or Abu Qatada without "tangible legal meaning"?

"The right of people anywhere in the world to resist invasion and occupation is legitimate." That is the standard defense of Palestinian suicide bombers. This argument is no different from that of Milan judge Clementina Forleo, who in 2005 released terrorist recruiters for Iraq on the grounds that "Recruiting mujahidin for the war in Iraq is not against the law. The serious charge of international terrorism can only be brought if there is proof of the organization of attacks 'aiming to spread indiscriminate terror in the civilian population in the name of a political and/or religious creed', in other words 'crimes against humanity'."[172] In other words, assisting in the kidnapping and murder of civilians in Iraq, or the murder of American (or Italian) soldiers, is no crime.

"Questioning the legitimacy of Israeli occupation is legitimate political expression." That is, legitimizing the destruction of Israel.

The proposal to ban the nonviolent organization *Hizb ut-Tahrir* is "unwarranted, unjust and unwise." Obviously, the fact that HuT calls for the destruction of all Muslim governments, as well as the West, does not matter, nor does its recruitment of future Salafi terrorists.

"Arbitrary closure of mosques may prevent legitimate political discourse in mosques, fuelling a radical subculture." This is the logic of self-defeat, copied from "human-rights" NGOs: Cracking down on radicalism is producing more of it; hence the implication is that it should be allowed (or encouraged?).

"Deporting foreign nationals to countries known for gross human rights abuses is abhorrent."[173] The implication is that terrorist ideologues and recruiters should be given free rein in Europe—a reality already, but most people don't find this a sensible policy.

The rest of the report follows the same flawed logic. Since Islam is not *per se* anti-democratic, the Netherlands and the EU were wrong when, in dealing with Muslim countries, they "primarily put ... hopes on non-religious movements and parties, even if these groups had little political support within the local population. It becomes increasingly apparent, however, that ignoring the political and juridical agendas of religious activism offers no solution and may even be counterproductive." The first part of the argument is basically correct, but the second is justified only if one accepts the authors' benign views on political Islam. Furthermore, as Morocco, Tunisia, Turkey, and, to some extent, post-civil-war Algeria have demonstrated, reform is possible within Islamic (but anti-Islamist) parameters, even if it is reached not via democratic means but through government fiat.

The conclusion of the study is the logical result of its combination of optimism and extrapolations of isolated facts:

> The EU and the Netherlands should no longer rule out in advance Islamic movements as potential interlocutors, but should be guided by the concrete political actions of these groups. They should strongly support groups moving towards the acceptance of democracy and human rights and condemn groups which move away from this goal. In addition, they must develop more positive incentives to be able to encourage and reward reforms. . . . Democracy and human rights cannot be permanently imposed from outside. The Netherlands and the EU should influence without lecturing and accept the fact that within an Islamic frame of reference democracy and human rights may sometimes (provisionally) be worked out in a manner different from that which is customary in Western countries.[174]

Why "provisionally"—is that not wishful thinking? And what does "different" mean in the context of democracy and human rights? Is that not accepting the "moderate" Islamists' disingenuous argument that "democracy" in Islam will not be identical to democracy in the West—just as democracy, in its details, is not identical in France, the United States, and Costa Rica? The issue—and it is doubtful that the report's authors do not understand this—is not whether the democratic system is federal or centralized, presidential or parliamentarian; whether the legislature has a Senate and a House; whether the electoral system is first-past-the-post or proportional. The issue is whether major issues are decided by voters or decided by imams; whether women have equal rights with men; whether non-Muslims have equal rights or are treated as *dhimmis*; etc. And on none of these matters do the authors have anything to say.

They do have something to say regarding the post–van Gogh situation in the Netherlands:

> In the Dutch situation, the formation of parties (partially) based on Islam or Muslim identity can offer a constructive contribution to political debate. Political parties inspired by Islam can give voice to those who do not feel themselves to be represented in the Muslim representative bodies. Such parties attest to the aspiration for participation in the existing institutions and according to the democratic rules that obtain.

Confessional Islamic, which inevitably means Islamist, parties are thus the solution to the growing rejection of integration by Muslims in the Netherlands—inevitably, because the currently recognized "Muslim representative bodies" are not radical, and the alternative to them is bound to be organizations influenced by radicals, whether religious or ethnic. The Arab European League (AEL) in neighboring Belgium is a case in point—although, obviously, the authors did not notice it.

Although *Dynamism in Islamic Activism* is quite typical of European academic and elite approaches to Islamism, the Dutch government was far from happy with the result of this taxpayer-funded study. Indeed, Ben Bot, the Dutch foreign minister, declared the report "unbalanced" and, regarding its suggestion that Hamas should be negotiated with, reiterated the EU position of no recognition or aid unless Hamas recognizes Israel.[175] The reason for the government's rejection of the report it paid for is, simply put, that the Netherlands is a democracy, and the opinion of voters matters more to politicians than the opinion of academics. That makes the other side of the argument, that of MP Geert Wilders, relevant, since he seems to have significant support precisely among voters.

Wilders's analysis and recommendations regarding Islam in the Netherlands should be seen in the light of that country's long and well-deserved reputation for tolerance and political blandness—or "consensus-based" politics. While many still make the (largely absurd) case that Germany and Austria, and even France, Spain, and Italy, still bear the "guilt" of past ideological commitments to or collaboration with fascism, Nazism, or Communism, that is a very hard case to make for the Dutch (or the now similarly inclined Danes). Nor is Wilders—a devotee of Margaret Thatcher and Ronald Reagan—an extreme "right-winger," let alone a "fascist": Conservative and patriotic is, it seems, the way most Dutch see him. While large numbers of Dutch agreed with him by 2006 (totally agree: 28 percent; partly agree: 37 percent; neutral: 7 percent; partly disagree: 12 percent; totally disagree: 13 percent), that does not necessarily translate into votes for his new party. In the same poll 62 percent did not intend to vote for it. That would seem to mean that many of Wilders's fellow countrymen agree him over the nature of the problem but disagree over solutions. And what are the problems and solutions, according to Wilders's "Declaration of Independence"?[176]

First, he defines his goal as a struggle "about the continuation of the Netherlands as a recognizable nation, a country that is on the point of kissing its roots goodbye and trading that for multiculturalism, cultural relativism and a European superstate, all under the leadership of a political elite that long ago lost its way." In that, he coincides with just about every populist and nationalist party in Europe, as well as with significant sectors of mainstream parties, from German Christian Democrats to British Tories to Gianfranco Fini's National Alliance (now part of the People of Freedom) in Italy.

Second, he wants the Netherlands to opt out of EU decisions on immigration laws, "just like the Danes and the British. We have to keep our autonomy on immigration affairs. Never

must we allow a civil servant in Brussels or a French politician
to decide how many immigrants we need to accept." Relatedly,
he states, "The European [Union] should not expand any further. Turkey in, the Netherlands out." Opposition to Turkey's
accession—mostly for unmentioned, and perhaps unmention-
able, cultural reasons, as well as for economic reasons—is
widespread among mainstream political parties in Europe. It is
the official policy of Angela Merkel's government in Germany
and was sharply expressed by former French president Valéry
Giscard d'Estaing ("Turkey is not a European country").

Third, Wilders demands harsh security measures against
Moroccan street crime in Dutch cities and the elimination of
the *de facto* "no-go areas"—a complaint often heard in Berlin
and in the French *banlieues* as well. In regard to public education, Wilders notes that

> Within Islam and the Muslim community the separation
> between state and church is not fully recognized. That is why
> the founding of Islamic schools cannot be seen as something
> other than a harbinger of segregation and backwardness,
> because these schools do not contribute to the development
> of Western citizenship values. Article 23 of the constitution
> [providing equal treatment for religious schools, e.g., Calvinist,
> Catholic, Jewish] will stay, but Islamic schools may not be
> founded. Different situations don't need to be treated equally.

But the most decisive criticism is directed at the problem
of Islam and democratic values. Expressing views quite similar
to de Villiers's belief that there is no moderate Islam, but most
Muslims are moderate, Wilders states:

> Islam and democracy are not compatible. But Muslims could
> be won over for our democracy. But I resist the abuse that
> groups of Muslims make of our rights and freedoms of our
> constitutional state. Some abuse the freedom of religion
> to spread hatred, the freedom of education to set our

children against our society, the freedom of association for activities that are meant to undermine our society. We have a jurisdiction that (until now) makes it impossible to arrest people (for example: potential perpetrators of terror attacks or youngsters who want to go attend a training camp in Afghanistan) preventively or to expel and denaturalize criminal culprits of violent crimes who have a dual nationality. This has to change.

The solution proposed is that "We have to deny the use of our civil rights to those (Islamic) radicals who want to eliminate our constitutional state and civil rights. That will not weaken our constitutional state but will strengthen it. This is already possible in Germany." Asylum should be restricted to no more than 5,000, and those only "political refugees that come from regions that have demonstrable lack of refugee capacity." Headscarves at public functions should be banned (as was already done in France and in a number of German states).

Regarding Islamists, "Not only should radical imams leave the country, we should also undertake much firmer action to close radical mosques (and dissolve their administration). Financing by radicals—such as Salafist groups out of Morocco or Wahhabist groups out of Saudi Arabia—should be prohibited." Expulsions of Salafi imams are by now almost routine in France, have occurred in Italy and Germany, and were proposed by Tony Blair's government in Britain.

Finally, the frontal assault on multiculturalism:

- Immigration for marriage and family reunion will be prohibited for five years; marriage between first cousins will never be facilitated by immigration.

- An immigrant can be naturalized only after working 10 years in the Netherlands, and only if he has not committed any criminal offense during those 10 years; meanwhile there can be no social-benefits claims.

- Non-citizens may not vote, even in municipal elections.
- Government documents will be done only in Dutch.

Political Taxonomy

Why was Pim Fortuyn, an avowed homosexual and activist environmentalist, regularly described as a "leader of the populist Right"?[177] For the same reason that all groups, personalities, or political parties opposed to unlimited immigration or skeptical about the possibility of Muslim integration—and regardless of their other ideas and opinions—are routinely labeled "racist," "right wing," or even "fascist": simply put, because the politically correct position of the Left is to shut down any rational debate on those issues.

For decades, "mainstream" European political parties have been loath to even mention the two related issues of immigration and terrorism, although they are known to have long been among the top priorities of their voters. Not surprisingly, voters have found alternative channels to express their opinions on those issues and their frustrations over the major parties' refusal to deal with them.

The French presidential elections of 2002 were a major example of what the results could be. The ruling Socialist Party's candidate, Lionel Jospin, was eliminated in the second round, to the advantage of the National Front's Jean-Marie Le Pen, after refusing even to recognize that crime and terrorism were problems. While it is true that the somewhat more conservative Chirac came in first (barely) in the first round and received 82 percent of the votes in the final one, Le Pen received 18 percent of the votes, and close to 20 percent of the voters abstained. That result was a shock in France, indeed throughout Europe, and in many ways opened the gates for a serious discussion on

immigration, integration, and association with Islamist terrorism. When mainstream politicians and parties still avoid the
issues, alternative parties pick them up and benefit politically.

If France 2002 was a political wake-up call, shocks of similar
or greater magnitude soon took place in the Netherlands, Spain,
and the UK, as well as in countries like Denmark and Austria,
which have had no victims of terrorism, Islamist or otherwise.
Some voters evidently decided that they did not have to wait
until "it happens here" but could act preventively. The dominant Socialist/Social Democratic parties, or in some cases the
Christian Democrats, were seen as obstacles to be defeated—
and they were.

Meanwhile, whether in Austria or Denmark, the Netherlands
or France, if a party raises questions about immigration, or
about links between Islam and terrorism, it doesn't matter
that it is democratic in its political and ideological platform,
and accepts all democratic conditions and regulations. Most
of the media, as we have seen, will nonetheless instantly accuse it of "fascism," "racism," "xenophobia," or, the latest label,
"Islamophobia," intended as the combination of all the others.
This is the fight of elite media, NGOs, and academics against
reality and voters' will. It mostly fails.

Indeed, most of these "far right" parties were and are nothing of the sort—though some are. There is no question that
the British BNP is indeed a racist and totalitarian party, but
it is also the smallest and least significant anti-immigration
party in a major European country. Some of the (East) German
regional parties also appear to be neo-Nazi, or at least totalitarian in nature. On the other hand, the Austrian, Danish, Dutch,
and Italian parties are anything but totalitarian, and many of
them are not "far right" by any rational definition, since they
do not challenge the welfare state or tolerance within nation-

al historical traditions. Indeed, in the case of Fortuyn's party in the Netherlands, it openly advocated everything the Left would normally applaud—homosexuality, legal prostitution and drug use, etc. Everything, that is, except the free admission of those who vocally and, as it turned out, violently oppose all those things.

NATIONAL DEBATE: THE UNITED KINGDOM

Following the July 2005 London bombings, Prime Minister Blair declared: "Let no one be in any doubt: the rules of the game are changing."[178] But that remains to be seen, considering the political strength of the leftist NGOs in Britain, their infiltration of the judiciary, the old British tradition of harboring "dissidents" of all colors and destructive ideas, and the largely self-imposed restraints airily accepted by the courts under the cover of European legislation.

Perhaps typical of the mentality behind the establishment of Londonistan is *The Guardian*'s editorial following a May 2006 speech by President Bush on immigration: "The debate raging in America is part of a necessary process by which the US is struggling to see itself as it really is—one increasingly multicultural nation in a world of such nations, not a divinely ordained exception to which normal rules do not apply. There is a long way to go before America's Latinos are accepted as they should be."[179]

Thus, for the voice of the British Left, the world is made up of "multicultural nations"—this at a time when nationalism in Latin America and Islamism in the Muslim world are growing in intensity and exclusivism, and when even in Europe (Britain included) popular dissatisfaction with multiculturalism and the loss of national identity is manifested on a daily basis. *The Guardian*'s editorial is, of course, an expression of the same Eurocentric narcissism that Brussels and the pro-EU supranational elites are criticized for, and guilty of, and which was soundly rejected by the French and Dutch votes against the proposed EU Constitution in 2005.

As for British judges, the story of David Hicks—the Australian convert to Islam who fought as a jihadist in Kosovo and Kashmir, and was captured while fighting on the Taliban's side in Afghanistan and turned over to the United States—is characteristic. Since his mother was English, he—or his "progressive" British lawyers and supporters—discovered that he had a "right" to British citizenship. They applied for it on his behalf in London, and the government rejected the application. The reason behind Hicks's sudden discovery of loyalty to the Queen is well known: Because of Britain's close ties to Washington, British citizens held at Guantanamo were released into London's custody—and promptly let go, free to sue the American and British governments for "mistreatment." Hence, as a newly minted British citizen, Hicks had good reason to hope he would avoid trial and other unpleasantness at American hands. A three-judge appeals court in London overruled the government's refusal to grant Hicks citizenship, and the judges' comments are another good example of what created and maintains Londonistan.[180]

Lord Justice Pill claimed that Hicks was not given a chance to make representations about his attitudes since he discovered he had the right to citizenship. "Where a person has the right to citizenship and takes, or is prepared to take, the appropriate oath and give the appropriate pledge, basic fairness requires an assessment of his state of mind when he has become a citizen before he can be deprived of the citizenship granted."

Translation: The admitted Al-Qaeda follower has not repeated that admission while asking for British citizenship, hence "basic fairness" demands that he be given the benefit of the doubt regarding present loyalties.

That bizarre line of "reasoning" was also used by Lord Justice Rix in arriving at his holding that Hicks "could not have been disaffected towards Her Majesty at a time when he was neither a British citizen nor owed in any other way any allegiance to Her Majesty other than in her right as Queen of Australia."

Amnesty International was true to form. Its campaign director, Tim Hancock, offered summary judgment of the United States:

> Rather than fighting David Hicks's claim for British citizenship, the UK authorities should concentrate on the fact that Mr Hicks and hundreds of others are being held without charge or trial at Guantánamo Bay. . . . After four years the Guantánamo Bay prison camp has become a byword for abuse and an indictment of the US government's failure to uphold human rights in the "war on terror."[181]

Another perfect example of the judicial attitudes that permitted the formation of Londonistan, and explain its persistence, was provided by the judges of the Special Immigration Appeals Commission in May 2007, in the case of Mouloud Sihali, an Algerian asylum seeker. Accused, and acquitted, in the 2002 plot to attack the London Underground with the poison ricin, Sihali admitted to possessing false passports and received 15 months' imprisonment, but was released owing to time spent on remand. When, on the basis of its memorandum of understanding with Algeria, the government wanted to deport him, the judges refused because "he had never engaged in anything beyond petty dishonesty," had "no significant skill which would be of use to terrorists in the future," and

> did not appear to be a practising religious person. . . . Our view is that he would not knowingly put his liberty, the possibility that he might be allowed to remain in the United Kingdom and

his perceived safety on return to Algeria, if deported, at risk
by further assistance to those who might be terrorists.

This amazing second guessing implied that an alien criminal's appearing to become less religious, and having "no significant skill" for terrorism, is enough to decide that "Whatever
the risk to national security which he may have posed in 2002,
the risk is now insignificant."[182]

Case study:

A former Taliban intelligence officer—the son of a senior minister of the regime—was given indefinite leave to remain in
Britain after entering the country illegally, hidden in a container ship. The reason? "He told the Home Office that his position in the Taliban made it impossible for him to return to
Kabul without fear of torture and even death."[183] To help with
his case, he received "free" (i.e., paid for by British taxpayers)
legal aid. Nor was he alone: At the time (early 2003) lawyers
disclosed that at least two other Taliban fighters' asylum applications were being processed—all this at a time when British
soldiers were in Afghanistan, fighting (and dying) against
Taliban remnants.

Case study:

In February 2000 an Afghan Ariana plane with 78 people on
board was hijacked in Afghanistan by nine armed men and
forced to land in Britain. The hijackers, who claimed persecution by the Taliban, received short sentences (between 27
months and five years), and upon their release a court decided
that they could not be deported to Afghanistan because "their
lives would be at risk" (why, the court did not say, since the
Taliban no longer ruled Afghanistan) and because they had
acted "under duress" in hijacking the plane. When the initial

convictions were voided on appeal, Lord Justice Longmore explained that

> The only reason this appeal has succeeded is that there was a misdirection in relation to the law as explained to the jury. . . . In the light of some of the newspaper comments on the announcement of our decision, we think it right to say that we do not for a moment accept that the success of this appeal is a charter for future hijackers."[184]

The government delayed accepting the hijackers' asylum applications, but in 2006 another court gave them the right to stay. Moreover, Judge Sullivan stated that the government's behavior was such that "It is difficult to conceive of a clearer case of conspicuous unfairness amounting to an abuse of power."[185] Meanwhile, the nine air pirates and their families were living on welfare in London.

In fact, despite their protestations, Justices Longmore and Sullivan were only half right. As Charles Moore mordantly put it in *The Telegraph*,

> Today we have the case of the Afghan hijackers. The judges hold that they have a right to remain here, even though they violently grabbed a plane to get here in the first place, because Article 3 of the Human Rights Convention says that they cannot be sent anywhere where they might face torture. Mr Blair says this decision is "an abuse of common sense", and so it is. But in upholding such an abuse, the judges are only doing what the law tells them, and the person most responsible for passing that law is Mr Blair. Physician—or rather, barrister—heal thyself.[186]

On the other hand, the judges also engaged in extra-judicial pontificating and denied the obvious implications of their action: *de facto* amnesty for hijackers combined with the arbitrary decision that somehow post-Taliban Afghanistan is unsafe for . . . alleged anti-Taliban militants.

Moore accurately described the problem as it exists in, and as a root cause of, Londonistan:

> In popular conversation now, "human rights" in this country is the subject of mockery. It is understood, essentially correctly, to be a system by which judges defend bad people from the consequences of their actions and impose duties upon good people which are unreasonable. . . . Every grumpy prisoner, second-rate employee, suspected terrorist, mixed-up transsexual, Muslim schoolgirl who wants to wear the most extreme forms of religious outfit—these, and countless others, know that they can get lawyers, attention, legal aid and, often, money out of "human rights".
>
> Human rights are also understood, also correctly, to be an arrangement by which British citizens derive no advantage from their citizenship and foreigners can ride on their backs. Because the laws of human rights regard most of those rights as being universal, you do not have to qualify for them by becoming a citizen of our country.
>
> All you have to do is get inside the perimeter fence. Then your rights to religious freedom and social security and privacy and founding a family and paid holidays and free health treatment are all there. And so is the delay that so much law involves, the public expense of keeping claimants and their dependents, the fees for people like Mrs Blair [Cherie Blair, a lawyer], and the virtual breakdown of all administrative systems— policing, immigration, criminal justice, prisons, deportation, extradition—which relate to the problems involved.[187]

One must remember that Britain is an extreme case. France, for instance, has found ways to protect its security and national policies, on issues ranging from deportation of radical imams to veiling, without running afoul of the European "human-rights" bureaucracy. There were even some signs that Prime Minister Blair—if not his Labour back bench or the opposition Liberal Democrats—realized that the balance between "human rights" and the citizens' safety had gone too far against the latter. Blair's attorney general, Lord Goldsmith, admitted that European "jurisprudence [incorporated into British law via the Human Rights Act of 1998] says you can't deport people where there is a serious risk of particular things happening to them—death, torture, for example—without taking into account the security considerations at home." Blair himself described the judges' decision on the hijackers' case as "an abuse of common sense."[188]

After the July 2005 bombings, the British government tried to tighten counter-terrorism rules, to expand pre-trial detention for suspects, and to make it possible to expel such prominent Islamist recruiters and enablers as Abu Qatada, mostly by obtaining official assurances from their countries of origin (Jordan, Egypt) that they would not be mistreated. Considering the watering down of some of those measures and the ferocious opposition to them, both in Parliament and among "human-rights" fundamentalists like Amnesty International, one has to say that if Londonistan has diminished in size and capability, it is far from being closed down.

CHAPTER EIGHT

Europe, Islam, and U.S. Security

"My dear brother, the greatest weakness of the European and Western authorities is the [public] frustration over the security measures . . . since the European nations, by their very nature, strive to free themselves of security limitations, thereby contributing to the weakness of the European authorities and facilitating the mobility of the mujahedeen."

—"Al-Murabit Al-Muwahhid," Islamist blogger, 2008[1]

If, despite many differences over Islamist terrorism, its causes, and appropriate methods to deal with it, there is a transatlantic consensus, it is that cooperation between Europe and the United States is not where both sides would like it to be. There have been a number of public conflicts on these issues between Washington and specific European governments, and many less-public conflicts, but ultimately the problem is more profound. It has to do with threat perceptions and cultural differences. While both sides understand that the jihadist threat is global, they see its nature very differently and have adopted divergent means to deal with it. The result, far too often, is that a single enemy is countered by a patchwork of different, even diverging, legal and security measures.

Does Europe's way of dealing with its Islamist presence have an impact on the security of the United States and on transatlantic relations? This is not a question easy to answer because, to begin with, there is no "Europe" yet in this respect. As we have seen throughout this study, for all the efforts of the EU bureaucrats, different nations still have different cultures and different laws, and some of them have sometimes reacted unexpectedly to traumatic events within their borders. There is no effective Europe-wide agreement on counter-terrorism efforts either. It is true that there are the beginnings of practical intra-European cooperation, but there is also a legal framework, formally established by the European Convention on Human Rights, that often makes counter-terrorism efforts ineffective. So, for the time being, European states have adopted disparate approaches to Islamist terrorism, determined by their distinct legal traditions, experience with the phenomenon, and perceived security needs.

The Threat: Definitions and Perceptions

The EU Council's 2002 "Framework Decision on Combatting Terrorism," which has informed a number of national legislative acts, is itself a demonstration of Europe's ambiguous approach to the terrorist phenomenon.

On the one hand, it accurately (Art. 1) describes the goals of terrorism: "seriously intimidating a population, or unduly compelling a government or international organization to perform or abstain from performing any act, or seriously destabilizing or destroying the fundamental political, constitutional, economic or social structures of a country or an international organization."[2] This description indicates that terrorists have little in common with bank robbers or rapists—in other words, with ordinary criminals.

On the other hand,

> [The following] shall be deemed to be terrorist offences:
> (a) attacks upon a person's life which may cause death; (b)
> attacks upon the physical integrity of a person; (c) kidnapping
> or hostage taking; (d) causing extensive destruction to
> a Government or public facility, a transport system, an
> infrastructure facility, including an information system, a
> fixed platform located on the continental shelf, a public place
> or private property likely to endanger human life or result in
> major economic loss; (e) seizure of aircraft, ships or other means
> of public or goods transport; (f) manufacture, possession,
> acquisition, transport, supply or use of weapons, explosives or
> of nuclear, biological or chemical weapons, as well as research
> into, and development of, biological and chemical weapons;
> (g) release of dangerous substances, or causing fires, floods or
> explosions the effect of which is to endanger human life; (h)
> interfering with or disrupting the supply of water, power or
> any other fundamental natural resource the effect of which is
> to endanger human life; (i) threatening to commit any of the
> acts listed in (a) to (h).[3]

This list includes ordinary crimes like murder and assault,
as well as typical acts of terrorism, like hijacking and use of
weapons of mass destruction, creating a mishmash of conflicting and inconsistent legal approaches to an already complex
phenomenon.

By contrast, the United States operates with a simple and
clear definition:

> Criminal acts dangerous to human life and apparently intended
> to: (i) intimidate or coerce a civilian population; (ii) influence
> the policy of a government by intimidation or coercion; or (iii)
> to affect the conduct of a government by mass destruction,
> assassination or kidnapping.

The United Kingdom uses a similar definition: "The use or
threat of action designed to influence the government or to
intimidate the public or a section of the public, for the purpose

of advancing a political, religious or ideological cause."[4] That doesn't mean, as we have seen, that British judges necessarily apply the definition in rational ways. But at least it is clear, and on the record.

For the EU as a whole, if not for all the individual states, the idea of banning terrorist groups wholesale was difficult to agree on. Thus, while the U.S. first established a list of 30 terrorist groups in October 1997, the UK did so only in March 2001 (21 groups), and the EU in December of that year (13 groups, including the Taliban and Al-Qaeda).[5]

Since many European countries based their post-9/11 anti-terrorism legislation on the EU Framework document, it is not surprising that the result was equally confusing, and allowed individual courts to decide terrorist cases according to their own preferences, legal or ideological. In January 2005, Milanese judge Clementina Forleo dismissed terrorism charges against three Tunisians and two Moroccans accused of recruiting suicide bombers and supporting terror activities in Iraq. Judge Forleo said the defendants had been engaging in wartime "guerrilla" activities, not terrorism.[6] The judge's decision, and arguments, were indeed strange. No European country considers terrorism "war" (unlike the United States), nor is there any valid legal distinction between "guerrilla" activities and "terrorism." Franco Frattini, security and justice commissioner of the European Union, commented: "This sends a devastating signal. Fundamentalist Islamic cells can now think that there are safe havens in Europe." But he was mistaken when he claimed that "The judge has interpreted the law wrongly."[7] The problem was less with an ideological judge than with the vague and contradictory European counter-terrorism laws themselves.

Given such a context, Judge Forleo's ruling, later overturned, that Italian-based Al-Qaeda recruiters for Iraq were not terrorists but guerrilla fighters was comprehensible. Desperately seeking some precedent in international law, she thought she had found one in the UN's Global Convention on Terrorism of 1999. Thus she held that

> "Violent or guerrilla activity taking place in the context of an armed conflict, even if conducted by armed forces different from institutional ones, cannot be prosecuted, not even at the level of international law, unless international humanitarian law is violated," and that "Terrorist activities which are relevant and prosecutable on the level of international law are those which are directed towards the dissemination of indiscriminate terror amongst the civilian population in the name of an ideological and/or religious creed, setting itself as a crime against humanity." According to her, punishing a guerrilla act done during a conflict "could inevitably lead to an unjustified taking of a position in support of one of the forces in the field."[8]

Leaving aside the fact that Judge Forleo must have been the only person in Europe unaware of the targets of foreign jihadis in Iraq and the nature of their activities, the fact remains that using UN documents as precedents allows decisions like hers to happen.

Counter-Terrorism and Human Rights

> "The Court's jurisprudence makes it clear that there is no balance to be struck between the right of the individual not to be exposed to such risks [of torture] and the national security interests of the sending state (see the European Court of Human Rights judgment in the case of *Chahal v. United Kingdom*)."
>
> —Amnesty International[9]

In many ways the debate over the proper balance between counter-terrorism and "human rights" is even more heated in Europe than in the United States, for at least two major reasons, one general and one practical. In general terms, European cultural trends are far more advanced into postmodern, post-democratic terrain than even San Francisco or Vermont would dream. Indeed, the notions and practice of "tolerance" and multi-culturalism have advanced far into the popular psyche of most European countries, making any reassessment very painful. Second, the political influence of the European Left, especially in the parallel universe of the mushrooming "human-rights" NGOs, is extraordinary and unmatched in the United States. Furthermore, European states have for so long surrendered so many of their sovereign attributes to the EU that, even when a large majority of voters demand, and elements of the political class try to implement, meaningful counter-terrorism or anti-immigration measures, bodies such as the European Court of Human Rights or the International Criminal Court are able to block, delay, or reject such measures.

The above quote from Amnesty International, the UK-based over-influential NGO, is accurate and should be highly disturbing. It precisely describes a series of decisions by the European Court (EC) in Strasbourg in terrorism cases, all of which repeat the same opinion: The rights of terrorists trump both the obligation of governments to provide security for their citizens and the latter's right to life.

It all originated in Article 3 of the Human Rights Convention, adopted by the Council of Europe back in 1950.

Article 3

No State Party shall expel, return or extradite a person to another State where there are substantial grounds for believing that he would be in danger of being subjected to torture.

For the purpose of determining whether there are such grounds, the competent authorities shall take into account all relevant considerations including, where applicable, the existence in the State concerned of a consistent pattern of gross, flagrant or mass violations of human rights.[10]

In *Chahal v. The United Kingdom* (1996), a majority ruled that

Article 3 of the European Convention may engage the responsibility of the State where substantial grounds are shown for believing there would be real risk to the deportee of torture or inhuman or degrading treatment or punishment in the receiving country. Article 3, said the Court, provides an absolute prohibition of torture; consequently in expulsion cases, if substantial grounds are shown for believing that the deportee would be at risk, his or her conduct cannot be a material consideration.[11]

Karamjit Singh Chahal was a Sikh militant and an illegal immigrant to Britain, who appealed his deportation to democratic India, claiming that he would be mistreated or tortured there. The EC ruled that the absolute prohibition of torture is more important than the British government's claim that Chahal was a security threat, and prohibited his deportation.

The 2005 *Ramzy v. The Netherlands* was a similar case, involving an Algerian engaged in terrorist activities in the Netherlands. Despite interventions by the governments of Italy, Lithuania, Portugal, Slovakia, and the UK on behalf of the Dutch, the European Court brought in a ruling similar to its *Chahal* ruling.[12] The British NGO Justice and Liberty weighed in on the court's side, claiming that "Each of the nongovernmental organisations intervening in this case consider that the judgment of the Court in *Chahal*, that the prohibition on return to face torture or ill-treatment is absolute under the ECHR, was correct and is the only position which is in accordance with other sources of international law."[13]

Of course, "torture" and "ill-treatment"—the prospect of which, in the view of the "human-rights" NGOs and the

European Court, is sufficient to forbid deportation of terrorist suspects—are subjective terms infinitely flexible and culturally varied. In fact, for German "human-rights" expert Dieter
Grimm, torture is whatever violates something he calls "human dignity" and defines as follows:

> . . . a quality that humans do not acquire by a worthy life or
> good deeds nor forfeit by an unworthy life or bad deeds. It
> is innate in every human being, and a violation of someone's
> dignity amounts to a negation of his or her quality as a person.
> . . . Thus dignity becomes the basis of all concrete liberties. *If
> there is anything that constitutes a violation of dignity it is torture.*
> [Emphasis added.] The world has reached a consensus that
> torture is prohibited under all circumstances. This consensus
> has found its expression in a number of documents of the United
> Nations as well as in the Geneva Convention. Nevertheless,
> under the threat of terrorism the number of voices justifying
> torture in certain extreme situations is growing. The argument
> is always proportionality. Torturing one person may save the
> lives of hundreds or thousands of others. It is a quantitative
> argument and it has a certain appeal.[14]

The immediate problem with this is that "dignity" is a culturally specific concept and not, as Grimm would have it, an innate quality. For an Islamist the wearing of the *niqab* or *burqa*
is a matter of dignity; use of police dogs is an insult to dignity;
and, of course, the Danish cartoons were an outrageous insult
to dignity. Should the French Parliament's ban on the *hijab*,
burqa, and *niqab* in schools, or the universal use of police dogs,
therefore be considered "torture"? Should the Danish publishers of *Jyllands-Posten* be accused of "torture"? For Amnesty
International—a major influence in European legal and intellectual circles—virtually any form of pressure on a detainee,
from sleep deprivation to loud music to threats, is "torture."

And Grimm's views are pervasive among the European
elites, as demonstrated when Hans Jürgen Papier, president of

the German Constitutional Court, offered the opinion that "The protection of human dignity will never be limited in any case"— hence the court's 2006 ruling that the military would never be permitted to shoot down a hijacked plane flying toward a skyscraper.[15] By contrast, in France such a decision would be taken by the prime minister; and in the U.S., following 9/11, the president delegated the decision to the Air Force.

The level of unreality is indicated by the further elucidation that shooting down civilian aircraft is always illegal because it violates the human rights of the civilians on board: *"By killing the passengers as a means to save others, they are treated as objects and at the same time deprived of their rights."* Even if it were clear that a hijacked plane was going to be crashed into a building and the passengers were doomed to die, the court wouldn't budge. In fact, its press release read: *"Human life and human dignity enjoy the same constitutional protection regardless of the duration of the physical existence of the human being."*

Commenting on this quagmire, the *Wall Street Journal* concluded:

> No doubt, the question of shooting down a civilian airliner in order to avert an even greater catastrophe poses a terrible moral dilemma that no government should consider lightly. But this is not an issue that judges should or can decide. Non-state actors who can inflict war-like casualties no longer fit into our traditional legal concepts. A constitutional judge has the luxury to base his decisions on absolute norms (killing innocents is always wrong) without having to assume responsibility for the consequences of his ruling. . . . The judges yesterday only looked at the innocent civilians on the plane but had little to say about the "human dignity" and "inalienable rights" of those innocent civilians the law was intended to protect.[16]

More recently, on February 28, 2008, the EC again decided, in *Nassim Saadi v. Italy,* that the claims of the human-rights lobby trump the safety of European citizens. Saadi was tried, found guilty of criminal conspiracy and of forgery, and sentenced in Italy, and was tried and sentenced to 20 years by a Tunisian military court. Using Amnesty International and Human Rights Watch reports, the court ruled that the prospect that Saadi might pose a serious threat to the community in Italy "did not diminish in any way the risk that he might suffer harm if deported."[17] The reaction of the human-rights establishment was triumphant:

> "This decision will be welcomed by anti-torture and human rights campaigners everywhere," said Sonya Sceats, an associate fellow at the international think tank Chatham House. "By affirming the absolute nature of the torture ban, the Strasbourg court has proved that basic rules of international human rights law cannot be sacrificed in the name of counter-terrorism."[18]

That despite the fact that the reason Italian authorities had sought to have Nassim Saadi deported was that he had played an "active role" in an organization providing support to fundamentalist Islamist cells in Italy and abroad.[19]

In desperation, when confronted with such decisions, European governments have searched for a solution and, as the United States has done, have looked to bilateral guarantees from the terrorists' states of origin—memoranda of understanding (MoUs), promising fair treatment for returnees. However, in the world of human-rights fundamentalists, that is not good enough.

The reactions ranged from furious to positively Kafkaesque when then Prime Minister Tony Blair stated:

> [W]e are today signalling a new approach to deportation orders . . . the circumstances of our national security have self-evidently changed, and we believe we can get the necessary assurances from the countries to which we will return the

deportees, against their being subject to torture or ill treatment contrary to Article 3. We have now concluded a Memorandum of Understanding with Jordan, and we are close to getting necessary assurances from other relevant countries . . . I had very constructive conversations with the leaders of Algeria and Lebanon. There are around 10 such countries with whom we are seeking such assurances.[20]

The British Parliamentary Joint Committee for Human Rights, the UN Human Rights Commissioner, the UN Special Rapporteur on Torture, the EU Network of Independent Experts, and the Commissioner for Human Rights of the Council of Europe all weighed in, stating that diplomatic assurances are no safeguard against torture.[21]

The Council of Europe's Commissioner for Human Rights claimed that "The weakness inherent in the practice of diplomatic assurances lies in the fact that where there is a need for such assurances, there is clearly an acknowledged risk of torture and ill-treatment. Due to the absolute nature of the prohibition of torture or inhuman or degrading treatment, formal assurances cannot suffice where a risk nonetheless remains."

This claim was repeated by the UN Special Rapporteur: "Diplomatic assurances are sought from countries with a proven record of systematic torture, i.e. the very fact that such diplomatic assurances are sought is an acknowledgement that the requested State, in the opinion of the requesting State, is practising torture."[22]

Louise Arbour, the UN High Commissioner for Human Rights, in her address on Human Rights Day 2005, pushed absurdity even further:

> Even if some post-return monitoring were functioning, the fact that some Governments conclude legally non-binding agreements with other Governments on a matter that is at the core of several legally binding UN instruments threatens to empty international

human rights law of its content. Diplomatic assurances basically
create a two-class system among detainees, attempting to
provide for a special bilateral protection and monitoring
regime for a selected few and ignoring the systematic torture
of other detainees, even though all are entitled to the equal
protection of existing UN instruments.[23] [Emphasis added.]

Thus, in her opinion, even if the rights of returned terrorist
suspects are monitored and protected, if such protections do
not extend to unrelated cases, that would "empty international
human rights law of its content"!

These court cases demonstrate that European states face
a very serious obstacle if they intend to try virtually any
method to deal with the hundreds, or thousands, of jihadis in
their midst—and that some basic legal formulations have to
be reconsidered. Tony Blair had a point when he described the
judge's decision to prevent the deportation of the nine Afghanis
who hijacked a plane to Britain as "barmy."[24] Equally direct was
British Home Secretary Charles Clarke, speaking in Washington
in October 2005: "The right to be protected from the death and
destruction caused by indiscriminate terrorism is at least as
important as the right of a terrorist to be free of torture and ill
treatment. . . . We cannot fight terrorism with one legal hand
tied behind our back."[25] As it has turned out, however, not just
Britain but other countries have had to do just that.

Human Rights and Counter-Terrorism: The Practical Impact

In practical terms, the European Court decisions on terrorist-
deportation cases mean that any Islamist terrorist or suspected
terrorist who manages to reach Europe is safe—since, at least
according to the human-rights groups the European courts
and governments take so seriously and subsidize so heavily,

virtually all Muslim countries practice "abuse'" and "torture." Thus Taliban leaders ask for asylum in Europe, pleading that if sent back home they will be persecuted. Thus, an individual like Omar Bakri Mohammed, expelled from Saudi Arabia for religious extremism, received asylum in London.[26]

In addition to the general constraints imposed by the EC, the various European countries have different perceptions, legal and intelligence tools, and competence in dealing with terrorism, and that fact implies varying levels, from country to country, of cooperation with the United States.

Local traditions and practices are sometimes pathetically in conflict with common sense and current necessities. Thus, Sweden does not apply serious sentences for terrorism; it has no death penalty or, in reality, life in prison. In order to get rid of a dangerous Egyptian terrorist and recruiter, it did allow U.S. operatives to move him from Sweden to Egypt—and then engaged in a bout of national hand-wringing over how it was done (why was he forced to wear a certain uniform?) and what happened to him in Egypt—after all, he was able to call and make allegations that he had been tortured.

In Italy, a judge decided that a similar proceeding against an illegal immigrant, an Egyptian jihadi, allegedly taken away and sent to Egypt by CIA operatives, was a crime, and decided to pursue the action against the CIA, rather than deal with the problem in Italy.

Most shocking of all, British judges managed to find reasons to prevent, for ten years (November 1995 to December 2005), the extradition of a major Algerian terrorist, Rachid Ramda, to France, because a fellow accused terrorist claimed that Ramda could be mistreated by the French. German and Dutch courts have let known terrorists go free because of technicalities and have rejected intelligence information as evidence. And then there is the case of Mohammed Haydar Zammar, a member of the European Syrian network, linked to Al-Qaeda generally and to the Hamburg group of 9/11 terrorists specifically. What makes Zammar interesting is what has happened to him since 9/11.

Interrogated by the Germans in 2002, he was captured—by the CIA, according to the German media—and sent to Syria, whose citizenship he holds (as well as, since 1982, Germany's). While talking to the Germans, Zammar admitted that he had traveled to Afghanistan five times between 1991 and 2000, and "identified other mujahidin in photographs"—intelligence the Germans shared with Syria. By the end of 2006 Zammar was on trial in Damascus, accused of being a member of the violent Attar wing of the Muslim Brotherhood, of "attending training camps in Afghanistan and Bosnia," and of having "jihadist ambitions"—all of which he admitted both in Germany and in Syria. He was sentenced to death, but the sentence was reduced to 12 years in prison.[27]

Instead of being seen as a rare instance of a jihadist receiving a deserved punishment, albeit in a country of dubious justice, the case made the Germans feel guilty for having provided evidence to Syria. The German Foreign Ministry sent an observer to witness Zammar's new trial, and German diplomats obtained an attorney for the accused terrorist, even offering to pay his legal fees.[28] All this, not because anyone had any doubts about Zammar's jihadist role, importance, or links to the 9/11 terrorists, but because his was a capital case—argument enough for Amnesty International to, once again, put emotions ahead of truth and justice. Amnesty thought Zammar would not get a fair trial, since "the judges on the Syrian court have no qualms in allowing confessions obtained through torture." According to Ruth Jüttner, a Middle East expert with Amnesty, "Sometimes the lawyers aren't even allowed to set foot in the courtroom, and sometimes the court bars them from reviewing the files ... and there is no appeal."[29]

Worse still, a case like Zammar's prevents intelligence personnel from doing their job—namely, trying to prevent terrorists from carrying out their lethal plots. The head of Italian intelligence was forced to resign in 2006 for cooperating with the United States.

Somewhat surprisingly, Britain finally decided, on the basis of an MoU with Jordan, to deport Abu Qatada to his country of citizenship, as the Special Immigration Appeals Commission (SIAC) decided that he was under "no real risk of persecution" if he was sent back to Jordan. The decision establishes the legal principle that foreign nationals may be deported on national-security grounds, if a diplomatic "no torture, no ill-treatment" pledge can be obtained.[30]

In a 2006 case, the SIAC "gave some weight" to the assurances of Algerian authorities when Britain was contemplating returning to his home country a man cleared of any involvement in the supposed ricin plot. Justice Ouseley stated, "We have concluded that they are acting in good faith; the political changes demonstrate their will and the level and consistency of the assurances support that."[31]

These rulings notwithstanding, it remains very difficult to deport suspects for national-security reasons. More typical was the case of two Libyan terrorists, "DD" and "AS." The judges described DD as "a global jihadist with links to the Taliban and al-Qaida" and identified him as the brother-in-law of Serhane ben Abdelmajid Fakhet, a.k.a. El Tunecino, a leader of the Madrid bombing cell.[32] The SIAC admitted the terrorists' appeals on the grounds that they might be tortured or even executed if returned to Tripoli. SIAC chairman Justice Moseley stated that the European Convention on Human Rights could be breached if the two men were removed to Libya, although he indicated there was no probable risk. Justice Mitting said that even keeping them in detention after they had won their appeal would be on the "cusp of legality."

Thus, the SIAC made decisions on the basis of European rather than British law; it also decided differently from case to case because, in its *political* judgment, Algeria has some credibility, Jordan is credible, and Libya is not. In no case were British security concerns given priority, despite the court's admitting that they are real. But even the SIAC's inconsistent approach was better than the consistent lack of concern for national safety on the part of Amnesty International's UK director, Kate Allen: "Amnesty has long argued that MoUs offer no protection from torture and are not worth the paper they're written on."[33]

It should be pointed out that even when judges do somehow manage to find ways to allow the deportation of prominent jihadis, the process is so protracted and costly that its deterrent effect is minimal. The fate of Abu Qatada is quite significant in this respect.

Considered by most analysts to be Al-Qaeda's main ideologue and recruiter in Europe, Abu Qatada issued a *fatwa* in 1995 justifying the killing of wives and children of "apostates," and in 1998 he asked for indefinite leave to remain in the UK. He received no decision. The following year he was convicted *in absentia* in Amman for conspiracy to commit terrorist acts and sentenced to life in prison, but that did not prevent him from declaring that jihad had begun. Already suspected of ties with German jihadi cells (Mohamed Atta possessed tapes of his sermons), he went into hiding after 9/11 and was finally arrested in October 2002. Throughout his stay in England he never held a job but lived, with his family, on public assistance.

Following a court decision, he was released on bail in

December 2004, but a "control order" (equivalent to house arrest) was imposed in March 2005. He was detained again in August 2005, and in February 2007 an SIAC court rejected his appeal against deportation. That ruling was overturned in 2008 and reaffirmed in 2009. Still, his lawyer, the sympathetic Gareth Peirce, has filed further appeals, including to the European Court of Human Rights, which infuriated Britons in February 2009 by awarding Abu Qatada £2,500 in compensation for his "unlawful detention."[34]

Another absurd case is that of Omar Khyam, the cell leader of the "fertilizer plot" in London ("Operation Crevice"), who was arrested on March 30, 2004. A week before his arrest, Sidique Khan and Shehzad Tanweer were seen in his company—a fact that should have aroused suspicions about those two, who a year later committed the worst terrorist attack ever in Britain.[35] What is more, the members of the fertilizer cell admitted dealing with Mohammed Quayyum Khan, a.k.a. "Q," who has sent many jihadis to Pakistan for training. A cell member turned informer claimed that "Q" was in direct touch with the core Al-Qaeda leadership through Abdul Hadi al-Iraqi, a senior leader captured by U.S. forces in 2006.[36] While Khyam and four other plotters were sentenced to life in prison, "Q" remains free in Britain for "lack of evidence." As for Sidique Khan and Shehzad Tanweer, MI5 gave the reason why they were not arrested or even put under surveillance after being seen together with Khyam and taped discussing with him methods of raising funds through fraud: To MI5, "they appeared as petty fraudsters in loose contact with members of the plot."[37] This suggests that the main British counter-terrorist agency made a sharp and unwarranted distinction between terrorist planners and the petty criminals providing logistical support—a distinction without a difference, as the two categories have repeatedly proved to overlap; everywhere in Europe, many, if not most, jihadis have a criminal background.

The awkward and discomfiting reality is that, with the partial exception of France, the prevailing European mentality—reflected in the major media outlets and, more importantly, in judicial decisions and legal texts—is incompatible with a serious approach to counter-terrorism. A potentially lethal and in the long term unsustainable combination of sentimentalism, "human-rights" fundamentalism, and unwillingness to adapt past legislation to the realities of today's Islamist terrorism has led to Europe's transformation into a *de facto* depository of some of the most dangerous jihadists anywhere—at the cost of not only European but world security.

PERCEPTIONS OF THREAT AND HUMAN RIGHTS

If there is an ultimate cause of many European countries' difficulties in cooperating with the United States in counter-terrorism—apart from the rampant anti-Americanism pervading the elites and, often, the public as well—it is their interpretation of human rights and their long-standing customs.

Most European countries have a decades-long tradition of tolerance for terrorists of the Far Left, especially when they come from the Third World. A particularly outrageous case is that of José María Sison, the founder of the Philippines' (Maoist) Communist Party, whose terrorist arm, the New People's Army, is still active. Sison fled to the Netherlands in 1987—after the return of democracy in Manila—and asked for political asylum. While he did not receive it, he has received welfare payments. He has been designated as a terrorist supporter by the U.S., the EU, and Manila since 2002, and he was accused of murdering a Filipino senator in 2001; his appeal was finally rejected by the European Human Rights Court in 2004. Nevertheless, as his supporters gloated, "whatever is the outcome of the litigation on the main issue of 'terrorist' status, Prof. Sison will continue to be protected by the [European Convention on Human Rights], especially by its Article 3, which prohibits his forcible transfer to any country where he is at risk of torture, degrading or inhuman treatment or punishment."[38]

Sweden has long been a host for terrorist leaders from around the world, but while *de facto* support for Marxist revolutionaries in Peru or the Philippines may perhaps be explained by European romantic views of such individuals, the issue takes on a greater urgency when similar tolerance is demonstrated for terrorists active against a European country, and one that is a candidate for EU membership.

The Kurdish PKK was long allowed to gather funds throughout Europe—mostly through racketeering and drug trafficking—despite being listed as a terrorist group by the U.S. and the EU. It took the shock of Pim Fortuyn's murder for the Dutch to discover a PKK training camp in their densely populated country.[39]

Fehriye Erdal of Turkey's Marxist-Leninist Revolutionary People's Liberation Party/Front (DHKP/C) was directly involved in the 1996 murder of prominent businessman Ozdemir Sabanci. Erdal fled to Belgium, where she was arrested for arms possession and using a false name. Brussels denied Turkey's extradition request, giving justifications including the standard (Turkey had the death penalty) and the legalistic (Brussels did not consider the DHKP/C a terrorist organization). When both these points became moot (Turkey renounced capital punishment and the EU listed the DHKP/C as terrorist), Erdal "escaped."[40]

And then there was the case of Metin Kaplan, head of the German-based *Hilafet Devleti* (Caliphate State) movement. The group, officially banned in Germany, was in fact long tolerat-

602 EUROPE, ISLAM, AND U.S. SECURITY

ed, despite its ties to Al-Qaeda and various associated groups and its fundraising for Islamists in Afghanistan, Bosnia, and Chechnya. In 1997 Kaplan was responsible for the murder of rival Halil Ibrahim Sofu in Germany, and the following year he was accused of planning to use a plane to destroy Atatürk's tomb in Ankara. Arrested for Sofu's murder in 1999, he was sentenced by a German court to just four years in prison. After lengthy legal delays, in 2004 he was finally extradited to Turkey, where he received a life sentence.[41]

Many Europeans, and not only leftists, stubbornly cling to the notion that the Geneva Conventions, which were never intended to apply to terrorist groups, should nevertheless apply to them, because, as British historian Niall Ferguson, now at Harvard, put it, "the tables could easily be turned."[42] This claim, common in Europe and often repeated in the United States—for instance, by presidential candidate John McCain—is simply illogical. Regular armed forces of a state engaged in a conflict with the United States will respect Geneva out of fear of retaliation and hope of reciprocal treatment. Indeed, fear of retaliation worked, at least in part, even in the case of Nazi Germany's *Wehrmacht*, which never used chemical weapons simply because of fear of an Allied response in kind. None of these arguments, however, apply to Islamist terrorists, whose moral, psychological, and legal conditioning makes them immune to the threat of retaliation or the notion of reciprocity with the infidel. For those routinely engaged in suicide bombings, beheadings, and torture of noncombatants, the very idea of international humanitarian law is simply alien and inapplicable.

Equally significant was the official reaction of Anna Lindh, then Sweden's foreign minister, to the killing of Yemeni Al-Qaeda terrorists by a U.S. armed drone in 2002:

> [Lindh] declared that the American military attack, even with
> Yemeni approval, "is nevertheless a summary execution that
> violates human rights." She added, "Even terrorists must be
> treated according to international law. Otherwise, any country
> can start executing those whom they consider terrorists."
> Amnesty International also questioned "the deliberate killing
> of suspects in lieu of arrest, in circumstances in which they
> did not pose an immediate threat."[43]

Those were extraordinary statements demonstrating a profound and deliberate misunderstanding of the nature of the
fight against jihadism throughout the world. Did Lindh and
Amnesty truly expect the Stockholm police to arrest Al-Qaeda
operatives in the wilds of Yemen, perhaps under the aegis of
the UN?

One example of the kinds of problems the EU human-rights
establishment raises for counter-terrorism authorities—and
a demonstration of the way rigid human-rights interpretations of law contravene real life—is a May 2007 "Point of
View" by Thomas Hammarberg, Human Rights Commissioner
of the Council of Europe, and formerly a Swedish diplomat.[44]
Hammarberg was particularly critical of profiling, because
"The underlying assumption of the current terrorist profiling is dangerous, namely that young men of Muslim faith or
Middle-Eastern appearance are particularly likely to be involved in terrorist activity." He was also upset because "The
risk of discrimination in carrying out such profiling exercises
is certainly high. Taking law enforcement decisions based on
grounds such as race or colour may violate the principle of
non-discrimination as enshrined in Article 14 of the European
Convention on Human Rights."

In fact, discrimination, in its true sense of critical sifting of
analytical elements, is necessary; and Muslims are neither a
"race" nor distinguished by their "color"—a fact that bears rep-

etition. Hammarberg's words are another indication of the extent to which Muslim and Islamist claims that any criticism of Islam or of any Muslim is *ipso facto* "Islamophobic," and hence "racist," have become common currency in Brussels.

The absolute priority given to the rights of individuals, terrorists included, over the community's vital interests has, as we have seen, led European judges to allow alien terrorists to stay in their country despite the public threat they pose. It also explains the uproar among European political and cultural elites over "extraordinary rendition" and Guantanamo.

THE GUANTANAMO AND RENDITION ISSUES

Nothing more clearly demonstrates the moral, political, and legal gap between Europe and the United States regarding terrorism than the issues of Guantanamo and "extraordinary rendition"— delivering suspected terrorists to their countries of origin or culturally related ones rather than keeping them in Europe (or the U.S.) for lack of legal requirements needed for prosecution.

The reactions to both are linked to a cultural phenomenon (anti-Americanism, often associated with pacifism) and a related legal one, with Europeans seeing terrorism purely as crime and the U.S. seeing it as a peculiar phenomenon, combining politics, military threat, and crime, and thus needing a new and still-undefined approach.

Indeed, if there is a perfect illustration of the gap between European elite attitudes and the interests of transatlantic cooperation, it is the treatment of rendition by the European Parliament.[45] Led by Dick Marty, a Swiss (and thus from a non-EU state), it underscores the convoluted way of thinking of European politicians—their mixing of anti-Americanism, emotionalism, arrogance, and misinterpreted international and domestic law—and, ultimately, their practical irrelevance.

The document in question observes that

> While the states of the Old World have dealt with these threats primarily by means of existing institutions and legal systems, the United States appears to have made a fundamentally different choice: considering that neither conventional judicial instruments nor those established under the framework of the laws of war could effectively counter the new forms of international terrorism, it decided to develop new legal concepts.[46]

The document then continues by bluntly declaring that "This legal approach is utterly alien to the European tradition and sensibility, and is clearly contrary to the European Convention on Human Rights and the Universal Declaration of Human Rights." It even condemns the Security Council's post-9/11 creation of a list of terrorist individuals and entities:

> It is frankly alarming to see the UN Security Council sacrificing essential principles pertaining to fundamental rights in the name of the fight against terrorism. The compilation of so-called "black lists" of individuals and companies suspected of maintaining connections with organisations considered terrorist and the application of the associated sanctions clearly breach every principle of the fundamental right to a fair trial: no specific charges, no right to be heard, no right of appeal, no established procedure for removing one's name from the list.

Naturally, Guantanamo, being a manifestation of precisely the attempt of the United States to develop a new legal framework to deal with the global terrorist threat, is strongly condemned. The Parliamentary Assembly of the Council of Europe (PACE) adopted a resolution (1433/2005) and a recommendation (1699/2005) urging Washington to "put a stop to this situation and to ensure respect for the principles of the rule of law and human rights."[47]

When, in December 2005, the House of Lords' justices decided that "information obtained under torture" could not be used in British courts, what they were saying was that all information sent from the U.S. to British law courts was *ipso facto* unacceptable—because the very same Law Lords had already decided that whatever came out of Guantanamo and Bagram (in Afghanistan), not to mention the undefined and undescribed "secret" U.S. camps elsewhere, was suspected to have been obtained through torture.

Simply put, according to Senator Marty and the Parliamentary Assembly, no change in the judicial approach to terror is necessary, even when approved by the Security Council—where EU member states have more than one-fifth of the seats, including two permanent ones. The fact that many EU member governments in fact cooperate with the United States suggests that Marty's views are not universally shared; the fact that they do so discreetly, and in defiance of official EU opinion, suggests the seriousness of the problem.

The European Parliament, an entity with few powers but an assertive political voice, engaged in what it called an investigation of renditions and, by a vote of 382 to 256, with 74 abstentions, approved a report accusing Britain, Germany, Italy, and other EU countries of turning a blind eye to CIA flights carrying terrorist suspects in Europe. The Parliament's committee on CIA activities in Europe claimed that 1,200 CIA-operated flights had used European airspace between 2001 and 2005. The allegations were that the CIA used European territory (e.g., Poland or Romania) for the transfer of prominent Al-Qaeda prisoners from their place of capture (Pakistan, Afghanistan, etc.) to alternative locations for interrogation, mostly in the Middle East.

The basis of the Parliament's vote was the strange report of Senator Marty, strange because its major complaint was the lack of proof of criminal acts due to various governments' refusal to provide it to him.[48] "It presumes there is one chief guilty party and that is the USA," said Jas Gawronski of the European People's Party. "That's why we don't like this report."[49]

Ultimately, of course, it is the great and growing gap between the dominant European culture and the American culture—with the former always looking for any reason to blame "the Americans" for Islamist terror—that determines the political tone of transatlantic cooperation.

The Atlantic gap is not likely to be bridged soon. One illustration of the difficulty is an exchange in 2006 between the State Department's legal adviser, John B. Bellinger III, and Gijs de Vries, the EU's counter-terrorism coordinator. Bellinger: "But is it clear that what all of our countries invented in 1949 [the Geneva Conventions] is the immutable legal holy grail as to what the rules ought to be in the 21st century?" De Vries: "Mr. Bellinger is suggesting that we should change the rules. The opinion of Europe's ministers is that respecting the rules, not bending them, is essential to our credibility and hence to our effectiveness in the fight against terrorism."[50] Leaving aside the intrinsic substance of the argument over the applicability of the Geneva Conventions to irregular combatants in a conflict in which they disregard all laws of war, de Vries's statement demonstrates a dangerous, stubborn, and reactionary inflexibility when the world is confronted with a radically new threat.

Jihad—A Crime without a Name

To go back to the European Parliament report, it also makes the argument, common in progressive circles, that by making the public aware of the nature and magnitude of the threat, the government makes the problem worse, by alienating the Muslim "community." Even assuming, wrongly, that Muslims in Britain, for example, are a single, homogeneous category, the implication is that by simply calling Islamist terrorism by its own name the government makes matters worse. This "analysis" is similar to that of self-appointed leaders of Islam in Britain, such as the MCB and MAB, interested in avoiding debate more than in helping to isolate and defeat the extremists.

Thomas Hammarberg, quoted above, concluded his remarks on profiling with the warning that focusing on "young men of Muslim faith or Middle-Eastern appearance" is particularly "dangerous since the police need the trust of the community for effective intelligence gathering."[51] In other words, for police to operate on the basis of facts and experience—for all Islamist terrorists in Europe are, by definition, Muslim; almost all are young; and many are of "Middle-Eastern appearance"—is dangerous. One may also note the presumptuousness of the claim that human-rights activists understand best how intelligence gathering should be conducted.

Similar views were expressed by Amnesty International:

> Many of the UK's three million Muslims and other minority communities have felt under siege in recent years. Like everyone else in the country, they experienced the fear associated with the attacks of 11 September 2001 and July 2005. But they also experienced increasing racism, fostered in part by the frequent linking by the government and media of the "terrorist threat" with "foreigners" and "Muslim extremists".[52]

The British government, for its part, has consistently tried to engage the Muslim community. One of its key initiatives in the struggle to win hearts and minds was the decision to fund, covertly, an Islamic website appealing for moderation. A classic of New Labour terminology, it is called the Radical Middle Way. Government documents disclose that the site is "run as a grassroots initiative by Muslim organizations." However, it has "most of its financial backing from the Foreign Office and Home Office." The site uses videos and podcasts to spread an "alternative message" to young Muslims. Around 100,000 CDs promoting moderation have also been funded by the government and distributed free to Muslim students as an antidote, apparently, to the jihadist CDs circulated at universities and colleges.[53]

Alternative Models or Cooperation?

Various EU countries have had distinct experiences with terrorist activities and have reacted accordingly. Thus Spain and France have developed legislation and intelligence/police capabilities far more effective than those in the UK, Germany, or Belgium, where popular attitudes are quite different.[54] The result is that even countries as apparently close, culturally and geographically, as Belgium and France, or the Netherlands and Germany, have serious difficulties in counter-terrorism cooperation—i.e., in legal, intelligence, police, and political coordination.

All these countries were late in introducing legislation specifically directed against terrorism—some as late as 2004—in most cases, because they viewed terrorism as a circumscribed criminal phenomenon, rather than as a largely political and international one. That, interestingly, was true even of Italy, Germany, and Belgium, all of which had experience with internationally connected Marxist terrorist groups during the 1960s and 1970s: the Red Brigades, the Baader-Meinhof gang (Rote Armee Fraktion), and the Communist Combatant Cells. It was only outside pressure, from Washington or Paris (in the case of Belgium), and UN and EU calls for change that finally led to new and specific legislation.

Just as 9/11 led to a flurry of counter-terrorism legislation—as if the jihadi threat had not existed before—the aftermath of the 2005 London attacks brought to the fore the contradictions between security and some of the EU's applauded successes, above all the 1990 Schengen agreement for the abolition of physical borders among European countries (excluding the United Kingdom and Ireland). The *de facto* territorial unity ratified in the Schengen agreement facilitates unlimited and uncontrolled mobility of residents—including Islamist militants, native born or legal as well as illegal immigrants—within most of the EU space. The borders remain open despite the lack of any common legal or intelligence arrangements among the EU states. Hence, membership in a designated terrorist group may bring an automatic jail sentence in France but not in the Netherlands; Belgium has tolerated, indeed legally protected, groups known to have acted against France, Turkey, or Spain; and the UK legal system still provides alleged terrorists a level of protection unavailable in France or Spain.

However, it was a specific event that triggered a rethinking of Schengen: the successful escape to Italy of Osman Hussain, one of the failed Somali bombers of July 21. Despite what Metropolitan police commissioner Sir Ian Blair described as "the largest ever investigation that the Met has ever mounted," Hussein, wearing a *burqa*, managed to get out of England; he crossed France and ended up among the Somali community in Rome, where he was arrested and extradited to the UK.

As a result, France reintroduced border controls, including passport checks, which had been scrapped under the Schengen agreement; Italy announced closer monitoring of its northern border and detained 174 people suspected of being involved in Islamic militant groups; Germany drew up plans for a national anti-terror database; and Britain asked the EU for better information-sharing among law-enforcement services—the same proposals first made following the 2004 Madrid bombings. As German counter-terrorism expert Rolf Tophoven put it, "We have to realize more and more that Schengen is a gift to terrorists. . . . It's difficult to give it up, but if I were a terrorist, I would see the Schengen agreement as a gift."[55] The fact that it took 15 years and two spectacular Islamist attacks in major capitals for some Europeans to understand reinforces the view that Europeans, far more than Americans, still consider the terrorist threat less of a danger than the loss of some conveniences, far too superficially treated as fundamental "rights." In fact, following France's reinstatement of border controls, Franco Frattini, while "respecting" Paris's decision, insisted that the EU should continue to guarantee "full freedom of circulation within the [EU] borders."[56]

NATIONAL DIFFERENCES

Different countries' experience, or lack thereof, is reflected in their legal and practical approaches to terrorism. France—which has the longest experience with Islamic terror, going back two decades—and Spain—targeted by the ETA since the 1960s—have developed capabilities and evolved attitudes very distinct from the traditionally terror-free Netherlands and Scandinavia. Italy, with its past experience with the Red Brigades, has adapted to the new threat faster than Britain, which, the protracted IRA terror campaign notwithstanding, is still searching for a balance between its tradition of tolerance and its distinct legal system on the one hand, and its grave Islamist presence on the other. Germany, still nursing the psychological wounds of its Nazi and Communist pasts, remains reluctant to adopt stern measures, although its federal system allows for significant differences among the *Länder*. And neither the Madrid bombings of March 2004 nor the London ones of July 2005 led to an effective increase in counter-terrorist cooperation at the EU level.

France has introduced a number of anti-terrorist laws since 1986, including laws on interception of electronic communications (Law #91-646, as amended), use of video surveillance (Law #95-73), and biometric checks (Decree #2005-556), and it now has a computerized database holding files on individuals. Most effectively, in 1986 a section within the Trial Court of Paris was created, involving prosecutors and examining magistrates (*juges d'instruction*) who would specialize in cases of terrorism. Acts of terrorism are a criminal offense as set out in Articles 421-1 et seq. of the Penal Code. Following the wave of Islamist terrorist attacks in the mid-1990s, those articles were amended by Law #96-647 of July 22, 1996, which specified that "criminal association [association de malfaiteurs] with a terrorist enterprise" is also a terrorist act.[57] That provision allows the arrest and imprisonment of terrorist accomplices and supporters prior to their passing to action.

Countries on the periphery of the EU, most particularly the Scandinavian members (Finland, Sweden, and Denmark), have legal, political, and police institutions and attitudes that are even more out of sync with reality than the rest of the EU. One may call such countries the weakest link in counter-terrorism. The 12 new EU members (Poland, Lithuania, Latvia, Estonia, Slovakia, the Czech Republic, Hungary, Slovenia, Malta, Greek Cyprus, Bulgaria, and Romania) are almost equally far behind.[58]

Fundamentally, there are different approaches to the issue of Islamist terrorism and radicalization of Muslims in Europe, with different levels of public support within countries and at the Union level. The two extremes in terms of effectiveness are

France and the pre–July 2005 UK. France, which was first targeted by Islamists with a series of bombings in February 1986,
has devised a rather effective system of both prevention and
punishment of Islamist terrorism. In January 2005 the government established the "regional poles of combat against radical
Islam" (*pôles régionaux de lutte contre l'islam radical*), under the
authority of the local prefects (regional appointed officials).
Ultimately, these engage in official forms of permanent harassment of Salafi and *Tablighi* imams, mosques, unauthorized
Islamic centers, and individuals, combining police and admin-
istrative measures. Thus, starting in 2005, the "poles" have kept
under surveillance 47 prayer halls, 473 commercial establishments, and 85 cafés and phone centers which could serve as
financing and proselytizing locations. Measures have included
expulsion or interdiction of activity. As the then director of the
intelligence service, Pascal Mailhos, stated, "the objective is to
destabilize radical Islam upstream, without disturbing services
in the framework of the anti-terrorist combat, nor interfering
with republican Islam."[59] Thus a mosque came under "control"
for illegal commerce in meat, a spokesman for a radical mosque
in Champagne-Ardennes was arrested, and other establishments were closed for overcrowding.

When, in October 2006, a number of Muslim baggage handlers at the Charles de Gaulle airport in Roissy, near Paris, lost
their access permits—and thus their jobs—Interior Minister
Sarkozy justified the measure as a matter of prudence, and the
local sub-prefect, Jacques Lebrot, stated that the terrorist risk is
great and that, "For us, someone who takes his vacations a few
times in Pakistan raises questions [even more so, one may add,
as one of those involved was Tunisian] and some of the handlers have gone through training camps."[60] Considering that all
of the many terrorist plots in Britain had direct ties to Pakistan,

and that some 400,000 persons fly annually from the UK to that country, applying the French approach there would make sense—but British lawmakers would not even consider it.

In the same statement, Sarkozy mentioned that in 2006 seven non-citizen imams or suspected Islamists had been deported, most of them to North Africa. Islamist religious venues, both legal and illegal, have been closed in the vicinities of the airports at Roissy and Orly, and 18 imams who have "expressed opinions perfectly incompatible with the values of the Republic" have been expelled.[61] Sarkozy's policy of expelling radical imams followed a long series of precedents. For instance, just between the beginning of 2004 and September 2005, the following imams were expelled from France:

- Two Turkish imams associated with the Kaplanci group, accused of anti-Semitism and anti-Western statements.

- Abdelkader Yahia Cherif, Algerian from Brest, accused of proselytism in favor of radical Islam and active relationships with Islamist movements favorable to terrorism.

- Chellali Benchellali, Algerian from Minguettes (discussed in Chapter 5), accused of "participation in an association of malefactors . . . with a view to the commission of one or more acts of terrorism."

- Abdelkader Bouziane, Algerian from Vénissieux (discussed in Chapter 3), accused of "complicity in defense of crime and direct provocation without effect against the integrity of a person," as well as of defending polygamy. He is widely seen as the "spiritual leader" of Salafis in France.[62]

- Ali Yashar, Iraqi from Argenteuil, seen as a Salafi propagandist.

- Midhat Güler, Kaplan follower, accused of "incitement to hatred for the West in his sermons, and glorification of jihad."[63]

The legal basis for these expulsions is the Ordinance of November 2, 1945, Article 26, modified in 2003. It is still contested by assorted "human-rights" NGOs in France, but increasingly used.[64]

What this suggests is that France has decided to take serious preventive measures against Islamism, rather than await violent developments—something being at least partially done in the United States since 2001, but not in the rest of Europe. In fact for most of Europe the French measures seem, if not a violation of human rights, at least arbitrary and excessive.

How important are specific characteristics of national legal systems—and political contexts—is best demonstrated by the contrasting cases of Britain and France. In France, for instance, radical imams, whether jihadists or just legitimizers of wife beating, can lose French citizenship and be summarily deported (usually to Algeria) by the local prefect, regardless of how long they had lived in France or what were their family circumstances. In Britain, far more important ideologues of Islamist terrorism, the likes of Abu Hamza and Abu Qatada, receive short sentences when tried and convicted (seven years for the former), and are virtually impossible to deport, even when initially admitted under false pretenses.

In France (and Spain) the existence of specialized prosecuting magistrates makes for a smooth relationship between police, intelligence agencies, and the judiciary; in Britain, as Prime Minister Blair and a series of home secretaries have discovered, the judiciary is a major obstacle to establishing an effective counter-terrorism system. Nowhere is that more obvious than in the courts' interpretation of Article 5 of the European Convention on Human Rights.

Article 5 states, *inter alia*, that

> 1. Everyone has the right to liberty and security of person. No one shall be deprived of his liberty save in the following cases and in accordance with a procedure prescribed by law:
>
> (a) the lawful detention of a person after conviction by a competent court;
>
> (b) the lawful arrest or detention of a person for non-compliance with the lawful order of a court or in order to secure the fulfillment of any obligation prescribed by law;
>
> (c) the lawful arrest or detention of a person effected for the purpose of bringing him before the competent legal authority on reasonable suspicion of having committed an offence or when it is reasonably considered necessary to prevent his committing an offence or fleeing after having done so; . . .
>
> (f) the lawful arrest or detention of a person to prevent his effecting an unauthorized entry into the country or of a person against whom action is being taken with a view to deportation or extradition.
>
> 2. Everyone who is arrested shall be informed promptly, in a language which he understands, of the reasons for his arrest and the charge against him.
>
> 3. Everyone arrested or detained in accordance with the provisions of paragraph 1(c) of this article shall be brought promptly before a judge or other officer authorized by law to exercise judicial power and shall be entitled to trial within a reasonable time or to release pending trial. Release may be conditioned by guarantees to appear for trial.[65]

What is clear about these provisions is that none is easily applicable to suspected terrorists. Releasing intelligence information leading to detention is virtually banned. In complex cases with extensive international links, evidence collection seldom allows a suspect to be "promptly" brought to trial, as the British debate on the topic (see below) abundantly demonstrates.

Moreover, as *The Economist* observed, although the ECHR is the same everywhere, the British adversarial legal system makes it peculiarly cumbersome.

> Defendants typically have the right to appeal at several stages of the legal process, with the result that in 2001, it took an average of eight months to extradite someone to Britain, but 18 months to send someone the other way. Contested hearings cost around £125,000 ($263,310 on 8 November 2007). In France, by contrast, deporting suspects to countries with patchy human rights records causes little fuss. Rights of appeal are more restricted and deportees may not be able to appeal until after they have left the country, by which time it might be too late. "Often you send a fellow back to Algeria and that's the last you hear of him."[66]

In Britain, pre-trial detention for terrorist suspects is 28 days—and that only after the Blair government fought a 2004 battle in Parliament to extend the period from the existing 14 days (the government was denied an extension to 92 days). A 2008 attempt by Blair's successor, Gordon Brown, to increase the period to 56 days was defeated in the House of Lords. In France, pre-trial detention for terrorist offenses can be as long as two years for crimes punishable by 10 years' imprisonment or less, and up to four years for crimes punishable by more than 10 years' imprisonment.[67] Considering the time needed to unravel the international connections of Islamist cells, that is an enormous difference.

Even more significant, considering Britain's history of tolerance of Islamist elements, is the Catch-22 situation the UK finds itself in now, when trying to change the circumstances that led to Londonistan. Following Parliament's adoption of the ECHR into national law, without any qualifications, judges began deciding terrorist cases upon a strict interpretation of the Convention's provisions.

As Prime Minister Blair complained toward the end of his time in office,

> After September 11, 2001, in common with many other nations, we passed new anti-terror laws. . . . We gave ourselves the ability, in exceptional circumstances, to detain foreign nationals who we believed were plotting terrorism but against whom there was insufficient evidence to prosecute. It was an important power. They were, of course, free to leave Britain. But we wouldn't let them be free here. The ability to detain foreign nationals gave our services the ability to focus even more resources on the surveillance of British nationals who were a threat. It also sent out a strong signal of intent. In December 2004 these laws were struck down by the courts. In his famous judgment Lord Hoffmann [sic] said there was a greater risk to Britain through the abrogation of the foreign suspect's civil liberties than through terrorism.[68]

What Blair was referring to was the issue of foreign nationals suspected of terrorism—ranging from Abu Qatada to various Algerian asylum claimants (usually associated with the GSPC)—who could neither be tried, for lack of admissible proof (usually intelligence but also telephone intercepts[69]), nor deported because of Article 3 of the ECHR. Since such individuals had not been convicted in the UK, instead of prison the government tried "control orders"—a lax type of house arrest. How lax? Enough for six of them to disappear in the spring of 2007 alone. And when London reached memoranda of understanding with Jordan (for Abu Qatada), Morocco, and Algeria, receiving written guarantees that returned nationals would be treated decently, it came under ferocious attack from Amnesty

International and similar groups. Indeed, AI was stinging, stating in its 2007 Annual Report that

> Thwarted in 2004 by the courts from pursuing its policy of detaining people indefinitely without charge or trial, the UK government has resorted increasingly to deportation, or to "control orders" that allow the Home Secretary effectively to place people under house arrest without criminal prosecution. Suspects are thus condemned without ever being convicted. The essence of the rule of law is subverted while its form is preserved.[70]

Unless they make a mistake, as Omar Bakri did when he left for Lebanon and was denied a return permit to Britain, Islamist radicals and other assorted questionable aliens in Britain could feel secure for a long time, thanks to infinite appeals. How far this problem could go was demonstrated by the case of Rachid Ramda.

Accused by a French court of being the financier and organizer of the 1995 wave of GIA terror in France, Rachid Ramda, a.k.a. "Elyas" and "Abu Farès," fled to Londonistan.[71] It took until the spring of 2005 for Britain to finally extradite him to France, a fellow EU member state, and that despite an international arrest warrant and repeated decisions by the British government to extradite. This may help us understand why the French at one time considered a plan to kidnap Abu Hamza from his comfortable nest at Finsbury Park. Such problems do not bode well for intra-European cooperation.

EU COOPERATION AND COORDINATION

A 2006 conference of counter-terrorism experts in Paris brought into focus the common threats Islamist terrorist activities pose in Europe, as well as some differences. Thus Thierry Matta of the Directorate of Territorial Surveillance (DST) explained that for France, the main Islamist grievances are seen as coming

from the Algerian spillover, via the GSPC, now an Al-Qaeda af-
filiate (he pointed out that "If Al Qaeda decides to hit in France,
its most natural arm would be the GSPC"[72]); the French involvement in Lebanon; and the headscarf issue.[73]

As for physical threats, in Matta's opinion the main one
comes from the Iraqi networks—individuals who go to Iraq,
acquire combat experience, and return to France to operate
there. Although those Muslims from Europe have been used as
cannon fodder by jihadists in Iraq and have high casualty rates,
the ones who survive are a problem. The figures Matta gives—
and he adds that they are far from complete—are significant:
Nine individuals who had been resident in France have been
killed in Iraq, a dozen are there now, two have been jailed there,
and over thirty have been arrested in France, either prior to
their departure or upon their return.

Spanish counter-terrorism expert and former government
advisor Fernando Reinares noted that although few Europeans
have been killed by Al-Qaeda or elements influenced by it, the
trends are not encouraging, as demonstrated by the first suicide action, at Leganés, and by the disproportionate impact
Islamists have had on national politics (in Spain) and in dis-
crediting the idea of multiculturalism (in the Netherlands).[74]
The main threat, Reinares explained, comes from radicalized
communities, whether first- or second-generation, among
which, he claimed, some 10 percent are receptive to Al-Qaeda
or Salafist ideas.

Reinares notes that the correlation between the Islamist threat
and a presence in Iraq is weak—countries in southern Europe,
especially Spain, are under greater threat than others, despite
being the least supportive of the Iraq war. (Spain is especially
threatened because of the jihadists' obsession with Al-Andalus,
going back to Abdullah Azzam, bin Laden's ideological mentor.)

Is there and can there be a common "European" response to Islamist terrorism? Beyond rhetoric, the answer to both questions has to be largely in the negative. First and foremost because member states have divergent experiences and attitudes toward Islamist terrorism—Reinares noted that only 10 percent of Europeans overall see it as the most important issue, and that figure is as low as 2 percent in the new EU member states—and also because Brussels does not want to have to "represent" the combination of those differences.

Even when the EU takes a common decision on counter-terrorism legislation, national courts are or see themselves as free to disregard it. Thus in July 2005 the German Constitutional Court decided to release Madrid bombing suspect Mamoun Darkazanli, a Syrian/German citizen with extensive terrorist links, including close ties to the 9/11 Hamburg group. At the time, Darkazanli was in custody awaiting extradition to Spain on the basis of the newly agreed EU arrest warrant. The court's argument was that German enabling legislation was unconstitutional because the subject was a German citizen. As a result, Spain decided to consider invalid any future German demand for extradition, thus considerably weakening the entire enterprise.[75]

Considering that the EU arrest warrant, instituted in June 2002, was intended as a fast track to extradition of terrorist suspects, and that Spain and Germany are both major jihadi targets, the German-Spanish spat is highly significant for intra-European cooperation. Since, thanks to the court's decision, Germany will retain its present system of dealing with extradition—which allows the extradition of German citizens to other EU nations only when they are accused of crimes committed on German soil—this means that the country remains a *de facto* safe haven for any German-based jihadi who manages to get back there, no matter what he did, or may be planning to do, in another EU country.

In short, the EU, despite the dreams of its apologists, remains a collection of 25 independent states, with different cultures and traditions and, most importantly, different experiences with terrorism in general and Islamist terrorism in particular. Since EU member states are all democratic, popular support would be essential for the dramatic legal, police, intelligence, immigration, and indeed cultural changes necessary for an effective and coordinated counter-terrorism policy. But, from a rational viewpoint, why should Poland, Lithuania, or the Czech Republic—all without a significant Muslim presence— engage in such costly and painful reforms? And why should one assume that Brussels could handle terrorism better than national governments?

The eight former Communist states of Central Europe never had any experience with international terrorism, and neither had Finland, Malta, Luxembourg, Denmark, or Portugal—more than half the EU members. Others (Sweden, Cyprus) had only experienced episodic spillovers of conflicts from elsewhere. Belgium, strategically located close to France, Germany, and the UK, and known for police and judicial laxity, has long served as a rear base for jihadis—especially Algerians of the GIA and GSPC and, with the support of a large Moroccan immigrant community, the GICM. As early as the mid-1990s, the first wave of Algerian terrorism in France received significant help from across the border in Belgium.[76]

On the other hand, the most important EU members— France, Germany, the United Kingdom, Italy, and Spain—have had extensive terrorist problems for decades. But even among those, their experience has been quite varied—and so were the responses. In the UK and Spain, and to a lesser extent France

(Corsica and the Basque region), the most lasting terrorist experience has been with ethnic, occasionally Marxist separatists—the IRA, the ETA, *Iparretarrak*, *Frontu di Liberazione Naziunalista Corsu*—and with violent Marxist-Leninist fringe groups, such as *Action Directe* in France, the Red Brigades in Italy, the Baader-Meinhof gang in Germany. Only France has experienced all of the above—and the differences are evident in performance and effectiveness.

With the exception of France, European anti-terrorism legislation, when it exists, is weak or under challenge. Even in France, some convicted terrorists receive mild sentences—and don't complete the sentences they receive. A recent example is that of the Algerian Safé Bourada, sentenced to ten years in February 1998 for membership in the GIA and involvement in the 1995 wave of bombings. Released in February 2003, he was arrested again in September 2005 for forming a terrorist cell planning to bomb major objectives in Paris, including the Orly airport.

The issue of torture and accusations thereof is not only a political problem with the United States and many Muslim countries—it is also a serious problem when suspected terrorists are brought to court. Indeed, most European courts reject testimony suspected of having been obtained through torture. And here the issue of definition is key. When, according to the human-rights NGOs and the European Parliament, even the United States engages in torture, not to mention dozens of Muslim countries, that means in practice that virtually all information from those countries is unacceptable. In Britain, Lord Justice Hoffman was even prepared to place on the government the burden of proving that no torture was used in obtaining evidence—in other words, trying to prove a negative.[77] The same kind of legal problem has come up in German and Dutch courts regarding the use of intelligence.

In Germany the judicial odyssey of Mounir el Motassadeq, a close Hamburg friend of Mohamed Atta accused of serving as the financier of the 9/11 group, lasted five years. At first, he was sentenced to 15 years in 2003, having been convicted of complicity in the death of the 3,000 victims of 9/11; however, the verdict was overturned by a federal court in 2004, because the U.S. did not make available testimony of captured Al-Qaeda figures. Retried for membership in a terrorist organization (Al-Qaeda), he was again convicted and sentenced to 15 years, a sentence confirmed on appeal.[78] However, while his appeals in Germany have been exhausted, his case is not over, as he can still appeal to the European Court of Human Rights.

In some countries (Portugal, Sweden) the maximum sentence possible is 15 years; French justice is generally tougher, although not faster, and in France a person of the prominence of Abu Hamza, of Finsbury Park and international fame, would have received far more than the seven years in jail the British courts gave him. One should bear in mind, however, the chilling fact that, because there is no death penalty in Europe, terrorists in Europe, even if convicted and imprisoned, will always be with us.

TRANSATLANTIC COOPERATION TODAY

The problems in intra-European cooperation on counter-terrorism are greatly multiplied when it comes to transatlantic cooperation. As Belgian analyst Rik Coolsaet observed

> Europeans seem to widely share the assumption that the root causes of jihadi terrorism in the rest of the world are mainly local—just as is the case in Europe itself. Whereas the US Global War on Terrorism considers local terrorist groups to be part of a global Islamist insurgency, the EU's point of departure—admittedly more implicit than explicit due to a lack of in-depth reflection—would be to consider international

terrorism to have returned to what existed before the rise of al-Qaeda in the 1990s: even if they use the same Salafist rhetoric and thrive on a more enabling international momentum, most terrorist groups are primarily driven by domestic grievances, which remain the main drive behind their actions.[79]

For Europeans the problem—although some, like the French, manage to discreetly avoid it—is that "morality"—i.e., political posturing or self-righteousness—trumps intelligence needs, and European courts and governments refuse to draw the appropriate conclusions from what even their own police and intelligence agencies tell them. Hence the repeated problems regarding extradition of known terrorists to the United States, where they might be sentenced to death, and hence the strange spectacle of CIA operatives being indicted in Germany or Italy for rendition of Islamists, including Al-Qaeda operatives involved in the 9/11 attacks, to countries like Syria, Egypt, or Jordan, which were accused of torturing them.

Since the definition of "torture" used by the Europeans is, as we have seen, vague, confusing, and overly friendly to "victims," and since the decision of what countries are guilty of it is ultimately left to groups like Amnesty International—groups whose purpose is to infinitely expand the definition—the result is typically that when choosing between transatlantic intelligence cooperation and their own security on the one hand, and "human rights" as defined by unelected NGOs on the other hand, many European politicians and governments, not to mention courts, choose the latter.

De Vries thought what was required for transatlantic cooperation was for the U.S. to "go back to a common definition" of human rights. For him, the CIA's extraordinary-rendition flights over Europe were "immoral, illegal and counterproductive." On the other hand, he pointed out that his powers were almost nonexistent, since he had no influence over national intelligence services, and that the terrorist threat remains— and has moved toward "the interior" of Europe. The solution? Cooperation between Muslims and non-Muslims, centered on the common value of human rights.[80] This obsession with "human rights" was demonstrated by the European Parliament's two-year hunt for "proof" that a majority of EU member states had engaged in violations of such rights by cooperating with the CIA. Dutch MP Kathelijne Buitenweg even blamed de Vries for "failing to inform the parliament accurately" and for "not trying to find out the truth"—as if that, rather than counter-terrorism, was his duty.[81]

It is impossible to separate the growing cultural differences between Europe and the United States, differences manifested in attitudes *vis-à-vis* economics, religion, and the use of military power, as well as specific foreign-policy issues (e.g., the Middle East), from the issues of Islamist terrorism, counter-terrorism, and general threat perceptions.

Most importantly, most Europeans still cling to the notion that pursuing Islamist terrorism is a matter of criminal law, in contrast to the prevailing U.S. opinion that Islamist terrorism is an enemy at war with the West. Hence the Europeans are pre-occupied with the legal aspects of counter-terrorism, while the Americans are interested in an effective response to terrorism.

The result has been that Europe today offers a puzzling and contradictory image as far as opinions on Islamism, terrorism, and cooperation with the United States are concerned. Thus Britain, America's closest ally in Europe, is also the most important center of Islamist radicalization and exporter of terror across the Atlantic, while France, the *bête noire* of American conservatives (and diplomats), is clearly the most effective in countering Islamism and is also (very discreetly) cooperative on counter-terrorism throughout the world. Ever since the 1980s, under Socialist and conservative governments alike, France has worked together closely with the American military in countering Libyan ambitions in the Sahel, especially Chad, and it is doing so to this day against Islamist activities spilling over from Algeria and Sudan, even accepting as a *fait accompli* the massive U.S. (and NATO) presence in Djibouti, traditionally seen as part of Paris's sphere of influence in Africa—and still the home of a major French military base.

Meanwhile, since 2002, French intelligence has established, in cooperation with the CIA, a joint counter-terrorist center in Paris ("*Alliance Base*"), focused on surveillance and ultimately capture of transnational terrorists.[82] Furthermore, well-established French intelligence ties with the services of such former French colonies as Algeria, Tunisia, and Morocco have opened many doors to American intelligence, as well as obtaining and transferring information to Washington. Overall, the French share the general American assessment of the threat posed by Islamism, have longer experience in combatting it, and have more legal and operational freedom than most, if not all, other European countries. In addition, a fact seldom noticed by most Americans—terrorism experts included—the French have an enormous intellectual advantage over their Anglo-American rivals, in the number and especially the quality of specialized publications on Islam, Islamism, and Islamist terrorism.

Equally important, perhaps, is the French ability to, discreetly or not so discreetly, put pressure on some neighboring countries to get serious about Islamist terrorism. Spain, to be sure, had its own complaints against Paris for decades of unofficial sympathy for Basque terrorists, but all of that ceased as soon as the ETA began operating, indeed created a new branch, on French territory, the now-defunct *Iparretarrak*. Ever since,

Spanish-French cooperation against Basque terrorism has been a true model. As for the Belgians, French intelligence, government, and social pressures forced Brussels to not only pass anti-terrorism legislation but also pay more attention to Islamist, especially GICM, activities in its country.

U.S.– European Cooperation: Problems and Challenges

Leaving aside, for a moment, the infinity of ties—cultural, economic, historical, and many other—between Europe and the United States, counter-terrorism requirements alone suggest that what happens in Europe is immediately relevant to the United States.

By virtue of its huge Muslim population, if nothing else, Europe is not just part of the global war on Islamic terrorism as a target and victim, but is also a net exporter of terrorists. Not only was 9/11 planned in Europe, but at least one failed attack against the United States was attempted by a British citizen (Richard Reid) and many other attacks were planned from Britain, including the destruction of transatlantic flights and the bombing of the New York Stock Exchange. Furthermore, traditional close ties and arrangements—including the ability of EU citizens to travel to the U.S. without visas—could facilitate further Europe-based attacks against the United States.

Many more Islamist terrorists or suspected terrorists have been arrested in Europe than in the United States—indeed more than anywhere else outside Afghanistan. Others, coming from Europe, have been captured or killed in Afghanistan, Iraq, Israel, Syria, Morocco, Canada, and the United States. In fact it appears that there is a common understanding among both intelligence services and the terrorist networks themselves that

Europe has become *the* main recruiting ground for Islamist terrorists operating in the West and against Western, especially American, interests throughout the world.

The cases of Richard Reid and Zacarias Moussaoui are best known to Americans because they were involved in anti-U.S. actions inside the U.S. But the number is much larger, as is the area of operations of Europe-based Islamists. Indeed, as we have seen, British citizens of Pakistani background have been involved in suicide attacks in Israel and the West Bank. At least five French citizens were mentioned by the *Direction Générale de la Sécurité Extérieure* (DGSE) as active or trying to become active in Iraq in 2004 against Iraqi and Coalition forces: Boubakeur el-Hakim, jailed in Damascus since August 2004; Redouane el-Hakim, killed on July 17, 2004; Tarek Ouinis, killed on September 17; Abdelhalim Badjoudj, involved in a suicide attack on October 20;, and Fawzi D., named as the "emir" (military leader) of some 20 "combatants" in Fallujah. True enough, some French observers try to minimize their numbers and significance. "One has to put this phenomenon in context ... the French network remains marginal," claimed *Le Monde*.[83]

Perhaps so, and this author's interviews in France suggest a strong and relatively effective effort on the part of the government to make this indeed a marginal phenomenon. But this is, again, a matter increasingly beyond the reach of Paris—it is an EU problem. As increasingly clear data suggest, the EU is thoroughly infiltrated by a number of interconnected networks of Islamists, many born in Europe and bearing EU passports; recruited in Europe (mostly in London); indoctrinated in places like Syria or Egypt or Yemen or Saudi Arabia; manipulated by or representing existing terrorist groups in Algeria, Morocco, Pakistan, or Yemen; and given religious legitimacy by imams living on welfare in London.

Interpol has the legal authority to concern itself in anti-terrorist matters, and that is an obvious form of intercontinental cooperation. However, most European-U.S. counter-terrorism links are by necessity multilateral, between Washington and London, Washington and Paris, Washington and Madrid, etc., rather than bilateral between Washington and Brussels. The reason is that intra-EU cooperation on such matters is itself still tentative, despite the rhetoric coming from Brussels, and despite the establishment of a (powerless) EU coordinator on counter-terrorism.

In Europe, both the type of Islamist threat and the quality of intelligence and police performance regarding that threat differ from those of the United States. In fact, they differ by orders of magnitude. As of 2006, the U.S. Justice Department, which had tightened the way it defines terrorism cases over the previous five years, cited a much higher rate of success than European authorities. Examining only those cases in which someone was actually charged, it reported in June 2006 that it had secured convictions or guilty pleas against 261 of the 441 defendants accused in connection with terrorism since 9/11.[84]

But those in Europe who have long been serious about fighting Islamist ideology are now less alone. The French were the first and are still the most effective in tackling this problem—especially with Sarkozy's "zero tolerance" approach for such things as explaining how to beat one's wife in the "correct Islamic way," calling Jews "apes," and inciting jihad.

As we have seen, even traditionally tolerant Belgium has created a *plan mosqué*, placing mosques under police surveillance; in Germany, "spiritual inciters of disorder" are to be prosecuted; in Austria, radical imams can now be expelled for "speeches threatening public security"; in Italy, radical imams can be expelled by the interior minister.[85] Even the UK is finally making an effort to deal with the radical imams in its territory. It is discussing criminalization of their acts and sermons, with conviction to be followed by extradition or expulsion, even to countries like Egypt, Jordan, or Saudi Arabia, traditionally the taboo "human-rights violators" of the powerful NGO lobbies and their supporters in the judiciary. On the other hand, with relatively few (but growing) numbers of Muslims in their midst and no terrorism (yet), Sweden and Finland are leading a Scandinavian resistance to the European crackdown on radical imams—although the recent attention focused on "honor killings" in their territory might ultimately weaken that resistance.

After decades of unthinking multiculturalism, most European countries are now actively working to ensure that resident imams help establish a European Islam, rather than the present Islam in Europe—hence the new (in Denmark, the Netherlands, etc.) insistence on imams' proficiency in those countries' languages, training in European institutions, familiarity with local/national traditions, and oaths of loyalty to the countries' respective monarchs.

In one remarkable development, the United States is joining France in implementing the strongest, and most realistic and practical, approach to Islamist "clerics" of all Western democracies. But where France often expels radical inciters to their unpleasant fate in North Africa, the United States is trying them and imposing stiff sentences at home. Sheikh Mohammed Ali Hassan al-Moayad, 57, a Yemeni recruiter, was sentenced in New York in July 2005 to 75 years in prison for conspiring to support and fund Al-Qaeda and Hamas. Sheikh Omar Abdel Rahman, blind and diabetic, got a life sentence in 1996 for legitimizing the 1993 World Trade Center bombing (in 2005 his sympathetic American lawyer, Lynne Stewart, was convicted of helping to smuggle messages from him to his terrorist group in Egypt and was also imprisoned). Ali Timimi, a northern Virginia "spiritual" leader, was convicted of encouraging others to attend terrorist camps and received a life sentence. The bottom line is that, under U.S. law, there are clear limits between freedom of expression and calls for mass murder. This bottom line is ultimately less "legal" than self-preserving: U.S. prosecutors, like French Interior Ministry officials, have to work around a legal system that is poorly designed for dealing with Islamist terror, in order to protect their citizens—against terrorists and, more difficult still, against anti-anti-terrorist human-rights fundamentalists.

The urgency of the need for cooperation is finally becoming clear, which bodes well if the relevant authorities on both sides of the Atlantic heed the alarms that come their way. The French claim that they had an "Osama bin Laden" unit within the DGSE as early as 1995, long before the Clinton administration took him seriously. They even claim that they had some information on a coming airplane attack against the U.S. by the fall of 2000—and that they informed Washington.[86]

How difficult cooperation with some Europeans, including NATO allies, can be was demonstrated by the case of Belgium and its extraordinarily lax attitude regarding passports. Until 1998, when the United States threatened to cancel Belgian citizens' visa-waiver privileges, Belgium was the world center of false passports—or, more accurately and dangerously, of legitimate blank passports that were stolen and used by terrorists. Thus Ahmed Ressam, the "millennium bomber" caught on the Canadian border, and the Tunisian Al-Qaeda assassins of Ahmed Shah Massoud in Afghanistan all used Belgian passports.

The reason is that blank passports were kept—and not kept securely—in every small-town city hall in the country and in numerous consulates abroad. As a result, between 1990 and 2001, 19,050 blank Belgian passports were stolen (and, one may add, so were 24,851 blank Italian passports), compared with 50 American passports. Since then, a database nicknamed Braingate has been created: It is the Belgian police's repository of information on 1.4 million stolen and fraudulent documents from all over the world.[87] Nevertheless, all is still not fine. On December 5, 2003, when Jamal Ahmidan ("El Chino")—the leader of the cell that carried out the Madrid attacks and one of the Leganés suicides—was stopped, fined, and released by traffic police near Madrid, he was carrying a false Belgian passport.[88]

Considering that since 1990, through the Schengen Accords, most EU states have eliminated intra-community border controls, and that most enjoy visa-waiver privileges with the United States, the illegal access to Belgian and Italian passports by terrorists means that they could not only travel unchecked between Lisbon and Helsinki but also between Brussels and New York. All this without mentioning the obvious: that many Islamist terrorists are legitimate European citizens. American requests that airlines flying to the U.S. provide personal data on their passengers in advance were accepted by the airlines, but met strong opposition from the European Parliament, in the name of "privacy."

In 2006, Italian judge Caterina Interlandi issued arrest warrants for 31 U.S. and Italian intelligence agents, including the director of the Intelligence and Military Security Service (SISMI), Nicolò Pollari (who resigned in November 2006), for their alleged role in the February 17, 2003, abduction and extraordinary rendition of Osama Moustafa Hassan Nasr in Milan. This, despite Nasr's own stated inability to describe his alleged "torturers" in Egypt.[89] Moreover Nasr, an Egyptian Jihad activist, was long known as a veteran of military training camps in

Bosnia and Afghanistan, and was a longtime surveillance target of Italian counter-terrorism police. Similarly, alleged CIA agents were indicted in Germany for the (admittedly mistaken) capture in Macedonia and interrogation in Afghanistan of one Khaled Masri (since interned in a psychiatric asylum for arson). In Stockholm, a parliamentary investigator concluded that CIA operatives violated Swedish law by subjecting two Egyptian nationals to "degrading and inhuman treatment" and by exercising police powers on Swedish soil during a rendition in December 2001. That rendition was carried out with the help of Swedish security police. Swedish prosecutors have not filed charges.[90]

In all these cases, spectacularly in Nasr's, it was clear that for some prosecutors and politicians (but not all: both the Italian and German governments quashed the CIA indictments), threatening cooperation with the United States is worth it when "human rights" are involved. It was also an open inhibition to their own counter-terrorism experts doing their jobs. Equally revealing, the fact that European laws protecting known jihadis may themselves be the reason for extra-legal extraditions, and thus should be revisited, was never brought up in the media or public discourse.

These are serious and long-term problems facing transatlantic relations. Politics do count, and anti-Americanism especially so. This author had very fruitful discussions with Spanish intelligence officers and police prior to the March 2004 terrorist bombings in Madrid and the radical change of government resulting from them, but he faced veritable mutes when meeting the same people afterwards.

To all these problems facing counter-terrorist cooperation, one should add another practical liability: The politics (and legislation) of many European countries alienate Muslim governments, whose cooperation is vital in combatting terrorism.

There are some exceptions. France has excellent relations with intelligence services in North Africa and, despite political differences, Syria. But in many cases politics and "human rights" are a clear obstacle. It is indeed hard for governments like those of Morocco, Algeria, or Egypt to cooperate with countries that give refuge to some of their worst Islamist enemies and whose courts and NGOs routinely accuse them of various violations of human rights. Even in the case of Spain, victim of the Atocha bombings and unwilling host of a large number of jihadi cells linked to the Moroccan GICM and the Algerian GSPC, intelligence cooperation with Morocco is sporadic (it is better with Algeria) due to longstanding political and territorial disputes.

That is another example of politics getting in the way of security and intelligence capabilities—and it is unnecessary. The French have managed to establish the best counter-terrorism organization in Europe, perhaps in the West, in large part because their political elites have long since reached a consensus about separating national-security interest from politics and rhetoric. Naturally, that has brought upon France accusations of cynicism and hypocrisy. But it explains why, despite its millions of Algerian and Moroccan immigrants, it has remained relatively safe—at least so far. It also explains why such Al-Qaeda satellite groups like the GICM and GSPC have preferred to concentrate their European presence in places like England, Spain, and Belgium, rather than France. It also explains the apparently contradictory relations with the United States during the Mitterrand and Chirac eras—very distant and, from Washington's perspective, often irritating politically, but excellent on matters of terrorism, whether in Europe, North Africa, or the Sahel. With the 2007 election of Nicolas Sarkozy, intelligence and counter-terrorism cooperation continues unchanged, while political ties are closer than they had been for decades.

On the other side of the coin, excellent political ties with Washington did not prevent John Major's and Tony Blair's Britain from becoming first a major rear base of global jihadism, then a danger for its friends, and more recently a target of the jihadis.

For the foreseeable future, barring catastrophic events, relations in the counter-terrorism field at the intelligence level will remain complicated and discreet, while political relations will remain rhetorically cool, reflecting the two different, even antagonistic, cultural perceptions of the common threat.

Dark Clouds—Lessons Learned and Avoided

"You say that it is your custom to burn widows. Very well. We also have a custom: when men burn a woman alive, we tie a rope around their necks and we hang them. Build your funeral pyre; beside it, my carpenters will build a gallows. You may follow your custom. And then we will follow ours."

—General Sir Charles James Napier,
British India Commander-in-Chief, 1849–51[1]

The Making of Europe's Islamist Ghost

The entire Muslim world is going through a process of religious radicalization, which, in the case of Muslims in Europe, is unthinkingly tolerated, indeed magnified, by multiculturalism and a generalized identity crisis among native Europeans. When faced with an increasingly assertive revival of Muslim identity in Europe, Europeans answered with "tolerance"—accepting their adversary's arguments as being as valid as their own, instead of asserting a European identity.

The unlearned lesson of the European experience with Islam is that excessive tolerance logically leads to intolerance, and intolerance inevitably leads to conflict. It is less than honest, or serious, for the multiculturalist Left to condemn or be surprised at the growing incidence of "honor" killing, wife beating, homophobia, anti-Semitism, and polygamy after decades of advocacy of immigrant "rights" and relentless attacks against national identity, Christianity, and "Eurocentrism." The very idea of obligations and responsibility on the part of immigrants and their descendants was allowed to become the monopoly of extremist nationalists. Moreover, Europe's identity problem—and it is a very serious one—does not lie in some alleged past and present "racism" or in a variety of largely invented or anachronistic crimes, but in self-inflicted renunciation of national traditions in favor of some undefined "European" or, even worse, "global" commonalities and, as human-rights radicals like to pretend, "international standards."

Common sense has been largely missing from the European discourse on Islamism and indeed Islam. When everything is "context," nothing is worth defending or deserving of condemnation, because there is no moral or cultural standard to defend. Polygamy, FGM, and wife beating are tolerated because they are thought to be from "Islamic" cultures, but they are supposed to stay out of public discourse, because to mention them may be insensitive to certain groups. There are only small and logical steps from viewing cultural differences as irrelevant or marginal, to their very mention being labeled as "racist," to giving such practices "equal treatment" under the law.

There is today a certain repetitive language indicating intellectual exhaustion on the part of the previously dominant multiculturalists, who are now under attack. The overused word "racism" and its still more absurd relation, "xeno-racism" ("racism" against foreigners)—which are never applicable to Muslims as a whole, who can be of any race—are no longer seen as valid by anyone except the human-rights fundamentalists of unelected NGOs and their supporters within the equally unelected EU and UN bureaucracies.

Not everything is negotiable or debatable, which makes Theo van Gogh's last words to his fanatical assassin—"Don't do it! Don't do it! Surely we can talk about this!" —so misguided. As van Gogh found out tragically late, not everything can be talked about, and two people cannot talk about anything when one uses words and reason, and the other a knife. And here lies one of Europe's main cultural problems with Islamists in general and jihadis in particular: There can be no dialogue when the two sides do not share the same language, literally and figuratively.

How, for instance, could the British authorities engage in a meaningful dialogue with parts of the Muslim community when a June 2007 survey of 500 British Muslims found that nearly a quarter don't believe the four men identified as the London bombers were responsible for the attacks?[2] That was despite the video testimony of two of the perpetrators themselves. Similarly, significant elements in Muslim communities in England and elsewhere still denied as late as 2007 that Osama bin Laden had anything to do with 9/11—his proud admission of responsibility notwithstanding—and even denied that those who perpetrated it were Muslims.

In some countries—Britain foremost, but also the Netherlands and Germany—the arrival of millions of Muslim foreigners and the birth of their descendants was never considered a potential problem by elites and governments. Even to see it as such, let alone deal with it, would have been "racist" and unfair. Most importantly, noticing a Muslim problem would have been seen as encouraging what was indiscriminately labeled the "Far Right."

One has to be pessimistic about Europe's ability to learn lessons from the past, even the recent past, with Spain's experience during the last few years a good example. By 1990 the country had c. 40 million people and a negative growth rate. Today it has 45 million, with all the net additions coming from immigration, largely by Muslims from North and sub-Saharan Africa. Until around 2006 the economy was growing rapidly and there was a clear need for low-skilled workers, especially in construction. Since then, the building industry has virtually come to a stop, and there are now masses of recent immigrants unemployed—and growing native resentment of their presence. In other words, in less than 20 years Spain has repeated the French, German, and Dutch experience since the 1960s—with similar results. Still, during the March 2008 electoral campaign, when the opposition Popular Party criticized the ruling Socialists' mass legalization of immigrants and proposed that immigrants be required to meet certain citizenship standards—including speaking Spanish and respecting national laws and customs[3]—it was successfully accused of "racism" and xenophobia, and lost the elections.

In time, with shocks like 9/11, the Dutch assassinations, and the Madrid and London bombings, popular perceptions forced their way, electorally, to the political front pages. Instead of serious examination of why those outrages happened, however, what one may read in newspapers like *The Independent* and *The Guardian, Le Monde* and *Libération,* and *El País* is references to Iraq and the American "invasion," or, more serious still, the "invasion" of Afghanistan by NATO. More serious, because if there ever was a legal, moral, or security reason to intervene in a country, it was Afghanistan under the Taliban, exporting jihad throughout the world. By criticizing the intervention, even implicitly, the pacifist, leftist, and anti-American forces of Europe play directly into the Islamists' main ideological theme: Islam as such is under attack. Add to this the persistent revisionism and anachronism of academic and media treatment of the

Crusades and of Western colonialism—non-Western colonialism, especially the Ottoman version, is never even mentioned—and it is difficult to avoid the conviction, shared by Islamists and their helpers in Europe, that "Al-Murabit Al-Muwahhid," quoted at the beginning of Chapter 8, was accurate in his assessment that Europeans are simply too comfortable to face the reality of jihad.

To this one may add the fact, recognized by authorities and noticed by most Muslims in Europe, that while even the "domesticated" organizations operating with government support ultimately defend some Islamist goals and perceptions (Muslims as "victims," Islam under global assault, etc.), they still do not "represent" ordinary Muslims. The reply of "Al-Murabit Al-Muwahhid" to the question, To what extent do Muslims in France support an attack? was likely accurate:

> As for [the Muslims'] loyalty to France, believe me that it is true only with regard to self-designated representatives of the Muslim diaspora, and not for [all Muslims]. After all, you see that nobody is condemning the groups of youths that are protesting the policy of racist discrimination. So we do not attribute much weight to the factor [of loyalty to France].[4]

The problem is that in Europe, immigrant alienation and youth criminality, common as they are everywhere, can find a justification in association with a greater cause: jihad. Whereas a gangbanger in Los Angeles is just that, a gangbanger in Saint-Denis, Slotervaart, or Brixton can always claim he is acting on behalf of oppressed Muslims everywhere, and can find a constellation of leftist politicians, multiculturalist academics, established Muslim leaders, and underground HuT or *Tablighi* preachers to defend him as a "victim."

The same realities make the search for the "root causes" of terrorism in general, and Islamist terrorism in or from Europe in particular, an exercise of dubious value. "Racism," economic deprivation, and social and legal discrimination are all either artificial inventions, slogans, or acts of Western self-flagellation. Equally important, it is not realistic to search for motivations for Islamism in Europe, since so many of them come from outside—whether through immigration or the Internet. Indeed, what *European* cause would push a British-born individual to blow himself up in a café in Tel Aviv? Or a French convert to freeze to death in the mountains of Afghanistan after fighting for Al-Qaeda, or to lead a group blowing up people in Casablanca? It should seem obvious that the "root cause" is an ideology coming from and aiming at goals beyond the boundaries of Europe. Yet that is precisely what most European politicians and intellectuals (and many of their American colleagues) avoid talking about, because of a pervasive fear of offending Muslim sensitivities.

Islamist terrorist actions in Europe, even from organizations whose main target is a specific regime in the Muslim world— Algeria, Morocco, Egypt, etc.—are likely to continue and increase in intensity for a number of reasons, starting with the re-Islamization of the young and the growing size of the immigrant groups, but also the specific circumstances of European societies. The publicity and thus propaganda value of a bombing in a European capital is infinitely greater than with a much larger attack against some Algerian town or even Sinai resort. Indeed, it is more likely that the Algerian or Egyptian population will learn about a GSPC bombing in Paris, London, or Amsterdam than about one in their own country, where the regime has a degree of control over the media. Without media access there is seldom terrorism—anywhere.

That, of course, flies directly in the face of the conventional (academic) wisdom, which looks for "root causes" of terrorism in the "injustice," poverty, and lack of democracy in the Third World. To the contrary, a principal factor is the favorable environment of Western democracies, with their free media, "human-rights" NGOs, and a strong political Left all too often prepared to find excuses for Islamists. Moreover, while radical imams originally from the Muslim world have played a key role in the indoctrination of Islamists everywhere, some indoctrination was facilitated by the cultural and political atmosphere in Europe itself.

In Britain in 2006, police arrested a group of Muslims on what turned out to be insufficient evidence and wound up apologizing to the "Muslim community"—something British authorities had never done for centuries to the Christian Scottish or Welsh "communities." Why the new need for apologies? Because the dominant political correctness—dominant in both the ruling Labour Party and the "new" Tory Party of David Cameron—insisted on it.

The reaction of the media—from the BBC to Fox News—to a terrorist attack is always, How could they do this to their own people? That was the reaction of most Canadians after the recent arrest of a group of "new Canadians" for Islamist terrorist planning, and it was the British and Spanish reaction to the July 2005 and March 2004 Islamist bombings: How could they do this to us, since they (supposedly) *are* us?

In fact, none of these events is about "our boys" trying to destroy "their own." The perpetrators are aliens among us, aliens we have tolerated and indeed encouraged to remain aliens, enjoying Western rights and freedoms but maintaining their alien mentalities, goals, and enemies—the latter being *us*. In short, they are the natural and inevitable products of the fashionable adoration of "diversity" and "tolerance."

The "boys" of London (the oldest of whom was a bit over 30) or of Toronto (the recruiter was over 40, some recruits less than 16) were mostly educated in officially "multicultural" environments—which is to say in politicized environments where the "West" (i.e., their own countries) means colonialism, oppression, capitalism, and victimization of undefined "peoples of color." And they had easy access to the Internet, which is especially poisonous for the lost teenagers of the West, with no identity or cultural knowledge—a void easily filled by Islamist websites.

Add the increasingly obvious connection between youth criminality and youth radicalism to the attraction of radical Islam as a legitimizer and identity provider, and *voilà!* here are "our boys."

They are *not* "our boys." They are our societies' self-marginalized losers, prepared to join forces with the main enemy. Yesterday Communism, or occasionally neofascism, and today radical Islam.

It should be no surprise that some far-Left groups and individuals, such as the remnants of the Red Brigades in Italy, proclaim their "solidarity" with Al-Qaeda. And then there is "Carlos the Jackal," the alias of Ilich (as in Lenin) Ramírez Sánchez, a global terrorist trained at the Soviet cadre factory known as Patrice Lumumba University. In 2003, newly wed (while serving life in a French prison) to an aristocratic "human-rights" lawyer, Carlos revealed himself as an Islamic convert and author of *L'Islam révolutionnaire*, where he explains how unstressful his transition from Marx and Lenin to Allah was.

But it is not just that the enemy of my (American-democratic-capitalist) enemy is my friend. Some of the remaining admirers of Lenin see the Islamists as the new vanguard of the world's oppressed. And indeed, al-Zawahiri sees Al-Qaeda as the "vanguard" of Islam in much the same way Lenin saw the Party as the vanguard of the proletariat. Without pushing the analogy too far—especially since, at least as yet, there is no big state behind international Islamism—there are similarities between Lenin's creation, the Comintern, with its branches in every country, and the Muslim Brotherhood, of whose wayward children Hamas and Al-Qaeda were born.

Al-Qaeda, as we have seen, is now less a terrorist organization than it is a global nebula, connecting various self-selected and self-financed groups, cells, and mosques (including basement ones). So was Communism in its 1930s heyday. Islamism is now a default position of the alienated in the West—witness the disproportionate role of converts—and the most active and growing element in the Muslim world, from Turkey to Nigeria to Indonesia.

To all of this, many in Europe and some American liberals answer as they did to Communism, by contradicting the dictum that democracy is not a suicide pact. The dubious rights of the terrorists at Guantanamo, and the need to punish the CIA (and its European accomplices) for the allegedly illegal flights carrying captured terrorists through European airspace, are given priority—absolute priority—over democracy and citizens' right to live. Similarly, if Palestinians are *ipso facto* victims, whatever they do is "understandable"—a big step toward *acceptable*. If Islamists target "imperialist America," misguided as they are in their methods, it is wrong to crack down on them—especially if that might imply giving government agents access to public-library records.

While speaking of *déjà-vu* all over again, remember how Communist insurgencies in Nicaragua and Guatemala were "explained" by alleged or real U.S. support for local juntas, oligarchies, and so on. Here we are again, with the cultural and media elites on both sides of the Atlantic explaining al-Zarqawi's beheadings by the American invasion of Iraq, or Al-Qaeda's atrocities in general by American support for heads of state of Muslim countries such as Egypt's Hosni Mubarak, Pakistan's Pervez Musharraf, and Saudi Arabia's King Abdullah. Once again, those who believed that Communist totalitarianism was the cure for military regimes in Ciudad de Guatemala or Managua seem to believe that bin Laden may be the solution to Saudi autocracy, or the Muslim Brotherhood to the Hashemites of Jordan.

On the moral and political plane, too many in the European elites believe that tolerance can solve any problem, without noticing that tolerance is both impotent and dangerous when faced with fanaticism—especially religious fanaticism, something Europe had not experienced since the 17th century, and thus has no antibodies to. In a postmodern, post-religious cultural era, Europe is simply unprepared, legally, culturally, or politically, to deal with fanaticism. One does not need to accept the dubious claims that Muslims will soon be a majority in some European states to understand that they are already a major political factor in certain localities (Amsterdam, the Paris suburbs, Berlin) and that, whatever the interpretation of what most "Muslims think," they do not accept some of the trends in European culture, whether it is homosexual rights and feminism, secularism, or aspects of foreign policy—especially regarding Israel.

While the danger of Europe's being submerged in a Muslim demographic tide is wildly exaggerated, Muslim birthrates in Europe, even declining as they are, are still higher than national averages, and immigration continues to increase the numbers of Muslims. Yet there are politicians who do not seem concerned by the implications of this, such as Swedish Social Democrat Jens Orback, former Minister for Democracy, Metropolitan Affairs, Integration and Gender Equality. Orback claimed in 2004 that "We must be open and tolerant towards Islam and Muslims because when we become a minority, they will be so towards us."[5]

Nor does it seem that the Islamist threat is taken seriously, even in countries shocked by its presence. Thus the Dutch Center–Left government, in the post–van Gogh era, saw no contradiction between the Islamists' rejection of integration and the government's appointing to ministerial posts two MPs who held dual citizenship. Danish intelligence chief Hans Jorgen Bonnichsen felt that the radical imams behind the cartoon episode "contributed to our domestic security."[6] Even when some measures are taken, they are often mild, like the sentences given by British courts to some of the most dangerous and influential terrorist recruiters and ideologues: Abu Hamza was sentenced to seven years, and the Brixton recruiter of Richard Reid and Germaine Lindsay, Abdullah el-Faisal, was similarly sentenced, served half his sentence, and was deported to his native Jamaica. And when Tony Blair claimed that it is a mistake to put the civil liberties of terrorist suspects first, *The Economist* qualified that statement as "authoritarian."

EUROPE'S IDENTITY CRISIS: A CIVILIZATIONAL PROBLEM

The Islamist ghost haunting Europe today is not accidental, nor is its timing due to some plot hatched by a clique of terrorists from a Pakistani or North African hideout. To the contrary, it is to a large extent the result of cultural and economic— in that order—developments long in the making both in Europe and in the Muslim world. These trends are heading in opposite directions, and it is this fact that makes the threat so serious, far more than legal and intelligence errors or misguided social policies.

The most important discordance between trends in Europe and the Muslim world is identity. Europe as a whole is going through a clear identity crisis at both national and individual levels. Politically, the nation-state—which Europe invented and which largely explains both its past political, cultural, military, and technological triumphs and the totalitarian disasters of the 20th century—is under persistent attack. It is threatened from above by supranational, largely unelected elite and bureaucratic forces, primarily the European Union and its associated institutions; and from below by the rise of regionalism and micro-nationalisms (Basque, Catalan, Flemish, Scottish, etc.), and by a general loss of national culture and traditions in favor of an undefined "multiculturalism" and promiscuous expansion of "human rights." Multiculturalism, however, is not a policy, a doctrine, or an ideology. It is escapism. Brussels is quite effective in diluting national identities, but what has it to offer in exchange? "Tolerance"? "Europeanness"? Obviously it has nothing, which is why its Constitutional Treaty was rejected by both the least nationally conscious Europeans and the most—the Dutch and the French. Do not even ask the Poles, Balts, or Romanians what they think of "post-nationalism," or "postmodernism"!

When legislation passed by national, elected parliaments on issues of major importance—membership in the military, counter-terrorism, immigration, or asylum, to name just a few—either is overridden by Brussels or by the ECHR in Strasbourg, or is harshly treated as a "gross violation" by self-appointed NGOs, the sense of lost control over the nation's life and identity is increased. Hence a still inarticulate, or insufficiently articulated, disappointment with the political system as a whole and the rise of anti-system populists, ranging from quasi-anarchic skinheads to xenophobic parties à la Le Pen's *Front National*.

European youth suffer from loss of identity, combined with widespread tolerance or justification of deviant behavior. They see the legalization of drugs and prostitution, the continual lowering of jail sentences for various kinds of crime, and the educational system's frowning upon or outright rejection of national cultural identity. Many of them are losing all moral and cultural standards, and live in a chaotic, disorderly, no-responsibility world. And here is the key difference between native Europeans and Muslim immigrants of the second or third generation: While both suffer the same loss of identity and aim, the former have no obvious exit, since both Christianity and mass ideologies are largely dead in Europe, while the latter do—and it is Islam, especially in its most simplistic, and poisonous, forms. It is hard to avoid drawing comparisons between British and German "skinheads"—who are opposed to an undefined "system" and are ready to blame their own problems on an undefined "other," and to borrow the slogans of fascist or Nazi ideologies they know nothing about—and young Muslims in Europe who cannot read or understand the Quran but accept in its entirety the Salafi interpretation of it because it gives them an identity and a goal: to fight the infidel "other." Doing so conveniently gives them a reason to reject a system they cannot or will not adapt to, and offers even the most ordinary petty criminal, be he a Muslim from birth or a convert, the opportunity to feel part of a large, indeed global, struggle—something that any psychologist would agree serves to create unconditional loyalty.

At the same time that Europe is suffering an extreme loss of national identity, the Islamic world, aware of its general backwardness but in denial of the local roots of that backwardness, seeks scapegoats abroad, and solutions in a return to the mythical "pure" Islam of the Prophet's times. While these factors are obvious in the case of Muslims born in Europe, they are even more acutely felt by Third World immigrants. For the latter the identity vacuum of Europe's metropolises adds to the double cultural shock of entry from a rural into a post-industrial world and from a conservative and structured moral universe into postmodern moral relativism and anarchic individualism.

To this, one has to add the impact of the political culture from the countries of origin, often imported wholesale to Europe and reinforced by the common pattern of marriage with partners from the original countries. That explains the disproportionate representation of individuals of Algerian, Pakistani, Moroccan, and Syrian background in Islamist activities—just as it partially explains the disproportionately low participation of Turks, Albanians, or Bosniaks in such activities. The former are products of radical or fast radicalizing Islamist environments, the latter of less radical or partially secularized Muslim societies. While this is just one element in the mixture of factors explaining the distribution of Islamism in Europe, it is an important one.

Europe, however, has by now created its own peculiar Islamic environment, in which Muslim immigrant ethnic and national identities are to some extent being submerged into an increasingly homogeneous "Muslim" whole, especially among the second and the growing third generation of immigrants. The best example of this is the joint presence of Algerian and Moroccan radicals in Islamist cells in Spain, of Pakistani and Algerian cooperation in Britain, of Pakistan-originated *Tablighi* recruitment among France's Maghrebi immigrants, and so on.

The neo-Wahhabi groups financed from, if not by, the *nouveaux riches* Gulf States are a different but not unrelated story.

And then there is the peculiar impact of globalization, especially via the Internet. It does not itself produce radicals, but it does offer the disaffected and alienated Muslim youths of Europe an "explanation" and a "solution" to their problems. How else could one explain why Muslims born in France or Britain, knowing nothing about Iraq, Kashmir, Chechnya, or Palestine but what *The Guardian, Le Monde,* or Salafi Internet sites tell them, decide to go there to fight and die?

It is said *ad nauseam,* by Muslims and Western politicians and academics, that terrorism is not Islam and attempts to associate the two are insulting, dangerous, and counterproductive. This is one of those partial truths made of two halves. In this case, the obvious one is that not all Muslims, not even a majority, are terrorists. The other is that, as the CEO of Al-Arabiyya courageously put it, "while most Muslims are not terrorists, most terrorists today are Muslims." Or as the German-Turkish Muslim author Necla Kelek explained,

> Politicians and religious scholars of all faiths are right in pointing out that there are many varieties of Islam, that Islamism and Islam should not be confused, that there is no line in the Koran that would justify murder. But the assertion that radical Islamic fundamentalism and Islam have nothing to do with each other is like asserting that there was no link between Stalinism and Communism.[7]

And the Islamist terrorists are Muslims. Neither the Quran itself nor prominent orthodox theologians today say otherwise. Indeed, the Quran is clear that all those who claim to be Muslims are. Thus, the real problem is not that somebody else—outsiders, non-Muslims—"insults" the followers of Islam by associating them with terrorists, but that most Muslims choose to hide behind emotions (feeling "insulted") rather than face the problem head on. Unfortunately, the genuinely moderate imams, few and mostly living in London, lack the legitimacy to reach the masses of nominal Muslims. The "moderates" *à la* Yusuf al-Qaradawi, and the Muslim Brotherhood in general, are anything but. Qaradawi is quite clear in his opinion: Al-Qaeda and its followers *are Muslims as long as Allah does not decide otherwise*—which is in His hands alone.

And here is the key dichotomy that Muslims living in Europe face (or, more often, avoid): either agree with the radicals, who are Muslims, that Islam is under threat globally and violence is the answer, or reject the main premise and admit that Islam has to *adapt* to different circumstances because Muslims now live under various circumstances. The latter, however, would be the end of feeling "insulted." It would require cooperating with the authorities and, most importantly, willingly accepting adjustments to traditional Islamic (or pseudo-Islamic) customs and beliefs: intolerance toward gays and denial of women's rights, but also practices such as polygamy, FGM, and honor killings. The alternative is grim: the continuous rise of populist, anti-immigrant demagogues, serious attempts to stop Muslim immigration, and eventually a general cultural clash in most, if not all, European countries. Of course, the creation of an Islam of Europe, adapted to the postmodern cultural environment, would solve all such problems. But that process is, at the very best, in its incipient, baby-steps stage.

In global terms, Europe has, as we have seen, moved during the past decade or so from being a favorite *R&R area* for radical Islamist ideologues, financiers, and recruiters, to being an *exporter* of Islamist terrorism, to being a *target* of such terrorism. As those changes took place, some European governments have started to understand and to act upon the implications—

Denmark, the Netherlands, France—while others are still in denial—Britain, Sweden, and especially Spain. Indeed, Socialist Madrid's idea of countering Islamism's spread is the woolly and discredited UN-sponsored notion of a "dialogue of civilizations," more on which below.

That Europe, with its cultural developments, government policies, and security problems, is important, indeed crucial, for the security of the United States goes without saying. On the one hand, American elites, from the Ivy League to the *New York Times* and *Time* magazine, share or indeed follow the behavior and mentalities of European elites, as do many politicians, especially on the West Coast and in the Northeast. On the other hand, the European governments have more extensive, and in some cases better, intelligence information on the Muslim countries and, at the intelligence and general law-and-order levels, more and longer experience with Salafist radicals.

There are some immediate problems, such as the obsessive European opposition to capital punishment—and the extraordinary and quasi-paranoiac attacks against the very idea of intelligence cooperation with the United States because of the allegedly illegal CIA rendition flights. Just consider: Here are U.S. planes flying through European airspace, taking CIA "captives" to Muslim states that mistreat Islamist terrorists (no *Miranda* rights!). Ultimately, human-rights groups, and the legislation they push for, threaten to be an obstacle to all kinds of intelligence cooperation between Europe and the United States.

There are additional institutional problems, especially with pan-European institutions, such as the Human Rights Court, the European Parliament, and the inertia-dominated European Commission, all of which are both unrepresentative of public opinion in most countries, and hard to reform.

One might think that, after numerous judges' refusals to uphold verdicts that were clearly valid, such as the Samir Azzouz case in the Netherlands and the Mounir el Motassadeq one in Germany, European authorities would conclude that existing legal rules and practices are simply inadequate to deal with Islamist terrorism. But one would be wrong. In fact, the EU is the major factor in pushing for greater UN involvement in terrorism cases; for the expansion of the reach of various tribunals such as the International Criminal Court in The Hague and the International Criminal Tribunal for Rwanda in Arusha (regardless of their failures so far); and generally a more legalistic approach to the issue of terrorism.

Interestingly, elite opinion, always in search of some deep "root cause" for any dysfunctionality in Third World peoples, refuses to look for such "root causes" for growing anti-immigrant hostility at home. One of the results of this is the rise of populist, occasionally xenophobic and racist, political parties, with the elites being "shocked" at this phenomenon (and yes, in Casablanca bars, they did engage in gaming!).

Is the European Union in decline, as many commentators suggested following the collapse of the European Constitutional Treaty and the June 2005 failure to agree on an EU budget for 2007–2013? What impact does that have on the European Muslim problem? Meanwhile, there are more and more Muslims in Europe, posing more, rather than less, of a security problem.

With that in mind, some issues are clear, as are their possible solutions:

- Any increase in the Muslim communities via immigration is dangerous and increasingly unpopular, as repeatedly demonstrated in both national and European Union elections.

- The radicalization of young, second-generation Muslims in Europe will continue unless it is interrupted by direct action. The only solution—a long-term one—is control over the imams. Imams—the natural leaders of the community—must be native (unlike the imported radicals of Londonistan) or, at the very least, speakers of the country's language.

- The attraction of Islamism, at least in the short term, is a problem that will continue to occupy European security and intelligence institutions.

- Most important, the problem—and here the U.S. and the EU share the same problem—is that Western-born or -educated Muslims increasingly see themselves as Muslims sojourning in the West rather than as Muslim citizens of a specific Western country. That makes the problem a cultural one—with all the implications of that.

Ultimately, however, as George Weigel has pointed out,[8] the European problem is a civilizational one. It is the problem of a society that has lost its moral and cultural bearings. What makes matters worse is that while the Europeans have lost their bearings, the growing Muslim communities in their midst have not. Many, perhaps most, Muslims in Europe today are religious, some strongly so, and the Europeans have nothing with which to counter those beliefs. One cannot counter something with nothing.

"Multiculturalism" in the West is widely practiced as tolerance, encouragement, and indeed subsidization of an archipelago of mutually incompatible, often mutually hostile, ethnic islands in countries which until a few decades ago were relatively homogeneous. Thus traditions, practices, and habits alien to Europe—polygamy, FGM, honor killings—are, if not tolerated, at least not systematically punished. Any serious Islamic scholar or imam would reject those practices as alien to his religion, but Europe's ruling circles see that as less important than "respect" for Islam. Their ignorance of Islam is never pointed out by national Islamic umbrella groups. Instead, the accusations from those circles are that Westerners choose not to understand Islam for "racist" reasons.

The basis of the West's self-defeating multiculturalism is the notion that all cultures, everywhere and at any time, are equal—except that Western culture is less so, as it is oppressive, guilty of past abuses, etc. Hence the pernicious "nonjudgmental" attitude so chic in London, Brussels, and New York. The fundamental change required is to accept and enforce the notion that any immigrant group in the West has some basic obligations, most prominent among them that of obeying the laws and traditions of its new country and learning the language. Until that happens, we will continue to see spectacles like that of an elected Manchester city councilman of Pakistani background who, after years of living in the UK, still needs a translator and claims the "right" to have that translator paid by the taxpayers.

A continued belief in multiculturalism by the elites suits Muslim radicals just fine. Unlike immigrants who come to America in pursuit of the American dream, many Muslims come to Europe determined not to assimilate into the local culture, which they despise. Many of their children, unlike second-generation Americans, hold to their traditional ways with greater tenacity than their parents. This is especially true of young Muslim men eager to maintain their traditional dominance over women, a role threatened by the fact that Muslim girls in Europe are outperforming boys in school and in the workplace. And yet Tony Blair thought he could reach this group through the mostly moderate Muslims who constitute the outreach "network" or "task force" he established.[9] Indeed, "official" Islamic organizations in Europe all suffer the same disabilities. They are not effective among the most dangerous elements of the Muslim communities, the impressionable youth; indeed, in the eyes of the youth, since they are sanctioned by the non-Muslim government, they cannot be "representative." They also are subject to the same divisions plaguing the Muslim communities themselves (along lines of ethnicity, sectarian differences, foreign influences). And this is leaving aside the fact that their leaders are seldom elected.

So far most European governments have chosen to avoid the problem, or to change the subject. Prime Minister José Luis Rodríguez Zapatero of Spain actually believes, as former French president Jacques Chirac claimed to, in the "dialogue of civilizations" mentioned above, and specifically in the "Euro-Mediterranean Partnership," a.k.a. the "Barcelona Process," launched at a conference in Barcelona in 1995. At the Barcelona meeting of 2005, however, the only Muslim leaders present were Recep Tayyip Erdogan of Turkey and Mahmoud Abbas (Abu Mazen) of the Palestinian Authority. Even if leaders like the kings of Morocco and Jordan, or the presidents of Egypt, Algeria, and Tunisia, had been there, they would only have complicated matters. They are all less tolerant of political Islam than most of the EU leaders present. Indeed, it is hard to see with which "Islamic civilization" Messrs. Zapatero et al. want to talk—a radical one like that of the Islamists in their midst? Or one where the Muslim Brotherhood is banned or barely tolerated (Egypt, Syria); where the veil is banned in schools and government offices (Turkey, Tunisia) because its political meaning is well understood; or where Islamists were killed by the tens of thousands (Algeria), while their ideologues and recruiters operated freely in Britain or Belgium?

On the other hand, some facts stubbornly remain. While EU economic growth as a whole has been modest to nil, that of the Maghreb has been nil or negative. Hence emigration is seen as a solution for social problems in Algiers, Rabat, Tunis, and beyond. Especially, one may add, if the emigrants are Islamists, as many are. Indeed, difficult as it would be to carry out, a detailed analysis of Moroccan or Algerian emigrants to Europe would almost certainly suggest that a disproportionate number are inclined toward Islamism, and that the GSPC and GICM may have more supporters among Algerians and Moroccans in Europe than they have at home.

And then there is the technical matter of security cooperation. At least in the case of France, as we have seen, counterterrorism and politics are largely separated, with the DGSE working well with its North African colleagues, despite official "human-rights" complaints and legislation. However, other European countries are less cooperative, and there are persistent Egyptian, Moroccan, Tunisian, and Algerian complaints about European tolerance of Islamists who are ensconced in Europe's welfare states while working hard to subvert the present regimes of their countries of origin, the Europeans' hoped-for partners in the "dialogue of civilizations."

When it comes to the U.S., on the one hand, the French provide needed military and intelligence cooperation to the United States' Trans-Sahara Counter-Terrorism Initiative (TSCTI) in the Sahel, as well as in Europe itself. On the other hand, the hysteria encouraged by the European Parliament over CIA rendition flights is clearly a problem—and a career threat to any European intelligence operative inclined to cooperate with the Americans.

The most important obstacle to transatlantic cooperation against Islamism remains cultural. And that is a problem that no "good will" or new governments and attitudes, whether in Washington or in the capitals of Europe, can change any time soon. The best sign of hope is that the realization of the problem of Islamism has now penetrated to the surface of Europe's politics. Even a few parliamentarians, such as Michael Gove in Britain and Gustavo de Arístegui in Spain (whose father was murdered by Islamists),[10] have written books criticizing European attitudes toward Islamists.

In 1974, French novelist and politician André Malraux stated: "Politically, the unity of Europe is a Utopia. The political unity of Europe would need a common enemy, but the only common enemy that could exist will be Islam." The current European actuality indeed gives the impression that in most countries Islam has become, if not the enemy, at least a common concern. Suddenly, tolerance no longer accepts what was accepted only a short time ago. The UK, which has lost its phlegm, does not want to have Salman Rushdie's books burned in Bradford. Germany is suddenly anxious about long-established prayers in the public gardens of Mannheim. Spain starts to condemn imams who are too literally inspired by the Quran.[11] Whether Malraux was prophetic or alarmist, the fact remains that the issue of Islam's role in Europe is finally open to debate after decades of silence, avoidance, or denial of the very existence of Europe's ghost.

And the need for this debate is urgent. Timothy Winter, a.k.a. Abdal Hakim Murad, a lecturer in Islamic Studies at Cambridge University, was quite representative of the opinion of many resident Muslims when he said, "The question facing British society, and society as a whole, is not how we encourage minorities to engage with western countries, but how those countries define themselves as a collage of different religious cultures."[12] Simply put, Winter believes that it is British society which should redefine itself to adapt to the Muslim presence, by ceasing to be British and resigning itself to being a "collage" of different cultures. Winter is a convert and thus more Muslim than some born Muslims, but his views are still the dominant ones—unlike their opposite, as expressed by the German-Turkish lawyer Seyran Ates, who optimistically believes that "We Western Muslim women will set off the reform of traditional Islam, because we are its victims."[13]

Admittedly, Muslims in Britain are more alienated and radicalized than most, but when a third of them would prefer to live under Sharia rather than British law, a similar number think Britain is decadent, and only a quarter see Britian as their country,[14] those figures suggest a problem that is serious indeed. Ultimately, Europe's Islamist ghost is its own creation.

Trends toward an Awakening?

There is a flourishing *décliniste* literature in France, spurred heavily by that country's consistently poor economic performance, diplomatic and military decline, and domestic instability, but also by the impact of the more than five million Muslims living there. There is also the beginning of a realization that England may actually deserve the label of "Londonistan," a trend manifested in books and articles by at least one politician, Tory MP Michael Gove, and by prominent journalists of both Right (Melanie Phillips) and Left (Martin Bright).[15] In Spain, the conservative MP Gustavo Arístegui understands the Islamist threat well,[16] and the respected scholar Serafín Fanjul García has demolished the prevailing Western academic and

Islamist utopian myths about the alleged *convergencia* during the Muslim rule of Al-Andalus.[17]

At the political level, it seems that the pattern of the 1990s—wherein the mainstream political parties largely avoided the connected issues of out-of-control immigration and Islamist terrorism, and thus opened the way to populist and xenophobic parties—has collapsed in many countries. Indeed in France important politicians of the governing party, and in Austria, Denmark, and the Netherlands non-extremist smaller parties or pressure groups, are taking all these issues seriously and acting upon public fears that the political elites have long disregarded. This obviously worked well in France, where Nicolas Sarkozy was elected president in 2007 by expressing some of the public's anxieties about Islam, Islamism, and immigration, and thus marginalizing the National Front.

At the operational level, new legislation against terrorism has been introduced in some European countries that had none before (Belgium, Greece), while in others, such as France, the UK, the Netherlands, Italy, and Denmark, existing counter-terrorism laws and the powers of intelligence agencies have been strengthened.

After all, the ideological tension between the European Left and most Muslims was such that sooner or later, the *de facto* mutual-support society of progressives and Islamists had to collapse under the weight of its own contradictions. Feminism, gay rights, freedom of expression, and secularism are just the most important factors counterbalancing the old alliance based on anti-Americanism, multiculturalism, and immigrant "rights." The fact that the conflict is now centered in Europe's most progressive countries—Denmark and the Netherlands—is highly significant.

As for the public at large, recent European voting patterns suggest a growing understanding that there is indeed an Islamist problem in Europe. That is demonstrated not just by the growing electoral success of anti-immigration and anti-Islamist parties, but also by the popularity of individual politicians associated with such views, people like Philippe de Villiers in France, Geert Wilders in the Netherlands, and Pia Kjærsgaard in Denmark, all elected and respectful of democratic rules.

Ultimately, for Europeans the main issues related to the presence of Islam in their midst and its inevitable association with the activities of Islamists are *national and cultural identity*, on which they are largely failing to identify solutions; and *security*, internal and external, on which some are worse than others, but none is satisfactory. For an American looking to Europe—and even more from the perspective of a transplanted European like this author—there is a clear logic to the old continent's becoming first a haven, then an exporter, and now a major target of jihadis. And it originates from a culture in flux: uncertain identity, ambiguous moral and legal standards, and misguided "tolerance."

For the United States, and especially its political elites, the fact that Europe is now a major incubator and exporter of Islamist terrorism should be a wake-up call. The Atlantic Ocean is wide. Nevertheless, European ghosts have ways of crossing the ocean.

TERMS AND ACRONYMS

AIVD: *Algemene Inlichtingen- en Veiligheidsdienst* (General Intelligence and Security Service)—Dutch intelligence service.

Al-Muhajiroun: ("The Emigrants")—Radical offshoot of HuT, founded by Omar Bakri Mohammed and Anjem Choudary in London in 1986; banned in 2006.

BfV: *Bundesamt für Verfassungsschutz* (Federal Office for the Protection of the Constitution)—German intelligence.

DGSE: *Divisione Investigazioni Generali e Operazioni Speciali* (General Directorate of External Security)—French foreign intelligence.

DIGOS: *Direction Générale de la Sécurité Extérieure* (Division of General Investigations and Special Operations)—Italian intelligence.

DST: *Direction de la Surveillance du Territoire* (Directorate of Territorial Surveillance)—French domestic intelligence.

ECHR: European Court of Human Rights—Established in 1950 and based in Strasbourg. Its decisions are legally binding on all member states of the Council of Europe—including non-EU members—and all their citizens have the right to appeal to it upon exhaustion of all appeals in national courts. (The acronym also stands for the European Convention on Human Rights.)

EIJ: Egyptian Islamic Jihad (*Al-Jihad al-Islami*, also called the Islamic Jihad, "al-Jihad," and the Jihad Group)—Jihadi splinter of the Muslim Brotherhood, led since 1991 by Ayman al-Zawahiri and formally merged with Al-Qaeda.

FNMF: *Fédération Nationale des Musulmans de France* (National Federation of the Muslims of France)—Umbrella organization of Muslim groups in France, Moroccan-dominated.

GIA: *Groupe Islamique Armé* (Armed Islamic Group; *al-Jamaah al-Islamiyah al-Musallah*)—Algerian Islamist terror group.

GICM: *Groupe Islamique Combattant Marocain* (Moroccan Islamic Fighting Group).

GSPC: *Groupe Salafiste pour la Prédication et le Combat* (Salafist Group for Preaching and Combat)—Algerian Islamist terror group, split off from the GIA in 1998.

HuT: *Hizb ut-Tahrir* (Party of Liberation)—A radical and secretive Islamist group, apparently based in London.

IAA: Islamic Army of Aden Abyan (*Jaysh Aden Abyan al-Islami*)—The Yemeni member of the Al-Qaeda nebula.

Islamic Caliphate (*Hilafet Devleti*): Formally known as the Association of Islamic Societies and Communities (*Verband islamischer Vereine und Gemeinden*), also present in France as the *Association Islamique de France* (AIF), it is a radical, ethnic-Turkish organization, led by the Kaplan family: Cemaleddin Kaplan until his death in 1995, and his son Metin since, based in Cologne. The group is in decline since Metin's extradition and trials in Turkey (2005, 2006).

IHRC: Islamic Human Rights Commission—Iranian-supported radical Shia organization based in London.

IslamOnline: Yusuf al-Qaradawi is the chairman of this highly popular Muslim website, heading a committee of scholars that oversees the site's content. Launched in Qatar in 1999 with support from that country's royal family, it often features comments and religious rulings by Qaradawi or his European Council for Fatwa and Research. It features a link to the anti-Semitic forgery *The Protocols of the Elders of Zion*.

Jamaat al-Tabligh Wal-Dawa, or ***Tablighi Jamaat*** (Proselytizing Group for Mission).

LeT: *Lashkar-e-Toiba* (Army of the Pure)—Pakistani jihadi organization active in Kashmir.

MB: Muslim Brotherhood—International network, founded in 1928 in Cairo, sometimes violent, sometimes not, according to local circumstances.

MCB: Muslim Council of Britain—National representative organization of Muslims in Britain

MRAP: *Mouvement contre le Racisme et pour l'Amitié des Peuples* (Movement against Racism and for Friendship among Peoples)—French left-wing "human-rights" group.

RG: *Renseignements Généraux* (General Intelligence)—The French police intelligence and counter-terrorism unit.

Salafi: "A follower of the Prophet Muhammad's immediate successors, the pious ancestors (*al-salaf al-salihin*). Salafi movements have sought to restore Islam on the basis of its seventh-century teachings—that is, Islam as it was under the Prophet Muhammad and his immediate successors. Salafis usually belong to one of several groups, most notably the Muslim Brotherhood and the Wahhabis."*

SISMI: *Servizio per le Informazioni e la Sicurezza Militare* (Intelligence and Military Security Service)—Italian military and defense intelligence service.

SOS: Supporters of Sharia (*Ansar al-Sharia*)—Jihadist group founded by Abu Hamza in 1994.

Takfir-wal-Hijra (Excommunication and Exodus)—Originally an Egyptian radical splinter of the Muslim Brotherhood, it is now a loose network active in Europe, especially in Britain, although banned in Germany, France, and Spain.

UOIF: *L'Union des Organisations Islamiques de France* (Union of the Islamic Organizations of France).

---

* Jonathan D. Halevi, "Al-Qaeda's Intellectual Legacy: New Radical Islamic Thinking Justifying the Genocide of Infidels," Jerusalem Viewpoints No. 508, December 1, 2003, http://www.jcpa.org/jl/vp508.htm.

BIBLIOGRAPHY

Monographs and Studies Available on the Internet

Alonso, Rogelio. *"Procesos de radicalización de los terroristas yihadistas en España."* ARI No. 31 (2007). http://www.realinstitutoelcano.org/wps/portal/rielcano/Convocatoria?WCM_GLOBAL_CONTEXT=/wps/wcm/connect/Elcano_es/Zonas_es/ARI%2031-2007.

Álvarez-Miranda, Berta. *"Aquí y allí: vínculos transnacionales y comunitarios de los inmigrantes musulmanes en Europa."* DT No. 9 (2007). http://www.realinstitutoelcano.org/wps/portal/rielcano/Convocatoria?WCM_GLOBAL_CONTEXT=/wps/wcm/connect/Elcano_es/Zonas_es/DT%209-2007.

Atran, Scott. "Genesis and Future of Suicide Terrorism." http://www.interdisciplines.org/terrorism/papers/1.

Bakker, Edwin. "Jihadi terrorists in Europe, their characteristics and the circumstances in which they joined the jihad: an exploratory study." Netherlands Institute of International Relations. Clingendael, The Hague. December 2006. http://www.clingendael.nl/cscp/publications/?id=6480&&type=summary.

Bar, Sarah, Sharon Marek, and Blair Mersinger. "An Investigation into the North African Crime-Terror Nexus, Transnational Crime and Terrorism." http://www.american.edu/traccc/resources/publications/students/bar01.pdf.

Blick, Andrew, Tufyal Choudhury, and Stuart Weir. *The Rules of the Game: Terrorism, Community and Human Rights.* A Report by Democratic Audit, Human Rights Centre, University of Essex. For the Joseph Rowntree Reform Trust. November 2006. http://www.statewatch.org/news/2006/nov/uk-rules-of-the-game.pdf. http://www.jrrt.org.uk/Terrorism_final.pdf.

Bonanate, Luigi. *"Democracia italiana y terrorismo internacional: ¿Quién vencerá el desafío? Algunas premisas."* Real Instituto. Elcano No. 6 (2007). http://www.realinstitutoelcano.org:9081/wps/portal/rielcano/Convocatoria?WCM_GLOBAL_CONTEXT=/wps/wcm/connect/Elcano_es/Zonas_es/DT%206-2007.

Bourseiller, Christophe. *"La faucille et le Coran."* *Le Meilleur des Mondes*. No. 3 (Spring 2007). http://www.denoel.fr/Denoel/collections/meilleur_sommaire_n3.jsp.

Bright, Martin. *When Progressives Treat with Reactionaries: The British State's Flirtation with Radical Islamism.* Preface by Jason Burke. Policy Exchange. London. July 2006. http:///www.policyexchange.org.uk/Publications. aspx?id=192.

"La Comunidad Musulmana en España." Informe Final, Estudio de Opinión realizado por Metroscopia para el Ministerio del Interior. Madrid. November 2006. http://www.realinstitutoelcano.org/materiales/docs/comunidad_musulmana_esp_novo6.pdf.

Coolsaet, Rik. "Between al-Andalus and a failing integration: Europe's pursuit of a long-term counterterrorism strategy in the post-al-Qaeda era." Egmont Paper 5. Royal Institute for International Relations (IRRI-KIIB). Brussels. May 2005. http://www.irri-kiib.be/paperegm/ep5.pdf.

Denécé, Eric. *"Le Développement de l'islam fondamentaliste en France: Aspects sécuritaires, économiques et sociaux."* Centre Français de Recherche sur le Renseignement. Rapport de Recherche No. 1. September 2005. http:// www.cf2r.org/download/rapports_recherche/RR1-Islam.pdf.

Drake, C. J. M. "The Role of Ideology in Terrorists' Target Selection." In *Terrorism and Political Violence*, vol. 10, no. 2 (Summer 1998), pp. 53–85. www.ciaonet.org/wps/drc01/.

Drukwerk, Zijlstra, and B. V. Rijswijk. "Violent Jihad in the Netherlands: Current Trends in the Islamist Terrorist Threat." Report for the General Intelligence and Security Service of the Netherlands (AIVD). March 2006. http://www.aivd.nl/contents/pages/65582/jihad2006en.pdf.

Dupont, Alain. *"El Islam de Francia: Sus Implicaciones Políticas y de Seguridad."* Unisci Discussion Papers. May 2005. http://www.ucm.es/info/unisci/ UNISCI-Review8.htm.

Echeverría Jesús, Carlos. *"La amenaza del activismo terrorista del Grupo Salafista para la Predicación y el Combate (GSPC) argelino."* ARI No. 20 (2007). http://www.realinstitutoelcano.org:9081/wps/myportal/rielcano/ Convocatoria?WCM_GLOBAL_CONTEXT=/wps/wcm/connect/Elcano_es/ Zonas_es/ARI%2020-2007.

Escobar Stemmann, Juan José. "Middle East Salafism's Influence and the Radicalization of Muslim Communities in Europe." *Middle East Review of International Affairs*, vol. 10, no. 3, (September 2006). http://meria.idc. ac.il/journal/2006/issue3/jv10no3a1.html.

European Monitoring Centre on Racism and Xenophobia. "Muslims in the European Union: Discrimination and Islamophobia." Vienna. 2006. http://eumc.europa.eu/eumc/material/pub/muslim/Manifestations_EN.pdf.

Europol. TE-SAT 2007. "EU Terrorism Situation and Trend Report 2007." http://www.europol.europa.eu/index.asp?page=news&news=pr070410.htm.

García Rey, Marcos. *"Del uso de referencias culturales islámicas para la acción yihadista en Europa."* ARI No. 48/2007. April 23, 2007. http://www.realinstitutoelcano.org/wps/portal/rielcano/contenido?WCM_GLOBAL_CONTEXT=/Elcano_es/Zonas_es/ARI+48-2007.

General Intelligence and Security Service of the Netherlands (*Algemene Inlichtingen- en Veiligheidsdienst).* "The radical dawa in transition: The rise of Islamic neoradicalism in the Netherlands." October 9, 2007. https://www.aivd.nl/contents/pages/90126/theradicaldawaintransition.pdf.

German Bureau for the Protection of the Constitution (*Verfassungsschutzbericht)* 2002. http://www.verfassungsschutz.de/de/publikationen/verfassungsschutzbericht/vsbericht_2002/.

Gerstenfeld, Manfred. "Radical Islam in the Netherlands: A Case Study of a Failed European Policy." Institute for Contemporary Affairs. Jerusalem Issue Brief. January 2, 2005. http://www.jcpa.org/brief/brief004-14.htm.

Grignard, Alain. *"L'Islam face au terrorisme."* http://www.mil.be/rdc/viewdoc.asp?LAN=nl&FILE=doc&ID=193.

Haqqani, Husain. "Jihad and Jihadism." *The Indian Express.* August 3, 2005. http://www.indian-express.com/columnists/full_column.php?content_id=75539.

Homeland Security Policy Institute and Critical Incident Analysis Group, Prisoner Radicalization Task Force. *Out of the Shadows: Getting Ahead of Prisoner Radicalization.* http://www.healthsystem.virginia.edu/internet/ciag/publications/out_of_the_shadows.pdf.

Home Office. *Report of the Official Account of the Bombings in London on 7th July 2005.* http://www.homeoffice.gov.uk/documents/7-july-report.pdf?view=Binary.

House of Commons, Foreign Affairs Committee. "Foreign Policy Aspects of the War against Terrorism." Fourth Report of Session 2005–2006. HC 573, incorporating HC 904–i. Published on July 2, 2006. http://www.publications.parliament.uk/pa/cm200506/cmselect/cmfaff/573/573.pdf.

Intelligence and Security Committee. *Report into the London Terrorist Attacks on 7 July 2005.* Presented to Parliament by the Prime Minister by Command of Her Majesty May 2006. http://www.cabinetoffice.gov.uk/intelligence/index.asp#reports#reports.

Jordán, Javier, Fernando M. Mañas, and Humberto Trujillo. *"Perfil socio-comportamental y estructura organizativa de la militancia yihadista en España. Análisis de las redes de Abu Dahdah y del 11-M."* http://www.jihadmonitor.org/.

Jordán, Javier, and Fernando M. Mañas. *"Indicios externos de la radicalización y militancia yihadista."* Jihad Monitor, Occasional Paper No. 4. January 10, 2007. http://www.jihadmonitor.org/.

Jordán, Javier, and Sol Tarrés. *"Movimientos musulmanes y prevención del yihadismo en España: Hizb ut-Tahrir."* Jihad Monitor, Occasional Paper No. 9. April 17, 2007. http://www.jihadmonitor.org/.

Jordán, Javier, and Humberto Trujillo. Tomás Navarro Blakemore, trans. "Favourable Situations for the jihadist recruitment: The neighborhood of Principe Alfonso (Ceuta, Spain)." Jihad Monitor, Occasional Paper No. 3. November 27, 2006. http://www.jihadmonitor.org/.

Jordán, Javier, and Robert Wesley. "The Threat of Grassroots Jihadi Networks: A Case Study from Ceuta, Spain." Terrorism Monitor, vol. 5, no. 3. February 15, 2007. http://www.jamestown.org/terrorism/news/article.php?articleid=2370249.

Kull, Steven (Principal Investigator). "Muslim Public Opinion on US Policy, Attacks on Civilians and al Qaeda." University of Maryland Program on International Policy Attitudes. April 24, 2007. http://www.worldpublicopinion.org/pipa/articles/home_page/346.php?nid=&id=&pnt=346&lb=hmpg2.

Lamo de Espinosa, Emilio. "A Difference That Makes a Difference? The US and Europe on Values and Culture." Working Paper, March 22, 2005. Real Instituto Elcano, Madrid. http://www.realinstitutoelcano.org/wps/portal/rielcano_eng/Content?WCM_GLOBAL_CONTEXT=/elcano/elcano_in/zonas_in/usa-transatlantic+dialogue/dt16-2005.

Lav, Daniel. "The Al-Qaeda Organization in the Islamic Maghreb: The Evolving Terrorist Presence in North Africa." MEMRI Inquiry and Analysis Series No. 332, March 7, 2007. http://memri.org/bin/latestnews.cgi?ID=IA33207.

Marret, Jean-Luc. *"Les Djihadistes en Occident: Approche comparée des exemples français et américains."* *Annuaire Français des Relations Internationales,* vol. 5, 2004. Editions Bruylant, Bruxelles. http://www.afri-ct.org/article.php3?id_article=885.

———. *"Évolution des profils jihadistes et des processus de radicalisation en Occident: Atomisation des réseaux et problèmes accrus de détection."* Notes de la Fondation pour la Recherche Stratégique, June 23, 2006. http://www.frstrategie.org/barreCompetences/secuInterieureTerrorisme/terrorisme.php.

———. *"Évolutions récentes du GSPC—'Al-Qa'ida au Maghreb islamique': Un redéploiement historique."* Notes de la Fondation pour la Recherche Stratégique, March 12, 2007. http://www.frstrategie.org/barreFRS/publications/notes/20070312.pdf.

———. *"Radicalisations et recrutements de l'islamisme radical dans l'Union européenne: L'exemple des prisons."* Notes de la Fondation pour la Recherche Stratégique, January 14, 2006. http://www.frstrategie.org/barreCompetences/secuInterieureTerrorisme/20060114.pdf.

Matta, Thierry. *"La menace vue de la France après le Livre Blanc,"* in *Cinq ans après le 11 septembre: Le point sur la lutte contre Al Qaida et le terrorisme international*, p. 12. Fondation pour la Recherche Stratégique, Paris, September 27, 2006. http://www.frstrategie.org/.

Ministry of the Interior and Kingdom Relations. "Saudi influences in the Netherlands—Links between the Salafist mission, radicalisation processes and Islamic terrorism." March 2004. http://www.minbzk.nl/bzk2006uk/subjects/public_safety/publications?ActItmIdt=13421.

Mirza, Munira, Abi Senthilkumaran, and Zein Ja'far. "Living Apart Together: British Muslims and the Paradox of Multiculturalism." Policy Exchange, London. January 29, 2007. http://www.policyexchange.org.uk/Publications.aspx?id=307.

Muslim Council of Britain Research & Documentation Committee, Commission on Integration and Cohesion. "Our stand on Multiculturalism, Citizenship, Extremism, & Expectations." MCB Briefing Paper, January 2007. http://www.mcb.org.uk/downloads/MCB%20ReDoc%20Briefing%20Paper%20PRINTRUN.pdf.

Nesser, Petter. "Jihad in Europe: Post-millennium patterns of jihadist terrorism in Western Europe." May 2–3, 2005. http://www.mil.no/felles/ffi/start/article.jhtml?articleID=103578.

———. *Profiles of Jihadist Terrorists in Europe*. http://www.mil.no/felles/ffi/start/FFI-rosjekter/Alfover/_TERRA/Publikasjoner/Books/#1.

Paz, Reuven. "The Non-Territorial Islamic States in Europe." www.e-prism.org.

Richards, Julian. "Terrorism in Europe: The local aspects of a global threat." Jihad Monitor Occasional Paper No. 7. April 10, 2007. http://www.jihadmonitor.org/.

Rupérez, Javier. Closing Remarks at "Jihadi Terrorism—Where Do We Stand?"
Second IRRI Conference on International Terrorism, Brussels, February
13, 2006. http://www.egmontinstitute.be/speechnotes/06/060213-jihad.
terr/Rup%C3%A9rez.htm.

Al-Suri, Abu Musab. *Primary Writings: Lessons Learned from the Armed Jihad
Ordeal in Syria*, Chapter 2. AFGP-2002-600080 (full translation). http://
www.ctc.usma.edu/aq/AFGP-2002-600080-Trans.pdf.

Taarnby, Michael. "Profiling Islamic Suicide Terrorists: A Research Report for
the Danish Ministry of Justice." Submitted November 27, 2003. http://
www.jm.dk/image.asp?page=image&objno=71157.

———. "Recruitment of Islamist Terrorists in Europe. Trends and Perspectives.
Research Report funded by the Danish Ministry of Justice." Submitted
January 14, 2005. http://www.jm.dk/image.asp?page=image&objno=73027.

Tarrés, Sol, and Javier Jordán. "*Movimientos musulmanes y prevención del
yihadismo en España: La Yama'a At-Tabligh Al-Da'wa.*" Jihad Monitor
Occasional Paper No. 6. March 27, 2007. http://www.jihadmonitor.org/.

Varghese, Peter. "Islamist Terrorism: The International Context." Canberra.
May 11, 2006. http://www.ona.gov.au/news.htm.

Vermaat, Emerson. "Bin Laden's Terror Networks in Europe." Mackenzie
Institute, May 26, 2002. http://www.mackenzieinstitute.com/commen-
tary.html.

Vidino, Lorenzo. "The Muslim Brotherhood in Holland." April 6, 2007.
http://counterterrorismblog.org/mt/pings.cgi/3860.

Warner, Carolyn M., and Manfred W. Wenner. "Religion and the Political
Organization of Muslims in Europe." Perspectives on Politics, vol. 4,
no. 3, pp. 457–479. September 2006. http://www.apsanet.org/imgtest/
POPSep06WarnerWenner.pdf.

VOLUMES AND MONOGRAPHS

Algar, Hamid. *The Society of the Muslim Brothers*. Oneonta, N.Y.: Islamic
Publications International, 2002.

———. *Wahhabism: A Critical Essay*. Oneonta, N.Y.: Islamic Publications
International, 2002.

Allam, Khaled Fouad. *Carta a un terrorista suicida: Islam contra la violencia*.
Barcelona: RBA Libros, 2005.

Allam, Magdi. *Kamikaze made in Europe: Riuscirá l'Occidente a sconfiggere i
terroristi islamici?* Milano: Oscar Mondadori, 2004.

———. *Bin Laden in Italia: Viaggio nell'Islam radicale*. Milano: Oscar Mondadori, 2002.

Arístegui, Gustavo de. *La Yihad en España: La obsesión para reconquistar Al-Andalus*. 6th edition. Madrid: La Esfera de los Libros, 2006.

Al-Ashmawy, Muhammad Saïd. *L'Islamisme contre l'Islam*. Paris: Editions la Découverte, 1989.

Ashtor, Eliyahu. *The Jews of Moslem Spain*, vols. 1–3. Philadelphia and Jerusalem: The Jewish Publication Society, 1992.

Aviles, Manuel, ed. *El Terrorismo Integrista: Guerras de religión?* Alicante: Editorial Club Universitario, 2004.

Bauer, Alain, and Xavier Raufer. *La Guerre ne fait que commencer*. Paris: Editions JC Lattès, 2002.

Bawer, Bruce. *While Europe Slept: How Radical Islam Is Destroying the West from Within*. New York: Doubleday, 2006.

Beckford, James A., Daniele Joly, and Farhad Khosrokhavar. *Muslims in Prison: Challenge and Change in Britain and France*. New York: Palgrave Macmillan, 2005.

Bell, Stewart. *Cold Terror: How Canada Nurtures and Exports Terrorism around the World*. Etobicoke, Ont.: John Wiley & Sons, 2004.

Bencheikh, Soheib. *Marianne et le Prophet*. Paris: Bernard Grasset, 1998.

Bergen, Peter L. *The Ossama bin Laden I Know. An Oral History of al Qaeda's Leader*. New York: Free Press, 2006.

Berlinski, Claire. *Menace in Europe: Why the Continent's Crisis Is America's Too*. New York: Crown Forum, 2006.

Al-Berry, Khaled. *Confesiones de un loco de Alá*. Madrid: La Esfera de los Libros, 2002.

Berthomet, Stéphane, and Guillaume Bigot. *Le jour où la France tremblera: Terrorisme Islamiste: les vrais risques pour l'Hexagone*. Paris: Ramsay, 2005.

Besson, Sylvain. *La conquête de l'Occident: Le projet secret des islamistes*. Paris: Seuil, 2005.

Bloom, Mia. *Dying to Kill: The Allure of Suicide Terror*. New York: Columbia University Press, 2005.

Borum, Randy. *Psychology of Terrorism*. Tampa: University of South Florida, 2004.

Bostom, Andrew, ed. *The Legacy of Jihad: Islamic Holy War and the Fate of Non-Muslims*. Amherst, N.Y.: Prometheus Books, 2005.

Brisard, Jean, with Charles Damien Martinez. *Zarqawi: The New Face of al-Qaeda*. New York: Other Press, 2005.

Bukay, David, ed. *Muhammad's Monsters: A Comprehensive Guide to Radical Islam for Western Audiences*. Green Forest, Ark.: Balfour Books, and Shaarei Tikva, Israel: ACPR Publishers, 2004.

Bunt, Gary R. *Islam in the Digital Age: E-Jihad, Online Fatwas and Cyber-Islamic Environments*. London: Pluto Press, 2003.

Burgat, François. *Face to Face with Political Islam*. London and New York: I. B. Tauris, 2005.

Burr, Millard J., and Robert O. Collins. *Alms for Jihad*. Cambridge, UK, and New York: Cambridge University Press, 2006.

Buruma, Ian. *Murder in Amsterdam: The Death of Theo van Gogh and the Limits of Tolerance*. New York: Penguin Books, 2006.

Canales, Pedro, and Enrique Montáchez. *En el nombre de Alá: La red secreta del terrorismo islamista en España*. Barcelona: Planeta, 2002.

Chalvidant, Jean. *11-M: La manipulación*. Madrid: Ediciones Jaguar, 2004.

Clarke, Colin, Ceri Peach, and Steven Vertovec, eds. *South Asians Overseas: Migration and Ethnicity*. Cambridge, UK: Cambridge University Press, 1990.

Courmont, Barthélémy. *Terrorisme et contre-terrorisme: L'Incompréhension fatale*. Paris: Le Cherche Midi, 2003.

Dambruoso, Stefano. *Milano-Bagdad: Diario de un magistrato in prima linea nella lotta al terrorismo islamico in Italia*. Milano: Mondadori, 2004.

Deloire, Christophe, and Christophe Dubois. *Les Islamistes sont déjà là: Enquête sur une guerre secrète*. Paris: Albin Michel, 2004.

Denécé, Eric, ed. *Guerre secrète contre Al-Qaeda*. Paris: Centre Français de Recherche sur le Renseignment, 2002.

Dennis, Anthony J. *The Rise of the Islamic Empire and the Threat to the West*. Bristol, Ind.: Wyndham Hall Press, 1996.

Devji, Faisal. *Landscapes of the Jihad: Militancy, Morality, Modernity*. Ithaca, N.Y.: Cornell University Press, 2005.

Djavann, Chahdortt. *Que pense Allah de l'Europe?* Paris: Gallimard, 2004.

Emerson, Steven. *American Jihad: The Terrorists Living among Us*. New York: Free Press, 2002.

Encel, Frédéric. *Géopolitique de l'apocalypse: La démocratie à l'épreuve de l'islamisme*. Paris: Flammarion, 2002.

Etienne, Bruno. *Les combatants suicidaires; suivi de Les Amants de l'Apocalypse.* La Tour d'Aigues: Editions de l'Aube, 2005.

Fanjul García, Serafín. *Al-Andalus contra España: La Forja del Mito.* Madrid: Siglo XXI de España Editores, 2002.

———. *La Quimera de Al-Andalus.* Madrid: Siglo XXI de España Editores, 2004.

Forestier, Patrick. *Confession d'un émir du GIA.* Paris: Grasset, 1999.

Fourest, Caroline. *Frère Tariq: Discourse, stratégie et méthode de Tariq Ramadan.* Paris: Bernard Grasset, 2004.

Fradkin, Hillel, Husain Haqqani, and Eric Brown, eds. *Current Trends in Islamist Ideology,* vols. 1–5. Washington D.C.: Hudson Institute, 2005.

Fregosi, Paul. *Jihad.* Amherst, N.Y.: Prometheus Books, 1998.

Gambetta, Diego, ed. *Making Sense of Suicide Missions.* Oxford: Oxford University Press, 2005.

Garzón, Baltasar. *Un Mundo sin Miedo.* Barcelona: Plaza Janés, 2005.

Gerges, Fawaz A. *The Far Enemy: Why Jihad Went Global.* Cambridge, UK, and New York: Cambridge University Press, 2005.

Ghandour, Abdel-Rahman. *Jihad humanitaire: Enquête sur les ONG islamiques.* Paris: Flammarion, 2002.

Gove, Michael. *Celsius 7/7.* London: Weidenfeld & Nicolson, 2006.

Griffith, Lee. *The War on Terrorism and the Terror of God.* Grand Rapids, Mich., and Cambridge, UK: William B. Eerdmans, 2002.

Gritti, Roberto, and Magdi Allam, eds. *Islam, Italia: Chi sono e cosa pensano i musulmani che vivono tra noi.* Milano: Guerini e Associati, 2005.

Guidère, Mathieu. *Al-Qaida à la conquête du Maghreb: Le terrorisme aux portes de l'Europe.* Paris: Editions du Rocher, 2007.

———. *Les "Martryrs" d'Al-Qaeda: Au cœur de la propagande terroriste.* Nantes: Editions du Temps, 2006.

Gunaratna, Rohan. *Inside Al Qaeda: Global Network of Terror.* London: Hurst & Co., 2002.

Haddad, Yvonne Yazbeck, ed. *Muslims in the West: From Sojourners to Citizens.* Oxford and New York: Oxford University Press, 2002.

Heffelfinger, Christopher, ed. *Unmasking Terror: A Global Review of Terrorist Activities.* Washington, D.C.: Jamestown Foundation, 2005.

Hunter, Shireen, et al. *Islam: Europe's Second Religion.* Westport, Conn.: Praeger, 2002.

Husain, Ed. *The Islamist.* London: Penguin Books, 2007.

Iannaccone, Laurence R., and Massimo Introvigne. *Il mercato dei martiri: L'industria del terrorismo suicida*. Torino: Edizioni Lindau, 2004.

Ibrahim, Raymond. *The Al Qaeda Reader*. New York: Doubleday, 2007.

Jacquard, Roland. *Les archives secrètes d'Al-Qaida*. Paris: Jean Picollec, 2002.

———. *Fatwa contre l'Occident*. Paris: Albin Michel, 1998.

Jacquard, Roland, and Atmane Tazaghart. *Ben Laden, la destruction programmée de l'Occident*. Paris: Jean Picollec, 2004.

Jordán, Javier, et al. *Los origenes del terror*. Madrid: Biblioteca Nueva, 2004.

Kaci, Rachid. *La République des laches: La faillite des politiques d'intégration*. Paris: Editions des Syrtes, 2003.

Kaltenbach, Jeanne-Hélène, and Michèle Tribalat. *La république et l'Islam*. Paris: Gallimard, 2002.

Kepel, Gilles. *Allah in the West: Islamic Movements in America and Europe*. Cambridge, UK: Polity Press, 1997.

———, ed. *Al-Qaeda dans le texte*. Paris: PUF, 2005.

———. *Les Banlieues de l'Islam*. Paris: Editions du Seuil, 1987.

———. *Jihad: The Trail of Political Islam*. Cambridge, Mass.: Belknap Press, 2002.

———. *The Revenge of God: The Resurgence of Islam, Christianity, and Judaism in the Modern World*. University Park: Penn State University Press, 1994.

———. *The Roots of Radical Islam*. London: Saqi Books, 2005.

———. *The War for Muslim Minds: Islam and the West*. Cambridge, Mass.: Belknap Press, 2004.

Khosrokhavar, Farhad. *L'Islam dans les prisons*. Paris: Balland, 2004.

———. *Quand Al-Qaïda parle: Témoignages derrière les barreaux*. Paris: Grasset, 2006.

Klausen, Jytte. *The Islamic Challenge: Politics and Religion in Western Europe*. Oxford: Oxford University Press, 2005.

Kohlmann, Evan F. *Al-Qaeda's Jihad in Europe: The Afghan-Bosnian Network*. New York: Berg, 2004.

Labevière, Richard. *Les coulisses de la terreur*. Paris: Bernard Grasset, 2003.

Labidi, Samia. *Karim: Mon frère ex-intégriste terroriste*. Paris: Flammarion, 1997.

Laidi, Ali, and Ahmed Salam. *Le Jihad en Europe: Les Filières du terrorisme islamiste*. Paris: Seuil, 2002.

Lamchichi, Abderrahim. *Géopolitique de l'islamisme*. Paris: L'Harmattan, 2001.

———. *Islam et musulmans de France: Pluralisme, laïcité et citoyenneté*. Paris: L'Harmattan, 1999.

Landau, Paul. *Le Procès d'un réseau islamiste*. Paris: Albin Michel, 1997.

———. *Le sabre et le Coran: Tariq Ramadan et les Frères musulmans à la conquête de l'Europe*. Paris: Editions du Rocher, 2005.

Mandaville, Peter. *Global Political Islam*. London and New York: Routledge, 2007.

Marchand, René. *La France en danger d'Islam*. Lausanne: L'Age d'Homme, 2003.

Maréchal, Brigitte, ed. *L'Islam et les musulmans dans l'Europe élargie: Radioscopie*. Louvain-la-Neuve: Academie AB Bruylant, 2002.

Marret, Jean-Luc. *Techniques du terrorisme*. Paris: PUF, 2002.

———, ed. *Les fabriques du Jihad*. Paris: PUF, 2005.

McDermott, Terry. *Perfect Soldiers: The Hijackers: Who They Were, Why They Did It*. New York: HarperCollins, 2005.

Meddeb, Abdelwahab. *La maladie de l'Islam*. Paris: Seuil, 2002.

Menocal, María Rosa. *The Ornament of the World: How Muslims, Jews and Christians Created a Culture of Tolerance in Medieval Spain*. Boston: Little Brown, 2003.

Millard, Mike. *Jihad in Paradise: Islam and Politics in Southeast Asia*. Armonk, N.Y.: M. E. Sharpe, 2004.

Mitchell, Richard P. *The Society of the Muslim Brothers*. New York and Oxford: Oxford University Press, 1995.

Moniquet, Claude. *Le Djihad: Histoire secrète des hommes et des réseaux en Europe*. Paris: Editions Ramsay, 2004.

———. *La Guerre sans Visage: De Waddi Haddad à Oussama ben Laden*. Neuilly-sur-Seine: Michel Lafon, 2002.

Nasiri, Omar. *Inside the Jihad: A spy's story—My life with Al Qaeda*. New York: Basic Books, 2006.

Nordmann, Charlotte, ed. *Le Foulard Islamique en questions*. Paris: Editions Amsterdam, 2004.

O'Neill, Sean, and Daniel McGrory. *The Suicide Factory: Abu Hamza and the Finsbury Park Mosque*. London and New York: Harper Perennial, 2006.

Pape, Robert A. *Dying to Win: The Strategic Logic of Suicide Terrorism*. New York: Random House, 2005.

Phillips, Melanie. *Londonistan*. New York: Encounter Books, 2006.

Pontaut, Jean-Marie, and Marc Epstein. *Ils ont assassiné Massoud: Révélations sur l'internationale terroriste.* Paris: Editions Robert Laffont, 2002.

Radu, Michael, ed. *Dangerous Neighborhood: Contemporary Issues in Turkey's Foreign Policy.* New Brunswick: Transaction Publishers, 2002.

Ramadan, Tariq. *Western Muslims and the Future of Islam.* Oxford and New York: Oxford University Press, 2004.

Ramírez Sánchez, Carlos. *L'islam révolutionnaire.* Monaco: Editions du Rocher, 2003.

Razavi, Emmanuel. *Frères musulmans dans l'ombre d'Al Qaeda.* Mayenne: Jean-Cyrille Godefroy, 2005.

Reinares, Fernando, and Antonio Elorza, eds. *El Nuevo Terrorismo Islamista: Del 11-S al 11-M.* Madrid: Temas de Hoy, 2004.

Roy, Olivier. *Les Illusions du 11 Septembre: Le débat stratégique face au terrorisme.* Paris: Seuil, 2002.

———. *L'Islam mondialisé.* Paris: Seuil, 2002.

Sageman, Marc. *Leaderless Jihad: Terror Networks in the Twenty-First Century.* Philadelphia: University of Pennsylvania Press, 2007.

———. *Understanding Terror Networks.* Philadelphia: University of Pennsylvania Press, 2004.

Al Sayyad, Nezar, and Manuel Castells, eds. *Muslim Europe or Euro-Islam: Politics, Culture, and Citizenship in the Age of Globalization.* Lanham, Md.: Lexington Books, 2002.

Sfeir, Antoine, et al. *Dictionnaire mondial de l'Islamisme.* Paris: Plon, 2002.

Sifaoui, Mohamed. *L'affaire des caricatures: Dessins et manipulations.* Paris: Editions Privé, 2006.

———. *La France malade de l'Islamisme: Menaces terroristes sur l'Hexagone.* Paris: Le Cherche Midi, 2002.

Sreedhar, Santhanam K., and Sudhir Saxena Manish. *Jihadis in Jammu and Kashmir: A Portrait Gallery.* New Delhi: Sage Publications, 2003.

Steyn, Mark. *America Alone: The End of the World as We Know It.* Washington, D.C.: Regnery, 2006.

Stora, Benjamín. *L'Algérie en 1995: La guerre, l'histoire, la politique.* Paris: Editions Michalon, 1995.

Ternisien, Xavier. *La France de mosquées.* Paris: Albin Michel, 2002.

Thomas, Dominique. *Les Hommes d'Al-Qaeda.* Paris: Editions Michalon, 2005.

———. *Le Londonistan: La voix du Jihad.* Paris: Editions Michalon, 2003.

Tibi, Bassam. *The Challenge of Fundamentalism: Political Islam and the New World Disorder.* Berkeley: University of California Press, 2002.

———. *Islam between Culture and Politics.* New York: Palgrave, 2001.

Touzanne, Jean-Pierre. *L'Islamisme Turc.* Paris: L'Harmattan, 2001.

Trigano, Shmuel. *La démission de la république: Juifs et Musulmans en France.* Paris: PUF, 2003.

Valenzuela, Javier. *España en el punto de mira: La amenaza del integrismo islámico.* Madrid: Temas de Hoy, 2002.

Vidal, Cesar. *España frente al Islam: De Mahoma a Ben Laden.* Madrid: La Esfera de los Libros, 2004.

Weigel, George. *The Cube and the Cathedral: Europe, America and Politics without God.* New York: Basic Books, 2005.

Weimann, Gabriel. *Terror on the Internet: The New Arena, the New Challenges.* Washington, D.C.: United States Institute of Peace Press, 2006.

Wiktorowicz, Quintan. *Radical Islam Rising: Muslim Extremism in the West.* Lanham, Md.: Rowman & Littlefield, 2005.

Ye'or, Bat. *Eurabia: The Euro-Arab Axis.* Madison, N.J.: Fairleigh Dickinsón University Press, 2005.

Zahab, Mariam Abou, and Olivier Roy. *Islamist Networks: The Afghan-Pakistan Connection.* New York: Columbia University Press, 2004.

Zarka, Yves Charles, Sylvie Taussig, and Cynthia Fleury, eds. *L'Islam en France.* Paris: PUF, 2004.

Zerrouky, Hassane. *La Nébuleuse islamiste en Europe et en Algérie.* Paris: Editions 1, 2002.

ENDNOTES

FOREWORD

1 "Hamas MP and Cleric Yunis Al-Astal in a Friday Sermon: We Will Conquer Rome, and from There Continue to Conquer the Two Americas and Eastern Europe," Middle East Media Research Institute (MEMRI) Clip No. 1739, April 11, 2008.

2 "New Muslim Brotherhood Leader: Resistance in Iraq and Palestine Is Legitimate; America Is Satan; Islam Will Invade America and Europe," MEMRI Special Dispatch Series No. 655, February 4, 2004.

3 *Europa wird am Ende des Jahrhunderts islamisch sein*," *Die Welt*, July 28, 2004.

4 "100 percent immigrants at Danish school," *DR Nyheder*, September 9, 2004.

5 Steve Harrigan, "Swedes Reach Muslim Breaking Point," Fox News, November 26, 2004.

6 "Bin Laden backer on his way to Oslo," *Aftenposten*, August 9, 2004.

7 "Qazi Hussain Ahmed refused to comment on capital punishment on blasphemy and homosexuality during visit to Norway," *Pakistan Christian Post*, September 9, 2004.

8 Jamie Pyatt, "Jail loos turned from East," *The Sun*, January 31, 2007.

9 Nick Britten, "Schoolboys disciplined for 'refusing to pray to Allah'," *The Telegraph*, July 5, 2008.

10 Frances Gibb, "Case dismissed: Lord Chief Justice lays down law on Sharia," *The Times*, July 4, 2008.

11 Christopher Hope and James Kirkup, "Muslims in Britain should be able to live under sharia, says top judge," *The Daily Mail*, July 4, 2008.

12 Ibid.

13 Gibb, "Case dismissed."

14 Hope and Kirkup, "Muslims in Britain should be able to live under sharia."

15 "Sharia law in UK is 'unavoidable'," *BBC News*, February 7, 2008.

CHAPTER ONE

[1] "Declassified Key Judgments of the National Intelligence Estimate, 'Trends in Global Terrorism: Implications for the United States'," April 2006 (released September 26, 2006); cf. *Wall Street Journal*, September 26, 2006.

[2] Eric Conan and Christian Makarian, "*Enquête sur la montée de l'Islam en Europe*," *L'Express*, January 26, 2006.

[3] For a copy of the poll, see http://online.wsj.com/documents/wsj-religion04-age.pdf.

[4] Conan and Makarian, "*Enquête sur la montée.*"

[5] Brian Moynahan, "Putting the Fear of God into Holland," *The Sunday Times*, February 27, 2005. See also George Weigel, *The Cube and the Cathedral: Europe, America and Politics without God* (New York: Basic Books, 2005), passim.

[6] Moynahan, "Putting the Fear of God into Holland."

[7] Quoted in Elisabeth Rosenthal, "A Poor Fit for an Immigrant: After 20 Years of Hard Work in Italy, Still Not Italian," *New York Times*, January 1, 2006.

[8] Jérôme Rivière, "*Le multiculturalisme des imbéciles,*" *Le Figaro*, December 30, 2005. The author is an MP from Alpes-Maritimes.

[9] Bernardo Cervellera, "Vatican says no to churches used as mosques," *Asia News*, April 29, 2004.

[10] Serafín Fanjul García, *Al-Andalus contra España: La forja del mito* (Madrid: Siglo XXI de España Editores, 2002); Serafín Fanjul García, *La Quimera de Al-Andalus* (Madrid: Siglo XXI de España Editores, 2004).

[11] Bassam Tibi, *Islam between Culture and Politics* (New York: Palgrave, 2001); Bassam Tibi, *The Challenge of Fundamentalism: Political Islam and the New World Disorder* (Berkeley: University of California Press, 2002).

[12] The vagueness of the numbers is largely due to the French law banning ethnic/religious questions on census questionnaires. Since France has the largest Muslim population in Europe, that skews the total numbers for the entire area.

[13] http://www.geocities.com/WestHollywood/Park/6443/Europe/, March 16, 2005.

[14] Conan and Makarian, "*Enquête sur la montée.*"

[15] http://euro-islam.info/pages/nether.html.

[16] Conan and Makarian, "*Enquête sur la montée.*"

[17] See the following overviews of Muslims in Europe: Shireen Hunter et al., *Islam: Europe's Second Religion* (Westport, Conn.: Praeger, 2002); Brigitte Maréchal, ed., *L'Islam et les musulmans dans l'Europe élargie: Radioscopie* (Louvain-la-Neuve: Academie Bruylant, 2002); Xavier Ternisien, *La France des mosquées* (Paris: Albin Michel, 2002); Nezar Al Sayyad and Manuel Castells, eds., *Muslim Europe or Euro-Islam: Politics, Culture, and Citizenship in the Age of Globalization* (Lanham, Md.: Lexington Books, 2002).

[18] "Reducing Immigration in Italy and Britain," *Migration News*, January 1996 at http://migration.ucdavis.edu/mn/comments.php?id=849_0_4_0.

CHAPTER TWO

[1] Nathalie Ferré, *"Uni(e)s contre une immigration jetable: L'immigré, un travailleur jetable,"* *L'Humanité*, May 6, 2006.

[2] See Gustavo de Arístegui, *La Yihad en España: La obsesion para reconquistar Al-Andalus*, 6th edition (Madrid: La Esfera de los Libros, 2006), pp. 232–233.

[3] Claude Imbert, *"Le bûcher d'une politique,"* *Le Point*, November 10, 2005, p. 3.

[4] Pew Forum on Religion & Public Life, "An Uncertain Road: Muslims and the Future of Europe," 2005, at http://pewforum.org/docs/index.php?DocID=60.

[5] Jean-Jacques Bozonnet, *"L'Italie s'ouvre aux travailleurs de l'Est et régularise 517,000 clandestins,"* *Le Monde*, July 22, 2006.

[6] "Spain's immigration amnesty ends," BBC News, May 7, 2005.

[7] Cf. http://www.cbs.nl/en-GB/menu/themas/mens-maatschappij/bevolking/publicaties/artikelen/2006-1886-wm.htm.

[8] Mark Steyn, *America Alone: The End of the World as We Know It* (Washington, D.C.: Regnery, 2006) and Bat Ye'or, *Eurabia: The Euro-Arab Axis* (Madison, N.J.: Fairleigh Dickinson University Press, 2005).

[9] Daniel Sandford, "Immigrant frustration for Malta," BBC News, October 21, 2005.

[10] Paco Pardo, *"Si las empresas europeas van a Africa, ¿porqué no nosotros a Europa?"* *Rebelión*, March 27, 2006

[11] Robert Rowthorn, "Never have we seen immigration on this scale: we just can't cope," *The Telegraph*, February 7, 2006.

[12] *"Immigration: la mobilisation des chrétiens contre les propositions de Sarkozy,"* lefigaro.fr (with Agence France Presse), April 24, 2006.

[13] Gregory Crouch, "A Candid Dutch Film May Be Too Scary for Immigrants," *New York Times*, March 16, 2006.

[14] Luke Harding, "Want a German passport? Then get revising, says state minister," *The Guardian*, March 16, 2006; "Merkel signals green light for controversial citizenship test," *Turkish Daily News*, March 20, 2006.

[15] Indeed, in Sweden, the Netherlands, Belgium, etc., pseudo-refugees or asylum seekers from a wide list of terrorist groups have found convenient refuge. Those include Peru's Sendero Luminoso and MRTA, Chile's MIR, the Philippines' PCP and NPA, Turkey's PKK, and Sri Lanka's LTTE.

[16] See http://www.unhcr.org/publ.html.

[17] Osman Hussain, *"Uno de los terroristas del 21-J: 'No queríamos matar, sólo sembrar el terror'."* *El Mundo*, July 30, 2005.

[18] Profiles of the five men in custody, *The Guardian*, July 30, 2005.

[19] "On Territorial Asylum," General Assembly resolution 2312 (XXII) of December 14 Declaration 1967, http://www.unhchr.ch/html/menu3/b/o_asylum.htm.

[20] "Wickedness in disguise," *The Telegraph*, December 20, 2006.

[21] Andrew Norfolk, "Police killer suspect fled Britain in a veil," *The Times*, December 20, 2006; Martin Wainwright, "Suspect snatched in Somali desert jailed for life for killing woman PC," guardian.co.uk, July 22, 2009.

[22] "Ex-Taliban spy granted asylum in UK," *The Daily Times* (Pakistan), February 24, 2003; Susan Bisset and Chris Hastings, "Taliban who fought British troops is granted asylum," *The Telegraph*, January 19, 2003.

[23] John Downing, "Taliban refugee still sees the UK as his enemy," *The Telegraph*, February 2, 2003.

[24] "Terror suspect deported from UK," *The Guardian*, September 15, 2006.

[25] In December 2006 the Dutch Parliament was still divided over the fate of 25,000 "asylum seekers" whose applications were rejected prior to 2001—yet another example of the magic impact the word "asylum" has, no matter how phony the claimant, on tolerant (and leftist) opinion.

[26] Henrik Bering, "The Good Terrorist: What happened when the Dane came back from Guantanamo," *The Weekly Standard*, October 18, 2004.

[27] Farhad Khosrokhavar, *Quand Al-Qaïda parle: Témoignages derrière les barreaux* (Paris: Grasset, 2006), pp. 136–137.

[28] Zacarias Moussaoui, to the U.S. District Court for the Eastern District of Virginia, February 14, 2006; see also John Rosenthal, "The French Path to Jihad," *Policy Review*, October/November 2006.

[29] Massoud Ansari and Andrew Alderson, *The Telegraph*, October 29, 2005.

[30] None of this should be particularly surprising to an American. This author remembers seeing signs of "We speak English" in the Astoria neighborhood of New York City during the late 1970s, and there are more people from certain villages of the Zacatecas state of Mexico in Cicero, Illinois, than in those villages.

[31] Muslim Council of Britain Research & Documentation Committee, "Our Stand on Multiculturalism, Citizenship, Extremism, & Expectations," from the Commission on Integration and Cohesion, MCB Briefing Paper, January 2007, www.mcb.org.uk/.

[32] Henryk M. Broder, "The West and Islam: 'Hurray! We're Capitulating'" *Spiegel Online*, January 25, 2007.

[33] Ferda Ataman, "Cologne's Turkish Spectacle: Erdogan's One-Man Show," *Spiegel Online*, February 11, 2008.

[34] "Merkel rejects Erdogan's call to resist assimilation," Radio Netherlands, February 11, 2008.

[35]   Michel Hoebink, "Morocco wants to reinforce ties with migrants," Radio Netherlands, February 15, 2008.

[36]   That is not the exact case everywhere. Barcelona's 14,000 Pakistani immigrants come from rural areas of the Punjab and have, at best, secondary-level education; large families and subsequent division of agricultural land forced them to emigrate. Salma Shakir, "Desi Salsa in Barcelona," http://www.pakistanlink.com/Letters/2004/July04/02/10.html.

[37]   http://www.middle-east-online.com/english/culture/?id=19226.

[38]   Matthias Bartsch, Andrea Brandt, Simone Kaiser, Gunther Latsch, Cordula Meyer, and Caroline Schmidt, "German Justice Failures: Paving the Way for a Muslim Parallel Society," *Spiegel Online*, March 29, 2007. It should be pointed out, however, that most of the "Turkish" women in Europe subjected to forced marriages are in fact Kurds from southeastern Anatolia, where a 2004 study found that "45.7 percent of women were not consulted about their choice of marriage partner and 50.8 percent were married without their consent." Those findings were confirmed by Yakin Erturk, the UN special rapporteur on human rights, in 2006. Cf http://www.islam-watch.org/AdrianMorgan/Women-Under-Islam2.htm.

[39]   Veit Medick and Anna Reimann, "Justifying Marital Violence: A German Judge Cites Koran in Divorce Case," *Spiegel Online*, March 21, 2007.

[40]   Ali Laïdi and Ahmed Salam, *Le Jihad en Europe: Les Filières du terrorisme islamiste* (Paris: Seuil, 2002), pp. 140–147.

[41]   Magdi Allam, "*Matrimoni misti? La sharia è già da noi*," *Corriere della Sera*, February 21, 2007.

[42]   "Dutch far-right party tries to block appointment of Muslims to Cabinet," *The Daily Telegraph*, March 1, 2007.

[43]   Mohammed el Ayoubi and Nicolien den Boer, "Dutch MP to serve as advisor to Moroccan king," Radio Netherlands, March 2, 2007.

[44]   Vikram Dodd, "Officer who accused Met of racism denied promotion," *The Guardian*, March 7, 2007.

[45]   Mahtab Haider and David Smith, "The Asian bride who died a lonely death in Britain," *The Observer*, October 15, 2006.

[46]   Ibid.

[47]   Ibid.

[48]   Sunny Hundal, "The secret violence that challenges Britain's Asians," *The Times*, February 26, 2007.

[49]   Directorate of Immigration, "Newest statistics," Helsinki, 2004; Elli Heikkilä and Selene Peltonen, *Immigrants and Integration in Finland*, Institute of Migration, Turku, 2002; Arno Tanner, "Finland's Prosperity Brings New Migrants," Finnish Directorate of Immigration, November 2004, http://www.migrationinformation.org/Profiles/display.cfm?id=267.

[50] Ibid.

[51] Ibid.

[52] Daniel Williams, "A French City and Its Underclass Drift Apart: Riots in Toulouse Reveal Gulf between Officials, Minorities," *Washington Post*, November 13, 2005.

[53] Thomas Lebegue, "*Des voix pour le vote des étrangers*," *Libération*, December 10, 2005.

[54] Ibid.

[55] "European lessons from the French riots," *The Economist*, November 10, 2005.

[56] "Immigrants in the Netherlands—Facts and Figures," http://islamineurope. blogspot.com/2005/11/immigrants-in-netherlands-fact-and.html.

[57] Marie-Claire Cécilia, "*La tolérance néerlandaise à l' épreuve de l'Islam*," in Alain Gresh, ed., *Islam de France, Islams d'Europe* (Paris: L'Harmattan, 2005), p. 93.

[58] Migration Watch UK, "Transnational Marriage and the Formation of Ghettoes," http://www.migrationwatchuk.org/frameset.asp?menu=researchpa pers&page=briefingpapers/other/transnational_marriage.asp.

[59] Charles P. Wallace, "Denmark's Closing Door: Parliament considers laws intended to discourage a flood of refugees hoping to find a dream life," *Time Europe*, February 25, 2002.

[60] Dipesh Gadher, Christopher Morgan, and Jonathan Oliver, "Minister warns of 'inbred' Muslims," *The Sunday Times*, February 10, 2008.

[61] "Arranged Marriages in Western Europe: A Comparative Analysis of Britain, France and Germany," at http://www.cas.lancs.ac.uk/papers/roger/; Mark Townsend, "Top judges in key ruling on sharia marriage," *The Observer*, February 10, 2008; Bruce Bawer, "Arranged marriages prevent integration: A trap for Muslim women in Europe," *International Herald Tribune*, June 27, 2003.

[62] Andrew Norfolk, "Despair as forced marriages stay legal," *The Times*, July 24, 2006.

[63] Ibid.

[64] Stéphane Kovacs, "*Les fiancées turques de Hambourg*," *Le Figaro*, October 29, 2005.

[65] Jonathan Wynne-Jones, "Multiple wives will mean multiple benefits," *The Telegraph*, February 4, 2008.

[66] Geneviève Oger, "France's Polygamy Problem," *Deutsche Welle*, July 31, 2005.

[67] Ibid.

[68] Ibid.

[69] Cécilia Gabizon, "*Davantage de Noirs chez les émeutiers*," *Le Figaro*, November 11, 2005.

[70] Cécilia Gabizon, "*Les enfants de familles polygames montrés du doigt*," *Le Figaro*, November 17, 2005.

[71] "*Polygamie: On ne pouvait pas faire un lien aussi étroit*," *Le Figaro*, November 17, 2005; see also John Lichfield, "Riots blamed on 'polygamous Africans'," *The Independent*, November 17, 2005.

[72] Jean-Michel Décugis, Christophe Labbé, and Olivia Recasens, "*Banlieues Emeutes: Les Blacks en première ligne*," *Le Point*, November 10, 2005.

[73] "Men who have embraced Islam: Abdur-Raheem Greene (formerly Anthony)," *Islamic Voice*, November 1997, at www.islamselect.com.

[74] "Berlin court convicts Turkish teen of killing sister, acquits two brothers," *Turkish Daily News*, April 14, 2006; Kerstin Rebien, "Man jailed for 'honour killing' that shook Germany," *The Guardian*, April 14, 2006; "Keeping count of 'honor' murders," Radio Netherlands, May 9, 2006; "Denmark: 9 Found Guilty in 'Honor Killing'," AP, June 28, 2006; Peter Popham, "Murder of Muslim girl 'rebel' by her father shocks all Italy," *The Independent*, August 20, 2006; "Father and sons guilty of honour killing," *The Telegraph*, November 4, 2005.

[75] Jonathan Wynne-Jones, "Study alleges 'honour killings conspiracy'," *The Telegraph*, February 3, 2008.

[76] http://islamineurope.blogspot.com/2007/12/norway-rape-and-muslims-study-much.html.

[77] "Muslim Rape Epidemic in Sweden and Norway—Authorities Look the Other Way," www.Abrahamic-Faith.com, February 20, 2005.

[78] Cf. Sharon Lapkin, "Western Muslims' Racist Rape Spree," FrontPageMagazine.com, December 27, 2005.

[79] "Pan-European Arab Muslim Gang Rape Epidemic," May 19, 2006, http://www.iris.org.il/blog/archives/757-Pan-European-Arab-Muslim-Gang-Rape-Epidemic.html.

[80] "Europe impotent in fighting female mutilation among African women," *Afrol News*, November 30, 2000.

[81] Franz Haas, "Don Camillo and the Imam," November 28, 2007, http://print.signandsight.com/features/1609.html.

[82] "Three African imams to be prosecuted by Norwegian state for promoting FGM," *Afrol News*, October 5, 2000.

[83] "*Texto íntegro de la sentencia a Mohamed Kamal Mustafa*," Juzgado Penal No. 3 de Barcelona Procedimiento Abreviado 276/03 C Sentencia N° 03104, Barcelona, January 2, 2004.

[84] Esther Hageman, "*Enkele feiten over de migrant in Nederland*," *Trouw*, November 9, 2005.

[85] "Muslim extremism in Europe: The enemy within," *The Economist*, July 14, 2005.

[86] Peter Schneider, "The New Berlin Wall," *New York Times*, December 4, 2005.

[87] Hageman, *"Enkele feiten over de migrant in Nederland."*

[88] Karen Schönwälder and Janina Söhn, "How Well Has Germany Performed in Integrating Immigrants into Society?" Goethe Institute, 2005.

[89] "Faith healing: Ignorance of Islam often stops Muslims receiving proper healthcare. But that may be changing, says Faisal Bodi," *The Guardian*, June 20, 2002.

[90] Hageman, *"Enkele feiten over de migrant in Nederland."*

[91] Murad Ahmed, "The day that I crossed the road to racism," *The Times*, December 18, 2006; Jennifer Carlile, "Islamic radicalization feared in Europe's jails," MSNBC, July 7, 2006.

[92] Tracy Wilkinson, "In a Prison's Halls, the Call to Islam," *Los Angeles Times*, October 4, 2005; Alan Travis and Audrey Gillan, "Bomb suspect 'became a militant' in prison," *The Guardian*, July 28, 2005.

[93] Travis and Gillan, "Bomb suspect 'became a militant' in prison."

[94] "Faith healing," *The Guardian*.

[95] Cécilia Gabizon, *"Emeutes: des meneurs au profil de récidivistes,"* Le Figaro, November 5, 2005.

[96] Axel Gyldèn, *"Danemark: L'envers du modèle,"* L'Express January 26, 2006.

[97] "Muslim extremism in Europe."

[98] "The Swedish model: Admire the best, forget the rest," *The Economist*, September 7, 2006.

[99] "Europe's Muslim Question: Dutch filmmaker's murder stirs integration debate," *Christian Science Monitor*, November 26, 2004.

[100] Jean-Pierre Stroobants, *"Le chômage frappe 40 percent des jeunes d'origine non-néerlandaise,"* Le Monde, January 18, 2006.

[101] Brian Moynahan, "Putting the fear of God into Holland," *The Sunday Times*, February 27, 2005.

[102] Jean-Pierre Touzanne, *L'Islamisme Turc* (Paris: L'Harmattan, 2001), pp. 115–117.

[103] Ibid.

[104] Leon de Winter, "Tolerating a Time Bomb," *New York Times*, July 16, 2005.

[105] Christopher Caldwell, "Stillstand in Deutschland: German voters choose stalemate," *The Weekly Standard*, October 3, 2005.

[106] *Libération*, December 16, 2002.

[107] "Turkey Slams German Immigration Law: Language Requirement 'Against Human Rights'," *Spiegel Online*, April 5, 2007.

[108] Vera Marinelli, "The Netherlands," in Jan Niessen, Yongmi Schibel, and Cressida Thompson, eds., *Current Immigration Debates in Europe: The European Migration Dialogue* (The Hague, September 2005, at http://www.migpolgroup.com/multiattachments/3009/DocumentName/EMD_Netherlands_2005.pdf).

[109] Ibid.

[110] Sabine Cessou, *"Les immigrés abandonnent les Pays-Bas," Libération*, January 10, 2006.

[111] Ibid.

[112] For a serious analysis, see Jeanne-Hélène Kaltenbach and Michèle Tribalat, *La République et l'Islam* (Paris: Gallimard, 2002.)

[113] "The Great Divide: How Westerners and Muslims View Each Other," Global Attitudes Project, released: 06.22.06 http://pewglobal.org/.

[114] Interview with Al Jazeera Host Yusuf Al-Qaradawi, "God Has Disappeared," *Spiegel Online*, September 27, 2005.

[115] David Harrison, "Government policy on multiculturalism has been left in tatters," *The Telegraph*, October 9, 2006.

[116] "Iranians integrate well," http://islamineurope.blogspot.com/; see also Marinelli, "The Netherlands."

[117] Abdul Diriye, "The ticking bomb: the educational underachievement of Somali children in the British schools," http://www.hiiraan.com/op/2006/feb/Abdull_Diriye190206_1.htm.

[118] For details on the PKK and its activities in Europe, see Michael Radu, "The Rise and Fall of the PKK," *Orbis*, Winter 2001, and Michael Radu, ed., *Dangerous Neighborhood: Contemporary Issues in Turkey's Foreign Policy* (New Brunswick, N.J.: Transaction, 2002).

[119] Blandine Grosjean, *"Les Noirs de France solidaires montent un Cran," Libération*, November 28, 2005.

[120] Décugis, Labbé, and Recasens, *"Banlieues Emeutes," Le Point*, November 10, 2005.

[121] Ibid.

[122] Ibid.

[123] Matthew d'Ancona, "This horror began with a literary row," *The Telegraph*, July 17, 2005.

[124] Barnie Choudhury, "Asian Vigilantes," http://www.bbc.co.uk/radio4/today/reports/archive/politics/oldham1.shtml.

[125] Tamara Jones, "Among the Young of Multiethnic Leeds, a Hardening Hatred," *Washington Post*, July 20, 2005.

[126] Isaac Kfir, "The Pakistan Connection," ICT, July 17, 2005.

[127] Khaleej Times Online, "Islamic leader criticizes Austrian interior minister for suggesting Muslims don't integrate," AP, May 15, 2006.

[128] Carsten Bleness, "Norway cabinet minister wants Islam 'modernized'," *Aftenposten*, November 4, 2003.

[129] Elif Safak, "London impressions," *Turkish Daily News*, May 21, 2006.

[130] Djebbi Nasreddine, "Turkish Communities in Europe: Societies within Socie-ties," December 29, 2005, http://www.islamonline.net/English/EuropeanMuslims/Community/2005/12/01.SHTML

[131] Schneider, "The New Berlin Wall."

[132] Moynahan, "Putting the fear of God into Holland."

[133] Alaa Bayoumi, "Recent laws to integrate European Muslims damaging," *Jordan Times*, April 4, 2004.

[134] Ibid.

[135] European Council for Fatwa and Research at http://www.e-cfr.org/eng/article.php?sid=9.

[136] Ibid.

[137] "Men who have embraced Islam."

[138] Paul Belien, "Muslim Radical Defends Freedom of Speech, Deplores Europe's Hypocrisy," at http://www.brusselsjournal.com/node/748.

[139] Timothy Garton Ash, "What young British Muslims say can be shocking—some of it is also true," *The Guardian*, August 10, 2006.

[140] Mark Steyn, "Making a pig's ear of defending democracy," *The Telegraph*, October 4, 2005.

[141] Aaron Hanscom, "Italian Beaches under Islamic Law," FrontPageMagazine.com, August 7, 2006.

[142] "Right Wing Pork Soup," *Spiegel Online*, January 25, 2006.

[143] Necla Kelek, "Mr. Buruma's stereotypes," in "Let's talk European," February 5, 2007, http://print.signandsight.com/features/1173.html. For a revealing look at multiculturalism and Islam in Europe, see the fascinating debate involving Pascal Bruckner, Ian Buruma, Timothy Garton Ash, Necla Kelek, Paul Courteur, and others at http://print.signandsight.com/features/1174.html.

[144] Pew Global Attitudes Project, "Muslims in Europe: Economic Worries Top Concerns about Religious and Cultural Identity. Few Signs of Backlash from Western Europeans," released July 6, 2006.

[145] Bat Ye'or, *Eurabia: The Euro-Arab Axis* (Madison, N.J.: Fairleigh Dickinson University Press, 2005).

[146] Keith Sinclair, "Scot's vision of Islamic Europe is condemned as 'alarmist'," *The Herald*, April 13, 2004.

[147] "Krekar claims Islam will win," *Dagbladet*, quoted in http://www.aftenposten.no/english/local/article1247400.ece?service=print.

[148] "Tales from Eurabia: Contrary to fears on both sides of the Atlantic, integrating Europe's Muslims can be done," *The Economist*, June 22, 2006.

[149] Joshua Rozenberg, "Sharia law is spreading as authority wanes," *The Telegraph*, November 29, 2006.

[150] Olivier Guitta, "Veiled Threat," TechCentralStation.com, April 4, 2005.

[151] Hassan M. Fattah, "Anger Burns on the Fringe of Britain's Muslims," *New York Times*, July 16, 2005.

[152] Ibid.

[153] Rachid Kaci, *La République des laches: La faillité des politiques d'intégration* (Paris: Editions des Syrtes, 2003).

[154] http://www.london.gov.uk/gla/publications/factsandfigures/factsfigures/diversity.jsp.

[155] *"Critiquée par certains pays africains, la loi Sarkozy sur l'immigration sera votée à l'Assemblée,"* lefigaro.fr (with AFP, AP), May 17, 2006.

[156] "Moroccan scholars to preach in Belgium mosques during Ramadan," at http://www.arabicnews.com/ansub/Daily/Day/031031/2003103121.html.

[157] "Belgium needs theology institute to train Islam teachers," at http://www.arabicnews.com/ansub/Daily/Day/040401/2004040120.html..

[158] "Minister Bot to Clean Up after Verdonk Visit to Morocco," *Dutch News Digest*, June 24, 2005.

[159] Besma Lahouri and Eric Conan, *"Ce qu'il ne faut plus accepter: La laïcité face à l'islam,"* *L'Express*, September 18, 2003.

Chapter Three

[1] Gilles Kepel, *The War for Muslim Minds: Islam and the West*, Carnegie Council, October 19, 2004.

[2] Ibid.

[3] Central Intelligence Agency, *The World Factbook 2004*.

[4] Mechthild Küpper, " 'Why not let them work?' Supporters say it would make sense to regularize the status of illegal immigrants," *Frankfurter Allgemeine Zeitung*, January 14, 2004.

[5] Bruno Etienne, *"Le danger arrive par Internet,"* Nouvelobs.com, July 29, 2005.

[6] Munira Mirza, Abi Senthilkumaran, and Zein Ja'far, "Living Apart Together: British Muslims and the Paradox of Multiculturalism," Policy Exchange, London, January 2007, p. 37, at http://www.policyexchange.org.uk/Publications.aspx?id=307.

[7] CSA/La Vie poll among French Muslims, "*Portrait des Musulmans,*" September 2006, http://www.csa-fr.com/dataset/data2006/opi20060823b.htm.

[8] Gerald Robbins, "Italy's Immigration Agita: Turin is an example of Italy's unsteady future," *The Weekly Standard*, November 9, 2007.

[9] Carolyn M. Warner and Manfred W. Wenner, "Religion and the Political Organization of Muslims in Europe," *Perspectives on Politics*, September 2006, pp. 457-479.

[10] Haas, "Don Camillo and the Imam."

[11] In addition to the specific sources given for each country, see also the BBC's "Muslims in Europe: Country Guide," December 23, 2005, and Felice Dassetto, Silvio Ferrari, and Brigitte Maréchal, "Islam in the European Union: What's at Stake in the Future?" Brussels, European Parliament, 2007.

[12] Austrian Society for International Understanding, http://islamineurope. blogspot.com/2007/12/austria-muslims-to-overtake-protestants.html.

[13] *Der Standard,* May 22, 2006; cf. http://www.militantislammonitor.org/article/ id/1929.

[14] "Muslims in Austria: Recognition is not the last stage," Shorok Press at http:// www.e-cfr.org/eng/article.php?sid=8. Sources: Total population: Statistics Austria, 2005 figures; Muslim population: Statistics Austria, 2001 figures.

[15] See Table 1, p. 41. Most of the other data are from the EU-supported website http://euro-islam.info/pages/about.html, which describes itself as a "a network on comparative research on Islam and Muslims in Europe, composed of scholars and doctoral students from Belgium, France, Germany, Italy, Spain, Sweden, The United Kingdom and The Netherlands." Data from other sources are quoted separately.

[16] http://euro-islam.info/pages/about.html.

[17] Personal interviews in Brussels, Brugge, and Gent, 2004.

[18] http://euro-islam.info/pages/belgium.html.

[19] Quoted in http://euro-islam.info/pages/about.html. See also Maréchal, ed., *L'Islam et les musulmans.*

[20] Lionel Panafit, "First for Islam in Belgium," http://mondediplo.com/2000/ 06/13belgium.

[21] Lionel Panafit, "*En Belgique, les ambiguïtés d'une représentation 'ethnique',*" *Le Monde Diplomatique*, June 2000, p. 12.

[22] See www.arabeuropean.org; see also Rosemary Bechler, "Everyone is afraid: the world according to Abou Jahjah," May 20, 2004, http://www.opendemocracy. net.

[23] "Vision of the AEL," at http://www.arabeuropean.org/vision.php.

[24] AEL Political Bureau, Brussels, "AEL Statement on the situation in the Netherlands and Belgium," November 20, 2004, http://www.arabeuropean.org/pressreleasedetail.php?ID=40.

[25] "Euro-letter," March 2003, http://inet.uni2.dk/~steff/eurolet/eur_105.pdf.

[26] Ibid.

[27] Axel Gyldèn, "*Danemark: L'envers du 'modèle'*," *L'Express*, January 26, 2006.

[28] http://www.euro-islam.info/pages/denmark.html.

[29] Ibid.

[30] "*48 percent des Danois se méfient de l'islam*," nouvelobs.com, September 4, 2006.

[31] Stephen Castle, "Tranquil nation at the centre of a clash of cultures," *The Independent*, February 4, 2006.

[32] http://euro-islam.info/pages/about.html.

[33] http://www.euro-islam.info/pages/france.html.

[34] "French Islam in the tent or out? When French Muslims quarrel, the establishment argues too," *The Economist*, October 28, 2004.

[35] Dassetto, Ferrari, and Maréchal, "Islam in the European Union."

[36] http://www.diyanet.gov.tr/english/default.asp.

[37] As a general proposition, based on this author's own travels to Eastern Anatolia and interviews in Berlin, Amsterdam, and Brussels, many Kurds also belong to the Alevi sect, considered non-Islamic by many Sunnis.

[38] Blandine Milcent, "*Allemagne: Allah enseigné à l'école*," *L'Express*, January 26, 2006.

[39] Philippe Broussard, "*Italie: Ces mariages qui divisent*," *L'Express*, January 26, 2006; Roberto Gritti and Magdi Allam, eds., *Islam, Italia: Chi sono e cosa pensano i musulmani che vivono tra noi* (Milano: Guerini e Associati, 2005), pp. 41–70. Sources: Total population: Italian National Statistical Institute.

[40] Patrizia Laurano, "*Il camino dell'intesa*," in Gritti and Allam, *Islam, Italia*, pp. 173–179.

[41] Sara Silvestri, "The Institutionalization of Islam in Europe: A Case Study of Italy," Council for European Studies, Columbia University, September 2005.

[42] Magdi Allam, *Bin Laden in Italia: Viaggio nell'islam radicale* (Milano: Mondadori, 2002), p. 124.

[43] Jean-Michel Demetz, "*Pays-Bas: De la tolérance à la méfiance*," *L'Express*, January 26, 2006. Sources: Total population: Statistics Netherlands, 2005 figures; Muslim population: Statistics Netherlands, 2004 figures.

[44] Jeffrey Schwerzel, "In the Aftermath of the Van Gogh Assassination: The Future of Islam in the Netherlands," ICT, May 15, 2005.

45 "Holland's New Greeting for Immigrants: 'If It Ain't Dutch, It Ain't Much',"
Spiegel Online, January 24, 2006.

46 http://www.islamawareness.net/Europe/Norway/.

47 Sources: Total population: Spanish National Institute of Statistics, 2005
figures; Muslim population: U.S. State Department, http://www.islamonline.
net/English/News/2004-05/09/article03.shtml; see also Dassetto, Ferrari, and
Maréchal, "Islam in the European Union."

48 That also means that a gate is open for Islamism. See Javier Jordán and
Humberto Trujillo, "Favourable situations for the jihadists' recruitment: the
neighborhood of Principe Alfonso (Ceuta, Spain)," Jihad Monitor, Occasional
Paper #3, November 27, 2006, http://www.jihadmonitor.org/.

49 Ben Sills, "Cathedral may see return of Muslims," *The Guardian*, April 19,
2004.

50 Abdennur Prado, "*La Islamofobia Es el Fascismo del Siglo XXI*," January 24,
2005, http://www.argenpress.info/nota.asp?num=017980.

51 Javier Monjas, "*No hay que temer que estados extranjeros financien al
islam en España*," Nuevo Digital, January 5, 2007, http://www.nuevodigital.
com/2007/01/05/mansur_escudero_junta_islamica_mezquita_.

52 http://euro-islam.info/pages/spain.html.

53 http://www.webislam.com/?idt=2719.

54 Jesús Bastante, "*La España que reza a Alá*," ABC.es, January 3, 2007.

55 Ibid. See also de Arístegui, *La Yihad en España*, pp. 215–216 and 267–269.

56 Dassetto, Ferrari, and Maréchal, "Islam in the European Union."

57 http://euro-islam.info/pages/sweden.html; Dassetto, Ferrari, and Maréchal,
"Islam in the European Union."

58 Sources: Total population: Swiss Federal Statistical Office, 2003 figures;
Muslim population: Swiss Federal Statistical Office, 2000 figures.

59 http://euro-islam.info/pages/swiss.html.

60 Marc Epstein, "*Royaume-Uni: Le multiculturalisme, parlons-en!*" *L'Express*,
January 26, 2006; it should be pointed out that although official figures
generally refer to the UK as a whole, the Muslim population of Scotland, Wales,
and Northern Ireland is less than 10 percent of the total. Sources: Total and
Muslim populations: Office for National Statistics, 2001 figures.

61 From MCB website, http://www.mcb.org.uk/downloads/MCB_acheivments.
pdf.

62 See Martin Bright, *When Progressives Treat with Reactionaries: The British
State's Flirtation with Radical Islamism*, preface by Jason Burke (London: Policy
Exchange, July 2006).

63 http://mcbwatch.blogspot.com/.

[64] Kevin Sullivan, "Denmark Tries to Act against Terrorism as Mood in Europe Shifts," *Washington Post*, August 29, 2005.

[65] http://dmoz.org/Society/Religion_and_Spirituality/Islam/Organizations/Europe/United_Kingdom/.

[66] Christophe Deloire et Christophe Dubois, *Les Islamistes sont déjà là: Enquête sur une guerre secrète* (Paris: Albin Michel, 2004), p. 193.

[67] Abdelkader Bouziane, *"L'imam Bouziane: Sarkozy en appelle au CFCM,"* Nouvelobs.com, June 22, 2005.

[68] Jon Henley, "France to train imams in 'French Islam'," *The Guardian*, April 23, 2004.

[69] A January 15, 2007, British Channel 4 series on radicalism in mosques suggests that a disproportionate number of radical imams have been trained in the Saudi universities of Medina and Riyadh. See "Undercover Mosque" on YouTube.com.

[70] Marc Semo and Brigitte Vitalle-Durand, *"L'Europe face aux prêcheurs de haine,"* *Libération*, July 30, 2005.

[71] Eva Vergaelen, "Looking for Imams for Belgian Mosques," IslamOnline.net, December 14, 2006.

[72] Ibid.

[73] Jean Chichizola, *"Onze religieux islamistes en instance d'expulsion,"* *Le Figaro*, September 27, 2006; Colin Randall, "France ejects 12 Islamic 'preachers of hate,'" *The Daily Telegraph*, July 30, 2005; *"Expulsion d'un Algérien ayant appelé à la guerre sainte,"* *Le Parisien*, July 30, 2005.

[74] Jamey Keaten, "Imams Facing More Scrutiny in Europe," washingtonpost.com, Associated Press, August 3, 2005; Seth Rosen, "European nations oust imams," *Washington Times*, August 4, 2005.

[75] "Italy deported imam 'illegally'," BBC, December 12, 2004; Ahmad Maher, "Italy Expels Imam for pro-Al-Qaeda Statements," *Islam Online*, November 18, 2003; Magdi Allam, *"L'imam espulso fanatico e minaccioso, voleva la guerra santa,"* *Corriere della Sera*, September 7, 2005; "Italy expels 'Islamic extremist'," BBC, September 8, 2005.

[76] "3 Imams to be expelled," http://dutchreport.blogspot.com/2005/02/3-imams-to-be-expelled.html; Sabine Cessou, *"Les Pays-Bas imposent des cours aux imams: Les nouveaux entrants doivent s'initier au néerlandais et à la culture occidentale,"* *Libération*, July 30, 2005.

[77] "Imam demands apology for 'humiliating' Mohammed cartoons," *Copenhagen Post Online*, October 13, 2005; Ian Black, "Denmark shuts out Muslim clerics," *The Guardian*, February 19, 2004; Henrik Bering, "Sex in the Park," *The Weekly Standard*, November 23, 2006.

[78] "Germany Bans Two Egyptian Imams," *Deutsche Welle*, September 27, 2005.

[79] Nick Britten, "Leading cleric rails at injustice of 'Muslim bashing'," *The Telegraph*, July 28, 2005.

[80] Henley, "France to train imams in 'French Islam'."

[81] Henri Astier, "French struggle to build local Islam," BBC, November 14, 2005.

[82] Xavier Ternisien, *La France de mosquées* (Paris: Albin Michel, 2004), pp. 103–106.

[83] "*La mosquée égyptienne Al-Azhar va former des imams français*," *Le Monde*, October 1, 2005.

[84] For other, mostly failed, efforts to train imams in France, see Jérôme Cordelier, "*Imams sous contrôle: Nicolas Sarkozy en guerre contre les 'prêcheurs radicaux'*," *Le Point*, July 28, 2005; Cécilia Gabizon and Jean Valbay, "*La formation des imams échappe au contrôle de l'État*," *Le Figaro*, December 7, 2005.

[85] See his essay in Yves Charles Zarka, Sylvie Taussig, and Cynthia Fleury, eds., *L'Islam en France* (Paris: PUF, 2004), pp. 93–105.

[86] http://www.e-cfr.org/eng/article.php?sid=8.

[87] Cessou, "*Les Pays-Bas imposent des cours aux imams*."

[88] "Belgium needs theology institute to train Islam teachers," MP, Morocco-Belgium, Religion, January 4, 2004, http://www.arabicnews.com/ansub/Daily/Day/040401/2004040120.html.

[89] Like the Danish Lutheran pastor denying the Trinity but still claiming a right to his government salary—all with public support.

[90] "*L'ex-imam de Vénissieux condamné à six mois avec sursis*," *Le Figaro*, October 14, 2005.

CHAPTER FOUR

[1] Jean-Pierre Touzanne, *L'Islamisme Turc* (Paris: L'Harmattan, 2001), p. 127.

[2] Interview with Al Jazeera host Yusuf al-Qaradawi, "God Has Disappeared," *Spiegel Online*, September 27, 2005.

[3] Romain Leick, Stefan Simons, and Gilles Kepel, "On the War on Terror," *Spiegel Online*, December 13, 2006.

[4] See George Weigel, *The Cube and the Cathedral: Europe, America, and Politics without God* (New York: Basic Books, 2005), passim.

[5] See Serafín Fanjul García, *La quimera de Al-Andalus* (Madrid: Siglo XXI de España Editores, 2004). For the idealistic and angelist view see most recently María Rosa Menocal, *The Ornament of the World: How Muslims, Jews and Christians Created a Culture of Tolerance in Medieval Spain* (Boston: Little Brown, 2003). For a rebuttal of the angelist view, see Dario Fernandez-Morera, "The Myth of

the Andalusian Paradise," *Intercollegiate Review*, Fall 2006. For the idealization of Salahaddin, the Hollywood movie *The Kingdom* (2007) is characteristic.

6 Thus former CIA analyst Graham Fuller claimed that "After all, what were the Crusades if not a Western adventure driven primarily by political, social, and economic needs? The banner of Christianity was little more than a potent symbol, a rallying cry to bless the more secular urges of powerful Europeans." Graham E. Fuller, "A World without Islam," *Foreign Policy*, January-February 2008.

7 Frantz Fanon, *The Wretched of the Earth* (New York: Grove Press, 1965). Translation (by Constance Farrington) of *Les damnés de la terre* (Paris: F. Maspero, 1962).

8 Olivier Roy, "Britain: homegrown terror," *Le Monde Diplomatique*, August 2005.

9 Soumaya Ghannoushi, "Islamophobia masquerading as free speech," Al Jazeera, March 4, 2006.

10 "Europe and the Shylock complex," March 3, 2006, http://www.arabeuropean. org/article.php?ID=105.

11 Abduljalil Sajid, "Islam and the middle way: extremism is a betrayal of Islam's essence, states Imam," *For a Change*, June-July, 2004.

12 http://www.mabonline.net/content/?page=9.

13 Christopher Caldwell, "After Londonistan," *New York Times Magazine*, June 25, 2006.

14 Nasreen Suleaman, "The mystery of 'Sid'," BBC News, October 19, 2005.

15 Robert Barr, "British Muslims shocked by video of bomber," AP, September 2, 2005.

16 Oliver King and agencies, "War on terror is a perpetual fight, says minister," *The Guardian*, August 22, 2006.

17 "Muslims in the European Union: Discrimination and Islamophobia," European Monitoring Centre on Racism and Xenophobia, Vienna, 2006, http://eumc.europa.eu/eumc/material/pub/muslim/Manifestations_EN.pdf.

18 Alan Cowell, "Britain Arrests 9 Suspects in Terrorist Kidnapping Plot," *New York Times*, February 1, 2007. It should be pointed out that those individuals later admitted guilt and were sentenced in January 2008.

19 "*Sobre el islam y la identidad europea*," Boletín No. 59-02/2007, http://www. islamyal-andalus.org/control/noticia.php?id=1339.

20 "Muslims in Europe: Economic Worries Top Concerns about Religious and Cultural Identity. Few Signs of Backlash from Western Europeans," released July 6, 2006, http://pewglobal.org/reports/pdf/254.pdf.

21 Hizb ut-Tahrir, "The Muslim Ummah will never submit to the Jews," http://archive.bibalex.org/web/20010305125154/hizb-ut-tahrir.org/english/leaflets/palestine31199.htm.

22 Nina Berglund, "Krekar threatens Norway," *Aftenposten*, November 25, 2006.

23 Lorenzo Vidino, "Is Italy Next in Line after London?" Jamestown Foundation, Terrorism Monitor, September 21, 2005; Magdi Allam, *Kamikaze made in Europe: Riuscira l'Occidente a sconfiggere i terroristi islamici?* (Milano: Oscar Mondadori, 2004), pp. 29–43.

24 Marcos García Rey, "*Del uso de referencias culturales islámicas para la acción yihadista en Europa,*" ARI No. 48/2007-23/04/2007, http://www.real-institutoelcano.org/.

25 Martin Bright, *When Progressives Treat with Reactionaries: The British State's Flirtation with Radical Islamism,* preface by Jason Burke (London: Policy Exchange, 2006), http://www.policyexchange.org.uk/.

26 Hamid Algar, *The Society of the Muslim Brothers* (Oneonta, N.Y.: Islamic Publications International, 2002); Sylvain Besson, *La conquête de l'Occident: Le projet secret des islamistes* (Paris: Editions du Seuil, 2005); Emmanuel Razavi, *Frères musulmans dans l'ombre d'Al Qaeda* (Mayenne: Jean-Cyrille Godefroy, 2005).

27 Cf. Lorenzo Vidino, "The Muslim Brotherhood in Holland," April 6, 2007, http://counterterrorismblog.org/mt/pings.cgi/3860.

28 There are literally hundreds of MB-controlled organizations and associations in all European countries, and many more charities—some separate, some ostensibly separate, and some overlapping with Saudi/Gulf groups. See Millard J. Burr and Robert O. Collins, *Alms for Jihad* (Cambridge, UK, and New York: Cambridge University Press, 2006), pp. 237–263; Abdel-Rahman Ghandour, *Jihad humanitaire: Enquête sur les ONG islamiques* (Paris: Flammarion, 2002).

29 Razavi, *Frères musulmans dans l'ombre.*

30 For two opposite views on the organization, see Algar, *The Society of the Muslim Brothers*, passim, and Richard P. Mitchell, *The Society of the Muslim Brothers* (New York and Oxford: Oxford University Press, 1995).

31 "Interior minister says he wants to take a close look at Italy's mosques and Islamic schools," *International Herald Tribune*, January 5, 2007.

32 "Fatwa (Scholarly Opinions): Questions about Palestine," The American Muslim Online, March 2002, http://web.archive.org/web/20060209135249/http:/www.americanmuslim.org/11palestine11e.html.

33 Ibid.

34 Intelligence and Terrorism Information Center at the Center for Special Studies (CSS), http://www.intelligence.org.il/eng/bu/britain/sib3_10_03.htm.

35 http://chris-kutschera.com/A/suburbs_islam.htm. See also Gilles Kepel, *Les Banlieues de l'Islam* (Paris: Editions du Seuil, 1987).

[36] Mahmmud Ezet, Secretary General of the Muslim Brotherhood, "The Muslim Brotherhood's Methodology of Reform," Ikhwan Online, November 7, 2005, www.ikhwanweb.com.

[37] Ian Johnson and John Carreyrou, "As Muslims call Europe home, isolation takes root," *Wall Street Journal*, July 11, 2005.

[38] Gilles Kepel, *Allah in the West: Islamic Movements in America and Europe* (Cambridge, UK: Polity Press, 1997), pp. 151 and 213.

[39] Sita Ram Goel, "The Tabligh Movement, or Millions of Bearded Militants on the March," in Sita Ram Goel, ed., *Time for Stock Taking: Whither Sangh Parivar* (New Delhi: Voice of India Books, 1996).

[40] "Questions about Jammat Tabligh," Islam Newsroom, June 2006.

[41] Quoted in http://www.allaahuakbar.net/tableegi_jamaat/final_fatwa_of_shaykh_bin_baaz.htm.

[42] http://www.islamicacademy.org/html/Articles/English/Tableeghee percent20Jma'at.htm.

[43] Goel, "The Tabligh Movement."

[44] Alex Alexiev, "Tablighi Jamaat: Jihad's Stealthy Legions," *Middle East Quarterly*, January 2005, http://www.meforum.org/article/686.

[45] Ibid.

[46] Richard Norton-Taylor, Sandra Laville, and Vikram Dodd, "Terror plot: Pakistan and al-Qaida links revealed," *The Guardian*, August 12, 2006.

[47] Zeyno Baran, "Radical Islamists in Central Asia," in Hillel Fradkin, Husain Haqqani, and Eric Brown, eds., *Current Trends in Islamist Ideology*, vol. 2 (Washington, D.C.: Hudson Institute, 2005), pp. 50–51.

[48] Quoted in http://www.parapundit.com/archives/001482.html. Interestingly, Tariq Ramadan also placed *Tabligh* in the same Islamic ideological category of "scholastic traditionalism" as the Taliban. Tariq Ramadan, *Western Muslims and the Future of Islam* (Oxford and New York: Oxford University Press, 2004), p. 24.

[49] Susan Sachs, "A Muslim Missionary Group Draws New Scrutiny in U.S.," *New York Times*, July 14, 2003.

[50] Alexiev, "Tablighi Jamaat."

[51] "*Selon la police, l'essor du mouvement salafiste en Essonne comporte des risques de dérives extrémistes*," *Le Figaro*, October 7, 2003; see also Eric Denécé, "*Le Développement de l'islam fondamentaliste en France: Aspects sécuritaires, économiques et sociaux*," Centre Français de Recherche sur le Renseignement, Rapport de Recherche No. 1, Paris, September 2005, p.16, http://www.cf2r.org/download/rapports_recherche/RR1-Islam.pdf.

[52] Deloire et Dubois, *Les islamistes sont déjà là*, pp. 43 and 314; Denécé, *Le Développement*.

53 Antoine Sfeir et al., *Dictionnaire mondial de l'Islamisme* (Paris: Plon, 2002), pp. 309–312.

54 Sandra Laville, "Suspects linked to hardline Islamic group," *The Guardian*, August 18, 2006.

55 Alain Grignard, "*L'Islam face au terrorisme*," http://www.mil.be/rdc/viewdoc. asp?LAN=nl&FILE=doc&ID=193.

56 http://www.hizb-ut-tahrir.org/english/english.html.

57 "Defending the Honour of the Prophet (SAW): A Message to the Muslim Community," Hizb ut-Tahrir Britain, February 4, 2006, www.hizb.org.uk.

58 KComLeaflet, http://www.khilafah.com/home/printable.php?DocumentID=12823.

59 Assaf Maliach, "Hizb ut-Tahrir al-Islami and the Cartoon Fracas," International Institute for Counter-Terrorism (ICT), March 1, 2006.

60 HuT press release, "Let Muslims establish the Shariah in their own lands!" February 11, 2008.

61 Shiv Malik, "The conveyor belt of extremism," *New Statesman*, July 18, 2005.

62 For an excellent analysis of HuT's ideology, see Peter Mandaville, *Global Political Islam* (London and New York: Routledge, 2007), pp. 267–271.

63 Malik, "The conveyor belt."

64 Emerson Vermaat, "Hizb ut-Tahrir: A dangerous anti-Semitic and terrorist organization," February 19, 2008, http://www.militantislammonitor.org/ article/id/3364.

65 For a comprehensive analysis of HuT's theologically unorthodox views, from a Sunni perspective, see http://www.htexposed.com/.

66 Javier Jordán and Sol Tarrés, "*Movimientos musulmanes y prevención del yihadismo en España: Hizb ut-Tahrir*," Jihad Monitor, Occasional Paper #9, April 17, 2007, http://www.jihadmonitor.org/.

67 M-F, "*Le Takfir au service de Ben Laden*," *Le Nouvel Observateur*, October 18, 2001; Sebastian Rotella, "Holy Water, Hashish and Jihad," *Los Angeles Times*, February 23, 2004; David Zucchino, "In 2 Strict Sects, Terror Suspects Find Inspiration," *Los Angeles Times*, December 22, 2001.

68 "Terrorism Special Report," *Time*, November 12, 2001.

69 M-F, "*Le Takfir au service de Ben Laden*."

70 Ibid.

71 Sebastian Rotella and David Zucchino, "Embassy plot offers insight into terrorist recruitment, training," *Los Angeles Times*, October 22, 2001.

72 Michael Elliott, "Hate Club," *Time*, November 12, 2001.

73 The most comprehensive study of the Islamic NGOs is Ghandour, *Jihad humanitaire*; see also Jean-Luc Marret, ed., *Les fabriques du Jihad* (Paris: PUF, 2005); Burr and Collins, *Alms for Jihad*.

74 "Muslim Community United against Blair's Denial," IHRC Press Release, September 27, 2005, http://www.ihrc.org.

75 "The Islamic Right," Awaaz—South Asia Watch, June 2006, www.awaazsaw.org.

76 The Stephen Roth Institute for the Study of Contemporary Antisemitism and Racism, http://www.tau.ac.il/Anti-Semitism/asw2002-3/uk.htm.

77 http://www.mpacuk.org/content/view/2014/44/.

78 Tom Moseley, "Iraq deputy prime minister's 'Blackburn mosque jibe'," The Blackburn Citizen, January 21, 2008.

79 Omar Nasiri, Inside the Jihad: A spy's story—My life with Al Qaeda (New York: Basic Books, 2006). Nasiri's book was challenged on many points, but his description of his British handlers as being single-mindedly preoccupied with London Islamist threats against Britain—and not the rest of the world—is confirmed by too many other sources and by British actions prior to 2005 to be dismissed. See also Melanie Phillips, Londonistan (New York: Encounter Books, 2006); Dominique Thomas, Le Londonistan: La voix du Jihad (Paris: Editions Michalon, 2003); Michael Gove, Celsius 7/7 (London: Weidenfeld & Nicolson, 2006).

80 Thomas, Le Londonistan; Phillips, Londonistan; Michael Radu, "The Problem of 'Londonistan': Europe, Human Rights, and Terrorists," Foreign Policy Research Institute E-note, April 12, 2002, at www.fpri.org.

81 Vikram Dodd and Fred Attewill, "UK orders Hamza's extradition to US," The Guardian, February 7, 2008.

82 "The judiciary should not patrol our borders," The Telegraph, July 30, 2005; Isaac Kfir, "House of Lords Ruling on Torture Evidence," International Institute for Counter-Terrorism, December 20, 2005.

83 "Muslim cleric denies terror link," BBC, October 19, 2001.

84 Interview in London's Al-Sharq Al-Awsat on August 22, 1998, quoted in http://www.jewishvirtuallibrary.org/jsource/biography/Bakri_Muhammad.html.

85 Jamie Doward and Gaby Hinsliff, "PM shelves Islamic group ban," The Observer, December 24, 2006.

86 "New Group replaces AL Muhajiroun," BBC News, November 18, 2005.

87 "Failed Plan to ban Hizb ut-Tahrir: Playing 'Politics with Security'," Press Release, London,December 24, 2006, www.hizb.org.uk.

88 Doward and Hinsliff, "PM shelves Islamic group ban."

89 Ibid. The Observer later noted that in this story, "we said Hizb ut-Tahrir 'campaigns for Britain to become a caliphate—a country subject to Islamic law'—and is 'banned in Germany, Russia, the Netherlands, Sudan and in almost every Arab country'. We should clarify that, while Hizb ut-Tahrir has lobbied for other nations to become caliphates, its UK wing does not campaign for Britain to become one. The movement maintains that it is not banned in

the Netherlands or Sudan. In Germany, HT's public activities are proscribed, but membership of the party is not. This is currently the subject of a legal challenge."

90 That fact did not prevent the British government from denying him an entry visa in February 2008.

91 Mahan Abedin, "A Saudi Oppositionist's View: An Interview with Dr. Muhammad Al-Massari," Terrorism Monitor, December 4, 2003.

92 "Controversial imams," The Telegraph, July 20, 2005; Thomas, Le Londonistan; for Abu Qatada, see also Dominique Thomas, Les Hommes d'Al-Qaeda (Paris: Editions Michalon, 2005), pp. 97–110; for Abu Bakri, see also Yotam Feldner, "Radical Islamist Profiles: Sheikh Omar Bakri Muhammad—London," MEMRI Inquiry and Analysis No. 24, October 2001; for Abu Hamza see Yotam Feldner, "Radical Islamist Profiles: London—Abu Hamza Al-Masri," MEMRI Inquiry and Analysis No. 72, October 16, 2001; for Massari, see Abedin, "A Saudi Oppositionist's View."

93 Kepel, Allah in the West; Lorenzo Vidino, "Aims and Methods of Europe's Muslim Brotherhood," Hudson Institute, November 1, 2006.

94 Sean O'Neill, "Radical cleric who has never been prosecuted," The Times, January 17, 2005; Feldner, "Sheikh Omar Bakri Muhammad."

95 Khaled Ahmed, "Is Islam in chains?" The Daily Times (Pakistan), September 16, 2005.

96 Ed Husain, The Islamist (London: Penguin Books, 2007), p. 83.

97 http://www.dailytimes.com.pk/default.asp?page=story_16-9-2005_pg3_2, September 16, 2005.

98 Feldner, "Abu Hamza Al-Masri"; BBC, "Sheikh Abu Hamza," April 26, 2003.

99 "Abu Hamza and the Supporters of Shariah," http://www.al-ab.com/yemen/hamza/hamza1.htm.

100 Ibid.

101 Patrick J. McDonnell, "Al Qaeda Camp in Oregon," Los Angeles Times, September 24, 2002.

102 Daniel McGrory, Richard Ford, and Michael Evans, "Bin Laden 'ambassador' arrested," The Times, October 25, 2002; David Bamber, "Bombers are linked to jailed cleric," The Telegraph, May 25, 2003.

103 Laïdi and Salam, Le Jihad en Europe, p. 55.

104 Baltasar Garzón, Sumario 00000/35 2001 E, Auto (Indictment), El Mundo (Madrid), September 17, 2003; Juan José Escobar Stemmann, "Middle East Salafism's Influence and the Radicalization of Muslim Communities in Europe," MERIA Journal, September 2006.

105 Quintan Wiktorowicz and John Kaltner, "Killing in the Name of Islam: Al-Qaeda's Justification for September 11," Middle East Policy Council Journal, vol. 10, no. 2, Summer 2003.

106 "Muslim cleric denies terror link," BBC, October 19, 2001.

107 "Controversial imams."

108 Evan Kohlmann, "Dossier: Majid al-Massari," http://www.globalterroralert. com/majidalmassari.pdf.

109 Zucchino, "In 2 Strict Sects."

110 http://www.jewishvirtuallibrary.org/jsource/biography/Bakri_Muhammad. html.

111 Abedin, "A Saudi Oppositionist's View."

112 "Muslim cleric denies terror link."

113 "These men are fanatics and must be beaten," *The Telegraph*, July 20, 2005.

114 http://www.jewishvirtuallibrary.org/jsource/biography/Bakri_Muhammad. html.

115 "Osama aide mocks 'lost glory' of United States," *The Daily Times* (Pakistan), October 7, 2002.

116 "Muslim cleric denies terror link."

117 "Abu Hamza and the Supporters of Shariah."

118 Feldner, "Abu Hamza."

119 Anton La Guardia, "Muslim radicals in Britain issue 'holy war' warning," *The Telegraph*, August 14, 2002.

120 http://www.jewishvirtuallibrary.org/jsource/biography/Bakri_Muhammad. html.

121 "Cleric demands cartoonists' death," Al Jazeera, February 6, 2006.

122 "Iraqi Ansar Al-Islam Commander Mullah Krekar in Norway: 'No Peace between West & Islam until Islamic Caliphate Is Re-established'," MEMRI Special Dispatch Series No. 1134, April 6, 2006.

123 La Guardia, "Muslim radicals in Britain."

124 Peter Ford, "Europe's rising class of believers: Muslims," *Christian Science Monitor*, February 24, 2005.

125 "Iraqi Ansar Al-Islam Commander Mullah Krekar."

126 Roy, "Britain: homegrown terror."

127 Thomas, *Le Londonistan*, pp. 122–125.

128 The following quotes are in "Controversial imams"; see also Thomas, *Les Hommes d'Al-Qaeda*.

129 Ibid.

130 Raymond Ibrahim, *The Al Qaeda Reader* (New York: Doubleday, 2007), pp. 281–282.

131 http://www.terrorism.com/modules.php?op=modload&name=Intel&file=inde x&view=649.

[132] "Cleric who poisoned the young drip by drip," *The Telegraph*, February 25, 2003; "Hate-preaching cleric jailed," BBC News, March 7, 2003.

[133] For details, see also Thomas, *Le Londonistan*, passim.

[134] "Abd Al-Rahman Al-Rashed, Director-General Al-Arabiyya TV, 'Why Do Islamist Extremists Who Incite against the West Insist on Living There?'" MEMRI Special Dispatch No. 1493, March 8, 2007, http://memri.org/bin/latestnews. cgi?ID=SD149307.

CHAPTER FIVE

[1] Zacarias Moussaoui testifying in the U.S. District Court for the Eastern District of Virginia, *Trial Transcript, United States of America* v. *Zacharias Moussaoui (February 14, 2006).*

[2] Peter Ford, "Europe's rising class of believers: Muslims," *Christian Science Monitor*, February 24, 2005.

[3] See Olivier Roy, *L'Islam mondialisé* (Paris: Seuil, 2002) and *Les Illusions du 11 Septembre: Le débat stratégique face au terrorisme* (Paris: Seuil, 2002). Roy tracks it to the 1980s in Muslim countries like Turkey, Egypt, and Morocco, later spreading to Bosnia.

[4] *"Les paradoxes de la réislamisation en Egypte"* in *Monde Arabe Maghreb Machrek*, January-March 1996, following S. Radi's *La réislamisation de la société égyptienne vue par les étudiants de l'Université du Caire*, Cairo, report to the Ford Foundation, 1995.

[5] See, e.g., Marfua Tokhtakhodzhaeva, *The Re-Islamization of Society and the Position of Women in Post-Soviet Uzbekistan*, Case 2007; Raphael Israeli, "From Bosnia to Kosovo: The Re-Islamization of the Balkans," in David Bukay, ed., *Muhammad's Monsters: A Comprehensive Guide to Radical Islam for Western Audiences* (Green Forest, Ark.: Balfour Books, and Shaarei Tikva, Israel: ACPR Publishers, 2004), pp. 143–166.

[6] Gilles Kepel, *The Revenge of God: The Resurgence of Islam, Christianity, and Judaism in the Modern World* (University Park: Penn State University Press, 1994).

[7] Xavier Bougarel, "How Panislamism Replaced Communism (Part 3)," http://www.ex-yupress.com/dani/dani10.html; for the phenomenon elsewhere, see, e.g., Tokhtakhodzhaeva, *The Re-Islamization of Society*; and Giuseppe Candela, "Spaces of social exclusion and the re-Islamization of Europe," http://kennedy.byu.edu/partners/CSE/rmesc/pdfs/candela.pdf.

[8] http://pewglobal.org/reports/display.php?PageID=813.

[9] Roy, *L'Islam mondialisé*, pp. 40–50.

[10] Dan Bilefsky, "Denmark Is Unlikely Front in Islam-West Culture War," *New York Times*, January 8, 2006.

[11] Saskia van Reenen, "Growing interest in radical Islam among young Dutch Muslims," Radio Netherlands, July 26, 2005.

[12] Stephen Castle, "Europe speeds up plan to clamp down on suspects," *Belfast Telegraph*, July 14, 2005.

[13] Jacques Myard, "Assez d'angélisme, adaptons nos méthodes répressives sans mollir," *Le Figaro*, November 4, 2005.

[14] Cécilia Gabizon, *"Emeutes: des meneurs au profil de récidivistes,"* Le Figaro, November 5, 2005.

[15] "Muslim extremism in Europe: The enemy within," *The Economist*, July 14, 2005; see also Denécé, *"Le Développement de l'islam fondamentaliste en France,"* http://www.cf2r.org/download/rapports_recherche/RR1-Islam.pdf.

[16] Hans de Vreij, "Terrorism—Dutch intelligence service reports," AIVD intelligence chief S. van Hulst speaks to Radio Netherlands, March 31, 2006.

[17] Audrey Gillan, "Pakistani intelligence and Americans 'abduct' Briton: Case part of trend in casual detention, say lawyers," *The Guardian*, March 9, 2002.

[18] Daniel Steinvorth, "'Never a Religious Necessity': Headscarf Researcher Condemns Turkey's Move to Lift Ban," *Spiegel Online*, February 14, 2008.

[19] Hearing of the Committee on International Relations, Subcommittee on Europe and Emerging Threats, U.S. House of Representatives, "The radicalisation of Muslim youth in Europe: The reality and the scale of the threat," testimony of Claude Moniquet, Director General of the European Strategic Intelligence and Security Center, April 27, 2005, http://www.agentura.ru/english/experts/euroislamism/.

[20] George Jones, "Blair wades into Muslim veil row," *The Telegraph*, July 17, 2006.

[21] Daud Abdullah, "Incitement to violence: The political and media onslaught on Muslims is already fuelling physical attacks on the streets," *The Guardian*, October 17, 2006.

[22] European Commission against Racism and Intolerance (ECRI), Third Report on the Netherlands, adopted on June 29, 2007, and made public on February 12, 2008, http://www.coe.int/t/e/human_rights/ecri/1-ecri/2-country-by-country_approach/netherlands/netherlands_cbc_3.asp#P593_112115.

[23] Andrea Brandt and Cordula Meyer, "Religious Divisions within Germany: A Parallel Muslim Universe," *Spiegel Online*, February 20, 2007.

[24] Quoted in "Belgium: Breeding Ground for Muslim Terror," March 15, 2005, http://fjordman.blogspot.com.

[25] Cécilia Gabizon, *"Ces jeunes Français qui se pressent à La Mecque,"* Le Figaro, January 4, 2006.

[26] Bruce Bawer, "Not all Muslims want to integrate," *Christian Science Monitor*, November 17, 2005.

[27] "Islamic Extremism: Common Concern for Muslim and Western Publics—Support for Terror Wanes among Muslim Publics," released July 14, 2005, at wwww.pewglobal.org.

[28] Ibid.

[29] *Saudi Aramco World*, January-February 1979.

[30] Ghandour, *Jihad humanitaire*, pp. 241–270.

[31] Jean-Yves Camus, "Islam in France," May 10, 2004, http://www.ict.org.il/.

[32] Juan José Escobar Stemmann, "Middle East Salafism's Influence and the Radicalization of Muslim Communities in Europe," *MERIA Journal*, September 2006; http://meria.idc.ac.il/journal/2006/issue3/jv10no3a1.html.

[33] Brian Eads, "Saudi Arabia's deadly export," *Australian Reader's Digest*, February 2003. For an analyisis of Saudi charities' role in radicalizing Muslims, see Jon Alterman's chapter in Jon B. Alterman and Karin von Hippel, eds., *Understanding Islamic Charities* (Washington, D.C.: CSIS Press, 2007), pp. 64–75.

[34] Ibid. See also Wendy Kristiansen, "'A visible statement of separation and difference': A patchwork of communities," *Le Monde Diplomatique*, November 2006.

[35] Murad Ahmed, "I'm angry, too. Angry with extremist nutcases," op-ed, *The Times*, February 5, 2007.

[36] Cf. *Wall Street Journal*, September 22, 2006.

[37] Mirza, Senthilkumaran, and Ja'far, "Living Apart Together: British Muslims and the Paradox of Multiculturalism," Policy Exchange, London, January 29, 2007, figures 3 and 4, at http://www.policyexchange.org.uk/Publications.aspx?id=307.

[38] Dounia Bouzar, "'*Les jeunes consomment de l'islam comme de la drogue*,' Propos recueillis par Cécilia Gabizon," *Le Figaro*, March 10, 2006.

[39] Gilbert Charles and Besma Lahouri, "*3,7 millions de musulmans en France: Les vrais chiffres*," *L'Express*, December 4, 2003; see also Jeanne-Hélène Kaltenbach and Michèle Tribalat, *La république et l'Islam* (Paris: Gallimard, 2002); an extensive analysis of the issue can be found in Yves Charles Zarka, Sylvie Taussig, and Cynthia Fleury, eds., *L'Islam en France* (Paris: PUF, 2004), pp. 21–66; Peter Schneider, "The New Berlin Wall," *New York Times*, December 4, 2005; Daniel Williams, "Immigrants Keep Islam—Italian Style," *Washington Post*, July 24, 2004.

[40] Scheherezade Faramarzi, "Decision to join Iraqi rebels fatal for French teens," WT/AP, November 26, 2004; Scheherezade Faramarzi, "French-Arab Slum Youths Joined Insurgency," WT/AP, November 25, 2004.

[41] David Cohen, "The rise of the Muslim Boys," *The Evening Standard*, February 3, 2005.

[42] Quico Chirino, "*Huelo que la 'Yihad' está muy cerca*," *Ideal* (Spain), November 13, 2007.

43 Marcos García Rey, "*Del uso de referencias culturales islámicas para la acción yihadista en Europa*," ARI No. 48/2007, April 23, 2007, www.realinstitutoelcano. org.

44 See Homeland Security Policy Institute (HSPI) and Critical Incident Analysis Group (CIAG), "Prisoner Radicalization Task Force, Out of the Shadows: Getting Ahead of Prisoner Radicalization," http://www.healthsystem.virginia.edu/ internet/ciag/publications/out_of_the_shadows.pdf.

45 Georges Malbrunot, "*Irak: les Américains mettent en déroute al-Qaida*," *Le Figaro*, February 12, 2008.

46 Sean O'Neill and Daniel McGrory, *The Suicide Factory: Abu Hamza and the Finsbury Park Mosque* (London and New York: Harper Perennial, 2006), pp. 66–75.

47 Farhad Khosrokhavar, *L'Islam dans les prisons* (Paris: Balland, 2004).

48 Craig S. Smith, "Islam in Jail: Europe's Neglect Breeds Angry Radicals," *New York Times*, December 8, 2004.

49 "*Justice: gain de cause pour les Belges*," http://www.aujourdhui.ma/nation-details53207.html.

50 Urban Fox, "Captive converts: What makes Islam so attractive to prisoners?" *Times Online*, August 11, 2005; see also Rémi Godeau, "*Les prisons anglaises, vivier de l'islam radical*," *Le Figaro*, April 14, 2007.

51 Theodore Dalrymple, "Our prisons are fertile ground for cultivating suicide bombers," *The Times*, July 30, 2005.

52 Piotr Smolar, "*L'antiterrorisme, selon le patron des RG*," *Le Monde*, November 24, 2005. Alan Travis and Audrey Gillan, "Bomb suspect 'became a militant' in prison," *The Guardian*, July 28, 2005.

53 Fjordman, "Muslim Rape Wave in Sweden," FrontPageMag.com, December 15, 2005.

54 Smith, "Islam in Jail."

55 "*Plus d'imams pour moins de prosélytisme*," Nouvelobs.com, January 13, 2006.

56 "*Le prosélytisme islamiste inquiète*," Nouvelobs.com, January 14, 2006.

57 Urban Fox, "Captive converts."

58 Travis and Gillan, "Bomb suspect 'became a militant' in prison."

59 Interview in Claire Chartier, "*Prisons: L'islam majoritaire*," *L'Express*, March 15, 2004.

60 Khosrokhavar, *L'Islam dans les prisons*, p. 146; see also James A. Beckford, Danièle Joly, and Farhad Khosrokhavar, *Muslims in Prison: Challenge and Change in Britain and France* (New York: Palgrave Macmillan, 2005), pp. 217–220.

61 Martin Samuel, "Jailbirds ripe for recruiting," *The Times*, October 3, 2006.

[62] http://www.lexpress.fr/express/info/monde/dossier/benladen/dossier.asp.

[63] For more details, see *"Document: Le rapport des RG sur les convertis à l'islam"*; *"Selon la police, l'essor du mouvement salafiste en Essonne comporte des risques de dérives extrémistes,"* *Le Figaro*, October 7, 2003; Peter Ford, "Why European women are turning to Islam," *Christian Science Monitor*, December 26, 2005; Jean-Pierre Stroobants, *"Les convertis sont devenus la cible des recruteurs d'Al-Qaida,"* *Le Monde*, December 8, 2005; Smolar, *"L'antiterrorisme"*; Craig Whitlock, "Trial of French Islamic Radical Sheds Light on Converts' Role," *Washington Post*, January 1, 2006.

[64] Godeau, *"Les prisons anglaises."*

[65] Jean Chichizola with Cécilia Gabizon and Feurat Alani, *"De jeunes djihadistes français envoyés en Irak via l'Egypte,"* *Le Figaro*, October 26, 2005.

[66] UN Office on Drugs and Crime, "Morocco Cannabis Survey 2003," http://www.unodc.org.

[67] Isambard Wilkinson, "Informer told police of Spanish bomb plot," *The Telegraph*, April 25, 2005.

[68] Nicolas Marmié and Jamal Zougam, *"Itinéraire d'un enfant de Tanger suspecté du carnage de Madrid,"* *Le Nouvel Observateur*, March 15, 2004.

[69] Khosrokhavar, *L'Islam dans les prisons*, examines only the significant, but still limited, case of France.

[70] Quoted in Pascale Combelles Siegel, "Radical Islam and the French Muslim Prison Population," Jamestown Foundation, Terror Monitor, July 27, 2006.

[71] Khosrokhavar, *L'Islam dans les prisons*, pp. 12, 279–280; Dominique Gaulme, *"Islam en prison: missions d'urgence pour aumôniers musulmans,"* *Le Figaro*, January 12, 2007.

[72] Samuel, "Jailbirds ripe for recruiting"; Beckford, Joly, and Khosrokhavar, *Muslims in Prison*, pp. 71–73.

[73] Jennifer Carlile, "Islamic radicalization feared in Europe's jails," MSNBC, July 7, 2006.

[74] Arístegui, *La Yihad en España*, pp. 208–211; Edwin Bakker, "Jihadi terrorists in Europe, their characteristics and the circumstances in which they joined the jihad: an exploratory study," Netherlands Institute of International Relations, Clingendael, The Hague, December 2006, p. 23.

[75] Hal Bernton, Mike Carter, David Hearth, and James Neff, "The Terrorist Within: The Story behind One Man's Holy War against America," *Seattle Times*, June 23–July, 2002; "Trail of a Terrorist," PBS Frontline.

[76] For details and criticism of Canada's role as a jihadi producer and exporter, see Stewart Bell, *The Martyr's Oath: The Apprenticeship of a Homegrown Terrorist* (Mississauga, Ont.: Wiley, 2005), and Stewart Bell, *Cold Terror: How*

Canada Nurtures and Exports Terrorism around the World (Etobicoke, Ont.: Wiley, 2004).

[77] Glenn Frankel, "From Civic Activist to Alleged Terrorist: Muslim Suspect in Dutch Director's Killing Was Caught between Cultures," *Washington Post*, November 28, 2004.

[78] See "Muslim extremism in Europe: The enemy within," *The Economist*, July 14, 2005; David Rennie, "Life for van Gogh killer fails to ease Dutch fears," *The Telegraph*, July 27, 2005.

[79] David Crawford, "New Terror Threat in EU, with Passports," *Wall Street Journal*, December 17, 2004.

[80] Alan Travis, "Fear of Islamist recruiting in jails," *The Guardian*, July 14, 2007; "Terrorism in Spanish prisons," http://www.athenaintelligence.org/index2. html; "Al-Qaeda threat to British prisons," *The Observer* February 10, 2008; Stephen Schwartz, "Radical Islam behind Bars. Islamist prison chaplains face renewed challenge," *The Weekly Standard*, November 9, 2007; Godeau, *"Les prisons anglaises."*

[81] Sally Neighbour, "Mates 'til the death: Terrorist cells are like cults whose members form close bonds and attack their own communities," *The Australian*, February 19, 2007.

[82] Molly Moore, "Rage of French Youth Is a Fight for Recognition," *Washington Post*, November 6, 2005.

[83] *"Les violences urbaines gagnent du terrain, 1300 véhicules incendiés,"* *Le Point*, November 6, 2005.

[84] Mohamed Sifaoui, *La France malade de l'Islamisme* (Paris: Le Cherche-Midi, 2002), pp. 78–80.

[85] C.G., *"L'islam ne joue pas un rôle déterminant dans la propagation des troubles,"* *Le Figaro*, November 5, 2005.

[86] Rik Coolsaet, "Between al-Andalus and a failing integration: Europe's pursuit of a long-term counterterrorism strategy in the post-al-Qaeda era," Egmont Paper No. 5, Royal Institute for International Relations (IRRI-KIIB), Brussels, May 2005, http://www.irri-kiib.be/paperegm/ep5.pdf.

[87] Jason Bennetto, "MI5 conducts secret inquiry into 8,000 al-Qa'ida 'sympathisers,'" *The Independent*, July 3, 2006; Anthony Glees, "Campus Jihad, " *Wall Street Journal*, October 23, 2006.

[88] Moniquet testimony, April 27, 2005.

[89] Andreas Ulrich, Holger Stark, Cordula Meyer, and Dominik Cziesche, "The Changing Threat of Al-Qaida: How widespread is terrorism in Europe?" *Der Spiegel*, July 11, 2005, http://www.spiegel.de/international/spiegel/0,1518,364661,00.html.

⁹⁰ Jean-Marie Amat and Yves Benoit, *"Néo-islamistes: Stratégies pour noyauter la République," L'Express*, April 17, 2003.

⁹¹ Ibid.

⁹² "The Reality of the Sect, Hizb-ut-Tahrir," http://htexposed.bizland.com/.

⁹³ *"Dinamarca, Italia, y España, a la cabeza de Europa en el riesgo de sufrir un ataque de Al Qaida,"* ABC.es, March 10, 2006.

⁹⁴ Anthony Glees and Chris Pope, "When Students Turn to Terror: How safe are British universities?" published by the Social Affairs Unit, London, October 2005.

⁹⁵ Matthew Taylor and Rebecca Smithers, "Extremist groups active inside UK universities, report claims," *The Guardian*, September 16, 2005.

⁹⁶ Glees, "Campus Jihad."

⁹⁷ Taylor and Smithers, "Extremist groups active inside UK universities"; Glees, "Campus Jihad"; Amat and Benoit, *"Néo-islamistes."*

⁹⁸ Ali Hussain, "'Stealth' Islamists recruit students," *The Sunday Times*, October 16, 2005.

⁹⁹ "Militant Islam lures many teenaged recruits," IndiaMonitor, May 27, 2005.

¹⁰⁰ Ibid.

¹⁰¹ Anne-Charlotte de Langhe, *"Enquête dans la nébuleuse de l'imam Benchellali," Le Figaro*, January 10, 2004.

¹⁰² Yves Bordenave, *"La 'filière tchétchène' devant le tribunal correctionnel," Le Monde*, March 21, 2006.

¹⁰³ Mourad Benchellali, "Detainees in Despair," *New York Times*, June 14, 2006.

¹⁰⁴ Patricia Tourancheau, *"Un ticket pour le jihad," Libération*, February 22, 2005; Mark Houser, "French Muslims battle internal, external strife," *Pittsburgh Tribune-Review*, May 29, 2005; Peter Taylor, "Radicalising Europe's young Muslims," BBC News, September 1, 2006; Jean Chichizola, *"Le nouveau visage des jeunes djihadistes," Le Figaro*, October 18, 2006.

¹⁰⁵ Denécé, *"Le Développement de l'islam fondamentaliste en France."*

¹⁰⁶ Mathieu Guidère, *Les "Martyrs" d'Al-Qaïda: Au cœur de la propagande terroriste* (Nantes: Editions du Temps, 2006); Gary R. Bunt, *Islam in the Digital Age: E-Jihad, Online Fatwas and Cyber-Islamic Environments* (London: Pluto Press, 2003).

¹⁰⁷ Chichizola, *"Le nouveau visage."*

¹⁰⁸ *Lashkar-e-Toiba* ("Army of the Pure"—LeT) is a Pakistani jihadi organization active in Kashmir.

¹⁰⁹ http://news.bbc.co.uk/2/hi/uk_news/4676577.stm.

¹¹⁰ Chichizola, *"Le nouveau visage."*

[111] Olivier Truc, "*Huit jours d'émeutes confrontent les Danois à leur modèle d'intégration*," *Le Monde*, February 19, 2008.

[112] Riazat Butt, Paul Lewis, and Sandra Laville, "We tried to keep out extremists, say leaders," *The Guardian*, August 14, 2006.

[113] "Profiles: Mohammed Hamid and his followers," *The Guardian*, February 22, 2008.

[114] Javier Jordán and Robert Wesley, "The Threat of Grassroots Jihadi Networks: A Case Study from Ceuta, Spain," February 15, 2007, http://www.jamestown.org/terrorism/news/article.php?articleid=2370249.

[115] Tony Thompson, Mark Townsend, Martin Bright, and Barbara McMahon, "Terror suspect gives first account of London attack," *The Observer*, July 31, 2005.

[116] Anne-Charlotte de Langhe, "*Les ex de Guantanamo et 'la mode' du djihad*," *Le Figaro*, July 4, 2006.

[117] Peter Varghese, "Islamist Terrorism: The International Context," Security in Government Conference, Canberra, May 11, 2006, http://www.ona.gov.au/news.htm.

[118] "Young Muslims and Extremism," FCO/Home Office Paper," London, April 6, 2004, in Robert Winnett and David Leppard, "Terror in London: Leaked No 10 dossier reveals Al-Qaeda's British recruits, Parts 1–4," *The Sunday Times*, July 10, 2005.

[119] Jean Chichizola, "*Comment les islamistes recrutent en France*," *Le Figaro*, June 3, 2006.

[120] Ibid.

[121] J.C., "*Safé Bourada avait créé un groupe terroriste derrière les barreaux*," *Le Figaro*, June 2, 2006.

[122] Geoff Pingree and Lisa Abend, "In Spain, dismay at Muslim converts holding sway," *Christian Science Monitor*, November 7, 2006; Whitlock, "Trial of French Islamic Radical Sheds Light"; Claire Chartier, "*La France des convertis*," *L'Express*, January 26, 2006; International Crisis Group, "France and Its Muslims: Riots, Jihadism and Depoliticisation Europe," Rapport Europe No. 172, March 9, 2006, at http://www.crisisgroup.org/home/index.cfm?l=1&id=4014; Denécé, "*Le Développement de l'islam fondamentaliste en France*;" *I numeri dell'Islam in Italia*, http://www.italiaplease.com/ita/megazine/ponderando/2002/02/islam.

[123] See Carlos Ramírez Sánchez, *L'islam révolutionnaire* (Monaco: Editions du Rocher, 2003).

[124] Ford, "Why European women are turning to Islam."

[125] For details and explanations, see Abd Samad Moussaoui and Florence Bouquillat, *Zacarias Moussaoui, mon frère* (Paris: Denoël Impacts, 2002).

[126] Magdi Allam, *Kamikaze Made in Europe*, pp. 36–37.

[127] Ibid.

[128] Murad al-Shishani, "Westerners Being Recruited by al-Qaeda," Terrorism Monitor, December 13, 2005.

[129] Carol Bigot, "Un symptôme de l'islamisation: les 'convertis du Djihad'," Voix des Français, March 2004.

[130] Craig Pyesjosh Meyer and William C. Rempe, "Terrorists Use Bosnia as Base and Sanctuary," Los Angeles Times, October 7, 2001.

[131] Françoise Dentinger, "L'islamiste Lionel Dumont devant ses juges," http://www.rfi.fr/actufr/articles/072/article_40254.asp.

[132] Jeremy Britton, "Rowe 'bore al-Qaeda hallmarks'," BBC News, September 23, 2005; Sandra Laville, "Terror suspect denies using his socks to clean mortar," The Guardian, September 15, 2005.

[133] "L'intervention contre les fanatiques de Roubaix," http://raid.admin.free.fr/roubaix.htm.

[134] Norimitsu Onishi, "Japan Arrests 5 Who Knew Man Possibly Tied to Qaeda," New York Times, May 27, 2004.

[135] "L'intervention contre les fanatiques de Roubaix."

[136] Dentinger, "L'islamiste Lionel Dumont devant ses juges."

[137] Ibid.; Pierre-Yves Glass, "Islamic gangsters 'served in Bosnia'," The Independent, April 8, 1996.

[138] Alice Géraud and Didier François, "Grand Angle: Le procès de Pierre Robert, alias Yacoub, doit s'ouvrir demain à Rabat," Libération, September 2, 2003; Martin Arostegui and Kim Willsher, "Middle-class Islamic convert masterminded suicide attacks," The Telegraph, July 20, 2003; Juan Avilés, "Una Amenaza Compartida: La Yihad Global en Europa y el Magreb," ARI No. 15, 2005, Análisis, February 1, 2005.

[139] "Interview: Quand les convertis passent au djihad. Propos recueillis par Philippe Broussard," L'Express, December 15, 2005.

[140] Whitlock, "Trial of French Islamic Radical Sheds Light."

[141] C-Span, February 21, 2006. See also Peter L. Bergen, The Osama bin Laden I Know: An Oral History of al Qaeda's Leader (New York: Free Press, 2006).

[142] "Dinamarca, Italia y España."

[143] Craig Whitlock, "Terrorists Proving Harder to Profile," Washington Post, March 12, 2007.

[144] Javier Jordán and Fernando M. Manas, "Indicios externos de la radicalizacion y militancia yihadista," Jihad Monitor, Occasional Paper No. 4, January 10, 2007, http://www.jihadmonitor.org/.

[145] Jane Perlez, "Briton Criticizes U.S.'s Use of 'War on Terror'," New York Times, April 17, 2007.

[146] James Slack, "Government renames Islamic terrorism as 'anti-Islamic activity' to woo Muslims," *The Daily Mail*, January 17, 2008.

[147] Among the best sources are *Al Qaeda Training Manual* (Philadelphia: Pavilion Press, 2006); Laura Mansfield, *His Own Words: A Translation of the Writings of Dr. Ayman al Zawahiri* (Old Tappan, N.J.: TLG Publications, 2006); Brad K. Berner, *Jihad: Bin Laden in His Own Words: Declarations, Interviews, and Speeches* (Charleston: BookSurge, 2006); Raymond Ibrahim, *The Al Qaeda Reader*, (New York: Doubleday, 2007).

[148] Quoted in Faisal Devji, *Landscapes of the Jihad: Militancy, Morality, Modernity* (Ithaca, N.Y.: Cornell University Press, 2005), p. 28; the entire text in Mansfield, *His Own Words.* The organization of the latter volume is, unfortunately, very reader-unfriendly.

[149] Devji, *Landscapes of the Jihad*, pp. 61–65.

[150] Alain Dupont, *El Islam de Francia: Sus Implicaciones Políticas y de Seguridad*, Unisci Discussion Papers, May 2005, http://www.ucm.es/info/unisci/UNISCI-Review8.htm.

[151] Touzanne, *L'Islamisme Turc*, pp. 125–131.

[152] Jean-Yves Camus, "Islam in France," ICT, May 10, 2004, http://www.ict.org.il/.

[153] Allam, *Bin Laden in Italia*, p. 65.

[154] While by 2005 some 400 Algerian fake asylum seekers had been expelled from the UK, some 9,000 remained. See Marret, *Les Fabriques du Jihad*, p. 50.

[155] Antonio Baquero and Jordi Corachán, "*Alerta por la vuelta a Catalunya de muyahidines de Irak y Afganistán,*" *El Periodico*, March 16, 2007.

[156] Kathryn Haahr, "Assessing Spain's al-Qaeda Network," Terrorism Monitor, July 1, 2005.

[157] "*L'importance de l'armement saisi à Casablanca et à Nador montre la détermination des terroristes,*" February 21, 2008, http://www.aujourdhui.ma/couverture-details59970.html; "*Liste des suspects arrêtés,*" February 21, 2008, http://www.aujourdhui.ma/couverture-details59970.html.

[158] "Belgium's Belliraj terrorist leader committed six murders," http://myflandersfields.blogspot.com/2008/02/belgiums-belliraj-terrorist-leader.html.

[159] Carlos Echeverría Jesús, "*Acoso al frente europeo del terrorismo salafista transnacionalizado,*" *Civilización & Dialogo*, January 6, 2006.

[160] "The Hama Massacre of 1982: Syria's regime brutally massacres it's [sic] own people," http://www.2la.org/syria/. See also "Armed Conflict. Events Data, Muslim Brotherhood in Syria 1965–1985," http://www.onwar.com/aced/data/sierra/syria1965.htm.

[161] Murad Al-Shishani, "Abu Mus'ab al-Suri and the Third Generation of Salafi-Jihadists," Terrorism Monitor, August 11, 2005.

[162] For English translations and analyses of al-Suri's writings, see Abu Musab al-Suri, *Primary Writings: Lessons Learned from the Armed Jihad Ordeal in Syria*, AFGP-2002-600080 (full translation); http://www.ctc.usma.edu/aq/AFGP-2002-600080-Trans.pdf; Brynjar Lia, "Al-Suri's Doctrines for Decentralized Jihadi Training—Parts 1 and 2," January 2, 2007, http://www.jamestown.org/news_details.php?news_id=217; al-Shishani, "Abu Mus'ab al-Suri and the Third Generation of Salafi-Jihadists"; http://jamestown.org/terrorism/news/article.php?articleid=2369766; Paul Cruickshank and Mohannad Hage Ali, "Abu Musab Al Suri: Architect of the New Al Qaeda," *Studies in Conflict & Terrorism*, vol. 30, nos. 1–14, 2007, http://www.lawandsecurity.org/documents/AbuMusabalSuriArchitectoftheNewAlQaeda.pdf.

[163] "Al-Bianoni: We neither use violence nor have a relation with Abo-Mus'ab al-Sori," September 1, 2006, http://www.ikhwan.tv/Home.asp?zPage=Systems&System=PressR&Press=Show&Lang=E&ID=5183.

[164] Henry Schuster, "The Mastermind," CNN, March 9, 2006.

[165] Ibid.; Shane Drennan and Andrew Black, "Fourth-generation warfare and the international jihad," September 26, 2006, http://www.janes.com/security/international_security/news/jir/jir060926_2_n.shtml.

[166] Lia, "Al-Suri's Doctrines for Decentralized Jihadi Training."

[167] Ibid.

[168] Ibid.

[169] Javier Jordán, "*El Yihadismo en España: Situación Actual*," ARI No. 93/2005, July 11, 2005, http://www.realinstitutoelcano.org/analisis/775.asp.

170 José A. Rodríguez, "The March 11th Terrorist Network: In its weakness lies its strength," Working Papers EPP-LEA, Grupo de Estudios de Poder y Privilegio, Departamento de Sociología y Análisis de les Organizaciones, Universitat de Barcelona, December 3, 2005, http://www.ub.es/epp/wp/11m.PDF.

[171] Ferry Biedermann, "Syrian mystery man sought in Van Gogh case," Radio Netherlands, December 3, 2004.

[172] Holger Stark, "The Forgotten Prisoner. A Tale of Extraordinary Renditions and Double Standards," *Der Spiegel*, November 21, 2005.

[173] John Crewdson, "CIA tried in 1999 to recruit associate of 9-11 hijackers in Germany," *Chicago Tribune*, November 16, 2002.

[174] Javier Jordán and Robert Wesley, "The Madrid Attacks: Results of Investigations Two Years Later," Terrorism Monitor, March 9, 2006.

[175] "Suspects in GIA Bombings on Trial in France," ICT, June 2, 1999, http://cfrterrorism.org/groups/gia.html.

[176] Hassane Zerrouky, *La Nébuleuse islamiste en Europe et en Algérie* (Paris: Editions 1, 2002); Moshe Marzuk, "Radical Islamic organizations announce merger with al-Qaida," ICT, October 3, 2003; Dan Darling, "Who Are Those Guys?

Understanding the ties between Ansar al-Islam, the GSPC, the Sudanese Islamic Army, and al Qaeda," *The Weekly Standard*, November 1, 2006.

[177] Malek Sohbi, "*Algérie. La résistance du maquis*," *Le Point*, November 10, 2005.

[178] Zerrouky, *La Nébuleuse islamiste*.

[179] O'Neill and McGrory, *The Suicide Factory*.

[180] Thomas Joscelyn, "The Algerian Plague: Going inside the terrorist group GSPC," *The Weekly Standard*, January 19, 2006.

[181] Jonathan Schanzer, "Algeria's GSPC and America's 'War on Terror'," Washington Institute for Near East Policy, PolicyWatch No. 666, October 2, 2002; see also Salim Tamani, "*Il représentait al-qaïda dans les pays du maghreb et du sahel: l'agent de Ben Laden est tombé à Batna*," *La Liberté* (Algiers), November 26, 2002.

[182] "*Ben Laden rebaptise le GSPC*," lefigaro.fr, January 26, 2007; Olivier Guitta, "Terror in the Maghreb: Al Qaeda linked groups are spreading from Algeria and Morocco into Tunisia," *The Weekly Standard*, February 14, 2007.

[183] Cf. Carlos Echeverría Jesús, "*La amenaza del activismo terrorista del Grupo Salafista para la Predicación y el Combate (GSPC) argelino*," ARI No. 20/2007, February 13, 2007.

[184] Stephen Ulph, "Arrests in Morocco Highlight the Expanding Jihadi Nexus," Terrorism Focus, November 29, 2005, http://jamestown.org/terrorism/news/article.php?articleid=2369838.

[185] For additional information, see Mohamed Darif, "*El Grupo Combatiente Marroquí*," ARI, March 23, 2004; Benjamin Keating, "In the Spotlight: Moroccan Combatant Group (GICM)," May 21, 2004, http://www.cdi.org/program/document.cfm?DocumentID=2227&from_page=./index.cfm.

[186] Ibid.

[187] Ulph, "Arrests in Morocco."

[188] "Unmasking Belgium's terror suspects," *Expatica*, November 3, 2005.

[189] Ali Lmrabet, "*Aux racines de l'islamisme marocain: 'Maman, je vais aller au paradis'*," *Courrier International*, May 13, 2004, http://quibla.net/mda/maroc5.htm. Medjati was the leader of a group of 15 radical Islamists killed by the Saudi antiterrorist forces in Al Ras, some kilometers north of Riyadh. Another member of the group was the Moroccan citizen Younes Mohamed Al Hayar; see Carlos Echeverría Jesús, "Radical Islam in the Maghreb Countries," Foreign Policy Research Institute, October 2005, http://www.fpri.org/pubs/200510.echeverria.radicalislammaghreb.pdf.

[190] Michel Zerr, "*Un cerveau des attentats de Casablanca arrêté*," *Le Figaro*, March 10, 2007.

[191] Stephen Ulph, "Jihad Declared on the Moroccan State," Jamestown Foundation, Terrorism Focus, October 31, 2005.

[192] Mathieu Guidère, *Al-Qaida à la conquête du Maghreb: Le terrorisme aux portes de l'Europe* (Paris: Editions du Rocher, 2007), pp. 185–190.

[193] Joseph Felter and Brian Fishman, "Qa'ida's Foreign Fighters in Iraq; A first look at the Sinjar Records," The Combating Terrorism Center, West Point, http://www.ctc.usma.edu/harmony/pdf/CTCForeignFighter.19.Dec07.pdf; Richard A. Oppel Jr., "Foreign Fighters in Iraq Are Tied to Allies of U.S.," *New York Times*, November 22, 2007.

[194] Daniel Lav, "The Al-Qaeda Organization in the Islamic Maghreb: The Evolving Terrorist Presence in North Africa," MEMRI Inquiry and Analysis Series No. 332, March 7, 2007.

[195] Ignacio Cembrero, "*La espada de Al Qaeda en el Magreb*," *El País*, March 11, 2007.

[196] "*Al-Qaida: Six ans de prison pour le 'Taliban espagnol*'," Nouvelobs.com, October 5, 2005.

[197] Al Jazeera, March 13, 2004, http://english.aljazeera.net/NR/exeres/2CDD53D6-7AF7-40C7-AF88-32A16072F81B.htm.

[198] Mark Hosenball, "Washington Wire: Online Face of Terror," *Newsweek*, June 12, 2006; Anton La Guardia, "Arrests reveal Zarqawi network in Europe," *The Telegraph*, December 22, 2005.

[199] Stewart Bell, "Probe had global dimension: Project Osage—One of several investigations underway in half a dozen countries," *National Post*, June 5, 2006.

[200] See Evan F. Kohlmann, *Al-Qaeda's Jihad in Europe: The Afghan-Bosnian Network* (New York: Berg, 2004); Nicholas Wood, "Bosnia: Haven for Islamic radicals?" *International Herald Tribune*, November 27, 2005.

[201] See Emerson Vermaat, *De Hofstadgroep*, pp. 89–93 ("Jihad training in Pakistan"), http://emersonvermaat.com/.

[202] "The 'Hofstad' group—background and profiles compiled by Saskia van Reenen," December 23, 2005, http://www2.rnw.nl/rnw/en/currentaffairs/region/netherlands/ned051222?view=Standard&version=1.

[203] Ibid.

[204] http://en.wikipedia.org/wiki/PimFortuyn.

[205] "Fortuyn ghost stalks Dutch politics," BBC News.

[206] E. S. M. Akerboom, "Counterterrorism in the Netherlands," http://www.fas.org/irp/world/netherlands/ct.pdf.

[207] Ibid.

[208] Eric Pelletier and Jean-Marie Pontaut, "*Les islamistes indésirables*," *L'Express*, August 1, 2002.

[209] Chichizola, with Gabizon and Alani, "*De jeunes djihadistes français*."

[210] "Jihadists Find Convenient Base in Bosnia," *Jihad Watch*, August 18, 2005; see also a more detailed analysis in Kohlmann, *Al-Qaeda's Jihad in Europe.*

[211] *"Los 35 presuntos miembros de Al Qaeda procesados por Garzón,"* El Mundo, September 17, 2003; *Conclusiones y Recomendaciones Finales de la Comisión de Investigación del 11-M*, Grupo Parlamentario de Izquierda Verde, Madrid, June 8, 2005, http://estaticos.elmundo.es/documentos/2005/06/08/iu_icv.pdf.

[212] *"Filières tchétchènes': aggravation des peines requise en appel,"* Le Monde, March 12, 2007.

CHAPTER SIX

[1] Shane Drennan and Andrew Black, "Fourth-generation warfare and the international jihad," *Jane's Defence Weekly*, September 26, 2006.

[2] Rogelio Alonso, *"Procesos de radicalización de los terroristas yihadistas en España,"* ARI No. 31/2007.

[3] Andreas Ulrich, "Terrorism In Germany: Failed Bomb Plot Seen as Al-Qaida Initiation Test," *Spiegel Online*, April 9, 2007.

[4] "Muslims in Western Europe: Dim drums throbbing in the hills half heard," *The Economist*, August 8, 2002; Roger Ballard, "Migration and kinship: the differential effect of marriage rules on the processes of Punjabi migration to Britain," in Colin Clarke, Ceri Peach, and Steven Vertovec, eds., *South Asians Overseas: Migration and Ethnicity* (Cambridge, UK: Cambridge University Press, 1990), pp. 219–249.

[5] For useful, if somewhat biased, information, see Santhanam K. Sreedhar and Sudhir Saxena Manish, *Jihadis in Jammu and Kashmir: A portrait gallery* (New Delhi: Sage Publications, 2003).

[6] "Inside the mind of a terrorist," *The Observer*, March 9, 2003.

[7] *Le Point*, February 15, 2003.

[8] Petter Nesser, "Jihad in Europe; Recruitment for Terrorist Cells in Europe," in Laila Bokhari, Thomas Hegghammer, Brynjar Lia, Petter Nesser, and Truls H. Tønnessen, *Paths to Global Jihad: Radicalisation and Recruitment to Terror Networks*, Proceedings from an FFI Seminar, Oslo, March 15, 2006, pp. 9–21, http://www.jihadmonitor.org/category/recruitment-and-processes-of-radicalization/.

[9] Jordán and Wesley, "The Madrid Attacks: Results of Investigations Two Years Later," Terrorism Monitor, March 9, 2006.

[10] José María Irujo, *"Los hombres de Abu Dahdah y el 11-M,"* El País, June 20, 2004.

[11] Jordán and Wesley, "The Madrid Attacks."

[12] *El País*, January 22, 2005.

¹³ Duncan Gardham, "Mohammed Hamid 'is evil personified'," *The Telegraph*, February 26, 2008; Duncan Gardham, "'Osama bin London' groomed 21/7 bombers," *The Telegraph*, February 26, 2008.

¹⁴ "Profiles: Mohammed Hamid and his followers," *The Guardian*, February 26, 2008.

¹⁵ Dominik Cziesche, Juergen Dahlkamp, and Holger Stark, "Syrian terror suspect: Aladdin of the Black Forest," *Der Spiegel*, August 15, 2005.

¹⁶ Selcan Hacaoglu, "Syrian charged with masterminding bombings," AP, February 10, 2006.

¹⁷ Cziesche, Dahlkamp, and Stark, "Syrian terror suspect."

¹⁸ Ibid.; Holger Stark, "Syrian Had Inside Knowledge of 9/11 and London Bombings," *Der Spiegel*, August 24, 2005; Ercan Gun, "Interesting Confession: I Provided 9/11 Attackers with Passports," *Zaman*, August 14, 2005; *"Le chef présumé d'Al-Qaida en Turquie a été inculpé pour des projets d'attentats anti-israéliens,"* lemonde.fr, August 11, 2005.

¹⁹ For biographical data, see Henri Haget, *"Lyon: Le vivier des banlieues,"* *L'Express*, September 14, 1995; Jean-Marie Pontaut, *"Khaled Kelkal. Itinéraire d'un terroriste,"* *L'Express*, September 26, 1996.

²⁰ Jérôme Dupuis, Sylvaine Pasquier, Jean-Marie Pontaut, and Djamel Zitouni, *"L'islamiste qui mène la guerre contre la France,"* *L'Express*, May 30, 1996; for more on the ties between France and Algerian terrorist networks see Patrick Forestier, *Confession d'un émir du GIA* (Paris: Grasset, 1999); Baya Gacemi, *Moi, Nadia, femme d'un émir du GIA* (Paris: Seuil, 1998); Paul Landau, *Le Procès d'un réseau islamiste* (Paris: Albin Michel, 1997); Benjamín Stora, *L'Algérie en 1995: La guerre, l'histoire, la politique* (Paris: Editions Michalon, 1995); Zerrouky, *La nébuleuse islamiste en Europe et en Algérie.*

²¹ Clara Beyler, "The Jihadist Threat in France," February 16, 2006, http://www.futureofmuslimworld.com/research/pubID.44/pub_detail.asp.

²² Haget, *"Lyon: Le vivier des banlieues."*

²³ *"Théâtre: Les Paravents de Jean Genet sont à l'affiche,"* http://www.humanite.presse.fr/journal/2001-01-15/2001-01-15-237980.

²⁴ Pierre Conesa, *"Aux Origines de la Guerre Antiterroriste: Al-Qaida, une secte millénariste,"* *Le Monde Diplomatique*, January 2002.

²⁵ Abdallah-Thomas Milcent, *"Mission d'Information à l'Assemblée Nationale Française sur la question du port des signes religieux à l'école,"* July 1, 2003, http://www.voltairenet.org/article11986.html.

²⁶ Pontaut, *"Khaled Kelkal."*

²⁷ For his profile, see Stéphane Durand-Souffland, *"Djamel Beghal ne reconnaît que sa foi en Allah: Le djihadiste français, interrogé sur ses convictions religieuses, a reproché à ses juges de se comporter comme ceux de l'Inquisition,"* *Le Figaro*,

January 4, 2005; "*Accusé de terrorisme, Beghal dénonce 'un tribunal d'inquisition',*" *Libération*, January 3, 2005.

28 "*Accusé de terrorisme.*"

29 Eric Pelletier, "*Les 'Afghans' français,*" *L'Express*, February 28, 2002.

30 "*Accusé de terrorisme.*"

31 Emerson Vermaat, "Bin Laden's Terror Networks in Europe," Mackenzie Institute, 2002.

32 Sean O'Neill, "Why France lived in fear of 'Londonistan'," *The Telegraph*, October 13, 2001.

33 Martin Bright, Antony Barnett, et al., "War on Terrorism—The secret war: Part 2," *The Observer*, September 30, 2001.

34 Vermaat ("Bin Laden's Terror Networks") claims that Abu Qatada told Beghal to leave *Takfir-wal-Hizra*. This is unlikely, considering that organization's nature, which does not provide members with the possibility of ever leaving.

35 For details on the Beghal network, see Patricia Tourancheau, "*Ambassade des Etats-Unis, Une Filière Tombe en France,*" *Libération*, September 26, 2001; Pascal Céaux and Fabrice Lhomme, "*Le Rôle des Sept Hommes Mis en Examen en France se Précise,*" *Le Monde*, September 27, 2001; Pascal Céaux and Fabrice Lhomme, "*Un Islamiste Franco-Algérien Interpellé à Dubaï a Confirmé qu'un Attentat Etait Projeté à Paris,*" *Le Monde*, September 20, 2001; Sebastian Rotella and David Zucchino, "Embassy plot offers insight into terrorist recruitment, training," *Los Angeles Times*, October 22, 2001.

36 Durand-Souffland, "*Djamel Beghal ne reconnaît que sa foi en Allah.*"

37 Bright, Barnett, et al., "War on Terrorism."

38 Ibid.

39 Rotella and Zucchino, "Embassy Plot."

40 Michel Deléon et Stéphane Joahny, "*Un islamiste français échappe à la police,*" *Le Journal du Dimanche*, September 23, 2001.

41 Pelletier, "*Les 'Afghans' français.*"

42 Bright, Barnett, et al., "War on Terrorism."

43 Vermaat, "Bin Laden's Terror Networks."

44 On Trabelsi, see Rotella and Zucchino, "Embassy plot offers insight"; Michael Taarnby, "Profiling Islamic Suicide Terrorists: A Research Report for the Danish Ministry of Justice," submitted November 27, 2003, Centre for Cultural Research, University of Aarhus, http://www.jm.dk/image.asp?page=image&objno=71157; Frédéric Delepierre, "*Trabelsi a été joueur de football professionnel,*" *Le Soir* (Brussels), September 19, 2001.

45 "Footballer 'swayed by bin Laden'," CNN, May 22, 2003; "Terror Verdict for Soccer Pro: Former German Player Found Guilty of Plot to Strike U.S. Base," CBS, September 30, 2003.

[46] Arnaud de la Grange, "*Le culte du martyre de la secte djihadiste*," *Le Figaro*, July 14, 2005.

[47] Michel Décugis, and Christophe Deloire, "*Islamistes: Les PV des épouses.*" *Le Point*, December 23, 2004.

[48] Taarnby, "Profiling Islamic Suicide Terrorists."

[49] Christophe Dubois, "*Procès des lieutenants de Ben Laden à Paris*," *Le Parisien*, January 3, 2005.

[50] Eric Pelletier and Jean-Marie Pontaut, "*Islamistes: La France menacée*," *L'Express*, September 27, 2001.

[51] Jean Chichizola, "*Les groupes djihadistes font souvent escale dans l'Hexagone: La France, une étape pour les terroristes en Europe*," *Le Figaro*, July 9, 2005.

[52] Rotella and Zucchino, "Embassy plot offers insight."

[53] Craig S. Smith, "Europe Fears Converts May Aid Extremism," *New York Times*, July 19, 2004.

[54] J. C., "*Trois suspects restent retenus*," *Le Figaro*, July 28, 2004.

[55] "*L'Italie doit renforcer la collaboration justice-police*," entretien avec Armando Spataro, procureur au parquet de Milan, *Le Monde*, March 2004.

[56] "*Dix ans d'emprisonnement requis contre Djamel Beghal*," lemonde.fr, February 10, 2005.

[57] Rotella and Zucchino, "Embassy plot offers insight."

[58] Dubois, "*Procès des lieutenants de Ben Laden à Paris*"; Décugis and Deloire, "*Islamistes: Les PV des épouses*"; Pelletier, "*Les 'Afghans' français.*"

[59] Décugis and Deloire, "*Islamistes: Les PV des épouses.*"

[60] For biographical data, see Jean-Pierre Stroobants, "*A Amsterdam, l'itinéraire de 'Mohammed B,' petit délinquant devenu djihadiste et meurtrier de Théo van Gogh*," *Le Monde*, November 9, 2004; Saskia van Reenen, "The 'Hofstad' group—background and profiles," December 23, 2005, radionetherlands.nl; Robert S. Leiken, "Europe's Angry Muslims," *Foreign Affairs*, July/August 2005.

[61] Van Reenen, "The 'Hofstad' group"; Craig S. Smith, "Dutch Try to Thwart Terror without Being Overzealous," *New York Times*, November 25, 2004.

[62] Ibid.

[63] Glenn Frankel, "From Civic Activist to Alleged Terrorist: Muslim Suspect in Dutch Director's Killing Was Caught between Cultures," *Washington Post*, November 28, 2004.

[64] Stroobants, "*A Amsterdam, l'itinéraire de 'Mohammed B.'*"

[65] Smith, "Dutch Try to Thwart Terror."

[66] According to Dutch journalists Kustaw Bessems and Elwin Verheggen, quoted by Stroobants, "*A Amsterdam, l'itinéraire de 'Mohammed B.'*"

[67] Michel Hoebink, "The Islam debate in the Netherlands," Radio Netherlands, November 3, 2005.

[68] Mohammed Bouyeri, "Open Letter to Hirsi Ali," translated from the original Dutch text, http://www.balder.org/articles/Theo-van-Gogh-Murder-Open-Letter-To-Hirsi-Ali.php.

[69] "The Multiculturalism Society is dead, long live multiculturalism," *Spiegel Online*, July 27, 2005.

[70] Norbert Both and Nabil Taouati, "Holland after van Gogh," http://www.project-syndicate.org/print_commentary/both1/English.

[71] See Emerson Vermaat, *De Hofstadgroep*, pp. 89–93 ("Jihad training in Pakistan") at http://emersonvermaat.com/; Massoud Ansari, "Pakistani arrested over prayer ritual for suicide bomber," *The Telegraph*, July 31, 2005.

[72] Ferry Biedermann, "*De Syrische connectie*," Radio Netherlands, December 3, 2004; van Reenen, "The 'Hofstad' group."

[73] Emerson Vermaat, "The Extremists' Art," FrontPageMagazine.com, December 19, 2005.

[74] Hans de Vreij, "Ominous letters," Radio Netherlands, November 5, 2004.

[75] David Crawford, "Police Seek Syrian Man Linked to Dutch Filmmaker's Murder," *Wall Street Journal*, November 12, 2004.

[76] Judit Neurink, "'Mujahideen of the Lowlands' on Trial in the Netherlands," Terrorism Monitor, December 20, 2005; see also Vermaat, "The Extremists' Art."

[77] Van Reenen, "The 'Hofstad' group."

[78] Elaine Sciolino, "Dutch Struggle to Prevent Terror and Protect Rights," *New York Times*, December 25, 2005.

[79] "Map of Islamic Terrorist Network in America: The Morocco File," http://www.maryschneider.us/.

[80] Stroobants, "*A Amsterdam, l'itinéraire de 'Mohammed B.'*"; Smith, "Dutch Try to Thwart Terror"; Leiken, "Europe's Angry Muslims"; Vermaat, "The Extremists' Art."

[81] Sebastian Rotella, "European Women Join Ranks of Jihadis," *Los Angeles Times*, January 10, 2006.

[82] Sciolino, "Dutch Struggle to Prevent Terror."

[83] Ibid.

[84] Smith, "Dutch Try to Thwart Terror."

[85] Emerson Vermaat, "Lawyers for EU Jihad," FrontPageMagazine.com, January 30, 2006.

[86] Ibid.

[87] Ibid.

[88] Sciolino, "Dutch Struggle to Prevent Terror."

[89] See Vermaat, *De Hofstadgroep*, pages 89–93.

[90] Annual Report 2004, Communications Department, General Intelligence and Security Service (AIVD), http://www.aivd2004-eng.pdf.

[91] Isaac Kfir, "Terror network recruiting suicide bombers in Europe," ICT, June 20, 2005; Jean-Pierre Stroobants, with Martine Silber and Eric Leser, "*Le réseau islamiste 'Hofstad' était solidement ancré en Europe*," *Le Monde*, December 9, 2004.

[92] "*24 Acusados, 18 Condenados: Quién es quién en el macrojuicio contra la célula de Al Qaeda*," *El Mundo*, September 26, 2005; "Map of Islamic Terrorist Network in America: The Morocco File," http://www.maryschneider.us/; Agence France Presse quoted by Craig S. Smith, "Dutch Police Seize 2 in Raid on Terror Cell after a Siege," *New York Times*, November 11, 2004.

[93] "*Garzón imputa a Abdeladim Akoudad, detenido en España en 2003, pertenencia a la célula que asesinó a Van Gogh*," November 16, 2004, http://www.lukor.com/not-por/0411/16153401.htm; Michael Radu, "Holland: Trouble in a Multiculturalist Utopia," FrontPageMagazine.com, November 30, 2004.

[94] "Terror arrests 'thwarted attack'," *Expatica*, November 12, 2004; María Jesús Prades, "Moroccan Charged in Europe Terror Probe," Associated Press, November 17, 2004; Stroobants, with Silber and Leser, "*Le réseau islamiste 'Hofstad'*."

[95] Ulph, "Arrests in Morocco Highlight the Expanding Jihadi Nexus," November 29, 2005, http://jamestown.org/terrorism/news/article.php?articleid=2369838.

[96] Vermaat, *De Hofstadgroep*, p. 138.

[97] Ibid.

[98] A.L.G. and Olivier Roy, "*Les djihadistes sont des déracinés*," *Le Figaro*, July 30, 2005.

[99] "Arab world condemns London blasts," Al Jazeera, July 7, 2005. See also Julian Glover, "Labour losing battle to convince public: Two-thirds believe London bombings are linked to Iraq war," *The Guardian*, July 19, 2005.

[100] Martin Bright and Paul Harris, "'Londonistan' no longer rings true," *The Observer*, July 17, 2005; Marc Semo, "*Le Londonistan repousse ses extrémistes*," *Libération*, July 23, 2005.

[101] Aaron Klein, "Palestinian Leader: London Attacks 'Different'. Official Warns Against Israel Using Events to 'Score Points'," WorldNetDaily.com, July 7, 2005.

[102] "Arab world condemns London blasts."

[103] "Arab Media Reactions to the London Bombing—Part II: 'The Attacks Were Anticipated Due to British Leniency to Extremists Acting in Britain'—'Expel Extremism Today'," MEMRI, Special Report No. 37, July 12, 2005.

[104] Paul Tumelty, "An In-Depth Look at the London Bombers," Jamestown Foundation, Terrorism Monitor, July 28, 2005.

[105] Both Daoudi and his fellow cell member, convert Jean-Marc Grandvisir, were employed as youth advisers—a perfect position for recruitment.

[106] Sudarsan Raghavan, "Friends Describe Bomber's Political, Religious Evolution; 22-Year-Old Grew Up Loving Western Ways and Wanting for Little," *Washington Post*, July 29, 2005.

[107] Ibid.

[108] Olivier Toscer, *"Des kamikazes made in England: Qui sont les terroristes de Londres?"* *Le Nouvel Observateur*, July 21, 2005.

[109] Raghavan, "Friends Describe Bomber's Political, Religious Evolution."

[110] Michael Evans, "MI6 knew of 21/7 bomb suspect," *The Times*, February 27, 2006.

[111] Sandra Laville and Ian Cobain, "From cricket-lover who enjoyed a laugh to terror suspect," *The Guardian*, July 13, 2005; Ian Cobain, "The boy who didn't stand out," *The Guardian*, July 14, 2005; Arifa Akbar and Ian Herbert, "Hasib Hussain: The boy who grew up to bomb the No. 30," *The Independent*, July 14, 2005; "London Attacks," BBC News, http://news.bbc.co.uk/1/shared/spl/hi/uk/05/london_blasts/html/bombers.stm.

[112] Ian Herbert, "Hussain's Story: Family struggle to understand why their gentle boy became a bomber," *The Independent*, August 2, 2005.

[113] Ibid.

[114] Tumelty, "An In-Depth Look."

[115] Terry Kirby, "The 'quiet, likeable' man who was the King's Cross bomber," *The Independent*, July 15, 2005.

[116] Armelle Thoraval, *"Samantha, veuve d'un kamikaze de Londres, témoigne dans le 'Sun': 'C'est atroce comme ces gens ont empoisonné son esprit',"* *Libération*, September 24, 2005; Jamie Pyatt, "From an angel to a devil," *The Sun*, September 24, 2005; for a comparison, see Terry McDermott, *Perfect Soldiers: The Hijackers: Who They Were, Why They Did It* (New York: HarperCollins, 2005), pp. 230–231.

[117] MEMRI TV, July 8, 2005.

[118] Kim Sengupta, Ian Herbert, Arifa Akbar, and Jonathan Brown, "Why four young men turned to terror," *The Independent*, July 15, 2005.

[119] Alan Cowell, "Britain Takes Step toward Deporting Radical Clerics," *New York Times*, July 20, 2005.

[120] Luke Harding and Rosie Cowan, "Pakistan militants linked to London attacks," *The Guardian*, July 19, 2005.

[121] Jacques Duplouich, *"Grande-Bretagne: De nombreuses pièces manquent encore au puzzle de l'enquête sur les quatre explosions du 7 juillet à Londres,"* *Le Figaro*, July 18, 2005.

[122] David Leppard, "MI5 knew of bomber's plan for holy war," *The Sunday Times*, January 22, 2006.

[123] Arif Jamal and Somini Sengupta, "Two Militants Place Suspect at a Camp in Pakistan," *New York Times,* July 26, 2005.

[124] That also led Pakistani President Musharraf to state: "The fault lies with the people of Pakistani origin," he said. "Why have your children not been assimilated into the society that you have adopted for yourselves?" Ansari, "Pakistani arrested over prayer ritual."

[125] "*Al-Qaida lance un ultimatum d'un mois aux pays européens,*" *Le Monde,* July 19, 2005; *Le Figaro,* July 9, 2005; for text and facsimile of letter, see Yassin Musharbash, "Terrorist Attack in London: Purported Al-Qaida Letter Claims Responsibility for Bombings," www.spiegel.de.

[126] Tumelty, "An In-Depth Look."

[127] Mouna Naïm, "*Grande-Bretagne: La piste islamiste,*" *Le Monde,* July 8, 2005.

[128] Raghavan, "Friends Describe Bomber's Political, Religious Evolution."

[129] "Suicide terrorism: a global threat," *Jane's Security News,* October 20, 2000; Mark Follman, "The enemy is closer than we think: A top counterterrorism expert says the London suicide bombers may not have acted alone—and America may be next," Salon.com, July 19, 2005.

[130] David Leppard, "British brigade of Islamists join Al-Qaeda foreign legion in Iraq," *The Sunday Times,* June 4, 2006; David Ward, "Shock at martial arts fan's suicide attack," *The Guardian,* November 17, 2003.

[131] Victor Homola, "Germany: Algerian Held in Bomb Plot," *New York Times,* August 5, 2003; Isaac Kfir, "British police hunt suicide network," ICT, June 22, 2005.

[132] Dominik Cziesche and Georg Mascolo, "Leaving for the Death Zone," *Der Spiegel,* December 8, 2003.

[133] Thierry Matta, "*La menace vue de la France après le Livre Blanc,*" in *Cinq ans après le 11 septembre: Le point sur la lutte contre Al Qaida et le terrorisme international,* Fondation pour la Recherche Stratégique, Paris, September 27, 2006, http://www.frstrategie.org/barreFRS/publications/colloques/20060927.pdf.

[134] Magdi Allam, "The historical truth," September 17, 2006, http://regimechangeiran.blogspot.com/2006/09/historical-truth.html.

[135] Robert A. Pape, *Dying to Win: The Strategic Logic of Suicide Terrorism* (New York: Random House, 2005), pp. 80–81.

[136] Peter Bergen and Michael Lind, "A Matter of Pride. Why We Can't Buy Off the Next Osama bin Laden," *Journal of Democracy,* Winter 2007.

[137] Nicola Smith, "Making of Muriel the suicide bomber," *The Sunday Times,* December 4, 2005; "*Muriel, de Monceau-sur-Sambre à Bagdad: L'histoire de la jeune terroriste se précise. Elle n'était pas la seule prête au martyre,*" *Le Soir,* December 2, 2005.

[138] Smith, "Making of Muriel."

[139] *La Razón* (www.larazon.es), December 22, 2004.

[140] Jorge A. Rodríguez, "*El sumario desvela que 'El Tunecino' ideó el 11-M por la guerra de Iraq,*" *El País*, January 20, 2005.

[141] Juan C. Serrano, "*El Tunecino se encargo de busca medio y terroristas para los attentions del 11-M,*" *La Razón*, March 11, 2006.

[142] José Sanmartín, *El Terrorista: Cómo Es, Cómo Se Hace* (Barcelona: Ariel, 2005), p. 132.

[143] Jean-Marie Pontaut, with Vanja Luksic and Cécile Thibaud, "*L'œil d'Al-Qaeda en Europe,*" *L'Express*, June 14, 2004.

[144] Rodríguez, "*El sumario desvela que 'El Tunecino' ideó el 11-M.*"

[145] Juan C. Serrano and F. Velasco, "*'El Chino' tenía televisión, móvil y fotos de Ben Laden en la cárcel de Marruecos,*" *La Razón*, April 23, 2005.

[146] Juan C. Serrano, "*La Policía sitúa el techo de la investigación del atentado en 'el Tunecino' y 'el Chino',*" *La Razón*, March 29, 2006.

[147] "Piecing together Madrid bombers' past," http://news.bbc.co.uk/1/hi/world/europe/3600421.stm.

[148] Paloma D. Sotero, "*'El Chino', a dos guardias civiles en la A-1: 'Racistas, os vais a enterar',*" elmundo.es, April 16, 2007; "*Guardias de tráfico admiten que no detuvieron a 'El Chino' pese a que llevaba ropa robada y cuchillos en el coche,*" elpais.com, April 16, 2007.

[149] "*El 'Chino' confesó a su hermano su participación en los atentados,*" ABC.es, April 9, 2007.

[150] Serrano, "*La Policía.*"

[151] Transcript in J.C.S., "*Uno de los suicidas de Leganés avisó a su hermano antes de inmolarse, 'Soy tu hermano Abdallah. Voy a encontrarme con Dios',*" *La Razón*, April 24, 2005.

[152] *El Mundo*, April 21, 2004.

[153] Scott Atran, Robert Axelrod, and Richard Davis, "Terror Networks and Sacred Values," March 2007, http://sitemaker.umich.edu/satran/files/synopsis_atran-sageman_nsc_brief_28_march_2007.pdf.

[154] Dale Fuchs, "Drug Money Paid for Attacks on Trains, Spain Says: News Conference Describes Alleged Planning by Suspects," *New York Times*, April 15, 2004.

[155] Nicolas Marmié, "*Jamal Zougam, itinéraire d'un enfant de Tanger suspecté du carnage de Madrid,*" *Le Nouvel Observateur*, March 15 2004, http://archquo.nouvelobs.com/cgi/articles?ad=etranger/20040315.FAP7865.html&host=http://permanent.nouvelobs.com/.

[156] "*Supuesto Responsable de la Célula Española de Al Qaeda 'Abu Dahdah' Declara ante Garzón,*" elmundo.es, March 18, 2004.

[157] In fact, allegations appeared in the Spanish media in August 2005 linking Ziyad Hashem, an alleged member of the Libyan Islamic Fighting Group (LIFG), as well as the group's imprisoned emir, Abdullah Sadeq, with Fakhet. The article, which cited a leaked Spanish police report, also claimed that Hashem was linked by marriage to al-Maymouni. Alison Pargeter, "LIFG: An Organization in Eclipse," Jamestown Foundation, November 3, 2005. See also *"La Policía Revela Conexiones de 'El Tunecino' con Terroristas Libios Asentados en China,"* ABC.es, August 1, 2005; María Jesús Prades, "Judge links suspect to Spain, 9-11 attacks: Moroccan accused of helping planning," Associated Press, April 29, 2004, http://www.spokesmanreview.com/local/story_txt.asp?date=042904&ID=s1514317.

[158] Lawrence Wright, "The Terror Web: Were the Madrid bombings part of a new, far-reaching jihad being plotted on the Internet?" *The New Yorker*, August 8, 2004.

[159] Irujo, *"Los hombres de Abu Dahdah y el 11-M."*

[160] D. Martínez and P. Muñoz, ABC.es, http://www.abc.es/informacion/11m/investigacion_01.asp.

[161] AGI, June 8, 2004, http://notizienl.blogspot.com/.

[162] Pontaut, Luksic, and Thibaud, *"L'œil d'Al-Qaeda."*

[163] For complete Spanish text, see *"Los terroristas suicidas amenazaban en un vídeo con continuar con su 'yihad' en España,"* ABC.es, April 13, 2004; for other documents left by the terrorists, see Jorge A. Rodríguez, *"11-M: Sumario de los Atentados de Madrid. La tercera cinta de los terroristas del 11-M vincula los atentados con Irak y con el 'trío de las Azores',"* El País, September 5, 2005.

[164] For an analysis and critique of such opinions, see Edurne Uriarte, *Terrorismo y Democracia tras el 11-M* (Madrid: Espasa, 2004), pp. 62–82.

[165] In September 2005 Abu Dahdah was sentenced to 27 years for terrorism.

[166] Irujo, *"Los hombres de Abu Dahdah y el 11-M."*

[167] D. Martínez and P. Muñoz, *"Prisiones ha ordenado ya la dispersión de 49 sospechosos de terrorismo islámico,"* ABC.es, October 21, 2004.

[168] Mark Townsend et al., "The secret war," *The Observer*, March 21, 2004.

[169] *"Un islamista asegura que los atentados del 11-M se gestaron en Valencia,"* EFE/ABC.es, May 4, 2007.

[170] D. Martínez and P. Muñoz, ABC.es, at http://www.abc.es/informacion/11m/investigacion_01.asp.

[171] Abdelhak Najib, *"Révélations américaines sur le 16 mai: Les Marocains d'Al Qaïda,"* La Gazette du Maroc, March 15, 2004.

172 Tito Drago, "Spain: Two Faces of Terrorism, One Thrives, the Other Agonizes," http://www.ipsnews.net/print.asp?idnews=23225.

[173] For details, see *"Grande-Marlaska procesa a 32 presuntos terroristas islamistas que querían atentar contra la Audiencia,"* ABC.es, March 21, 2006; *"Se Retracta de Su Declaración en 2004. Un imputado en el 11-M declara que la Policía le forzó a vincular la masacre de Madrid con Irak,"* El Mundo, August 29, 2005; *"Islamistas: El imputado por el 11-M Faisal Allouch cedió su domicilio para que se reuniera la célula de Madrid,"* November 8, 2004, http://www.lukor.com/not-esp/terrorismo/0411/08174121.htm; "Madrid Breaks Up Terror Plot," October 19, 2004, http://www.cbsnews.com/stories/2004/05/06/terror/main616051.shtml.

[174] Driss Bennani, Abdellatif El Azizi, Ismaïl Bellaouali, and Lahcen Aouad, *"Enquête: Au-delà de la panique,"* TelQuel, May 1, 2007.

[175] *"Los detenidos en la 'operación Nova',"* El Mundo, March 21, 2006.

[176] Paul Lewis and Sandra Laville, "Ordinary friends who grew devout together," *The Guardian*, August 12, 2006.

[177] Adam Fresco, Russell Jenkins, Lewis Smith, and Nicola Woolcock, "Terror plot: Arrests included baker, salesman and book-keeper," *The Times*, August 12, 2006.

[178] "Italian Intelligence Fears Latest Al-Masri Brigade Statement a Call to Arms in Italy," BBC, July 23, 2005; "Second Group, Abu Hafs al-Masri Brigade, Claims Responsibility for London Bombings," AP, July 9, 2005.

[179] Al Jazeera, March 13, 2004.

[180] Guidère, *Al-Qaida à la conquête du Maghreb*, p. 242.

[181] Aidan Kirby, "Toward the Far Enemy: N. Africa's GSPC Joins the Global Qaida," World Politics Watch, April 18, 2007; Roland Jacquard and Atmane Tazaghart, *"Terrorisme: La stratégie guerrière d'al-Qaida au Maghreb,"* Le Figaro, April 27, 2007; Javier Jordán, "Al Qaeda in Maghreb: Terrorist groups join forces in Northern Africa," *Safe Democracy*, April 23, 2007.

[182] See Jean Brisard with Charles Damien Martinez, *Zarqawi: The New Face of al-Qaeda* (New York: Other Press, 2005).

[183] Javier Jordán, *"La cadena de mando del 11-M,"* El Correo, February 25, 2007.

[184] Catherine Simon, *"Maroc: Kamikazes sans testament,"* Le Monde, May 4, 2007; Jacquard and Tazaghart, *"Terrorisme: La stratégie guerrière d'al-Qaida au Maghreb"*; Bennani, El Azizi, Bellaouali, and Aouad, *"Enquête."*

[185] For text of indictment, see http://www.abc.es/informacion/pdf/auto_olmo.pdf.

[186] Craig S. Smith, "8 Sentenced in Morocco for Plotting Terror Attacks," *New York Times*, March 3, 2007. As late as 2007 an Italian analyst still claimed that in the case of the San Petronio bomb plot, "Later investigation proved without any doubt that the entire episode was the result of wrong information and incorrect interpretations of some phone intercepts." Luigi Bonanate,

"Democracia italiana y terrorismo internacional: ¿Quién vencerá el desafío? Algunas premisas," February 20, 2007, http://www.realinstitutoelcano.org/wps/portal/rielcano/contenido?WCM_GLOBAL_CONTEXT=/Elcano_es/Zonas_es/Terrorismo+Internacional/DT6-2007.

187 For the links between those groups and Al-Qaeda, see Mike Millard, *Jihad in Paradise: Islam and Politics in Southeast Asia* (Armonk, N.Y.: M. E. Sharpe, 2004); Sreedhar and Manish, *Jihadis in Jammu and Kashmir.* For LeT's ties with Al-Qaeda and Iraq, see also South Asia Intelligence Review at http://www.satp.org/satporgtp/countries/india/states/jandk/terrorist_outfits/lashkar_e_toiba.htm; for Al-Qaeda ties with LeT in Europe see also B. Raman, "Al Qaeda's Threat to UK," ICT, December 24, 2006, http://www.ict.org.il/apage/8291.php.

188 Husain Haqqani, "Jihad and Jihadism," *The Indian Express,* August 3, 2005.

189 Massoud Ansari, "The Pakistan Connection," Newsline, September 2006.

190 Ibid.

191 Antonio Baquero and Jordi Corachán, *"Catalunya es la base europea de una filial paquistaní de Al Qaeda,"* El Periódico (Barcelona), February 2, 2007.

192 *"Willie Brigitte condamné à neuf ans de prison,"* Nouvelobs.com, March 15, 2007.

193 Jason Burke, "Al Qaeda recruiting more Westerners faster via internet—UK most vulnerable to attack because of Pakistani citizens," *The Observer,* March 10, 2007.

194 *"'El Egipcio' cambia de opinión y accede a responder sólo a preguntas de su abogado en el juicio por el 11-M,"* ABC.es, February 15, 2007; *"'El Egipcio,' presunto autor intelectual de la masacre,"* elmundo.es, February 15, 2007.

195 Javier Jordán and Robert Wesley, "The Threat of Grassroots Jihadi Networks: A Case Study from Ceuta, Spain," Terrorism Monitor, February 15, 2007.

196 Coolsaet, "Between al-Andalus and a failing integration," Royal Institute for International Relations, Brussels, May 2005, http://www.irri-kiib.be/paperegm/ep5.pdf.

197 Kevin Sullivan, "No Proof of Al-Qaeda in '05 London Transit Blasts: Two Government Reports Find Evidence of Contact, Not Aid," *Washington Post,* May 12, 2006; Alan Travis and Richard Norton-Taylor, "Evidence points to al-Qaida link to 7/7 bombs," *The Guardian,* May 12, 2006.

198 See, e.g., "Madrid Bombings Probe Finds No Direct Link to al Qaeda," Associated Press/*Wall Street Journal,* March 10, 2006.

199 Daveed Gartenstein-Ross, "Al Qaeda's Resurgence," *The Weekly Standard,* February 29, 2008, http://frontpagemag.com/Articles/Read.aspx?GUID=C8555807-8408-46D5-99BC-21F9B8F317BB; Peter Bergen, "The Return of al Qaeda," *The New Republic,* January 29, 2007, http://www.peterbergen.com/bergen/services/print.aspx?id=288.

[200] Dana Priest, "British Raids Net a Leader of Al Qaeda: Official Connects Suspect to Terror Alert Data," *Washington Post*, August 5, 2004.

[201] D. Martínez, "*'El Chino' recibió instrucciones desde un campo de entrenamiento 'on line' de Arabia Saudí*," ABC.es, March 10, 2006; "'Al-Battar': Al Qaeda's Leading Online Publication on Terrorist Techniques." "Al-Battar" is the leading publication extending the training mission of Al-Qaeda online. "The first issue of the publication, called Al-Battar Training Camp, concludes with an emphasis on the virtual program's convenience. 'Oh Mujahid [holy warrior] brother, in order to join the great training camps you don't have to travel to other lands,' the magazine states. 'Alone, in your home or with a group of your brothers, you too can begin to execute the training program. You can all join the Al-Battar Training Camp'." http://www.camerairaq.com/2004/07/al_battar_al_qa.html.

[202] D.M., "*Los musulmanes tienen una venganza pendiente con España*," ABC.es, March 10, 2006.

[203] Abdel Bari Atwan, *The Secret History of Al Qaeda* (Berkeley: University of California Press, 2006), p. 117.

[204] See, e.g., Gary R. Bunt, *Islam in the Digital Age: E-Jihad, Online Fatwas, and Cyber-Islamic Environments* (London: Pluto Press, 2003); Guidère, *Les "Martyrs" d'Al-Qaeda*; Gabriel Weimann, *Terror on the Internet: The New Arena, the New Challenges* (Washington, D.C.: United States Institute of Peace Press, 2006).

[205] *World Internet Usage and Population Statistics, 2006*, assesses population penetration at 70 percent for North America, 38.7 percent for Europe (obviously much higher for Western Europe), but only 10.2 percent for the Middle East. In Iraq only 0.1 percent of the population has access. http://www.internetworldstats.com/stats.htm..

[206] For an analysis of Islamist Internet sites directed toward French Muslims, see Nathalie Szerman, "Islamist Sites in French—An Overview," MEMRI, Inquiry and Analysis Series No. 308, December 21, 2006; MEMRI, Islamist Website Monitor No. 29, Special Dispatch Series No. 1375, December 1, 2006. The most important are http://news.stcom.net/index.php; http://www.ribaat.org/; and http://www.quibla.net/echos/lesechos.htm.

[207] Nick Fielding, "Encyclopaedia of Terror: Revealed: the bloody pages of Al-Qaeda's killing manual," *The Times*, November 4, 2001; "Web of Terror: Nadya Labi discusses the murky world of online jihad," *Atlantic Unbound*, June 5, 2006.

[208] This works both ways. Internet surveillance has helped French intelligence unravel Islamist cells. See J.C., "*La piraterie informatique, nouvelle arme des djihadistes*," *Le Figaro*, September 27, 2006.

[209] Audrey Gillan, "Militant groups in the UK," *The Guardian*, June 19, 2002.

[210] Nasiri, *Inside the Jihad*; see also O'Neill and McGrory, *The Suicide Factory*.

[211] The Al-Battar Training Camp," January 6, 2004, at Middle East Information, http://middleeastinfo.org/article3820.html.

[212] "UK al-Qaida man 'hoped to kill thousands'," *The Guardian*, November 6, 2006.

[213] Adam Fresco and Sean O'Neill, "British Muslim 'wanted to blow up Tube train under Thames'," *Times Online*, November 6, 2006.

CHAPTER SEVEN

[1] "Leading Sunni Sheikh Yousef Al-Qaradhawi and Other Sheikhs Herald the Coming Conquest of Rome," MEMRI, Special Dispatch Series No. 447, December 6, 2002.

[2] See, e.g., François Burgat, *Face to Face with Political Islam* (London and New York: I. B. Tauris, 2005).

[3] Abd Al-Rahman Al-Rashed, Director-General Al-Arabiyya TV, "Why Do Islamist Extremists Who Incite Against the West Insist on Living There?" MEMRI Special Dispatch Series No. 1493, March 8, 2007.

[4] Bruce Thornton, *Decline and Fall: Europe's Slow-Motion Suicide* (New York: Encounter Books, 2007), p. 83.

[5] Bernhard Zand, "The Cartoon Wars: The Inciters and the Incited," *Der Spiegel*, February 13, 2006; Andrew Higgins, "How Muslim Clerics Stirred Arab World against Denmark," *Wall Street Journal*, February 7, 2006.

[6] See Michael Taarnby, "Recruitment of Islamist Terrorists in Europe: Trends and Perspectives," research report funded by the Danish Ministry of Justice, submitted January 14, 2005, http://www.jm.dk/image.asp?page=image&objno=73027.

[7] *"Les propos de Jack Lang sur les 'crimes' commis par la France en Algérie suscitent la polémique," Le Monde*, with AFP, February 5, 2007.

[8] Henryk M. Broder, "The West and Islam: 'Hurray! We're Capitulating!'" *Spiegel Online*, January 25, 2007.

[9] Hugh Muir, "Livingstone decries vilification of Islam," *The Guardian*, November 20, 2006.

[10] Michael Meacher, "This war on terrorism is bogus: The 9/11 attacks gave the US an ideal pretext to use force to secure its global domination," *The Guardian*, September 6, 2003.

[11] Nicola Smith, "Burqa ban splits Holland," *The Sunday Times*, November 19, 2006.

[12] "Islamophobia on the rise in the Netherlands," Radio Netherlands, February 12, 2008.

[13] Stephen Castle, "Dutch Muslims condemn 'populist' burqa ban move," *The Independent*, November 20, 2006.

[14] "Minister Welcomes Sharia in Netherlands if Majority Wants It," NIS News Bulletin (Netherlands), September 13, 2006.

[15] John Vinocur, "Nudging to Consensus over Dutch Muslims," *International Herald Tribune*, November 21, 2006.

[16] Magdi Allam, "*'Il velo legge di Dio'*," *Corriere della Sera*, October 22, 2006; John Hooper, "Veils gag falls flat: An imam's 'death threat' to an Italian MP has not stopped her speaking out on Islam and feminism," *The Guardian*, October 27, 2006.

[17] Allam, "*'Il velo legge di Dio'*."

[18] Daud Abdullah, "Incitement to violence: The political and media onslaught on Muslims is already fuelling physical attacks on the streets," *The Guardian*, October 17, 2006.

[19] "IHRC Statement in Response to New Government Guidelines Which Give Head Teachers the Right to Ban Face Veil in Schools," March 20, 2007, http://www.Islamophobia-watch.com/Islamophobia-watch/.

[20] *"La Junta Islámica se muestra contraria al uso del 'niqab' en las escuelas europeas,"* ABC.es, March 21, 2007.

[21] Jean-Marie Amat and Yves Benoit, *"Néo-Islamistes: Stratégies pour noyauter la République,"* L'Express, April 17, 2003.

[22] *"Sarkozy fait un tabac dans un sondage,"* Libération, November 16, 2005; Jon Henley, "Rising from the ashes: The aftermath of France's worst rioting since 1968 has seen both Dominique de Villepin and Nicolas Sarkozy's popularity soar," *The Guardian*, November 16, 2005.

[23] "Les catholiques avec Sarkozy . . . *les musulmans avec Royal*," Le Figaro, April 23, 2007; Jean Chichizola, *"La candidate socialiste fait un tabac à Clichy-sous-Bois,"* Le Figaro, April 22, 2007.

[24] Nick Britten, "Leading cleric rails at injustice of 'Muslim bashing'," *The Telegraph*, July 28, 2005.

[25] Paul Belien, "In bed with Islamists," *Washington Times*, April 11, 2007.

[26] Ibid.

[27] Carlos Rangel, *Del Buen Salvaje al Buen Revolucionario*, introduction by Jean-François Revel (Caracas: Monte Vila, 1976), passim.

[28] Henryk M. Broder, "Shariah Is for Everyone!" *Spiegel Online*, February 12, 2008.

[29] Herman De Ley, "Imagining the Muslims in Belgium: 'Enemies from Within' or 'Muslim Fellow-Citizens'?" Center for Islam in Europe, 1998.

[30] Michael Evans, "Britain is a 'soft touch' for terrorism, defence institute says," *Times Online*, February 15, 2008.

³¹ Baltasar Garzón, *Un Mundo sin Miedo* (Barcelona: Plaza Janés, 2005), pp. 279–283.

³² See also William Chislett, *"El antiamericanismo en España: el peso de la historia,"* November 14, 2005, http://www.realinstitutoelcano.org/documentos/imprimir/228imp.asp.

³³ Al Jazeera, November 8, 2005.

³⁴ Jean-Baptiste Naudet, *"L'Amérique tortionnaire: Apres le 11-Septembre, plus de gants . . . ,"* *Le Nouvel Observateur*, March 24, 2005.

³⁵ "U.S. Image Up Slightly, but Still Negative: American Character Gets Mixed Reviews," http://pewglobal.org/reports/display.php?ReportID=247.

³⁶ "How others see Americans: Still not loved. Now not envied," *The Economist*, June 25, 2005.

³⁷ Hans Hoyng, "Goodbye Uncle Sam?" *New York Times*, May 4, 2005 (original in *Der Spiegel*).

³⁸ Karl Vick, "In Many Turks' Eyes, U.S. Remains the Enemy: Hostility Bodes Ill for Efforts to Boost Americans' Image," *Washington Post*, April 10, 2005; for a general analysis of anti-Americanism, see Paul Hollander, ed., *Understanding Anti-Americanism: Its Origins and Impact at Home and Abroad* (Chicago: Ivan R. Dee, 2004).

³⁹ Christophe Boltanski, Didier Arnaud, and Renaud Lecadre, *"Du procès de 'Charlie' à celui de l'intégrisme,"* *Libération*, February 9, 2007.

⁴⁰ *"Un Français sur trois se déclare raciste,"* Nouvelobs.com, March 21, 2006.

⁴¹ Charles Moore, "How Livingstone turned a racist remark into a cause célèbre," *The Telegraph*, March 3, 2006.

⁴² "Young Muslims and Extremism," FCO/Home Office Paper (Restricted), April 6, 2004, in Robert Winnett and David Leppard, "Terror in London: Leaked No. 10 dossier reveals Al-Qaeda's British recruits," *The Sunday Times*, July 10, 2005.

⁴³ Bruce Bawer, *While Europe Slept: How Radical Islam Is Destroying the West from Within* (New York: Doubleday, 2006).

⁴⁴ Tawfik Hamid, "The Trouble with Islam," *Wall Street Journal*, April 3, 2007.

⁴⁵ Interviewed in *"La gauche fait-elle le lit de l'Islamisme? Propos recueillis par Jacqueline Remy, Anne Vidalie,"* *L'Express*, November 17, 2005. Fourest is the author of *La tentation obscurantiste* (Paris: Grasset, 2005).

⁴⁶ Ibid.

⁴⁷ Burgat, *Face to Face with Political Islam*, passim.

⁴⁸ Dan Bilefsky, "Danish wake-up call on Islam," *International Herald Tribune*, September 25, 2006; Ignacio Cembrero *"Hay que plantar cara con nuestros valores,"* *El País*, September 28, 2006.

⁴⁹ Ibid.

50 Ibid.

51 Christopher Hitchens, "Muslims at the French Embassy in London complain about cartoons," *Vanity Fair*, June 2007.

52 *"L'immigration serait perçue très différemment selon les pays,"* *Le Point*, May 25, 2007.

53 Interview with Cardinal Walter Kasper, "Islam Is a Different Culture," *Der Spiegel*, September 18, 2006.

54 Ndeye Andújar, *"Ni Putas Ni Sumisas 'y la instrumentalización política de la batalla contra el velo,"* *Rebelión*, February 26, 2007.

55 "Kelly urges 'honest debate' on multiculturalism," *The Independent*, August 24, 2006.

56 Leo McKinstry, "Dis-United Kingdom," *The Weekly Standard*, November 28, 2005.

57 Timothy Garton Ash, "What young British Muslims say can be shocking—some of it is also true," *The Guardian*, August 10, 2006.

58 Letter, *The Guardian*, March 22, 2007.

59 Rupert Darwall, "Vintage Blair Attempt to Talk Terror Away," *Wall Street Journal*, July 26, 2005.

60 Matthew d'Ancona, "This horror began with a literary row," *The Telegraph*, July 17, 2005.

61 Anthony Glees, "Campus Jihad," *Wall Street Journal*, October 23, 2006.

62 Nathalie Szerman, "Reformist Thinker Abdennour Bidar Makes the Case for Individual Islam and Poses Questions to France's 2007 Presidential Candidates," MEMRI, Inquiry and Analysis Series No. 350, May 1, 2007, http://memri.org/bin/articles.cgi?Page=archives&Area=ia&ID=IA35007.

63 "Sharia Law in Britain Unavoidable: Archbishop," *New York Times*, February 7, 2008.

64 "Civil and Religious Law in England: a religious perspective. The full text of the Archbishop of Canterbury's lecture in London," *The Guardian*, February 7, 2008.

65 "Our stand on Multiculturalism, Citizenship, Extremism, & Expectations," MCB Research & Documentation Committee, Commission on Integration and Cohesion, Briefing Paper, January 2007, http://www.mcb.org.uk/downloads/MCB percent20ReDoc percent20Briefing percent20Paper percent20PRINTRUN.pdf.

66 David B. Rivkin Jr. and Lee A. Casey, "Toleration and Islamic Law," *Wall Street Journal*, February 12, 2008.

67 Riazat Butt, "Archbishop backs sharia law for British Muslims," *The Guardian*, February 7, 2008.

[68] Rowan Williams BBC interview, February 7, 2008, at www.bbc.co.uk.

[69] Butt, "Archbishop backs sharia law."

[70] Dipesh Gadher, Abul Taher, and Christopher Morgan, "Rowan Williams faces backlash over Sharia," *The Sunday Times*, February 10, 2008.

[71] David Harrison, "Sharia in Britain: Unease in Oxford," *The Telegraph*, February 10, 2008.

[72] Gadher, Taher, and Morgan, "Rowan Williams faces backlash."

[73] Mark Townsend, "Top judges in key ruling on sharia marriage," *The Observer*, February 10, 2008.

[74] Jonathan Wynne-Jones, "Sharia law may result in 'legal apartheid'," *The Telegraph*, February 10, 2008.

[75] James Sturcke and Hélène Mulholland, "Bishop condemns 'shameful' sharia outcry," *The Guardian*, February 8, 2008.

[76] Ibid.

[77] Will Woodward and Riazat Butt, "Williams defiant over Islamic law speech. Archbishop insists his remarks were 'well-researched'," *The Guardian*, February 9, 2008.

[78] "*Sarkozy: 'No hay sitio en Francia para el velo en las escuelas'*," ABC.es, January 8, 2008.

[79] Graham E. Fuller, "A World without Islam," *Foreign Policy*, January-February 2008.

[80] Steven Runciman, *A History of the Crusades*, vols. 1–3 (Cambridge, UK: Cambridge University Press, 1987); Christopher Tyerman, *God's War: A New History of the Crusades* (Cambridge, Mass.: Belknap Press, 2006).

[81] Karen Armstrong, quoted in www.DiscoverTheNetwork.org, February 19, 2008.

[82] http://www.Islamfortoday.com/karenarmstrong02.htm; Karen Armstrong, *Holy War: The Crusades and Their Impact on Today's World* (New York: Anchor Books, 2001), pp. 458–465.

[83] Ron Barkai, *El Enemigo en el Espejo: Cristianos y Musulmanes en la España Medieval* (Madrid: Ediciones Rialp, 2007), pp. 76–81.

[84] See, e.g., Menocal, *The Ornament of the World*; for a convincing rebuttal, see Serafín Fanjul, *La Quimera de Al-Andalus;* for a Jewish view, see Eliyahu Ashtor, *The Jews of Muslim Spain*, vols. 1–3 (Philadelphia and Jerusalem, The Jewish Publication Society, 1992), passim.

[85] Fanjul, *Al-Andalus contra España*; Fanjul, *La Quimera de Al-Andalus.*

[86] Vincent Lagardere, *Les Almoravides: Le djihad andalou (1106–1143)* (Paris: L'Harmattan, 1998); Jane S. Gerber, *The Jews of Spain. A history of the Sephardic Experience* (New York: Free Press, 2002).

[87] Marie Simon, *"Redeker: l'auteur des menaces arrêté,"* *Le Figaro*, January 9, 2007; *"L'Affaire Redeker: l'auteur présumé des menaces de mort arrêté,"* *Libération*, January 9, 2007.

[88] "French thinker called a racist for comments," *Jewish Exponent*, December 15, 2005.

[89] Dror Mishani and Aurelia Smotriez, "What sort of Frenchmen are they?" *Bella Ciao*, November 25, 2005.

[90] *"Le racisme à l'honneur,"* *Le Monde Diplomatique*, December 15, 2005.

[91] "Berlin Opera on Its Knees before Terrorists," *Der Spiegel*, September 27, 2006.

[92] Philip Willan, "Al-Qaida plot to blow up Bologna church fresco," *The Guardian*, June 24 2002.

[93] "Fear of Muslim Backlash," *Der Spiegel*, September 26, 2006.

[94] Devika Bhat and agencies, "Opera reignites Islam row after cancelling production," *The Times*, September 28, 2006.

[95] Josep Pons Fraga, *"Mezquita primero, catedral después,"* *Última Hora* (Menorca), January 4, 2007; cf. Jesús Bastante, *"El principal grupo islámico exige a la Iglesia el patrimonio musulmán español,"* ABC, January 4, 2007.

[96] Fraga, *"Mezquita primero."*

[97] José Antonio Zarzalejos (Director of ABC), *"Provocación en Córdoba,"* January 7, 2007.

[98] An issue exacerbated by the Socialist government's encouragement and acceptance of nationalist, quasi-secessionist developments in Catalonia, País Vasco, and elsewhere, including failed talks with Basque Marxist terrorists of ETA.

[99] Javier Salado, *"Córdoba, ¿capital cultural de Europa?"* December 29, 2006, http://www.webIslam.com/?idt=6484#.

[100] Ben Sills, "Cathedral may see return of Muslims," *The Guardian*, April 19, 2004.

[101] "Muslims ask to worship at Córdoba," Al Jazeera, December 26, 2006.

[102] Jesús Bastante, "El principal grupo islámico exige a la Iglesia el patrimonio musulmán español," ABC.es, January 2, 2007.

[103] Ibid.

[104] The imam of Fuengirola was sued by Spanish feminists for advocating wife beating. Cécile Thibaud, *"Espagne. Des immigrés si loin, si près,"* *L'Express*, January 26, 2006.

[105] "Muslims of Al-Andalus (Now Spain) Still Mark Every Year in Anguish," *Saudi Gazette*; cf. *Saudi Daily*: "Andalusian Muslims Recall Mass Exodus," MEMRI Special Dispatch, March 4, 2005.

[106] Ibid. Sephardic Jews have retained Ladino, a Spanish dialect, for centuries, some until today. One may question Hakim's expertise, although not his anti-Semitism.

[107] Serafín Fanjul, *"Inmigrantes y moriscos,"* ABC.es, January 4, 2007.

[108] Elizabeth Nash, "Spanish bishops fear rebirth of Islamic kingdom," *The Independent*, January 5, 2007. One may add that all three cities have Socialist mayors, sympathetic to Muslim "grievances."

[109] *"Los terroristas suicidas amenazaban en un vídeo con continuar con su 'yihad' en España,"* ABC.es, April 13, 2004. A plot to bomb buildings in New Jersey in 2006 was led by Assem Hammoud, a.k.a. "Emir Andalusi" ("Prince of Andalus").

[110] Osama bin Laden, "The betrayal of Palestine," December 29, 1994, in Bruce Lawrence, ed., *Messages to the World: The Statements of Osama bin Laden* (London: Verso, 2005), pp. 4–14.

[111] Barkai, *El enemigo en el espejo*, p. 263.

[112] "Spanish Fatwa against Terrorism," Islamic Commission of Spain, *The American Muslim*, March 26, 2005.

[113] For complete Spanish text, see *"Los terroristas suicidas amenazaban en un vídeo con continuar con su 'yihad' en España,"* ABC.es, April 13, 2004.

[114] Elaine Sciolino, "Terror Threat from Pakistan Said to Expand," *New York Times*, February 10, 2008.

[115] Caroline Fourest, Corinne Lepage, and Pierre Cassen, *"Contre un nouvel obscurantisme,"* *Libération*, April 28, 2006; see also www.petitiononline.com/2104/petition.html..

[116] Quoted in Sandro Magister, "Oriana Fallaci Has Enrolled in the Society of Jesus," April 10, 2006, http://chiesa.espresso.repubblica.it/articolo/48741?&eng=y.

[117] Jonathan Laurence, "The Prophet of Moderation: Tariq Ramadan's Quest to Reclaim Islam," *Foreign Affairs*, May-June 2007.

[118] Tariq Ramadan, *Western Muslims and the Future of Islam* (Oxford and New York: Oxford University Press, 2004), p. 216.

[119] Ian Buruma, "Tariq Ramadan Has an Identity Issue," *New York Times*, February 4, 2007.

[120] For such sharp criticisms see Caroline Fourest, *Frère Tariq: Discourse, stratégie et méthode de Tariq Ramadan* (Paris: Bernard Grasset, 2004); Paul Landau, *Le sabre et le Coran: Tariq Ramadan et les Frères musulmans à la conquête de l'Europe* (Paris: Editions du Rocher, 2005).

[121] Tibi, *Islam between Culture and Politics*; Tibi, *The Challenge of Fundamentalism*.

[122] "Muslim Americans: Middle Class and Mostly Mainstream," May 22, 2007, http://people-press.org/reports/display.php3?ReportID=329; "The Great Divide," http://pewglobal.org/reports/display.php?ReportID=253.

[123] Flemming Rose, cultural editor at *Jyllands-Posten*, "Why I Published the Muhammad Cartoons," *Der Spiegel*, May 31, 2006.

[124] James Sturcke, "Muslims being demonised, says Livingstone," *The Guardian*, October 24, 2006.

[125] Quoted in Liz Fekete, "The emergence of xeno-racism," Institute of Race Relations, September 28, 2001, http://www.irr.org.uk/2001/september/ak000001.html.

[126] Interview with Bassam Tibi, "Europeans Have Stopped Defending Their Values," *Der Spiegel*, October 2, 2006.

[127] Soumaya Ghannoushi, "Religious hatred is no more than a variety of racism," *The Guardian*, November 16, 2006.

[128] Nathalie Szerman, "Reformist Thinker Abdennour Bidar Makes the Case for Individual Islam and Poses Questions to France's 2007 Presidential Candidates," MEMRI, Inquiry and Analysis Series No. 350, May 1, 2007.

[129] "Most foul. De Menezes shooting," *The Economist*, July 20, 2006.

[130] http://www.Islamophobia-watch.com/Islamophobia-a-definition. For text see "Islamophobia: A Challenge for Us All," http://www.runnymedetrust.org/publications/currentPublications.html#Islamophobia.

[131] http://www.salaam.co.uk/maktabi/Islamophobia.html.

[132] Amir Taheri, "Muslim Matryushka," *Wall Street Journal*, July 7, 2006.

[133] Conan and Makarian, "*Enquête sur la montée de l'Islam en Europe*," *L'Express*, January 26, 2006.

[134] Frank Furedi, "Phobias," *Spiked*, May 21, 2007, http://www.spiked-online.com/index.php?/site/article/3382

[135] Bruno Jeudy, "*Sarkozy remet 'l'identité nationale' au coeur du débat*," *Le Figaro*, March 10, 2007.

[136] See full text at http://www.unhcr.org/cgi-bin/texis/vtx/protect?id=3c0762ea4.

[137] Text at http://findarticles.com/p/articles/mi_m1309/is_v22/ai_3581827.

[138] "Abu Qatada Ruling Threatens Absolute Ban on Torture. Assurances by Jordan Won't Protect Terrorism Suspect from Torture," Human Rights Watch UK, March 1, 2007; see also Amnesty International, "UK must stop deportations to torture states," March 1, 2007.

[139] Ruth Gledhill, "Protest over school's stand on halal meat," *The Times*, February 9, 2007.

[140] Sabine Cessou, "*La Belgique indignée par le meurtre raciste d'Anvers. Une fillette belge de 2 ans et sa nourrice malienne abattues par un skinhead*," *Libération*, May 13, 2006; "*Un proche du 'Blok' tue deux fois*," *Le Soir*, May 12, 2006.

[141] Gaby Hinsliff, "Challenge to Cameron over BNP: MP blames rise of the extreme right on political correctness," *The Observer*, April 23, 2006.

[142] Will Woodward, "Immigration level unsustainable, warns former Labour minister," *The Guardian*, June 29, 2006.

[143] *"Villiers: 'L'Islam n'est pas compatible avec la République',"* AFP/*Le Monde*, April 23, 2006.

[144] *"Pour Nicolas Sarkozy, 'Si certains n'aiment pas la France, qu'ils ne se gênent pas pour la quitter',"* Lemonde.fr, April 23, 2006.

[145] *"Villiers accuse Sarkozy d'avoir copié le slogan du MPF,"* Nouvelobs.com, April 23, 2006.Ð

[146] *"Jack Lang dénonce le 'fonds de commerce' de l'immigration,"* *L'Express*, April 23, 2006.

[147] Gündüz Aktan, "Legal battles," *Turkish Daily News*, May 11, 2006.

[148] Laetitia Van Eeckhout, *"En 2005, les opinions racistes ont gagné du terrain en France,"* *Le Monde*, March 21, 2006.

[149] Ibid.

[150] Alain Ruscio, *"Des Sarrasins aux Beurs, une vieille méfiance,"* *Le Monde Diplomatique*, February 2004.

[151] Ibid.

[152] E.V. (with AFP, Reuters), *"Amsterdam enterre Van Gogh sur fond de xénophobie: Deux églises attaquées en représailles aux attentats contre des mosquées,"* *Libération*, November 10, 2004.

[153] See text at http://memri.org/bin/latestnews.cgi?ID=SD85605.

[154] Clare Dyer, " 'There is no war on terror': Outspoken DPP takes on Blair and Reid over fear-driven legal response to threat," *The Guardian*, January 24, 2007.

[155] Andrew Blick, Tufyal Choudhury, and Stuart Weir, *The Rules of the Game: Terrorism, Community and Human Rights*, A Report by Democratic Audit, Human Rights Centre, University of Essex, for the Joseph Rowntree Reform Trust, http://www.jrrt.org.uk/Terrorism_final.pdf.

[156] "Intelligence and Security Committee Report on the London Terrorist Attacks on 7 July 2005," p. 8, text at http://www.guardian.co.uk/.

[157] " 'War on terror' phrase unhelpful, UK tells US," *The Guardian*, April 16, 2007.

[158] Cf. Sam Knight, "British minister dumps 'War on Terror' in New York speech," *The Times*, April 16, 2007.

[159] Mark Trevelyan, "EU lexicon to shun term 'Islamic terrorism'," Reuters, April 11, 2006.

[160] David Rennie, "EU draft calls to reject 'Islamic terrorism' term," *The Telegraph*, April 12, 2006.

[161] Ibid.

[162] Nicholas Watt and Leo Cendrowicz, "Brussels calls for media code to avoid aiding terrorists," *The Guardian*, September 21, 2005.

[163] Stephen Castle, "Europe speeds up plan to clamp down on suspects," *Belfast Telegraph*, July 14, 2005.

[164] For more comments and abundant quotations on the issue, see Tibi, *The Challenge of Fundamentalism*; Andrew Bostom, ed., *The Legacy of Jihad: Islamic Holy War and the Fate of Non-Muslims* (Amherst, N.Y.: Prometheus Books, 2005).

[165] Ian Buruma, *Murder in Amsterdam: The Death of Theo van Gogh and the Limits of Tolerance* (New York: Penguin Books, 2006), p. 245.

[166] Ibid., p. 246.

[167] Interview with Bassam Tibi, "Europeans Have Stopped Defending Their Values."

[168] Scientific Council for Government Policy (the Netherlands), *Dynamism in Islamic Activism: Reference Points for Democratization and Human Rights* (Amsterdam: Amsterdam University Press, 2007). (Main authors: Jan Schoonenboom and Wendy Asbeek Brusse. Translation: Kate Delaney.)

[169] Geert Wilders, "Declaration of Independence," http://dutchreport.blogspot.com/.

[170] Some comments are based on the author's interview with Mr. Wilders in Philadelphia, in 2005.

[171] Quoted in "Controversial imams," *The Telegraph*, July 20, 2005.

[172] Paolo Biondani, "Recruiting Combatants for Iraq Is Not a Crime," http://www.corriere.it/english/articoli/2005/01_Gennaio/25/militanti.shtml.

[173] "Muslim Community United against Blair's Denial," Islamic Human Rights Commission press release, September 27, 2005, http://www.ihrc.org/.

[174] *Dynamism in Islamic Activism*.

[175] Jean-Pierre Stroobants, "*L'aversion injustifiée' des Néerlandais pour l'Islam*," *Le Monde*, April 15, 2006.

[176] Wilders, "Declaration of Independence."

[177] Stroobants, "*A Amsterdam, l'itinéraire de 'Mohammed B'*," *Le Monde*, November 9, 2004.

[178] "Dealing with traitors," *The Economist*, August 11, 2005.

[179] "The sound of hope," *The Guardian*, May 3, 2006.

[180] "Clarke loses appeal over Guantanamo inmate," *The Guardian*, April 12, 2006.

[181] Ibid.

[182] Emma Henry and agencies, "Judge rejects terror suspect's deportation," *The Telegraph*, May 14, 2007.

[183] "Ex-Taliban spy granted asylum in UK," *The Daily Times* (Pakistan), February 24, 2003.

[184] "Hijack convictions 'a mistake'," BBC, June 6, 2003.

[185] "Afghan hijackers 'not spongers'," BBC, May 13, 2006; Lee Glendinning, "Judge allows hijackers to stay in UK and attacks ministers," *Times Online*, May 10, 2006.

[186] Charles Moore, "Blair's Major moment: Why Human Rights are like the ERM," *The Telegraph*, May 20, 2006.

[187] Ibid.

[188] "UK seeks human rights law review," BBC News, May 20, 2006.

CHAPTER EIGHT

[1] "Participants in Islamist Forums Discuss Proposal for Terrorist Attack in Paris," MEMRI Special Dispatch Series No. 1816, January 18, 2008, http://memri.org/bin/latestnews.cgi?ID=SD181608.

[2] "Council of European Union Framework Decision on Combatting Terrorism," June 13, 2002, http://www.tamilnation.org/terrorism/eu/020613eu_council_framework_decision.htm.

[3] Ibid.

[4] http://www.statewatch.org/terrorlists/listschallenges.html.

[5] Ibid.

[6] Elaine Sciolino, "French Detain Group Said to Recruit Iraq Rebels," *New York Times*, January 26, 2005.

[7] Ibid.

[8] Faheem Hussain, "A Historic Judgement: Guerilla War Is Not Terrorism," ZNet, February 3, 2005, http://www.zmag.org/content/print_article.cfm?itemID=7166&sectionID=1.

[9] http://www.amnesty.org/en/library/asset/EUR45/004/2006/e2c79946-a368-11dc-9d08-f145a8145d2b/eur450042006en.html.

[10] http://www.hrweb.org/legal/cat.html.

[11] *International Journal of Refugee Law*, 9(1):1997, pp. 86–121, http://ijrl.oxfordjournals.org/cgi/content/abstract/9/1/86.

[12] http://www.echr.coe.int/eng/press/2005/Oct/ApplicationlodgedRamzyvNetherlands.htm.

[13] Ibid.

[14] Dieter Grimm, "Civil Liberties in an Age of Terror. How to Balance Freedom and Security," *Spiegel Online*, April 26, 2007.

[15] Pierre Bocev, "*La Luftwaffe n'abattra pas les avions détournés*," *Le Figaro*, February 16, 2006.

[16] "Who Makes the Call?" *Wall Street Journal*, February 16, 2006.

[17] http://english.aljazeera.net/NR/exeres/DA87DE76-E24B-4645-9A4C-C3EA6ECC6055.htm.

[18] Clare Dyer, "Court bans deportation of terror suspect," *The Guardian*, February 28, 2008.

[19] Richard Ford, "European judges thwart attempts to deport foreign terrorist suspects," *The Times*, February 29, 2008.

[20] Statement by Prime Minister Tony Blair, August 5, 2005, quoted at http://www.amnesty.org/en/library/asset/EUR45/004/2006/e2c79946-a368-11dc-9d08-f145a8145d2b/eur450042006en.html.

[21] http://hrw.org/backgrounder/eca/uk0607/4.htm.

[22] http://www.amnesty.org/en/library/asset/EUR45/004/2006/e2c79946-a368-11dc-9d08-f145a8145d2b/eur450042006en.html.

[23] "UN High Commissioner for Human Rights Louise Arbour delivers statement for Human Rights Day," December 6, 2005, http://un.op.org/node/2763.

[24] Ned Temko and Jamie Doward, "Revealed: Blair attack on human rights law," *The Observer*, May 14, 2006.

[25] Tom Carter, "Official defends hard line on terror," *Washington Times*, October 7, 2005.

[26] Even when he temporarily renounced asylum the British authorities had it reinstated because they could not deport him to his native Syria for the reasons described above. Ultimately he left for Lebanon on his own, in August 2005.

[27] Holger Stark: "A German Islamist Faces Death Penalty in Syria," *Der Spiegel*, November 27, 2006; The Syrian Human Rights Committee, "Mohammed Haydar Zammar Sentenced Pursuant to Article 49/1980," February 13, 2007; http://www.shrc.org/data/aspx/d2/3052.aspx.

[28] Ibid.

[29] Ibid.

[30] Alan Travis, "Reid wins key legal victory as judges say radical cleric may be deported, despite risk of assault," *The Guardian*, February 27, 2007.

[31] Ibid.

[32] James Sturcke and agencies, "Libyan terror suspects win deportation appeal," *The Guardian*, April 27, 2007.

[33] Ibid.

[34] Richard Ford, "Radical cleric loses deportation battle," *The Times*, February 27, 2007; Jenny Percival, "Abu Qatada gets £2,500 compensation for breach of human rights," guardian.co.uk, February 19, 2009.

35 "Timeline: Fertiliser bomb plot," *The Times*, April 30, 2007; for more on the links between the two cells, see Sean O'Neill, Michael Evans, and Nicola Woolcock, "British bombers and the lost links to 7/7," *The Times*, May 1, 2007.

36 Ian Cobain and Jeevan Vasagar, "Free—the man accused of being an al-Qaida leader, aka 'Q'," *The Guardian*, May 1, 2007.

37 "Links between the 7 July Bombers and the Fertiliser Plot," http://www.mi5.gov.uk/output/Page602.html.

38 http://www.josemariasison.org/legalcases/Documents/01-AECJvsTL/ECjudgmentDefendstmnt.html.

39 "*Démantèlement d'un camp du Kongra-Gel, ex-PKK, aux Pays-Bas*," Lemonde.fr, November 12, 2004; "Dutch arrest 20 in training camp raid," *The Guardian*, November 12, 2004.

40 "Erdal's Lawyers Take Initiatives to Take Erdal Out from Prison," http://www.hri.org/news/turkey/anadolu/2000/00-05-27.anadolu.html#27; Grigor Arshakyan, "The Murder of Ozdemir Sabanci and Turkish-Belgian Tension," November 9, 2005, http://www.newneighbors.am/news.php?cont=3&rg=2&date=09.11.2005&month=12&year=2005.

41 "Germany extradites Islamist leader to Turkey," ICT, October 13, 2004; Wolfgang Günter Lerch, "A Totalitarian State Working within a Democratic One," *Frankfurter Allgemeine Zeitung*, December 13, 2001.

42 Niall Ferguson, "Don't flout Geneva—or the tables could easily be turned," *The Telegraph*, October 1, 2006.

43 Quoted by Seymour M. Hersh, "Manhunt: The Bush Administration's New Strategy in the War against Terrorism," *The New Yorker*, December 23, 2002.

44 Thomas Hammarberg, "Racial and religious profiling must not be used in the combat against terrorism," May 29, 2007, www.commissioner.coe.int.

45 "Alleged secret detentions and unlawful inter-state transfers involving Council of Europe member states," draft report—Part II, Committee on Legal Affairs and Human Rights, June 7, 2006. Rapporteur: Mr. Dick Marty, Switzerland, http://news.bbc.co.uk/2/hi/europe/5056614.stm.

46 Ibid.

47 Ibid.

48 http://jurist.law.pitt.edu/paperchase/2007/02/eu-parliament-condemns-member-states.php.

49 "EU countries ignored CIA terror suspect flights, report says," *The Guardian*, February 14, 2007. The Romanians, indirectly accused, also reacted negatively—see "*Fara dovezi, PE cere Romaniei sa-si probeze nevinovatia*" ("With no proofs, the EP asks Romania to prove its innocence"), *Romania Libera*, January 23, 2007.

50 Ariane Bernard, "European Faults U.S. Official for Remarks on Geneva Rules," *New York Times*, September 23, 2006.

51 Hammarberg, "Racial and religious profiling."

52 http://www.amnesty.org/en/library/asset/EUR45/004/2006/e2c79946-a368-11dc-9d08-f145a8145d2b/eur450042006en.html.

53 Patrick Hennessy and Melissa Kite, "Al-Qa'eda is winning the war of ideas, says Reid," *The Telegraph*, October 22, 2006.

54 "Counter-Terrorism Legislation and Practice: A Survey of Selected Countries," *The Guardian*, October 12, 2005.

55 Mark Rice-Oxley, "How far will Europe go to stop terror? European Union officials agreed Thursday to begin storing phone and Internet records," *Christian Science Monitor*, July 15, 2005.

56 Piotr Smolar, "*Le ministère de l'intérieur veut améliorer le repérage des islamistes radicaux sur le territoire français*," *Le Monde*, July 15, 2005.

57 "Counter-terrorism Legislation and Practice."

58

59 Piotr Smolar, "*Les lieux de prosélytisme de l'islam radical mis en difficulté*," *Le Monde*, April 10, 2006.

60 "*Nicolas Sarkozy justifie, au nom de la sécurité, les mesures contre des bagagistes musulmans de Roissy*," *Le Monde*, with Reuters and AFP, October 21, 2006.

61 "*Nicolas Sarkozy justifie des retraits de badges à Roissy et Orly*," *Libération*, October 21, 2006.

62 Claire Chartier, "*L'homme qui veut instaurer l'islamisme en France*," *L'Express*, October 18, 2004.

63 Denécé, "*Le Développement de l'islam fondamentaliste en France*."

64 Ibid.; Xavier Ternisien, "*L'ordonnance de 1945, fondement contesté des expulsions d'imams*," *Le Monde*, August 21, 2004, p. 5.

65 The European Convention on Human Rights, http://www.hri.org/docs/ECHR50.html#C.Art5.

66 "Watch your mouth," *The Economist*, August 11, 2005.

67 "Counter-Terrorism Legislation and Practice."

68 Tony Blair, "Blair: shackled in war on terror," *The Sunday Times*, May 27, 2007.

69 Which even Liberty, a vocal human-rights NGO, considered absurd. See "Extending pre-charge detention for terror suspects will make us less safe," February 1, 2007: "Remove the bar on intercept (phone tap) evidence in criminal trials because its inadmissibility is a major factor in being unable to bring charges." http://www.liberty-human-rights.org.uk/news-and-events/1-press-releases/2007/pre-charge-detention.shtml.

70 "Freedom from Fear," http://thereport.amnesty.org/eng/Download%20the%20Report.

[71] Eric Pelletier and Jean-Marie Pontaut, "*Les attentats de 1995: Le scandale Ramda*," *L'Express*, September 26, 2002; "*Un 'intellectuel' de la mouvance islamiste algérienne radicale*," *Le Figaro*, November 17, 2005; "*Le parcours judiciaire de Rachid Ramda*," *Le Figaro*, November 17, 2005; "*La justice britannique autorise l'extradition de Rachid Ramda*," *Le Figaro*, November 17, 2005.

[72] Ibid.

[73] Matta, "*La menace vue de la France après le Livre Blanc*," in *Cinq ans après le 11 septembre*, pp. 12–16, http://www.frstrategie.org/barreFRS/publications/colloques/20060927.pdf.

[74] Fernando Reinares, "*La menace vue d'Europe*," in *Cinq ans après le 11 septembre*, pp. 18–22.

[75] Robin Niblett, "Islamic Extremism in Europe," statement before the Senate Foreign Relations Committee, Subcommittee on European Affairs, April 5, 2006, http://www.senate.gov/~foreign/testimony/2006/NiblettTestimony060405.pdf; "Spain and Germany Feud over EU Arrest Warrant," September 23, 2005, http://counterterror.typepad.com/the_counterterrorism_blog/2005/09/spain_and_germa.htm; "*Alemania no entrega a sus nacionales*," http://www.levante-emv.com/secciones/noticia.jsp?pIdNoticia=137559&pIndiceNoticia=4&pIdSeccion=6.

[76] See, e.g., Claude Moniquet, *La Guerre sans Visage: De Waddi Haddad à Oussama ben Laden* (Neuilly-sur-Seine: Michel Lafon, 2002), pp. 311–318.

[77] Isaac Kfir, "Briefing Note: House of Lords Ruling on Torture Evidence," ICT, December 20, 2005.

[78] "Sept. 11 Conviction Upheld by German Court, Motassadeq Loses Appeal," *Der Spiegel*, May 11, 2007.

[79] Coolsaet, "Between Al-Andalus and a failing integration," Royal Institute for International Relations, Brussels, May 2005, http://www.irri-kiib.be/paperegm/ep5.pdf.

[80] Jean-Pierre Stroobants, "*Gijs de Vries: 'La lutte antiterroriste doit être menée dans le respect des lois'*," *Le Monde*, February 17, 2007.

[81] Vanessa Mock, "EU 'terror tsar' bowing out amid criticism," Radio Netherlands, February 14, 2007.

[82] Dana Priest, "Help from France Key in Covert Operations. Paris's 'Alliance Base' Targets Terrorists," *Washington Post*, July 3, 2005.

[83] Gérard Davet, "*Les filières de recrutement de la 'guerre sainte' sont en place*," *Le Monde*, December 15, 2004.

[84] Eric Lichtblau, "Study Finds Sharp Drop in the Number of Terrorism Cases Prosecuted," *New York Times*, September 4, 2006.

[85] Marc Semo and Brigitte Vitalle-Durand, "*L'Europe face aux prêcheurs de haine*," *Libération*, July 30, 2005.

[86] Guillaume Dasquié, "*11 septembre 2001: Les Français en savaient long,*" *Le Monde*, April 16, 2007; "*La DGSE aurait été informée début 2001 des projets d'Al Qaïda,*" *Le Point*, April 16, 2007.

[87] Jeff Goodell, "How to Fake a Passport," *New York Times*, February 10, 2002.

[88] Paloma D. Sotero, "*'El Chino', a dos guardias civiles en la A-1: 'Racistas, os vais a enterar',*" Elmundo.es, April 16, 2007; "*Guardias de tráfico admiten que no detuvieron a 'El Chino' pese a que llevaba ropa robada y cuchillos en el coche,*" ELPAIS.com, April 16, 2007.

[89] "Italy judge indicts 31 in CIA kidnapping case," February 16, 2007, http://jurist.law.pitt.edu/paperchase/2007/02/italy-judge-indicts-31-in-cia.php; http://english.aljazeera.net/NR/exeres/85F028B7-EB30-452D-B427-67179998A1F0.htm.

[90] Craig Whitlock and Dafna Linzer, "Italy Seeks Arrests of 13 in Alleged Rendition," *Washington Post*, June 25, 2005.

Conclusion:

[1] Cf. Steyn, *America Alone*, p. 193.

[2] http://www.channel4.com/news/media/images/articles/2007/06/04_muslims_survey2.doc.

[3] "*Rajoy quiere que los inmigrantes 'respeten las costumbres de España',*" ABC.es, February 6, 2008.

[4] "Participants in Islamist Forums Discuss Proposal for Terrorist Attack in Paris," MEMRI Special Dispatch Series No. 1816, January 18, 2008.

[5] Quoted in Fjordman, "Jihad Destroys the Swedish Model," JihadWatch.org, May 1, 2007.

[6] Mohamed Sifaoui, *L'affaire des caricatures: Dessins et manipulations* (Paris: Editions Privé, 2006), p. 151.

[7] Quoted in Peter Schneider, "The New Berlin Wall," *New York Times*, December 4, 2005.

[8] Weigel, *The Cube and the Cathedral*.

[9] Irwin M. Stelzer, "Letter from Londonistan: Britain still thinks it's 1999," *The Weekly Standard*, August 1, 2005.

[10] See Gustavo de Arístegui, *La Yihad en España: La obsesion para reconquistar Al-Andalus,* 6th edition (Madrid: La Esfera de los Libros, 2006); Michael Gove, *Celsius 7/7* (London: Weidenfeld & Nicolson, 2006).

[11] Conan and Makarian, "*Enquête sur la montée de l'islam en Europe,*" *L'Express*, January 26, 2006.

[12] http://www.melaniephillips.com/diary/?p=1538..

[13] Quoted in Schneider, "The New Berlin Wall."

[14] Patrick Basham, "The Spread of Homegrown Terror: Are British Muslims really a threat?" *National Review Online*, August 11, 2006.

[15] Bright, *When Progressives Treat with Reactionaries*.

[16] Aristegui, *La Yihad en España*.

[17] Fanjul, *Al-Andalus contra España*; Fanjul, *La Quimera de Al-Andalus*.

INDEX